Note to Students

Hello, Writer.

I know. Maybe no one's ever addressed you like that before. But a college writer you are, and a better college writer you'll be after this course. The advice, examples, and activities in *Hello, Writer* are all designed to help you build the skills and habits you will need to write well and to write confidently in your composition course. The book will also help you to adapt when facing new and challenging writing situations in other courses and outside of college.

The book emphasizes a few fundamental skills. First, you'll practice reading and analyzing college-level texts. *Hello, Writer* gives you strategies for doing so and offers interesting and challenging readings. Second, you'll use a writing process to write a range of coherent works driven by a thesis. The assignments in Part Two are, of course, "English assignments," but in other courses and in your life, you will be asked to take a position, propose a solution, and evaluate any number of objects, events, and activities. Third, you'll gather, assess, use, and cite sources as you research a topic or a problem that matters to you. Finally, as you draft and edit, you'll be invited to think and learn about conventions or *rules* of English—when to follow them and when to bend them, depending on your purpose, audience, and genre.

So those are the "skills." *Hello, Writer* teaches the core composition skills your school expects you to develop. In addition, I am asking you, writer to writer, to develop a few good habits of mind—and this book will help you to do that, too. Here's what I mean:

Engage with the entire college community. Your instructor will play a role in your learning experience, and fellow students may end up playing a bigger part in your success than you thought possible. Outside of the classroom, many people are devoted to helping you reach your goals: academic counselors, career counselors, financial aid personnel, tutors, health services professionals, and others. *Hello, Writer* will return again and again to the idea that the strongest students are those who reach out to others. ▶

Set goals, commit, and persist. There is no magic solution to writing well or doing well in college. Success takes planning and hard work. And grit. Grit, according to psychology professor Angela Duckworth, is "passion and perseverance for very long-term goals." Having grit means "sticking with your future, day in, day out, not just for the week, not just for the month, but for years, and working really hard to make that future a reality." This book will help you to set goals and priorities and to demonstrate perseverance.

Be open and flexible so that you can see setbacks and outright failures as opportunities. You'll see in the early chapters of this book the value of what psychology professor Carol Dweck calls a "growth mindset," which is a way of thinking that helps a person thrive rather than buckle in the face of a challenge.

Reflect, always, on your choices and decisions, your successes and failures, your past experiences and present opportunities. *Hello, Writer* is based on research that argues that success comes from taking time to think back on a learning experience (and by "learning," I don't necessarily mean "school") and building connections among your different learning experiences to help you transfer knowledge (again, not only in school) from one situation to the next.

So welcome. I wish you great success in becoming the curious, creative, committed college writer you want to be. You belong here. You can do it. And *Hello, Writer* will be with you every step of the way.

David Starkey

Hello, Writer.
An Academic Writing Guide

David Starkey

Santa Barbara City College

bedford/st.martin's
Macmillan Learning

Boston | New York

For my wife, Sandy, and my parents,
Betty & Frank

For Bedford/St. Martins
Vice President, Humanities: Leasa Burton
Program Director, English: Stacey Purviance
Senior Executive Development Editor: Michelle M. Clark
Assistant Editor: Paola García-Muñiz
Director of Content Development: Jane Knetzger
Director of Media Editorial: Adam Whitehurst
Media Editor: Sarah Gatenby
Marketing Manager: Amy Haines
Senior Director, Content Management Enhancement: Tracey Kuehn
Senior Managing Editor: Michael Granger
Senior Manager of Publishing Services: Andrea Cava
Senior Content Project Manager: Pamela Lawson
Lead Workflow Project Manager: Paul Rohloff
Production Supervisor: Robert Cherry
Director of Design, Content Management: Diana Blume
Interior Design: Claire Seng-Niemoeller
Cover Design: William Boardman
Text Permissions Editor: Allison Ziebka-Viering
Text Permissions Researcher: Elaine Kosta, Lumina Datamatics, Inc.
Photo Permissions Editor: Alexis Gargin
Photo Researcher: Richard Fox, Lumina Datamatics, Inc.
Director of Digital Production: Keri deManigold
Advanced Media Project Manager: Rand Thomas
Project Management: Lumina Datamatics, Inc.
Project Manager: Vanavan Jayaraman
Editorial Services: Lumina Datamatics, Inc.
Composition: Lumina Datamatics, Inc.
Printing and Binding: LSC Communications

Library of Congress Control Number: 2021933691

ISBN 978-1-319-21453-1 (paperback)
ISBN 978-1-319-42605-7 (loose-leaf edition)

Printed in the United States of America.
1   2   3   4   5   6   26   25   24   23   22   21

Acknowledgments

Text acknowledgments and copyrights appear at the back of the book on page 525 which constitutes an extension of the copyright page. Art acknowledgments and copyrights appear on the same page as the art selections they cover.

For information, write: Bedford/St. Martin's, 75 Arlington Street, Boston, MA 02116

Preface for Instructors

Hello, Colleagues.

Thank you for exploring *Hello, Writer: An Academic Writing Guide,* a book I developed after more than three decades of teaching composition, developmental composition, and corequisite composition, primarily at Santa Barbara City College. The book assumes that *all* first-year college students—whatever their assessment level or preparedness—can benefit from clear and specific advice about how to compose an academic essay and from practicing the skills and habits of mind of experienced writers. *Hello, Writer* draws on composition and rhetoric research, learning science research, and the research that brought about the accelerated learning movement in the United States (see p. vi), though always through the filter of a friendly, respectful approach.

I have organized the writing instruction by purposes—with chapters on making an evaluation, arguing a position, proposing a solution, analyzing a text, and presenting research. I have chosen readings that are diverse and challenging. And since both writing and reading are foundational competencies for college success—not to mention an engaged human experience—I have made sure to include plenty of coverage of active and critical reading. *Hello, Writer* encourages writing process *and* reading process. If you're breathing a sigh of relief, that's good. This all sounds familiar, yes? I have used backward design to foster success with the SLOs/ outcomes of many first-year writing programs: Students will be able to read and analyze college-level texts; compose thesis-driven works that are coherent and compelling; develop and deploy rhetorical knowledge; gather, evaluate, use, and cite evidence; and edit for grammar, style, and word choice. Check, check, and check.

Here's where *Hello, Writer* may differ from texts you have used before. This text offers the high-challenge, high-support instruction that the corequisite/ALP movement has called for—instruction that expects all composition students to perform on-level and achieve college-level outcomes but that also features robust support for developing writers. So, what does "robust support" look like? ▶

Robust support means consistent scaffolding and guided practice throughout the text. High-support teaching begins with an emphasis on **reflection**. Each chapter starts with a "Write Before You Read" prompt that will help students make the most of skills and knowledge they already possess and guide them toward areas where they may need to work the hardest. I find that these reflection prompts work for low-stakes writing opportunities and can be conversation starters for class. Reflection has been shown to build confidence and make learning "sticky." Second, apprentice

A Corequisite Composition Timeline, or, *What's Behind This Book?*

New thinking by Peter Adams
Peter Adams, writing program director at the Community College of Baltimore County, realizes that while success rates for students in developmental composition classes look acceptable, only a small percentage of less prepared students are moving through the entire composition sequence, and even fewer students are transferring to four-year colleges. After analyzing data, Adams comes to believe that rather than preparing students for the college-level composition course, remediation ultimately waylays students.

A pivotal study introduces "accelerated learning"
Peter Adams, Sarah Gearhart, Robert Miller, and Anne Roberts, all CCBC faculty, publish "The Accelerated Learning Program: Throwing Open the Gates" (*Journal of Basic Writing*), in which they argue that mainstreaming developmental writers decreases stigma and exclusion and promotes the idea that these writers are "college material." The authors close with recommendations for cohort learning, small class size, heterogeneous grouping, and attention to noncognitive issues.

Gates Foundation and the *Complete College America* program
Focused on helping students not only gain access to college but achieve a degree, the Complete College America program recommends "guided pathways to success." Features of the pathways model include clear and coherent programs of study; milestone courses that track a student's progress; and "intrusive, just-in-time advising."

‖‖‖ **1990s** ‖‖‖‖‖‖‖‖‖‖‖ **2008** ‖‖‖‖‖‖‖‖‖‖‖ **2009** ‖‖‖‖‖‖‖‖‖‖ **2010** ‖‖‖‖‖‖‖‖‖‖ **2011** ‖‖‖‖‖‖

Advances in learning science by Carol Dweck
A psychology professor at Stanford, Carol Dweck publishes two important works related to "fixed mindset" versus "growth mindset": "Brainology: Transforming Students' Motivation to Learn" and *Mindset: The New Psychology of Success.* She points out that learners with a fixed mindset assume that they either have or don't have a certain ability and often see failure as an endpoint. She looks to the potential of growth mindset, which sees failure as *opportunity* and which "portrays abilities as acquirable."

Another corequisite model
In California, home to more community colleges than any other state, Katie Hern and Myra Snell form the California Acceleration Project, which transforms approaches to college remediation. They respond to the "poor outcomes of students placed" in non-credit-bearing basic writing programs with "high-challenge, high-support pedagogy."

Express to Success begins at Santa Barbara City College
Developed by Kathy Molloy, SBCC's Express to Success Program (ESP) includes support sections for college-level composition, a noncognitive curriculum with attention to habits of mind, dedicated ESP counselors, and peer tutoring. Both the author of this book and his wife teach in this program, committed to the promise of a high-challenge, high-support environment.

writers benefit from a range of **activities**—hands-on, collaborative, and just-in-time opportunities to reinforce and extend their learning. I include many Do-it-yourself (DIY) prompts throughout each chapter and a series of activities and additional prompts at the ends of the chapters. I have used some DIYs in my anchor sections and others in the corequisite sections. Similarly, the chapter-ending "Making It Stick" activities are flexible enough to be used in primary instruction or for practice and support.

"Grit" becomes a thing

Angela Duckworth, a former 7th-grade math teacher and now psychologist at the University of Pennsylvania, delivers a highly influential TED Talk about "grit," a "passion and perseverance for very long-term goals," a hallmark trait, she concludes, of successful people, and a far more accurate predictor of success than IQ. She builds on Carol Dweck's growth mindset ideas and links them to grit. Grit becomes a guiding idea in education.

Two influential books promote redesign

Thomas Bailey et al.'s *Redesigning America's Community Colleges* and Keith Witham et al.'s *America's Unmet Promise: The Imperative for Equity in Higher Education* argue for redesigning curriculum to emphasize *guidance* by making outcomes and options clearer and *equity* by recognizing "differences in students' aspirations, life circumstances, ways of engaging in learning and participating in college, and identities as learners," and make adaptations for those differences.

Corequisite composition continues to grow

In states such as Tennessee and Texas, writing programs offer composition courses alongside corequisite support. Various corequisite models are implemented in Arkansas, Colorado, Connecticut, Indiana, Michigan, and West Virginia. Hundreds of writing programs around the U.S. report corequisite pilot programs starting in the new decade.

2013 **2014** **2015** **2018** **2019**

Then things get "sticky"

Many composition instructors embrace offering developing writers a high-challenge curriculum, one supported by ideas in Peter C. Brown et al.'s *Make It Stick: The Science of Successful Learning*. The authors contend that learning isn't better when it's easier. Instead, "when the mind has to work, learning sticks better."

More state legislation

California's Assembly Bill 705 (AB705) prohibits a college "from requiring students to enroll in remedial coursework that lengthens their time to complete a degree unless placement research that includes consideration of high school grade point average and coursework shows that those students are highly unlikely to succeed in transfer-level coursework." A lively debate ensues about how we can know whether a student is "highly unlikely" to succeed in a college-level class, but in the meantime, community college faculty energetically revise their curricula, applying considerable passion and experience in an effort to help all writers and learners succeed in a college composition course. One such faculty member writes a new corequisite composition textbook. Meet David Starkey's *Hello, Writer*.

Hello, Writer supports the development of not only writing skills but also **writing habits and noncognitive skills**. The early chapters present "grit" and "growth mindset" as key traits of successful learners; this learning psychology angle is one my student writers have responded to positively. I also weave discussion of time management, etiquette, wellness, and community through the early chapters and emphasize that these concerns are every bit as crucial to their success as knowing how to write a thesis statement. I let students know that whether or not they are enrolled in a corequisite course, they will benefit from working with support staff outside the writing classroom—academic counselors, personal and career counselors, tutors, health services professionals, and so forth—in order to have a successful college experience.

Finally, *Hello, Writer* supports writers through the powerful writing tools in **Achieve**, a platform built on everything we know about writer development and designed to make writing and writers, revision, reflection, and peer review central to the course (see pp. ix–x). It also functions as a space for guided practice and the reinforcement of skills in the corequisite or support section, which I hope you and your colleagues will find helpful.

I have spent my teaching career being inspired by students—their stories, their struggles, and their successes. As I finished up work on this book in 2020, students all over California and the country were facing real challenges: an emergency move to online learning with an abundance of access problems; lost and lowered incomes due to pandemic fears and realities; racial tensions, protests, and unreliable news; and climate-driven catastrophes that affected health, housing, and hope for the future. Through *Hello, Writer*, we tell beginning college writers that we hear their stories, support their struggles, and celebrate their successes—successes made all the more meaningful by adverse circumstances.

Hello, Writer makes learning challenging yet achievable. Support for first-year writing assignments sits side by side with support for first-year writers. Finally, wherever possible, I have tried to find ways to encourage writers' curiosity, openness, and creativity, inviting them to see themselves and their experiences reflected throughout what I believe is an exciting new guide to writing.

Features

Hello, Writer: An Academic Writing Guide, developed for the first-year corequisite composition course, combines familiar academic writing and reading topics with a fresh and flexible approach that works in multiple teaching and learning contexts and with a range of college writers.

Achieve is an exciting and comprehensive set of interconnected teaching and assessment tools. It integrates the most effective elements from the Bedford/St. Martin's digital content you may be familiar with (LaunchPad and LearningCurve) with writing tools built for engagement and based on research—all in a single powerful, easy-to-use platform that works for face-to-face, remote, and hybrid learning scenarios. **Achieve with Hello, Writer** offers the following benefits for teachers and learners in composition and corequisite composition courses.

- **Superior content, developed in the Bedford/St. Martin's way.** David Starkey's approach and advice are evident in the interactive e-book and engaging activities—all designed to deliver a coherent learning experience and to make prep, practice, and review easy.

- **Writing tools that keep writing and revision at the center of your course.** Achieve with *Hello, Writer* gives teachers deeper visibility into students' writing processes to target instruction and feedback and help writers grow across drafts, across assignments, and across courses. Students do the work of the course in a contained and active writing space that promotes revision, reflection, and review.

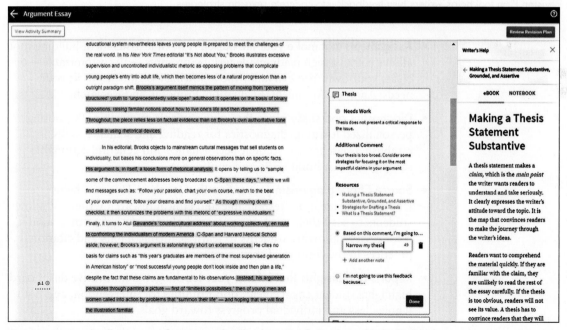

Commenting tools allow you to focus your feedback on Draft Goals and link to e-book content.

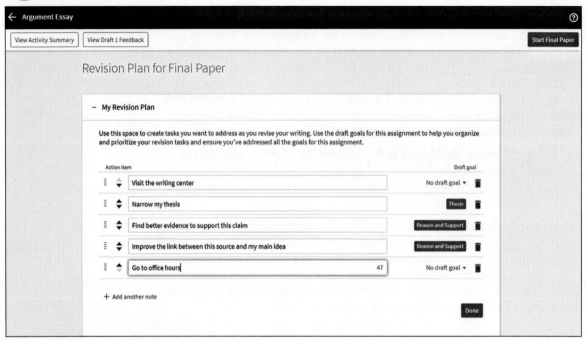

The Revision Plan tool helps writers turn feedback into concrete revision strategies.

- **Assignments that make your life easier.** A flexible assignment building tool allows you to assign ready-made writing prompts—all customizable—or create your own. You can tailor the following assignments to fit your needs: Analysis, Argument, Evaluation, Proposal, and Research.

- **Diagnostics and study plans that give students ownership.** Promoting personalized learning, diagnostics for reading and sentence skills establish a baseline for student performance and generate actionable study plans that build skills and confidence.

- **Source Check plagiarism prevention that teaches.** This tool helps students become more responsible and ethical research writers. It allows students to scan their work for potential plagiarism *before* they submit it for review, allowing students to learn academic habits and citation practices in the context of their own writing.

- **Reports and insights that inform your teaching.** An innovative dashboard highlights student engagement, opportunities for intervention, and both whole-class and individual progress toward goals.

Comprehensive coverage of composition topics provides support for students as they complete common assignments such as analyzing a text, arguing a position, and presenting research; as they build rhetorical awareness and develop strategies around writing and revision; as they develop skills as reviewers and editors of their own work and that of others; as they read college-level texts actively and critically; and as they develop useful habits of mind that will transfer to the writing and reading they do in other courses and contexts. The instruction is example driven, relevant, and class tested.

- **Part One, *Becoming a College Reader and Writer*,** introduces the book's approach, familiarizes students with the research that informs the book—research on developing grit and a growth mindset—and includes chapters on the reading process and writing process that teachers and students would expect to see in a composition text. A substantial editing chapter supports students as they learn and use sentence-level conventions.

- **Part Two, *Strategies for Academic Writing*,** focuses on common assignments that students are asked to complete in composition and beyond. Each chapter includes both professional and student readings by diverse authors and on topics students care about. Chapter 14 covers both analyzing and producing multimodal works.

- **Part Three, *Writing with Research*,** supports students in both Composition I and II by offering an overview of the research process as well as specific advice for developing a research strategy, setting goals, finding sources, evaluating sources, integrating sources, and using either MLA (2021) or APA (2020) citation style. Sample annotated research essays are included.

Flexible, scaffolded instruction allows instructors to tailor support to fit students' needs. Within each chapter, students will progress from basic understanding to gradually more sophisticated understanding of the material with a combination of instruction, examples, and practice. Structured and intentional prompts provide frequent opportunities for discussion, collaboration, and writing practice. Chapters feature the following elements:

- **Chapter-opening reflection prompts** The book encourages students to activate prior knowledge and reflect on prior reading and writing experiences in "Write Before You Read" prompts. These low-stakes reflections get students thinking about the chapter content in the context of their own experience.

- **Invitations to read** Most chapters include challenging high-interest and diverse readings, made accessible with apparatus that facilitates understanding and critical thinking. The topics are relevant (race, e-cigarettes, sex trafficking, voter apathy), and the readings act as writing models, discussion motivators, and opportunities to apply reading strategies.

- **DIY prompts** Since apprentice writers benefit from hands-on activities, every chapter features six to ten Do-it-yourself (DIY) activities that

---

DIY 4.1 Summarize Your Essay Prompt

Write a paragraph summarizing the main expectations for your essay based on the prompt your instructor has given you for your first assignment. Make sure you include each aspect of the assignment that you *must* cover. What do you think is the purpose of the assignment? Who is your audience, real or imagined? What are the key features of a successful draft? What requirements do you need more information about?

DIY activities provide just-in-time support.

5.6 Making It Stick

How will you craft a thesis and organize your essay?

Working Together

5.6a Narrow, Claim, Outline First, form groups of three or four students. Then choose one of the broad topics below and (1) narrow it down, (2) create a working thesis, and (3) write a scratch outline. You have a limited amount of time to complete this exercise (your instructor will tell you how much), but there are no "rules," per se. Your only goal is to make the best use of the knowledge and skills of the people in your group.

Because the topics are intentionally broad, you will need to do quite a bit of work to quickly narrow down the one you choose and to come up with a thesis that, most likely, will argue in favor of, or against, a certain approach to the topic.

Broad Topics

Gun control

Legalizing suicide

Censoring social media

Regulating junk food

Mandatory military service at age eighteen

Tuition-free college

When you're finished, respond to the following questions, first in your small group, then as part of a full-class discussion:

1. How did you go about narrowing the broad subject down to a topic that could be realistically addressed in a short academic essay? What strategies were effective or ineffective?

2. What were the most productive aspects of your collaboration? How could you reproduce those successes in future collaborations?

3. In what areas was your collaboration less productive? What could you do differently next time to achieve better results?

Applying What You Know

5.6b A Two-Minute Talk Imagine that you are giving a speech about your chosen topic, but you have only two minutes to state your argument and provide your most compelling evidence. Write out your thesis statement and make a list of the most important elements of your essay. Then organize and edit your material so that you can tell people everything they need to know in the compressed time frame.

When you're ready, give your two-minute speech to a few of your classmates. If you are taking your class remotely, enlist a friend or family member to be your audience.

5.6c Organizing Nonacademic Arguments Think about an argument you've made recently in a social or personal situation ("You should watch this Netflix show . . ."; "Supporting this candidate is the smartest choice . . ."; "The accident wasn't my fault because . . ."). Write notes about how you "organized" your argument. Were your choices successful? If you had the chance to make that argument again, what would you do differently to achieve your purpose?

Each chapter ends with a robust and flexible cluster of activities.

---

reinforce the chapter concepts and, in the case of the chapters in Part 2, help students make progress through a specific assignment. DIY prompts can be completed individually or collaboratively and are designed with learning science in mind—designed to provide an immediate, just-in-time scenario to test a skill or apply a strategy so that the learning sticks.

- **Chapter checklists** offer quick tools for students to manage their efforts and recall important chapter information.

- **"Making It Stick" chapter activities** Each chapter ends with a collection of optional prompts and practices that teachers can choose to assign to help students apply new learning and make the most of the material. "Working Together" activities invite students to collaborate and build community while building chapter skills. "Applying What You Know" activities reinforce, apply, and extend students' understanding of chapter material. And finally, "Invitations to Write" are paired writing prompts—with a shorter option and a longer option—that provide additional writing opportunities related to the chapter topic.

Substantial reading strategies and practice are integrated throughout the text. In addition to a full chapter on college reading (Chapter 2, "Becoming a College Reader"), *Hello, Writer* includes readings, reading instruction, and reading activities throughout. The text fosters proficiency in reading nonfiction selections for discussion and analysis, source material for research, peers' drafts, and students' own drafts. Diagnostic tests and personalized study plans in Achieve help students establish a baseline and build skills in reading comprehension and critical reading strategies. Twenty-two reading selections in the book, a combination of professional and student-written essays, deliver opportunities for students to get inspired, get fired-up, and get thoughtful.

Diversity and inclusion from cover to cover helps students see themselves represented in the writers, ideas, and imagery throughout *Hello, Writer*. Of the readings and model student writing, ten of the twenty-two are by authors of color; and coverage of visual argument features Oreo's "Pride" campaign and the notion that advertisements can sell ideas as well as products. The editing chapter, too, acknowledges that students will come from a range of linguistic backgrounds and will speak and write in many Englishes. Finally, the instructor's manual offers support for teaching with a pedagogy tuned in to diversity, equity, and inclusion.

Attention to noncognitive skills helps students become independent learners and adapt to college expectations. Coverage of time management, growth mindset, classroom etiquette, interacting with peers and professors, managing anxiety, and more rests on the assumption that when students fail or give up, it can be for reasons unrelated to academic performance. *Hello, Writer* acknowledges that fear of failure is real and encourages students to commit themselves to a set of habits that will help them to succeed in an academic environment.

A student-friendly tone and relatable narrative grow out of a veteran classroom teacher's desire to make learning challenging yet achievable, to respect the varied life experiences of the individuals in his class, and to encourage students' curiosity, creativity, and commitment in the writing course. David Starkey writes with patience, clarity, and humor—even as he challenges students to adjust their habits, achieve outcomes, produce college-level writing, and—occasionally—surprise themselves.

A practical instructor's manual offers implementation guidance and additional resources for teachers of composition and corequisite composition. Our *Instructor's Manual for Hello, Writer,* written by experienced composition teacher, curriculum designer, and corequisite pioneer Margie Nelson Rodríguez (El Paso Community College), covers a range of topics. Both novice and veteran instructors will benefit from tips and best practices, an overview of David Starkey's approach, and chapters on planning a corequisite course, teaching online, building community, strengthening college reading skills, developing inclusive pedagogy, addressing noncognitive skills, designing a corequisite composition syllabus, and more. The IM is available online at **macmillanlearning.com** and in Achieve.

Bedford/St. Martin's Puts You First

From day one, our goal has been simple: to provide inspiring resources that are grounded in best practices for teaching reading and writing. For forty years, Bedford/St. Martin's has partnered with the field, listening to teachers, scholars, and students about the support writers need. We are committed to helping every writing instructor make the most of our resources in any learning scenario.

How can we help you?

- Our editors can align our resources to your outcomes through correlation and transition guides for your syllabus. Just ask us.
- Our sales representatives specialize in helping you find the right materials to support your course goals.
- Our learning solutions and product specialists help you make the most of the digital resources you choose for your course.
- Our curriculum solutions team can help you design a custom product to meet your needs and even deliver a royalty to your department. You can choose from trade title excerpts with our MAP program, brief skills chapters from our ForeWords content, or add original content.
- Our *Bits* blog on the Bedford/St. Martin's English Community (**community.macmillan.com**), which features posts by David Starkey, publishes fresh teaching ideas weekly. You'll also find easily downloadable professional resources such as the *Instructor's Manual for Hello, Writer* and links to author webinars on our community site.

Contact your Bedford/St. Martin's sales representative for additional information or visit **macmillanlearning.com** to learn more.

Ordering information

Digital

- Achieve with *Hello, Writer* (six-month access): ISBN 978-1-319-40647-9
- Achieve packaged with the paperback version of *Hello, Writer*: ISBN 978-1-319-40648-6
- Achieve packaged with the loose-leaf version of *Hello, Writer*: Contact your Bedford/St. Martin's sales representative.
- *Popular e-book formats.* For details about our e-book partners, visit **macmillanlearning.com/ebooks**.

Inclusive Access. Enable every student to receive their course materials through your LMS on the first day of class. Macmillan Learning's Inclusive Access program is the easiest, most affordable way to ensure all students have access to quality educational resources. Find out more at **macmillanlearning.com/inclusiveaccess**.

Print

- *Hello, Writer: An Academic Writing Guide* (paperback): ISBN 978-1-319-21453-1
- *Hello, Writer: An Academic Writing Guide* (loose-leaf): ISBN 978-1-319-42605-7

Contact your Bedford/St. Martin's sales representative for additional pricing and packaging information.

Acknowledgments

It certainly takes a village to raise a textbook, and I am grateful for the many fellow teachers of writing who offered candid reviews and suggestions during the process of development: Lisa Bamber, Otero Junior College; Jessica Best, Adirondack Community College; Sarah Boggs, Santa Barbara City College; Cheryl Cardoza, Truckee Meadows Community College; Rebecca Cash, Adirondack Community College; Jackson Connor, University of Rio Grande; Howard Cox, Angelina College; Sharon Down, Gateway Community and Technical College; Clark Draney, College of Southern Idaho; Jason File, Santa Barbara City College; Megan Fischer, Angelina College–Lufkin; Lisa Gannon, College of Southern Nevada; Kendra Griffin, Aims Community College; Joel Henderson, Chattanooga State Technical Community College; Candice May Hill, Anne Arundel Community College; Nikkina Hughes, Tarrant County College; Donald Jacob Hutchinson, Arkansas State University Mid-South; Elizabeth Johnston, Monroe Community College; Kimi Kelley, Otero Junior College; Emily King, Truckee Meadows Community College; Tiffany LaPeer, Oakland Community College; Aaron Leff, Front Range Community College; Melissa Long, Porterville College; Helaine Lubar, Onondaga Community College; José Maldonado, Oxnard College; Molly Maynard, Truckee Meadows Community College; Jennifer McCann, Bay College; Gary McIlroy, Henry Ford College; Darren Meritz, University of Texas San Antonio; Jessica Nastal Dema, Prairie State College; Margie Nelson Rodríguez, El Paso Community College; Rachel Pannell, Community College of Philadelphia; Jay Peterson, Atlantic Cape Community College; James Reed, Trinity Valley Community College; Dixie Shaw-Tillmon, University of Texas San Antonio; Allyson Smith, North Georgia Technical College; Angela Spires, College of South Nevada; Sandy Starkey, Santa Barbara City College; John Stevens, Temple College; Pamela Mathis Stone, North Arkansas College; Melissa Strong, Community College of Philadelphia; Wendy Swyt, Highline College; Roberta Tragarz, Santiago Canyon College; Joel Wilson, Walters State Community College.

I also thank a number of students for generously granting permission to reprint their essays as models: Ian Byrne, Angela Edwards, Ethan Fischer, Oliver Hernandez, Curran McCrory, Larissa Moss, and Zoe Rojas.

And I'm especially grateful to the team at Macmillan for shepherding *Hello, Writer* from an idea I proposed at the 2017 ALP conference to the book you have before you. Thank you, Leasa Burton, Vice President of Humanities, for believing in the book in its earliest stages; Stacey Purviance, Program Director for English, who took over midstream and handled the transition seamlessly; Karita dos Santos, Program Manager, for her enthusiasm and the tough love she gave the manuscript in its early incarnations; Amy Haines, Marketing Manager, and Azelie Fortier, Market

Development Manager, for their unflagging good sense and good spirits; Adam Whitehurst, Director of English Media Editorial; Sarah Gatenby, Media Editor; Pamela Lawson, Senior Content Project Manager; Vanavan Jayaraman, Senior Project Manager; and Alexis Gargin, Permissions Editor.

The look of a book can be as integral to its success as its content, and I want to give special thanks to Diana Blume, Art Director, and Claire Seng-Niemoeller, Book Designer. I've also been lucky to have the brilliant William Boardman create the cover designs for all of my books with Macmillan.

To Assistant Editor Paola García-Muñiz, I've often said the company would stop running without you. I still believe that's true.

It was also my great good fortune to work on a day-to-day basis with two of the best editors in the business. During the drafting and initial revision of the book, Gillian Cook, Senior Development Editor, answered my every question and assuaged my every fear. Gill, whose career has been devoted to working with authors of developmental composition textbooks, was the perfect editor for the first stages of *Hello, Writer*. It is immeasurably better thanks to her many suggestions. When Gill left the project, I knew she was irreplaceable, and I had no right to expect an editor of similar intelligence and creativity. Yet, suddenly, there she was: Michelle Clark, Senior Executive Development Editor. Michelle scrutinized every aspect of what I thought was already a strong manuscript and made everything better. Her attention to both the big picture and the smallest detail never wavered. Like Gill, Michelle is a more than honorary coauthor of *Hello, Writer*.

A key team member and author of the instructor's manual for *Hello, Writer*, Margie Nelson Rodríguez (El Paso Community College) conceived a flexible, practical, pedagogically sound teaching program for users all over the country.

Finally, I want to acknowledge the invaluable experience I gained as an instructor in SBCC's Express to Success (ESP) program, which was developed and helmed for many years by Kathy Molloy. I am also grateful to my smart, funny, and dedicated colleagues in the English Division at Santa Barbara City College, and especially to my wife and fellow SBCC professor, Sandy Starkey, who taught in the ESP program from its inception. Whenever I hit an obstacle and was sure I couldn't move forward, a few minutes of conversation with Sandy always solved the problem. She, too, is a coauthor, and her intelligence, experience, advice, and good sense permeates—if I have been successful—the entire book.

David Starkey
Santa Barbara, CA

How *Hello, Writer* and Achieve Support WPA Outcomes for First-Year Composition

This chart aligns *Hello, Writer* with the latest WPA Outcomes Statement (2014). As revisions to the WPA Outcomes occur, we will update the chart and post updates to **macmillanlearning.com**

WPA Outcomes	Relevant Content in *Hello, Writer.*
Rhetorical Knowledge	
Learn and use key rhetorical concepts through analyzing and composing a variety of texts.	• **Section 4.1** gives students rhetorical grounding as they prewrite, plan, and draft—focusing on the rhetorical situation. • **Sections 5.1** and **5.2** encourage students to start with purpose and audience in the early stages of every writing task: For what reason(s) am I writing? For what readers? And in what form and format? • **Section 15.2** covers purpose, audience, genre, and delivery in the context of writing with sources. • *Hello, Writer* helps students compose and analyze essays, advertisements, multimedia and visual texts, narratives, online sources, and peer review commentary.
Gain experience reading and composing in several genres to understand how genre conventions shape and are shaped by readers' and writers' practices and purposes.	• Students are invited to read and view a psychology book chapter (**3.2**), traditional nonfiction essays (**10.1**), TED Talks (**3.3**), advertisements (**14.3**), a multimodal reflective work (**14.5**), data (**2.1**), and more. • Students write traditional essays but are invited to remix ideas in multimodal ways in **Chapter 14** and in **section 17.8**. • **Activities 2.7c** and **2.7d** ask students to analyze websites, textbooks, and data. • Attention to audience is emphasized in **sections 5.2, 11.3**.
Develop facility in responding to a variety of situations and contexts, calling for purposeful shifts in voice, tone, level of formality, design, medium, and/or structure.	• More than 130 **DIY** (Do-it-yourself) **activities** offer just-in-time low-stakes writing opportunities that ask students to write in a number of different contexts with varying levels of formality and tone. • Attention to multimodal writing and creative nonfiction in **Chapter 14** ensures students have experience with shifts in design and medium as they compose.
Understand and use a variety of technologies to address a range of audiences.	• *Hello, Writer* assumes students are learning in a variety of classroom contexts (face-to-face, remote, and hybrid) and using different platforms (LMS, Zoom, social media, Google suite, YouTube, etc.) to communicate with peers, instructors, mentors, counselors, and others.

WPA Outcomes	Relevant Content in *Hello, Writer.*
Match the capacities of different environments (e.g., print and electronic) to varying rhetorical situations.	• Most chapters assume that students are composing and sharing their writing online—sometimes just within their course and other times in more social contexts. There is some attention given to the affordances of print for different rhetorical and logistical purposes.

Critical Thinking, Reading, and Composing

Use composing and reading for inquiry, learning, thinking, and communicating in various rhetorical contexts.	• **Chapter 2**, Becoming a College Reader, teaches active, critical reading for various purposes and promotes the relationship between being a thoughtful reader and an effective writer. **Section 2.4** covers reading rhetorically. • **Section 15.1** encourages students to tap into their natural curiosity in the service of academic and everyday purposes. **Section 15.2** addresses writing and reading to explore. • The 132 **DIY** prompts in *Hello, Writer* offer abundant write-to-learn opportunities.
Read a diverse range of texts, attending especially to relationships between assertion and evidence, to patterns of organization, to interplay between verbal and nonverbal elements, and how these features function for different audiences and situations.	• A group of twenty-two diverse readings, some annotated, demonstrate skillful use of evidence, effective deployment of verbal and nonverbal elements, and a range of organizational patterns. • Texts range from essays and articles to podcasts, TED talks, and advertisements. See **Sections 2.1, 3.2–3.4, 10.1, 10.6, 11.1, 11.5, 12.1, 12.6, 13.1, 13.4, 14.3,** and **14.4**.
Locate and evaluate primary and secondary research materials, including journal articles, essays, books, databases, and informal Internet sources.	• **Section 2.4** covers distinguishing fact from opinion. • **Section 15.4** encourages students to "quick-search" in an effort to focus their research efforts. • See **Section 16.3** for coverage of finding and using primary and secondary sources. • **Chapter 16** offers robust coverage of finding scholarly, popular, and multimedia/visual sources on the web, in databases, through field research and lived experience, and elsewhere. • **Section 16.10** covers annotated bibliography.
Use strategies—such as interpretation, synthesis, response, critique, and design/redesign—to compose texts that integrate the writer's ideas with those from appropriate sources.	• **Section 17.4** covers organization with an emphasis on audience's needs. • **Section 17.5** encourages students to balance interpretation, synthesis, and discovery.

WPA Outcomes	Relevant Content in *Hello, Writer.*
Processes	
Develop a writing project through multiple drafts.	• *Hello, Writer* assumes students are using a process approach for composing texts for the course. **Part 1** helps students build skills in prewriting, drafting, revising, editing, and seeking feedback. • **Achieve** facilitates drafting, review, and revision through innovative writing tools.
Develop flexible strategies for reading, drafting, reviewing, collaboration, revising, rewriting, rereading, and editing.	• **Section 2.6** covers the SQ3R reading strategy. • **Chapter 2** offers students a flexible reading process. • **Achieve**'s writing tools include, with each assignment, Draft Goals that help students target their reviewing and revising.
Use composing processes and tools as a means to discover and reconsider ideas.	• **Section 4.3** presents multiple prewriting strategies as a means of discovering ideas for writing and preparing to write. • **Achieve** encourages multidraft writing through an innovative writing tools platform that emphasizes **reflection** and **revision**.
Experience the collaborative and social aspects of writing processes.	• **Working Together** (collaborative) activities are a feature of every chapter. See **1.6**, for example. • Many chapter **DIY** prompts encourage working with a peer (see **Section 3.5a**, for example, a collaborative activity on rhetorical reading).
Learn to give and act on productive feedback to works-in-progress.	• **Working Together** (collaborative) activities are a feature of every chapter. See **1.6**, for example. • **Achieve** helps students give productive feedback with Draft Goals that target their reading and review of drafts. • **Achieve** allows students to make an actionable revision plan from the feedback they receive from reviewers.
Adapt composing processes for a variety of technologies and modalities.	• **Applying What You Know** activities in each chapter invite students to extend and apply composing processes in other contexts, for other purposes, and in other modalities (see **Section 14.6** for examples).
Reflect on the development of composing practices and how those practices influence their work.	• Each chapter begins with a reflection prompt, **Write Before You Read**, that asks students to reflect on their processes, practices, and prior writing and reading experiences. • **Achieve** is powered by reflection pedagogy—with metacognition built into writing assignments and all peer review tasks.

WPA Outcomes	Relevant Content in *Hello, Writer.*
Knowledge of Conventions	
Develop knowledge of linguistic structures, including grammar, punctuation, and spelling, through practice in composing and revising.	• **Chapters 8**, Revising, and **9**, Editing, present sentence-level structures and conventions. The **DIY** activities in each chapter give students practice applying and bending conventions in their own projects.
Understand why genre conventions for structure, paragraphing, tone, and mechanics vary.	• **Section 4.1** covers the rhetorical considerations of drafting and covers purpose, audience, genre, and structure. • **Section 15.2** address genre conventions in the context of research writing.
Gain experience negotiating variations in genre conventions.	• **Chapter 14** introduces the notion of negotiating conventions in various visual genres.
Learn common formats and/or design features for different kinds of texts.	• **Section 14.3** covers writing with visuals. • **Section 17.8** presents advice for designing and presenting research.
Explore the concepts of intellectual property (such as fair use and copyright) that motivate documentation conventions.	• **Section 17.6**, which covers integrating sources, teaches students to weave the voices of others into their own writing fairly, respectfully, and accurately. • **Section 17.7** offers a rationale and guidance for documenting sources and avoiding plagiarism—arguing that plagiarism "substitutes for learning."
Practice applying citation conventions systematically in their own work.	• **Chapters 18** (MLA) and **19** (APA) offer guidelines for citing and formatting works.

Contents

7 Composing Introductions, Conclusions, and Titles   144

Write Before You Read

PART TWO Strategies for Academic Writing   215

10 Making an Evaluation   216

Write Before You Read

PART 1

Becoming a College Reader and Writer

1

Knowing Yourself and Your Community

Write Before You Read   Think for a minute: How do you see yourself fitting into a college environment? What are your goals for college? What do you already know about the school you are attending? What is your opinion of colleges and universities in general? What will make you feel like you belong? Write a paragraph or two discussing yourself as a college student and the college community you are entering.

1.1 Embracing Adaptability

Since you're here—right now—in this class, it's clear you want to succeed. One key to achieving success in college is adaptability, which is the willingness to try something new when things don't turn out how you hoped they would. If a particular study habit isn't working, for instance, you'll want to try another one—and soon. If you can't solve a problem on your own, you'll need to acknowledge the problem and identify people who can help you—and fast. In short, quitting when you first hit a roadblock just isn't an option if you want to succeed.

Understand Habits That Support Academic Growth

While you might be wondering what a discussion of college success has to do with writing papers in your English class, it's worth remembering that if you don't pass your courses, you won't be writing any papers! So, let's take a look at some habits and strategies experts recommend to help students achieve their academic goals.

Growth Mindset

One aspect of embracing adaptability is trusting that you have the potential to grow and become a better, more successful person. That might sound easy enough—after all, most of us, at some point in our lives, have witnessed the power of believing in ourselves. However, too many people give up when things get hard, blaming themselves or others for their lack of success.

In an article entitled "Brainology," Stanford psychology professor Carol Dweck examines how students in a study reported dealing with setbacks. She reports that having a setback, such as receiving a low grade on an exam, affected different students in different ways. Students with a fixed mindset—fixed on the idea that their abilities are static—tended to say the low grade made them "feel dumb" and want to "study *less*" or even cheat. Those with growth mindsets tended to look toward the next exam and the opportunity to "study more or study differently." The fixed mindset students in the study had "no good way to bounce back and be successful." However, students with a growth mindset could "make a plan of positive action" as a follow up.

Not surprisingly, the concept of a "growth mindset" has been an inspiration for many composition students. Believing that failure is an opportunity to improve rather than a final decision about the limits of your abilities is a liberating experience. In addition, adopting a growth mindset not only frees you from constant self-doubt, but it also encourages you to form specific plans to overcome the challenges you face.

Grit

Like Carol Dweck, University of Pennsylvania psychologist Angela Duckworth insists that it is "critically important—and not at all easy—to keep going after failure." This persistence, or *grit*, is especially important when the challenges a person faces outpace their abilities. In other words, you most need grit or a growth mindset when you are least likely to have it—when you've just failed and success can seem impossibly far away. Duckworth also connects grit with self-control and the ability to steer clear of the "temptations" that might derail active pursuit of a challenge (like binge-watching Netflix, binge-reading social media feeds, and gaming and texting compulsively). Just as a person can adopt a growth mindset, a person can also develop grit as a habit of mind.

You may be starting to see a pattern here—successful people embrace a philosophy of welcoming challenges and becoming more adaptable, qualities that can help you succeed in this course and the others you are taking this semester.

Make-It-Stick Mentality

When you think of "practice," what comes to mind? Soccer drills? Guitar chords? Lines for a play? In their book *Make It Stick: The Science of Successful Learning*, Washington University psychologists Henry Roediger and Mark McDaniel and journalist Peter Brown spend a good deal of time discussing "neuroplasticity" and the science of the brain. One of their insights is that learning is an active process that requires constant practice. The more you practice something, the more a substance called *myelin* thickens fibers in your brain.

According to learning psychologists, practicing something within twenty-four hours after you first learn it can increase your memory of how to do that task by up to 80 percent. Ultimately, practice becomes "reflexive" so that while it begins as "actions we teach ourselves in pursuit of a goal," it becomes "automatic." If you've mastered a musical instrument or excelled in a sport, you've already experienced this transformation from practice into automatic action.

Habits of Mind

Being both positive and deliberate in your mental approach to challenges is important. Educators Arthur Costa and Bena Kallick identify sixteen habits of mind for problem solving in their book *Learning and Leading with Habits of Mind*. Their success strategies include approaches that you might anticipate after reading Dweck and Duckworth, like "persisting," "managing impulsivity," and "applying past knowledge to new situations." However, they also encourage habits of mind that you might not expect, like "listening with understanding and empathy" and "finding humor." The Council of Writing Program Administrators have published a *Framework for Success in Postsecondary Writing*, in which they argue that eight habits of mind are key to successful writing in college:

> According to learning psychologists, practicing something within twenty-four hours after you first learn it can increase your memory of how to do that task by up to 80 percent.

- Curiosity
- Openness
- Engagement
- Creativity
- Persistence
- Responsibility
- Flexibility
- Metacognition (or Reflection)

You may have seen the acronym (an abbreviation created from the first letters of a series of words) that turns "FAIL" into "First Attempt in Learning." That clever way of converting something negative into something positive is characteristic of the way positive habits of mind and growth mindsets work. Whenever something doesn't go as planned, don't think of it as an excuse to give up, but instead as an opportunity to do better next time.

DIY 1.1 See Failure as a Learning Experience

On your own or with a partner, write notes about some recent "FAIL moments" each of you have had. Identify and describe a time when you realized that an experience that initially felt like a failure turned out to be just the first step in the learning process.

1.2 Developing Time Management Skills

To reach larger academic goals with the help of growth mindset and grit, you will need that commodity that often seems precious and elusive to a college student: time. Managing your time well can be the difference between floundering and failing or moving through your day with confidence and calm.

Prioritize and Avoid Procrastination

The most essential skill in time management is *prioritizing*—deciding what you need to do right now and what can wait until tomorrow. Often that decision means buckling down and doing something you really don't want to do.

Say, for instance, you are generally successful in math but less so in English. It's Saturday morning, and on Monday you have a math quiz that's worth just a few points and an English essay that's worth 15 percent of your total grade. Let logic guide you: Almost all of your study time should be spent working on the English essay, even though reviewing for the math quiz is so much easier. When you become adept at prioritizing, you'll turn your attention to your English essay right away, devoting just enough time to studying for your math quiz—and hardly even thinking about all the episodes of *Rick and Morty* or *The Crown* that you haven't seen yet.

Of course, following through on your priorities is easier said than done. One of the greatest enemies of prioritizing is procrastinating. Holding distractions at bay so you can do the work you know you need to do will keep you productive.

A planner can be a useful learning tool.
Andriy Popov/AGE Fotostock

Use a Planner

Many schools provide students with free planners at the beginning of the term, and nearly all school bookstores sell planners suitable for your college's schedule.

Monthly and weekly calendars are useful for plotting out due dates for homework, essays, quizzes, in-class tests, and so on. Being able to look down on your day or week or semester, especially if you are a spatial learner, will give you a stronger sense of when you need to build extra time for studying into your calendar.

DIY 1.2a *Start Using a Planner*

Using a planner or the calendar app on your smartphone, make a note of the significant academic events you have coming up. This could be anything from a quiz to a major essay to an important advising session. When you're finished, go back and add in work, home, and personal obligations.

Finally, identify any flashpoints you may have coming up in your life, such as days (or weeks) when you're going to have to do some extensive juggling because so many things are happening at once, then decide how you're going to successfully navigate all those demands.

Take Advantage of Your "Best Time"

When it comes to studying, not all times are equal, so think about *when* you are setting time aside to do your schoolwork. Dan Ariely, a professor of psychology and behavioral economics at Duke University, recommends working your hardest in the first two hours after you are fully awake: "One of the saddest mistakes in time management is the propensity of people to spend the two most productive hours of their day on things that don't require high cognitive capacity (like social media). If we could salvage those precious hours, most of us would be much more successful in accomplishing what we truly want."

Of course, not everyone works best in the morning, but being able to identify your own most productive hours and finding a way to protect them so that you can actually do your work afterward is crucial. This might mean changing your class or work schedule, or it could mean finding your "second best" time of the day for studying. In any event, remember that maintaining a growth mindset requires adapting productively to new information.

DIY 1.2b *Identify Your Best Time to Work*

Take a few minutes to think back over the past few weeks. When did you do your best work, especially in your role as a student? When were you most accurate, creative, productive, or focused? Brainstorm ways to open up more of that time for completing your schoolwork. Make notes for yourself: If your best time is early in the morning, how can you make more time to study? If you work best late at night, what sacrifices can you make to claim that time as your own?

1.3   Staying Healthy

It would be difficult to overemphasize how important staying healthy is during your college years. If you're living at home with family, you may be able to tap into some of the positive strategies you've developed for staying healthy—and avoid those that are harmful.

However, if you're living on your own for the very first time, you may be tempted to indulge in behaviors that feel good in the moment, but not so good the day after. There's nothing wrong with blowing off some steam, but consistently eating well, exercising, getting enough sleep, and avoiding drugs and alcohol can boost your academic progress. For fun, you might try keeping track of your sleep or your food intake with your smartphone or other device and then looking—for better or worse—at how your academic performance tracks with your health habits.

Manage Anxiety

One of the most common student (and human) responses to stress is anxiety. In fact, a little anxiety can actually help you prepare for change. A lot of anxiety, however, can stand in the way of your academic success. Fortunately, the same behaviors that keep you healthy can also be used to reduce anxiety. Whenever possible, remain on a regular schedule, exercise and eat well, avoid drugs and alcohol, and get a good night's sleep.

In the midst of an anxiety attack, try using the strategies psychologists recommend: relaxing, breathing deliberately, thinking about what's happening and why, distracting yourself, and remembering that anxiety attacks always come to an end. That extra cup of coffee you had this morning to get you going may also play a surprisingly big role in your anxiety. (You can find additional strategies by visiting the website of the Anxiety and Depression Association of America at adaa.org.)

Access Personal Counseling and the Student Health Center

Treatment for severe anxiety calls for more than just deep breathing and avoiding caffeine, and if you're feeling stressed and stretched to the breaking point, now may be the time to make an appointment to visit a personal counselor. If your situation feels like an emergency, say so when you call or drop in for an appointment.

Personal counselors are often located at the student health center—another resource to help keep you on track, whether you're battling the common cold or something much more serious. You may be able to receive quicker and cheaper initial treatment at your student health center than you would at an urgent care or emergency facility, so the campus health facility is always worth checking out when your body or mind isn't feeling quite right. If possible, call first or register online, as students with appointments generally have priority over walk-in patients.

1.4 Getting to Know Your Professor

In upcoming chapters, you'll learn more about your professor as an audience for your writing, but for now just focus on the first impressions you and your professor will make on each other.

Practice Classroom Etiquette

You may associate the word *etiquette* with proper behavior in high society—how to address wedding invitations, for instance, and when it is permissible to dig through a box of chocolates—but etiquette simply refers to polite behavior in a group; adhering to good classroom behavior will not only make your life easier, but it will also be greatly appreciated by your instructor and your classmates.

As you know, it doesn't take long to get a sense of the etiquette a teacher expects in a face-to-face class. One instructor may value a loose and friendly atmosphere where everyone feels free to share ideas and opinions, the sort of class where teachers from other rooms drop by to ask the instructor to quiet things down. Other professors run a tighter ship: Classroom time is planned down to the minute, and discussions are curtailed if they threaten to sidetrack the day's lessons. For online classes, teachers will likely share expectations about participation, communication, and interaction. No doubt you have your own notions of what constitutes the ideal class, but for the duration of this course at least, it's best to try and tailor your behavior to the conduct your instructor finds most productive.

Incidentally, if this is one of your first college classes, you may be wondering what to call the teacher. Sure, some teachers will ask you to use their first names, but if your instructor doesn't explicitly make that offer, it's best to use "Professor + Last Name."

Follow Your Syllabus

The course syllabus is the map of the class you are taking. Whether your professor hands out a paper copy of the syllabus or links to a digital version, this is one document you should refer to frequently and carefully. Here, you'll find out how much each assignment is worth, when it's due, what the policy is on absences, which courseware or online platforms will be used, when your professor is available to meet with you during office hours, and more. If you're using a daily planner, be sure to import key due dates from the syllabus.

The syllabus not only tells you what assignments you must complete, it also gives you a sense of who your professor is as a person. What habits of mind does the professor emphasize? Do they value punctuality and politeness, or are they someone who privileges creativity? The tone of the syllabus probably echoes your professor's own speaking voice, so read closely and use what you learn to plan your approach to the class. Even a simple thing like referencing the syllabus during a conversation with your professor—"I notice that our third essay is due just before our midterm. . . ."—will mark you as a serious and attentive student.

By the way, you may have noticed that in the previous paragraph, the grammatically singular "the professor" was, in the next sentence, referred to with the grammatically plural pronoun "they." While your instructor may reasonably request that you use a singular pronoun when referring to a singular noun, in *Hello, Writer* we will be using **singular "they"** when the referent's gender is not clear. As *New York Times* columnist Farhad Manjoo eloquently states, the singular "they" is a "perfect pronoun" because "it's flexible [and] inclusive" and avoids "the risk of inadvertent misgendering," which is disrespectful and can be hurtful.

DIY 1.4a Get to Know Your Syllabus

Think of your syllabus as the rules for a game you'll be playing. With that concept in mind, reread the syllabus and try to answer the following questions:

- **What activities earn you the most points?** What are the major grades for? When are high stakes activities due? How much work seems to be expected for each one?

- **Which actions result in the biggest penalties?** How important is attendance, and what happens if you're consistently late or fail to show up for class? When you turn in your essays, will your instructor deduct points if the work is late? Too short? Doesn't meet all the requirements?

- **Which activities or actions might you expect to be rewarded for, but which don't seem important in this "game"?** For example, many students enter an English class believing that perfect grammar will result in an "A" grade, when sentence-level correctness may not be your instructor's top priority. The beginning of the semester is the time to synch your expectations of the course with your instructor's.

Learn to Accept Criticism — and Let Go

When you're willing to admit that you don't know everything, you can grow both as a person and as a student. Some people are naturally more open to hearing criticism and putting it to good use. They think of the advice they receive from an instructor not as a put-down but as an opportunity to improve.

These students are like the young children who initially inspired Carol Dweck: they "love a challenge" and can't wait to learn something they didn't know.

Other students, unfortunately, may hear that same criticism and blame themselves, giving up altogether. If you fall into this category, tell yourself that it's okay if the work you take on seems too challenging at first. The authors of *Make It Stick* remind us that you shouldn't assume that "you're doing something wrong if the learning feels hard." Learning *is hard*, and that's why it's so satisfying. Trying harder, thinking harder, and putting in more effort after a FAIL (first attempt in learning) will result in deeper, more useful knowledge.

Still, other students hear criticism and rather than blaming themselves, they blame their teachers. These students often complain because they can't admit that a perspective other than the one they hold could possibly be right. They also have trouble separating the criticism of a *task* they are performing inadequately (like writing an essay) from the *person* who is performing the task (themselves).

Most professors welcome thoughtful questions and comments about classroom policies and activities; these interactions show that you're engaged. However, if you find yourself questioning and quibbling with every classroom decision, your relationship with your professor may suffer. If you have a complaint, visiting your instructor during office hours will give you an opportunity to be heard. Make sure you're as well informed as you can be about the activity, assignment, or policy you want to discuss. Such preparation will help the instructor see you as mature and committed. If you must make a public complaint during class time, do so respectfully.

Still, sometimes you're going to find that you just don't like the person running your class. What do you do? The answer, of course, is to let it go. (Cue *Frozen*.) Even the most popular instructor on ratemyprofessor.com isn't going to click with every student, and that's okay. Remember that you're going to see your professor only for a few hours each week for a couple of months. You can succeed in your class without being best friends with the instructor.

> **DIY 1.4b** Profile Your Professor
>
> Write a one-paragraph profile of your professor that *only you will see*. Don't be mean-spirited but do be honest. What seem to be the pet peeves of your instructor? What aspects of the course have they emphasized? What do the two of you have in common? What do you anticipate will be your biggest challenges to getting along together? If your instructor inspires fear or anxiety in you, what strategies can you think of that might help you get past those negative emotions?

1.5 Getting to Know Your Classmates

Many students find they work best when they become part of a community of learners. When you can turn to your classmates to ask questions about the homework, ask for someone to read a draft of your essay, or collaborate on a revision, you're in much better shape than if you were going it alone.

You will want to provide the same sort of support for your classmates that they give to you, and chances are that your instructor has already tried to get everyone working together as a group toward the common goal of success. Many instructors use icebreaker activities on the first day of class, which help students meet and introduce one another. Try to remember the names and something about at least a few of your classmates; knowing just a few people can make a classroom much more inviting. Even in online writing classes, instructors try to design get-to-know-you opportunities.

Admittedly, building a positive group dynamic isn't always easy. Some students in your class may have vastly different personalities, political views, or life experiences, and you may not be crazy about the idea of spending extra time with them. Remember, though, that keeping the group harmonious will make it easier for you to find help when *you* need it, and building a community will make your class the sort of place where you, your peers, and your instructor want to be.

DIY 1.5a Learn Your Classmates' Names

It's always helpful to be able to refer to your classmates by name. Knowing and using someone's name creates a pathway between you. In an online/video class, you can easily take a screen shot to study faces and names. In a traditional class, try making a seating chart and listening carefully as the instructor takes attendance or calls on students. See if you can learn everyone's names by week 3 or 4.

An Invitation to Read

The following profile of Binghamton University student Julio Reyes was written in 2017 by *New York Times* staff writer John Otis as part of a series about students in need who have benefited from a direct assistance fund set up by the newspaper. As you will see, Reyes has overcome a number of obstacles that would have thwarted less persistent students: He clearly has both grit and a growth mindset.

Becoming a Confident College Student, With the Help of an "Angel"

JOHN OTIS

1   The police came to the door on the family's cleaning day. Julio Reyes, then 13, remembers that the apartment was spotless; his mother was a stickler for cleanliness.

2   After the authorities forced their way into the Lower East Side home, they scoured the place looking for drugs. Furniture was flipped over,

clothing tossed around, debris strewn everywhere, and somehow the toilet ended up broken.

3 "I was like, 'Really? We just cleaned,'" said Mr. Reyes, now 21, recalling the day, which ended with him being placed in foster care.

4 He and a brother eventually ended up in the custody of an aunt who had raised Mr. Reyes until he was 4. Though he called her "tia," Spanish for aunt, he considered her a mother. He took on adult responsibilities and was like a parent to many of his siblings.

5 "If you go back and ask my brothers and sister who raised them, they would tell you it was me," Mr. Reyes said.

6 Though Mr. Reyes was a leader at home, his tumultuous childhood left him more reserved at school. He saw himself as a geek, preferring the company of action figures or puzzles to other people. He was known as the student who played chess with the teachers and spent hours mastering solitary games like Sudoku and KenKen, and puzzles like Rubik's Cube.

7 In high school, Mr. Reyes began to shed his meek demeanor. "That's when I started figuring out who I am as a person," he said. "I started becoming more outgoing."

8 He nurtured a passion for dance, something he had previously enjoyed only if he could avoid being seen by others. "I stopped caring what people thought," he said. "People looked at me. I don't know if they judged me, but if they did I was like, 'This is what I like to do.'"

9 Despite the strides he made in building confidence, Mr. Reyes's plans beyond high school were murky. Family members had told him and his siblings how critical college was to their future.

10 During Mr. Reyes's junior year, he met Alex Blaise, a counselor with the Children's Aid Society. Mr. Blaise encouraged Mr. Reyes to apply to college and helped him with the process.

11 "He was an angel in disguise," Mr. Reyes said.

12 With Mr. Blaise's help, Mr. Reyes was accepted at Borough of Manhattan Community College. He balanced his studies with two jobs, one at a moving company and the other waiting tables at a diner.

13 "Sleeping was not a thing," he said.

14 After two years, a desire for change, motivated in part by a breakup, turned Mr. Reyes's attention to colleges outside New York City. He decided on Binghamton University and has been taking classes there since fall 2015.

15 A more self-assured person has emerged since he moved to the Binghamton area. "At first, I was in this bubble," he said. "And nobody was allowed in my bubble. Now, I don't have a bubble. I'm very open to meeting people."

Julio Reyes.
Heather Ainsworth/The New York Times/Redux

16   Mr. Reyes is working toward a bachelor's degree in accounting and expects to graduate in May 2018. He plans to become a certified public accountant or financial analyst.

17   "I am the best at math—the best," he said.

18   Mr. Reyes is also a member of the campus dance team, Quimbamba. Dancing will never be a career, he said. It is purely an expression of his heart, one that enlivens him. He brings the same discipline to his workout routine, waking at 5 a.m. to go to the gym, part of his effort to continually better himself and his life.

19   While on his way to accomplishing more than he may have thought possible a few years ago, Mr. Reyes refuses to accept congratulations for his successes.

20   "I prefer to get the job done, then celebrate its accomplishment when it is completely done," Mr. Reyes said. "It has more meaning and value when it's celebrated at the end, rather than at every minor step."

DIY 1.5b Think about Julio Reyes and a Growth Mindset

On your own, write notes in response to each of the following questions. Your instructor may also ask you to discuss your responses in a small group.

1. What challenges did Julio have as a boy and a young man? How, specifically, did he overcome them?

2. How has your own experience getting to college differed from that of Julio Reyes? How is it similar?

3. Using specific examples from the article, demonstrate that Julio Reyes has repeatedly demonstrated grit and a growth mindset.

Chapter 1 Checklist
Knowing Yourself and Your Community

☐ **As the semester begins, have you identified your strengths and weaknesses as a student?**

Knowing what you're good at and where you need improvement are important starting points for a successful academic career. Being aware of your strengths and weaknesses not just now, but also throughout the semester and your academic and work career, will help you to become a more successful person.

☐ **Do you have a plan to stay healthy this semester?**

Staying physically and mentally healthy during your college career is crucial. If you have health issues that need addressing, now is the time to do so. If you anticipate possibly having concerns later in the term, it's always reassuring to know in advance where you can go to deal with them.

☐ **Have you introduced yourself to your professors and alerted them to any special issues you will face this term?**

While it's still early in the semester, it's never too early to get to know your professors, to make a good impression, and to alert them to any unusual challenges you will be facing. That sometimes involves sending an email, staying a few minutes after class, or, better yet, stopping in for a visit during your professor's office hours. If you have a specific question, dropping by for even a few minutes is a good way to show you care about the course.

☐ **Have you begun meeting your classmates?**

Building community is a big part of college English classes, so your instructor has probably already begun this process. Now it's up to you to chat—at appropriate times, of course—with your fellow students. If you're shy, take advantage of small group situations to begin making a place for yourself among your peers.

1.6 Making It Stick

How will you get to know yourself and your community?

Working Together

1.6a Making Connections   Talk to five people in your class and try to find a similarity with each person. You can do that by asking questions that are general in nature or that relate to you specifically. Here are a few questions to get you started:

- Do you have a favorite sports team?
- What are your hobbies?
- What other classes are you taking?
- Do you speak a language other than English?

- Do you have a full-time or part-time job?
- What goals do you have after graduating from college?

Once you find a connection with one person, write down the person's name and what you have in common, then move on to another classmate. When you've finished, reassemble as a full group and discuss some of the commonalities among the students in your class.

1.6b Campus Services Field Trip   On your own or with a partner, visit *one* of the following campus resources (either in person or online):

- Academic Counseling
- Campus Bookstore
- Career Center
- Computer Lab
- Financial Aid
- Health and Wellness Center
- Main Library
- Student Services Center
- Writing/Learning Resource Center

Take a campus map with you (paper or digital), and do the following:

1. introduce yourself to whoever is behind the front desk or in charge of welcoming online students
2. find out the hours and services provided
3. take notes and bring back any information that is provided
4. be prepared to show your classmates where the service is, how to get there, and what to do when you arrive

Applying What You Know

1.6c What Am I Doing Here?   Answer the question, "What am I doing here?" This prompt is deliberately open ended, so feel free to respond to this question however you wish. However, be sure to provide concrete and specific examples to illustrate your response.

1.6d Who Am I as a Writer?   Describe yourself as a writer. Do you write quickly or slowly, happily or grudgingly? Do you tend to prefer academic writing or creative writing? Writing that focuses on other writing or writing that looks out directly to the world? Talk about the one or two most impactful and memorable events that have shaped you as a writer. Describe those events using appropriate sensory details — sight, sound, smell, touch, and taste — so that your reader can envision being right there beside you.

When you've finished, share your responses with a partner, a small group, or the entire class.

Invitations to Write

1.6e Growth Mindset

Shorter: In your own words, describe the difference between a growth mindset and a fixed mindset. Then describe one area of your life where you are currently demonstrating a growth mindset — that is, where your persistence is paying off in the retraining and reorganizing of your thinking and behavior.

Longer: Think of other areas in which you demonstrate a growth mindset. When do you see challenges as opportunities? When do you learn from your mistakes by adapting and being open to constructive criticism?

Then, write a bit about the areas of your life where you are more likely to demonstrate a fixed mindset. Which challenges cause you to give up or see your mistakes as permanent? When do you shun criticism, sticking with what you know instead? Give examples of both behaviors and discuss specific ways in which you can promote a positive mindset and eliminate negative thinking.

1.6f Your Academic Challenges

Shorter: Make a list of all the academic and life challenges you face this term, then choose the single most pressing issue on your mind — that is, the one you will have to face the soonest — and write a paragraph about how you will overcome that challenge. If ideas for coping with the problem don't occur to you right away, refer to the student success strategies described in this chapter.

Longer: Expand your list of academic and life challenges to the *two or three* that are the most pressing, then problem-solve ways to meet those challenges. Go online to investigate the campus resources you have available to you. If you have time, call or visit the resources you think will benefit you most. Ask staff members for additional resources for dealing with your issues. Report what you learned about your plans to meet these challenges.

1.6g Your Career Starts Now

Shorter: Research indicates that knowing what you want to do when you begin college is a strong incentive to completing your degree. However, many students enter their first year with only a vague idea of the career they want to pursue after college. To help you begin thinking about your ultimate goal, write a paragraph about the career you would most like to pursue if you had to choose it *right now.*

Longer: Do some research on your career of choice. Visit your campus's career center. Go online and see what people in that field are talking about. What qualifications do people need, and what are the big issues of the day? What educational background will you need to enter your career? What additional skills are required and how can you acquire some of them *before you graduate*?

1.6h Student Profile

Shorter: Briefly interview a classmate, then write a one- or two-paragraph profile of that person. Make sure to learn some specific facts about the person's life and reasons for wanting to attend college. Try to discover at least one or two interesting and unusual facts about your interviewee.

Longer: Delve further into the life of the person you are profiling. Find out about the person's college major, career goals, challenges, and achievements. Take careful notes and think about the "hook" you might open with to get readers interested in the subject of your profile. Use concrete and specific details from your interview to illustrate why particular people, beliefs, and dreams matter so much to your interviewee.

If you're writing a longer profile, reread John Otis's profile of Julio Reyes in this chapter (p. 12); notice how much ground Otis covers in less than seven hundred words and how he feels no obligation to stick to a five-paragraph formula. Instead, he allows each paragraph just as much space as it needs to explore its main idea. Otis also frequently uses direct quotes from Reyes to allow him to tell his story in his own words, and you may want to follow his lead when writing your own profile.

2

Becoming a College Reader

REFLECT

Write Before You Read | Activity to connect what's new with what you already know 19

READ & PRACTICE

DIY (Do-it-yourself) activities offer just-in-time support for all the skills in this book.

REFLECT

Write Before You Read What makes a strong reader? Drawing on any instruction you've received, the experiences you've had with reading, and any practical strategies you may have developed on your own, write a short letter of two or three paragraphs that gives advice to students who are just entering college and have some anxiety about the reading that they will face. If the previous sentence happens to describe you, too, that's fine. In that case, the letter might be especially useful!

2.1 Preparing to Read

Preparing to read might sound little mystifying for a college student. After all, what's involved besides cracking open a book or magazine, turning on your phone, or booting up your computer? Words appear and you read them. Simple, right?

That method of reading works pretty well some of the time, especially when you're scrolling through someone's social media feed or catching up on the latest sports or celebrity gossip. In those cases, you don't have much responsibility for remembering or interpreting the texts in front of you. Unless you're posting something yourself, if you misunderstand or forget what you've read, it doesn't really matter.

However, when you're reading assignments for your college classes, it *does* matter whether you've understood the material, and you will frequently be responsible for not just hearing and talking about readings in class, you'll also be writing in response to them.

Because active reading is such an important skill to master, we'll tackle it in this chapter and then keep coming back to it throughout the book.

> **Good to know:**
> 85 percent of college learning depends on active, careful reading. —Simpson & Nist, *Handbook of College Reading*

Know Yourself as a Reader

Even students who are solid readers can continue adding new and necessary skills to their toolkits. Indeed, the word "toolkit" is used quite a bit by reading experts. The idea is that having a set of strategies you can draw on whenever you face a new reading situation will better enable you to handle it. In discussions of new readings, you'll also often hear reference to the **text**, which typically means the body of the reading—the words on the page or screen or, in other cases, the combination of words and images. You can read an article or an essay—but you can also "read" an ad, a photo, or an infographic.

Even if you don't consider yourself a strong reader, chances are that you already have the makings of one. You know how to read the people and situations in your life, and you inevitably get better at interpreting them the more practice you have. Granted, you're not always going to correctly interpret the moods of your best friend or the warning signs in a video game. Over time, though, you *will* get better. Yes, learning can be hard work, but don't give up. Acknowledge the difficulty and confusion you face when engaging with a challenging reading, then sort through the challenges and push on. That's grit. As in every endeavor you face in college, the more questions you ask, the more you'll realize that the answers are all around you.

> **DIY 2.1a** Describe Yourself as a Reader
>
> Take a few minutes to describe yourself as a reader. How old were you when you learned to read? What sort of texts do you like and dislike? Are you a good "reader" of situations and people? Whether or not reading is a strength of yours, try to think of some situations in which being a good reader might make you more in control of your own life.

Find a Time and Place to Read

> Acknowledge the difficulty and confusion you face when engaging with a challenging reading, then sort through the challenges and push on. That's grit.

Before thinking about when and where you'll be doing the reading for your classes, take a minute to decide where you're going to stash your phone. If you are the type of person who needs to check in with your device every few minutes, your phone needs to be out of reach, preferably in another room. Granted, if your assigned reading is on a computer or a tablet, it will be tempting to wander off into the wired world, so you may want to print out short assignments and disconnect from the web altogether.

If you anticipate having a lot of reading this semester—and what college student doesn't?—try to find a time and place you can retreat to where you don't get distracted and you feel comfortable immersing yourself in someone else's words. For some people, the ideal is a crowded coffee shop in the middle of the day; they find the dull hum and occasional shouts of "Venti Mocha Frappuccino!" soothing. Most people, though, need silence to concentrate, making the quiet area of the campus library a preferable sanctuary for generations of college students. If the weather's pleasant, some people prefer public parks; others roll down their windows and study in their cars. During a global pandemic, your bedroom may be that quiet place.

However, if you can't escape to an ideal location at an ideal time, you'll need to create that space yourself as best you can. In a noisy environment, look for the least noisy corner and consider buying noise-canceling headphones, which you may want to connect to a device playing ambient music or electronically-generated noise.

Preview

Previewing a text is like watching a movie trailer—you don't expect to have the experience of seeing the whole film, but you do want to come away knowing the subject and some highlights. Granted, if you are previewing a long passage in a chemistry textbook, especially if you aren't a chemistry major, you may or may not feel much like "watching the movie," but at least you know what you're in for.

Tips for Previewing an Assigned Reading

- **Read the title and introduction.** The title will alert you to the topic of the reading, and if an editor has provided an introduction, you'll be given a mini-preview of what's to come.

- **Read the first paragraph.** Reading the first paragraph not only gives you a window into the topic, it also familiarizes you with the author's style. Informal or formal, personal or full of jargon—how an author writes will give you a clue about how they may be planning to approach the subject matter.

- **Skim the text.** While you're mostly letting your eyes glide over the page, it's good to drop into the text every few paragraphs and read an entire sentence that catches your eye. Again, skimming is like watching the preview for a movie or a video game—you miss the nuances, but you do get the big picture.

- **Look for headings and visuals.** Headings announce important subtopics. Visuals highlight or reinforce significant points, people, or data and can help bring the subject to life.

- **Read the final paragraph, then look to see if any discussion questions follow.** Authors tend to sum things up in their final paragraphs, giving you a bite-sized synopsis of what the reading has been about. The questions that follow the reading in the textbook indicate what the author wants you to learn from the reading.

Ask Questions

Between previewing the text and reading it, ask a few important questions to ensure that you're as prepared as possible when heading into the reading:

- **How does the reading relate to you personally?** Are you generally interested in the topic? Why or why not? Even if you don't have an immediate connection with the reading, try and find points of connection between you and the text as you go along; the more you can imagine yourself in the world of the text, the easier it will be to understand.

- **What do you already know about the topic?** Has your instructor mentioned anything in class that offers some insight into the reading? Have you ever read, or heard, about the topic in any previous context? Even a shred of previous knowledge can make a difficult topic slightly less daunting.

- **Who wrote the piece and why (and for whom)?** Especially in textbooks, there is often a short introduction, sometimes called a "headnote," about the author and the reading. While you don't necessarily need to know this information to understand a text, it does give you a clue about the writer's background and interests and helps you situate the reading in a larger context.

- **Does the structure of the piece look familiar or unfamiliar?** Even if you don't know the first thing about the topic, reading about it in a recognizable format can make learning more about it much easier. If you were to skim through this textbook, for instance, with its headings and questions and assignments, you'd probably feel like you were in familiar territory. If the structure of a piece looks unusual or unconventional, think about how it specifically differs from the types of readings you are normally assigned.

- **What is your responsibility toward the reading?** What will you have to do after you finish the reading? Will you be discussing it in class? Is there a quiz? On a deeper level: What does your instructor want you to learn? How can you use the material in your current class? In other classes? In the larger world?

DIY 2.1b Preview "Is College Worth It?"

The rest of this chapter will introduce additional suggestions for engaging with a text; most of them will be based on the following essay by David Leonhardt. For now, though, practice what you've just learned by previewing the reading:

- Read the title and introduction.
- Read the first paragraph.
- Skim the text.
- Read the final paragraph, then look to see if any discussion questions follow; write a few preview notes before you move on.

An Invitation to Read

Neilson Barnard/Getty Images

David Leonhardt is an Opinion-Editorial columnist and associate editorial page editor at *The New York Times*. Prior to
joining the Opinion department, Leonhardt was the founding
editor of The Upshot section, which emphasizes data visual-
ization and a graphics approach to news. Leonhardt has also
served as Washington bureau chief of the *Times* and wrote
"Economic Scene," a weekly economics column. In 2011,
he won the Pulitzer Prize for Commentary for his columns. Leonhardt wrote
"Is College Worth It?" in May 2014, but the following includes an updated graph.

Is College Worth It? (Clearly, New Data Say)

DAVID LEONHARDT

1   Some newly minted college graduates struggle to find work. Others
accept jobs for which they feel overqualified. Student debt, meanwhile, has
topped $1 trillion.

2   It's enough to create a wave of questions about whether a college
education is still worth it.

3   A new set of income statistics answers
those questions quite clearly: Yes, college is
worth it, and it's not even close. For all the
struggles that many young college graduates face, a four-year degree has probably
never been more valuable.

4   The pay gap between college graduates
and everyone else reached a record high last
year, according to the new data, which is
based on an analysis of Labor Department
statistics by the Economic Policy Institute
in Washington. Americans with four-year
college degrees made 98 percent more an
hour on average in 2013 than people without a degree. That's up from 89 percent five
years earlier, 85 percent a decade earlier
and 64 percent in the early 1980s.

5   There is nothing inevitable about
this trend. If there were more college

The singer Jill Scott, who was being given an honorary
doctorate, at graduation ceremonies at Temple University in
Philadelphia this month. The pay disparity between those with
college degrees and those without continues to grow.

AP Photo/The Philadelphia Inquirer, David Swanson

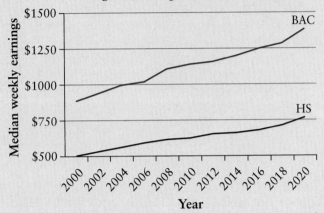

Median weekly earnings by education level, bachelor's degree (BAC) vs. high school diploma (HS), 2000–2020

College graduates earn more than those without a degree, and the gap in earnings is growing.

Data from Bureau of Labor Statistics 2020.

graduates than the economy needed, the pay gap would shrink. The gap's recent growth is especially notable because it has come after a rise in the number of college graduates, partly because many people went back to school during the Great Recession. That the pay gap has nonetheless continued growing means that we're still not producing enough of them.

6 "We have too few college graduates," says David Autor, an M.I.T. economist, who was not involved in the Economic Policy Institute's analysis. "We also have too few people who are prepared for college."

7 It's important to emphasize these shortfalls because public discussion today—for which we in the news media deserve some responsibility—often focuses on the undeniable fact that a bachelor's degree does not guarantee success. But of course it doesn't. Nothing guarantees success, especially after 15 years of disappointing economic growth and rising inequality.

8 When experts and journalists spend so much time talking about the limitations of education, they almost certainly are discouraging some teenagers from going to college and some adults from going back to earn degrees. (Those same experts and journalists are sending their own children to college and often obsessing over which one.) The decision not to attend college for fear that it's a bad deal is among the most economically irrational decisions anybody could make in 2014.

9 The much-discussed cost of college doesn't change this fact. According to a paper by Mr. Autor published Thursday in the journal *Science*, the true cost of a college degree is about negative $500,000. That's right: Over the long run, college is cheaper than free. Not going to college will cost you about half a million dollars.

10   Mr. Autor's paper—building on work by the economists Christopher Avery and Sarah Turner—arrives at that figure first by calculating the very real cost of tuition and fees. This amount is then subtracted from the lifetime gap between the earnings of college graduates and high school graduates. After adjusting for inflation and the time value of money, the net cost of college is negative $500,000, roughly double what it was three decades ago.

11   This calculation is necessarily imprecise, because it can't control for any pre-existing differences between college graduates and nongraduates—differences that would exist regardless of schooling. Yet other research, comparing otherwise similar people who did and did not graduate from college, has also found that education brings a huge return.

12   In a similar vein, the new Economic Policy Institute numbers show that the benefits of college don't go just to graduates of elite colleges, who typically go on to earn graduate degrees. The wage gap between people with only a bachelor's degree and people without such a degree has also kept rising.

13   Tellingly, though, the wage premium for people who have attended college without earning a bachelor's degree—a group that includes community-college graduates—has not been rising. The big economic returns go to people with four-year degrees. Those returns underscore the importance of efforts to reduce the college dropout rate, such as those at the University of Texas, which Paul Tough described in a recent *Times Magazine* article.

14   But what about all those alarming stories you hear about indebted, jobless college graduates?

15   The anecdotes may be real, yet the conventional wisdom often exaggerates the problem. Among four-year college graduates who took out loans, average debt is about $25,000, a sum that is a tiny fraction of the economic benefits of college. (My own student debt, as it happens, was almost identical to this figure, in inflation-adjusted terms.) And the unemployment rate in April [2014] for people between 25 and 34 years old with a bachelor's degree was a mere 3 percent.

16   I find the data from the Economic Policy Institute especially telling because the institute—a left-leaning research group—makes a point of arguing that education is not the solution to all of the economy's problems. That is important, too. College graduates, like almost everyone else, are suffering from the economy's weak growth and from the disproportionate share of this growth flowing to the very richest households.

17   The average hourly wage for college graduates has risen only 1 percent over the last decade, to about $32.60. The pay gap has grown mostly because the average wage for everyone else has fallen—5 percent, to about $16.50. "To me, the picture is people in almost every kind of job not being able to see their wages grow," Lawrence Mishel, the institute's president, told me. "Wage growth essentially stopped in 2002."

18   From the country's perspective, education can be only part of the solution to our economic problems. We also need to find other means for lifting living standards—not to mention ways to provide good jobs for people without college degrees.

19   But from almost any individual's perspective, college is a no-brainer. It's the most reliable ticket to the middle class and beyond. Those who question the value of college tend to be those with the luxury of knowing their own children will be able to attend it.

20   Not so many decades ago, high school was considered the frontier of education. Some people even argued that it was a waste to encourage Americans from humble backgrounds to spend four years of life attending high school. Today, obviously, the notion that everyone should attend 13 years of school is indisputable.

21   But there is nothing magical about 13 years of education. As the economy becomes more technologically complex, the amount of education that people need will rise. At some point, 15 years or 17 years of education will make more sense as a universal goal.

22   That point, in fact, has already arrived.

DIY 2.1c Ask Questions about the Reading

Answer the following questions about "Is College Worth It?"

- Who wrote the text and why?
- Does the structure of the text look familiar or unfamiliar?
- What is your responsibility toward the reading?
- Which paragraph or passage made the most vivid impression on you? Why did you find it so memorable?

2.2   Reading Actively

If you've ever sprawled out on a couch and stared at a TV program without really watching it, you know the feeling of *passive* viewing. Rather than becoming engaged in what is happening, predicting what will happen next, questioning the characters' motives, and discussing your reactions with another viewer, you simply sit there like a bump on a log.

Passive reading is a lot like passive TV watching. Your eyes run across the words on the page or screen, and you have a dim idea of what they're saying, but you're not really engaged in the material. By the time you finish passively reading a text of any length, you can barely recall what it was about, and you'd have a hard time explaining its finer points to anyone.

Passive reading won't help much when you're facing a college-level reading assignment. Instead, you'll want to adopt the *active* reading strategies outlined in the coming pages. When you read actively, you are in a constant conversation with the author. *Sure*, you think, *I can see your point, but I'm not sure why you said* x. Or: *Yes, you're correct about* y, *but why in the world would you think that about* z? Rather than waiting passively to be "filled up" with information, you assume that you're going to have to go out and actively get what you need from the reading.

The following active reading strategies should help you engage with any text you are reading:

- predicting
- questioning
- challenging the text
- making connections
- visualizing
- summarizing as you read
- thinking out loud

Predict as You Read

When you actively watch a TV show, you anticipate what will happen next. You base your predictions on what you know about the type of program you're viewing, as well as whatever has previously happened in the series and in the particular episode you're in the middle of watching. Similarly, when you're reading and predicting what will happen next in a written text, you take what you know of the particular article—the title, the author's biography, and whatever you've read up to that point—and you combine that with what you know about the topic overall.

If you're familiar with the topic and the author, you'll probably be able to predict what comes next with some accuracy. However, even if the text presents you with entirely new material, once you begin reading, you'll almost certainly begin making assumptions about what's ahead.

Question as You Read

Earlier in the chapter, there was a discussion of the sort of questions you might ask about a text before you begin reading it: Who wrote it, and why? How does the reading relate to you? What are you supposed to do with it after you've finished reading? As you read, you may continue to ask, and answer, those questions, but you'll also be coming up with questions you had no idea you wanted to ask. In fact, the more you practice being an active reader, the more frequently your response to an author's statement will begin with one of the following words: *Who? What? When? How? Where?* And, most important, *Why?*

Challenge the Text

As you read, you will often identify a problem in the text. The difficulty may not be the fault of the author—it may just be a piece of information you don't understand—but if you stop and think, *How can that be?* or *That doesn't makes sense to me*, then you're at a place where you are challenging the text.

> **If you stop and think, *How can that be?* or *That doesn't makes sense to me*, then you're at a place where you are challenging the text.**

At this stage of your reading, you'll be playing what Peter Elbow, author of the provocatively titled book *Writing without Teachers*, calls the "doubting game." According to Elbow, "[b]y trying hard to doubt ideas, we can discover hidden contradictions, bad reasoning, or other weaknesses in them—especially in the case of ideas that seem true or attractive. We are using doubting as a *tool* in order to scrutinize and test."

While Elbow goes on to praise "the believing game," in which readers look for ways to embrace the text they are reading, it's useful to understand that uncritical acceptance of an author's ideas and arguments on a first reading generally leads readers to disengage intellectually from the text.

Make Connections

Obviously, not every reading assignment will have a deeply personal resonance for everyone. If you're a STEM major, a poem in your literature textbook may not have quite the same zing as it will for an English major. And English majors who somehow find themselves reading a report about fragmentation of polystyrene exposed to sunlight may not go wild learning about the chemistry of marine pollution. Nevertheless, it pays to try and connect with the reading in front of you, no matter how far afield it is from your core interests. Even when you're not making personal connections between the text and your own life, you can always try and situate the reading in the context of the larger world or use it to practice academic questions: What problem is this author trying to solve?

Visualize as You Read

Visualizing what you read is a great way to remember it. This may be more difficult in subjects like math, but even there, you are always "picturing" equations. Indeed, authors often go out of their way to use what literary critics call "images"—words and phrases that relate not only to things you can see but also to things that you can touch, hear, smell, and taste.

Psychologist Donna Wilson argues that transforming the nonfiction material you are reading into a "mini-film," or a "brain movie," will lead to a better understanding of the material and foster the habit of reading "with more care and concentration."

Summarize as You Read

To summarize a reading is to give a brief statement of an author's main point(s). Indeed, you have probably been summarizing as you read this book, whether you realized it or not. Granted, those summaries were probably very brief ("Play the doubting game," "Visualizing is good," etc.) and mostly unconscious, but they did serve the function of encapsulating what you perceived to be the main points of a sentence or paragraph or section.

Not surprisingly, summarizing on a more consistent and formal basis can make a very big difference in how much of a reading you retain over time, which is why we will take a closer look at this activity later in the chapter (see p. 33).

Think Out Loud

One of the best strategies for improving your reading skills is to develop your "metacognition," that is, thinking about how you think. To do that, you'll need to know what it "sounds" like when you think, which will require you to think out loud. This approach, used extensively in the Reading Apprenticeship program described in Schoenbach, Greenleaf, and Murphy's book *Reading for Understanding*, doesn't *exactly* reproduce the type of thinking you do in your head—for one thing, it's usually much slower—but it's a very helpful tool in giving you, and others, an insight into your thought processes as you read.

There's no single "correct" way to think out loud while reading, but it is useful to employ the active reading strategies we've just been discussing. As an example, take another look at the opening paragraphs of "Is College Worth It?" and imagine how a reader might respond to the text. The active reading strategies are named in the margin, Leonhardt's text is in regular font, and the reader's thoughts are in italics.

30

CHAPTER 2
Becoming a College Reader

Questioning

Visualizing/Making Connections

Predicting

Challenging the Text

Summarizing

Some newly minted college graduates struggle to find work. Others accept jobs for which they feel overqualified. [True, but isn't that always the case?] Student debt, meanwhile, has topped $1 trillion. [Wow! It's such a huge figure I don't even really know what it means. Like if you stacked a trillion dollar bills would it reach the moon?]

It's enough to create a wave of questions about whether a college education is still worth it. [Catchy intro. At this point I don't know what the answer to the question is, even though the subtitle seems to be giving it away. But since the opening made it sound like college isn't worth it, I'm guessing the author is going to go against my expectations and say it is.]

A new set of income statistics answers those questions quite clearly. [What are "income statistics"? Why doesn't he just say "income" or "annual salary"?] Yes, college is worth it, and it's not even close. For all the struggles that many young college graduates face, a four-year degree has probably never been more valuable. [College is worth it—I knew it! And this sounds a lot like a thesis statement to me.]

DIY 2.2 Actively Read "Is College Worth It?"

Practice reading and thinking out loud and record yourself doing so on your phone or computer. Read paragraphs 4 and 5 of the article "Is College Worth It?" out loud and interrupt your reading anytime you have a thought about the text. Say your thoughts out loud, too.

Write notes about the experience after you've listened to the recording a couple times. What active reading strategies did you use to make sense of Leonhardt's article? What is the hardest part of thinking out loud about a reading? How did you overcome it? If you didn't have much to say about the reading, how can you improve your thinking-aloud skills in the future?

2.3 Annotating to Record Your Active Reading

"Annotations" are explanatory notes or comments added to a text, and experienced readers move from thinking out loud to thinking with a pen or pencil or keyboard. One huge advantage of annotating is that it's permanent—you can go back later on and see what you thought. Annotating is just another way of having a conversation with a text. Like thinking out loud, annotating forces you to slow down and be responsible for and attentive to the material you are reading.

In high school, you may have been told not to write in your textbook, since it was owned by the school. In college, however, instructors strongly encourage writing in your books—or making notes in digital texts and e-books. The longer and more complicated the reading, the more likely you will want to leave behind substantial signs that you've been there, interacting with the work. You might even think of your annotations as the early stages of a draft—your earliest responses to a text.

All of the active reading strategies you learned about earlier in this chapter also apply to annotation: predicting, questioning, challenging the text, making connections, visualizing, and summarizing. Here's how these actions might take shape.

Underline Important Passages

The sentences you linger over when you're reading—whether silently or aloud—are the very sentences you'll want to underline in an annotation. Underlining important passages also enables you to quickly revisit them when you're hunting for material for an essay or trying to remember what to study for in an exam. It's important not to overdo it, though; if you underline too much, you may have trouble locating passages later. That means sometimes you'll want to underline only significant phrases or words, rather than underlining entire sentences.

If you have successfully wielded a neon highlighter in the past, that may continue to work for you. However, know that overenthusiastic highlighting can drown the really important material in a sea of yellow or orange or blue. Even selective highlighting tends to overwhelm the page.

Circle Unfamiliar Words or Ideas

Part of the fun of encountering a new text is the strong possibility that you'll meet new words and ideas. (Hello, new idea.) Close reading nearly always involves *rereading*, so when you first encounter these unfamiliar items, circle them and move on. If you stop to look up every unfamiliar word or idea, particularly in a difficult text, especially on a first reading, you may lose track of the main points that the author is making.

Instead, do your best to figure out the words or ideas mean by thinking about the context in which they occur. After you've completed the reading, spend some time learning about those new words and concepts, making sure to write their definitions in the margins of your text. Then give the text another read, knowing you can now fill in those earlier gaps.

Draw a Picture

Even if you're not artistically inclined, sometimes a picture is still worth a thousand words. Making your own drawing of ideas in a text keeps the visual in your head; you're unlikely to forget a passage you associate with even the most rudimentary sketch.

In the first paragraph of "Is College Worth It?," for instance, we find this sentence: "Student debt, meanwhile, has topped $1 trillion." To emphasize the enormity of that amount of money, you might draw a stack of dollar bills reaching from Earth toward the Moon. (One trillion one-dollar bills would reach almost one-quarter of the way to the Moon.) The simple act of putting a pencil to paper might make that almost incomprehensible amount of money more concrete and real.

Some readers sketch to remember ideas or make connections.

> **DIY 2.3a** Draw to Visualize a Term or Idea from the Reading
>
> Choose a memorable concept or term from "Is College Worth It?" or any text you are currently reading and make a drawing that reflects that concept or term. Don't worry about your artistic skills — stick figures are okay.

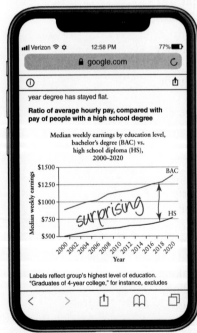

You can often annotate a digital text on a smartphone or a tablet.

Alexey Boldin/Shutterstock.com

Write in the Margins

As you begin to annotate, you'll notice that many textbooks have deliberately wide margins to allow for student comments. If you're lucky enough to have those wide spaces, take advantage of this built-in opportunity to converse with the text. If the margins of a brief assigned reading are narrow, consider making photocopies that allow you to shrink the size of the font and increase the size of the margins. If you are renting or borrowing your book and you feel you just can't write in it, another common workaround is to use sticky notes.

You may be reading this book or a class reading on your tablet, laptop, or phone. If so, some e-readers and apps allow you to make digital annotations. A few of these programs permit annotators to go well beyond what they can do on paper, allowing readers to highlight text and link it to the Internet. You might also be able to add audio commentary and images. For an online reading, it is easy to take screenshots of key passages, visuals, or data and mark up the text, as in the example here.

But what, exactly, are you writing in the margins? In her *English Journal* article "Beyond the Yellow Highlighter," Carol Porter-O'Donnell recommends that students do the following:

- summarize

- make predictions

- formulate opinions

- make connections

- ask questions

- write reflections/reactions/comments

- look for patterns/repetitions

As Porter-O'Donnell points out, using these strategies for interacting with a text "slow[s] down the reading," thereby helping to bring to light "the complex thought process involved in making sense of text."

Not all marginal annotations need to take the form of extended comments, of course. Often, you'll simply jot down a keyword or phrase. And some students like to keep a cheat sheet or key to the highlighting marks they frequently make. A check mark (√), for instance, could mean that the author made a good point, while an asterisk (*) might indicate that a passage needs rereading, and so on. Obviously, graphic marginal annotations don't require the same depth of thought as written comments, but they do help you to return quickly to key parts of the text.

If you have room, use lines or arrows to connect related ideas. Your text shouldn't look like it's been taken over by a mad scientist, but you want to be able to easily connect ideas that go together or that contradict one another.

See below for a sample annotated reading, paragraphs 9 through 11 of "Is College Worth It?" Again, there's no single correct way to annotate a reading, but this one does use many of the tools we've just been discussing. In general, the more fully and intelligently you mark the page, the more you will take away from the reading *and* the more you will have to come back to when you need to review it and respond to it.

Sample annotated paragraphs

9   The much-discussed cost of college doesn't change this fact. According to a paper by Mr. Autor published Thursday in the journal *Science*, the true cost of a college degree is about negative $500,000. That's right Over the long run, college is cheaper than free. Not going to college will cost you about half a million dollars.

Wow!

Reputable source?

If this is true, it's a very convincing argument

Find out more about Autor – is he biased in any way?

Important: you have to graduate from, not just attend, college

Good - Leonhardt admits that ½ a million is a guesstimate - that makes him more credible IMO

10   Mr. Autor's paper—building on work by the economists Christopher Avery and Sarah Turner—arrives at that figure first by calculating the very real cost of tuition and fees. This amount is then subtracted from the lifetime gap between the earnings of college graduates and high school graduates. After adjusting for inflation and the time value of money, the net cost of college is negative $500,000, roughly double what it was three decades ago.

This sounds impressive but I'd like to see the actual numbers

11   This calculation is necessarily imprecise, because it can't control for any pre-existing difference between college graduates and nongraduates—differences that would exist regardless of schooling. Yet other research, comparing otherwise similar people who did and did not graduate from college, has also found that education brings a huge return.

What other research? At least name the sources

These 3 paragraphs are the core of Leonhardt's argument in favor of graduating from college

---

DIY 2.3b Annotate "Is College Worth It?"

Review the active reading strategies in section 2.3. Then, using the "Sample annotated paragraphs" as a model, annotate the next three paragraphs (12–14) of "Is College Worth It?" (p. 25).

Summarize After You Read

A summary is a concise statement of the main points of a text; it provides a brief recap. While summarizing *as* you read happens quickly, in real time, summarizing *after* you read is a more deliberate and thoughtful process. In order to summarize well, you first need to identify the main points and separate them from the supporting details. As an example, let's take another look at paragraph 3 of "Is College Worth It?," which is jam-packed with statistics:

Original text

3   The pay gap between college graduates and everyone else reached a record high last year, according to the new data, which is based on an analysis of Labor Department statistics by the Economic Policy Institute in Washington. Americans with four-year college degrees made 98 percent more an hour on average in 2013 than people without a degree. That's up from 89 percent five years earlier, 85 percent a decade earlier and 64 percent in the early 1980s.

The paragraph's topic sentence provides us with the crucial point that the discrepancy between pay for college graduates "and everyone else" has reached record highs. However, we don't realize how big that gap is until the next sentence, when we learn that it is "98 percent more an hour." The paragraph's final sentence indicates that the figure has gone up considerably in recent years, but all those numbers are merely supporting details, the very things we *don't* want to get in the way of our summary.

Here is one student's first try at summarizing this paragraph's main point, which does leave the details out:

Student's draft summary

Data analysis shows that the disparity in pay between those with and without college degrees has grown so much in the past thirty years that college graduates now receive almost twice as much per hour as those without degrees.

That's a good start, but it's almost as long as the original passage. A more effective summary would be shorter and focused on the two main elements of the paragraph: (1) college graduates and (2) their superior pay. The student's second try results in a much tighter summary:

Student's revised summary

College graduates earn almost twice as much as those without degrees.

If you were introducing this summary into an essay, you'd want to identify its source. You can do so with signal language that mentions the author or by including the author's name in parentheses after your summary. Citing the source in this way—even when it's just the source of an idea that you've put into your own words—means you'll steer clear of **plagiarism,** or the unacknowledged use of someone else's words or ideas. (See 17.7 for more on avoiding plagiarism.) Here's that same summary attached to its source:

Student's final summary

According to David Leonhardt, college graduates earn almost twice as much as those without degrees.

Tips for Writing a Summary

As you practice writing summaries, remember the following tips:

- A short summary uses only your own words.

- Longer summaries may very briefly borrow the writer's language, but you must place those words and phrases in quotation marks.

- A summary should include only the main points of a text and few, if any, supporting details.

- A summary should be accurate and objective—you're telling only what is in the text, *not* what you feel about it.

- In many cases, a summary should indicate its source, including the piece's author and title.

Note that while many summaries in academic essays are single sentences, a good summary doesn't necessarily have to be just one sentence, but a summary is usually significantly shorter than the original.

Chunk Ideas

One reading and learning skill that you may already be practicing is the ability to "chunk" material together by grouping smaller parts into a larger whole. As Terry Doyle and Todd Zakrajsek note in their book *The New Science of Learning*, "[If] you can find patterns in material you are studying, and thus create chunks, it is much easier to learn and remember."
    Chunking is a particularly valuable skill to have when you are summarizing, as it forces you to understand each small part before having to account for the whole. In the book *Reading for Understanding*, chunking is compared to eating a pizza: "Even if you're really hungry, you can't eat a whole pizza at once. You have to eat it a little bit at a time, in slices. Understanding text is similar to eating pizza. Though you may want to read a large amount at once, you may not be able to understand it unless you take it in bits and pieces."

DIY 2.3c Write One-Sentence Summaries

Choose any paragraph from *the second half* of "Is College Worth It?" — that is, paragraphs 12 to 22 (pp. 25–26) — and write a one-sentence summary of that paragraph.
    Then practice your chunking skills by writing one-sentence summaries for two or three continuous paragraphs in Leonhardt's essay. What ideas are easier to understand once you have the smaller bits?

Make a Reverse Outline

While you will often want to summarize an entire article, or a longer work like a report, in a single sentence, there will also be times when it's important to understand a work in detail. In that case, you may decide to summarize the reading in a "reverse outline."

When you make an outline prior to composing an essay, you're only projecting what you *think* will appear on the page. Fortunately, in a reverse outline you already have a text—the reading you are trying to understand. All you need to do is briefly state what is there on the page. It's best to look at the reading paragraph by paragraph, grouping similar paragraphs together whenever possible.

The first half of a reverse outline of "Is College Worth It?" follows. Note that special emphasis is given to the thesis, and each summary is a complete sentence.

Sample reverse outline

Para. 1–2: Many college graduates are un- or underemployed and in a great deal of debt, which leads to the question: Is college worth it?

Para. 3: Thesis: New statistics comparing employees with and without degrees show that college is, indeed, more valuable than ever.

Para. 4: A huge pay gap exists between those with and without a college degree.

Para. 5–6: America is not producing enough college graduates for the workforce.

Para. 7–8: The media undervalues the importance of college degrees.

Para. 9–11: People who graduate from college will, over the course of their careers, earn approximately $500,000 more than those who don't.

As you can see from this sample, a reverse outline not only requires you to understand and summarize the article, but it also provides you with a clear synopsis of your assigned reading. This document will come in very handy if you are asked to write about the work.

DIY 2.3d Complete a Reverse Outline of "Is College Worth It?"

Complete the reverse outline that begins in the sample above, creating summaries of paragraphs 12 to 22 of "Is College Worth It?"

2.4 Reading Critically

After musing over the difference between active reading and critical reading, one of my students said that critical reading is "active reading on steroids." That phrase has stuck in my head all these years because there's a certain truth to it. Reading critically, like reading actively, means engaging with the text in a hands-on way, but it also means looking harder at the text, posing tougher questions, and not accepting easy, unproven answers.

When you encounter a difficult text for the first time, you're going to be focused mostly on comprehension—deciphering what the text is trying to tell you. However, as you return to the text with more and more confidence, you'll begin to challenge the author when necessary. Even when you agree with the author's position, you'll be concurring because you have examined and validated the ideas that support the text's argument.

As you might imagine, reading critically is closely aligned with thinking critically. This means that you'll want to remain open to new ideas and new theories, but only when there is evidence to support them. Critical readers are always digging deeper into a text as they try to understand the author's rhetorical situation. They investigate

- *why* the piece was written

- *who* it was written for

- *how* the writer sees the world

- to *what* extent the text relies on fact rather than opinion

Identify the Writer's Purpose

When you read a piece of writing, you can usually discern its primary purpose(s). To take a basic example, the instruction manual for assembling a bookcase is writing that informs or explains. A textbook's main purpose is also to *inform* and *explain*, but learning how to write an academic essay can be a much more complex task than attaching the sides to the shelves of a bookcase. An article like "Is College Worth It?" informs its readers about the size of the wage gap between those with and without a college degree; however, its primary purpose seems to be to *persuade* readers to believe that college is worth the investment of money and time.

Of course, any piece of writing more sophisticated than an instruction manual is likely to have multiple purposes. While the primary purpose of *Hello, Writer* is to *inform* you about how to write an academic essay, throughout the book, I'm also trying to *persuade* you to accept my particular version of how to accomplish that goal.

Purposes for writing can include the following:

informing	explaining
persuading	reflecting
analyzing	evaluating
proposing	synthesizing
inspiring	action

Identify the Writer's Audience

Usually, the writer's audience is dictated by the writer's purpose. The audience of a manual explaining how to put together a bookcase, for instance, is clearly people who have purchased the unassembled bookcase. The audience for *Hello, Writer* is equally clear: college-age composition students. However, there is another, perhaps equally important, audience for this book, and that is the instructors who have asked their students to read it. After all, if instructors don't find the book useful, they won't assign it to their students.

The specific audience for Leonhardt's "Is College Worth It?" is less clear. On the one hand, it appears to be directed at people who are considering dropping out of college and need both encouragement and concrete reasons to stick it out. On the other hand, the article originally appeared in the data-driven "Upshot" section of the *New York Times*, which may not be the go-to site for people struggling to complete a degree. You might come to the conclusion that the audience could include college administrators or parents of high school students or recent college graduates looking to justify their decisions.

If Leonhardt genuinely wants to reach those about to drop out of college, is he really publishing in the best venue? And if his real audience is readers of the *New York Times*, how does he expect them to react to his article? There may be no easy answers, but asking questions about audience is a good first step to discerning which readers Leonhardt is really writing for.

Identify the Writer's Point of View

Even when they try and maintain strict objectivity, all writers are inevitably affected by the details of their own life stories, which include where and when they grew up, the level and orientation of their education, their work experiences, the opinions of their friends and family members, how much

> **Critical Reading Tip 1: Purpose**
> As you read, identify the writer's motivations, which may shift from paragraph to paragraph. Is the text merely informative, or does the writer want to justify an opinion or persuade you to adopt a certain belief?

> **Critical Reading Tip 2: Audience**
> Try to identify clues indicating the author's likely audience. Are you among the intended readers? If not, how effective is the writer at persuading you to adopt the text's argument? If there are multiple audiences, do the writer's goals seem at cross-purposes in any way?

sleep they had the previous night, and so on. All writers make *assumptions* about the world: even without direct proof, they believe that certain things are true. In making these assumptions, writers necessarily betray their biases, their own partiality for a particular opinion or point of view.

In our politically charged times, when everyone appears to be on one side of a fence or the other, impartiality can seem harder than ever to find. Nevertheless, while bias has a way of creeping in no matter how hard a writer tries to prevent it, many readers still value the work of authors who at least *strive* for objectivity.

Usually, you can tell when writers are taking a biased approach toward a topic. Be wary of an author's objectivity if you notice the following qualities in a piece of writing:

- The language is inflated and extreme.

- Only one side of the story is being told.

- Important facts are left out.

- Complex arguments are generalized in such a way that they only prove the speaker's argument.

And, of course, readers, too, have their assumptions and biases. We can't help seeing a subject through the lens of our own beliefs and experiences. While that reality may make finding the "truth" of any nonfactual issue a challenge, knowing that both writers and readers are swayed by their own imperfect judgments helps us understand why it is so easy to disagree with someone whose way of thinking is different than our own.

Distinguish Fact from Opinion

A fact is something that is indisputable; it can be empirically proven to be true. An opinion is a belief or view or judgment that is weaker or stronger, depending on the evidence used to support it. "The earth is round" is a fact. "The earth looks flat, so it must be flat" is an opinion based on faulty evidence. "The earth is flat because I saw a video about it on Instagram" is an opinion based on even faultier evidence.

In the rapid-fire pace of much contemporary writing, especially unedited online personal writing, it can be difficult to separate fact from opinion. Fortunately, there are reliable, nonpartisan fact-checking sites, such as Snopes and PolitiFact, that will help you assess the truth of many of the most common—and outrageous—claims being made online at any given time. And even when you haven't checked a claim being made by a writer, you can frequently detect the tilt toward opinion and away from fact when you recognize the biased tone described in the previous section. Again, be wary of writing that exaggerates, seems to be leaving out important information, only presents one side of an argument, or presents opinions as facts.

Critical Reading Tip 3: Point of View

When information about the author is presented alongside a reading, read it. Perhaps also do an online search to learn a few details about the author. As you read, take note of the author's point of view, always remaining aware of any biases that may be shaping what and how the material is presented. Be aware, also, of your own preexisting assumptions and biases about the topic.

Critical Reading Tip 4: Fact versus Opinion

As you read, remain skeptical. Play the doubting game (see page 28). Don't believe something just because it has been published in print or online. While people have a right to their own opinions, simply stating something doesn't make it true.

The term "fake news," for instance, which came into common use in 2015, was supposedly a straightforward term for news that wasn't true. However, its real meaning soon became clear: Most people who labeled something "fake news" did so not because the news was inaccurate but because they did not like the facts that were being presented.

DIY 2.4a Practice Critical Reading

Take another look at "Is College Worth It?" (p. 23) and practice critical reading by answering the following questions based on the strategies we've just discussed:

1. What is Leonhardt's purpose in writing "Is College Worth It?"
2. Who is the audience for "Is College Worth It?" (Be more specific than just "readers of *The New York Times*.")
3. Describe Leonhardt's point of view in the article.
4. Make a list of what you regard as *facts* in "Is College Worth It?" Then list those statements that seem to represent Leonhardt's *opinion*.

Use a Double-Entry Journal

Try using a double-entry journal to focus your critical reading skills on a specific quotation. Rather than responding to a general impression you have of the reading, you must locate the exact place in the text that you want to engage with, which helps prevent you from exaggerating or misrepresenting the writer's position.

As you can see from the following example, the double-entry journal is formatted simply as two columns. On one side is a quotation that represents an important idea from the text. On the other side is your response to that quotation. This format allows you to respond to ideas at much greater length than you can in the margins of a book page.

Quotation	Response
"Some newly minted college graduates struggle to find work. Others accept jobs for which they feel overqualified. Student debt, meanwhile, has topped $1 trillion."	This is a really smart opening for an essay trying to convince students to graduate from college. It comes right out and states the sort of things you hear all the time: that college grads can't find work, or they have to take low-wage jobs that don't have anything to do with what they studied. And to top everything off, college graduates are in a ton of debt when they almost certainly could have got the same lousy jobs without ever attending college. The fact that Leonhardt doesn't hide from potential counterarguments makes him seem honest and trustworthy.

(Continued)

Quotation	Response
"Over the long run, college is cheaper than free. Not going to college will cost you about half a million dollars."	This is an interesting way to phrase Leonhardt's point about college grads making $500,000 more over their lifetimes than high school graduates. Instead, he makes it sound like you're actually going to have to pay a half million dollars—although he doesn't say to whom—if you don't graduate from college. That's a scary thought.

DIY 2.4b Respond to Quotations from "Is College Worth It?"

Draw a line down the center of a piece of paper or make two columns in a digital document. Then choose two or three quotations that you want to explore further from "Is College Worth It?" or another assigned reading. Write the quotations on the left, leaving plenty of space between them so that you can comment in the right-hand column, keeping your focus on identifying the writer's purpose, audience, and point of view, and distinguishing between fact and opinion.

2.5 Focusing on Vocabulary

In your first reading of a new text, as mentioned earlier in the chapter, it's best not to get too caught up in knowing the exact meaning and nuance of every unfamiliar word. Instead, read through to the end, circling any unfamiliar words and phrases and making guesses about their meaning.

Unless the reading is highly technical or full of jargon, you can often figure out what a word means by the context in which it occurs. How, for instance, would you define the made-up word "blugstenfrejo" in the following sentence: "I need to blugstenfrejo my homework before I go out to dinner tonight"?

In this case, you might guess the meaning of the word was something like "finish," "complete," or "do," as those are the most logical synonyms. Just to be sure, you might circle the word and jot down a question in the margin, but it wouldn't be worth interrupting your reading to confirm the meaning of a word you were 95 percent sure you could define correctly.

Of course, if one unknown word keeps reappearing, and you have no idea what it means, you may want to take the time to look it up. Fortunately, if you're reading on a computer or an e-reader, the definition of a word is usually just a right-click or finger-tap away.

Use Strategies for Improving Vocabulary

If you want to improve your vocabulary, you have options. Reading specialists have developed several strategies to help students understand and use new words. The following are among the most frequently cited approaches:

1. **Make and use flash cards.** Using blank index cards or a flashcard app, write a new word on the front and the definition on back. Practice learning the definitions, always adding new cards into the mix and returning to older words, even when you think you've learned their meaning.

2. **Learn the prefixes, roots, and suffixes of common words.** Becoming familiar with even a few dozen prefixes, roots, and suffixes will add tremendous power and potential to your vocabulary, as you realize that the parts of a word are often clues to its meaning. Take the word *incredible*, for example. The prefix *in* means "not"; the root *cred* means "to believe"; and the suffix *ibile* signifies "being capable of." Put them together and you have "not capable of being believed": *incredible*. A quick online search will reveal numerous helpful charts listing word parts and their meanings, which you can bookmark or print out for future reference.

3. **Visualize new words.** Creating a mental picture associated with the meaning of each new word increases your memory of the word. For instance, when I hear or read the word "coagulate," which means to "change from a fluid to a semisolid or solid state," I always picture a pool of drying blood. It's an unpleasant image, but I never forget the meaning of the word.

4. **Use new words in conversation.** Try to use new words when speaking to friends and family. If you and someone you know are dedicated to improving your vocabularies, set aside time to talk together using as many new words as possible.

5. **Play games.** Crosswords provide you with often comic and slightly misleading clues, while games like Scrabble require you to come up with words on your own. In both cases, an element of fun makes the learning easier. An added bonus is that some vocabulary-building games—Freerice and Magoosh Vocabulary Builder are among the most popular—can be downloaded as apps on your phone.

6. **Read.** Of course, the single best way to increase your vocabulary is to read. Rereading after looking up and writing down the definitions of new words increases your memory of them, as does reading aloud. In addition, learning words through reading places them in context, which increases your retention and recall.

DIY 2.5 Learn Five to Ten Vocabulary Words a Week

Choose one or more of the vocabulary strategies above and set yourself a goal of learning five to ten new words each week for the rest of the semester. Be sure to keep a list or a log.

2.6 Using the SQ3R Strategy

One popular way to ensure that you've thoroughly read the material you were assigned is to follow the SQ3R protocol, which stands for "Survey, Question, Read, Recite, Review." Here's how it works

START ▶ **Survey**

Preview the reading. See what you can learn from the title. Pay attention to the headnote about the author (if there is one). Quickly read the introductory and concluding paragraphs for an overview. Look closely at images or graphs in the text.

 Question

Ask yourself, *What do I want or expect to learn from the text?* Look for question marks in the reading to see what the author is asking. Use *Who? What? When? Where? How? Why?* to prompt your own queries. You might also change the headings, subheadings, and topic sentences into questions and look for answers to them as you read.

SQ3R

Review

After you've finished reading, look back over your notes and summarize the overall argument and the important points. Think, too, about how the text connects with things you already know or are learning about.

 Read

Read carefully to understand each main idea. Reread if needed. Read the captions for any images and relate the images to the text. Annotate as you read and summarize in the margins.

 Recite

After each section, repeat what you've read. Speaking aloud is the best method here, as it accesses two brain functions: talking *and* listening. Write your summaries after you recite them.

DIY 2.6 Practice Using SQ3R

Choose a reading and practice the SQ3R method. How does this method compare with other reading strategies you've tried? If the overall method doesn't work as well for you, are there one or two parts of it that you still found especially useful?

Chapter 2 Checklist
Becoming a College Reader

☐ **Have you identified a place where you can comfortably complete your reading?**

College-level reading requires you to concentrate, and it's difficult to do that if you are constantly being distracted. If you haven't already located a quiet, pleasant place that you can visit easily and often, make an effort to find your "reading nook" right now.

☐ **Have you annotated this chapter?**

Flip back through Chapter 2. If none of the text has been circled or underlined, if the margins of the pages are as clean as newly fallen snow, then you need to go back and leave some evidence of your active engagement with the material. If you're reading a book, keep a pen or pencil in hand. If you're reading in a digital format, use the tools available with that software to mark and comment on the text.

☐ **Do you know who you will turn to if you have trouble with reading in this class?**

Asking for help can be hard, especially if you're not used to it. Try reading on your own first, of course, but remember that the most successful students are often the ones who are most active in seeking help—from their instructors, their tutors, their classmates, and their family and friends. If you believe talking about a text will help you better understand it, remember that the person you're talking to doesn't necessarily have to have read the material for *you* to benefit from a discussion.

How will you become a confident college reader?

Working Together

2.7a Reading with a Partner Practice reading aloud with a new partner, this time using the following passage from *Your College Experience: Strategies for Success* by John Gardner and Betsy Barefoot. Partner 1 should read through the end of the second bullet point, while Partner 2 should pick up at "Consider a word's parts."

Again, all you need to do is read slowly and deliberately, stopping each time you have a thought about the reading. That could mean stopping mid-sentence, but at the very least, you'll want to pause after every couple of sentences to sum up what you're thinking and to articulate any questions or confusions you might have. The idea is to try and mirror through spoken words what you are thinking silently in your head.

Remember that when you are actually reading the passage, your partner should remain absolutely silent. You can talk to one another after the two of you have completed reading the entire piece.

Excerpt from *Your College Experience: Strategies for Success*

JOHN GARDNER AND BETSY BAREFOOT

Developing Your Vocabulary

Textbooks are full of new words and terms. A **vocabulary** is a set of words in a particular language or field of knowledge. As you become familiar with the vocabulary of an academic field, reading the texts related to that field becomes easier.

If words are such a basic and essential component of our knowledge, what is the best way to learn them? The following are some basic vocabulary-building strategies:

- **Notice and write down unfamiliar terms while your preview a text.** Consider making a flash card for each term or making a list of terms.

- **Think about the context when you come across challenging words.** See whether you can guess the meaning of an unfamiliar term by using the words around it.

- **Consider a word's parts.** If context by itself is not enough to help you guess the meaning of an unfamiliar word, try analyzing the term to discover its root (or base part) and any prefixes (parts that come before the root) or suffixes (parts that follow the root). For example, *transport* has the root *port*, which means "carry," and the prefix *trans*, which means "across." Together the word means "carry across" or "carry from one place to another." Knowing the meaning of prefixes and suffixes can be very helpful. For example, *anti* means "against," and *pro* means "for."

- **Use the glossary of the text or a dictionary.** Textbook publishers carefully compile glossaries to help students learn the vocabulary of a given discipline. If the text has no glossary, have a dictionary on hand. If a given word has more than one definition, search for the meaning that fits your text. The online Merriam-Webster's Dictionary (**merriam-webster.com**) is especially helpful for college students.

- **Use new words in your writing and speaking.** If you use a new word a few times, you'll soon know it. In addition, any flash cards you have created will come in handy for reviewing the definitions of new words at exam time.

Once you and your partner have finished reading the passage, take some time to talk it over. If your conversation doesn't take off on its own, consider asking each other these questions:

- Which parts of the reading were the easiest to understand? What strategies did the authors use to make the reading easier?
- Where did you have the most difficulty? Why?
- In this passage about developing your vocabulary, did you learn any new words? What were they?
- Based on your own experience learning new vocabulary, which pieces of advice from Gardner and Barefoot are the most useful?
- Have you used other strategies in the past that have helped improve your vocabulary?

Share your discussion of the passage in a small group or in the full class. Talk about both (1) what you learned from the reading and (2) how you approached it as a reader, separate from the passage's subject matter.

Applying What You Know

2.7b Practicing Active Reading

1. Choose any section from this chapter and annotate it.
2. Write a one-sentence summary of the section you just annotated.
3. Write a two- or three-sentence summary of the entire chapter.

When you've finished, form a group of three or four students and compare your annotating/active reading process. What steps did you take that your classmates didn't? What can you learn from the way others in your group approached this assignment?

2.7c Annotating for Fun
Visit a website that you normally read just for fun. Copy and paste the text of a short article into a Google document or a Word document that has margins that are at least two and a half inches on both sides. Then, annotate it using the active reading strategies discussed in this chapter:

- Predicting
- Questioning
- Challenging the Text
- Making Connections
- Visualizing
- Summarizing

Compare the process of annotating this textbook with annotating the text you read for fun. What attitudes or strategies can you borrow from annotating the "fun text" to make annotating the "serious text" more enjoyable?

2.7d Annotating Data
An infographic represents information in visual form. Infographics are often used to make data more easily scannable and digestible and to help users see relationships between different datapoints. Do an online search using the terms "census.gov infographic." Browse visuals related to housing, employment, health, military spending, same-sex marriages, technology use, and more. Find an infographic about a topic that you're curious about. Write notes about how the strategies from this chapter helped you to "read" the visual text. Which specific strategies worked best?

2.7e Sharing Your Assigned Reading for Another Class

In a small group of three or four people, share a particular assigned reading *that you have already completed* from one of your other classes. Talk with your groupmates about the process of finishing this reading. You might address the following questions about the reading:

- What were the most interesting and exciting parts of the text? Why?
- Where did you get most confused or bored? Why?
- How does or did the text fit into the overall picture of what's happening in the class?
- What, if anything, had your instructor said about the text ahead of time?
- What background information were you missing that would otherwise have helped you better understand the text?

If you're a listener in the group, be respectful and pay attention as your classmate talks about the reading. While it is unlikely that you will be familiar with a reading from another course, after the person has finished discussing the reading, you can still contribute by doing the following:

- Asking questions about the text
- Pointing out connections and ideas the reader made when discussing the text
- Explaining how they might approach the reading of the text
- Making suggestions for supplementary materials — websites, videos, audio recordings — that the reader might consult

2.7f Writing a Letter about Reading

Write a letter to your instructor identifying your strengths and weaknesses as a reader. Be as specific as possible. Maybe you have a fairly strong vocabulary, but you worry you don't have the stamina to tackle longer readings, or you're still not sure about the best ways to annotate a text. End by letting your instructor know (1) what your plans are for becoming a better college reader and (2) how your instructor can help you achieve your goals.

Make sure to sign your name. Then give or send the letter to your instructor.

Invitations to Write

2.7g Profiling Another Reader

Shorter: Interview a classmate or someone you know well, and write a one- or two-paragraph profile of that person as a reader. Among the questions you might ask the person are the following:

- What do you remember about your early reading experiences?
- How would you describe yourself as a reader currently?
- Why are you the sort of reader that you are?
- What types of things do you mostly read now, and why?

Longer: Learn more about the reading habits of the person you are profiling by asking more nuanced questions. *Listen* carefully to what your interviewee is saying, and follow up on interesting responses you haven't anticipated by asking questions inspired by the conversation (and which you may not have written down). Here is a list of initial queries (some of which are adapted from *Reading for Understanding*) to help get you going:

- About how many books are in your home (or on your e-reader)?
- How many books do you personally own?

- Do you ever read books at home besides for school assignments? If so, what are they?
- When and where do you do most of your reading?
- How long do you spend on reading assignments during the average day? How long during the day do you spend reading *in total*, including reading such content on your phone as news stories and social media posts?
- How focused are you when you read? What sort of things tend to get you distracted? How do you deal with those distractions?
- When you're reading, do you use any of the strategies described in this chapter: previewing, annotating, summarizing, and so on?
- Do you ever talk to anyone you know about what you're reading — books or other reading materials?
- What do *you* think it takes to become a strong reader?

After you've taken notes on the answers to your questions, rewrite your profile using the new, fuller picture you have of your interviewee's reading habits.

2.7h Writing about Reading

Shorter: Write a paragraph describing the one or two *most important* strategies you learned in this chapter.

Longer: Write a page or so in which you give advice to new college students about how to become better readers of academic writing. Highlight and explain the strategies you personally find most useful, providing concrete and specific examples of how they worked for you. (If you responded to the "Write Before You Read" prompt at the beginning of the chapter, you might want to incorporate some of that material.)

Assuming that you found some of the strategies discussed in this chapter less useful than others, you might end your advice to new students by explaining why those strategies didn't work for you.

2.7i Is College Worth It?

Shorter: Write a paragraph or two in which you describe why you *either* agree or disagree with David Leonhardt's argument that college is worth it.

Longer: Make a double-entry journal, then jot down two or three specific quotations from "Is College Worth It?" that you think deserve a fuller response on the right-hand side of the journal.

After completing your double-entry journal, rewrite and expand your material about whether or not college is worth it by using the quotes and your responses in the double-entry journal to flesh out your reasoning.

3

Investigating a Topic: Growth Mindset, Grit, and College Success

REFLECT

Write Before You Read | Activity to connect what's new with what you already know 51

READ & PRACTICE

DIY (Do-it-yourself) activities offer just-in-time support for all the skills in this book.

REFLECT

Write Before You Read   How do you respond to challenges? In Chapter 1, we looked at some proven strategies for overcoming the difficulties faced by many college students. Among the strategies mentioned for college success were "growth mindset" and "grit" (see section 1.1). Take another look at these strategies, then write a paragraph reflecting on how each success strategy might help you *right now* in a specific college class or with a problem outside the classroom.

3.1 Investigating a Topic

To help students dig deeper into thought-provoking topics, instructors often assign a cluster of related materials, like those in this chapter. This chapter focuses on the ideas in the following three selections to help you dig deeper into important college success strategies:

- **Carol Dweck, excerpt from *Mindset: The New Psychology of Success.*** When we believe we can do better, and we pursue our goals with dedication and hard work, we do, indeed, get better, according to Dweck, a Stanford professor of psychology. In fact, our brains physically change when we have what she calls a "growth mindset." However, when we don't have confidence in our ability to improve, we can become stuck with a "fixed mindset."

- **Angela Duckworth, "Grit: The Power of Passion and Perseverance" [VIDEO].** Duckworth's theories about "grit" have some similarities with Dweck's work, so it's not surprising that a growth mindset and grit are related ideas or that Duckworth acknowledges Dweck in her TED Talk. Both psychologists argue that hard work and persistence are better predictors of success than any other factor, including talent, intelligence, and wealth.

- **Kurt Streeter, "South L.A. Student Finds a Different World at Cal."** Streeter profiles Kashawn Campbell, an academic standout at Jefferson High School in Los Angeles, who faced serious struggles in his first year at the University of California at Berkeley. While the words "growth mindset" and "grit" never appear in Streeter's article, it's clear that Kashawn demonstrates both qualities, even as he realizes that hard work alone may not always be enough to succeed in a demanding college environment.

When you immerse yourself in a topic, you want to get to know it as thoroughly as possible. Therefore, read and reread Dweck and Streeter carefully. Watch the Duckworth video, which is easy to find on the web, several times. The instruction in Chapters 4 to 8 frequently references the selections in this chapter, so it will be useful to know them well.

3.2 Reading an Excerpt from Carol Dweck's *Mindset*

Many students begin kindergarten with what Carol Dweck calls a *growth mindset*—a belief that success is always possible with effort and commitment. Throughout their early months in school, they learn their numbers and letters. With an enthusiastic teacher and a confident group of classmates, a growth mindset is contagious, and these young students feel comfortable taking risks and challenging themselves. Unfortunately, not every child has the same experience. Students with a *fixed mindset* see themselves as inadequate, often because they don't receive substantial feedback supporting the idea that they will ever be otherwise. When they are frustrated, they feel a sense of despair, or they simply give up.

Why does one group of children embrace difficulties while others are floored by them?

Stanford psychologist Carol Dweck's work began with just such a question, and an excerpt from her book *Mindset: The New Psychology of Success*, included in this section, you can see how fruitful that question has been for her research. Take special note of Dweck's emphasis on "perseverance and resilience," as those qualities are important in all three of the works discussed in this chapter.

DIY 3.2a Preview and Annotate an Excerpt from *Mindset*

Keeping in mind what you learned in Chapter 2 about approaching a new text, take a few minutes to complete the following activities before and as you read this selection.

Preview

- Read the biographic note about Carol Dweck.
- Read the article headings to get a feel for the main areas that Dweck will cover.
- Then skim over the text, slowing down to read the first paragraph more carefully after each new heading.

Annotate

- If you're reading a paper copy, read with a pen or pencil in hand; if the essay is in a digital format, make sure you have some way of marking it up.
- As you read, mark words or phrases you don't understand or that seem particularly important.
- Make brief notes or annotations in the margins. Ask short questions. Challenge the author if you disagree with her argument or evidence.

An Invitation to Read

Courtesy Stanford News Service

Widely regarded as one of the world's leading researchers in the fields of personality, social psychology, and developmental psychology, Stanford professor Carol Dweck is also an excellent writer. She presents her research and strategies in a way that is clear, positive, and approachable. The following excerpt from "The Mindsets," Chapter 1 of Dweck's *Mindset: The New Psychology of Success*, demonstrates how much we can learn about ourselves, and our potential, from this gifted educator.

From *Mindset: The New Psychology of Success*

CAROL DWECK

1   When I was a young researcher, just starting out, something happened that changed my life. I was obsessed with understanding how people cope with failures, and I decided to study it by watching how students grapple

with hard problems. So I brought children one at a time to a room in their school, made them comfortable, and then gave them a series of puzzles to solve. The first ones were fairly easy, but the next ones were hard. As the students grunted, perspired, and toiled, I watched their strategies and probed what they were thinking and feeling. I expected differences among children in how they coped with the difficulty, but I saw something I never expected.

2   Confronted with the hard puzzles, one ten-year-old boy pulled up his chair, rubbed his hands together, smacked his lips, and cried out, "I love a challenge!" Another, sweating away on these puzzles, looked up with a pleased expression and said with authority, "You know, I was hoping this would be informative!"

3   *What's wrong with them?* I wondered. I always thought you coped with failure or you didn't cope with failure. I never thought anyone loved failure. Were these alien children or were they on to something?

4   Everyone has a role model, someone who pointed the way at a critical moment in their lives. These children were my role models. They obviously knew something I didn't and I was determined to figure it out—to understand the kind of mindset that could turn a failure into a gift.

5   What did they know? They knew that human qualities, such as intellectual skills, could be cultivated through effort. And that's what they were doing—getting smarter. Not only weren't they discouraged by failure, they didn't even think they were failing. They thought they were learning.

6   I, on the other hand, thought human qualities were carved in stone. You were smart or you weren't, and failure meant you weren't. It was that simple. If you could arrange successes and avoid failures (at all costs), you could stay smart. Struggles, mistakes, perseverance were just not part of this picture.

7   Whether human qualities are things that can be cultivated or things that are carved in stone is an old issue. What these beliefs mean for you is a new one: What are the consequences of thinking that your intelligence or personality is something you can develop, as opposed to something that is a fixed, deep-seated trait?

What Does All This Mean for You? The Two Mindsets

8   For thirty years, my research has shown that the view you adopt for yourself profoundly affects the way you lead your life. It can determine whether you become the person you want to be and whether you accomplish the things you value. How does this happen? How can a simple

belief have the power to transform your psychology and, as a result, your life?

9   Believing that your qualities are carved in stone—the fixed mindset—creates an urgency to prove yourself over and over. If you have only a certain amount of intelligence, a certain personality, and a certain moral character—well, then you'd better prove that you have a healthy dose of them. It simply wouldn't do to look or feel deficient in these most basic characteristics.

10   Some of us are trained in this mindset from an early age. Even as a child, I was focused on being smart, but the fixed mindset was really stamped in by Mrs. Wilson, my sixth-grade teacher. Unlike [French psychologist] Alfred Binet, she believed that people's IQ scores told the whole story of who they were. We were seated around the room in IQ order, and only the highest-IQ students could be trusted to carry the flag, clap the erasers, or take a note to the principal. Aside from the daily stomachaches she provoked with her judgmental stance, she was creating a mindset in which everyone in the class had one consuming goal—look smart, don't look dumb. Who cared about or enjoyed learning when our whole being was at stake every time she gave us a test or called on us in class?

11   I've seen so many people with this one consuming goal of proving themselves—in the classroom, in their careers, and in their relationships. Every situation calls for a confirmation of their intelligence, personality, or character. Every situation is evaluated: Will I succeed or fail? Will I look smart or dumb? Will I be accepted or rejected? Will I feel like a winner or a loser?

12   But doesn't our society value intelligence, personality, and character? Isn't it normal to want these traits? Yes, but . . .

13   There's another mindset in which these traits are not simply a hand you're dealt and have to live with, always trying to convince yourself and others that you have a royal flush when you're secretly worried it's a pair of tens. In this mindset, the hand you're dealt is just the starting point for development. This growth mindset is based on the belief that your basic qualities are things you can cultivate through your efforts. Although people may differ in every which way—in their initial talents and aptitudes, interests, or temperament—everyone can change and grow through application and experience.

14   Do people with this mindset believe that anyone can be anything, that anyone with proper motivation or education can become Einstein or Beethoven? No, but they believe that a person's true potential is unknown (and unknowable); that it's impossible to foresee what can be accomplished with years of passion, toil, and training.

15   Did you know that Darwin and Tolstoy were considered ordinary children? That Ben Hogan, one of the greatest golfers of all time, was completely uncoordinated and graceless as a child? That the photographer Cindy Sherman, who has been on virtually every list of the most important artists of the twentieth century, failed her first photography course? That Geraldine Page, one of our greatest actresses, was advised to give it up for lack of talent?

16   You can see how the belief that cherished qualities can be developed creates a passion for learning. Why waste time proving over and over how great you are, when you could be getting better? Why hide deficiencies instead of overcoming them? Why look for friends or partners who will just shore up your self-esteem instead of ones who will also challenge you to grow? And why seek out the tried and true, instead of experiences that will stretch you? The passion for stretching yourself and sticking to it, even (or especially) when it's not going well, is the hallmark of the growth mindset. This is the mindset that allows people to thrive during some of the most challenging times in their lives.

A View from the Two Mindsets

17   To give you a better sense of how the two mindsets work, imagine — as vividly as you can — that you are a young adult having a really bad day:

> One day, you go to a class that is really important to you and that you like a lot. The professor returns the midterm papers to the class. You got a C+. You're very disappointed. That evening on the way back to your home, you find that you've gotten a parking ticket. Being really frustrated, you call your best friend to share your experience but are sort of brushed off.

18   What would you think? What would you feel? What would you do?

19   When I asked people with the fixed mindset, this is what they said: "I'd feel like a reject." "I'm a total failure." "I'm an idiot." "I'm a loser." "I'd feel worthless and dumb—everyone's better than me." "I'm slime." In other words, they'd see what happened as a direct measure of their competence and worth.

20   This is what they'd think about their lives: "My life is pitiful." "I have no life." "Somebody upstairs doesn't like me." "The world is out to get me." "Someone is out to destroy me." "Nobody loves me, everybody hates me." "Life is unfair and all efforts are useless." "Life stinks. I'm stupid. Nothing good ever happens to me." "I'm the most unlucky person on this earth."

21 Excuse me, was there death and destruction, or just a grade, a ticket, and a bad phone call?

22 Are these just people with low self-esteem? Or card-carrying pessimists? No. When they aren't coping with failure, they feel just as worthy and optimistic—and bright and attractive—as people with the growth mindset.

23 So how would they cope? "I wouldn't bother to put so much time and effort into doing well in anything." (In other words, don't let anyone measure you again.) "Do nothing." "Stay in bed." "Get drunk." "Eat." "Yell at someone if I get a chance to." "Eat chocolate." "Listen to music and pout." "Go into my closet and sit there." "Pick a fight with somebody." "Cry." "Break something." "What is there to do?"

24 *What is there to do!* You know, when I wrote the vignette, I intentionally made the grade a C+, not an F. It was a midterm rather than a final. It was a parking ticket, not a car wreck. They were "sort of brushed off," not rejected outright. Nothing catastrophic or irreversible happened. Yet from this raw material the fixed mindset created the feeling of utter failure and paralysis.

25 When I gave people with the growth mindset the same vignette, here's what they said. They'd think:

26 "I need to try harder in class, be more careful when parking the car, and wonder if my friend had a bad day."

27 "The C+ would tell me that I'd have to work a lot harder in the class, but I have the rest of the semester to pull up my grade."

28 There were many, many more like this, but I think you get the idea.

29 Now, how would they cope? Directly.

30 "I'd start thinking about studying harder (or studying in a different way) for my next test in that class, I'd pay the ticket, and I'd work things out with my best friend the next time we speak."

31 "I'd look at what was wrong on my exam, resolve to do better, pay my parking ticket, and call my friend to tell her I was upset the day before."

32 "Work hard on my next paper, speak to the teacher, be more careful where I park or contest the ticket, and find out what's wrong with my friend."

33 You don't have to have one mindset or the other to be upset. Who wouldn't be? Things like a poor grade or a rebuff from a friend or loved one—these are not fun events. No one was smacking their lips with relish. Yet those people with the growth mindset were not labeling themselves and throwing up their hands. Even though they felt distressed, they were ready to take the risks, confront the challenges, and keep working at them.

People with a growth mindset see opportunity in failure. People with a fixed mindset
see only the failure.
Studio_G/Shutterstock

Self-Insight: Who Has Accurate Views of Their Assets and Limitations?

34 Maybe the people with the growth mindset don't think they're Einstein or
Beethoven, but aren't they more likely to have inflated views of their abilities and
try for things they're not capable of? In fact, studies show that people are terrible
at estimating their abilities. Recently, we set out to see who is most likely to do
this. Sure, we found that people greatly misestimated their performance and their
ability. But it was those with the fixed mindset who accounted for almost all the
inaccuracy. The people with the growth mindset were amazingly accurate.

35 When you think about it, this makes sense. If, like those with the
growth mindset, you believe you can develop yourself, then you're open to
accurate information about your current abilities, even if it's unflattering.
What's more, if you're oriented toward learning, as they are, you need accurate information about your current abilities in order to learn effectively.
However, if everything is either good news or bad news about your precious
traits—as it is with fixed-mindset people—distortion almost inevitably
enters the picture. Some outcomes are magnified, others are explained away,
and before you know it you don't know yourself at all.

36 Howard Gardner, in his book *Extraordinary Minds*, concluded that
exceptional individuals have "a special talent for identifying their own
strengths and weaknesses." It's interesting that those with the growth mindset seem to have that talent.

37   The other thing exceptional people seem to have is a special talent for converting life's setbacks into future successes. Creativity researchers concur. In a poll of 143 creativity researchers, there was wide agreement about the number one ingredient in creative achievement. And it was exactly the kind of perseverance and resilience produced by the growth mindset.

DIY 3.2b Focus on Growth Mindset

On your own or with a classmate, make notes about the following questions:

1. Think of all the people you know personally who have a growth mindset. Choose one of those people, describe that person, and give specific examples of how their growth mindset has helped them succeed. If you're doing this activity with another person, what traits do the people you've identified have in common? How are they different? Make lists or a Venn diagram.

2. Talk about which type of mindset you generally have — fixed or growth. Describe how that mindset has played out recently in your life. In which areas can you cultivate a stronger growth mindset to help you overcome the challenges you currently face?

DIY 3.2c Use a Double-Entry Journal to Respond to Dweck's ideas

Reread the excerpt from *Mindset* and find two or three direct quotations that you would like to discuss further. Then create a double-entry journal (see p. 41 for details).

3.3 Viewing "Grit: The Power of Passion and Perseverance"

In his pamphlet series *Poor Richard's Almanack*, Benjamin Franklin offers a number of proverbs that seem to echo today's emphasis on grit: "Have you something to do tomorrow? Do it today." "Diligence is the mother of good luck." "There are no gains without pains."

(Yep, you heard it here: "No pain, no gain" comes from Ben Franklin.)

There's nothing new about the idea that people who possess courage, strength of character, purpose, and above all, determination are likely to succeed. However, University of Pennsylvania psychologist Angela Duckworth gave the concept of *grit* a whole new life in the digital age. Duckworth's 2013 TED Talk became a YouTube sensation: "Grit: The Power of Passion and Perseverance." In her talk, Duckworth argues that while talent and a growth mindset are necessary for success, those who are truly successful display extreme grit.

Duckworth's TED Talk persona is funny, charming, bright, and determined, and her belief in persistence and hard work struck a chord with both educators and businesspeople. According to Duckworth, people who are "unusually resilient and hardworking" and know "in a very, very deep way" what they want are much more likely to achieve their goals than people who are merely talented or lucky.

You can see why Duckworth and her ideas have been so popular by watching the TED Talk yourself in an Invitation to View in this section. But first, complete the following DIY activity.

DIY 3.3a Actively View Duckworth's TED Talk on Grit

When you read a difficult article in a textbook, you mentally prepare yourself for the experience, then you annotate the text and look up new words and concepts as you read. Watching a video, in contrast, may seem like the most natural thing in the world; after all, you do it all the time. However, when you are viewing a video, TV episode, or film for a college class, you need to give it the same focused attention that you would give a piece of writing.

You can focus yourself by writing as you watch. As Duckworth speaks,

- make predictions

- ask questions

- make comments

- look for patterns and repetition

- challenge ideas and evidence that you don't find persuasive

- rewind to rewatch and note sections that seem important or difficult

- annotate the transcript (available on TED.com), which can be displayed in languages other than English

---

An Invitation to View

Angela Lee Duckworth is a 2013 MacArthur Genius Fellow and professor of psychology at the University of Pennsylvania. She has advised a number of organizations, including NBA and NFL teams, Fortune 500 CEOs, the World Bank, and members of the White House. She completed her BA in neurobiology at Harvard, her MSc in neuroscience at Oxford, and her PhD in psychology at the University of Pennsylvania. As a researcher, she studies competencies unrelated to a person's IQ. Her book *Grit: The Power of Passion and Perseverance* was a New York Times bestseller.

Keith Morris/Hay Flotos/Alamy Stock Photo

Grit: The Power of Passion and Perseverance

ANGELA DUCKWORTH

To watch the video, simply search online for **"Angela Duckworth" and "TED Talk."** In just six minutes, you may find yourself, like so many others, persuaded that *grit* is the key element in any drive toward success.

DIY 3.3b Answer Questions about Duckworth's TED Talk

Answer the following questions on your own or with a peer.

1. How would you describe Duckworth's presentation on *grit*? Did you find it exciting and inspiring? If so, what was it about the talk that fired up your engines? If you didn't like it, what are your reservations?

2. Duckworth is clearly a good public speaker. What qualities does she have that help her connect with her audience? How does she stand while speaking? What does she do with her hands? What are her facial expressions? How would you describe her voice? Overall, how important is her physical presentation?

3. Now, take out your computer or phone and look at the TED Talk's transcript. Identify one passage that catches your attention. Write notes about the key idea and explain why it matters.

3.4 Seeing Growth Mindset and Grit in Action

Carol Dweck and Angela Duckworth provide numerous short examples to support their arguments. In support of a growth mindset, Dweck tell us that "Darwin and Tolstoy [who made major contributions in science and literature] were considered ordinary children"; "Ben Hogan, one of the greatest golfers of all time, was completely uncoordinated and graceless as a child"; and "photographer Cindy Sherman, who has been on virtually every list of the most important artists of the twentieth century, failed her first photography course." Similarly, Duckworth talks about grittiness not only in regard to teaching math to seventh graders in public schools and studying with elementary school children competing in the National Spelling Bee but also working with cadets at West Point Military Academy.

In contrast, the following reading focuses on the experience of one individual: Kashawn Campbell, a first-generation college student struggling to succeed at the University of California, Berkeley. In his 2013 profile of Campbell, Kurt Streeter never uses the words "growth mindset" or "grit," yet it's clear that Campbell has both qualities in abundance.

Indeed, the fact that Streeter's profile is not responding to either Dweck or Duckworth makes it more interesting as a case study in not only the power of growth mindset and grit but also their potential limitations.

In addition to previewing the article, you should also do the following:

- **Read actively.** Engage with the text; make sure you're tracking the author's ideas and argument from one paragraph to the next.

- **Annotate.** Underline; write in the margins; use commenting tools if annotating digitally.

- **Read critically.** If you find one of the author's points unconvincing, make a note of it.

- **Recite and review after reading.** Much of reading is *re*reading and reviewing to make sure that you've fully understood the text.

DIY 3.4a Preview "South L.A. Student Finds a Different World at Cal"

Preview Kurt Streeter's "South L.A. Student Finds a Different World at Cal'"; pay special attention to the photographs by Bethany Mollenkof (you can find even more photos by viewing the article on the *LA Times* website). What can you learn about Kashawn Campbell, the subject of Streeter's profile, by looking at Mollenkof's photographs and reading the captions?

An Invitation to Read

Earl Wilson/The New York Times/Redux

Currently a reporter for *The New York Times*, Kurt Streeter has also worked for ESPN, the *Los Angeles Times*, and the *Baltimore Sun*. While Streeter often writes about sports, he has also reported on politics, race, religion, education, dance, music, and architecture. A former tennis pro, Streeter attended the University of California, Berkeley, graduating with a degree in political science in 1989. In 2013, he won an award for "Best Feature" writing from the California Newspaper Publishers Association for a series of articles about life and death in a hospice for prison inmates.

Bethany Mollenkof/Los Angeles Times

Bethany Mollenkof is a Los Angeles–based photographer and filmmaker. For three and a half years she was a staff video journalist for the *Los Angeles Times*, where she was also part of the Pulitzer Prize–winning team that covered the 2016 San Bernardino terrorist attack.

South L.A. Student Finds a Different World at Cal

Kurt Streeter

Bethany Mollenkof/Los Angeles Times

Kashawn Campbell grew up in one of the toughest neighborhoods in South Los Angeles. He became a straight-A student at Jefferson High School, but at UC Berkeley, he found challenges far greater than he anticipated.
Bethany Mollenkof/Los Angeles Times

1   School had always been his safe harbor.

2   Growing up in one of South Los Angeles' bleakest, most violent neighborhoods, he learned about the world by watching "Jeopardy" and willed himself to become a straight-A student.

3   His teachers and his classmates at Jefferson High all rooted for the slight and hopeful African American teenager. He was named the prom king, the most likely to succeed, the senior class salutatorian. He was accepted to UC Berkeley, one of the nation's most renowned public universities.

4   A semester later, Kashawn Campbell sat inside a cramped room on a dorm floor that Cal reserves for black students [as part of the African American Theme Program]. It was early January, and he stared nervously at his first college transcript.

5   There wasn't much good to see.

6   He had barely passed an introductory science course. In College Writing 1A, his essays—pockmarked with misplaced words and odd phrases—were so weak that he would have to take the class again.

7   He had never felt this kind of failure, nor felt this insecure. The second term was just days away and he had a 1.7 GPA. If he didn't improve his grades by school year's end, he would flunk out.

8   He tried to stay calm. He promised himself he would beat back the depression that had come in waves those first months of school. He would work harder, be better organized, be more like his roommate and new best friend, Spencer Simpson, who was making college look easy.

9   On a nearby desk lay a small diary he recently filled with affirmations and goals. He thumbed through it.

10   "I can do this! I can do this!" he had written. "Let the studying begin! … It's time for Kashawn's Comeback!"

11   This is the story of Kashawn Campbell's freshman year.

––––––––––––––––––

12   Nothing had ever been easy for Kashawn.

13   "When I delivered him, I thought he was dead," said his mother, Lillie, recalling the umbilical cord tight around his neck. "He was still as stone but eventually he came to. Proved he was a survivor. Ever since, I've called him my miracle child."

14   A single mom, she often worked two jobs to make ends meet, at times as a graveyard shift security guard. Someone needed to care for her baby, so she paid an elderly neighbor named Sylvia to house, feed and care for Kashawn.

15   "Me and Kashawn always had a strong connection," Lillie said. "But Sylvia raised my boy, yes she did."

16   Sylvia didn't read many magazines, newspapers or books. Only rarely did she take Kashawn outside their neighborhood. Still, she was kind and loving, and he loved her in turn, as if she were his grandmother.

17   "I used what she taught me and expanded it," Kashawn said. That meant deciding early on that the life he was surrounded by wasn't what he wanted his future to be. "I had to be the one to push myself to do beyond well…. If I didn't do that, nothing was going to ever change."

18   Jefferson, made up almost entirely of Latinos and blacks, had a woeful reputation. His freshman year, just under 13% of its students were judged to be proficient in English, less than 1% in math.

19   "It was so rare to have a kid like Kashawn, especially an African American male, wanting that badly to go to college," said Jeremy McDavid, a former Jefferson vice principal. "We got together as a staff and decided that this kid, we cannot let him down."

20   By the end of his senior year, Kashawn's 4.06 grade point average was second best in the senior class. Because of a statewide program to attract top students from every public California high school, a spot at a UC system campus waited for him.

21 But when he got his acceptance letter from Berkeley, he couldn't celebrate like he always thought he would. It was Sylvia. She was losing a battle with cancer.

22 He sat near her hospice bed on a muggy day to give her the news. "I'm going to Cal, grandma," he said. She could barely open her eyes. "I'm going up there and I'm going to keep working hard and doing great. Nothing's going to change."

23 Sylvia died later that day.

---

24 A month later, when his mother drove him to Berkeley and dropped him off at his dormitory, Kashawn still crumbled into tears at the thought of Sylvia.

25 Yet he did everything he could to fit in. He lived at the African American Theme Program—two floors in Christian Hall housing roughly 50 black freshmen, an effort to build bonds among a community whose numbers have dwindled over the last two decades.

26 He filled his dorm room with Cal posters, and wore clothes emblazoned with the school's name. Each morning the gawky, bone-thin teen energetically reminded his dorm mates to "have a Caltastic day!"

27 "It was clear that Kashawn was someone who didn't know about, or maybe care about, social norms," said one of his friends. "A lot of people would laugh at first. They didn't understand how someone could be that enthusiastic."

28 But as the semester got going, he began to stumble. The first essay for the writing class that accounted for half of his course load was so bad his teacher gave him a "No Pass." Same for the second essay.

29 "It's like a different planet here," he said one day, walking down Telegraph Avenue through a mash of humanity he'd never been exposed to before: white kids, Asian kids, rich kids, bearded hipsters and burnt-out hippies. Many of them jaywalked. Not Kashawn. Just as he'd been taught, he only used crosswalks, only stepped onto the street when the coast was clear or a light flashed green. His shoulders slumped.

30 "I'm not used to the people. Not used to the type of buildings. Definitely not used to the pressure I feel."

31 Part of the pressure came from race. After peaking at 7% in the late 1980s and early '90s, the undergraduate African American population at Cal had been declining for years, especially since Proposition 209 had banned affirmative action in admissions to California public colleges. When Kashawn arrived, 3% of Berkeley undergraduates were African American.

32 The low numbers were the source of constant talk on the theme program floors, the symbolic center of black life for Cal freshmen.

33 "Sometimes we feel like we're not wanted on campus," Kashawn said, surrounded at dinner table by several of his dorm mates, all of them nodding in agreement.

34 "It's usually subtle things, glances or not being invited to study groups. Little, constant aggressions."

35 He also felt a more personal burden.

36 He couldn't let his mother down. She kept a box stuffed with each of his perfect report cards. She swore that he was going to be a lawyer, maybe even the president. Back home her bank account was running low, and he sent some of his scholarship money home to keep her going.

37 He'd never been depressed. Now clouds of sadness descended every few weeks. When they did he was barely able to speak, even to Spencer, his roommate.

38 The biggest of his burdens was schoolwork. At Jefferson, a long essay took a page and perfect grades came after an hour of study a night.

39 At Cal, he was among the hardest workers in the dorm, but he could barely keep afloat.

40 Seeking help, he went at least once a week to the office of his writing instructor, Verda Delp.

41 The more she saw him, the more she worried. His writing often didn't make sense. He struggled to comprehend the readings for her class and think critically about the text.

42 "It took a while for him to understand there was a problem," Delp said. "He could not believe that he needed more skills. He would revise his papers and each time he would turn his work back in having complicated it. The paper would be full of words he thought were academic, writing the way he thought a college student should write, using big words he didn't have command of."

43 At the end of the first semester, after he turned in a final portfolio of revised essays, Delp asked Kashawn to come to her office. She told him this last batch of work was better. After reviewing his writing, though, it was clear to her that he had received far too much help from someone else.

44 Both remember the meeting, recalling Kashawn's shock, his admission that friends and a tutor had offered suggestions and made edits, his insistence that the bulk of the writing was his own.

45 Delp reviewed his record: None of his essays had been good enough to receive passing grades. Still, instead of failing him, she gave a reprieve: His report card would show an "In Progress." The course wouldn't count against his grade point average, but he would have to take it again.

---

46 Before the start of the second term, hoping for a head start, Kashawn moved back into the dorm before anyone else on his floor. He imagined how different things were going to be from his first semester.

47 He couldn't wait to see Spencer. "We're both going to do very well this semester," he said. "I believe I can follow his lead and ace all my classes." They hadn't known each other before the year began. Now they were like brothers, partly because they shared so much. Spencer was raised in a tough

L.A. neighborhood by a single mom who had sometimes worked two jobs to pay the rent. Spencer had gone to struggling public schools, receiving straight A's at Inglewood High. Spencer didn't curse, didn't party, didn't try to act tough and was shy around girls.

48   As much as they had in common, they were also different. Spencer's mother, a medical administrator, had graduated from UCLA and exposed her only child to art, politics, literature and the world beyond Inglewood. If a bookstore was going out of business, she'd drive Spencer to the closeout sale and they would buy discounted novels. She pushed him to participate in a mostly white Boy Scout troop in Westchester.

49   To Spencer, Berkeley was the first place he could feel fully comfortable being intellectual and black, the first place he could openly admit he liked folk music and punk rock.

50   He was cruising through Cal, finishing the first semester with a 3.8 GPA despite a raft of hard classes. "I can easily see him being a professor one day," said his political theory instructor, noting that Spencer was one of the sharpest students in a lecture packed with nearly 200 undergraduates.

51   In the second term, Kashawn and Spencer volunteered for the same student organizations, and walked each Friday night to a job washing dishes at a nearby residence hall.

52   They even took a class together, African American Studies 5A, a survey of black culture and race relations. It was key for Kashawn: A top grade could ensure he would be invited back to Cal.

53   They sat together in the front row. One teacher noticed that Kashawn subconsciously seemed to mime his roommate: casually cocking his head and leaning back slightly as he pondered questions, just like Spencer.

54   Kashawn reveled in the class in a way he hadn't since high school. He would often be the first one to speak up in discussions, even though his points weren't always the most sophisticated, said Gabrielle Williams, a doctoral student who helped teach the class.

55   He still had gaps in his knowledge of history. But, Williams said, "you could see how engaged he was, how much he loved being there.... You could also see that he was struggling with his confidence, partly because this whole experience was so overwhelming."

56   Although the African American studies class was a bright spot — Kashawn had received an A on an essay and a B on a midterm, the best grades of his freshman year — the writing course he'd been forced to repeat wasn't going well. He knew that another failing effort in the class could doom his chances to return to Cal, so he worked as closely with his new instructor as he had with Delp.

57   There was little to show for the effort. On yet another failing essay, the instructor wrote how surprised she was at his lack of progress, especially, she noted, given the hours they'd spent going over his "extremely long, awkward and unclear sentences."

58 He told only Spencer and a few dorm mates how devastating this kind of failure felt, each poor grade another stinging punch bringing him closer to flunking out. None of the adults in his life knew the depth of his pain: not his professors, his counselors, any of the teachers at his old high school. He spoke vaguely about depression to his mother. She told him to read the Bible.

59 Spencer looked out for Kashawn; he was the first person Kashawn would turn to when depression came. Sometimes in the dorm room, Spencer would look over at Kashawn and see him sitting in front of his computer, body frozen and face expressionless, JVC headphones wrapped over his ears, but no music playing.

Spencer Simpson, left, and Kashawn Campbell chat before their African American Studies class.
Bethany Mollenkof/Los Angeles Times

60 One night Kashawn walked briskly from his room, ending up alone in a quiet, beige-walled lounge at Christian Hall. His mind raced. He chastised himself for his college grades, for being too sensitive, too trusting, too naive.

61 "Why was I even born?" he wondered. It felt like he was outside his body, looking at himself from above. "Is life really worth living under these conditions?"

62 He tried to calm down. "The way I was stressing myself out, it wasn't good, it wasn't healthy at all," he would recall later. "I just had to find my way out of that lounge. Had to get help, because this was a monster I needed to tame."

63 It wasn't long before he found himself sitting for the first time in a campus psychologist's office. The counselor urged him to put his life in better perspective. Maybe he didn't have to be the straight-A kid he'd been in

high school anymore. Maybe all that mattered was giving his best. The visit seemed to change him. His dorm mates had been so worried about his dark moods that some had called their parents, asking advice on how best to help their friend. As weeks passed and his smile returned, everyone breathed a little easier.

64 "I've learned the hard way that academics are not who you are," Kashawn said as he walked through Sproul Plaza, heading back to the dorm one day in May. "They are something you need to learn to get to the next level of life, but they can't define me. My grades at Cal are not Kashawn Campbell."

———————————————

65 Finals week. The school year was nearly over. After staying up all night to finish, Kashawn turned in the final portfolio for his writing course.

66 "I'm proud of you," his instructor said, as he handed her the essays in a black folder. "You've tried as hard as anyone I've ever seen."

67 Soon he'd taken his last test, turned in his last report. He stood on a sidewalk outside the dorm, saying goodbye to Spencer, stifling tears. Then he was on a Greyhound bus, heading home to Los Angeles, where he slept on the floor in his mother's apartment and waited for his grades.

68 Would he flunk out?

69 "All I can do is pray," he said.

70 One morning this summer he walked slowly to the kitchen table, sat in a black chair and cracked open his laptop. Cal's website had just posted grades.

71 He scrolled down the page and saw the results for College Writing. His teacher said he'd improved slightly, but not enough. She gave him an incomplete. To get a grade he'd have to turn in two more essays, if he came back to school.

72 His heart raced. He saw that he'd passed a three-unit seminar. He scanned further, his eyes resting finally on a line that said African American Studies 5A. There was his grade.

73 A-.

74 "Yes!" he exclaimed. An A- lifted his GPA above a 2.0.

75 He wasn't a freshman anymore. He would return to Cal for his sophomore year.

DIY 3.4b Practice Critical Reading

Practice your critical reading skills by answering the following questions about Kurt Streeter's "South L.A. Student Finds a Different World at Cal."

1. What is Streeter's central purpose in writing this article (other than simply doing his job as a journalist)?

2. Who is the article's primary audience? Other than the main audience, who else might be interested in reading it? Why?

3. To what extent is Streeter biased in favor of or against his subject? What evidence do you have for your belief?

4. To what extent does Streeter depend on verifiable facts to tell Kashawn's story? Where do you find the article relying primarily on his opinion?

Chapter 3 Checklist
Growth Mindset, Grit, and College Success

☐ **Have you thoroughly annotated the three selections in Chapter 3?**

It's important that you annotate both the readings in this chapter, as well as a transcript of Duckworth's TED Talk, as repeated reference will be made to this material in Chapters 4 through 8.

☐ **Have you looked up all the words and terms you didn't know?**

While it's often a good idea to skim past short, difficult words and sentences when you're first reading a piece, after you're done, be sure to follow up and fill in the gaps in your knowledge.

☐ **Can you summarize the main points of each piece without referring to the text or your notes and annotations?**

Reciting and reviewing assigned readings *without looking at them* gives you a stronger, more lasting grasp of the material (see the discussion of the SQ3R reading strategy in Chapter 2).

☐ **If your instructor has given you an essay assignment, do you understand everything that will be required?**

The most important element of an essay assignment is its focus, but you also want to be aware of practical issues like how long the essay should be and when it's due. (Chapters 4 through 8 will address these concerns in detail.)

3.5 | Making It Stick

How will you develop grit and a growth mindset?

Working Together

3.5a Reading Rhetorically   The following activity asks you to take another look at the two readings (Dweck's *Mindset*, p. 53, and Streeter's article about Kashawn Campbell, p. 63) and the video (Duckworth's TED Talk about grit, p. 60) discussed in this chapter.

1. Partner up with a classmate and make a list of the two or three most *memorable examples* in each piece. You might, for instance, have a vivid memory of one of the responses to Dweck's "really bad day" or a startling statement by Duckworth, or you might remember a particularly grueling challenge faced by Kashawn Campbell. There are no right answers — trust your own recall and retention.

2. Now think about *why* certain examples made such a strong impression on you. What rhetorical techniques did the writer or speaker use to catch your attention? Vivid imagery? Believable dialogue? An unexpected comparison or analogy? A bold claim?

3. Finally, discuss each piece as a full class. As you find out which examples made the biggest impression on your classmates, take note of *how* the writer or speaker achieved a certain effect so that you can emulate it in your own writing later on.

Applying What You Know

3.5b Thinking Out Loud about Grit   Practice the Thinking Out Loud activity described in

Chapter 2 (p. 29) on one of the two readings in this chapter.

1. Select what you consider to be the *most difficult* passage in your chosen reading.

2. Read and think aloud to a partner, stopping to comment on the material every sentence or two. Take your time. The material *is* difficult — that's why you chose it. If you've been having trouble coming up with ways to express your questions and ideas, the following list of suggestions could be useful:

   - I think in the next section the author will talk about . . .
   - The picture I have in my mind when I read this is . . .
   - My main question here is . . .
   - I don't see why . . .
   - I got stuck or bored when . . .
   - I need to learn more about . . .
   - I need to reread this passage because . . .
   - The main point of the reading is . . .
   - If I could talk to the author, I would ask . . .

3. Write notes about how reading aloud and thinking aloud helped you make some meaning of the passage.

3.5c I Don't Understand/I Understand

1. Your instructor will ask you to focus on one of the two articles in this chapter or will direct you to a transcript of Duckworth's speech. As you read the assigned piece, place a question mark in the margin next to each sentence or passage that you don't completely understand. When you finish

reading, go back and write a specific question about the text every time you see a question mark.

2. Find a partner and exchange work. (If you're completely online, scan and share a file — or take pictures with your phone.) Locate your partner's questions and see how many of them you can answer. In turn, give your partner a chance to try and answer your questions.

3. Write notes about how the collaborative reading experience helped develop your understanding of the text.

Invitations to Write

3.5d Writing about Your Own Growth Mindset and Grittiness

Shorter: Write a paragraph or two in which you describe a time when you demonstrated what Carol Dweck calls the "perseverance and resilience produced by . . . growth mindset" and the "passion and perseverance" that Angela Duckworth says are the hallmarks of grittiness. Focus on a *specific* accomplishment: learning how to read, working a difficult job, passing a specific class, making a team, and so on. Use concrete details highlighting any or all of the five senses — sight, sound, smell, taste, and touch — to make your readers feel as though they are there with you.

Longer: Explore the growth mindset and grittiness you described in the shorter assignment. Where does it come from? To what extent are you working to overcome a fixed mindset? Is grit an essential part of your character — or something you feel you need to develop? What is the *passion* that drives your *perseverance* in a particular area of your life?

3.5e Comparing and Contrasting Growth Mindset and Grit

Shorter: While both Carol Dweck and Angela Duckworth would acknowledge that their theories share several similarities, there *are* some differences between having a growth mindset and having grit. Review the excerpt from *Mindset* and the transcript of Duckworth's TED Talk, then write a paragraph describing what the two success strategies have in common. Write a second paragraph in which you identify the differences between the two theories.

Longer: Watch Carol Dweck's TED Talk video on growth mindset, "The Power of Believing that You Can Improve." You can find it online using the search terms **"Carol Dweck"** and **"TED Talk."** Then, read through the Questions & Answers about Grit on Angela Duckworth's homepage (angeladuckworth.com/qa/). Write an additional paragraph or two explaining how this added information deepens or changes your understanding of the two concepts.

3.5f Kurt Streeter and Kashawn Campbell

Shorter: As his biographical note indicates, Kurt Streeter, like Kashawn Campbell, was a student at Berkeley, although many years earlier. While Streeter's path to Cal wasn't quite as difficult as Kashawn's, he, too, came from a single-family home, and his life wasn't always easy. Read Streeter's *Los Angeles Times* article, "French Final Is Family Matter" (articles.latimes.com/2009/jun/07/sports/sp-streeter7), then write a paragraph describing a few ways that Streeter, too, demonstrated grittiness.

Longer: Compare Streeter's grittiness with Kashawn's. What experiences do they have in common? How were their lives different? What can they learn from one another?

3.5g Additional Essay Prompts on Growth Mindset and Grit

1. Many educators believe that a growth mindset and grit can help their students become more successful. Based on the material in this chapter, as well as any outside research you conduct, write an essay in which you explore how growth mindset and/or grit might improve student success. Be as specific as possible when discussing the ways these two concepts might manifest themselves in the lives of college students. Does having a growth mindset, for example, enable students to become stronger college readers? If so, how? In what ways might grittiness help a student who is struggling to complete a college essay?

2. While a growth mindset and grit can unquestionably help students succeed, these concepts aren't without their flaws — otherwise, every gritty person with a growth mindset would be successful. Critics like David Denby, who wrote an article in the *New Yorker* entitled "The Limits of 'Grit,'" point out that human nature is "complex and wavering" and that other factors besides grit, such as genetics or creativity, may be responsible for a person's success or failure. Find and read Denby's article "The Limits of 'Grit'" online, then write an essay in which you address some of the limitations of growth mindset and/or grit in ensuring student success.

3. Choose *either* growth mindset *or* grit as your focus, and write an essay in which you respond to this question: To what extent do you think a growth mindset *or* grit account for a person's success? Use Kashawn Campbell's experience, as described in Streeter's profile, as the main example of your chosen concept's strengths and limitations. However, you may also bring in credible outside research and draw on your own experiences and those of people you know.

4. Compare Kashawn's Campbell's experiences at Jefferson High and UC-Berkeley with your own high school and college experiences. In what ways was Kashawn grittier than you and vice versa? How did you both persist in the face of difficulties? — *every* high school student faces some difficulties. Conclude your essay by drawing on both Kashawn's and your own experience to offer other students advice on how to succeed academically.

5. Dweck, Duckworth, and Streeter all seem to suggest that "success" is equivalent to economic or educational or career achievement. Write an essay in which you explore other definitions of success. Many people with little education and backbreaking jobs, for instance, still manage to be happy because of the pride and joy they take in their families and friends, or because of a passion they have for an activity outside their work. Reference the readings when appropriate, but focus on examples of success that aren't necessarily money-, school-, or work-related.

4

Prewriting

Write Before You Read   How do you get started writing an essay? Are you someone who jumps in without even an outline, or do you prefer to meticulously plan everything before you actually begin drafting? Write a paragraph or two about your typical approach. Write a bit, too, about the strategies you use to generate material. Do you freewrite, map ideas, or make a list? Have you ever faced writer's block? If so, how did you get past it?

4.1   Getting Started

"Zest. Gusto," Ray Bradbury says in *Zen in the Art of Writing*: "How rarely one hears these words used. How rarely do we see people living, or for that matter, creating by them. Yet if I were asked to name the most important items in a writer's make-up, the things that shape his material and rush him along the road to where he wants to go, I could only warn him to look to his zest, see to his gusto."

While many of us might pause over Bradbury's outdated use of masculine pronouns to describe everyone, we can still share his passion for creativity. Ideally, whatever assignment your instructor sets before you will inspire zest, gusto, and the burning desire to write. However, even if the assignment you're currently facing doesn't exactly light your fire, you can still enjoy writing it. In fact, as you gain experience as a writer, you may welcome the challenges of a difficult assignment. As with any activity, the more you practice, the better you will become—and the more you will want to push yourself to get even better.

As noted earlier in the book, there's no single best way to read or write—or do anything, really. However, respected organizations like the Council of Writing Program Administrators tell us that being flexible and adaptable are crucial mindsets for students who want to succeed as academic writers. A textbook such as this one offers suggestions that have worked for many student writers for a long time. Ultimately, though, the purpose of any set of guidelines is to help you find your own best practices as a writer—to channel your own gusto.

> As with any activity, the more you practice, the better you will become — and the more you will want to push yourself to get even better.

Develop a Writing and Learning Mindset

One reason you'll want to develop multiple strategies for composing is that *what* you're writing often dictates *how* you write. For example, it would be silly to go through all the prewriting strategies in this chapter before composing a text message. And while you might use one or two prewriting activities to generate material for an in-class essay, you certainly wouldn't have time to use them all.

On the other hand, it would be foolish to put the same amount of effort into composing a formal academic essay as you do when you text a friend. Unfortunately, some students type their essays almost as quickly as they respond to messages on their phones. They may not think carefully about their purpose, their audience, or the readers' expectations and instead convince themselves that turning in *something*, no matter how confusing or careless it may be, should earn them a passing grade. "If wishes were horses," the old Scottish proverb goes, "beggars would ride," which implies that if all it took were a wish, even people with nothing would get whatever they desired. That's not the case, of course, since most times success is possible only with effort.

Granted, writing an essay comes easy on occasion, especially if you're engaged in the topic; but more often than not, it's a lot of hard work. All writers face opportunities to give up, but if you want to succeed in college, and in life, you know that's not an option. The next time you hit a stumbling block, remember the research described in Chapter 1; our brains actually change and grow when they are confronted with new and difficult tasks. Believing in your own mind's growth is the first step to making that growth actually happen, according to Carol Dweck, a learning psychologist (Chapter 3). Two more key points from Dweck's research should be emphasized:

1. When you don't succeed, remember that failure is just another opportunity to become better at the skill you are practicing.

2. When you *do* succeed, make sure you understand *how* and *why* so you can repeat those processes and strategies in the future.

Keep Writing Tasks Manageable

Still, no matter how much effort you put into your writing, and no matter hard you try to have a growth mindset, sometimes it can all seem overwhelming. If it's any comfort, you're not alone. Every writer, no matter how successful, periodically feels hopelessly stuck and unable to write another word ever. In her book *Bird by Bird: Instructions on Writing and Life*, Anne Lamott explains how she came up with her unusual title:

> Thirty years ago my older brother, who was ten years old at the time, was trying to get a report written on birds that he'd had three months to write, which was due the next day. We were out at our family cabin in Bolinas, and

he was at the kitchen table close to tears, surrounded by binder paper and pencils and unopened books about birds, immobilized by the hugeness of the task ahead. Then my father sat down beside him, put his arm around my brother's shoulder, and said, "Bird by bird, buddy. Just take it bird by bird."

The experience of Lamott's brother speaks to a lot of writers—and a lot of people in general. Our task seems impossible when we procrastinate until the day before an assignment is due and consider how little time we have left. But the larger message is that writing—or at least good writing—doesn't normally flow out all at once, like water from a tap: Instead, it's a *process* that typically involves a series of separate steps. And this is true for even the most experienced writers.

Composing an academic essay can seem like a tremendous challenge, but as long as you take it "bird by bird"—breaking the task into manageable parts—you will be able to find your way to the end.

Read and Reread the Prompt

A while back, the administrators at my college asked me to develop a Writing across the Curriculum handbook. I spent the academic year talking to colleagues, holding workshops, and collecting written responses to a questionnaire from every department on campus. Three pieces of advice emerged again and again. My fellow professors wanted college-level writers to do the following:

1. Be clear.

2. Address the appropriate audience.

3. Stay on task.

One of the best ways of following that third piece of advice and staying on task is *reading and rereading the prompt*. A "prompt" is the part of your assignment that specifically states the expected outcome of your essay. (As a verb, "prompt" means to "cause someone to take action"—in this case, the action is writing.) Understanding and responding to the writing prompt that you've actually been given—not the one you wish you had—is important to writing a successful essay.

To see how responding to a specific prompt plays out in the essay-composing process, in the next few chapters, you'll see responses to a single prompt related to the readings in Chapter 3. Therefore, while instructors typically provide multiple prompts for each essay assignment, for clarity's sake, let's say there is only one prompt, and this is it:

Sample essay prompt

Using "growth mindset" **or** "grit" as your focus, discuss the high school and college experiences of Kashawn Campbell and compare them with your own. Focus your discussion by referring *specifically* to either Carol Dweck's *Mindset* reading **or** Angela Duckworth's TED Talk.

- Aim for 1,000 to 1,500 words.

- Include a strong thesis and a clear argument.

- Support the thesis with concrete and specific evidence in each body paragraph.

- Use MLA-style formatting and documentation.

- Any outside research should be limited and relevant.

- Carefully edit and proofread your essay before turning it in.

  If you have questions at any time during the writing process, don't hesitate to contact me, our class tutor, or the campus writing center.

The first step in responding to a prompt like this is to immediately go back and read it again. So, even though you've just read the prompt, please take a minute and read it a second time right now, keeping your eyes open for details you didn't fully register the first time around.

Now, go back to the prompt for a third time and annotate the prompt. If you have questions, now is the time to ask them. Do you know what "MLA-style formatting and documentation" are? What does the professor mean by "outside research"?

Analyzing the Sample Essay Prompt

- **Determine the focus.** The first sentence typically signals the main emphasis of your essay. The sample prompt gives straightforward guidelines, indicating that that there will be three main areas for a writer to cover: (1) a growth mindset or grit, (2) Kashawn Campbell's high school and college experiences, and (3) your own experiences in high school and college.

- **Pay special attention to instruction verbs (which communicate your *purpose*).** Note the verbs "discuss" and "compare" in the sample. In discussing Campbell's experiences, you will examine the details that the reading presents and draw conclusions. When you compare them to your own, you will explore both similarities and differences between your experiences and Campbell's.

- **Look for limits.** It's important to remember the word "or" at the beginning of the first sentence. Here, your instructor is letting you know that it's okay to discuss *either* Dweck's work on growth mindset *or* Duckworth's exploration of grit. However, you should not discuss both. To make a good choice, you may need to know both *Mindset* and the TED Talk well.

- **Know the scope.** The assignment indicates the word count for the essay: 1,000 to 1,500 words. This is about four to six pages, double-spaced in a standard font, and should give you some flexibility in the length of your response.

- **Note any required features.** The assignment also details other specific aspects that the instructor will be looking for, including "a strong thesis" and "concrete and specific evidence."

- **Use the required style.** We learn that the essay should be written using MLA-style formatting and documentation. If you didn't use MLA style in high school, make a note to find out more about this. (MLA is covered in Chapter 18 of this book.)

- **Stay in your lane.** The assignment sounds a note of caution: "Any outside research should be limited and relevant." Your instructor *is* permitting you to do outside research if you think it's warranted, but it's clear that the focus of this essay should be on the material that has already been assigned and discussed in class.

- **Note details about submission.** The prompt ends by reminding you to edit and proofread your essay before turning it in. That may seem like a long way off now, which is one more reason to keep returning to the prompt even when you're almost ready to turn your essay in.

- **Ask for help.** The instructor signals a willingness to meet with students and also encourages them to talk with the class tutor or tutors in the writing center. Doing so is not mandatory, but it does indicate that if you have specific questions, help is available.

Prompts differ from instructor to instructor, of course. Some professors write multipage assignments that require a great deal of scrutiny on the part of students. And instructors aren't always as succinct as they might be. The longer the prompt, the more you want to be able to zero in on what's *most* important.

Conversely, other professors may provide you with only the bare essentials, offering something as basic as this: "Write an essay about the relative value of a growth mindset." If your prompt is brief or seems vague, ask questions to get more guidance from your instructor. At the very least, begin paying careful attention in class to the elements of writing your instructor seems to value.

Ask Key Questions Before You Draft

To begin, take stock of your complete writing situation — sometimes called your *rhetorical situation*. Normally, you will want to be able to answer the following key questions before you begin drafting.

- **What is your purpose?** If you are assigned to write an argument but you turn in a description instead, or if you're supposed to be reviewing a film but you end up writing a summary, you've mistakenly written for the wrong purpose. Be sure to identify this critical piece of information—your reason for writing.

- **Who is the audience?** The person grading your work is one audience for an assignment, but it's important to be aware of other real or imagined audiences. The assignment may ask you to address students on your campus or residents of the town you live in, even though you might not actually share your work with them. You might also be asked to address readers of a certain blog, for example, and to upload your work as a comment to a certain post. Don't assume that your professor is your only, or even your first, audience.

- **What should the final product look like?** When instructors create an assignment, they generally envision the finished product containing certain elements and looking a certain way. As much as possible, you'll want your essay to align with what your instructor is expecting to see. Multimodal essays—those that may incorporate images, sound, and video—are discussed in Chapter 14, but even traditional academic essays vary from discipline to discipline and instructor to instructor. Make sure you know what you're supposed to be creating before you begin writing. If your instructor points to a model to follow, study the features of the model.

- **How long should it be?** The length of an essay is traditionally determined by word count rather than number of pages, although multimodal essays often have different length requirements. Think of the length as the level of detail and complexity your instructor expects.

- **How much, if any, research is required?** Research requirements will differ depending on the discipline and the instructor. You may be expected to consult many sources or a few or zero. If research is required, it may be that you're asked to conduct traditional library or online research; to conduct field research using observations, interviews, or surveys; or to use a combination of methods.

- **Are there models—either professional or by other students—that you can study?** Some instructors use similar assignments from one academic term to the next, saving exceptional papers for use as models the following semester. If your instructor has provided model student papers, study them carefully. If none are available, ask to see *something* that resembles the essay you are expected to write. If your instructor doesn't have any models for you to read, the student essays in this book may serve as acceptable examples.

DIY 4.1 Summarize Your Essay Prompt

Write a paragraph summarizing the main expectations for your essay based on the prompt your instructor has given you for your first assignment. Make sure you include each aspect of the assignment that you *must* cover. What do you think is the purpose of the assignment? Who is your audience, real or imagined? What are the key features of a successful draft? What requirements do you need more information about?

4.2 Making a Schedule

Prioritizing in college is largely a matter of deciding on the urgency and importance of any particular assignment. In a perfect world, you could give every assignment its proper due, but few of us live in a perfect world, and as a college student you'll need to make decisions about time management constantly.

One of the most effective ways to prioritize your work is to create a schedule. Whether you make a schedule on paper, online, or on your phone, it's helpful to code each of your classes and nonacademic activities, with its own font or color. For example, one student created a daily schedule with an iPhone app:

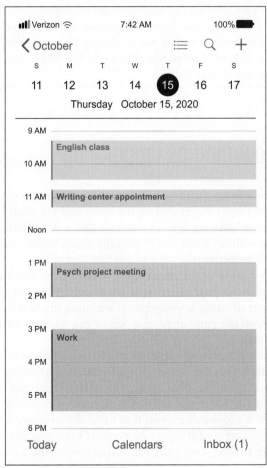

Calendar apps can help with planning.

Your schedule should be realistic, accounting for assignments that are due in other classes and acknowledging that college isn't all work; you need to set aside some time for exercise and fun. It's also a good idea to build in some time for things to go wrong. If you procrastinate, get called into work, or have a family emergency, you'll want to have some back-up time built into your timetable. Very early in your college career, you'll begin to see how important planning is and how critical it is to take advantage of every hour in the day available to you.

DIY 4.2 Make a Schedule

Make a schedule for completing your essay. Include activities that will keep you from working on your essay, such as other classes, work, family obligations, or time you need for staying healthy and happy. Be sure to build in time for things to go wrong. Start your work earlier than necessary so that you can adjust and adapt as life keeps coming at you. Many colleges and universities make daily planners available to students — either free or at deep discounts. Microsoft Word includes a calendar among its templates, or you may find that it's most convenient to use the calendar app in your phone.

4.3 Prewriting as Preparation

After you've carefully read and reread the prompt, what do you do next? Some writers will simply begin writing the essay and see what happens. That's not always a bad idea, but if you think about your rhetorical situation before you draft—about *what* you're actually going write, and *why*, and for *whom*—you will be better off.

Think of prewriting as the preparation necessary to begin the hard work of writing a good essay. Just as an experienced runner wouldn't head off on a 10K run without dressing appropriately, warming up, and hydrating, you don't want to go on the equivalent of a decent run without first preparing yourself for the task.

The following prewriting activities can act as idea starters and represent a range of directed, low-stakes ways to begin generating the material that will ultimately become your essay. The words "directed" and "low-stakes" are key here. When the activity is directed, you know exactly what to do. And when it's low stakes, you don't feel the pressure of *Oh no, I'm writing an entire essay and it better be perfect!* Like warming up before a run, prewriting before you begin your essay makes the actual writing easier.

Give all the following activities a try and then decide which ones work best for you. The more you use a particular strategy successfully, the more likely you will be successful with it when facing future writing assignments.

Freewrite

Freewriting in North American composition classes was made famous by Professor Peter Elbow. In *Writing Without Teachers*, Elbow describes the practice this way:

> The idea is simply to write for ten minutes. . . . Don't stop for anything. Go quickly without rushing. Never stop to look back, to cross something out, to wonder how to spell something, to wonder what word or thought to use, or to think about what you are doing. If you can't think of a word or a spelling, just use a squiggle or else write "I can't think what to say, I can't think what to say" as many times as you want; or repeat the last word you wrote over and over again; or anything else. The only requirement is that you never stop.

For some students, freewriting feels liberating; they love to write, but they hate rules, and freewriting's sole rule is to keep writing. Ideas pour forth, and moving a pen across a sheet of paper, or tapping on the keys of a keyboard as fast as possible, becomes a deeply satisfying physical act. Ten minutes seems far too little time—they want to go on and on.

For other students, ten minutes will seem like ten hours. They write for the first couple of minutes, but then they just run out of gas. Rather than writing continuously, they stare out the window or sneak a look at their phones.

As tempting as it might be, don't quit early. The real value often comes in those final minutes of a freewrite. The first things we jot down are the most obvious, but if your freewriting is working, you begin to dig deeper under the surface of your thoughts. Ideas you didn't quite know you had suddenly become words.

> **DIY 4.3a** Practice Freewriting
>
> If your instructor has already assigned the topic for your first essay, freewrite in response to your essay prompt. If not, practice freewriting in response to the reflection prompt from the beginning of the chapter: "How do you get started writing an essay?"

Question

Questioning often works well after a freewrite, when your "brain muscles" have limbered up. As its name implies, questioning is simply the act of forming questions about your topic. It's helpful to start with the basics: *Who? What? When? Where? How? Why?* These are often called the "reporter's questions," as reporters on the scene of a story are taught to find the answers to each of them. That last one—*Why?*—is often the most difficult to answer, but it's also the question that's most likely to yield the richest responses in an academic essay.

It doesn't matter if you don't know the answers to your questions when you ask them. In fact, it's probably better if you don't—questions that need answers often lead to the freshest, most exciting writing you will do on a topic. As an example, here are three quick questions about the excerpt from Carol Dweck's book *Mindset* (see Chapter 3):

- What are some of the differences between a fixed mindset and a growth mindset?

- What are the biggest challenges to adopting a growth mindset?

- How persuasive is Dweck's evidence?

Not every question you ask yourself will need to be answered in your essay, but the questions that come flying off your fingertips frequently point you in the direction you need to go.

DIY 4.3b Practice Questioning

Generate a list of questions inspired by the essay prompt given to you by your instructor. (If you don't yet have a prompt, you can practice with the sample assignment for this chapter on page 77.) It helps to begin with one of the question words. Write out *Who? What? When? Where? How?* or *Why?* — then don't overthink what comes next.

If you're having trouble getting started, set the timer on your phone for one minute and tell yourself you have to come up with three questions about your topic in that time. Don't be critical of your questions — just write down whatever comes into your head.

Write a List

When you're planning a trip to the grocery store or just thinking about all the things you need to get done this week, there's something satisfying about seeing each item take shape on a piece of paper or in a notes app and then—even more satisfying—being able to cross off or delete those items once they've been addressed.

As with freewriting and questioning, listing works best if you work quickly and write down *everything* that occurs to you. Don't censor yourself. If the items generally respond to the assignment you've been given, then consider any item that appears on your list as potentially useful. A prewriting list for an essay, therefore, might take many forms. For the prompt in this chapter, you might list all the people you know who have demonstrated a growth mindset, or all the instances of a growth mindset demonstrated by Kashawn Campbell or yourself.

After you've finished listing, it's useful to look for patterns in what you've written. These patterns represent ways you might group the material into possible paragraphs for your essay. You might also look for items that suggest areas needing further exploration. Often, in fact, one item on your list will inspire you to make another list altogether.

The first three items on a list responding to the prompt about mindset might look like this:

- Get a copy of Dweck's book online and see what her research is based on.

- Email Summer Bridge director and ask if there were any times that I had a growth mindset.

- Make a list of all the examples of Kashawn Campbell's growth mindset in Streeter's article.

DIY 4.3c Practice Listing

Make your own list of ideas and items relevant to the prompt you've been given. If you don't yet have an essay assignment, practice with a prompt such as this one: "What does it take to succeed in a class you don't like?"

You may be able to see now how doing multiple prewriting activities on the same topic helps you find out what you are most interested in while at the same time expanding the material you will have to draw on in the writing of your essay. Ideally, after a freewrite, a question set, and a list, you will begin thinking about how to organize your essay, which we will talk more about in the next chapter.

Write a Letter

Writing a letter may sound like an odd way of preparing to write an essay. However, for many of us, connecting with another human being—even if the connection is imaginary—encourages a more honest and direct approach.

In a letter, you have the following:

1. a specific audience

2. something concrete to convey that audience

3. the need to keep your audience engaged

Trying different prewriting strategies can help you get more comfortable *preparing* to write.
PeopleImages/Getty Images

If that description sounds a lot like a good essay, then don't be surprised if you end up using revised parts of your letter in your actual essay. As with most types of writing, the more concrete and specific details you draw on, the stronger your writing is likely to be.

As an example, here are the first two paragraphs of a letter to Kashawn Campbell as he is profiled in the article "South L.A. Student Finds a Different World at Cal" (see page 63).

Sample prewriting in letter form

Dear Kashawn,

I read the article about you in the LA Times, and I was really moved by not only all the things you've been through in your life but also by the ways you've managed to cope with stuff — hard stuff — that would have made a lot of people shrug their shoulders and quit. You truly have what Carol Dweck calls a "growth mindset"!

Actually, I'm getting in touch with you today because I've been assigned to write an essay that talks about how having a growth mindset allowed you to overcome many obstacles in high school and college. I noticed in Kurt Streeter's article that there were times when just trying really, really hard didn't seem to work for you. You seemed to be at a pretty low point after your first semester at Berkeley, but you ended up making it through the year. So, I'd like to ask you: What strategies do you recommend for developing a growth mindset, especially when it would be so easy to have a fixed mindset instead?

DIY 4.3d Write a Letter to an Expert

Write a letter to an expert on the topic of your essay, someone who can help you respond to your prompt. (If you were writing about growth mindset or grit, that expert could be Carol Dweck or Angela Duckworth. Or an "expert" in this case, could be someone with relevant lived experience, as Campbell is in the letter above.) While the tone of the letter may be relatively informal, don't go *too* far in that direction; remember that the main purpose of the letter, which you may never actually send, is to help you generate ideas for your essay.

Make a Map or Cluster

Mapping or clustering is particularly helpful for learners who are visually and spatially motivated. In the following map, which responds to the essay prompt we've been discussing, you see "Kashawn Campbell"—whose experiences are meant to be one of the main focuses of the essay—in the center. Lines reach out from Campbell to "High School" and "UC Berkeley" toward the top of the map, and "Growth Mindset" and "Grit" toward the bottom. From each of those circles, lines extend to related circles.

In *The Writer's Way*, Jack Rawlins and Stephen Metzger call the central word or phrase in a map the "seed." "Work out from the seed in all directions," they advise, "letting bits cluster as they will. Try to connect everything in the map to something else in the map." Seen from this perspective, the map is a kind of visual freewrite, where the goal is to generate as much material as possible, before finding ways the various clusters might connect.

Other versions of mapping see it as a slower, more methodical process. In this approach, you're not so much freewriting as drafting an early outline. This type of mapping is a particularly good way to imagine the relationships among your ideas and what your essay will look like on the page, with the main clusters serving as paragraph topics and the connecting circles acting as supporting evidence.

Sample prewriting in the form of mapping

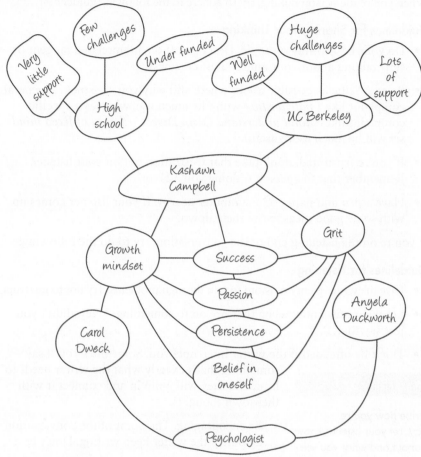

Mapping, one prewriting strategy, can help writers who are visual learners.

Talk and Listen

Not just at the beginning, but throughout the composing process, you will benefit from sharing your thoughts, ideas, and questions with someone else. Particularly when you get stuck, it's helpful to be able to try and articulate *why* you're having trouble. Often, simply describing the problem for someone else will help you see the solution.

Ideally, whoever you're talking to has some stake in your success. That could mean the person is a friend or family member, a classmate, or your instructor or tutor. Your listener doesn't have to be a whiz at English, but they do need

---

DIY 4.3e Practice Mapping

Make your own map for the essay prompt assigned by your instructor. If you don't yet have an essay topic, use a topic that you choose.

to be willing to listen to what you have to say and offer commonsense responses. When you're the person talking, try to adhere to the following guidelines:

Guidelines for Sharing Your Thinking

- Do your best to stay on topic. Don't go off on an unrelated tangent or start talking about your aunt's latest craziness.

- Be as specific as possible about where and why you are stuck. A general complaint like *I hate writing* won't be much use, whereas a specific complaint like *I don't understand Carol Dweck's theory of fixed mind-set* will be much more useful.

- If you're frustrated, don't take that frustration out on your listener. Remember that the person is doing you a favor.

- Have a pen and paper or a computer nearby. If your listener comes up with some good ideas, write them down.

If you're on the listening end of the conversation, try to do the following:

Guidelines for Listening

- Give the writer plenty of room to talk through problems. Try not to interrupt.

- Let the writer know when they are on to something: "Hey, didn't you just say that. . . ."

- Don't be offended if the writer interrupts you. Sometimes you'll say something that's exactly what the writer needs to hear, and they will jump in and connect it with their own thoughts.

- Be encouraging. The point of the conversation is to help the writer keep writing. Don't be a naysayer.

- Be honest. If you truly think the writer is going down the wrong path, say so. However, always temper your honesty with kindness and encouragement.

DIY 4.3f Practice Talking and Listening

Find a willing listener and describe how you're planning to approach your essay. Let your listener know both what you're most excited about and what you see as potential problems.

Then, take a turn listening to someone else who is working on a piece of writing; use the tips in 4.3 to guide the writer toward a resolution of issues they face. If possible, record your conversations.

4.4 Conducting Preliminary Research

Generating your own ideas is an essential part of taking ownership of the topic that you have been assigned to write about. At some point, however, you're going to want to seek out ideas that others have about your topic. You'll need, therefore, to do a bit of research.

Think of research as listening in on the conversations of others. You're learning what's been thought about your topic by experts in the field, and you're taking note of the specific things they have said or specific findings from their investigations. In short, you're beginning to look for the sort of "concrete and specific evidence" that our sample prompt—like most prompts you will be assigned—requires you to discover.

Do a Quick Search

The quickest way—and for many of us the most natural way—to find out about a topic is with an Internet search, usually through a popular search engine such as Google.

Later in the book, you'll hear quite a bit about the many ways you can go off track by searching only on the web—your college library's database of newspapers, magazines, and peer-reviewed scholarly journal articles is usually a much safer bet—but for now, you're simply looking for ways to come up with more ideas.

Most search engines return the most relevant results first, but it never hurts to put quotation marks around names and key phrases. Let's say, for instance, that you want to see if anyone has had reservations about Duckworth's theories on grit. If you type "Angela Duckworth" and "grit" into Google, you'll come up with more than a half million results.

Typing "Angela Duckworth" and "grit" and "review" narrows that down considerably. Among the first five results in a recent search were David Denby's compelling "The Limits of 'Grit'" in *The New Yorker*, as well as reviews of Duckworth's book in reputable sources like *The New York Times*, on the blog of *Scientific American*, and in the literary magazine *Ploughshares*.

If you want to narrow your search down even further, you can go to Google News (news.google.com), where—at the time of this writing—a search for "Angela Duckworth" and "grit" and "review" returned only a handful of results. Deleting the word "review" from the search brings in more results, most of which have to do with how businesses can use the concept of grit when hiring and retaining employees.

Again, a quick search is just that: quick. Think of it as the Internet equivalent of a freewrite: You'll be generating a lot of ideas, but you'll only be using a few. Right now, you're only looking for concrete ideas to move yourself closer to writing your essay.

When you do find potentially strong sources, you'll want to save them. If you're on your own computer, bookmark the pages. If you're searching on your phone, copy relevant links to a notes file. Use labels to keep clear which sources go with which search or project.

Another way to make sure you don't forget the location of a potentially valuable source is to create a citation using the formatting style (MLA or APA, for example) specified in your assignment. Here's a Works Cited

90

CHAPTER 4
Prewriting

list-in-progress of three sources found during a quick search that might be useful later on. The list uses the Modern Language Association, or MLA, style guide (see Chapter 18 for more):

Works Cited

Kaufman, Scott Barry. Review of *Grit: The Power of Passion and Perseverance*, by Angela Duckworth. *Scientific American Blog*, 10 May 2016, blogs.scientificamerican.com/beautiful-minds/review-of-grit-the-power-of-passion-and-perseverance.

Review of *Grit: The Power of Passion and Perseverance*, by Angela Duckworth. *Kirkus Reviews*, 3 May 2016, www.kirkusreviews.com/book-reviews/angela-duckworth/grit-power.

Sommers, Aaron. Review of *Grit: The Power of Passion and Perseverance*, by Angela Duckworth. *The Ploughshares Blog*, 30 Sept. 2016, blog.pshares.org/index.php/review-grit-the-power-of-passion-and-perseverance-by-angela-duckworth.

DIY 4.4a Practice Quick Searching

Do a quick Internet search on the essay topic assigned by your instructor. If your first search terms don't yield any results, try adding or deleting key terms such as "review," "debate," or "background" until you find what you're looking for. (Use "growth mindset" or "grit" for practice if you don't yet have an assignment.)

Save significant search items so you can find them again easily. If you're already familiar with the citation style your instructor requires, try saving your sources as citations. If not, bookmark them or simply cut and paste the web addresses and save them in a document, knowing that you will have to format proper citations in your final draft.

Curate Quotations

In the past, a "curator" was usually thought of as someone who selected the works of art for a museum. More recently, though, the term "curating" has come to be applied to the selection and organization of just about anything—from songs on a particular theme to items of clothing that are compatible with one another.

This newer concept of curating will be used here to help you begin gathering materials for your essay. One of the most persuasive types of evidence you can offer in support of an argument is a smart quotation from a credible source. Therefore, as you skim through the content of websites pertinent to your topic, be open to passages that jump out at you. Look for sentences or even short phrases that might enrich a discussion of your topic or introduce an important perspective.

Granted, this early in the composing process, it may be hard to know if the quotations you find in a quick online search will ultimately be the ones you use. (And in fact if the quotations you find do look promising, you'll want to read the entire works in which they appear.) However, if you get into the habit of "curating" your quotations—that is, selecting, organizing, and presenting them as though they will, indeed, be used in your essay—you'll not only get an idea of the big picture of your topic, you'll also begin to think about how you might want to group recurring ideas and arguments. Moreover, you'll find that you might have material you can use in your essay even before you begin writing the essay itself.

Once you have a suitable quotation, give it some context by creating a signal phrase to introduce it. In a **signal phrase**, you identify one or more of the following:

1. The author

2. The credentials of the author if relevant

3. The title of the source

4. The place where the source was published

Here are sample quotations, with signal phrases, from each of the three articles found in the earlier Quick Search on grit:

Reviewing Grit in Ploughshares, Aaron Sommers is "left wondering how teachers in underfunded districts can put her ideas to practice" as "Duckworth offers us little in terms of practical applications."

Psychologist Scott Barry Kaufman, who acknowledges that Duckworth is "a valued friend and colleague," resents criticism that Duckworth's work is overly focused on grit. He points out, in a recent review on the Scientific American Blog, that she also "mentions the importance of cultivating other character strengths (e.g., humility, social intelligence, kindness, etc.) for success in life."

An anonymous author writing in Kirkus Reviews believes that "[i]n the nature vs. nurture controversy, [Duckworth] sides with nurture, and there's more than a little of the tiger mom in the prescriptions she dispenses for education. . . . For Duckworth, there should be no trophies for just showing up."

Details on quoting sources are discussed in Chapter 6, but for the moment, you may have noticed the following conventions:

Conventions for Quoting

- Place quotation marks around only the *exact words* of your source.

- Use your own words in between quotations to help them flow as smoothly as possible.

- Quotations can be introduced as part of a sentence, without any punctuation, or with punctuation marks like commas and colons.

- A quotation *within* another quotation is indicated by single (rather than double) quotation marks.

- A quotation that eliminates one or more sentences in the middle of the quotation is indicated by four spaced periods at the end of the sentence before the omission (a four-dot ellipsis).

DIY 4.4b Find and Contextualize Quotations

Curate a quotation from each of the sources you found during your quick search. Provide context for the quotations by introducing them with a signal phrase that tells the reader who is being quoted and where the quotation originally appeared.

Chapter 4 Checklist
Prewriting

☐ **Have you read and reread the prompt?**

Knowing what your instructor wants to see in your essay is the first and most important task you face with each assignment. From beginning to end in the composing process, you can't be *too* familiar with the prompt.

☐ **Have you made a tentative schedule for the completion of your essay?**

Sketch out your initial plan for when you will complete the various stages of your essay, ideally on an academic calendar. Remember that setting and meeting interim deadlines will help make completing the assignment easier.

☐ **Have you experimented with each of the prewriting activities?**

Often, a certain prewriting activity will look boring or impractical on the surface, yet when you actually try it, that activity turns out to be one of your favorite and most useful methods for generating ideas. Try *every* prewriting or invention activity you come across.

☐ **Have you "curated" at least a few direct quotations that may be appropriate for your essay?**

Smart, to-the-point quotations by experts commenting on your topic are among the most valuable materials you can take away from your prewriting. Make sure you have at least a couple of quotations "in your pocket" as you move to the next stage of the writing process.

☐ **Have you read through your prewriting and thought about where your essay seems to be heading?**

As you begin to think about crafting an argument and organizing your essay, you'll want to be aware of what you've already written down. Look over everything you've written and consider the direction your prewriting seems to be taking you.

4.5 Making It Stick

How can you get going on an academic essay?

Working Together

4.5a "Yes, and" The "Yes, and" approach to collaborative writing was developed by composition professor and improv performer Lauren Esposito, who takes her idea from a theatre game in which the rule is always (1) to agree with whatever your scene partner says and (2) to add something new to that statement or claim.

For instance, suppose you and I are improv partners on stage, and you say, "I went to school today and our professor was giving out 'A's to everyone in our class." My response has to begin, "***Yes, and*** . . . he was also giving out 'A's to everyone who had to miss class to go work."

Then it's your turn: "***Yes, and*** all the bosses were giving huge raises to their employees."

My turn: "***Yes, and*** the bosses said the employees didn't even have to show up to work anymore." And on and on.

The idea is that rather than shutting down someone else's ideas — "Come on now, that it's impossible" — you're looking to bolster and enhance them. It's essentially another version of Peter Elbow's "believing game" (p. 28).

Try the game yourself. In order to heighten the energy, Esposito recommends limiting the collaborative exercise to two or three minutes, so choose a very short time frame for each person's topic. You'll generate a lot more ideas if you're not writing them down as you talk. Instead, have the person whose topic you are improvising on record the conversation on their phone. Many recording apps have speech-to-text capability; therefore, the ideas you generate orally can be right there waiting for you when you begin crafting your thesis and writing your paragraphs.

If there's time, try collaborating with a second or third partner. You never know when you're going to match up with someone who is full of ideas about your topic.

Applying What You Know

4.5b Scheduling Your Essay, Scheduling Your Life
Make a schedule for however much time there is between now and whenever your essay is due. Let's say you have two weeks before you must turn it in. Locate or create a Daily Planner and list all your major commitments.

4.5c "Speed-Dating" Your Writing Topics
As you probably know, speed dating is a way of meeting lots of people in a short amount of time. Each "date" lasts only a few minutes, then the daters move on and meet someone else. (The classic scene on film is in *The 40-Year-Old Virgin*.)

Try "speed-dating" your essay topics by freewriting for a short time on each one. (Normally, you will be given at least a couple of prompts for every essay assignment, and some instructors may practically overwhelm you with choices.) Then choose a short span of time — seven minutes is probably more than enough — to read the prompt and write. You'll quickly find that some "dates" are bad — you run out of things to say well before time's up — while others are quite interesting, and you want to continue writing even when you've been told to stop. Those "dates" will point you to the topics you are most likely to want to pursue in the form of a full essay.

4.5d Freewriting Revisited
Whatever your initial experience with freewriting is, try it again. It could even be in support of a writing assignment for another class — not English. In his book *Telling Writing*, professor Ken Macrorie says:

> If you didn't amaze yourself in your freewriting, go back and try more. It's a guaranteed activity: if you write fast—without thinking of spelling, grammar, punctuation or form—and try to tells truths, sooner or later you will write something that moves you and others. Then you will become more confident and begin to respect your own experiences because you realize they are different from every other person's in the world—and so [are] the ultimate sources of your power as a writer.

Choose an aspect of your writing prompt that interests you, then let it rip. For at least ten minutes, follow Macrorie's advice and "try to tell truths," never stopping, even when you don't have anything to say. (In this case, writing "I don't know the truth, I don't know the truth" is better than writing nothing at all.) When you've completed your freewrite, take a breath and clear your head, then try and find at least one "true" sentence or thought that you can use in your essay.

Invitations to Write

4.5e Discovering Your Go-to Prewriting Strategy

Shorter: Read through the prewriting you've just done, then write a paragraph describing which activity worked best for you and why you think that is.

Longer: Write a few paragraphs describing your *least* favorite prewriting strategy and speculate about why it didn't work for you. Finish with a paragraph about what your prewriting preferences might say about you as a writer overall.

4.5f Prewriting Collage

Shorter: A collage is an assemblage of various shorter pieces placed against one another in odd and interesting ways. You may be most used to seeing visual collages, where one image is pasted next to, or sometimes partially on top of, another one.

However, you can also make a written collage, where you contrast pieces of writing — your own prewriting, quotations from your sources, or a combination of the two — instead of images. Take another look at the prompt for the assignment you are working on, then go back through the prewriting you've done for this chapter and make a collage of three or four of your invention activities, including your curated quotes. You can use the whole prewriting activity, or just the most interesting parts. While you might want to arrange your pieces of writing in a logical order, it can also be illuminating (and fun) to choose a random arrangement.

Ultimately, your goal is not to create an actual essay, but to see the prewriting you've been doing in a new, and hopefully productive, light.

Longer: Reread your collage and comment on it *as though it were written by someone else.* What's most interesting about the collage? Where does it *not* work? Overall, what do you learn about the essay topic from the collage?

4.5g Prewriting into Paragraphs

Shorter: Turn one of your freewriting activities into a paragraph you can envision appearing in an academic essay. Start with a topic sentence stating the paragraph's focus, then provide evidence to support the paragraph's main idea. Use as much of your prewriting as is practical, but feel free to add, delete, and move around whatever you came up with during that particular prewriting activity.

Longer: Choose another *two* of your prewriting activities and transform each one into a paragraph with a clear and focused topic sentence followed by supporting evidence. Arrange the three paragraphs in the order you think is most effective.

5

Generating a Thesis and Organizing Your Essay

REFLECT

Write Before You Read | Activity to connect what's new with what you already know 97

READ & PRACTICE

DIY (Do-it-yourself) activities offer just-in-time support for all the skills in this book.

MAKING IT STICK

Write Before You Read   Think back to a conversation you've had when it seemed like your conversation partner started rambling and you were left wondering, *What's the point?* or *Where are we going with this?* Use that memory of your digressive friend to write a paragraph explaining why starting with a clear point and following an outline might be smart strategies for drafting a college essay.

5.1   Starting with a Point

Once you annotate your assigned readings and generate some useful material with prewriting strategies, it's time to focus on drafting the essay. Some people like to start drafting with the first paragraph, and you might be wondering why the chapter after the discussion of prewriting isn't about introductory paragraphs. Shouldn't your first order of business be coming up with a catchy "hook"? The truth is, crafting a hook often distracts from the much more pressing task of crafting a strong thesis—a sentence or two that presents your main point or position. Introductions and conclusions *are* significant elements of academic writing, but those will be examined in detail in Chapter 7.

To write a strong thesis that presents your main point, you need to consider your audience and narrow your topic to one that is manageable within the scope of your assignment. Before reading about the important process of writing a strong thesis, take another look at the writing prompt we'll refer to throughout Chapters 4 to 8:

Sample essay prompt

Using "growth mindset" **or** "grit" as your focus, discuss the high school and college experiences of Kashawn Campbell and compare them with your own. Focus your discussion by referring *specifically* to either Carol Dweck's *Mindset* reading **or** Angela Duckworth's TED Talk.

- Aim for 1,000 to 1,500 words.

- Include a strong thesis and a clear argument.

- Support the thesis with concrete and specific evidence in each body paragraph.

- Use MLA-style formatting and documentation.

- Any outside research should be limited and relevant.

- Carefully edit and proofread your essay before turning it in.

If you have questions at any time during the writing process, don't hesitate to contact me, our class tutor, or the campus writing center.

5.2 Identifying Your Audience

Often a writing prompt indicates not only your purpose or what you need to accomplish in your essay; it also tells you *for whom* you are accomplishing those goals. While you may initially assume the most obvious audience for a college essay is your instructor and classmates, your instructor may indicate another explicit audience for whom you are writing or may invite you to imagine posting your writing in a social media space.

In a marketing class, for example, you may be targeting a specific product for a very specific audience—teen athletes or recent retirees; while in a journalism class, you may be writing a piece that the entire campus and, if it's posted online, potentially anyone in the world might read. In the case of the sample prompt, no specific audience has been named, which is not uncommon in college essay assignments. If no specific audience for your writing is designated in your prompt, it's usually safe to assume your readers are

- reasonable, that is, more persuaded by evidence than inflammatory rhetoric

- open to learning about your topic

- members of the general academic community (rather than your church, athletic team, Reddit group, and so on)

Sometimes, however, the audience for your essay will be a specific group of people about whom you don't know. In that case, you'll want to research their shared beliefs and biases and imagine what a person is expecting when they begin to read your work. Even if your reader is just your professor and classmates, "[t]he more you can drill down to the bare bones of what your typical reader wants," editor Robert Lee Brewer suggests, "the easier it becomes to appeal to them."

Ask Questions about Audience

Because the tone you employ and the evidence you select will be affected by your audience, it's never a bad idea to take notes about your readers. If they aren't familiar to you, ask yourself the following questions:

- **What are your readers likely to know, or not know, about your topic?** Presumably, your instructor is informed about your topic but of course doesn't know everything about it. As you begin generating ideas for your essay, try to avoid repeating information your audience is probably already aware of; instead, search for information your reader may not have but needs to know.

- **What is your relationship to your audience?** Most of the time you're trying to persuade your audience to adopt your ideas about your topic, so you'll want to be respectful and open-minded. Depending on the audience, however, the level of formality and the types of examples you provide could swing from the relatively casual to the proper and reserved.

- **What biases might your audience bring to the reading of your work?** If your audience is likely to be opposed to your argument—say you are conservative, and your instructor has consistently voiced liberal opinions in class—think about what tactics you will need to find common ground with someone who may not have a great deal of sympathy for your point of view. Don't be antagonistic unless the assignment specifically dictates that you take that approach.

- **What do you want your audience to do or think after reading your work?** *Give it a good grade*, you might respond, which is a perfectly legitimate goal. Often, though, there is some real or imaginary goal integrated into the prompt itself. In an essay that is primarily evaluative, for instance, you might have to convince your readers to see a particular movie or *not* download a certain recording. When you're writing in the workplace, you typically want your boss and coworkers to take, or avoid, certain actions. In the case of the prompt we've been working on, you might want to persuade your audience that your interpretation of how Kashawn Campbell employs a growth mindset to become a successful student is the most intelligent and logical one.

- **In what mode is your work most likely to be read,** and how will that affect how your readers process the essay? Many instructors, especially earlier in the academic term, will ask for no more than a text-only black-and-white version of your essay. However, in other classes, and in the workplace, you're probably going to have to provide more than straight text to keep your reader engaged. (There is more about multimedia and design in Chapters 14.) As you compose your essay, think about where and how it is going to be read. Will your readers expect everything to be communicated in words alone, or will they also be looking for images, video, and sound?

Ultimately, remember that there will indeed be at least one careful reader for your work: your instructor. Sure, your professor is getting paid to read what you turn in, but be respectful of the time involved in the task, and do your best to craft an essay that repays the time it takes to read it.

DIY 5.2 Create a Clear Picture of Your Audience

Chances are that you are reading this chapter in conjunction with an essay assignment that your instructor has already given you. Write answers to the five bulleted questions above ("Ask Questions about Audience") as they relate to the audience for the essay you are writing. Remember Robert Lee Brewer's suggestion: "The more you can drill down to the bare bones of what your typical reader wants, the easier it becomes to appeal to them."

5.3 Narrowing Your Topic

When you're given a broad topic, your instructor will expect you to narrow it down to a manageable size. A broad topic such as "anxiety disorders" would be difficult to tackle in a brief college paper, for example, but a narrower topic like post-traumatic stress disorder (a specific anxiety disorder) among migrant children might be better suited to a short essay.

Broad topic: Anxiety disorders

Narrowed topic: Post-traumatic stress disorder

Even narrower: Post-traumatic stress disorder among migrant children

If you're visually oriented, it might be helpful to think of this narrowing process as moving from the edge to the center of what's called a "stacked Venn diagram," as seen here. You may remember from your math class that a

- Broad topic
- Major sub-topic
- One aspect of major sub-topic

A diagram like this one can help you narrow a broad topic.

Venn diagram is made up of overlapping circles, each representing a particular aspect or set of the problem under discussion. The place where those circles intersect shows what the different elements have in common. As its name suggests, a stacked Venn diagram "stacks" those circles on top of one another, with the circle in the middle containing all the qualities of all the circles.

The sample prompt we've been using to illustrate the writing process has already narrowed the topic somewhat, so let's instead imagine a more general assignment on growth mindset. Suppose your professor has simply said "Write an essay about growth mindset" and has given you maximum flexibility within those broad parameters. What would you do next? Most likely, you'd begin doing some of the quick online searches discussed in Chapter 4. What have other people said about growth mindset? Do you find any of their comments interesting? A few quick searches might lead you to the discovery that growth mindset has been especially embraced by five groups: parents, educators, businesspeople, athletes, and those wanting to improve their personal relationships.

As a college student, you might find the educational aspect of growth mindset intriguing. If so, it would be time to do some prewriting. After freewriting, listing, and mapping, you might come up with a stacked Venn diagram that looks something like this:

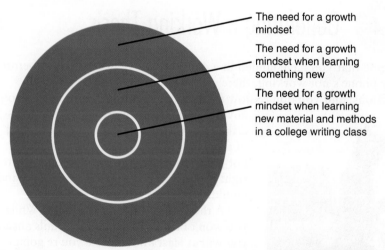

The need for a growth mindset

The need for a growth mindset when learning something new

The need for a growth mindset when learning new material and methods in a college writing class

Finding the "sweet spot" – the right scope for your essay – will keep your project manageable.

You can keep moving in toward the center of that circle, making your topic more and more specific; but at some point, you will go from having *too much* to say to *not enough*. Learning how to find that sweet spot where your topic is narrow enough that it doesn't feel like you're trying to explain the world in four pages, yet broad enough that you aren't repeating the same few points over and over, is one of the most useful skills you can develop as an academic writer.

DIY 5.3 Narrow Your Topic

If you've been assigned a broad topic for your essay assignment — one that differs from the fairly restricted prompt we've been working with — narrow that topic down until you feel you can comfortably write about it.

If your instructor has already sufficiently narrowed your topic, practice moving from the edge of the stacked Venn diagram to the center by choosing one of the broad topics below and narrowing it down to a manageable scale:

- Write an essay about tuition-free college education.
- Write an essay about professional sports.
- Write an essay about body positivity.
- Write an essay about racial justice.

5.4 Generating a Working Thesis

Imagine that you have landed in a country you've never been to before. Your phone's not working, there are no people around to give you directions, and you don't know the language; you certainly don't know anything about the highway system. Nevertheless, you have to get to the other end of the country in a single day, and you're not going to make it if you don't get started right now. A map would sure come in handy, wouldn't it?

A thesis is like a good road map. While you won't be able to see all the details ahead, you will at least know where you're going. That's an advantage for both writer *and* reader, as your reader will ultimately be following the same roads you take. Once you have the map, you can return to it whenever you need guidance.

You'll need a strong thesis no matter what sort of academic writing you're doing.

A good thesis is like a road map for both a writer and a reader.

Photostriker/Shutterstock

Your writing might be primarily persuasive, analytical, or evaluative. You could be writing a traditional words-only essay, or your "essay" might take the form of a podcast or a presentation. The essay is an elastic form, but having a well-crafted and concise argument is important to staying focused.

When you first begin writing, your thesis, or map, will be a work in progress. If your essay is like an unfamiliar country, it may turn out that this new country has a fairly unstable landscape. Sandstorms sometimes cover a highway, making it impassable; other times rivers flood a freeway, forcing you to take a back route to your goal. Because so much can change while you write your essay, you should begin with a working thesis. The more you write, the more you will discover about your topic, and the better your sense of direction will become. However, it's probably not going to be a straight line from your starting point to your destination. Commit yourself to this principle: As your ideas evolve, your thesis will need to evolve along with them.

> A thesis is like a good road map. While you won't be able to see all the details ahead, you will at least know where you're going.

Understand the Elements of a Strong Thesis

Sitting down to write your thesis is a pivotal moment in composing your essay because a strong thesis nearly always leads to a strong essay. Once you have a rough, working thesis in front of you, you'll want to subject it to a number of tests before you use it to begin writing your essay. As you read though this section, think about how the working thesis you're starting with might be revised and strengthened.

A Thesis Is Focused and Specific

If you've ever had an eye exam, you know what it's like when the optometrist puts a series of lenses into what's called a "phoropter" and asks you which one makes the eye chart look more or less clear. If your vision isn't great, you'll be moving from very blurry to blurry to clear. It's a great feeling when you reach that point of perfect vision, but in order to make sure it's the correct prescription, your optometrist will keep trying lenses, and soon *clear* will become *too clear*. In fact, an overly powerful lens will turn your vision blurry again.

Think of a visit to the optometrist when you're focusing your thesis. You certainly don't want it to be too broad and blurry, but if you narrow it down too far, it may become just as useless as if it were too broad.

As an example of how you might narrow a thesis, consider possible responses to the following question: "What does it take to get into the college of your choice?" Assume the thesis you are drafting needs to generate an essay of about 1,000 to 1,500 words (four to six double-spaced pages).

Too broad: It takes a lot to get into the college of your choice.

Still too broad: It takes money and intelligence to get into the college of your choice.

In focus: To get into the college of your choice, you need strong grades, a compelling personal story that sets you apart from other applicants, a complete application, and a little bit of luck.

Too narrow: It takes a weighted GPA of 4.95 to get into the college of your choice.

An effective thesis offers a specific and clear preview of the entire essay.
andresr/Getty Images

As you can see, the length of the assignment plays a big part in determining when a thesis statement is too broad and when it starts to become too narrow. "It takes a lot to get into the college of your choice" is vague and obvious, and, in any case, is much too general for a short academic essay. Even the narrower "It takes money and intelligence to get into the college of your choice" suggests a treatment of the subject matter that is too broad for 1,000 to 1,500 words allotted for the assignment.

On the other end of the spectrum, "It takes a weighted GPA of 4.95 to get into the college of your choice" is so specific and so limiting, and in fact is most likely untrue, that it would be difficult to argue that this particular criterion applies to more than a very small percentage of successful college students. In contrast, the "In Focus" thesis is specific, without being too limited, and clearly suggests the particular areas that will be covered in each of the essay's main paragraphs.

A Thesis Is Not a Statement of Fact

"Carol Dweck has written about growth mindset" is a simple statement of fact. There is abundant evidence—including her book, *Mindset*—to prove that Professor Dweck has addressed this topic in detail. Since no reasonable person could argue that Carol Dweck has *not* written about growth mindset, the statement does not work as a thesis.

However, things would change significantly if the wording and focus were shifted to the following: "Having a growth mindset is the single most important factor in determining a student's success." Suddenly, there's an argument and a defensible—if still somewhat broad—thesis statement.

"Why is growth mindset more important than economic security?" a reader might ask. "On what evidence are you basing your opinion?" The writer might respond that Dweck has conducted numerous experiments on a range of learners to reach her conclusions. "But what about a person's race and gender?" the reader might reply. "Surely those elements are just as important as growth mindset." On and on the dialogue could continue. Whatever your beliefs about growth mindset, it's clear that this conversation is much richer than any that a statement of fact might generate.

In high school, you may occasionally have been warned away from expressing your personal opinion on a topic. Usually, that's because teachers are worried that the essays they will receive will be *all* opinion with no substantive evidence to back up those beliefs. In college, though, your instructors will assume that you're going to provide concrete evidence, and, especially in humanities and social science classes, they will want to know what you think about the material you are discussing and why you hold that opinion.

A Thesis Contains a Topic and a Claim

Because it's so important to have an opinion about your topic, academic thesis statements normally announce their subject matter and make a claim about it. The following thesis statement can serve as an example:

Sample thesis with a topic and a claim		
	Topic	Claim
Thesis	Having a growth mindset	is the single most important factor in determining a student's success.

Just remember: Readers should be able to identify quickly *what* you are writing about and *your attitude* toward the subject matter.

A Thesis Answers a Question

As you've already discovered in your prewriting, asking questions inevitably encourages you to look for answers. In the diagram on page 101, a broad assignment about growth mindset was narrowed down to this topic: the need for growth mindset when learning new material in college composition classes. Here are some reporter's questions—*Who? What? How? When? Where? Why?*—that you could ask about that topic that might result in an interesting thesis:

- *Who* is responsible for ensuring that college composition students demonstrate growth mindset?

- *What* would be the major features of a curriculum that emphasizes growth mindset?

- *How* will these students demonstrate that they have a growth mindset?

- *When* must college composition students demonstrate a growth mindset?

- *Where* else, other than in their composition course, should students be taught how to develop a growth mindset?

- *Why* is a growth mindset necessary for college composition students to succeed?

Not all of these questions will result in an equally rich essay response. Nevertheless, each one suggests a particular avenue for a thesis. The *Why* question, for instance, might result in a thesis like this:

Sample thesis that answers a *Why* question

College composition students need a growth mindset to wrestle with complex and unfamiliar ideas, to navigate the difficult and time-consuming process of composing academic essays, and to persist to the end of a course despite encountering periodic failures.

If you worry that the questions you've come up with aren't likely to generate a strong essay, consider combining some of the questions. Asking, for example, "*Who* is responsible for ensuring that college composition students demonstrate growth mindset, and *how* will those people demonstrate that students actually possess it?" might result in a more complex thesis (and essay) than if only a single question were posed.

A Thesis Is Arguable and Worth Arguing

We've already seen that a thesis is not a statement of fact. If you write "Carol Dweck has written about growth mindset," you are not writing a thesis. That statement is not arguable, and it's not *worth arguing*. Many failed thesis statements have a similar lack of purpose.

Imagine, for instance, how your reader might respond to this sentence as a thesis statement:

Sample thesis that is not arguable

In my essay I will discuss growth mindset.

In addition to "announcing" itself as a thesis, this sentence doesn't hold up as a thesis statement because it is not arguable. Rather than making a claim a reader might dispute, the sentence simply *describes* what the essay is about. And what would be the value in "arguing" with a statement of fact?

A sentence like "In my essay I will discuss growth mindset" can't succeed because it has nowhere to go. There's no plan, no direction. Turning the sentence into a thesis would require actually thinking about *what* is going to be in the essay and *why* it will be there. Here's another sample thesis statement—this one has high potential for both objection and agreement:

Sample thesis that is arguable

Focusing on growth mindset in education distracts us from far more important factors that determine student success, such as high school preparation, economic security, and consistent access to support services.

Suddenly, as you can see, something is at stake. The writer has gone "against the grain," arguing a point of view about growth mindset that might not be popular. In addition, the sentence lists three particular elements the writer believes are more important than growth mindset, each of which is arguable—there are good points to be made for and against each one—and, as education is such a fundamental part of our democracy, is certainly worth arguing about.

A Thesis Is Often Longer Than a Single Sentence

A college essay often requires you to respond to multiple issues. Trying to cram everything you have to say into a single-sentence thesis statement—no matter how concisely you do it—can sometimes make for an unwieldy and confusing statement. When you have a complex prompt, allow yourself two or three sentences to summarize your argument.

Let's take one more look at the first paragraph of the essay prompt before envisioning a possible response:

Using "growth mindset" **or** "grit" as your focus, discuss the high school and college experiences of Kashawn Campbell (as described in Kurt Streeter's article) and compare them with your own. Your discussion should refer *specifically* to either Carol Dweck's *Mindset* reading **or** Angela Duckworth's TED Talk.

That's a lot of ground to cover in a single sentence. The following two-sentence thesis statement allows the writer room to make a concise, but not constricted, argument:

Sample multi-sentence thesis

Some college students' experiences suggest that Dweck's theory about the relationship between growth mindset and success is valid. However, it is equally important to have an external support system for those times when our individual efforts aren't quite enough.

The first sentence in the thesis responds to the three most important elements in the opening sentence of the sample prompt: It states that the essay's focus will be on the experiences of real college students—Kashawn Campbell *and* the writer himself—and it indicates specifically how Dweck's ideas will be used as a lens for the discussion about the relationship between growth mindset and success. The second sentence of the thesis qualifies and expands the previous material, alerting the reader to the writer's belief that while a growth mindset is important, "an external support system" is also important for student success.

As it stands, a great deal of information is conveyed in just two sentences. Trying to stuff all this information into *one* sentence might be like trying to squeeze a bunch of clowns into a MINI Cooper.

A Thesis Provides a Plan for the Rest of the Essay

Students sometimes fret that they're losing the element of surprise if their thesis is *too specific* and *too clear* about its plans. Don't worry about that. Essays that begin with a vague claim rarely get any clearer. For all the reasons we've been discussing, signaling *exactly* where your essay will go is the right move for most college classes in North America.

Outlines are discussed later in this chapter, but you can see how a strong thesis does much of the work for you by signposting the topic of each body paragraph. The sample prompt indicates that the writer must discuss both Kashawn Campbell's and their own "high school and college experiences," and the sample thesis tells us the writer will talk about growth mindset *and* the need for "an external support system." It doesn't take much imagination to quickly sketch out one possible form the essay might take:

> **Body Paragraph 1:** During high school, Campbell benefits from growth mindset and external support systems.
>
> **Body Paragraph 2:** During his first year of college, Campbell struggles with his growth mindset but continues to benefit from external support systems.
>
> **Body Paragraph 3:** During high school, the student writer *does not* benefit from either a growth mindset or external support systems.
>
> **Body Paragraph 4:** During the first year of college, the student writer benefits from external support systems, which ultimately lead to a growth mindset.

While the sample prompt suggests a logical way to organize this essay's paragraphs, other prompts may make the paragraph order feel less predetermined. One tried-and-tested method is to arrange paragraphs so that your *second* strongest argument comes first, your weakest argument or arguments come in the middle, and your *strongest* argument comes at the end, just before the conclusion. In an essay with three main arguments, that might look like this:

First section of the body: Stronger argument

Second section of the body: Strong argument

Third section of the body: Strongest argument

One important point, sometimes forgotten by busy writers, is that the order of the argument should correspond to the order in which the ideas are mentioned in the thesis statement. The organization of an essay will be further affected by the audience's needs and expectations. Your "strongest argument" will be the one for which you have the best evidence *and* which is most likely to connect with your reader.

See section 11.4 for a graphic organizer for an argument essay.

A Thesis Doesn't "Announce" Itself as a Thesis

You learned earlier that a thesis is not a statement of *fact*, but it is a statement. When you finally have a thesis that you think can guide and sustain an entire essay, don't be shy—come right out and say it.

You saw how "In my essay I will describe growth mindset" became the much richer "Focusing on growth mindset in education distracts us from far more important factors determining student success, such as high school preparation, economic security, and consistent access to support services." Now, here's another example of the difference between an announcement and a statement, using our other sample thesis:

Draft announcement thesis (not arguable)

My essay is based on Carol Dweck's theory about growth mindset and success and how it applies to college students. I also write about how students need an external support system to succeed.

Revised thesis statement (arguable)

Some college students' experiences suggest that Dweck's theory about the relationship between growth mindset and success is valid. However, it is equally important to have an external support system for those times when our individual efforts aren't quite enough.

The phrase "My essay is" immediately makes the reader step back from your argument because it suggests the writer is detached from their subject. We want to read work by people who *care* about their topics, not those who are only writing because they have to turn in an essay.

Elements of a Strong Thesis Statement

- Focused and specific

- Not a statement of fact

- Includes a topic and a claim

- Answers a question, whether specifically asked or implied

- Arguable and worth arguing

- Can be longer than a single sentence

- Provides a "plan" for the essay

- Is a statement, not an announcement

DIY 5.4 Write a Working Thesis Statement

Revise the working thesis you wrote earlier so that it follows the guidelines for a strong thesis statement. When you've finished, trade thesis statements with a classmate and see if you can make suggestions that help the writer strengthen their thesis. Double-check your partner's thesis against the "Elements" list in this section, making sure that the thesis includes all the qualities of a strong thesis and avoids the pitfalls of a weak one.

5.5 Outlining Your Ideas

One of the many reasons for beginning the composing process with a strong thesis statement is because doing so will suggest how the parts of your essay might come together. Drafting an outline based on your thesis will help you confirm whether your thesis is, indeed, capable of generating an entire essay. If there's a flaw in your thesis, an outline will often expose it. An outline is also an easy way to share the plan for your essay. If you want feedback from your instructor or tutor, it's much easier for them to give you a useful response if they are looking at a plan, rather than simply listening to you talk about your unwritten essay.

Remember, too, that just as you begin with a *working* thesis, you also begin with a *working* outline. Nothing is written in stone; everything can be changed. Your outline is a guide, but it's not the only possible version of that guide.

Write a Scratch Outline

A scratch outline is pretty much any initial plan you draft; it often looks much like a list. Working from the two-sentence thesis statement on page 107, you might come up with a scratch outline as basic as this:

--Intro hook about growth mindset

--Explain "growth mindset" using Dweck's terms and maybe an outside source

--Acknowledge the importance of growth mindset for Campbell and me, but point out in thesis that you can't do it alone

--Then go through Campbell's high school years — he had a lot of support from teachers and staff *and* his classes were really easy

--Talk about Campbell and Berkeley — still has a lot of support, but classes are much harder and just having a growth mindset wasn't enough to succeed

--Transition to me in high school: no support, even though I think I was pretty smart, so I had a fixed mindset and did terrible

--Last main paragraph: big turnaround for me — summer bridge program, where I learned skills and attitudes and had a support system in place for when I actually started college

--Value of/argument for a support system?

--Conclusion: Growth mindset is important but it's probably not enough on its own; maybe find a good outside quote to end with

Think of a scratch outline as the first phase of outlining, just something to get the ideas bubbling in your brain onto the page. A scratch outline is also very handy when you're writing an in-class essay and you want to remember your main points. And again, having a scratch outline to discuss with your professor or tutor will make their comments much more on-point as you continue the composition process.

> **DIY 5.5a** Write a Scratch Outline for Your Essay
>
> Write a scratch outline for the essay you are currently writing. Use your working thesis statement to help generate the main points of the outline.

Write a Topic Outline

If you've taken a high school English course, chances are you've made, or at least seen, a traditional topic outline for an essay. A topic outline highlights your most important points, moving from the general to the more specific.

A topic outline for a typical body paragraph looks something like this:

I. Topic
   A. Subtopic
      1. Supporting evidence
      2. Supporting evidence
   B. Subtopic
      1. Supporting evidence
      2. Supporting evidence

Using that as a model, here's a possible **topic outline** for a first body paragraph supporting the sample thesis we've been working with:

I. Growth Mindset and External Support in Kashawn Campbell's High School Experience *(Main Topic)*
   A. Growth Mindset *(Subtopic)*
      1. Grew up in very bad neighborhood, yet managed to "will himself" to become straight "A" student *(Supporting evidence)*
      2. Encouraged by mother to believe in his own potential *(Supporting evidence)*
   B. External Support *(Subtopic)*
      1. Teachers and other students name him prom king, salutatorian, most likely to succeed, etc. *(Supporting evidence)*
      2. One unexpected (ironic?) avenue of support is the fact that his classes are so easy *(Supporting evidence)*

Write a Sentence Outline

While a sentence outline will take considerably more time to complete, it also brings you much closer to the actual draft of your essay. Here is a **sentence outline** for the paragraph that was just outlined in topic form:

I. As a high school student, Kashawn Campbell demonstrated a growth mindset, but he also benefitted from outside support and the fact that his academic work was not very challenging. *(Main Topic)*
   A. Despite growing up "in one of South Los Angeles' bleakest, most violent neighborhoods," Campbell—like other people with a growth mindset—never turns away from a challenge or gives up. *(Subtopic)*
      1. Campbell's growth mindset is demonstrated by the fact that he "willed himself to become a straight-A student." *(Supporting evidence)*
      2. Throughout his childhood, Campbell was encouraged by mother to believe in his own potential. *(Supporting evidence)*
   B. At Jefferson High, he received support and positive reinforcement from teachers, staff, and other students. *(Subtopic)*
      1. By the time he graduated, Campbell was "named the prom king, the most likely to succeed, [and] the senior class salutatorian." *(Supporting evidence)*
      2. Campbell's path forward was made smoother by an unexpected piece of external support: his schoolwork was fairly easy. *(Supporting evidence)*

Notice how, unlike the scratch outline, the sentence outline includes specific information, including short quotations, and demonstrates care with the construction of the sentences themselves.

DIY 5.5b Write Topic and Sentence Outlines

1. Write a topic outline for the essay you are currently writing.
2. Transform at least one paragraph of that topic outline into a sentence outline.
3. Take notes. Are there areas, you want to cover that seem neglected? Does anything appear to be receiving *too much* attention?

Create a Sequence Chart

A sequence chart can serve several functions, but in this case, it is simply being used as a graph arranged in the order in which the essay material will be discussed. While it doesn't allow for as much detail as a topic or sentence outline, a chart does provide writers who are more spatially oriented with a clearer overview of their essay plan. It also forces writers to select and highlight what they think is really important.

As with the thesis statement and the topic and sentence outlines, the sequence chart is a useful reference point when you're actually composing your essay, because you can always check to make sure that what you are writing is relevant to the appropriate box on the chart.

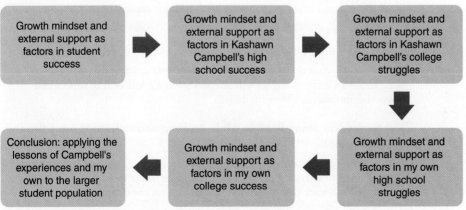

A sequence chart for an essay on the role of growth mindset in students' academic careers.

DIY 5.5c Create a Sequence Chart

Turn your traditional outline into a sequence chart. You can find the shapes necessary to create a chart in the Insert tab in Word or the shapes feature in a Google Slide. If you don't have such programs, or your computer isn't handy, just draw boxes and connect them with lines.

Chapter 5 Checklist
Generating Your Thesis and Organizing Your Essay

☐ **Have you identified and considered how to address the most likely audience, or audiences, for your essay?**

You'll want to identify not only who your readers are likely to be but also your relationship to them, the biases they may have, and how you want them to respond after reading your work.

☐ **Is your thesis narrow enough that you can comfortably discuss it within the scope of your assignment, while being broad enough to keep you from repeating the same few points over and over?**

The more you know about your topic, the narrower you will want your thesis to be. If you're still finding your way around your topic, be sure your thesis is broad enough to sustain a full and interesting essay.

☐ **Does your thesis meet all the criteria of a "strong thesis statement" listed on page 110?**

A strong thesis is focused and specific; is not a fact; includes a topic and a claim; answers a question, whether asked or implied; is arguable and worth arguing; is sometimes more than a single sentence; provides a plan for the essay; and is a statement, not an announcement.

☐ **Have you used an outline or sequence chart to develop your thesis?**

Developing your thesis with an outline not only ensures that you can generate an essay, doing so will also save you a great deal of time when you begin to write the essay itself.

☐ **Are you remaining flexible while drafting and redrafting your thesis and outline?**

As important as it is to have a plan for your essay, it's equally important to be open to changing that plan as new ideas occur to you. Be willing to modify both your thesis and outline throughout the composing process.

5.6 Making It Stick

How will you craft a thesis and organize your essay?

Working Together

5.6a Narrow, Claim, Outline First, form groups of three or four students. Then choose one of the broad topics below and (1) narrow it down, (2) create a working thesis, and (3) write a scratch outline. You have a limited amount of time to complete this exercise (your instructor will tell you how much), but there are no "rules," per se. Your only goal is to make the best use of the knowledge and skills of the people in your group.

Because the topics are intentionally broad, you will need to do quite a bit of work to quickly narrow down the one you choose and to come up with a thesis that, most likely, will argue in favor of, or against, a certain approach to the topic.

Broad Topics

Gun control

Legalizing suicide

Censoring social media

Regulating junk food

Mandatory military service at age eighteen

Tuition-free college

When you're finished, respond to the following questions, first in your small group, then as part of a full-class discussion:

1. How did you go about narrowing the broad subject down to a topic that could be realistically addressed in a short academic essay? What strategies were effective or ineffective?

2. What were the most productive aspects of your collaboration? How could you reproduce those successes in future collaborations?

3. In what areas was your collaboration less productive? What could you do differently next time to achieve better results?

Applying What You Know

5.6b A Two-Minute Talk Imagine that you are giving a speech about your chosen topic, but you have only two minutes to state your argument and provide your most compelling evidence. Write out your thesis statement and make a list of the most important elements of your essay. Then organize and edit your material so that you can tell people everything they need to know in the compressed time frame.

When you're ready, give your two-minute speech to a few of your classmates. If you are taking your class remotely, enlist a friend or family member to be your audience.

5.6c Organizing Non-academic Arguments Think about an argument you've made recently in a social or personal situation ("You should watch this Netflix show . . ."; "Supporting this candidate is the smartest choice . . ."; "The accident wasn't my fault because . . ."). Write notes about how you "organized" your argument. Were your choices successful? If you had the chance to make that argument again, what would you do differently to achieve your purpose?

Invitations to Write

5.6d Writing against the Grain

Shorter: When you sit down to write your essay, you may be tempted to respond to the prompt by going with whatever first comes into your mind. Be careful, though: The most obvious path isn't always the easiest. Sometimes you'll find it's a lot more interesting to turn received wisdom on its head. For example, rather than argue that college students spend too much time on social media, you might reverse conventional thinking and argue that young people spend *too* little time networking on their devices.

Try this strategy with your currently assigned topic. Generate a thesis that is unexpected and argues the opposite of what most people would consider to be common sense.

Longer: Use your new, controversial thesis to begin writing an essay. Make sure that you have at least two main points that will sustain full paragraphs. For instance, if your argument is that college students need to spend more time on social media, you might say something like, "Instagram is a powerful tool for making new friends, and college students need as many friends as they can get. Moreover, for those students who go away to college, Snapchat is a valuable way of maintaining networks of friends that might otherwise be lost." Granted, it would be easy to make counterarguments in favor of face-to-face contacts rather than digital contacts, but one of the benefits of trying to write from a challenging thesis is that you quickly realize whether or not your argument is likely to be defensible for an entire essay.

5.6e Wait . . . What?

Shorter: Reread your thesis statement and write a list of questions from the perspective of someone who has never heard of your subject at all. Try to write *at least ten questions* about the topic.

Longer: Choose two or three questions from the list that you think *most* readers would want to have answered in your actual essay. Then write a paragraph answering each question, providing specific examples to support your answers.

5.6f The Sentence Outline

Shorter: Earlier, you were asked to turn one paragraph of your traditional outline into a "sentence outline." That is, instead of using short phrases to suggest where your essay might go, you write out complete sentences, which you may end up using in your essay itself. Try writing a sentence outline for another of your body paragraphs.

Longer: Finish the entire outline in sentence form. Again, while this will require some work on your part, it will also make drafting your essay much easier. What's more, you will discover which areas of your essay are the strongest and which are likely to need more development.

6

Composing Paragraphs

REFLECT

Write Before You Read | Activity to connect what's new with what you already know 118

READ & PRACTICE

DIY (Do-it-yourself) activities offer just-in-time support for all the skills in this book.

→

REFLECT

Write Before You Read   In your own words, how would you describe the "body paragraphs" of an essay? What difficulties have you had composing these sorts of paragraphs? Do you remember times when you felt especially comfortable and self-assured writing the main part of an essay? If so, what accounted for that experience? If not, what kept you from writing with confidence?

6.1 Understanding What It Takes to Compose Paragraphs

Once you have your thesis and outline in place, the essay practically writes itself—doesn't it? It would be nice if that were the case, but most writers find that, even when they begin with a strong plan and some solid supporting evidence for their thesis, the most challenging part is still ahead.

That's okay, though; writing can be hard even for professional writers. Anne Lamott remarks in her book *Bird by Bird*: "Almost all good writing begins with terrible first efforts. You need to start somewhere. Start by getting something—anything—down on paper." Lamott describes a first draft as "the down draft—you just get it down. The second draft is the up draft—you fix it up. You try to say what you have to say more accurately." The third draft is "the dental draft, where you check every tooth, to see if it's loose or cramped or decayed, or even, God help us, healthy."

If you're used to writing only one draft of an essay, writing three may sound like a lot. But when you're first finding yourself as a writer, you may well compose more than three drafts—or you may write several overall drafts of your essay but take six or seven or eight (or more) passes through a particularly difficult paragraph.

The many tips in this book are designed to help you make your way through the composing process step by step by step. However, when you actually *are* on a roll and the writing is coming freely, put everything else out of your mind and give yourself over to inspiration. Unless you're writing an in-class exam, you'll nearly always have a chance to come back and make your essay better.

6.2 Composing Body Paragraphs

Flexibility in writing, as in most things, is key. Education professor and literacy researcher Mike Rose has written about how students with too rigid a set of internalized writing rules can find themselves blocked. Rose argues that such unalterable directives as "always make three or more points in an essay" or "craft a solid first paragraph before going on" can lead students straight into a wall when the subject matter they're working on doesn't fit a formula they have in their heads.

Being able to think flexibly and question what else might work in a writing scenario is important. Keep in mind, then, that the instruction in this chapter about composing body paragraphs is simply a starting place, a guideline for basic strategies that have worked for many students. Your own writing plan will inevitably evolve, and part of that evolution will come from your thoughts about the advice you receive from other writers.

Because introductions and conclusions are special types of paragraphs, they are discussed separately in Chapter 7. Keeping Rose's ideas about flexibility in mind, let's talk about the biggest and probably most time-consuming task you will face when writing an essay: composing body paragraphs, the paragraphs that make up the main part or "body" of your essay.

> **Being able to think flexibly and question what else might work in a writing scenario is important.**

Understand the Elements of a Paragraph

While expectations for the content of body paragraphs inevitably varies from professor to professor and from discipline to discipline, most composition instructors expect a well-developed paragraph to have the following elements:

- **A topic sentence.** A good topic sentence introduces the main idea in a paragraph in such a way that it continues the argument made in the thesis statement. Experienced writers may simply *imply* the topic without ever stating it. In a first-year composition class, however, it's a good idea to directly state what you'll be doing in your paragraph, which will also help keep you, the writer, on track. (Note: Topic sentences should not begin with unnecessary prefaces such as "In this paragraph I'll be discussing . . .".) See the sample body paragraph later in this section; it starts with an effective topic sentence.

- **Supporting evidence.** It's easy to make a claim about a topic: "You can't make it without a growth mindset!" "Growth mindset is totally unimportant!" However, without evidence to support your claim, there's little reason for readers to believe what you're saying. Often, evidence takes the form of quotations, paraphrases, and summaries from the readings you are discussing or from the opinions of informed experts.

- **Analysis and commentary.** Having evidence to support the claim you are making in your topic sentence is crucial, but if you plop the evidence down in your paragraph and don't say anything about it, readers may wonder: *So what?* Analyzing and commenting on your evidence provides context and connections and lets your reader know that you understand the material's significance.

- **A concluding sentence.** You don't want to just repeat what you've said in your topic sentence, but you do want to indicate the progress your argument has made over the course of the paragraph. What have readers just learned? Note: It's important *not* to introduce the subject of your next paragraph in your concluding sentence—that often confuses the reader.

Before discussing each of these elements in detail, as a reminder, here is the prompt we first saw in Ch 4:

Sample essay prompt

Using "growth mindset" or "grit" as your focus, discuss the high school and college experiences of Kashawn Campbell and compare them with your own. Focus your discussion by referring *specifically* to either Carol Dweck's *Mindset* reading or Angela Duckworth's TED Talk.

- Aim for 1,000 to 1,500 words.

- Include a strong thesis and a clear argument.

- Support the thesis with concrete and specific evidence in each body paragraph.

- Use MLA-style formatting and documentation.

- Any outside research should be limited and relevant.

- Carefully edit and proofread your essay before turning it in.

And here, again, is the thesis statement generated in response to that prompt:

Working thesis statement

Some college students' experiences suggest that Dweck's theory about the relationship between growth mindset and success is valid. However, it is equally important to have an external support system for those times when our individual efforts aren't quite enough.

Again, there is no "one-size-fits-all" structure for the paragraphs in an academic essay, but there *are* general guidelines you can follow. The following paragraph, which discusses Kashawn Campbell's need for more than just a growth mindset to succeed at UC Berkeley, is one example of a solid body paragraph. The topic and concluding sentences are in italics; between the two sentences is a combination of supporting evidence and the writer's analysis and commentary.

Sample body paragraph

While Kasahwn Campbell rarely faced serious academic challenges in high school, once he began attending UC Berkeley, his growth mindset alone wasn't enough for academic success. It's true that Campbell would never have made it into Berkeley without a belief that "human qualities, such as intellectual skills, could be cultivated through effort" (Dweck 54). Once he arrives, his growth mindset is still apparent as he tries to stay upbeat, always telling his dorm mates to "have a Caltastic day!" (Streeter 65). However, when he realizes how ill-prepared he is for college, a belief in himself isn't enough and "depression [comes] in waves" (64). In his second semester, when Campbell is still struggling academically, he tells only a few close friends "how devastating this kind of failure felt, each poor grade another stinging punch bringing him closer to flunking out" (68). Fortunately, Campbell has a good friend, Spencer Simpson, who provides both academic and moral support: Spencer is "the first person Kashawn would turn to when depression came" (68). Campbell also benefits from the encouragement of his professors at Berkeley, especially his writing instructors, who work hours with him on each assignment. And when the depression is nearly overwhelming, Campbell is able to turn to the campus psychologist's office, which brings him much needed mental relief. *Ultimately, while Kashawn Campbell is an inspiring example of someone with a growth mindset, he is just as much an example of someone who benefitted from reaching out to people who could help him.*

Topic sentence

The writer combines supporting evidence with his own analysis and commentary.

Concluding sentence

Different assignments call for different approaches, and paragraphs inevitably vary in length and purpose. In fact, toward the end of the chapter, we'll look at how you can incorporate two very different types of paragraphs—descriptive and narrative—into an academic essay. That said, *most* body paragraphs in *most* academic essays—at least the sort that you are likely to write in a composition class—will include a topic and a concluding sentence, with the bulk of the paragraph made up of analysis and commentary based on concrete supporting evidence.

Keeping in mind that no single strategy works all the time, let's look at some of the basic qualities of the body paragraph above to see how you might incorporate those elements into your own work.

Understand Topic Sentences

A topic sentence expresses a paragraph's main idea. Like a good thesis statement, a strong topic sentence lets readers know what's coming and keeps the writer from straying from the paragraph's central focus. Returning to our analogy from the previous chapter, if an effective thesis is like a roadmap, then a topic sentence is like one of the signs announcing where the road turns.

Here are six important pieces of advice to follow when writing topic sentences: three things you should do and three things to avoid.

Your Topic Sentence Should . . .

1. **Echo the appropriate part of your thesis statement.** It's important that topic sentences clearly reference the corresponding places in the thesis statement where the topic was mentioned. Again, here's the thesis we've been working with. Words emphasized in **bold** are echoed—closely, or exactly—in the topic sentence.

    > **College students' experiences** suggest that Dweck's theory about the relationship between **growth mindset** and **success** is valid. However, it is equally important to have an external support system for those times when our individual efforts **aren't quite enough.**

    And here's the topic sentence from the paragraph discussing how Kashawn negotiates "the rules of the game":

    > While Campbell rarely faced serious academic challenges in high school, once he began **attending UC Berkeley,** his **growth mindset** alone **wasn't enough** for academic **success.**

Although the topic sentence doesn't mimic the exact words of the thesis, there are more than enough markers here for the reader to know exactly which specific element this paragraph will address.

2. **Transition from the previous paragraph.** Normally the transition from the previous paragraph occurs early in the sentence. It may take the form of a contrasting transition word like "however" or "nevertheless," or, if the paragraph continues in a similar vein as the previous paragraph, you might turn to transition words showing continuation—like "moreover" and "furthermore." Frequently, too, a word or phrase in the topic sentence specifically alludes to the previous paragraph.

You can see both the elements in play in the beginning of the topic sentence we've been looking at:

> **While** Campbell rarely faced serious academic challenges in **high school**, once he began attending UC Berkeley....

The sentence opens with the contrastive word "While" and references the topic of the previous paragraph (high school).

3. **Signal a shift in focus to a new subtopic.** The third important function of a topic sentence is to introduce the subject of the new paragraph. Because the transition at the beginning of the model paragraph begins with "While," we know right away that this new paragraph will contrast in some way with the previous one. The topic sentence continues as follows:

> ...**once he began attending UC Berkeley**, his growth mindset alone wasn't enough for academic success.

We know at this point that, in keeping with the corresponding part of the thesis statement, the paragraph will focus on Campbell's academic difficulties as a college student.

Your Topic Sentence Should NOT . . .

1. **Be missing.** Omitting a topic sentence is a common mistake for new academic writers. Including topic sentences helps you focus your reader's attention and makes your progress through the essay coherent.

2. **Be an observation masquerading as a topic sentence.** Another frequent mistake is to begin your paragraph with a sentence that sounds like it could be a topic sentence but is in fact just an observation that doesn't

focus the paragraph. Suppose, for example, that you began the model paragraph on page 122 with this sentence:

> At the beginning of the article, Campbell is a freshman at Berkeley.

That observation is certainly true, but it is not related to do the real topic of the paragraph—Kashawn Campbell's struggles at UCB. Look carefully at the sentences that start each of your body paragraphs: Are they only marginally related to the content of the paragraph? Or do they actually do the work they're supposed to be doing?

3. **Be "announced."** In the same way that you wouldn't "announce" your thesis statement, you shouldn't announce your topic sentence. In other words, avoid writing topic sentences that begin with *In this paragraph, I will discuss . . . .*

DIY 6.2 Write Topic Sentences for Your Essay

If you are currently working on an essay assignment, look carefully at the thesis statement for your essay, then write out provisional or "working" topic sentences for each of the body paragraphs you plan to write. Make sure those sentences actually reflect what you intend to include in the paragraphs and check them against the six pieces of advice in section 6.2. (If you haven't yet started an essay, use the prompt on page 120 to generate a thesis and working topic sentences.)

6.3 Including Evidence and Commentary

To persuade readers to accept their arguments and interpretations, academic writers rely on a balance of evidence and commentary. Like evidence in a court trial, the evidence in an academic essay provides proof that the argument being put forth is a sound one. Similarly, just as trial lawyers interpret evidence to support the best interests of their clients, academic writers use commentary to frame evidence in ways that reinforce their own analysis of an issue.

Use Concrete Evidence

Throughout this book, using *concrete* supporting evidence is discussed as the best way to support an argument. But what is "concrete" evidence, anyway? It's not literally concrete, of course. Instead, concrete evidence is a kind of metaphor: It's something that has weight and solidity, something specific that you can point to, unlike an abstract or vague statement.

Here is an example from the criminal justice system:

Concrete: On the basis of new DNA evidence, seventy-year-old Craig Cooley was released from prison in 2017 after serving thirty-nine years on a double-murder charge.

Abstract: An innocent man received justice.

Which one of these sentences will you more likely remember? The abstract one where the "innocent man" receives generic "justice"? Or the sentence telling us that a seventy-year-old man named Craig Cooley was released due to DNA evidence "after serving thirty-nine years on a double-murder charge"? While you may not retain all the details of the concrete example, you are much more likely to hold on to *something* from that sentence.

Moreover, concrete evidence is verifiable in a way that abstractions aren't. If I tell you that an innocent man received justice, how are you going to check on that? But if I provide the name of the innocently convicted man, his age, the year of his release, and the length of his sentence, you can easily corroborate my claim, which is given additional substance due to the number and accuracy of its details.

When you're working on your essay, keep in mind how much more powerful and convincing concrete evidence is than abstraction, speculation, and opinion. Outside research for a variety of types of concrete evidence is discussed in detail in Part 3 of this book; for now, the focus is on paraphrasing and quoting from texts that have already been assigned to you by your instructor. When looking for concrete evidence to support your own ideas, concentrate on the following:

- **Paraphrases, summaries, and quotations from assigned readings.** Paraphrases and summaries (summary is covered in Chapter 2) provide concrete evidence and demonstrate the writer's understanding of and engagement with the text. Short, relevant quotations can provide impact and the flavor of the author's actual words.

- **Personal experience and observations.** While college-level writing classes tend to focus on argument rather than narrative, that doesn't mean that you can never reference your own experience. Indeed, lived experience is often one of the richest resources you will have to draw on, which is why the final sections of this chapter are devoted to discussions of description and narrative. Always check with your instructor about the kind of evidence they expect, but your own life—all the things you've seen and done—may well provide exactly the sort of concrete evidence you need.

- **Data and visuals.** Concrete evidence can come from data and statistical tables, graphic representations of data, multimedia sources, photos, and other nontextual sources.

DIY 6.3a List Concrete Evidence to Support Your Topic Sentences

Use the topic sentences you wrote for DIY 6.2a as headings. Then list the concrete evidence you have to support each of those topic sentences. If you don't have any evidence right now, indicate the type of support that would be most useful for each paragraph and where you might find it.

Paraphrase Evidence

While summarizing material is one of the most useful and portable skills you will learn in a composition class, you will also frequently want to take advantage of a related strategy: paraphrasing. When you **paraphrase**, you put the writer's language into your own words and structure. Although it's sometimes effective to use a little of the writer's own language (in quotations marks, of course) in the paraphrase, don't borrow more than a word or very short phrase. Ideally, the words you use should be your own.

Paraphrasing can be a challenge: Finding just the right words and reworking the presentation takes time, and it's hard not to inadvertently borrow the writer's own language. As an example of how to try, and try again, at paraphrase, let's take a look at a passage from *Narrative of the Life of Frederick Douglass, An American Slave.*

NARRATIVE

OF THE

LIFE

OF

FREDERICK DOUGLASS,

AN

AMERICAN SLAVE.

WRITTEN BY HIMSELF.

BOSTON:
PUBLISHED AT THE ANTI-SLAVERY OFFICE,
No. 25 CORNHILL.
1845.

University of North Carolina

Original Passage

The idea as to how I might learn to write was suggested to me by being in Durgin and Bailey's ship-yard, and frequently seeing the ship carpenters, after hewing, and getting a piece of timber ready for use, write on the timber the name of that part of the ship for which it was intended.

Here's a student's first try at a paraphrase:

First Draft Paraphrase

In Chapter Seven of his *Narrative*, Frederick Douglass explains that he developed the concept of <u>how</u> he <u>might learn to write</u> after hanging around where ships were being built, <u>and frequently seeing the ship's carpenters</u> constructing the parts of the ship, then inscribing <u>on the timber the name of that part of the ship</u> where it was going to be used.

Unfortunately, this is still too close to the original, even though the writer changed from the first-person "I" used by Douglass to the third-person "he." Those places where Douglass's original words are still in use are underlined.

Here's a better paraphrase, one that manages to say essentially what Douglass is saying while staying away from *most* of his actual words:

Revised Paraphrase

In Chapter Seven of his *Narrative*, Frederick Douglass explains that he developed the concept of learning to write after hanging around where ships were being built and watching the carpenters constructing the parts of the ship; he learned by studying the labels they put on each plank of timber, which showed where on the ship the wood would be used.

One of the main advantages of paraphrasing is that you can refer directly to the work you're discussing without overquoting the author. If the writer's style is much more elevated than your own, which is likely to be the case with this example, you can bring the language more in line with the rest of your essay. And if the opposite is the case—that is, the reading you're referring to contains material that is valuable to your argument but is poorly or carelessly worded—a paraphrase allows you to acknowledge your source while giving the author's words some much-needed polishing.

DIY 6.3b Practice Paraphrasing

Choose a sentence from a book or article published long ago, like Douglass's *Narrative*, then write a paraphrase that (1) acknowledges the source of the paraphrase and (2) uses your own words and structure to capture the author's ideas.

Use Quotations

Although they can certainly be taken out of context, quotations are perhaps the most concrete of concrete evidence. A quotation comes right from the horse's mouth. Granted, you don't want your essay to be one giant, unanalyzed patchwork of block quotations. On the other hand, if you employ *only* paraphrase and summary, and you never include brief quotations in your work, your essay won't be as lively and diverse as it might have been.

Signal Phrase, Quotation, Comment

Chapter 16 covers more ambitious methods of quoting, such as the use of block quotes and ellipses; but for now, let's stick with the basics. In academic essays, a signal phrase or sentence introduces a quotation, summary, or paraphrase. That signal phrase should include at least two of the following elements:

- The title of the work being cited

- The author's name

- The author's profession or some other indication of credibility

The following example includes a quotation with an MLA-style page reference at the end. In addition to using quotation marks, the writer signals the use of a different voice in the essay by including the source's name and credentials and the work in which the quotation appeared. (See Chapter 18 for more MLA guidance and Chapter 19 for APA guidance.)

> In his book *How Children Succeed: Grit, Curiosity, and the Hidden Power of Character*, journalist Paul Tough notes, "whether you're utilizing your self-control in the emotional realm or the cognitive realm, that ability is crucially important to getting through the school day, whether you're in kindergarten or your senior year of high school" (19).

Readers of quotations in an academic essay are also interested in your analysis or opinion of the material you've just quoted. Here's an example showing how these three elements—introduction of source, quotation, comment—work together.

The source
The direct quotation

In her book *Fact and Artifact: Writing Nonfiction*, English professor Lynn Bloom advises, "Whether your sources are written or oral, make sure you represent both the words and the music accurately" (311). Bloom is right to mention the "music" of a quotation, as the sound and intention of how someone

The student's analysis

says something are often as meaningful as what the person actually says.

Many teachers of writing use the popular phrase "quotation sandwich" when referring to this structure. The introduction and the analysis of the quotation are the two slices of bread, while the quotation itself is the meat (or the soy patty, if you're a vegetarian).

Not every quotation needs to be as fully introduced as our example, especially once you've established the author's credibility. And you don't always need to comment on the quotation; sometimes it will be more powerful if the quotation speaks for itself. Nevertheless, it's good to remind yourself never to drop a quotation in the middle of your essay without any explanation of who said it or why it's there. Readers need to get a sense of how the quoted material helps you make your point.

Synonyms for "Says" and "Writes"

When quoting sources, you may fall into the pattern of writing something like "Angela Duckworth says . . . ," or "Carol Dweck writes. . . ." While those attributions can get a bit monotonous, it's usually better to be bland than odd. "She writes . . ." is better than "She expostulates . . ." However, if you want to put some variety into the verbs you choose to attribute quotations, a few of the most common synonyms for "says" and "writes" are shown in the following chart. Make sure to choose a verb that keeps the focus on the quotation and that shows what role the quotation is playing. *Foster explains…* suggests, for example, that you are using Foster to define a term or give background information. *Foster warns…* may suggest an objection or counterargument (see p. 130).

Signal Verbs

acknowledges	emphasizes	proposes
adds	explains	reveals
admits	implies	shows
affirms	indicates	speculates
argues	insists	states
believes	maintains	suggests
claims	notes	thinks
concedes	objects	warns
concludes	observes	wonders
contends	points out	worries

One error you don't want to make is using the word "quoted" as a synonym for "says" or "writes." To quote someone is to repeat the person's words; therefore, when a source is speaking, you would not write, "Angela Duckworth quoted, 'Without effort, your talent is nothing more than your unmet potential.'" Angela Duckworth is not quoting anyone; she is stating the results of her research. If Professor Duckworth wants to quote another psychologist, that's fine, of course, but be careful how you use the words "quote" and "quoted."

DIY 6.3c Practice Making Quotation Sandwiches

Practice using a signal phrase, a quotation from one of your assigned readings, and a sentence or two of commentary to make a "quotation sandwich." Ideally, you will be working with the quotations that you plan to use in your essay. However, if you don't yet have an essay assignment, just take quotations from any handy source (including this book).

Consider Counterarguments

When you're really looking into a topic, you will want to introduce not only your own analysis, but also other writers' commentary. Like the trial lawyer we mentioned earlier, you'll need to sincerely weigh the evidence of opposing viewpoints rather than dismissing it outright. Ideas that contradict those you hold are often called **counterarguments**. When you anticipate and respond to counterarguments, you show yourself to be trustworthy and tuned in to your readers. Responding to counterarguments involves two basic moves:

1. Acknowledging your readers' concerns

2. Refuting their objections

Acknowledge Your Readers' Concerns

Everybody likes to be heard, and recognizing that an opposing viewpoint has merit is one of the most effective ways to convince readers of your own *ethos*, or credibility. After all, if you're willing to listen to the objections of others, it's only fair that they give you a listen as well.

When you acknowledge ideas that contradict your own, try following these guidelines:

-   **Mention specific instances when the counterargument is strong.** Pointing to the very same evidence that your opponents might use in support of their position means that you've not only carefully examined their side of the argument, but you've also identified its legitimate strengths.

-   **Don't be condescending or dismissive.** Readers can tell when you are writing down to them, so give the other side a fair hearing.

-   **Don't concede *too* much.** If you sound too sympathetic to your opponents' argument, readers will wonder why you haven't adopted that position rather than your own.

Address Your Readers' Objections

Once you've shown that you are reasonable and open to opposing ideas, it's time to turn the argument in your favor. Gently but firmly point out the error of your opponents' understanding of the topic and demonstrate clearly and concretely why your way of thinking is more reasonable.

-   **Provide specific examples as evidence.** If you include concrete evidence from your opponents' argument, it is more important that you highlight stronger evidence for your own side.

- **Don't be overly aggressive.** Avoid name-calling or contempt for the other side. Instead, emphasize the rationality of your argument.

- **Conclude on a firm and confident note.** Don't leave any doubts in your readers' minds about who has the stronger argument.

Find a Place for the Counterargument

Putting your opponent's point of view to work in the wrong part of your essay can undercut your own argument, so it's smart to look for a place where the counterargument doesn't receive too much weight. Generally, it's best to address and refute a counterargument early in a paragraph so that your focus will be on your own arguments.

If you feel it's necessary to include a full paragraph dealing with counterarguments in your essay, it should appear no later than the next-to-last body paragraph so that you have time to emphasize your own main points.

DIY 6.3d Identify and Address Counterarguments

Make sure you have a clear, concise thesis, with a list of the main arguments with which you plan to support it. (Use the thesis and arguments for the essay you are currently writing; if you haven't yet been assigned an essay topic, continue responding to the prompt on p. 120.) Then present what you have to a friend or classmate. After you explain how you plan how to proceed with your essay, ask the friend or classmate to tell you two counterarguments they foresee. Write notes on your plans to respond to these objections — and any others you can think of on your own.

6.4 Using Transitions

"Whenever one sentence comes after another, readers need to see a connection between them," Steven Pinker writes in his book *The Sense of Style*: "It's the hunger for coherence that drives the entire process of understanding language."

One way to show the connection between sentences or paragraphs and to appease your reader's "hunger for coherence" is to make effective use of transition words and phrases. The best topic sentences in body paragraphs often include a brief transitional phrase or word, such as "also" or "despite."

Here's a chart that shows some of the most common transitions, categorized by the ways in which they are normally used:

Transition Types	Examples
Addition/Emphasis	also, and, further/furthermore, in addition, in fact, indeed, moreover
Cause and Effect	as a result, because, consequently, therefore
Comparison	also, in comparison, likewise, similarly, too

→

Transition Types	Examples
Concession	admittedly, granted, certainly, I concede that, of course, it's true
Contrast	although, but, by contrast, despite, however, nevertheless, nonetheless, on the contrary, still, while, yet
Examples	consider, for example, for instance, in particular, specifically, to illustrate
Interpretation	fortunately, interestingly, significantly, surprisingly
Summary	ultimately, finally, basically, fundamentally, in the end

Use Transitions within Paragraphs

If transitions are often most noticeable at the beginning of a topic sentence, that doesn't mean that they don't appear throughout the body of an essay. Just look at how frequently transitions are used in the following model paragraph:

Contrast

Concession

Contrast

Interpretation

While Kashawn Campbell rarely faced serious academic challenges in high school, once he began attending UC Berkeley, his growth mindset alone wasn't enough for academic success. **It's true** that Campbell would never have made it into Berkeley without a belief that "human qualities, such as intellectual skills, could be cultivated through effort" (Dweck 54). Once he arrives, his growth mindset is still apparent as he tries to stay upbeat, always telling his dorm mates to "have a Caltastic day!" (Streeter 65). **However**, once he realizes how ill-prepared he is for college, a belief in himself isn't enough and "depression [comes] in waves" (64). In his second semester, when Campbell is still struggling academically, he tells only a few close friends "how devastating this kind of failure felt, each poor grade another stinging punch bring him closer to flunking out" (68). **Fortunately**, Campbell has a good friend, Spencer Simpson, who provides both academic and moral support: Spencer is "the first person Kashawn would turn to when depression came" (68). Campbell also benefits from the encouragement of his professors at Berkeley, especially his writing instructors, who work hours with him on each assignment. When the depression is nearly overwhelming, Campbell is able to turn to the campus psychologist's office, which brings him much needed mental relief. **Ultimately,** while Kashawn Campbell is an inspiring example of someone with a growth mindset, he is just as much an example of someone who benefitted from reaching out to people who could help him.

Readers of academic essays want to know where they are in a writer's argument, and they want to be reassured that the writer also knows where they are. Transition words and phrases serve that crucial function in smoothly moving the reader from one part of the essay to the next.

6.5 Writing Concluding Sentences

The final sentence of your paragraph reinforces the paragraph's main idea. In doing so, it echoes the corresponding part of the thesis statement, although it probably won't repeat the exact words in the thesis. For example, the model paragraph in the previous section ends this way:

> Ultimately, while Kashawn Campbell is an inspiring example of someone with a **growth mindset,** he is just as much an example of someone who **benefitted from reaching out to people who could help him.**

You can hear in this sentence a clear echo of the relevant portions of the thesis, which are in bold below:

> College students' experiences suggest that Dweck's theory about the relationship between **growth mindset** and success is valid. However, it is equally important to have an **external support system for those times when our individual efforts aren't quite enough.**

Tips for Writing Concluding Sentences

Concluding or summary sentences are fairly straightforward in their purpose, although you'll want to be cautious of potential missteps when writing a body paragraph's final sentence:

- **Reflect the journey.** Your paragraph should have taken the reader on a journey. You began with the claim you made in your topic sentence, which was based upon a relevant portion of your thesis statement. If your paragraph has succeeded, then, by the final sentence, the evidence and commentary will have convinced your reader that your argument was a sound one. Let the concluding sentence reflect that journey.

- **Stating is preferable to announcing.** Just as you want to avoid announcements in your thesis statement and topic sentences, so should you refrain from announcing the conclusion of your paragraph: "This paragraph has shown that. . . ." Instead, simply state what you have to say.

- **Stay on topic.** Finish what you have to say in one paragraph, before you begin transitioning to the next paragraph. Starting your transition too early—that is, before the first sentence of the following paragraph—is both confusing to readers and undercuts the momentum of the paragraph.

DIY 6.5 Practice Writing Concluding Sentences

Read through the topic sentences you wrote earlier and write a concluding sentence for one of them, even if you're not entirely sure yet what will go in the middle of the paragraph.

6.6 Using Description and Narrative

Description and narration offer two significant ways to turn observation and personal experience into persuasive concrete evidence. How much description and storytelling you use in your essay will depend a great deal on your audience and on the assignment you've been given. Many instructors will favor the traditional academic paragraphs described earlier in this chapter. Nevertheless, having description and narrative in your writer's toolbox, even if you only use them occasionally, will provide you with the means to bring otherwise unexciting paragraphs to life and to think differently about your subject when you're blocked or uncertain about where to head next.

Use Description

The following paragraph is from Tara Westover's *Educated: A Memoir*, which describes Westover's passage from a childhood with survivalist parents in rural Idaho to her journey as a college student at Harvard and Cambridge University. The paragraph itself is a description of a scrap metal-cutting machine purchased by her father for use in severing leftover iron into pieces small enough to sell to salvage companies.

A few days later Dad came home with the most frightening machine I've ever seen. He called it the Shear. At first glance it appeared to be a three-ton pair of scissors, and this turned out to be exactly what it was. The blades were made of dense iron, twelve inches thick and five feet across. They cut not by sharpness but by force and mass. They bit down, their great jaws propelled by a heavy piston attached to a large iron wheel. The wheel was animated by a belt and motor, which meant that if something got caught in the machine, it would take anywhere from thirty seconds to a minute to stop the wheel and halt the blades. Up and down they roared, louder than a passing train as they chewed through iron as thick as a man's arm. The iron wasn't being cut so much as snapped. Sometimes it would buck, propelling whoever was holding it toward the dull, chomping blades.

While you may not be describing heavy machinery in your own essay, you can pick up several tips from Westover's vivid, well-crafted paragraph.

Choosing and Using Descriptive Details

- **Capture your reader's attention.** One of the most useful features of a descriptive paragraph is the way it can bring your reader directly into your piece of writing. Westover does an excellent job of this with her first sentence: "A few days later Dad came home with the most frightening machine I've ever seen." That's quite a claim, and most readers are going to want to know more about this terrifying apparatus.

- **Select the most vivid and specific details.** As in any type of writing, vague generalities tend to leave us bored, while concrete particulars capture our attention and increase our focus. Describing the Shear, a fairly complex piece of machinery, isn't easy, so Westover only provides us with details that will help us picture it: "The blades were made of dense iron, twelve inches thick and five feet across." We learn later that their "great jaws [were] propelled by a heavy piston attached to a large iron wheel," with the wheel being "animated by a belt and motor." We may not be able to envision its full functions *exactly*, but this is more than enough detail for a short paragraph in the middle of a much longer passage.

- **Write with polish and care.** In addition to selecting vivid details, Westover takes the extra time to present them with style. Her verbs are especially precise and evocative. We learn that the Shear operates on sheer strength, as it "cut not by sharpness but by force and mass." Indeed, the "iron wasn't being cut so much as snapped." This paragraph clearly passes the style test: These nine well-crafted sentences can easily stand apart from the material that precedes and follows them.

- **Be creative.** Creative writers often think outside the box to help readers visualize their subject matter. Westover, for instance, makes excellent use of analogy—a comparison between two things for the purpose of explanation or clarification. She begins by asking us to imagine the Shear as a giant pair of scissors, a move that does a lot of descriptive work for her. She then tells us that the Shear "roared, louder than a passing train," and that the iron being "chewed through" was "thick as a man's arm."

Use Narrative

"Narrative" is another word for "story," and stories, in all their many forms, are at the heart of most human communication. Indeed, many students initially refer to the essays they read for college, as well as the essays they write, as "stories."

The academic essays you write may focus more on analysis and argument than dialogue and action. Nevertheless, stories are everywhere in academic writing, whether the subject be business, science, or sociology. It's important to note that in this context, "stories" are true; they are not made up. We might call such stories the events of human experience. Writing expert Helen Sword argues, "Every research project is made up of stories—the researcher's story, the research story, the stories of the individual subjects and participants, the backstory—each of which contains various plot twists." It's important to keep in mind that behind every academic subject, there are human stories to tell; the task for writers is to figure out *which* stories to tell—and how and why to tell them.

In first-year composition, brief stories—even stories of a single sentence—may be your most effective use of narrative. That's not to say, though, that in certain circumstances a full paragraph of nonfiction storytelling, like the one below, can't have a positive impact on your essay. Sometimes a story can be told *in the service of* a larger point or argument. You'll notice that the following narrative, written by LA gang-intervention activist and Homeboy Industries founder Father Greg Boyle, is taken from the author's personal experience and works in the service of an anti-gang message.

Boyle describes a troubled young man named Lalo, who is attempting, with mixed success, to disengage from gang life:

> One of the classes [Lalo] had agreed to attend was the Monday morning meditation class. Father Mark, who ran it, would shake his head at Lalo as he texted or talked during the quiet periods, distracting others. Mark tried to ignore him, hitting the gong and breathing in deeply. Then one day it just changed. Lalo began to breathe as deeply and as placidly as any

Sometimes a story can be told *in the service of* a larger point or argument.

Zen master. Four months into his time with us, he dropped by my office to tell me if it weren't for Homeboy he'd be dead. "Not locked up," he is determined to emphasize. "Dead."

While it is only one hundred words long, Boyle's paragraph tells a moving and persuasive story about the power of joining Homeboy Industries. To do so, he employs narrative elements such as description and dialogue.

Choosing and Using Narrative Elements

- **Report the sequence of events.** In a story, one thing happens and then another happens as a result. In this paragraph, (1) Lalo attends classes; (2) he goofs off and annoys the priest in charge; (3) he is suddenly changed, perhaps by meditation, perhaps—Boyle might argue—through the grace of God; (4) he becomes an expert at meditation; and finally, (5) he visits Boyle's office and tells the priest that if he hadn't joined Homeboy Industries, he'd be dead.

- **Set the scene.** If primarily descriptive paragraphs often contain some storytelling, then storytelling paragraphs will almost always contain some description. Boyle is rather light on description in this paragraph, although we know the story takes place in a classroom and an office, which allows us to create a general picture of the setting. And Boyle does incorporate several details that make the scene more vivid. We can, for instance, "see" Father Mark shaking his head and "hear" him hitting the gong. We see and hear Lalo talking during quiet periods, then breathing "as deeply and placidly as a Zen master" once he changes.

- **Introduce the "characters."** Lalo is introduced in the previous paragraph as someone who talks tough and has only "one foot in the door" of Homeboy Industries. For the purposes of this anecdote, that's really all we need to know about him. All we know of Father Mark is what we learn in the paragraph: He is patient and runs the Monday morning meditation class. Again, it's not much, but it's enough to make him seem like a real person.

- **Use dialogue (sparingly).** When people talk in a story, they come to life; we can begin to hear their voices. In a fictional story, you can make up as much dialogue as you need but in a non-fiction academic essay, you are responsible for telling the truth. So—especially if the event happened a while ago—you don't want to use any more dialogue than you could realistically remember. Typically, that dialogue—like the talk in this paragraph—will have been remembered precisely because it is unusual and *memorable*.

DIY 6.6 Practice Writing Description and Narration

Write two or three sentences of description and two or three sentences of narration that you might be able to use in the essay you are currently composing.

6.7 Overcoming Writer's Block

Of course, *wanting* to write doesn't always mean that you can just sit down and do it. Even if you've given yourself permission to write a lousy first draft, you may still find yourself facing what all writer's dread: writer's block. However, there's some evidence that being blocked isn't all bad; it's often a way for your brain to slow down and catch up with material that it's not quite ready to handle. Take a breath the next time you're stuck and feel sure you'll never write another word. Hang in there. As Carol Dweck's growth mindset model tells us, getting smarter is often hard work.

Try Strategies for Getting Unstuck

This chapter is full of time-tested advice about how to write body paragraphs for academic essays. Ideally, every suggestion worked perfectly for you. In reality, of course, it's more likely that everything didn't go exactly according to plan; facing adversity is part of being a writer. If you found yourself encountering writer's block—that awful feeling of not being able to get anything on the page—consider some of the following strategies for getting yourself back on track:

Don't get up. While you probably don't want literally to chain yourself to your desk (as more than one writer has done), if you have a habit of getting up before you get much work done, you need to do *something* to give yourself a chance to get some words on the page. One strategy is to put something heavy in your lap, such as a large textbook. It's not that you can't pick it up and move it, but the physical weight reminds you that you need to sit there and write.

Use a timer. Many writers set a timer and write more or less nonstop until the timer goes off. You can set the timer on your smartphone or use an app like Pomodoro, which is meant specifically for timed bursts of focused energy; such apps even have built-in breaks between the timed tasks.

Write to music or repeated noise. Plenty of evidence suggests writing in silence allows for maximum concentration. However, sometimes silence can be overwhelming, particularly if you aren't used to it. Writing to music can be inspirational, although you should be careful about your choice of tunes. Listening to songs you know well, songs that you want to sing along with, can be too distracting. Instead, consider playing instrumental or electronic music softly in the background—something that doesn't distract you from thinking through ideas and composing sentences.

If there are distractions all around you, you might consider putting on headphones and listening to repeated noise (there are plenty of free apps available). While the sound of rain puts some people to sleep, others find it soothing and reassuring. It doesn't matter *what* you're listening to as long as it keeps you at your writing desk.

Speak your writing. Talk into any device that turns speech into text. Most smartphones have the capacity to capture speech and transcribe it into text. There is also a speech-to-text feature in Word. Different platforms and versions of the software require different methods to enable this feature, but you should be able to find the how-to for your specific version with a quick Google or YouTube search. You can also have Word or Google Translate speak selected text back to you, a feature that's especially helpful when you aren't sure how your writing will sound when read aloud by others.

In addition, there are professional software manufacturers, like Dragon, devoted solely to learning the nuances of your voice and rendering your speech into text as accurately as possible. (Despite student discounts, some of these programs can be pricey.) No matter how accurate the software is, however, you're going to have to go back and correct what's on the page.

Another version of speaking your writing is a bit more low-tech. In this method, you simply say aloud what's in your mind and type what comes out of your mouth. For people who are primarily used to conveying their ideas orally, this is almost like having a typist transcribe your ideas. Some students even find that having to slow down and type the words as they say them aloud actually fosters clearer, more deliberate thinking.

Write about your writing. If the writing you have on the page doesn't measure up to what you were hoping for, if you're frustrated or depressed by your drafting, it might be time to do some writing about writing. Education specialists call this "metacognitive thinking," or thinking about thinking, but that sounds fancier that it needs to. Try to self-diagnose your block by asking yourself the following questions:

- What is the most frustrating thing about your essay so far?

- What habits and circumstances can you change to get around the problem?

- Is there another way to accomplish the same goal?

- What happens if you tackle the problem by beginning on a blank page or screen?

- If you could ask your instructor or tutor one question right now, what would it be?

Not only does writing about your writing problems help you solve the problems, but *by writing*, rather than talking, you're actually engaged in the process that's blocking you.

Take a break. All the advice up to this point about overcoming writer's block has emphasized facing the page and gutting it out, no matter how badly you want to flee. However, when you've been trying to write for a long time and you find yourself truly stuck, it may be time to step back from your writing desk, clear your head, and get some perspective. Try working out, listening to music, or grabbing lunch with a friend, all of which may be better in the long run than stewing over your writing problem.

Don't give up. Whatever strategy you try, remember that ultimately you do have to get back to work. As Angela Duckworth emphasizes in her work on grit, it's important to just keep at it, even if the going is rough and slow.

DIY 6.7 Practice Overcoming Writer's Block

Take another look at any place in the composition of your essay where you got stuck. Reread what you have so far, then try one or more of the strategies in section 6.6 to try and get your creativity "unstuck."

Chapter 6 Checklist
Composing Paragraphs

☐ **If you've been having trouble getting started, or finishing once you have started, have you carefully reread the many strategies for overcoming writer's block at the end of the chapter?**

From using a timer, to speaking your writing aloud, to writing about your frustrations with the writing process, there are many different ways to combat writer's block. If one doesn't work for you at this particular moment, try another, and another, until you are writing again.

☐ **Does each body paragraph begin with a clear topic sentence that advances a part of the corresponding section of your thesis statement?**

A topic sentence signals the content of the paragraph to your reader. It should be clearly connected to the thesis statement and should accurately represent the content of the paragraph itself.

☐ **Are your body paragraphs supported with an effective mix of concrete evidence and intelligent commentary?**

Whether you're using quotations from your assigned readings or analysis by other writers, your evidence should be specific and credible. In addition to providing persuasive evidence, you should reflect, if only briefly, on the significance of each piece of evidence in your paragraph.

☐ **Have you carefully acknowledged and refuted your readers' most likely counterarguments?**

If you believe your reader will have reservations about your argument, be sure to acknowledge those reservations, then politely, but firmly, demonstrate why their position is not as persuasive as your own beliefs.

☐ **Do your paraphrases accurately represent your source material, and are they almost entirely in your words?**

Double-check all of your paraphrases to make sure that you are faithfully conveying the meaning of the original, while doing so in language that does not repeat the author's own words.

☐ **Have you followed the major conventions for using direct quotations in your essay?**

If you come across a type of quotation not addressed in this chapter, ask your instructor or tutor, or consult the resources offered by your campus writing center.

☐ **Have you made effective use of transitions, both inside the body of your paragraph, and as connectors from one paragraph to another in your topic sentences?**

Transition words and phrases let your reader know where you're going and where you've been. Consult the list of transition words in this chapter to ensure that your transitions are serving the purposes you intend.

☐ **Does your concluding sentence summarize your paragraph's contents without simply repeating your topic sentence?**

As you sum up the contents of your paragraph, remember not to (1) simply repeat your topic sentence, (2) announce your concluding sentence, or (3) start talking about your next paragraph.

☐ **Have you made use, where appropriate, of description and narration?**

Not every essay will benefit from description and narration but keep these tools at the ready in your writer's toolbox. They can often revive a paragraph that feels dull and lifeless.

6.8 Making It Stick

How will you compose paragraphs?

Working Together

6.8a Revising paragraphs Do this activity in four parts.

1. Take another look at the model paragraph in the Composing Body Paragraphs section on page 119. Annotations indicate the topic sentence, the concluding sentence, and the mix of supporting evidence and commentary in the middle of the paragraph.

2. Now, choose an essay you are currently working on, then find a partner and exchange the body paragraph that is giving you the most trouble. (Google Docs is an easy way to exchange digitally.)

3. Use a styling system to mark up your partner's paragraph (your partner should do the same for yours): Highlight all the sentences in the paragraph using **bold**/*italics*/regular font/<u>underline</u> for **topic sentence**, *supporting evidence*, analysis and commentary, and <u>concluding sentence</u>.

4. Return the marked body paragraph to your partner and offer suggestions about how to strengthen the paragraph's content and organization. When you look at your own paragraph, ask yourself: Do you agree with your partner's markings? Do you have too much of one type of marking and not enough of another? Is one marking missing altogether?

Applying What You Know

6.8b Writing to/with Your Fellow Writers Form a group with two other writers in your class. Have one partner open a Google Doc and invite the other two writers to share it. Once you're all logged in, have everyone choose a different type font and color; identify yourself at the top of the page with your font type and color.

Then simply start writing about your experience composing your current essay. If someone else has already begun writing, start wherever there is some empty space in the document. Don't hold back. Tell your group where you've been having problems. If you've managed to solve those problems, then explain how. If you have a suggestion for someone else, let them know by commenting below their remarks.

If you can't think of anything to write about, pause and read what others are saying, then dive back in. The process will look chaotic, with words appearing out of nowhere and ideas flashing all over the place. Don't let that bother you; embrace the chaos and keep on writing until you are written out.

When your group feels done, go back through your crazy quilt of ideas and have everyone underline what they think are the most important problems and solutions. Share your ideas with the rest of the class.

6.8c Monitoring Your Quotations

If you're worried that you have either too many, or too few, quotations, go through your essay as it exists so far and highlight every quotation. You'll immediately see the balance between your own work and those of the sources you are quoting.

If you have too many quotations, try paraphrasing or summarizing instead. On the other hand, if you see little or no highlighting in your essay, take another look at your major points to identify which need the support of evidence, and then select one or two smart and striking quotations to strengthen your case.

6.8d Just Read

With your instructor's permission, take fifteen or twenty minutes of class time and just read. Your reading can be an assignment for this class, or another class, or simply something you've been wanting to read online. When you're finished, write a few notes about (1) what you've been reading and (2) how you responded to it: with pleasure, bafflement, frustration, anger, or another response. Speculate (3) why the reading evoked those particular feelings in you, and (4) what that says about you as a reader. Finally, (5) write a bit about the similarities and differences between you as a reader and you as a writer.

Invitations to Write

6.8e Strengthening a Paragraph with Evidence

Shorter: Choose one of the topic sentences you have written while doing the chapter's DIY activities. Then, write a body paragraph using only your own words (i.e., no quotations from your readings). Just do your best to convey what you want the paragraph to convey. Think of this more as a directed freewrite than a carefully crafted paragraph.

Longer: Now go back and look at what you have and underline every unsupported assertion that needs evidence. Then, scour your assigned readings to locate evidence supporting each assertion you made in your paragraph. Write one or two "quotation sandwiches" (p. 128) to give your quotes authority and context.

6.8f Writing a Description

Shorter: Describe a person, place, or thing that is essential to your essay.

Longer: Now see if you can pass "the style test" by writing a description that is worth reading on its own merits. Use the descriptive elements described on pages 134 to 136 to help you craft your work:

- Capture your reader's attention.
- Select the most vivid and specific details.
- Write with polish and care.
- Be creative.

6.8g Using Narration (a Story)

Shorter: Tell a story related to your topic. It can either be a personal story, or one about someone you know or have heard about. Don't worry too much about the writing — just get the story out of your brain and onto the page.

Longer: Now develop your story by introducing the narrative elements described on pages 136–137:

- Report the sequence of events.
- Set the scene.
- Introduce the "characters."
- Use dialogue (sparingly).

7

Composing Introductions, Conclusions, and Titles

Write Before You Read   Think about the last time you wanted someone to think, feel, or do something after a conversation. How did you start that conversation? Why did you choose to introduce the conversation that way? Imagine you have been asked to tell a fellow student — someone new to academic writing — everything you've learned about introductory paragraphs. Write a list, a letter, a diagram — whatever feels comfortable — to share your knowledge. If possible, work in what you know about conclusions as well.

7.1 Considering the Role of Introductions, Conclusions, and Titles

While it's important to write from a thesis statement, which will likely appear at the end of your introduction, your introductory paragraph may not be the first paragraph you write. In fact, you might not write your opening paragraph until after you've completed the rest of your essay. However, since your introduction will be the first thing your readers encounter, it's important not to rush through it on your way to the body of your essay. As you plan your approach, think about how you might capture your reader's interest and make your reader want to keep reading.

Another important but often overlooked element of an academic essay is the conclusion. Even more than with introductions, some writers tend to rush through their final paragraph. Yet the concluding paragraph is the last one your audience reads before deciding what to think, feel, or do in response to your ideas, so taking some extra time and effort to compose a memorable (or inspiring!) ending often works to your benefit.

Finally, we'll pay some attention to titles in this chapter. The title is a surprisingly powerful way to get your essay's point across. Titles can guide the reader through the essay, and experienced readers, like your instructor, will be in the habit of keeping the title in mind throughout the essay, even if it's only as a subdued melody playing over your words.

7.2 Writing Introductions

You will want to craft introductions that draw your reader into the essay and then provide a brief overview of how you will approach the essay topic before ending with your thesis statement.

Hook the Reader

You might have heard the expression, "Don't bury the lead"; it's what editors say to reporters when they fail to mention the most interesting and enticing part of the story right up front. While you won't be writing a journalist's lead in an academic essay, you are still responsible for capturing your reader's interest right out of the gate. You do this, of course, with what you might know as a "hook," the catchy beginning of your essay that hooks your reader the way a fisherman catches a fish.

Types of Openings

There are, of course, as many types of openings as you can imagine, but the following list and examples should help if you've having trouble beginning your essay.

- **Tell a story.** In a short academic essay, an introductory story is more likely to be brief and anecdotal than richly descriptive. Nevertheless, adopting a few of the narrative strategies discussed in section 6.6 can be a good way of placing your readers in the middle of your topic, as in the following example:

  "Grit?" my father yelled at me, his sunburned forehead bathed in sweat. "If you want to know what grit really means, then try growing up on a failing farm in Oklahoma in the 1960s."

- **Set the scene.** Readers always want to know where they are when beginning a new piece of writing. While the bulk of your essay may focus on the analysis of one or more texts, there's no reason why you can't briefly immerse your readers in a vivid setting relevant to the rest of the essay, as in this potential opening for an essay on growth mindset:

  When Kashawn Campbell looked around his South Los Angeles neighborhood, all he saw was crumbling sidewalks, iron bars on the windows, and young men—hopeless and angry—loitering on street corners.

- **Include a persuasive quotation from an expert.** One of the invention activities mentioned in Chapter 4 is curating quotations (p. 90). While the focus in Part I is on quoting from your assigned readings, you may come across a quotation by an expert that fits in well with your intro-duction, as in the following example:

Iowa State University psychologist Marcus Credé argues, "Grit as a predictor of performance and success and as a focus of interventions holds much intuitive appeal, but grit as it is currently measured does not appear to be particularly predictive of success and performance and also does not appear to be all that different [from] conscientiousness" (35).

- **Provide a specific date connected to a notable fact or event.** Anchoring the opening of your essay in a specific time and place not only gives you credibility—this writer has got the *facts*—it also gives your reader some idea of the general context for your essay. And readers want context, especially when they are deciding whether to commit themselves to an essay. Imagine this opening sentence in an essay focusing on growth mindset:

In February 2006, Carol Dweck published a book that would change the way many people evaluate human potential for growth.

- **Write a short declarative sentence.** Often, students are tempted to write a long, complicated opening with the goal of encompassing everything they have to say in a single sentence. Frequently those sentences get tangled up before they make their point. Rather than trying to cram everything into one long sentence, consider the impact you can make with just a few well-chosen words. Consider, for instance, the opening of two of the articles you've read in this book. David Leonhardt's "Is College Worth It?" begins like this:

Some newly minted college graduates struggle to find work.

And Kurt Streeter starts his profile on Kashawn Campbell like this:

School had always been his safe harbor.

We know that both of these essays will go on to address complex subjects, but these authors start short not because they can't write more complex sentences—they can—but because brevity provides their openings with a sharp *snap* that engages a reader's interest.

- **Use an analogy.** An analogy is a comparison between two different things. An essay on growth mindset, for instance, might begin this way:

Just as a car without fuel will not move forward, so a person without growth mindset cannot succeed.

- **Present an uncomfortable truth.** We don't always like to hear the truth, especially if it goes against our own views on a topic; however, confront-ing your readers head-on with a troubling fact or observation may make them want to hear what you have to say in defense of your argument. How, for instance, would you respond to the following claim in an essay on grit?

No one wants to say it, yet the reality is staring us all in the face: grit alone is not enough to guarantee a person's success.

- **Present an eye-opening fact or statistic.** If you were writing on grit, and you wanted to demonstrate the extreme improbability that every single person who is poor lacks grit, you might begin with a statistic showing just how many people are impoverished:

According to the Center for Poverty Research at the University of California, Davis, in 2019, nearly eleven percent of the United States population, or thirty-four million people, lived in poverty.

- **Introduce a claim that you intend to disprove.** Suppose you began an essay on growth mindset like this:

To hear some educators talk, no student without growth mindset has ever been successful.

Readers might initially think that you agree with the claim, which would make a move in a different direction unexpected and interesting:

However, there are a number of factors besides growth mindset that one should consider.

- **Make an interesting list.** Lists provide easily scannable information—they give a quick overview of a topic that allows you to feel like you know what's ahead. An opening list on grit might look like this:

Seventh-grade math students in Chicago Public Schools, West Point Military cadets, National Spelling Bee champions—the one thing these very different people all have in common is grit.

- **Ask an intriguing question.** Asking a genuinely interesting question—as opposed to one that is dull or obvious—is a time-tested way to open an essay. A piece on growth mindset might start this way:

Have you ever wondered what all successful people have in common?

- **Amuse your reader.** Humor doesn't work in all situations, of course, so be sure that your instructor appreciates a good chuckle and that this move is appropriate for the assignment.

What do you get when you cross grit with grits? Why, a Southern-fried success story, of course.

- **Write from an image.** You can get your reader's attention without even writing a word by inserting an arresting image between your title and your first paragraph. To see how journalists are using images in the space between the headline and first sentence, click on Google News and read through several stories. You can learn more about reading and writing about visuals in 14.2 and 14.3.

One tactic you emphatically *don't* want to take is providing the dictionary definition of a word or phrase. If a definition can be found in the dictionary, then assume that your instructor already knows it or is capable of looking it up.

If one of these strategies doesn't seem to be working on its own, consider combining several different approaches. While the focus here has been only on the very first sentence, there's no reason why you can't think of your opening as a cluster of related sentences. Your ultimate goal is drawing your reader into your essay. The strategies described earlier have worked in other essays, but they are by no means the only possibilities. Indeed, your opening is one of the best places in an essay to give your creativity and imagination free reign.

> **DIY 7.2a Write an Engaging Opening Sentence (or Sentences)**
>
> Using the models in section 7.2 for inspiration, write two to three opening sentences for your current essay assignment. Your goal is to craft something that will immediately make your readers want to keep reading. Reflect on the benefits of each of your draft openings.

Move from Hook to Thesis

Assuming you've captured your reader's attention with a strong opening, what do you do next? The middle of the introductory paragraph can become kind of a dead zone for writers. After an exciting introduction, your essay can grind to a slow crawl if you squander the momentum that you've generated with your hook.

It doesn't have to be that way. Moving from your opening hook to your thesis statement normally takes only a couple of hundred words at most, but that space can be put to excellent use. Consider the following strategies for getting from your hook to your thesis.

- **Explain more fully a concept introduced in your hook.** Often your opening sentence won't fully make sense until you "unpack" it a bit. By the time readers get to your thesis, the relevance of your hook should be clear.

- **Finish telling the story that you began in your opening sentence.** Sometimes a compelling story takes three or four sentences to complete. If you have a good story to tell, go ahead and tell it, but don't spend so much time that you forget the story's function as a bridge to your thesis.

- **Summarize key readings that you will return to later.** If your essay focuses on specific readings—or a film, work of art, podcast, or piece of music—very briefly summarize or describe those works so that they will be familiar to someone who is not familiar with them.

- **Introduce information that connects your hook with your thesis.** This could be a statistic that bolsters your argument or a quotation from an expert on your topic. The information should serve to make the thesis clearer and more persuasive.

The passage between your hook and your thesis may, of course, employ several of these strategies. As you draft the middle part of your introductory paragraph, keep these other tips in mind.

- **Make a clear connection between your hook and your thesis.** A catchy opening sentence is useless if it doesn't link clearly to your thesis and your essay overall. As you move beyond your opening sentences, be conscious that you are always writing *toward* your thesis statement.

- **Make sure each sentence connects with the next.** The sentences in this part of your introduction form a path from your opening to your thesis. Be certain that each new sentence connects logically with the one that precedes it.

- **Be concise.** Don't rush, but don't linger over the middle of your introduction, especially if you've written a strong opening. You don't want to lose momentum by getting tangled up in the minute details of your topic.

- **Revise your thesis as necessary *throughout* the composition process.** Until you turn in your final copy, your thesis is always a "working thesis" subject to change.

Sometimes it can be just as important to know what not to do as to do. As you're heading toward your thesis, keep two points in mind: First, don't introduce irrelevant material. It's never a good time to go off on an unrewarding tangent in an academic essay; but wandering away from your main point is particularly noticeable in your introductory paragraph. Second, try not to "tread water." Repeating the same idea over and over in slightly different guises strongly suggests that you don't have anything interesting to say about your topic.

DIY 7.2b Check Introductory Sentences Against Chapter Advice

Write a passage for your current essay assignment that takes readers from your opening sentence to your thesis statement, and then reread the "From Hook to Thesis" section of this chapter. Use the chapter advice to revise your opening paragraph.

End with Your Thesis

The placement of the thesis at the end of the introductory paragraph is common in academic writing in the United States and will be second nature to some students. However, you may resent the idea that your introduction must always end with your thesis statement, especially if you are passionate about pushing boundaries or feel that your audience or purpose calls for something else. Therefore, it's worth asking if your instructor is open to a thesis that appears in one of a variety of places throughout an essay. If you do choose an alternative placement, be certain of that flexibility before you turn in your essay.

Benefits of Conventional Thesis Placement

In a first-year class, ending your opening paragraph with your thesis serves three important functions:

- **It signals that you are aware of the conventions of academic writing.** Granted, there are disciplines, like creative writing and journalism, where innovative approaches to essay structure are rewarded. That may be the case in your class, too. But if it's not, or if you're unsure, it is better to err on the side of a more traditional approach.

- **It provides your reader with a clear roadmap of your essay.** It is also a smart way to ensure that you stay on track as you write.

- **It helps your instructor or a peer reviewer to quickly locate your essay's main points.** Knowing that a thesis will be found at the end of the opening paragraph allows busy readers to quickly identify and assess your argument before moving on to the other elements of your essay.

Thesis Check

Often when you are writing your introductory paragraph, you'll realize that the wording of your thesis needs some tweaking. That may be because the focus of your essay has changed during its composition, or it could simply be because you now see a way to make your thesis statement leaner, cleaner, and clearer.

While you will want to retain your focus on the material you've written about in the body of your essay, don't hesitate to revise your thesis so that it's more accurate, or simply because a few small changes would ensure that it flows more smoothly with the rest of the introduction.

Read a Sample Introductory Paragraph

As with body paragraphs, there is no single formula for introductory paragraphs. However, here's one possible way to introduce the essay on mindsets we've been working on. The paragraph opens with a fairly short declarative sentence (a simple informative sentence) followed by an illustrative quotation. It then provides a brief overview of the topic that transitions to the thesis statement, which concludes the paragraph. Notice that the working thesis statement from **Chapter 6** has been slightly revised. A transition phrase has been added—"It seems clear, therefore, that"—and a now-unnecessary word—"that" after "suggest"—has been dropped. Last-minute adjustments of phrasing are common: Again, don't ever feel that just because you've written a sentence, it can't be changed.

Declarative sentence followed
by a persuasive quotation

Stanford psychology professor Carol Dweck's ideas have a lot of people re-thinking their potential. In an article in *The Atlantic,* Christine Gross-Loh says that Dweck's "findings brought the concepts of 'fixed' and 'growth' mindset to the fore for educators and parents, inspiring the implementation of her ideas among teachers—and even companies—across the country." Kashawn Campbell, the student profiled in Kurt Streeter's *LA Times* article "South L.A. Student Finds a Different World at Cal," may never have heard of Carol Dweck, but he clearly has a growth mindset, as he is "ready to take the risks, confront the challenges, and keep working at them" (Dweck 58). Unlike Campbell, I was a failure in high school. Fortunately, the summer before my freshman year in college, I attended a program that has helped me develop a growth mindset. It seems clear, therefore, that college students' experiences suggest Dweck's theory about the relationship between growth mindset and success is valid. However, it is equally important to have an external support system for those times when our individual efforts aren't quite enough.

Transition from hook to thesis

Thesis statement

7.3   Writing Conclusions

CONCLUSION

End an essay on a strong, memorable note — the way you would a job interview.

If a strong introduction is like a good lead for a news story, a good conclusion is more like the final minutes of a job interview. You hope you've made a positive impression on your potential employer—that is, your reader—and you want to reinforce that impression by highlighting your strengths without simply repeating what you've already said.

As eager as you may be to finish your essay, resist the impulse to hurry through your final paragraph as quickly as possible. Instead, give your closing sentences as much thought as you gave your opening hook. It can help to take an extended break after writing the body of your essay. However, if you're on a deadline, even a snack break or a walk around the block can help reboot your imagination and energy.

While your conclusion is important, it doesn't have to do as much work as your introduction, so it's likely to be shorter. Think lean and strong. Stuffing your conclusion with irrelevant or redundant statements may pad your word count, but it will almost certainly make for a decreased impact on your reader—and may even lead to a lower grade.

Craft an Effective Conclusion

Many of the strategies that work for an opening hook can be used with equal success in a concluding paragraph. Of course, you may not want to use the same type of tactic in both your introduction and your conclusion, but reconsider these options when you're concluding your essay:

- **Tell a story.** Good storytelling nearly always makes us perk up and pay attention. Don't go overboard, but if a brief narrative dovetails with your overall message, use it to your advantage in your concluding paragraph.

- **Reset the scene.** Just as a vivid use of some or all of the five senses—sight, sound, touch, taste, and smell—nearly always draws readers in at the beginning of an essay, their use in a concluding paragraph can leave readers with an intense impression of the world you've been describing in your essay.

- **Include a persuasive quotation from an expert.** Quotations from authorities are often powerful, and a well-chosen quotation can cement your argument just as your reader is finishing your essay.

- **Provide a specific date connected to a notable fact or event.** Again, the actual date of an event often carries a lot of emotional weight. Think, for instance, of your response to the Fourth of July or September 11th or January 6th.

- **Use an analogy.** Metaphors and similes, which show surprising likenesses between apparently unlike things, can be as effective at the end of your essay as they are at the beginning.

- **Present an uncomfortable truth.** One of the main functions of academic essays is opening readers' eyes to difficult realities. However, if the evidence and analysis in your essay has been sufficiently persuasive, readers may no longer able to ignore those uncomfortable truths.

> While your conclusion is important, it doesn't have to do as much work as your introduction, so it's likely to be shorter. Think lean and strong.

- **Present a startling fact or statistic.** Because they can be proven objectively, well-chosen facts and statistics have persuasive power, wherever they appear in your essay.

- **Ask a provocative question.** Be sure that your question ties directly to the work that you have done in your paper. You *do* want your question to make people think, but you *don't* want it to be so open-ended that it makes readers feel as though they have learned nothing.

- **Amuse your reader.** Once again, humor doesn't work in all situations, but if your subject matter seems to demand a light touch at the end, there are far worse ways for readers to end an essay than with a smile on their faces.

- **Write from an image.** Sometimes you will find that a single image sums up everything you have been trying to say in your essay. Creating a "language picture" can be a very efficient way of helping to drive home your main points.

Here are two other time-tested strategies that are more relevant to conclusions than introductions.

- **Issue a reasonable call to action.** If you have convincingly made the case for your thesis, your reader may well want to know what, specifically, they can do next. The more specific and practical you are in your recommendations, the more likely your readers will look for ways to follow those suggestions. Don't ask your readers to change the world in one day, but do offer some modest suggestions that can help them along that journey.

- **Reconnect with your opening hook.** Returning to your opening hook is one of the most successful strategies for a conclusion in an essay. Doing so lets your reader know that your opening sentences were there for a reason, making the essay feel thorough and complete.

You want to be sure that your conclusion influences readers—and that it's clear what they should think, feel, or do in response to your essay.

Read a Sample Concluding Paragraph

It's important, yet again, to emphasize that there is no single correct strategy for composing a concluding paragraph. However, like the introductory paragraph, the conclusion serves as a kind of bookend for the essay. It sums up the main points, and may even expand on them somewhat, but its primary function is to bring the essay to a satisfying closure.

The following sample represents just one possible attempt to finish an essay using growth mindset to discuss the academic success of Kashawn Campbell and the essay writer. The paragraph opens with a quotation from the reading by Carol Dweck and then applies that quote to Campbell and the essay author. The next sentence reintroduces the essay's second main point—that an external support system is also necessary for student success—and is followed by a quotation by academic experts indicating the importance of support in the classroom. Finally, the paragraph concludes with a sentence that succinctly sums up the argument of the entire essay.

> Carol Dweck writes in her book *Mindset*, "The passion for stretching yourself and sticking to it, even (or especially) when it's not going well, is the hallmark of the growth mindset. This is the mindset that allows people to thrive during some of the most challenging times in their lives" (56). Both Kashawn Campbell and I have benefited from having a growth mindset. We believe in ourselves, and we know that challenges and failures are really just opportunities to become smarter and better. Just as important, we have not been shy about asking for help. Unfortunately, not every student is quite so confident, which is why the authors of *Teaching Men of Color in the Community College* point out how essential it is for professors to create "conditions in the class where students feel welcome to ask questions, respond to questions, and inquire about their progress" (Wood et al. 25). Succeeding in college, and in life, isn't always easy, but if we have a growth mindset and a supportive environment for our efforts, we all have the chance to become our best possible selves.

Quotation from an assigned reading

Quotation applied to essay subjects, Campbell and the student author

Further discussion

Additional quotation reinforces the writer's thesis

Final summary and a note of hope

DIY 7.3a Write or Revise a Conclusion

You've now seen a number of possible options for writing a conclusion. If you are currently working on the draft of an essay, write, or rewrite, your own final paragraph using the ideas above. (If you aren't working on anything at the moment, pull out an essay you've written in the recent past; try out one or two of the strategies from this chapter to revise the conclusion.) If your conclusion seems thin, consider combining several of the strategies listed in section 7.3.

Avoid Common Pitfalls

The suggestions above represent only some of the ways you might conclude your essay. Your main focus should be on making the conclusion feel *necessary*. A concluding paragraph with nothing new or significant to say is almost as bad as not having a conclusion at all, and even a good essay can be marred by a tedious ending. Here are a few final tips for what to avoid.

- **Don't simply repeat what you've already said.** This is by far the most common error you can make in a concluding paragraph. A highly repetitive conclusion makes it seem as though your readers are incapable of remembering what they read a few minutes ago, especially if your essay is just a few pages long. You want readers to feel as if they've been on a journey and have learned something.

- **Don't use a random quotation.** While a relevant quote from an expert on your topic is a compelling way to conclude an academic essay, don't settle for some arbitrary remark spat out by a quotation-generator. Also, avoid using a quotation for the final sentence. You want to leave your reader with *your* idea.

- **Don't conclude with "In Conclusion . . ."** It might seem natural to begin your final paragraph with the phrase "In conclusion . . ." However, just as readers assume you're talking about "today's society" unless you say otherwise, they will be able to see with their own eyes that this is your last paragraph.

DIY 7.3b Evaluate Your Conclusion

A good way to evaluate your conclusion is to look at it separately from the rest of your essay, as though it were its own paragraph. If you are currently working on an essay draft, print out your concluding paragraph or put it on its own page in a Google doc. (If you don't have an essay assignment right now, use the conclusion you wrote or revised for DIY 7.3a.) Write notes to answer the following review questions:

- Does the conclusion stand on its own as a good piece of writing? Point to specific examples in the paragraph supporting your evaluation.

- Does the conclusion employ one or more of the strategies suggested here in section 7.3? If so, which ones? If not, does it still engage your interest? If so, how does it accomplish this?

- Would the conclusion make someone want to read the essay? Explain why or why not.

 ## 7.4   Creating Titles That Work

While the title is the first thing that your reader will see, it is also often the very last thing many students think of before turning in their essays. Naturally, a great title paired with a lousy essay isn't going to earn you points with your readers (literally or figuratively speaking), but you'd be surprised how much readers value a good title. The very fact that you've taken the time to think it over and call your paper something other than "Essay #1"

or "Research Paper" suggests that you're attending to every last detail of your essay, that you want to get it just right. If you're writing something you plan to repurpose for or publish online—a blog post, perhaps—the right title can drive traffic to your ideas.

In her book *Stylish Academic Writing*, Helen Sword notes that "Among the many decisions faced by authors composing an academic title, the most basic choice is whether to *engage* the reader, *inform* the reader, or do both at once." Ideally, of course, your title will do both, but if you must decide on one or the other, re-read the assignment for any indication of your instructor's preference.

Write Engaging and Informative Titles

Using some recently published magazine articles as examples, let's take a look at some effective ways to craft titles.

- **Allude to a crucial moment in the essay.** Referring to a specific moment in the essay, especially if it comes toward the end, has the virtue of adding suspense to your essay. Readers want to know what the title is all about, so they read until the answer is revealed. Erin Vachon's "Rain on the Wind," for instance, refers to the lyrics in a Kris Kristofferson song that her father-in-law sings on the other side of a thin wall while she experiences painful medical issues.

- **Ask a question.** The answer to the title of Maureen Dowd's bitingly critical "Will Mark Zuckerberg 'Like' This Column?" is almost certainly no, and it can sometimes be effective to pose a question whose answer is obvious right from the start. More common, though, are titles with questions that don't have easy answers: "Should We Abandon Our Smartphones?" or "Can the United States Bridge Its Political Divides?" In either case, the question posed in the title must be intriguing. Readers should want to know the answer, whatever it may be.

- **Employ a pun.** A pun is a joke exploiting the various meanings of a word, phrase, or fact. Punning in titles is especially popular in magazine writing, but you'll want to check with your instructor to see if a pun is appropriate for the essay you're writing for class. Among some recent examples of titles with clever puns are Ellen Ullman's essay about women in software coding, "Gender Binary"; Barbara Ehrenrich's piece about the premium placed on healthy good looks among older people, "Running to the Grave"; and Elizabeth Royte's "Drinking Problems," which is not about alcoholism, but instead about polluted groundwater.

- **Be as direct as possible.** It would be hard to get any more straightforward than Rick Moody's "Seven Years of Identity Theft," an essay on exactly that topic. You see that same impulse to let readers know just what they're getting in Cheri Blauwet's "I Use a Wheelchair. And, Yes, I'm Your Doctor." These authors assume that the subject matter of their essays—the widespread danger of identity fraud and the notion that your doctor can be a brilliant practitioner and have a disability—is intrinsically interesting. Therefore, their titles state the content of the essays as precisely as possible.

- **Use a colon.** Many, if not most, titles in articles published in academic journals employ a colon in the middle of the title. Typically, the first part of the title provides the sort of catchy phrase we've just been talking about. On the right side of the colon, verbal playfulness is clarified by a more neutral and descriptive explanation of what the essay is actually about. We can see that dynamic at work in Katie Roiphe's "The Other Whisper Network: How Twitter Feminism Is Bad for Women." "The Other Whisper Network" piques our interest, and "How Twitter Feminism Is Bad for Women" provides us with the essay's focus.

The first title that pops in your head may be a good one, but more likely you will want to jot down several possibilities. Fiction writer Ernest Hemingway would draft dozens of titles for each book and then gradually discard those he didn't like. According to one critic, Hemingway would choose a title, in part, for its "potential impact on the browsing customer." You're likely not selling your work, but you are trying to convince a browsing reader to read on. *Listening* carefully to your title and *feeling* that it functions just as you want it to may be the best tests of whether or not you've got it right. Don't rule out "market testing" possible titles with peers or with a writing center tutor.

Once you have decided on your title, follow these rules for formatting it:

Basic Rules for Titles

- Titles are centered.

- In a double-spaced essay, the title is just two spaces above the beginning of your essay. There should not be any extra space.

- All the main words in a title are capitalized, while minor words are in lowercase. In a title, a minor word like "a" or "the" following a colon is also capitalized (*Hello, Writer: An Academic Writing Guide*).

- Do not use quotation marks around your own essay title (although if you are referring to a shorter work by someone else, you put the title inside the quotation marks).

DIY 7.4 Generate Titles for Your Essay

Using the title-generating strategies suggested here, as well as your own creativity, to write as many titles for your essay-in-progress as you can. Then narrow your list down to two titles and reflect on which may be best for your purpose and audience — and why.

Chapter 7 Checklist
Introductions, Conclusions, and Titles

☐ **Does your opening sentence (or sentences) immediately draw your reader into your essay?**

Hello, Writer provides a number of specific suggestions for "hooking" your reader into your essay. Be sure to try several different strategies before settling on one.

☐ **Have you made a clear and logical connection between your opening hook and your thesis statement at the end of the introductory paragraph?**

Be concise and clear in your transition, making sure that each sentence logically follows the preceding one and that all move cohesively toward the argument outlined in your thesis.

☐ **If your working thesis needs revision, have you modified it so that it is more effectively incorporated into your introductory paragraph?**

While you will want to retain your focus on the material you've written about in the body of your essay, don't be shy about changing the wording of the thesis to ensure the "flow" of the introduction.

☐ **Does your concluding paragraph bring closure to your essay without simply repeating what's already been said?**

Again, this book contains multiple strategies for writing conclusions that avoid vague and boring redundancies. Remember that the conclusion forms one of the last impressions your instructor will have before grading your essay.

☐ **Have you selected the best possible title for your essay?**

Use the tips in *Hello, Writer* for generating titles that, to use Helen Sword's phrase, "*engage* the reader, *inform* the reader, or do both at once."

7.5 Making It Stick

How will you introduce, wrap up, and title the essays you write?

Working Together

7.5a Revising Introductions Form a group of four or five students and have everyone send their introduction to another person in the group.

On the bottom of the document, each person in the group should ask one specific question about the paragraph. If someone has already asked the question you were planning to ask, think of another one.

Be as specific as possible with your questions. Rather than asking, "What's the point of your introduction?" ask something like, "What emotion do you want the reader to feel after reading the third sentence?"

When everyone has responded to all the introductions, read through the questions on your own introduction, make sure you can understand each one, and then try to answer them all.

7.5b Revising Conclusions   Now try the same exercise with your conclusion (see 7.5a). Share your conclusion with your group, and make sure each person asks a question about each concluding paragraph. Again, if anyone has already asked the question you were planning to ask, think of another one. Finish by trying to answer the questions written on the back of your own concluding paragraph.

Applying What You Know

7.5c Favorite Sentences   Browse a few online opinion pieces, paying particular attention to the opening and concluding paragraphs. Search online for "Sacramento Bee opinion" or "Miami Herald opinion" or "Chicago Tribune opinion" — or any other newspaper title plus the word "opinion." Read carefully and choose one or two of your favorite sentences from the essays you read. Write brief notes on two of your favorite sentences. What appeals to you about the sentences?

7.5d "Quick-Searching" Your Introduction
Do some quick research on your topic to help bridge the opening sentences and your thesis statement. Remember that while you don't want to go into great detail at this point, a specific example or two may be just what you need

to strengthen the middle of your paragraph. Remember to cite any ideas or language that you borrow for your introduction (see Chapter 18 for MLA, 19 for APA). (Note: If you uncover any research that doesn't work for your introduction, but might be useful elsewhere in your essay, be sure to file it for easy retrieval later on.)

7.5e "Quick-Searching" Your Conclusion
Do some quick research to strengthen your concluding paragraph. When you find a specific fact or relevant example, incorporate it into your conclusion, citing any material that comes from another writer. Again, if you uncover any research that doesn't work here, but might be useful elsewhere in your essay, be sure to hold on to it.

Invitations to Write

7.5f Writing Opening Sentences

Shorter: Take your favorite opening sentence from any essay you've ever written, and make it better. If it's long-winded, cut it down. If it doesn't have enough pizzazz, add some. In short, make what you thought was good even better.

Longer: Extend your opening so that it consists of two or three sentences rather than one. Your new sentences should (1) connect with the first sentence, and (2) move toward the argument you will be making in your thesis statement.

7.5g Writing Conclusions

Shorter: Write the last sentence of your essay, the one you think will have the most impact on readers as they finish your paper.

Longer: Back up a little and write the entire concluding paragraph so that it leads directly to your final sentence. Make sure each sentence in the paragraph follows logically from the one that precedes it.

7.5f Writing Titles

Shorter: Read through the titles of the Modern Library's list of the 100 Best Nonfiction Books ever written: modernlibrary.com/top-100/100-best -nonfiction/. If you had to choose one title from the Modern Library's list for the essay you are writing,

which one would it be? (Feel free to modify the title a bit to make it work better for your essay.) Write a short paragraph explaining why you chose the title that you did.

Longer: Now, look at the title you are actually using for your essay. Write a paragraph describing why this is the perfect title for your essay. If you begin your paragraph and realize that your title isn't so great after all, compose a different title and write a paragraph about your new, improved version.

8

Reviewing and Revising

REFLECT

Write Before You Read | Activity to connect what's new with what you already know 163

READ & PRACTICE

DIY (Do-it-yourself) activities offer just-in-time support for all the skills in this book.

MAKING IT STICK

Working Together | Collaborative and community-building activities 186

Applying What You Know | Activities to reinforce chapter content 186

Invitations to Write | Brief writing prompts 187

162

Write Before You Read   Write a paragraph describing what you normally do after you finish the first draft of an essay. Do you take some time off before looking at again? Do you ask a friend for feedback? Do you meet with your instructor or a writing center tutor? Or do you simply turn the first draft in to be graded? Overall, how well has your "post-first-draft" writing process worked for you in the past?

8.1   Taking Another Chance to Get It Right

If you've ever seen the 1990s movie *Groundhog Day*, you may be familiar with the idea of a time loop; the main character, Phil Connors, relives the same day over and over, using knowledge from each day to change and improve (and ruin, at times) the next. He is released from the time loop's monotony only after he chooses to change himself for the better. What if you could go back in time and undo the mistakes you made and improve the outcome? What if you had a second, third, and even fourth chance to get it right?

Think of revision as the power to remake the past, to change something that you wanted to forget into something you'll be proud to remember. In this case, of course, what you're changing isn't your life, but an earlier draft of your essay. Revision is your opportunity to get it right.

Revision involves looking at the big picture, at global issues like the essay's overall argument and structure. When you revise, you reread to see if your thesis adequately guides what comes afterward. You ask yourself if something crucial is missing or if something big has to go.

Editing, on the other hand, tends to take place mostly on the sentence level (see Chapter 9). When you sit down to edit, you should be fairly confident that the essay is already structurally sound. At this point, you're deleting words, phrases, and sentences that don't work and adding others that do. You're moving things around but mostly within the paragraphs themselves.

That said, revising can quickly turn into editing and vice versa. If you're lucky, you may set out to do a full-scale revision, only to discover that your essay mostly just needs sentence-level editing. A far more common experience, however, is sitting down to review your work and realizing that it's not just the sentences that need attention. At that point, editing halts, and you begin to think globally again. While the instruction in this book is sectioned off into "Revision" (Chapter 8) and "Editing" (Chapter 9), if you give your essay the full attention it deserves, you will very likely move back and forth from one to the other.

Moving from one draft to the next involves reviewing what you've written, seeking feedback, reflecting on the feedback, and revising. Writing a good essay is a complex endeavor; it's worth emphasizing, therefore, that while this chapter explains a number of strategies for giving your essay another chance, revision, like the composing process itself, can be a messy and scattered (and dare I say *exciting*) undertaking that involves commitment, grit, and a growth mindset (see section 3.1).

8.2 Reviewing Your Draft

Most experienced writers give a draft a bit of time to sit before they begin to revise. During this time, the mind often continues to work on the draft, even though the laptop is closed and the writer takes a break. With practice, you will come upon the best review and revision processes for you.

In addition to managing your time, you'll need to manage your files as well. Because discovering the best form for your essay is just as likely to require eliminating old material as generating new material, it's always a good idea to keep previous drafts in separate files so that you can go back to review and retrieve material that initially seemed to be irrelevant or in the wrong place, but which turns out to be useful after all. The more you write, the more you'll get used to going back and forth between files with older and newer drafts. The rest of this section discusses a variety of strategies you can use as you review your draft and plan a revision.

A full revision case study appears in section 8.5.

DIY 8.2a Revisit Your Essay Prompt

To make sure your essay has accomplished what your prompt is asking for, try this: Annotate the prompt like you would any other reading, underlining what's important, highlighting anything you need to question your instructor about, and making marginal comments about matters you still need to attend to.

Reread the Prompt

Before you reread your essay, carefully review your assigned prompt one more time. You may be amazed how often you come to assume that the assignment is asking you to do something that you're not required to do at all. Luckily, you may also notice on a reread that, somehow, you've forgotten to address a key element of the prompt.

Revisit Active Reading Strategies

An essential component of revising your work is stepping back and looking at it as though it were written by someone else. It helps if you pretend that the draft you are about to look at is a reading that your instructor has assigned. To make sure you approach it with the same focus and detachment you'd give a reading in your textbook, it's worth recalling some of the college reading strategies previously discussed in Chapter 2:

- **Consider reading a hard copy of the essay.** Most writers do the bulk of their composing, revising, and editing on a computer. Seeing your essay only in this format may keep you from noticing issues that might otherwise jump out at you. A hard copy can allow you to see things that you missed when the essay was only on your computer screen.

- **Find a quiet place and allow plenty of time to read.** If you only give yourself fifteen or twenty minutes to reread your essay, and you do so in a place where you are likely to get distracted, you're not likely to come away with a clear, fresh perspective on your material. Plan on at least an hour of quiet and concentration and on multiple rereadings of your draft. If you find yourself rushing through your essay, physically point to each word as you read it.

- **Annotate.** Engaging with a text through writing is one of the best ways to understand it. Note the places in your essay where you're confused or unconvinced by your own argument, but don't forget to reward yourself when you've made an especially good point.

- **Challenge the text.** While it might seem odd to be challenging something you yourself have written, that's actually one of the strategies experienced writers most often employ when they are revising their work. You're a different person now that you've finished your draft, someone who understands the subject better and has almost certainly written sentences or passages that can be made better. Don't let yourself get away with an idea or argument that you wouldn't accept if someone else were the author.

- **Ask why the text was written.** Yes, it was written because you were given a specific assignment by your instructor. But what other purpose does the essay serve? Make sure each sentence can answer the "So what?" challenge. Why should a reader care about what you've written?

- **Visualize.** If you are unable to "see" your argument in the form of images, it probably means you don't have any concrete information and supporting details. Make marginal notes anywhere the essay seems particularly hazy and vague.

- **Look for headings and visuals.** Is your essay one long expanse of nothing but words, or have you divided it into shorter sections, each with its own heading, to make it easier to read? If you have graphics or images, are they both striking and important to the argument you are making? (See Chapter 14 in Part 2 for a discussion of visuals.)

- **Keep reader responses in mind.** If you're revising *after* you've received peer review comments or instructor feedback, keep those responses in mind as you look for what's working and what still needs work.

Read Aloud

One way to ensure that you reread your draft at a slow and deliberate pace is to read aloud, a strategy followed by many professional writers and a technique that can, in the words of writing expert Peter Elbow, "intensif[y] our own experience of our own words."

If reading aloud makes you feel awkward, find a quiet, safe space, and make sure you have a pen or pencil to take notes. Basically, you're listening for both a flow and naturalness of speech. It's important, too, that what you've written still interests you. If your writing makes you sleepy and apathetic, imagine how your readers are going to feel.

DIY 8.2b Revise Your Essay with Reading Strategies

Working with the essay you are currently writing or an essay you wrote earlier in the semester or for another class, slowly read the piece annotating as you go, and employing the other reading strategies discussed above. Highlight every place where you stumble or get distracted or bored.

Then, send or share an unmarked copy of the essay with another student and ask that student to share an unmarked copy of their essay with you. Follow the same strategy with your partner's essay: annotating, challenging, visualizing, and marking the places where the writing loses energy or where the argument loses momentum.

Return the marked copies and compare the responses of you and your partner. Those areas that both of you identified as needing improvement will be especially good places to begin thinking about your revision.

Make a Reverse Outline

You'll recall that Chapters 2 and 3 discussed the value of reverse outlines when attempting to understand and summarize work by another writer. The same tool that helps you recap important readings is just as effective at presenting your own work in condensed form. Because a reverse outline summarizes *what is actually on the page*, it not only provides you with a synopsis of your essay; it also forces you to see what you've really written, rather than what you'd thought was there or what you'd hoped to write.

DIY 8.2c Create a Reverse Outline

Write a reverse outline of the essay you are currently writing. (If you aren't in the process of composing an essay, write a reverse outline of an essay that you have written in the past.) Make sure you identify the thesis, topic sentences, and main pieces of supporting evidence. Typically, the summary in a reverse outline takes the form of one sentence per paragraph. If you've forgotten what a reverse outline looks like, reread the sample reverse outline in section 2.3.

8.3 Seeking and Evaluating Feedback

Experienced writers often learn that feedback from others is critical to setting and meeting revision goals. Having an outside reviewer to help you think about your ideas, your organization, and your language can be very valuable, whether or not you decide to use the reviewer's advice. As a college student, you will most often seek feedback from your instructor, a writing center tutor, or a peer/classmate.

Work with Instructor Feedback

While some students are eager to hear everything that their instructors have to say about their essay, others cringe at the idea of reading their professor's feedback.

Assuming you have your instructor's written feedback on an earlier draft of an essay, the smartest first move is to read and evaluate those comments carefully. Pay attention to what your instructor *actually* said, not what you *wish* they had written. Often students will have a sense that one thing was wrong with an essay, when, in fact, their instructor is much more concerned with something else entirely. Don't waste your time correcting spelling mistakes if you're being asked to rethink a major part of your essay.

Don't, however, focus only on what you perceive to be the negative comments, which your instructor likely considers constructive criticism. Remember Carol Dweck's advice that "[p]eople in a growth mindset don't just *seek* challenge, they thrive on it. The bigger the challenge, the more they stretch." To improve, try to see each failure as simply another opportunity to get better. Every essay, no matter how rough it is, has some moments worth praising. Take consolation in those places where your instructor praised your writing or where you simply feel you've done a good job.

While it would be ideal if every essay you turned in received lavish attention and comments, instructors can't always comment as thoroughly as they would like. If the feedback you receive seems cryptic or brief, make an appointment with your instructor to go over your essay in a conference.

Guidelines for a Writing Conference

When you meet, whether in person or online, maximize your conference time by doing the following:

- **Think globally before you think locally.** Ask to work on larger issues, such as thesis, organization, and support, rather than fussing over one isolated error. On the other hand, if you find you are making a *pattern* of errors, then it's worth learning more about those errors and how to eliminate them.

- **Be specific whenever you can.** The best conferences tend to be those in which a writer starts with a few specific questions. Don't expect your instructor to have a perfect memory of your essay. Instead, provide a copy and direct your questions to those places where you need help. A broad question like, "How can I make this essay better?" *may* result in some useful feedback, but you are much more likely to receive a satisfactory and useful answer to a question such as, "How can the topic sentence of my second body paragraph be more in line with the evidence in that paragraph?"

- **Don't waste time—yours, or your instructor's.** If your instructor was checking emails when you walked in for your conference, that doesn't mean that they're necessarily waiting for a student to come in and kill the next hour with some friendly gossip. When you've received an answer to your question or questions, assume the conference is over, say thank you, and depart.

If you can't attend office hours, be realistic about what you can accomplish through other means, such as email. If you email asking your instructor, "What did you mean on p. 2?" you might want to send a photo or screeenshot of the page to refresh the instructor's memory and increase your chances of getting useful feedback.

Visit the Writer Center

If you can't reach your professor, or if the draft you're revising hasn't yet received any instructor comments, take advantage of the campus writing center. Just as you would when meeting with your instructor, maximize your time by having specific questions and working as expeditiously as possible. *Always* bring your assignment with you, along with any other writing you've done, such as outlines or previous drafts. If your essay has already been graded and you're looking for additional feedback, make sure to bring the copy that includes your instructor's comments.

Most writing centers tell students that they are not fix-it shops or editing factories. Instead, you will receive guidance and what's called "nondirective instruction," where the ultimate responsibility for coming up with the right answers falls back on you.

While tutoring sessions at a writing center are usually very productive, if you have one that doesn't go well, don't give up on the idea of visiting again. It's also okay to tell your tutor in the middle of a session if you feel that they're spending too much time on material that you already understand or on something that your instructor has specifically said is unimportant. Ultimately, it's up to you to advocate for yourself by letting the tutor know what you think you need to learn and why.

Be Open to Peer Review

Depending on past experiences with peer review or peer editing, you may be eager for or anxious about the task in a college setting. Peer review can be nerve-wracking, but it also provides distinct opportunities: getting to compare notes about assignment expectations, seeing skills or moves that you may want to try in your writing, and experiencing another person's worldview.

When your essay is under discussion—either in person or online—listen respectfully to everyone's evaluation and comments. Be open to receiving useful feedback from classmates you may not personally like but who nevertheless have good ideas. Likewise, know that you don't have to blindly embrace feedback from any reader. Try to weigh each bit of commentary against your purpose and your goals.

When it's time for you to exchange your draft with one or more of your classmates, be sensitive, and try to adhere to the following guidelines for constructively evaluating and discussing one another writer's work.

> **Peer review provides distinct opportunities: getting to compare notes about assignment expectations, seeing skills or moves that you may want to try in your writing, and experiencing another person's worldview.**

Guidelines for Peer Review

- **Be polite.** Treat others with kindness and respect.

- **Keep your focus on the text rather than the person.** Remember that the person who wrote the essay is *not* the essay itself. Your comments should be text-based and objective and should avoid personal comments about the author.

- **Be specific in your comments.** For example, instead of saying, "I thought your essay was kind of vague," point to paragraphs and sentences that could be strengthened by using concrete supporting examples.

- **If you are a more accomplished writer than your peer, be a generous mentor.** This isn't the time to gloat about your advanced skills.

- **If you are a less accomplished writer than your peer, be a listener and a learner, but do comment on issues you feel need attention.** There's a great deal of research showing that articulating your thoughts about the work of other writers can improve your own writing.

Peer Review Questions

Try to keep from focusing on editing and proofreading issues rather than revision: Unless they are numerous and distracting, don't worry too much about sentence-level errors at this point. Instead, look at the questions in the following checklist, and try to focus your attention on these important areas.

Peer Review Checklist

☐ **Audience and Purpose**
  - Does the essay meet the specific guidelines of the prompt? If not, where does it go off track?
  - If the prompt indicates the essay should be directed at a specific audience, how well has the writer addressed that audience?

☐ **Thesis**
  - What is the essay's thesis?
  - Is the thesis statement specific, arguable, and appropriate to the prompt?

☐ **Organization**

- What are the main points of each body paragraph?
- Are the paragraphs arranged in the most logical and effective order? If not, how might the paragraphs be reordered?
- Is the material *within* the paragraphs arranged logically and effectively? If not, what suggestions do you have for adding, deleting, or repositioning individual sentences?
- Are the introduction and the conclusion interesting and thoughtful? If not, what can the writer do to make them more compelling?

☐ **Evidence**

- Are the body paragraphs supported by concrete, specific, and convincing evidence? If not, what evidence is needed and where?

☐ **Overall Interest and Clarity**

- Where do you find yourself most interested?
- Where do you find yourself most bored or distracted?
- Where do you find yourself most confused?
- What one question about the topic would you still like the writer to answer?

Though questions like these are helpful, a peer review session should always respond to the actual work you have in front of you. If an essay has one huge problem—a lack of supporting evidence, for example, or a vague thesis—then it's a waste of time to focus on recrafting something relatively minor like the opening hook until the group addresses the larger issues.

If you have been assigned to use **Achieve,** a digital tool available with this book, your instructor may have identified **Draft Goals**—areas or skills to focus on for each draft. The Draft Goals are meant to focus early writing efforts and feedback. "Topic sentences," "Thesis statement," "Audience awareness," "Evidence," and "Integration of sources" are all examples of Draft Goals in Achieve.

Take Charge

It's easy to put off revising your essay and even easier not to revise it at all. Don't fall prey to that temptation. Instead, take charge of getting the work done.

Sometimes students will avoid revising because they think that their original grade

DIY 8.3 Form a Peer Review Group

Form a peer review group of three to five people and share your essay through the file-sharing platform used at your school. Then use the questions in section 8.3 as a starting place for a revision discussion. Don't get sidetracked by minor errors, and make sure you have a copy of your own essay during the discussion.

should have been better or that the professor just doesn't understand what they are trying to do. While those are both possibilities, dwelling on resentments rather than getting back to your essay isn't productive.

Ultimately, investing yourself in the writing and revision of not just your current essay but of all your future essays—and business letters and lab reports and marketing assessments—is empowering and liberating. Artists David Bayles and Ted Orland approach revision with both seriousness and humor in their book *Art & Fear*: "It's . . . called doing your work. After all, *someone* has to do your work, and you're the closest person around."

8.4 Revising for Focus, Support, and Organization

With some feedback from reviewers and the perspective you have gained from stepping back from your draft—even if only for a day—you can begin to revise with three questions in mind:

- Is my writing focused?

- Do I have enough support for my major and minor points?

- Is my writing organized?

One word of caution: When you revise, take care not to overwrite your draft file. Copy the draft file but add a new filename. For example, if your original file name included your name, the assignment, and the draft date,

PiaJackson_Argument_10.04.21

you may want to revise in a different file with a different date—preserving the work you've already done and making it easier to draw from the draft as you revise:

PiaJackson_Argument_rev10.15.21

Clarify the Introduction and Thesis

It's important to immediately engage your reader's interest with a hook that leads succinctly and intelligently to a clear and arguable thesis statement. Your opening sentences play an important part in convincing your reader that you will be a trustworthy guide to your subject matter, so let's take another look at how those elements might be addressed in your introductory paragraph:

Guidelines for Clarifying the Introduction and Thesis

- **Engage readers with your opening sentence or sentences.** You can review different types of openings in section 7.2; but remember that your ultimate goal in the first sentence or two is to write something so fascinating that readers feel compelled to read more. Strive toward that goal rather than settling for the first thing that pops into your head.

- **Move logically and concisely from your opening hook to your thesis.** Once you've captivated your reader with your opening sentence or sentences, you need to maintain that interest while shifting the focus to your thesis statement. Think of the middle part of the first paragraph as a pathway connecting the hook and thesis: Keep the route clear and short, and don't introduce material that sidetracks readers from your main argument.

- **Test the strength of your thesis.** Readers, and especially college professors, want to know your position on a topic, which is why succinct and confident thesis statements are crucial to so much of the writing you will do. Time spent refining your thesis statement is never wasted, so it's worth rechecking your current thesis against the elements described in section 5.4. A strong thesis

  is focused and specific

  is not a statement of fact

  answers a question, whether specifically asked or implied

  is arguable and worth arguing

  provides a plan for the essay

And don't forget that if your thesis explores a complex subject, it may well be longer than a single sentence.

- **Be certain that your thesis reflects the actual content of your essay.** While drafting and redrafting an essay, you will often find yourself moving away from your original thesis toward areas that are more interesting and productive. That process is normal, but make sure that the thesis in your final draft mirrors what you've written in the body of your essay.

DIY 8.4a Clarify the Introduction and Thesis

Using the guidelines in 8.4, carefully read and reread your opening paragraph to confirm that it meets all the requirements for an academic essay, paying special attention to your thesis statement. Be honest with yourself. If your opening hook is dull or your thesis is vague, now is the time to revise them.

Develop Ideas and Add Support if Needed

Revision is about developing your ideas, not simply correcting the ones you've already generated. As you flesh out your initial thoughts on a topic, your first ideas will need further thought and elaboration. Then, as those concepts become essential to your essay, you'll want to make sure you have sufficient evidence—in the form of summary, paraphrase, a direct quotation, data, or a visual—to support each main idea.

Guidelines for Developing Ideas and Adding Support

- **Make room for new ideas.** Many writers get their best ideas during the revision process. As you revise, be open to learning new things and possibly changing the organization of your essay—and even your opinion on your topic.

- **Support each claim with concrete and persuasive evidence.** Just as you might be skeptical that a friend had won the lottery until you saw some direct proof, your readers have every right to demand evidence for every significant assertion you make in your essay. Whether you provide facts, statistics, textual or visual evidence, or expert opinions, be ready to support all your major claims.

- **Include commentary on your evidence.** Simply depositing a quotation or statistic in the middle of a paragraph without commenting on it may leave readers almost as baffled as if you didn't provide any evidence at all. As a rule of thumb, every piece of evidence should be accompanied by explanatory material that is at least as detailed as the evidence itself.

- **Write to your audience.** Different audiences will be swayed by different ideas and evidence. The more skeptical your audience, the more rigorous your ideas and evidence will need to be. However, even a sympathetic audience will expect you to fully develop your main points and assemble detailed and appropriate support for each idea.

- **Consider counterarguments.** As discussed in section 6.3, you'll want to sincerely weigh the opinions of those who disagree with you. As you revise, make sure you have acknowledged the legitimate concerns of dubious readers, then firmly and politely offer evidence that demonstrates the strength of your own position.

DIY 8.4b Develop Ideas and Add Support

To ensure that all the ideas in your essay are fully developed and that each claim you make is supported by persuasive evidence, reread your essay, and each time you make a claim that someone could argue with — that is, the statement is not purely factual — highlight the sentence. Then go back and see if each of those claims is followed by persuasive supporting evidence. If the evidence is weak or nonexistent, either eliminate the claim, or generate some support that will convince even the most skeptical of readers.

Optimize Organization

Once you feel confident that you have sufficiently clarified your introduction and thesis and fully developed and supported each of your main ideas, it's time to make sure you are making the most effective use of your material.

Take another look at how your paragraphs are arranged and then how the sentences within those paragraphs are arranged. You should have the sense of a puzzle coming together, with each piece fitting in just the right place. Ultimately, optimizing organization is about achieving coherence, the sense that everything in the essay connects and works toward the greater good of the overall piece.

Guidelines for Optimizing Organization

- **Reflect on the content of your essay.** To make the most effective use of the material you are revising, you need to have a clear sense of what's actually there. Set aside some quiet time, take a deep breath, then slowly and consciously read through your essay, taking careful note of what you have done, and what you may still need to do.

- **Consider changing the order of your paragraphs.** Sometimes you have just about everything you need, but the main parts are arranged illogically. As you review the contents of your essay, maintain an attitude of flexibility and openness to new connections. If you do make changes in the order of your paragraphs, don't forget to reflect that fact by revising the order that those points appear in your thesis statement.

- **Write each body paragraph from a clear topic sentence.** Both readers and writers find it helpful to have the goals and focus of each paragraph encapsulated in a single sentence. While a topic sentence isn't always the first sentence in a body paragraph, it is often found in that slot. Wherever your topic sentence appears, you should remain conscious of it as you write, ensuring that each sentence in your paragraph is relevant and necessary.

- **Move, add, or delete sentences as necessary.** Rearranging the order of the paragraphs in an essay is common practice for writers, and rearranging—and adding or deleting—individual sentences is an even more integral part of the revision process. Try not to be overly attached to particular sentences, especially if they aren't working for your essay. Just because you've written a good sentence, that doesn't mean it belongs in the paragraph—or even the essay—where it is currently positioned.

- **Use clear transitions.** You know where you are going with your essay, but first-time readers won't. Help them out by employing words and phrases that signal when, and how, you are connecting ideas or moving on to new ones. See section 6.4.

- **Add headings when appropriate.** Even a relatively short essay can often benefit from headings; the longer your essay, the more helpful they are in letting readers know exactly what's going on. Moreover, headings have the added benefit of making sure that you, the author, know exactly where all of your material is.

- **Allow the process of organizing to lead to further revision.** As we've emphasized throughout this chapter, revision often doesn't follow a neat pattern. New ideas occur to you and you want to get them down while they're still in your head. Reorganizing your paragraphs, for instance, might inspire you to add a supporting example, just as discovering an exciting new piece of evidence might lead you to significantly change your thesis. Experienced writers take this sometimes-disruptive process in stride, and you should try your best to follow their lead.

DIY 8.4c Optimize Organization

Use the guidelines in section 8.4 to optimize both the overall organization of your essay as well as the individual sentences in each paragraph. Each point that you make — both major and minor — should lead clearly and logically to the next one. You may still need to do some serious rearranging at this point in your revision, so don't be afraid to dig in and get your hands a bit dirty. And if you suddenly have a great new idea along the way, don't be shy; welcome it into your essay.

8.5 Learning from a Revision Case Study

This section presents one student's revision experience. You can see the draft Oliver Hernandez wrote in response to a prompt, one peer reviewer's comments, and Oliver's own post-draft reflection. Oliver's revised essay appears on pages 179–184.

As you read through the first draft of Oliver Hernandez's essay in this section, think back on the most important things you have learned about writing academic essays, and make notes in the margins where you think Oliver's essay can be improved.

Study One Writer's First Draft

The following draft responds to the essay prompt given on page 77. Oliver Hernandez's assignment is to write an MLA-style argument essay of about 1,000 words in which he focuses on either growth mindset or grit and discusses his own school experiences and those of student Kashawn Campbell.

Sample Student Draft with Peer Comments

Hernandez 1

Oliver Hernandez

Professor Starkey

English 110

24 September 2020

Essay about Growth Mindset

My focus in this essay is on discussing how UC Berkeley
student Kashawn Campbell and myself had different
experiences in high school and college. I will use Carol Dweck's
growth mindset theory as my focus. Campbell did great in
high school, but not so great in college. So far, I have been the
opposite—crappy in high school but pretty good in college.
Irregardless, I believe Dweck is correct that having a growth
mindset is essential to a person's success.

As a high school student, Kashawn Campbell had a growth
mindset. He grew up in a tough neighborhood but he did very well
in high school. Campbell, like other people with a growth mindset,
is not someone "labeling themselves and throwing up their hands."
Instead, he was passionate about his own success: he "willed
himself to become a straight-A student." By the time he graduated,
Campbell was "named the prom king, the most likely to succeed,
[and] the senior class salutatorian." Having a growth mindset
pushed him through to the top level of success at Jefferson High.

Once Campbell began attending UC Berkeley, his growth
mindset was really tested. He still believed what Dweck
wrote, that "human qualities, such as intellectual skills, could
be cultivated through effort." For instance, when he first
starts college, he tries to stay upbeat with his dormmates.
Unfortunately, his bad grades force him to admit he isn't
prepared for college, and he gets depressed. In his second
semester, his growth mindset is just hanging on by a thread.
He only tells a few close friends how bad he feels. Fortunately,
Campbell has a good friend, Spencer Simpson, who jacks up

Pia Jackson
Oliver, it seems like you'll
have many points of
comparison with Campbell.
Your thesis seems a little bland.
I can't tell from the thesis
where your essay is going.

Pia Jackson
Maybe you should say here
what a "growth mindset" is.

Hernandez 2

Campbell's growth mindset. Ultimately, Kashawn Campbell is an inspiring example of someone with a growth mindset.

Like Campbell, I was not often challenged in my high school. My school doesn't have quite as a "woeful reputation" as Jefferson High, where "just under 13% of its students were judged to be proficient in English, less than 1% in math," but my high school in Sacramento does not have a good record of sending students off to college. I was lucky that I liked to read, which should have given me a growth mindset. However, all the people around me, including, unfortunately, my teachers and family members, assumed that I would end up in a blue-collar job like my dad. I have to say that even if I'd had a growth mindset, as maybe I did when I was a kid, the experience of high school killed it off. Like the people with a fixed mindset in Dweck's study, even though nothing really happened to me, I usually felt like a failure. I barely graduated with a 2.2 GPA.

My time in college has been better than I expected. Although my high school years were different from Campbell's, it all turned around for me when I attended a summer bridge program prior to my first semester of college. I was especially lucky in my mentor, Edgar Martinez, who sometimes sounded like he was channeling Carol Dweck. Throughout the summer, he asked different versions of Dweck's questions:

> Why waste time proving over and over how great you are, when you could be getting better? Why hide deficiencies instead of overcoming them? Why look for friends or partners who will just shore up your self-esteem instead of ones who will also challenge you to grow? And why seek out the tried and true, instead of experiences that will stretch you?

In the summer bridge program, we learned how to be successful.

Carol Dweck writes in her book *Mindset*, "The passion for stretching yourself and sticking to it, even (or especially) when it's not going well, is the hallmark of the growth mindset. This is

---

Pia Jackson
Develop this idea a bit more? You make a big leap from Campbell being down and depressed to being an inspiring example.

Pia Jackson
Remember that we have to cite our sources in the final draft.

Pia Jackson
I like how you include Dweck's 4 important questions. Would it be useful to talk about how mentors play a role in people's success? I would like to hear more about that kind of support.

Hernandez 3

the mindset that allows people to thrive during some of the most
challenging times in their lives." Both Kashawn Campbell and
I have benefited from having a growth mindset. We believe in
ourselves, and we know that challenges and failures are really just
opportunities to become smarter and better. Succeeding in college,
and in life, isn't always easy, but if we have a growth mindset, we
all have the chance to become our best possible selves.

Oliver's Comments on His Revision

Oliver's first draft was graded and returned to
him. He had two weeks to turn in a revised version of the essay. The next prompt was essentially
the same, with the following additions:

- Your revised essay may be up to 2,000 words
  in length, not including your Works Cited page.

- Conduct research, as necessary, to fill in the gaps in your earlier draft.

- Document your sources using MLA formatting and style.

- Write a brief reflection on your revision process.

   Here's what Oliver had to say about reviewing and revising his essay:

DIY 8.5a Use a Checklist to Peer Review a
First Draft

Begin by using the Peer Review Checklist on
page 170 to evaluate the success of Oliver's first
draft. Be as specific as possible in your response to
each question. Then, write a paragraph *to Oliver*
summing up your revision advice.

Sample Reflection

The most challenging parts of this assignment were hooking the reader
and developing my ideas. My first paragraph just restated the prompt, and
I didn't have any hook at all. One of my peer reviewers said my thesis was
"bland." When I went back to reread, I could see the draft was a little boring/
generic. Adding material on the need for a support system made my paper
more accurate, more interesting, and longer. Adding quotations from Dweck's
work and Streeter's article, and citing them the right way, made my own
writing stronger.

   Now read Oliver's revised essay, which includes marginal comments
noting significant differences between the two drafts.

Revised Essay

MLA-style heading gives the name, professor, class, date, and page number.

Title, centered, draws readers in.

Introductory hook features a quotation from a relevant outside source.

Names a key source that is central to the essay.

The writer uses MLA style to cite two sources throughout the essay.

Two-sentence thesis statement presents the writer's position and previews the essay.

Topic sentence shows that the student is responding to the writing prompt.

Hernandez 1

Oliver Hernandez

Professor Starkey

English 110

8 October 2020

Carol Dweck, Kashawn Campbell, and Me:

Two Growth Mindset Success Stories

Stanford psychology professor Carol Dweck's ideas have a lot of people re-thinking their potential. In an article in *The Atlantic*, Christine Gross-Loh says that Dweck's "findings brought the concepts of 'fixed' and 'growth' mindset to the fore for educators and parents, inspiring the implementation of her ideas among teachers—and even companies—across the country." Kashawn Campbell, the student profiled in Kurt Streeter's *LA Times* article "South L.A. Student Finds a Different World at Cal," may never have heard of Carol Dweck, but he clearly has a growth mindset, as he is "ready to take the risks, confront the challenges, and keep working at them" (Dweck 57). Unlike Campbell, I was a failure in high school. Fortunately, the summer before my freshman year in college, I attended a program that has helped me develop a growth mindset. It seems, therefore, that some college students' experiences suggest that Dweck's theory about the relationship between growth mindset and success is valid. However, it is equally important to have an external support system for those times when our individual efforts aren't quite enough.

As a high school student, Kashawn Campbell demonstrated a growth mindset, but he also benefitted from outside support and the fact that his academic work was not very challenging. Despite growing up "in one of South Los Angeles' bleakest, most violent neighborhoods" (Streeter 63), Campbell—like other people with a growth mindset—is not someone "labeling themselves and throwing up their

Hernandez 2

hands" (Dweck 57). Instead, he was passionate about his own
success: he "willed himself to become a straight-A student"
(Streeter 63). Campbell was also lucky to have a loving
caretaker named Sylvia and a devoted mother who encouraged
him to believe in his own potential to succeed. At Jefferson
High, he received support and positive reinforcement from
many people. By the time he graduated, Campbell was "named
the prom king, the most likely to succeed, [and] the senior
class salutatorian" (63). Having a growth mindset was part of
the reason he succeeded, but Campbell's path forward was
made smoother by an unexpected piece of external support:
his school work was fairly easy. Considering his troubled life
environment, continuous long nights of homework might have
been difficult for Campbell to complete. Fortunately for his
high school career, "[a]t Jefferson, a long essay took a page
and perfect grades came after an hour of study a night" (66).
Academically speaking, Kashawn Campbell wasn't pushed very
hard, which allowed his growth mindset to flourish in a way it
might not have at a more demanding high school.

   While Campbell rarely faced serious academic challenges
in high school, once he began attending UC Berkeley, his
growth mindset alone wasn't enough for academic success.
It's true that Campbell would never have made it into Berkeley
without a belief that "human qualities, such as intellectual
skills, could be cultivated through effort" (Dweck 54). Once he
arrives, his growth mindset is still apparent as he tries to stay
upbeat, always telling his dorm mates to "have a Caltastic
day!" (Streeter 65). However, when he realizes how ill-
prepared he is for college, a belief in himself isn't enough and
"depression [comes] in waves" (64). In his second semester,
when Campbell is still struggling academically, he tells only
a few close friends "how devastating this kind of failure felt,
each poor grade another stinging punch bringing him closer

Adds direct quotations
from featured article.

Incorporates specific
details from one of the
two key readings.

Topic sentence is tied
directly to the thesis.

Writer uses brief quotations
from both readings to
advance his arguments.

Hernandez 3

to flunking out" (68). Fortunately, Campbell has a good friend, Spencer Simpson, who provides both academic and moral support: Spencer is "the first person Kashawn would turn to when depression came" (68). Campbell also benefits from the encouragement of his professors at Berkeley, especially his writing instructors, who work hours with him on each assignment. And when the depression is nearly overwhelming, Campbell is able to turn to the campus psychologist's office, which brings him much needed mental relief. Ultimately, while Kashawn Campbell is an inspiring example of someone with a growth mindset, he is just as much an example of someone who benefitted from reaching out to people who could help him.

Like Campbell, I was not often challenged in my high school, but unlike him, I received very little outside support, which resulted in my having a fixed mindset. My high school in Sacramento doesn't have as much of a "woeful reputation" as Jefferson High, where "just under 13% of its students were judged to be proficient in English, less than 1% in math" (Streeter 64), but my school does not have a good record of sending students off to college. I was lucky that I liked to read, which should have given me a growth mindset. However, all the people around me, including, unfortunately, my teachers and family members, assumed that I would end up in a blue-collar job like my dad. While Kashawn Campbell had people like his vice principal and the school staff who "decided that this kid, we cannot let him down" (64), no one was really there for me during high school. My parents are divorced, and I pretty much fell through the cracks at my school, although I feel I'm reasonably intelligent. Like the people with a fixed mindset in Dweck's study, even though "[n]othing catastrophic or irreversible" happened to me, I sometimes had "the feeling of utter failure and paralysis" (Dweck 57). If I had had someone

Writer uses summary to conclude his argument.

Transition ties the ideas in the previous paragraph to those in the current one.

Makes a direct comparison relevant to the thesis.

cheering me on the way Kashawn did, maybe I would have
been able to develop a growth mindset and connect with my
coursework. As it was, I barely graduated with a 2.2 GPA.

Whereas Campbell's first year was incredibly difficult, my
time in college has been better than I expected, thanks in part
to what I learned about growth mindset and academic support
systems during my summer bridge program. The lack of success
during his first year, and especially during his first semester, left
Kashawn Campbell depressed and flailing. Luckily for Campbell,
Berkeley provided him with plenty of support. Although my high
school years were much different than Campbell's, it all turned
around for me when I attended a summer bridge program prior
to my first semester of college. The program gives advice about
financial aid, helps with housing, and provides tips on how to
succeed in college. I was especially lucky in my mentor, Edgar
Martinez, who was in the summer bridge program the previous
year. Sometimes Edgar sounded like he was channeling Carol
Dweck. Throughout the summer, he asked different versions of
Dweck's questions:

> Why waste time proving over and over how great you are,
> when you could be getting better? Why hide deficiencies
> instead of overcoming them? Why look for friends or partners
> who will just shore up your self-esteem instead of ones who
> will also challenge you to grow? And why seek out the tried
> and true, instead of experiences that will stretch you? (56)

In the summer bridge program, we learned two important
lessons. The first was that "a simple belief" in yourself has
"the power to you transform your psychology and, as a result,
your life" (Dweck 54). But our mentors emphasized that the
second lesson was just important: you have to ask for help
whenever you need it, and in your first year of college that may
be practically all the time.

Topic sentence connects to the
thesis and provides a clear
preview of the paragraph.

Includes relevant personal
details to advance the essay.

Sets off a long quotation
in MLA style and places the
parenthetical citation outside of
the final mark of punctuation.

Hernandez 5

Carol Dweck writes in her book *Mindset*, "The passion for stretching yourself and sticking to it, even (or especially) when it's not going well, is the hallmark of the growth mindset. This is the mindset that allows people to thrive during some of the most challenging times in their lives" (56). Both Kashawn Campbell and I have benefited from having a growth mindset. We believe in ourselves, and we know that challenges and failures are really just opportunities to become smarter and better. Just as important, we are not shy about asking for help. Unfortunately, not every student is quite so confident, which is why the authors of *Teaching Men of Color in the Community College* point out how essential it is for professors to create "conditions in the class where students feel welcome to ask questions, respond to questions, and inquire about their progress" (Wood et al. 25). Succeeding in college, and in life, isn't always easy, but if we have a growth mindset and a supportive environment for our efforts, we all have the chance to become our best possible selves.

Closes with another expert's perspective and a hopeful idea.

Hernandez 5

Works Cited

Dweck, Carol. *Mindset: The New Psychology of Success*.
     Ballantine, 2007.
Gross-Loh, Christine. "How Praise Became a Consolation Prize."
     The Atlantic, 16 Dec. 2016, www.theatlantic.com/education
     /archive/2016/12/how-praise-became-a-consolation-prize
     /510845/.
Streeter, Kurt. "South L.A. Student Finds a Different World at Cal."
     Los Angeles Times, 16 Aug. 2013, https://www.latimes.com
     /local/la-me-c1-cal-freshmen-20130816-dto-htmlstory.html.
Wood, J. Luke, Frank Harris, and Khalid White. *Teaching Men
     of Color in the Community College: A Guidebook*. Center
     for Organizational Responsibility and Advancement, 2015.

List of works cited begins on a new page with the heading Works Cited centered.

Sources are arranged in alphabetical order by author's last name.

DIY 8.5b Assess One Writer's Revisions

Make a list of what you believe are the most effective revisions in Oliver's new
version of his essay, "Carol Dweck, Kashawn Campbell, and Me: Two Growth
Mindset Success Stories." Are there any elements missing from the revision that
you found valuable in the original draft?

Chapter 8 Checklist
Reviewing and Revising

☐ **Does your essay meet all the requirements of the prompt?**

While you may be tired of rereading your prompt by the time you turn
your revision in, you will at least be in the habit of knowing how crucial
it is to the success of your essay. Pay particular attention to the audience
designated by your assignment.

☐ **Is your opening paragraph engaging? Does it provide a clear sense
of the overall scope of the essay?**

Your opening paragraph is the first impression that readers will have of
your essay. Your introduction should be lively and knowledgeable and
make the reader want to keep reading.

☐ **Is your thesis clear, arguable, and capable of sustaining a full-length
essay?**

Your thesis is the fulcrum of your essay—its most pivotal part—so make
sure you've scrutinized it as carefully as your instructor will. It should meet
all the tests described in Chapter 5 and should accurately reflect what is in
the essay.

☐ **Does each body paragraph have a clear topic sentence?**

Topic sentences are the equivalent of thesis statements on the paragraph
level. They should be clear, focused, and directly applicable to the material
in the rest of the paragraph.

☐ **Does each body paragraph support the topic sentence with concrete,
detailed, appropriate, and persuasive specific examples and
analysis?**

Short quotations from credible sources make some of the best concrete
evidence in an academic essay. In addition to compelling evidence, you'll
want to intelligently analyze and comment on the evidence in each body
paragraph.

☐ **Have you discarded the writing in your essay that is no longer needed?**

Revision is as much about deleting unnecessary or confusing material as it is about generating new writing. Keep previous copies of your revisions, and always have an open file in which to store "extras"—stray sentences and paragraphs cluttering up your new draft. You never know when they may come in handy.

☐ **Is your conclusion satisfying?**

Just as you want to make a good first impression in your introduction, you also want to exit leaving your reader with a positive opinion about your essay. The suggestions in section 7.3 provide several proven strategies for concluding your essay.

8.6 Making It Stick

How will you revise your work?

Working Together

8.6a Revising Collaboratively   Share your latest revision with two other writers. Take time to read through the two drafts you've been given, marking sentences you're not sure about and annotating in the margins.

When all three of you are done, begin a collaborative revision of each of the essays. (If you're not sure what to address, take another look at the Peer Review Checklist on page 170.) Discuss what you think is working, what still needs work, and how that work can be successfully accomplished. Be as specific as possible when offering constructive criticism, and focus on the draft, *not* the writer, when offering suggestions.

When your group discusses your essay, take careful notes, asking group members to slow down or pause if you haven't yet written down their ideas. Each writer should take their own notes, even if the person assessing the revision also made careful written comments.

Applying What You Know

8.6b Responding Like an Instructor
Read through the sample final essay by Oliver Hernandez, "Carol Dweck, Kashawn Campbell, and Me: Two Growth Mindset Success Stories" in section 8.5. Then imagine you are a composition instructor commenting on the essay.

1. Read through the essay once to get an overall sense of its strengths and weaknesses. Don't leave any comments the first time through.

2. Now read the essay again, this time looking for aspects that you think deserve *praise*. Make a list of positive comments in the margins. Note: The current marginal

comments point out some of Oliver's successes. Don't just copy those; instead, try to come up with your own ideas.

3. In your third and final reading, look for areas where you think the student can improve. Make a list of constructive criticism.

4. Finally, look over your two lists and write an *end comment* of three or four sentences that sums up your overall response to the essay.

Invitations to Write

8.6c Summarizing Your Revision

Shorter: List the three most important revisions you've made to your essay, writing a sentence or two to reflect on each revision.

Longer: Expand your list to cover all the major revisions you've made to your essay. In a brief reflective essay, discuss why you made the decisions you made and how you feel the final draft is stronger than your early drafts. Note: Your instructor may ask you to submit this short reflection with your completed essay.

8.6d Getting Help with Your Revision

Shorter: Imagine a frustrated student enrolled in a first-year college writing course. That person asks: "How in the world am I supposed to know what's wrong? If I knew it was wrong, I wouldn't have done it in the first place." Write a paragraph responding to the frustrated student by summarizing some of the ways a student at your college can receive help with a revision.

Longer: Write several additional paragraphs in which you discuss, in detail, two or three experiences you've personally had by taking advantage of campus resources. If you have not yet accessed any resources during your revision, write about why that is the case.

9

Editing and Proofreading

REFLECT

Write Before You Read | Activity to connect what's new with what you already know 189

READ & PRACTICE

DIY (Do-it-yourself) activities offer just-in-time support for all the skills in this book.

9.1   Editing for Grammar 189

> **DIY 9.1a** Correct Comma Splices, Run-Ons, and Fragments in Your Writing 193

> **DIY 9.1b** Use a Grammar Log 198

9.2   Editing for Punctuation 198

> **DIY 9.2** Find and Correct Comma Errors 200

9.3   Editing for Style 201

> **DIY 9.3a** Use Active Voice in Your Writing 203

> **DIY 9.3b** Edit for Directness 204

> **DIY 9.3c** Edit for Accuracy 205

> **DIY 9.3d** Add Variety to Your Writing 207

> **DIY 9.3e** Replace Biased Language 208

9.4   Proofreading 209

> **DIY 9.4** Proofread Your Essay 210

CHECKLIST for Chapter 9 212

MAKING IT STICK

Working Together | Collaborative and community-building activities 213

Applying What You Know | Activities to reinforce chapter content 213

Invitations to Write | Brief writing prompts 214

Write Before You Read   While revision involves deep rethinking of your organization, support, and thesis, editing has you looking to correct and strengthen individual sentences. If we compare essay writing to song writing, revision is changing the chords and rewriting the chorus, while editing is more like sound mixing, auto-tuning, and bass level adjustment.

Think of your own analogy to distinguish revision from editing by comparing essay writing to another creative activity. The endeavor could be something from the arts — like painting or photography — or your analogy might draw on activities as diverse as sports or cooking. If you get stuck, try using the following formula: Revision is like _____, while editing is like _____.

As you begin transitioning to editing, your focus will shift to sentence-level matters of grammar, punctuation, and style. In colleges in the United States, academic English is the widespread expectation, but some instructors may also encourage other Englishes as part of your writing process and in response to your rhetorical situation (your purpose and audience). This chapter focuses on uses of formal academic English.

While your instructor certainly doesn't expect you to know everything about writing, they will expect that you ask questions when you need help—with editing as well as with any other stage of the writing process.

If English is one of multiple languages you speak, you may not hear trouble spots as you edit, so you'll be more reliant on peers, tutors, and your instructor to help you locate and correct the types of errors you habitually make. Use resources when you can: Read widely, listen to and talk with native speakers, visit the campus writing center, and keep track of your errors and your progress as you write more in English.

9.1 Editing for Grammar

Since writing is one way in which we present ourselves to the world, most writers take care not to appear sloppy or careless. Careful editing ensures that good, well-organized ideas are presented in their best possible light.

> Careful editing ensures that good, well-organized ideas are presented in their best possible light.

The next sections address a few of the most common sentence-level errors. The intent is to make you a better editor of your own work and to give you enough terminology to commit yourself to improving your writing at the sentence level. This chapter is not meant to be a comprehensive grammar course. Consider *Hello, Writer* as one resource for grammar concerns, but know that you have others.

- Your college's writing center probably has useful handouts, both paper and online, and many college and university writing center websites offer free print and video instruction in grammar and style to all students.

- Along with this book, you may have been assigned Achieve, which includes instruction and practice in most sentence-level matters.

- If you use Microsoft Word, the grammar-check tool is fairly sophisticated; that doesn't mean, of course, that you should change something just because there's a line under it if you're using Word. Consider *why* the program is suggesting something and whether you have a better understanding of your sentence than your software's algorithm.

- Finally, consider keeping a personal error log (see p. 197).

Throughout Chapter 9, the symbol ✖ indicates an incorrect or ineffective sentence, and ✔ indicates a correct or effective sentence.

> **Throughout chapter 9, the symbol ✖ indicates an incorrect or ineffective sentence, and ✔ indicates a correct or effective sentence.**

Write Complete Sentences

One grammar skill a good writer must have is an awareness of sentence boundaries. You will need to know, for the writing you do in college and beyond, where a sentence legitimately starts and stops. Being able to identify these boundaries begins with knowing the difference between an independent clause and a dependent clause.

An **independent clause** has a **subject** (a person, place, or thing that is the focus of the sentence) and a **predicate** (the completion of the sentence, which tells what the subject is like or what it does). In short, an independent clause can stand alone as a simple sentence that expresses a complete thought. Take the following sentence as an example:

I am writing an essay.

The subject—the focus of the sentence—is "I"; the predicate—the description of what the "I" is doing—is "am writing an essay."

A **dependent clause**, by contrast, is only part of a sentence; there's not enough to stand alone. Let's take the previous sentence and add a few words:

✔ I am writing an essay because I have an assignment due.

At the end of the sentence is the dependent clause "because I have an assignment due." As its name suggests, a dependent clause *depends* on an independent clause to make sense. Take a look at the clause trying to act as its own sentence:

> ✖ Because I have an assignment due.

Sure, these six words begin with a capital letter and end with a period, but that doesn't mean they have the necessary components to make a complete sentence. The words would confuse any reader, who may think "*Huh?*" because some information is missing. While you may not be able to articulate grammar rules and definitions, you may have a *sense* of what makes a complete sentence if you pay careful attention to the sentence itself.

Proper punctuation is one of the keys to fixing the three most common sentence boundary errors: the comma splice, run-on, and fragment, which are discussed in the following sections.

Comma Splice

In a **comma splice**, the writer uses only a comma to join two independent clauses (i.e., two grammatically complete sentences). A comma is not strong enough to tie the two ideas together.

> ✖ I just had a good session with a writing tutor, I want to revise my essay today.

Once you identify a comma splice, you have several editing options.

1. Instead of using just a comma, use a comma along with a **coordinating conjunction** (*for, and, nor, but, or, yet,* and *so*) to connect two complete sentences.

2. Separate the independent clauses with an appropriate mark of punctuation, such as a period, semicolon, colon, or dash instead of a comma.

3. Turn one of the sentences into a dependent clause — that is, a grammatically *incomplete* clause — by using a **subordinating conjunction** (a word such as *after, although, because, until, when,* or *while*).

Comma and a Coordinating Conjunction:

> ✔ I just had a good session with a writing tutor, **and** I want to revise my essay today.

Appropriate Punctuation (a semicolon):

☑ I just had a good session with a writing tutor; I want to revise my essay today.

Making a Dependent Clause:

☑ Because I just had a good session with a writing tutor, I want to revise my essay today.

Run-On or Fused Sentence

A **run-on sentence** is the result of another punctuation error and is a close cousin of the comma splice. In a run-on sentence—sometimes called a *fused sentence*—the writer places two complete sentences side by side with no punctuation.

☒ I have read many books I learned more from writing.

As with a comma splice, you can correct a run-on by choosing among a few editing strategies:

1. Use a comma and a coordinating conjunction to separate the independent clauses.

2. Separate the independent clauses with a period, semicolon, colon, or dash.

3. Turn one of the sentences into a dependent clause by using a subordinating conjunction (such as *after, although, because, until, when,* or *while*).

Note: Some people use "run-on" to mean an overly long sentence, but that's grammatically inaccurate. A sentence can be pages long and still, technically speaking, not be a run-on.

Comma and a Coordinating Conjunction:

☑ I have read many books, yet I learned more from writing.

Appropriate Punctuation (a semicolon):

☑ I have read many books; I learned more from writing.

Making a Dependent Clause:

☑ While I have read many books, I learned more from writing.

Fragment

A **fragment** is a group of words written with an initial capital letter and followed by a period. Although the word group may include a verb or a subject, it does not constitute a complete thought.

> ✗ Searching the nearby forest.

Professor Diana Hacker describes the sentence fragment as "a word group that pretends to be a sentence," and looking for fragments in your essay is a bit like trying to expose impostors and pretenders.

Here are the most common ways to correct a fragment:

1. Attach the fragment to the sentence before or after it.

2. Transform the fragment into an independent clause.

Joining to an Independent Clause:

> ✔ Searching the nearby forest, rescuers located the toddler within an hour.

Converting into Independent Clause:

> ✔ Rescuers searched the nearby forest. They located the toddler within an hour.

DIY 9.1a Correct Comma Splices, Run-Ons, and Fragments in Your Writing

If you are currently in the editing stages of composing an essay, review your writing for sentence boundary errors, and use the information in section 9.1 to correct any comma splices, run-ons, or fragments that you see or that have been marked by your instructor or tutor.

Avoid Other Common Grammar Errors

This section covers a number of errors that may slow readers down or cause confusion for them as they read:

- Subject-verb agreement 193
- Pronoun-antecedent agreement 194
- Pronoun reference 194
- Incorrect tense shifts 195
- Wrong verb ending or missing verb 195
- Dangling or misplaced modifiers 196

Subject-Verb Agreement

The subject of a sentence must agree in number with its verb. A singular subject needs a singular verb, and a plural subject needs a plural verb. In the following examples, "essay" is a singular subject, and "students" is a plural subject.

❌ My essay <u>focus</u> on the development of plant-based burger patties.

✔️ My essay <u>focuses</u> on the development of plant-based burger patties.

❌ Students who accept a co-op position <u>reports</u> to their employer on June 1.

✔️ Students who accept a co-op position <u>report</u> to their employer on June 1.

Most compound subjects are plural.

❌ Trauma and creativity <u>is</u> often connected.

✔️ Trauma and creativity <u>are</u> often connected.

Most indefinite pronouns (*anyone*, *each*, *neither*, *one*, for example) are singular.

❌ <u>One</u> of her parents <u>are</u> from El Paso.

✔️ <u>One</u> of her parents <u>is</u> from El Paso.

Pronoun-Antecedent Agreement

In this error, the pronoun (*she*, *her*, *he*, *him*, *it*, *they*, etc.) doesn't correctly agree with the noun to which it refers (called the antecedent). In the following pair of sentences, "it" correctly refers to "the building."

❌ The <u>building</u> is unique; all of <u>their</u> windows face east.

✔️ The <u>building</u> is unique; all of <u>its</u> windows face east.

For people, it is respectful to use the pronouns they use to refer to themselves when you know that information. For indefinite pronouns that don't refer to specific people, it is acceptable to use "they" even when the antecedent is singular, as are most indefinite pronouns. Using "he or she" or "his or her," while grammatically correct, is now widely considered noninclusive.

Noninclusive: <u>Each</u> student should submit <u>his or her</u> course requests by 9 p.m.

Inclusive: <u>Each</u> student should submit <u>their</u> course requests by 9 p.m.

Pronoun Reference

Pronouns should refer clearly to a specific antecedent. When clarity is missing, your reader may become confused. In the following sentence, it may not be clear who was sprayed by the skunk—the boys or the dogs.

✖ The boys found the dogs just after <u>they</u> were sprayed by a skunk.

✔ The boys found the dogs just after <u>the dogs</u> were sprayed by a skunk.

When you use pronouns such as "it," "this," "which," "you," and "they," be sure the antecedent is specific. Otherwise, your reader may ask "What's the *it*?" or "Who's the *they*?"

✖ The speakers demanded justice and called for action. <u>It</u> was inspiring. [Ask: *What* was inspiring?]

✔ The speakers demanded justice and called for action. <u>The speakers' passion</u> was inspiring.

✖ In Amazon's job ads, <u>they</u> promote themselves as an "equal opportunity employer." [Ask: *Who* promotes themselves?]

✔ In its job ads, <u>Amazon</u> promotes itself as an "equal opportunity employer."

Incorrect Tense Shifts

Shifts in verb tense can sometimes result from the quick writing we do in an early draft. Somewhere in the middle of a paragraph or sentence, you may mistakenly change the tense from the one you were using initially—from past to present, or vice versa. Once you choose a tense in your essay, be consistent throughout, unless of course a tense shift makes logical sense.

✖ The president <u>signed</u> the executive order last month. Then yesterday he <u>contradicts</u> his own order and <u>tweets</u> about the need for rethinking the solution.

✔ The president <u>signed</u> the executive order last month. Then yesterday he <u>contradicted</u> his own order and <u>tweeted</u> about the need for rethinking the solution.

Logical Tense Shift: The president signed the executive order last month. He is rethinking the solution with advisers this week. He will issue a statement next Monday at noon.

Wrong Verb Ending or Missing Verb

Most verbs are regular verbs, and they form the past tense with a *–d* or *–ed* ending. The present tense verbs "ask" and "decide," for example, become "asked" and "decided," respectively, in the past tense. If you typically don't say these endings when you speak, you may also not add them when you write.

✘ She <u>introduce</u> me to her friend when we went got to the rally.

✔ She <u>introduced</u> me to her friend when we got to the rally.

Similarly, if you speak a dialect or language that allows you to leave out verbs occasionally, you may forget to add verbs when you edit your writing for different audiences.

✘ <u>They angry</u> about the changes in the program.

✔ <u>They are angry</u> about the changes in the program.

Of course depending on your readers and your reason for writing, you may decide to bend or even ignore the rules of academic English. In your class, you may find your teacher discussing how different English usages reflect our identity and our writing persona—and how your writing situation may call for different Englishes.

Dangling or Misplaced Modifiers

Sentence **modifiers**—words or groups of words that alter how we perceive an object—should come directly before or after the object they are modifying; otherwise, the reader may become confused. A **dangling modifier** is a phrase that doesn't refer logically to the word or words that it appears to modify. The effect on the reader is usually one of bafflement, as the real object being modified appears nowhere in the sentence. A dangling modifier often results in unintended comedy. See the example below: Software companies don't go to college!

Like a dangling modifier, a **misplaced modifier** doesn't really modify the word or words around it. However, the words it does modify *can* be found somewhere in the sentence.

Dangling Modifier

✘ After graduating from college, the software company made a surprisingly generous offer.

✔ After Paolo graduated from college, the software company made him a surprisingly generous offer.

Misplaced Modifier

✘ We watched her slide show about African elephants on the back deck.

✔ On the back deck, we watched her slide show about African elephants.

Keep a Grammar Log

An efficient way of tracking and eliminating your own error patterns is to keep a grammar log or an editing log. Rely on feedback from instructors, tutors, and peers, as well as your own memories of the types of errors you've made in the past.

If your instructor is marking the same *type* of error over and over in your essays, you'll be pleasantly surprised how effective a remedy keeping a grammar log can be if you do the following:

1. Write out an actual error that you've made.

2. Name the error.

3. Explain the reason for the error *in your words*.

4. Correct the error.

While it can take any form you wish, a grammar log might look like the following example:

Example of Error	Name of Error	Explanation of Error in Your Own Words	Corrected Sentence
Working for years, the new bridge was completed in 2017.	Dangling modifier	The word that is being modified isn't in the sentence. The "new bridge" wasn't "working for years." The work was done by the city's department of public works.	Working for years, **the city's department of public works** completed the new bridge in 2017.
Its a victory for the urban planners.	Missing apostrophe in a contraction	When you have a contraction, like it + is, you put an apostrophe where the missing letter would have been.	**It's** a victory for the urban planners.
Once the bridge was completed residents could easily access the city's economic hub.	Comma missing after introductory clause	If there would normally be a small pause after an introductory clause, or if not having a comma is confusing, you need to show the pause and clear up the confusion with a comma.	**Once the bridge was completed,** residents could easily access the city's economic hub.

If you conscientiously keep a grammar log throughout the semester, before you know it, you will eliminate most errors from your writing.

DIY 9.1b Use a Grammar Log

Start your own grammar log. If you have one or more marked drafts of previous essays, use those as your starting place. If not, swap drafts with a partner and, in a separate document, list all the types of errors you *think* you see in your partner's draft. Discuss what you've found in each other's writing and ask for help from classmates, your tutor, or your instructor if you don't know the error's name.

9.2   Editing for Punctuation

Punctuation in English is a system writers use to signal meaning to their readers. Although many of us read and write in social media spaces, where punctuation is often omitted, English in academic settings requires punctuation to improve clarity and avoid confusion. This section covers three important pieces of punctuation: commas, apostrophes, and quotation marks.

Know the Major Comma Rules

You might have seen this bit of humor in your school's writing center.

> Let's eat Grandma.
>
> Let's eat, Grandma.
>
> Commas save lives.

The absence of one little comma makes an enormous difference in how we read and respond to two otherwise identical sentences.

We've already looked at one major comma error—the comma splice (see p. 191)—and how to fix it, and you may be sensing that when it comes to comma errors, the most frequent mistakes are forgetting to put a comma where it is needed (as in the example above) and inserting a comma where it is not necessary. Below are a few more examples of how commas can go wrong.

Commas to Separate Items in a Series

When you make a list, separate the items in the list with commas. (While some writers choose not to use a final comma before a conjunction like "and," including a comma between all items in the series is a good idea for clarity.)

✘ The textbook contains information about comma splices fragments and run-ons.

✔ The textbook contains information about comma splices, fragments, and run-ons.

Comma after Introductory Words

A comma after an introductory word, clause, or phrase signals to the reader that the principal part of the sentence is coming up.

✘ Driven to win championships Michael Jordan often put his play above his politics.

✔ Driven to win championships, Michael Jordan often put his play above his politics.

✘ Before voting the committee will hear citizens' concerns.

✔ Before voting, the committee will hear citizens' concerns.

Commas to Set Off *Nonrestrictive* (Nonessential) Elements

A **restrictive clause** is an adjective clause that is essential to the meaning of a sentence. As such, it should not have any commas around it. In the example below, the words "that crashed my computer" are essential for the meaning of the sentence.

✘ The video game, that crashed my computer, was infected.

✔ The video game that crashed my computer was infected.

In contrast, a nonrestrictive clause is not essential to the meaning of the sentence, so it has commas before and after it. In the example below, it is not essential to know Jeremy's videogame preferences to understand the meaning of the sentence.

✘ Jeremy who loves *Fortnite* asked to borrow my car.

✔ Jeremy, who loves *Fortnite*, asked to borrow my car.

Commas to Set Off an Appositive

An appositive is a word or phrase that follows the noun it modifies. Generally, it acts as a kind of synonym for the word (or words) it is describing.

✘ Your textbook a useful resource is sitting unopened in your backpack.

✔ Your textbook, a useful resource, is sitting unopened in your backpack.

Use Commas for Direct Address

When you're directly addressing someone in a piece of writing, use a comma to separate their name from the rest of the sentence.

✗ Senator Warren how might we lower student debt?

✓ Senator Warren, how might we lower student debt?

Overall, common sense helps more than it hurts, as does reading a lot and seeing where other writers put their commas. Moreover, the spelling-and-grammar check on sophisticated word-processing programs like Word will alert you to a possible misuse of commas, even if it doesn't always get it right. Above all, writing and receiving feedback on your own work will gradually give you a sense when and where commas are necessary.

DIY 9.2 Find and Correct Comma Errors

Open an essay you are currently editing — or, if you don't yet have an assignment, open an essay you have previously written. First, use the Find feature on your word-processing program to look for comma errors. On a Mac, press command + F; on a PC, press ctrl + F. Type a comma into the search box, then look at *each* time you use a comma in your essay. Even if you don't know the exact rule for its use, can you explain why it is there? Correct any errors you find.

Now that you've thought about why each comma is where it is, go back and reread your essay, looking for places that don't currently have a comma but which you now think might need one. Again, even if you don't have the technical term at hand, try to explain to yourself why a missing comma is necessary.

When you've finished, talk your decisions over with a tutor or instructor — someone who has some expertise in this area.

Use Apostrophes Correctly

Apostrophes are used in a few important ways:

- **To show possession.** *This is Sharon's essay. The men's lacrosse team visited the veterans' hospital.*
- **To form a contraction.** *It's Sharon's essay.* (It is Sharon's essay.) *You're late for class.* (You are late for class.)
- **To signal omitted numbers.** *The levee built in '07 is already damaged. '90s grunge music was a response to the excesses of the '80s.*

Note the difference between the possessive "its," which doesn't need an apostrophe, and the contraction "it's" ("it is" or "it has"), which does. With careful proofreading, you will catch this error.

✖ <u>Its</u> his essay. His writing is known for <u>it's</u> style.

✔ <u>It's</u> his essay. His writing is known for <u>its</u> style.

Also take care not to use apostrophes to make nouns plural.

✖ Many <u>doctor's</u> now see <u>patient's</u> online.

✔ Many <u>doctors</u> now see <u>patients</u> online.

Use Quotation Marks Correctly

When you want to use the exact language of another writer or speaker in your writing, use quotation marks to signal the words you're borrowing.

✔ Melissa Goodblanket, a Cherokee mother whose son was killed by police, praises the Black Lives Matter movement, saying "[P]eople are waking up and standing together."

Note that periods and commas usually go inside quotation marks. If you are citing a source that has page numbers, however, and if the quotation appears at the end of your sentence, place the period after the in-text citation.

✔ In the 1960s, Motown Records was America's "most successful black-owned business" (Brackett 167).

When you use a quotation of four lines or more, set it off from the text by indenting the entire quotation, and don't use quotation marks (see Section 18.4).

For titles of short works (magazine and newspaper articles, internal webpages, poems, short stories, TV or podcast episodes, book chapters), use quotation marks.

✔ In his article "Silent Sting," Walsh raises concerns about the dying honeybee population.

9.3 Editing for Style

Style, which basically means "a way of doing something," has an even wider range of definitions than grammar. Because style covers a broader area of writing, correcting errors isn't always as cut and dried as changing a pronoun or inserting a comma. In writing for academic purposes, you will not only edit sentences so that they are correct, but also consider editing sentences so that they are effective and easy to read. Developing your own style as a writer often takes time, practice, and plenty of reading.

Create Effective Structures

One of the most satisfying aspects of developing your own style is creating sentence structures that do exactly what you want them to do. Parallel structure provides sentences with balance and proportion. The active voice often generates livelier and more concise sentences. Together, these two structures can help ensure that your writing is well formed and inviting to read.

Parallel Structure

When parts of a sentence are balanced, they are almost always easier to read. When you have two or more words or phrases that are similar in meaning, use the same grammatical form to keep them parallel. Faulty parallelism can occur in a list, as in the following example:

> ✖ I enjoy weight training, dancing, and <u>to sing</u>.

> ✔ I enjoy weight training, dancing, and <u>singing</u>.

Faulty parallelism can also happen when the structure of your sentence fails to highlight paired ideas.

> ✖ She started the fund to <u>raise</u> awareness, <u>appeal</u> to donors, <u>and she wanted to improve</u> people's lives.

> ✔ She started the fund to <u>raise</u> awareness, <u>appeal</u> to donors, and <u>improve</u> people's lives.

Active Voice

In the past, your teachers, especially in English classes, may have asked you to use the "active voice" rather than the "passive voice." Active voice makes your writing tighter, clearer, and easier to read. Here's a refresher about how you can tell the difference between the two.

In the **active voice**, the subject performs the action indicated by the verb.

Active Voice: <u>Franco wrote</u> the essay.

"Franco" is the subject performing the action of writing.

In the **passive voice**, by contrast, the subject of the sentence is acted on by the verb.

Passive Voice: The essay <u>was written by Franco</u>.

In this case, the person performing the action has been relegated to the end of the sentence, and the result of the action, "the essay," has been moved to the front. The active voice example has more energy, partly because it's shorter and partly because of the emphasis on the action itself.

Here's another example:

Passive Voice: A mistake was made.

Active Voice: The financial aid office made a mistake.

In this instance, the passive voice allows the writer to avoid naming the party responsible for the mistake, while the active voice tells us who is accountable.

Sometimes the passive voice more effectively conveys information; you may *want* to shift the focus away from the actor in the sentence.

Appropriate Passive Voice: Stella was awarded Most Improved Athlete of the Year by the athletic department.

In this example, Stella, the recipient of the award, is the most important person in the sentence. Changing to the active voice (*The athletic department awarded Stella . . .*) wrongly shifts the focus to the athletic department and away from Stella.

In some disciplinary writing, passive voice is sometimes expected when writers need to focus readers on a subject under study.

Appropriate Passive Voice: The participants' reactions were recorded and categorized.

DIY 9.3a Use Active Voice in Your Writing

Read through the essay you are currently writing (or one that you've composed in the past) and look for linking verbs like "was" and "were" and "is." Then go back through and read your work aloud, seeing if you can make simple changes to the sentences that tighten up and activate them. Don't feel obliged to make every sentence active, but do liven up your writing when the passive voice seems to be making your writing dull. Heed Strunk and White's admonition that many "a tame sentence of description or exposition can be made lively and emphatic by substituting . . . the active voice for some such perfunctory expression as *there is,* or *could be heard.*"

Choose Words Wisely

Early in the writing process, you're often simply doing your best to get your ideas down on the page. At that stage, using the wrong word or too many words isn't that big a deal. However, as you move closer to completing a final piece of writing for an audience that will read it with care, you'll want to revisit each of your sentences and make sure you've chosen every word with care.

Avoid Redundancy and Overwriting

Instructors use the word "redundant" to indicate when writers are needlessly repeating material. Have you ever written a sentence like the one below? Since thinking takes place in one's mind and the word "merging" means "coming together," editing makes the sentence more effective.

> ✘ I <u>thought in my mind</u> that the companies would profit once they <u>merged together</u>.

> ✔ I <u>thought</u> that the companies would profit once they <u>merged</u>.

Sometimes in an effort to fill pages or sound philosophical, we go overboard and overwrite an idea when being direct is much more effective.

> ✘ In spite of the fact that each and every year of my life has dealt its challenges, 2020 was an example of what I would call a particularly challenging year.

> ✔ Although my life has had challenges, 2020 was a particularly challenging year.

DIY 9.3b Edit for Directness

Reread your current essay (or one that you've previously written), this time focusing on clarity. Delete unnecessary words and replace unclear words and phrases with those that are concrete and direct.

Use Accurate and Concrete Language

Writing that is clear and straightforward becomes even stronger when it is also accurate and concrete. If you were writing a paper on coronaviruses, for example, you might refer to one of your sources as a "scientist," which would be generally correct. But the person's credibility—and our belief in your authority as a writer—increases if you note that the scientist is an researcher of infectious diseases. In general, the more concrete and specific you are, the more authority your writing will have.

Vague: Coronavirus research has had a big impact on public health.

Concrete: Coronavirus research has led to drastic decreases in ICU hospital stays.

Sometimes when you're in a rush, when the deadline for an essay is closing in, you may not take the time to go back and make sure each word you've selected is the best one. However, appropriate **diction**, your choice of words and phrases, can have a big impact on readers. "Style means the right word. The rest matters little," French author Jules Renard wrote in his journal in 1893, and you should be unflagging in your quest for the most accurate word.

Above all, don't say something that isn't true. If you make a claim, especially one that's controversial (*Everyone should carry a gun*) or outrageous (*Elvis Presley is alive and living on the moon*) or that goes against generally accepted facts (*The earth is flat*), you need to support that claim with evidence so strong that it will stand a chance of convincing your biggest skeptic.

> **DIY 9.3c** Edit for Accuracy
>
> Scan the essay you are in the process of writing — or reread a previous essay if you don't have a current assignment. Look for words that either (1) could be more precise or (2) don't say what you want them to say. Replace those errant words with better choices.

Wrong Word

If your instructor marks "wrong word" on your draft, the word you have chosen may not function in the way the sentence requires. Sometimes the words *sound* similar but have different meanings, as in the example below. Other times, you've simply chosen a word that doesn't mean what you think it means.

- ✘ I <u>past</u> the bank yesterday.

- ✔ I <u>passed</u> the bank yesterday.

- ✘ The children were <u>defiantly</u> excited to be reunited with relatives after the long journey.

- ✔ The children were <u>definitely</u> excited to be reunited with relatives after the long journey.

It's not uncommon to confuse words because they sound alike or have similar meanings. Here are a couple of common examples:

Then/Than: *Then* shows cause and effect or the passage of time: "He left, and *then* she left." *Than* indicates comparison and difference: "He's bigger *than* she is."

Lose/Loose: *Lose* is a verb: "Don't *lose* your shirt." *Loose* is an adjective: "That shirt looks *loose* on you."

Anyway/Anyways: In academic essays you should use *anyway*, not the informal *anyways*.

It can help to keep a list of the words you most often confuse and to use the search function in your word processing program to locate them in your essays so that you can check for and correct any usage errors.

Add Variety to Sentences

You can add variety and style to your writing by mixing things up—by combining sentences, adding quotations, and occasionally including visuals where helpful.

✖ John Lewis was a civil rights icon. He was one of the original Freedom Riders in the 1960s. He urged people to end racial inequality. John Lewis was a member of the U.S. House of Representatives for thirty-three years.

✔ A civil rights icon, one of the original Freedom Riders of the 1960s, and longtime member of the U.S. House of Representatives, John Lewis urged us all to "make some noise" and "get in good trouble" to end racial inequality.

As you edit your essay, look for opportunities to combine different types of sentences. While short, simple sentences can have an impact on your reader, they do so because they differ from the sentences around them. More than two or three simple sentences in a row tend to make you look like you're incapable of writing something more elaborate. Longer sentences, on the other hand, allow you to examine an idea in more depth and demonstrate your skills as a writer. However, an entire paragraph of nothing but extended sentences can have just as deadening an effect as a paragraph of very short ones. Essentially, you're trying to get a rhythm going with occasional "journey sentences" that, according to journalist Roy Peter Clark, "create a flow that carries the reader down a stream of understanding." You punctuate the journey sentences with brief ones that help a reader assess or take stock of the journey.

Another way to mix it up is to include the voices of others, as I included the voice of Roy Peter Clark in the previous paragraph. We've all had the experience of listening to someone monologue, without interruption, for a long time. Think of your most boring friend or teacher: What wouldn't you have given during one of their extended speeches to have heard some other voices chiming in? How refreshing would it have been to have heard a new opinion?

Think of the quotations you use from outside sources as equivalent to the fresh voices that spice up an otherwise lackluster talk. Of course, your own voice should be just as animated and interesting.

A third way to mix it up is to include something besides text in your essay—something that helps you shape an argument or make a point. A well-chosen photograph or a particularly compelling chart can re-engage a reader who is starting to check out, and headings always make for a nice break between pages and pages of text.

DIY 9.3d Add Variety to Your Writing

Reread your current essay draft (or one that you've previously completed) and mark those places where your interest begins to lapse when you read it. In the margins or in a comment bubble, jot down any thoughts you have about how you might add variety to what you currently have on the page. A new combination of long and short sentences? A quotation? A photograph?

Avoid Biased Language

It's easy to write as though everyone else in the world were exactly like you and to forget about members of your audience who may have different worldviews, different life experiences, and different ways of naming and claiming their identity. However, the world is a gloriously diverse place, and your language should always strive to avoid bias or prejudice. Therefore, as you go back and edit your essay, make sure you haven't inadvertently offended potential readers. In addition to using your own good judgment, here are a few guidelines worth following:

How to Write with Respect and without Bias

- Never assume your reader shares your race, religion, gender identity, sexuality, political party, or economic status, even if you know that your primary reader will be your instructor. Be careful with words like "obviously" or "certainly" or "everyone"—words that might indicate that you assume a reader shares your thinking.

- Whenever possible, use a plural pronoun rather than a singular pronoun to avoid possible misgendering: Writing "A student must show his ID" excludes female students. Writing "A student must show his or her ID" excludes some transgender and gender non-conforming students. Instead, write "A student must show their ID" or "A student must show an ID," both of which are inclusive and gender neutral.

- Use gender-neutral words like "person/people," "human/humanity," and "individual." When referring to occupations, replace the word "man" with the actual function of the job. "Fireman" would become "firefighter," for example, and "congressman" would be "lawmaker" or "member of Congress."

- Think carefully before using "we/they (and us/them)" in divisive ways. A sentence such as "We value democracy in America; when we look at Muslims, we see that they have a different set of values" ignores the fact that more than three million Americans are Muslims who practice and value democracy.

- Use language that groups use to refer to themselves, when possible. In general, the more precise you can be, the better. For example, "First Nations Peoples of Canada" or just "First Nations" would be appropriate, but Squamish or Anishinaabe might be even more accurate.

- When referring to people with conditions or different abilities, focus on the person first: "people who are blind" and "a child with autism" are often preferred to "blind people" and "autistic children." Putting the condition first defines the person too narrowly. A child who is autistic may also be a child who plays violin, goes to summer camp, and dislikes social media.

An easy rule of thumb is to follow a variation of the Golden Rule: "Do unto others as you would have them do unto you." Put yourself in the place of the people you are talking about. If someone referred to you in the language you are using, how would you feel about it? If you're not completely comfortable with a possibly offensive word or assumption, do the right thing and think of another way to say it.

DIY 9.3e Replace Biased Language

Read through the essay you're currently working on (or one that you've already written) and each time you mention a person or group of people, try to read what you've written through their eyes. Replace any biased language or assumptions with words that won't hurt or mischaracterize others.

9.4 Proofreading

If you've ever watched the preparations of dog owners just before they bring their pets out for a big show, you've seen something resembling the close attention a writer devotes to proofreading an essay. The exhibitors trim their dogs' nails, clean their ears, bathe and blow-dry and brush their fur, and snip every hair that's out of place. It's a fastidious routine, but the owners know that their dogs are going to be examined with great care, and they want to be ready for that scrutiny.

Proofreading is a bit like the final grooming before a show, but of course the dog is your essay, and the judge is your reader. Be ready for the "show" by making sure that your essay is as immaculate as you can make it before you turn it in.

Guidelines for Proofreading

- **Print out and proofread a *paper* copy of your essay, if possible.** We see things differently on the printed page than we do on the screen. Errors that were invisible on your computer suddenly stand out when they are on a printed page.

- **Read aloud, slowly.** Deliberately reading aloud the words that are actually on the page—not the words you *imagined* writing—is another method of alerting you to errors that might have hidden themselves from you earlier.

- **Read with a pen in hand (or with the comment function open in your digital document).** Mark everything you're uncertain about. Ask questions in the margins. Be ruthless with errors.

- **Look for the type of errors you tend to make.** You were looking for these errors while editing, but they may still appear when you are proofreading. If you've been keeping a grammar log, double-check it before you begin proofreading.

- **Read one sentence at a time.** One time-tested trick to slow yourself down and increase your focus is to place a blank sheet of paper directly below the line you are reading so that your eyes can't skip ahead.

- **Read backwards.** While it can be helpful to locate spelling and punctuation errors by reading word by word from the end of your essay to the beginning, generally this method works best if you start at the end and read individual sentences from finish to start. Reading the sentences without looking at what's come before them forces you to focus on each sentence as a standalone unit.

210

CHAPTER 9
Editing and Proofreading

- **Make sure your essay is double-spaced.** Unless your instructor specifically tells you otherwise, double-space your essay, whether you are turning in a print or digital copy. Most instructors will make comments in the margins—and on the text itself—and having this extra room gives them the space they need to comment.

- **Have someone you trust proofread your essay.** We all know someone who is better at a specific activity than we are. Seek out one or two people who have stronger writing skills than you and ask them to proofread your essay.

Proofreading isn't the time for big changes. You will have addressed those in your revision, and, hopefully, you will have caught most of your grammar and style errors while editing. Granted, sometimes what you anticipate will be a quick proofreading turns into a full-on editing session. If you have sufficient time for further editing, your essay will benefit from the extra attention. However, if your deadline is fast approaching, do your best to correct all the surface errors you can in the time you have left.

DIY 9.4 Proofread Your Essay

Use all or most of the proofreading tips listed in section 9.4 before submitting the final draft of your current essay. (If you're not working on an essay at the moment, proofread an essay that you've already written.)

Recognize Common Correction Symbols

To save space on the page, the names for the sort of errors we've been discussing are usually abbreviated. Some teachers will provide you with a key to the correction symbols they make in the margins of your essay. Sometimes, however, your instructor may assume you know the shorthand for common errors from previous classes. It can get a bit confusing, so here's a chart of correction symbols to give you a sense of what these correction symbols often look like and what they mean.

Common Correction Symbols		
Symbol	**Error**	**Definition/Correction**
cs	comma splice	A comma is joining two independent clauses (i.e., two complete sentences). Use, instead, a period or a semicolon or, less often, a colon.
dang mod	dangling modifier	The phrase or clause is not clearly related to the word or words that come directly after it.

Common Correction Symbols

Symbol	Error	Definition/Correction
frag	fragment	A dependent clause is acting as an independent clause. Typically, the fragment must be joined to a complete sentence, normally by a comma.
pro agr	pronoun agreement	The pronoun must agree with its antecedent.
punc	punctuation	The mark of punctuation is incorrect.
red	redundancy	Words, phrases, or sentences are repeated unnecessarily.
pro ref	pronoun reference	It is unclear to whom or what the pronoun is referring.
r-o	run-on	There is no punctuation between two complete sentences.
sp	spelling	The word is misspelled.
s-v	subject-verb agreement	The subject and verb do not agree; both should be plural or singular.
ten	tense	The verb tense does not correspond appropriately to the rest of the sentence or paragraph.
ww	wrong word	The word is inaccurate; it does not function in the way that the sentence requires.
^	insert	A missing character, word, or phrase needs to be inserted in the sentence.
℘	delete	This material is unnecessary.
¶	paragraph	Begin a new paragraph here.
//	parallelism	Successive constructions must correspond in their grammatical structure.
#	add a space	There should be a space between the two words or characters.

Common Correction Symbols

Symbol	Error	Definition/Correction
⊔	transpose	Change the order of the words or characters.
～～～	rephrase for clarity	The phrase or sentence is confusing to the reader.
???	meaning unclear	Generally, the more question marks in the margin, the less clear the phrase or sentence is.

Chapter 9 Checklist
Editing and Proofreading

Editing

☐ **Have you run a grammar and spell check on your essay?**

Not every underlined sentence or word will need to be corrected, but running a full check on your grammar and spelling before you begin editing will highlight issues you may need to address.

☐ **Have you identified and corrected the types of errors you most frequently make?**

Work on aggressively identifying and eliminating the errors you make most frequently. If you are keeping a grammar log, review the errors you have made earlier before you start editing.

☐ **Have you scoured your draft looking for opportunities to replace dull, inaccurate, and vague words and phrases with language that is stronger and more effective?**

While it's important to write grammatical English, it's just as important to make your sentences and paragraphs as vivid and compelling as they can be. When editing, don't settle for the first, most obvious expression that occurs to you. As you make the final changes to your essay, focus on style and correctness as they relate to your specific writing situation.

☐ **Are you using unbiased language? That is, have you eliminated potentially offensive words and phrases?**

Put yourself in the place of people who are different from you; write to include, and write to show respect.

Proofreading

☐ **Have you proofread a printed copy of your essay slowly and carefully?**

Remember the proofreading tips described on page 209, which include reading one sentence at a time, reading with a pen or pencil in hand, looking for the errors you tend to make, and reading—sentence by sentence—from the end to the beginning of your essay.

☐ **Have you allowed a trusted person to proofread your essay?**

Professional writers rarely send their work out into the world without getting another pair of eyes to look at it. Follow their example and take advantage of the perspective of someone who can see the errors you may have been missing.

9.5 Making It Stick

How will you edit and proofread the essays you write?

Working Together

9.5a It's All in the Details Editing for style helps make your writing come to life for readers. One sure way to do this is to incorporate vivid and specific details rather than easy generalizations.

Practice this skill by bringing in a passage of writing from a current or recent essay that you feel is vague or dull. Work with a small group of writers from your class to identify opportunities to replace generalizations and abstractions with concrete details. Before you begin, look at the example below to give you an idea of the sort of changes you might make in your own essay.

Original: The protestors against police violence marched down the street.

Revision: Carrying signs that read "There Comes a Time When Silence Is Betrayal" and

"I Can't Breathe," and chanting slogans such as "No Justice, No Peace" and "Black Lives Matter," the multiracial group of more than two thousand protestors—the majority of whom appeared to be in their twenties and thirties—began marching down State Street yesterday afternoon at three o'clock.

Applying What You Know

9.5b Making an Appointment with a Tutor There's never a bad time to consult with a writing tutor. These experienced writers can help you when you're struggling to come up with an idea and when you're early in the writing process. However, the closer you are to completing your essay, the more your tutor can help you put the finishing touches on it — the polish! — to ensure the work you turn in is something you'll truly take pride in.

Right now, stop what you're doing and make an appointment to see a writing center tutor. Go online and find out how best to contact the writing center, then clear some time in your schedule *before your next essay is due* and meet — in-person or virtually — with one of the most helpful people you're likely to encounter on your college campus. Bring your copy of *Hello, Writer* in case you need to consult this chapter as you and the tutor talk.

Invitations to Write

9.5c Knowing Your Words

Shorter: Reread your current or most recent essay and underline every word you aren't 100 percent sure means exactly what you think it does. In a separate document, make a list of these words, then look up and write out each word's definition. Note: You're a lot more likely to remember the definition if you type it yourself rather simply cutting and pasting it from an online dictionary.

Longer: After you've identified all the words in your essay that you used inaccurately, spend some time with the dictionary and thesaurus finding a replacement for each of those words. Then go back and replace the old words with the new, correct ones. Often, a new word will require you to revise or edit the sentence in which it is placed, so make sure to read your work aloud and share it with another writer if you have any doubts about what you've written.

9.5d Rethinking Your Approach to Editing

Shorter: Summarize your own philosophy toward editing *prior* to reading this chapter. (Take a look at your "Write Before You Read" response if you have one.)

Longer: Write about how your editing philosophy has changed or might change as a result of what you've read, in particular, Editing for Grammar (Section 9.1) and Editing for Style (Section 9.3). Be specific as you describe the strategies you've used, or that you'd like to use in the future, to achieve the best results.

PART TWO

Strategies for
Academic Writing

10

Making an Evaluation

Write Before You Read   Write a paragraph or two about the last time you relied on an evaluation or review by someone else to make a decision. What form did the evaluation take? A customer review of an item of clothing you were about to buy online? A recommendation from a friend about a new series to binge watch? What information were you looking for to help make your decision? Explain how and why the other person's evaluation did, or didn't, help you to make a particular choice.

10.1   Seeing Evaluation All Around Us

We live in a world that is constantly evaluated; everyone with a smartphone or a computer is a reviewer. Many people won't buy a product if it has poor reviews on Amazon's customer reviews, and you can rate just about anything you want on Yelp.

In fact, there are few aspects of our lives that aren't evaluated somewhere. People needing plumbers and electricians evaluate their experiences on Angie's List, just as travelers go to TripAdvisor for information about where to stay and what to see. Readers seeking their next good book visit Goodreads; potential employees check out Glassdoor; and students looking for classes visit RateMyProfessors.com. Even the meal you photograph with your cellphone and post on Instagram is likely to have some commentary attached, either by you or those who view the pictures—"Delicious!" or "Ew!" or "Are you kidding me?"

And if you evaluate and judge and critique all the time when you're outside of class, you also do it frequently when you're in school. English instructors often ask you to assess the effectiveness of a piece of writing, and they nearly always insist on detailed reasoning for your judgment. Courses in the arts require frequent evaluation—of plays, musical performances, gallery exhibits, and so forth. In business, you review marketing plans; in the sciences, you evaluate the methodology of the studies you are discussing. In short, being able to judge the effectiveness of a thing or an idea is one of the most important skills you can have—not just as a college student, but also as a citizen making your way through the world.

Because reviews are probably the most direct and condensed way of practicing your evaluating skills—and because you've probably done quite a bit of informal reviewing already—this chapter will focus on reviews, with the understanding that the types of evaluations you make in a review are similar to those you would make in any evaluative essay. We'll discuss the following strategies:

- Writing to your audience
- Generating appropriate criteria
- Organizing for maximum impact
- Employing language effectively
- Playing fair

UP FRONT: Evaluate a Subject

The Assignment

Write an essay in which you evaluate a subject of your choice. The chapter guidance, examples, and DIY prompts will help you complete the assignment. Follow your instructor's notes about length and formatting. Keep these guidelines in mind as you choose a subject.

Keep the focus of your evaluation narrow. If you're writing a music review, focus on a specific album or a song rather than the entire body of work by the musician. If you're evaluating a smartphone, keep your emphasis on the current version of the device.

Make sure you have some expertise on the subject. This is not a good time to become a specialist on a new topic. Instead, choose something you can write about with ease and assurance. If you're stuck, imagine you are going out on a first date. On what subjects could you talk about most entertainingly to the person you're with?

Choose a subject you really love. If your instructor has given you free rein to review anything you want, why not take advantage of this freedom to explore something that you really, *really* want to write about—a song or album, a film, an app, a podcast, a place, a performance, a product, an event, a venue, a restaurant, an attraction, a service, a policy, or something else.

DIY 10.1
Summarize What You Intend to Evaluate

Identify the subject of your evaluation. What are you planning to review? Write a paragraph in which you summarize the thing that you have chosen to evaluate. If you are evaluating a song or podcast, for example, what is it about? For an event or a service, give key details that an unfamiliar audience would need to know.

An Invitation to Read: A Movie Review

Manohla Dargis began writing about movies professionally in 1987 while earning her MA in cinema studies at New York University. After writing about avant-garde cinema for *The Village Voice*, she became the co-chief film critic for *The New York Times* in 2004. The following review is of *King Arthur: Legend of the Sword*, directed by Guy Ritchie and starring Charlie Hunnam and Jude Law. Like many reviewers, Dargis focuses at least as much on *how* she says something as on what she says—film reviewing, after all, is meant to be entertaining. As you'll see, Dargis isn't particularly fond of *King Arthur*, but she does attempt to find merit in what she sees as a deeply flawed movie.

Critical Reading Tip

Experienced movie reviewers help readers "see" the film they are evaluating, an important skill when the movie is new and readers are unlikely to have already watched it. As you read Manhola Dargis's review, try to visualize the scenes she describes so that you feel, to an extent, that you've been to see *King Arthur*.

Before He Was 'King Arthur,' He Was a Guy Ritchie Lad

MANOHLA DARGIS

Charlie Hunnam as Arthur in Guy Ritchie's film *King Arthur: Legend of the Sword*
Warner Bros/Alamy Stock Photo

1   The galumphing digital elephants crashing through the hectic, murky opening of *King Arthur: Legend of the Sword* are an early sign that this isn't meant to be your granddad's Arthurian legend. And, well, why should

it be or how could it be, given who's behind the camera? The director Guy Ritchie likes his action fast and frenetic, and he's more focused on how things look—mostly, he's chasing that certain something called cool—than in narrative coherency or plausibility. And, anyway, those angry elephants are magical, just like the dragons swooping through the HBO show *Game of Thrones*.

2   It's hard not to attribute the existence of this new Arthurian tale in part to the global success of *Game of Thrones*, which has hooked legions on its epic soap opera, clashing swords, spurting blood and unending intrigue. (That show's Aidan Gillen pops up here too.) The Arthur story has played out differently across the centuries, from the Middle Ages to T. H. White's novel *The Sword in the Stone* to Disney's 20th-century cartoon take, and each moment in time shapes the way it's told. In this case, that means something old, something blockbustery and that Guy Ritchie *je ne sais quoi*.

3   Put differently, this variation on the Arthurian legend fleetingly brings to mind *Game of Thrones* but mostly plays out according to the Ritchie template: a self-amused, endlessly resourceful laddish hero gets in and out of trouble with winks, smarts and brute force, sometimes in the company of Jude Law. This time the resident rogue is Arthur, played with easy, low-wattage charisma by Charlie Hunnam, who has a gift for delivering nonsense without seeming embarrassed. Mr. Law, who played Watson in Mr. Ritchie's "Sherlock" flicks, takes on mustache-twirling duties as Vortigern, a louche pouter who skulks around in black, doubtless dreaming of Richard III.

4   Arthur and Vortigern mix it up amid a lot of shenanigans, detours and filler, some bad, some good and all of it disposable. Written by Mr. Ritchie, Joby Harold and Lionel Wigram, the movie is mostly about establishing Arthur's origin story, which turns on the usual reluctant hero coming to terms with his destiny, meaning Dad (Eric Bana) and Dad's mighty sword. This lineage and its burdens take a while to work through, primarily because this movie plays like the first installment in a hoped-for series. Merlin scarcely makes the scene, and Guinevere and Lancelot have yet to arrive to stir up trouble.

5   The opener is a clotted visual mess, which isn't surprising. But it is disappointing just because the whole thing—the landscape, castle and so forth—is so drearily fake and ugly, even if the elephants are kind of amusing and it's always nice to see Mr. Bana. The movie improves once Mr. Ritchie moves closer to his actors, a pleasantly diverting crew that includes Djimon Hounsou as a fixer extraordinaire and Astrid Bergès-Frisbey as a witchy woman of some type. They help sell the generic goods—basically, a band of merry, dirty dozen (or so) smarty-pants renegades giving it to the Man—and the results are easy enough to watch, especially if, like Mr. Hunnam, you don't embarrass easily.

1. If, back in 2017, you had been considering seeing *King Arthur*, would you still want to see it after reading Dargis's review? Why or why not? What does she say, *specifically*, that would have confirmed your desire to go, or changed your mind?

2. Without looking at the review, jot down anything about it that you can recall from memory alone. What made an impression on you? Why?

3. Using Dargis's review as your model, what would you say a film review has in common with other types of reviews — books, restaurants, consumer products, hotels, and so on? How is it different?

10.2 Writing to Your Audience

No matter what you are evaluating, when you write a review, you are doing so to convey your impressions of the subject *to other people*. It's crucial, therefore, that you are aware of the audience reading your review, and that you keep their expectations in mind.

Granted, *King Arthur* didn't do very well at the box office, but Manohla Dargis, writing for one of our most important news outlets, is still aware that hundreds of thousands of people might consult her work. Dargis also knows that not everyone is going to be interested in an epic version of *King Arthur*, and she identifies the expectations of the audience most likely to see it several times. In the first paragraph, for instance, she points out that the use of digital elephants suggests that the movie "isn't meant to be your granddad's Arthurian legend." At the end of that paragraph, and in the beginning of the second, she namechecks the HBO television series *Game of Thrones*, implying that the audience for that "epic soap opera" with its "clashing swords, spurting blood and unending intrigue" is being targeted by the *King Arthur* filmmakers.

Therefore, while Dargis makes plenty of snarky comments befitting a reviewer who once specialized in avant-garde cinema, she nevertheless does take the film seriously, attempting to view *King Arthur* through the eyes of the people who are most likely to watch it.

Audience awareness is a key consideration for any writing task (see Chapter 5). In a different sort of evaluation, Michael Pollan's *In Defense of Food: An Eater's Manifesto*, Pollan assesses the impact of "food science" and the food industry on our health and finds them to be extremely negative. In the opening chapter, he addresses his audience directly:

A writer addresses his
audience directly

I started on this quest to identify a few simple rules about eating after publishing *The Omnivore's Dilemma* in 2006. Questions of personal health did not take center stage in that book, which was more concerned with the ecological and ethical dimensions of our eating choices. (Though I've found that, in most but not all cases, the best ethical and environmental choices also happen to be the best choices for our health—very good news indeed.) But many readers wanted to know, after they'd spent a few hundred pages following me following the food chains that feed us, "Okay, but what should I *eat*? And now that you've been to the feedlots, the food-processing plants, the organic factory farms, and the local farms and ranches, what do *you* eat?"

Picturing your audience like this—as people interested in what you have to say and eager to learn more—is a useful focusing device. As you write your own evaluation, imagine one or two people who are likely to read your essay. Your instructor might well be one of those, of course, but if, for instance, you were evaluating the financial aid services available on your campus, the person you would most probably imagine reading your essay is a fellow student in need of money to get through college. As you write, keep your audience in mind.

Tips for Writing to Your Audience

- **Identify the people most likely to read your evaluation.** Throughout the writing process—from your first freewrite to your final proofreading—you should picture the audience you imagine reading your work. Who are they *specifically*? How are they responding to a particular point you are making? If they're skeptical, what can you do to convince them to believe you? If they're getting bored, what can you do to recapture their attention?

- **Tell your audience what it didn't know.** While audiences for particular types of evaluations, like film reviews, have fundamental assumptions about what areas are going to be discussed, they also expect to be given new information about the subject. Dargis, for instance (see Section 10.1), provides all sort of details about the film—from the description of its star's "low-wattage charisma" to the fact that it features digital elephants—that readers would not have known otherwise. Leave your audience feeling smarter and better informed than when they began reading your evaluation.

- **Provide a recommendation, either stated or implied.** The audience for an evaluation expects you to come down on one side or the other: Does your subject perform its task effectively, or is it something readers should avoid? While Dargis never directly says, "Don't go see this movie," it's clear that she doesn't think *King Arthur* is very good. More complex evaluations obviously require more complex responses. If you are evaluating policy initiatives to increase voter turnout, for example, your recommendations aren't going to be as simple as thumbs up or thumbs down.

DIY 10.2 Analyze Your Audience

Write three short paragraphs answering the following three questions about your evaluation:

1. Who is your audience?

2. What do they need to know about your subject that they don't know now?

3. What do you want your audience to do or think after reading your evaluation?

Hold on to those paragraphs and see if some, or all, of what you've written can become part of your essay.

10.3   Generating Criteria for an Evaluation

Identifying audience expectations will help you generate your evaluation criteria—that is, the principles or standards by which you will judge your subject. Ideally, you'll have some expertise in the subject you are evaluating, as will at least some of your readers. Ask yourself: What particular aspects of your subject will these well-informed readers want to see covered? Of equal importance, what *doesn't* need to be discussed? Keep in mind that if you're reviewing a restaurant, you'll employ much different criteria than you would if you were evaluating a Supreme Court decision. Therefore, generating criteria *specific* to your subject is critical.

Ignoring essential review criteria can undercut your authority among those who also value your subject. Manohla Dargis, for instance, expressed her frustration with film reviewers who evaluate movies as though they were books: In a recent interview, she said, "They pay very little if any attention to the specifics of the medium, to how a film makes meaning with images—with framing, editing, mise en scène [the scenery or setting], with the way an actor moves his body in front of the camera. To read most film critics in the United States you wouldn't know that film is a visual medium." Notice how, in the course of her critique of other reviewers, Dargis identifies four criteria she thinks movies *should* be judged by: "framing, editing, mise en scène . . . [and] the way an actor moves his body in front of the camera."

As you write, imagine that some of your readers are just as savvy about your subject as Dargis is about hers.

Of course, the more complex the subject of the evaluation, the more criteria you will have to consider, and the more you will have to prioritize those criteria you think are essential and disregard areas you think are less important. In addition, evaluations vary greatly from discipline to discipline. An art history student evaluating a painting by the Italian painter Bronzino will be using entirely different criteria than a chemical engineering student performing a critical data evaluation of vapor-liquid equilibria. Moreover, the amount of leeway each student has for their evaluation will be considerable, with the art history student's professor probably encouraging speculative leaps, while the chemical engineering professor insists on adherence to data. Still, each of these writers would begin by generating a list of criteria to focus their evaluation.

Tips for Generating Appropriate Criteria

- **Identify the criteria by which your subject is normally judged.** Readers of movie reviews want to know who is in the film (actors/acting), who directed it (visual storytelling), what it's about (plot), and, above all, whether or not it's any good. In a little over 500 words, Dargis answers all those questions. Whatever the subject you are evaluating, think carefully about the essential elements your reader will expect you to attend to, and make sure you cover those areas.

- **If your subject is often judged by numerous criteria, focus on those most relevant to your evaluation.** Manohla Dargis, for instance, believes that director Guy Ritchie is "more focused on how things look . . . than in narrative coherency or plausibility." Her own focus, therefore, is on the visual; among the cinematic elements she might have discussed but decided to ignore is the film's score. In the small space allotted to her, the music just wasn't important enough a criterion to address. As the criteria for your own evaluation begin to come into focus, think carefully about which you will use in your essay and which you will need to leave out.

DIY 10.3 Identify Criteria Relevant to Your Subject

Make a list of all the criteria typically associated with evaluations of your subject. If you are reviewing a film, for instance, you might jot down directing, editing, soundtrack, acting, cinematography, screenplay, and so on. Try to write down *more* criteria than you actually intend to discuss. Then, read through your list and choose the criteria most relevant to the particular subject you are evaluating. Finally, make a new list of criteria, leaving plenty of room after each item for discussion and examples.

10.4   Organizing for Maximum Impact

Different subjects demand different organizational plans. The structure of your evaluation will depend on how in depth you plan to go and what purpose you want the evaluation to serve. Evaluations often evolve more organically than other essays, so don't try and shoehorn yours into a certain format. If your evaluation takes the form of something other than a review, you will probably want to make an outline to unjumble all the ideas and examples that are swirling around in your brain. (See Section 5.5 on outlining.)

Don't feel obliged to make each paragraph the same length. Most evaluations spend more time on certain aspects of a subject than others. If you have some good ideas, but only a couple of sentences' worth of observations for each one, consider grouping two, or even three, *related* criteria together in a single paragraph. Manohla Dargis doesn't employ traditional topic sentences in her review of *King Arthur*, but she does group related observations together. Again, an evaluation gives you more flexibility than many essay forms, but it is almost always a good idea to use topic sentences to bring coherence to your paragraphs.

While Dargis's review is significantly shorter than a full essay that you might write for a class, she nevertheless follows a recognizable structure for film reviews, which looks something like this: Hook> Thesis> Summary> Examples> Closing.

Hook Readers from the Start

Readers of reviews are often flipping casually through a print source or skimming the first sentences in a Google search. In either case, they need a catchy opening to draw them in. Dargis's first sentence, her hook, about the "galumphing digital elephants crashing through the hectic, murky opening" of *King Arthur* is just that—a visual and linguistic wallop that can't help but make you want to read more.

Include a Thesis

Readers want to know what the reviewer thinks about the subject—in other words, the reviewer's judgment or position—very early on. Dargis makes clear in her opening paragraph that she attributes the failures and occasional successes of *King Arthur* to its director: "Guy Ritchie likes his action fast and frenetic, and he's more focused on how things look—mostly, he's chasing that certain something called cool—than in narrative coherency or plausibility." Dargis makes a number of other points along the way, but this sentence encapsulates her argument that Ritchie focuses on style over substance.

Summarize Briefly

A reader who is unfamiliar with the work under review will need a summary to provide grounding for understanding the rest of the evaluation. What is the film about? Dargis provides a nutshell version when she refers to Arthur's "origin story" and introduces the central problem of "Arthur's lineage and its burdens."

Use Examples, Examples, Examples

Readers are generally skeptical of reviewers who don't provide solid, specific examples to support their evaluation and illustrate their evaluation criteria. In Dargis's review, the examples are clear, well-chosen, and numerous. Indeed, she provides an example of why she finds *King Arthur* silly but kind of fun in just about every sentence of her review.

Make a Closing Statement

In an evaluation essay, your conclusion may well take up an entire paragraph, as in Dargis's review. However, it's crucial that you not repeat what you've already said. That's a bad idea in a traditional academic essay, and it's an even worse one in a review, where a major part of your job is to keep your readers engaged and entertained. Notice how, even as she's wrapping things up, Dargis is still giving us new and useful information about the minor actors and how Richie's directing improves as he "moves closer to his actors."

Here are some tips for how to organize your review for impact on your readers.

Tips for Organizing for Maximum Impact

- **Begin and conclude your evaluation memorably.** Reviewers must get their readers on board right away, and you should, too, no matter what you are evaluating. You might think your assessment of a program to help homeless people in your community is so important that no one should ignore it—and you'd be right—but if the topic is that important to you, then commit to making it *immediately* important to your readers.

- **Write from a working thesis.** You might think a "thesis statement" doesn't have a place in a movie or music review, but read the first paragraph of a piece by any first-rate critic and you'll have a pretty good idea of how that person feels about the movie or album or book. Although you have more flexibility when writing about popular culture, you still need a focusing statement early in your essay.

- **Begin with your strongest material.** In an evaluation, it's generally best to begin with your most convincing evidence and save your less persuasive arguments for the end. Dargis's fourth and fifth paragraphs, for instance, while important and entertaining, aren't as critical to her argument as her assessment of how Ritchie's version of the King Arthur story will play to contemporary viewers. In Chapter 5, I suggested that you save your strongest point for your last body paragraph, but that advice doesn't hold for an evaluation.

DIY 10.4 Plan Your Evaluation with a Graphic Organizer

Most writers benefit from (1) the process of writing something out and (2) being able to see what their thoughts look like on the page. See where you are with your evaluation by organizing your points graphically; make sure to lead with your most persuasive material. (For more on outlining, see Section 5.5.)

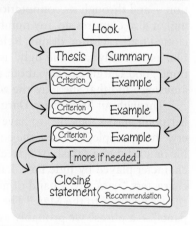

10.5 Using Language Effectively

When you describe something clearly and effectively, you bring it to life for your readers. Professional film reviewers are among the most gifted writers when it comes to description, and Dargis is one of the best. Just listen to her one-sentence description of Jude Law's acting in *King Arthur*:

> Mr. Law, who played Watson in Mr. Ritchie's *Sherlock* flicks, takes on mustache-twirling duties as Vortigern, a louche pouter who skulks around in black, doubtless dreaming of Richard III.

Her allusion to Shakespeare's *Richard III* may go over some readers' heads, yet even if we don't know Shakespeare and have never seen *King Arthur*, we can still *picture* the character: his mustache-twirling (even if that's only metaphorical), his pouting and skulking around in black. And what a precise and evocative verb "skulks" is. A big part of effective description involves choosing the most precise word. "Skulks," for instance, is not only incredibly specific—it means "to keep out of sight, typically with a sinister or cowardly motive"—it is also onomatopoetic—that is, is *sounds* like what it means.

Indeed, Dargis is clearly, and joyfully, in love with words. Take another look at the first two sentences of her final paragraph:

> The opener is a clotted visual mess, which isn't surprising. But it is disappointing just because the whole thing—the landscape, castle and so forth—is so drearily fake and ugly, even if the elephants are kind of amusing and it's always nice to see [actor Eric] Bana.

What a phrase: "clotted visual mess"! The adjective "clotted" literally refers to something that is thick, soft, and lumpy—already an unpleasant description—and through its connotation (the feeling evoked by its literal meaning), it also conjures up any number of disagreeable images: clotted blood, clotted traffic, clotted drains. Referring to the landscape and castle in the film as "drearily fake and ugly" is another kick in the shins. In fact, the only thing good Dargis can say about the scene is that "the elephants are kind of amusing" and that she likes the actor Eric Bana.

Throughout her review, Dargis uses unusual vocabulary not just to get her point across, but also to have fun. She makes up the word "blockbustery," for example, and uses the comic French word "*louche*" ("disreputable or sordid in a rakish or appealing way"), which exactly describes the character played by Jude Law. Later in the review, Dargis calls the film's characters "basically, a band of merry, dirty dozen (or so) smarty-pants renegades giving it to the Man." The comedic pairing of the adjective "smarty-pants"—a phrase we probably associate with bratty children—and its more formal noun "renegades" is just the sort of unlikely combination of words that reviewers love to play with.

If movie reviewers love making good sentences, their colleagues who review popular music are often even more flamboyant in their use of language. You may already have a favorite music website where the reviewers' funny, cleverly phrased opinions are at least as much an attraction as the artists they review. If not, check out Pitchfork.com, HipHopDX.com, or Rollingstone.com.

Granted, not every instructor will appreciate words like "smarty-pants" and "blockbustery" in an academic essay. Even professors who value language like Dargis's may find it inappropriate for a particular assignment. Nevertheless, it goes almost without saying that writing instructors love good writing. Therefore, show your professor that you care about the language that you put on the page.

Tips for Using Language Effectively

- **Craft your sentences carefully, paying attention to each word you use.** Whether you're assessing a Guy Ritchie movie, a new smartwatch, or a political ad, a thoughtful evaluation requires thoughtful language. Read, reread, and read again what you've written. Look for throwaway words such as "amazing" and "huge" and "crazy" and replace them with words that communicate your meaning more precisely. Was a benefit concert "amazing"? Or was it "a raucous and colorful display of human generosity"? Was the impact of the coronavirus "huge" or was it "an unprecedented public health alarm"?

- **Employ concrete details whenever possible.** As noted in the previous section, "Examples, Examples, Examples" are the way to persuade readers that an evaluation is a sound one. The more specific an example is, the more convincing your evidence will be (see Concrete Evidence in section 6.3).

- **Read professional examples of the type of evaluation you are making.** You can't become a good writer without reading lots and lots of work by more experienced writers. Whenever you feel a lack of focus or inspiration, read the work of writers who have already confronted, and surmounted, the challenges you are facing.

DIY 10.5 Supercharge Your Language

Cut and paste a paragraph of your evaluative essay into a separate document. Then go through it — sentence by sentence, word by word — looking for ways to supercharge your language. (*Visiting X is a great way to spend a day* might become *Visiting X provides an eye-opening and meaningful history lesson,* for example.) If you don't immediately see opportunities for making the paragraph better, take another look at the editing strategies discussed in Section 9.3, "Editing for Style." In particular, remember the suggestions to be aware of the passive voice and vary your sentences.

10.6 Playing Fair

Because it can be so much fun to go over the top with language in a review, we need to be careful of abandoning what is ultimately an evaluator's most important quality: impartiality. The moment readers sense you aren't playing fair with your subject, you'll begin to lose them. Think, for instance, of the escalating war of words you've seen so many times in the comments section of a YouTube video, or the back-and-forth remarks about a politically charged story on a news site. When people exaggerate or make claims without evidence to back them up, we can't help recoiling or becoming dismissive or angry, especially if we disagree with their point of view.

Movie reviewers know there will always be people who will argue with their judgment, so they usually attempt to anticipate or predict the most valid counterarguments. Despite the fact that Manohla Dargis clearly thinks *King Arthur* is often silly and overblown, she nevertheless makes a real effort to show that she can find some good in the movie. The digital elephants of the opening scene are "magical, just like the dragons swooping through the HBO show *Game of Thrones*," and the movie does benefit in some ways from popular director Guy Ritchie's "*je ne sais quoi*," that is, his indescribable quality. Star Charlie Hunnam has an "easy, low-wattage charisma," and "the movie improves once Mr. Ritchie gets closer to his actors." Even in her final sentence, while she is still calling *King Arthur* "generic goods," she admits that it is "easy enough to watch."

When you write, it's important to maintain a sense of fair play.

Tips for Playing Fair

- **Make a real effort to see both sides of the case**—even if you have strong positive or negative feelings about your subject. With our world divided so sharply, taking on someone else's perspective can be a very difficult thing to do. Nevertheless, it *is* important to at least try to imagine other ways of viewing a subject, especially if it is controversial and given to polarizing opinions. This kind of open mindedness is more important when you review a public policy than it is when you review a posh new restaurant, but know that most readers appreciate a reviewer capable of valuing another perspective.

- **Discuss any alternative views that have special merit.** If you *do* find elements that, in all fairness, you feel you must address in your evaluation, give them the attention they deserve. Acknowledge the positive attributes of your subject, even if you are mostly critical of it. The more you appear to be an impartial judge of your subject, the more readers will trust your overall opinion.

- **Seek feedback from a friend or peer.** You may not be able to see it when your draft starts to become biased but another reader may be able to. Before your work is due, be sure to share it with at least one other person (writing center tutor, teammate, coworker, friend, parent) and see whether they think you're playing fair.

DIY 10.6 Consider an Alternative Point of View

Close your eyes, take a deep breath, let it out — now pretend that your opinion of your subject is the *opposite* of what it really is. As quickly as you can, write down what is effective and accomplished about your subject (if you *really* think it is unsuccessful and unpolished), or vice versa. When you're finished, read through what you've written. Has your alter ego made any good points that should be addressed in your evaluation?

An Invitation to Read: An Album Review

A 20-year veteran critic who writes about hip-hop music and other genres, Gary Suarez spent at least part of his COVID-19 quarantine enjoying new music by "Puerto Rican superstar" Bad Bunny. His review of the artist's surprise 2020 album includes a careful evaluation of the tracks through multiple lenses — collaborations, lyrics, and mixing — and includes the sort of humor he knows will appeal to his reading audience. His evaluation of Bad Bunny's album as "intimately comforting" is, overall, a positive one.

Bad Bunny's *Las Que No Iban a Salir* Turns Self-Isolation into a Global Party

GARY SUAREZ

1   Of all of Bad Bunny's many gifts — his charmingly nasal vocal delivery, his apparent good nature, his preternatural ability to pull off a manicure — his finest attribute may be his knack for pleasant surprises.

2   As the modern música urbana industry's predilection toward unexpected album drops often reflects disorganization more so than imagination, the Puerto Rican superstar's ingenuity and affability has more than carried him through four such releases, beginning with the *Nochebuena* 2018 blessing of his full-length debut *X 100pre*. Still, fans had at least some inclination that last year's J Balvin team-up for mini album *Oasis* and this past February's *YHLQMDLG* were coming with some degree of imminence.

3   Not so for *Las Que No Iban a Salir*, a 10-song dive into Bad Bunny's hard-drive of set-aside, previously discarded, or otherwise unreleased songs unveiled on Mother's Day. Though the specific origins of this material remain unclear, most of these tracks appeared in some form during his Instagram Live quarantine event in early May. As he virtually teased hundreds of thousands of viewers with snippets, lip-syncing and even singing over some of them with a wood spoon substituting for a microphone, it was unlikely that many anticipated an actual release would come so soon.

4   Though the absence of an Anuel AA feature heard during the social media twerk-in has sparked some online snark, guest appearances from the likes of Jhay Cortez, Yandel, and Zion & Lennox that did make the cut certainly won't leave listeners wanting. And, after *YHLQMDLG* so plainly revealed a near-sacred devotion to reggaeton, it makes perfect sense that such perreo piety would persist here. To that end, Bad Bunny plucks Don Omar—urbano's proverbial King of Kings himself—from a state of semiretirement for the hedonistic thump of "Pa' Romperla." With enduring veteran Nicky Jam in tow, Bad Bunny time travels through decades of genre history for "Bad Con Nicky," in a move not unlike what he undertook for *YHLQMDLG*'s still-smoldering single "Safaera." A nod to the days when Jamaican dancehall inspired the earliest of reggaetoneros, the sample of Daddy Yankee's refreshed *Playero 37* cut "Donde Mi No Vengas," from 2003's *Los Homerun-es,* is an especially nice touch.

5   Of course, as we've seen with signature singles like "Estamos Bien" and "Vete," Bad Bunny certainly doesn't need fancy features to prop himself up. With lyrics that indicate recording during self-isolation, "Bendiciones" kills his haters with kindness while offering empathy and hugs for those affected by the virus and natural disasters that have imperiled his home country. The quarantine theme continues for "En Casita," a duet with girlfriend Gabriela Berlingeri that stresses the need for social distancing even with the emotional costs.

6   While some persnickety audiophiles might bristle at the unmixed and unmastered nature of the project, *Las Que No Iban a Salir* sounds more than acceptable by today's home-streaming standards. After all, there's

no place else most listeners will get to hear the record apart from their rechargeable devices, thanks to the global pandemic going on outside. Instead, it plays out like the Instagram Live DJ sets and password-protected Zoom parties occurring nightly all over the world, something intimately comforting and oddly unifying when people so desperately need it.

Reading Questions

1. Assuming that the first sentence of this short review acts as a kind of thesis statement, locate examples in the body of the review that demonstrate Bad Bunny's "knack for pleasant surprises." What other claims and evidence does Suarez use to support his judgment that the new album is worth listening to?

2. Are there musical references in the review that you find confusing? If so, identify them and explain how Suarez might have made the references clearer to someone who is unfamiliar with Bad Bunny and reggaetón.

3. Identify your favorite sentence in the review, and then explain why that particular sentence appealed to you.

An Invitation to Read: A Student Essay

When Santa Barbara City College student Larissa Moss decided to visit the 9/11 Memorial and Museum on a trip to New York City, she had no idea the impact the museum would make on her. Larissa had been having a hard time deciding on a subject for her evaluation, but she says that the moment she left the museum, she suddenly knew "what I was going to review and how I was going to describe it. The criteria and organization came later, but I knew I was off to a productive start."

Moss 1

Larissa Moss

Professor Starkey

Eng 110

17 February 2019

Intense and Spectacular:

A Review of the 9/11 Memorial and Museum

When I mentioned buying tickets to the 9/11 Memorial and Museum for an upcoming trip to New York City, my friend Emily warned me, "Don't stay more than three hours! And

The writer engagers readers immediately.

Moss 2

book a lighthearted Broadway show for later that night. The place is harrowing." I took her advice about the play, mostly because I wanted to see Kevin Kline in a Noel Coward farce. I also booked the 9/11 tickets, thinking she was probably exaggerating about its effect on museum-goers. She wasn't. The experience flattened me; some visitors, including the friend I was with, were openly sobbing. However, despite the emotional intensity of the experience, I still recommend a visit to both the memorial and the museum. Though the exhibits emphasize the tragic loss of life, the curators took pains not to sensationalize the subject or descend into the macabre.

The memorial is both emotionally intense and spectacular. It consists of two large, deep pools where the north and south towers once stood. Water cascades into the pools, which has a strange effect. On the one hand, the rushing falls have a soothing quality, but they also remind us of the endless tears that come with such a loss, especially for the surviving family members. Around the sides of the pool, the victims' names are engraved in granite. Some of the most heartbreaking ones include a woman's name, along with "her unborn child." Roses are placed next to some of the names; family members put them there each year to commemorate their loved ones' birthdays. Perhaps partly because they are outside, the twin pools felt less suffocating and tragic than the exhibits inside the museum.

The museum itself is underneath the pools, which gives the visitor a terrifying feeling of being physically trapped. The exhibit that made the strongest impression on me was a room covered with photographs of the victims, both those in the towers and on the planes (see fig. 1). Suddenly, the engraved names became faces, real people, each of whom was cherished by their family and who died horribly. It was very difficult to look at some of these photos, especially the ones of children. Two little girls are pictured, along with their

The thesis makes the writer's judgment clear.

A summary grounds the reader in the place being evaluated.

The writer begins to spell out her criteria: Memorials should make a strong impression on visitors.

Reference to a visual in MLA style.

Moss 3

Anadolu Agency/Getty Images

Fig. 1. Cem Ozdel. *National 9/11 Memorial Museum.* May 2014.
Getty Images, www.gettyimages.com/detail/news-photo/
people-visit-the-national-9-11-memorial-museum-in-new-york-
news-photo/493896763.

dad; they were on the plane to Los Angeles so they could visit
Disneyland. In an adjacent room, an endless slideshow plays.
The show has pictures of each victim, along with audio of
family members describing their loved one.

At this point, my friend wanted to leave the museum, so I
agreed to meet her later, outside. I was also tempted to leave,
but I thought about all the victims who hadn't had that option
and forced myself to stay a little longer. Many, many of the
dead were firefighters and I kept thinking about how much
courage it must have taken to run into those towers while
everyone else was fleeing. The last part of the exhibit I visited
showed video of those who jumped from the towers. It was
terrifying and just unbearably sad because they obviously
had no other option. One woman was even holding down
her skirt as she jumped, trying to be modest. Little details
like that are the most impactful because they humanize the
victims and force us to face the fact that this person could
easily have been us. Some visitors might view this segment
as sensational or even exploitative, but as hard as it was

Full publication information
for the visual is given in
the caption, so no works
cited entry is needed.

Specific examples strengthen
the writer's evaluation.

Moss 4

to watch, the video tells an important truth about what happened that horrible day.

I couldn't help but be reminded of another 9/11 exhibit, one that doesn't quite measure up, at the Washington D.C. Newseum. At the Washington D.C. site, many of the victims' possessions are displayed, such as wallets, checkbooks and receipts. This feels voyeuristic and even disrespectful, especially when I contrast it to the 9/11 museum, which does an excellent job of humanizing the victims. The Newseum exhibit feels cluttered and maybe tacky, but the 9/11 Museum has a classical feel. There is even a quote from Virgil that is prominently placed and suggests that people who are gone will not be erased from memory.

Many visitors to New York may decide to avoid the 9/11 Memorial and Museum because of its intensity. Though I understand this reflex, I believe people must find the courage within to face the horrors of history such as the 2001 bombing of the World Trade Center. Turning a blind eye means choosing to ignore rather than honor the victims of terrible suffering. However, as my friend Emily suggested, book tickets to a light-hearted play or movie for a bit of relief afterward. You'll need it.

Another specific criterion — memorials should humanize victims — anchors this paragraph.

Reading Questions

1. Find two concrete and detailed descriptions of the 9/11 Memorial and Museum and explain how they further Larissa's argument that while "the exhibits emphasize the tragic loss of life, the curators took pains not to sensationalize the subject or descend into the macabre."

2. What purpose is served by the comparison between the 9/11 Memorial in New York and the Newseum in Washington, DC?

3. Larissa Moss's essay is bookended by references to a comic play on Broadway that she plans to attend. Do you find this technique effective, or does it undercut the seriousness of her visit to the museum? Explain your reasoning.

CHAPTER 10 Checklist
Making an Evaluation

☐ **Have you chosen the best subject for your evaluation?**

Your instructor may assign a subject, but if you've been given some choice, have you selected a subject that will draw on expertise you already possess? Is the subject something that truly makes you excited to write about it?

☐ **Have you considered your audience's expectations for your evaluation?**

Always imagine the people for whom you are writing. What do they want to read? What will keep them interested? What will make them turn away?

☐ **Have you generated appropriate criteria for the evaluation?**

Different subjects require different criteria. Make sure you address the areas your readers expect you to cover, focusing on those that are most relevant to the subject you are evaluating.

☐ **Is your evaluation organized in such a way that it will have maximum impact on your readers?**

Most reviews are structured like an academic essay: hook, thesis, supporting evidence, and conclusion. Use what you have learned about essay writing in this book to guide your moves, knowing that the length of your evaluation and a specific audience may cause you to modify your approach.

☐ **Have you carefully described what you are evaluating?**

Meticulous, detailed description provides the evidence for your opinion. Don't waste your time generalizing; be specific instead.

☐ **If you are writing a review, have you spent as much time crafting the language of your review as you have advocating for or recommending against your subject?**

This is not an assignment to rush through. Slow down and enjoy the possibilities of language, the way it can bring a topic to life.

☐ **Have you tried to be fair and impartial in your evaluation, and have you conveyed that impartiality to your reader?**

Even if your likely readers are already biased in favor of the judgment you are making, they still want to feel that you (and they) have been fair in that judgment. Readers who are skeptical of your evaluation will require even more evidence to demonstrate that you have carefully considered potential counterarguments.

10.7 Making It Stick

How will you produce a strong and successful evaluation?

Working Together

10.7a Reviewing a Draft Evaluation Exchange a draft of your evaluation essay with another student; use the following questions to guide your peer review:

1. Has the writer carefully followed *all* the instructions for the evaluation provided by your professor? Were any draft goals listed in the assignment prompt? Reread the prompt, sentence by sentence, and make sure the essay meets all the assignment's requirements.

2. Does the writer have a clear thesis statement that succinctly summarizes the evaluation's argument? If the evaluation is a review, the thesis may have a playful element, but it should still ensure that a reader can quickly determine how the writer feels about the subject and understand why the writer feels that way. Take a close look at the criteria being used to evaluate the subject. Are any of them unnecessary, or underdeveloped in the essay? Is it possible to combine several related criteria? Has the writer forgotten an important element of the subject that needs to be addressed?

3. Has the writer offered sufficient concrete and detailed evidence to support the essay's opinion about the subject? To find out, take a highlighting pen or, if you are working online, use the highlighter function on your word processing program, and highlight all the evidence that supports the writer's judgment. If, for instance, you

choose yellow to highlight the evidence, half or more of the review should light up in yellow. If not, suggest ways the writer can generate more support for their argument.

4. Does the final paragraph fall into the trap of dully recapping everything the writer has already said, or does it maintain reader interest, adding new information as necessary? If the writer has gone into repeat mode, make suggestions for aspects of the subject that the writer hasn't covered or about which more can be said.

Applying What You Know

10.7b Video Life On your own or with a classmate, generate a list of things that make a music video good — aside from the song itself. Come up with five to seven elements you typically notice as you judge whether a music video is effective or not. Then choose a video and watch it.

Afterward, discuss how well the video held up to the criteria. If you were evaluating the video, which criteria would you use? Which would you delete? What criteria would you add that you didn't think about before watching the video?

10.7c Mulling It Over Reflect on your draft by focusing on the strategies for writing an evaluation discussed in this chapter. Write notes on how well your draft illustrates the chapter concepts.

- Writing to your audience
- Generating appropriate criteria
- Organizing for maximum impact
- Employing language effectively
- Playing fair

If you can, share your draft with a classmate and offer to read that classmate's draft. In a 20-minute in-person or video conversation, focus on how well each writer carried out the chapter's five concepts.

Invitations to Write

10.7d Joining a Reviewers' Conversation

Shorter: Choose a popular movie you have seen, an album you have listened to, or a book that you have read. Your encounter with the work should be recent, as you will initially be relying on your memory. Once you've made your choice, without consulting anyone else's opinion, write what you think about your subject.

Longer: Now that you know what you think about your subject, find out what other reviewers have said. If you read their reviews online, cut and paste their most striking comments into a document, making sure to carefully record who said what and where it was published. Once you have three or four quotes that make you want to respond, go ahead and write back to the other reviewers, praising them for what they got right and letting them know where they went wrong.

If this prompt leads to an essay, be sure to reread this chapter and include all the major features of a review: an awareness of audience expectations; appropriate review criteria; a clear and compelling thesis that guides a series of well-organized paragraphs being supported by plenty of concrete, specific, and well-written examples; carefully crafted sentences; and a sense that the reviewer is impartial and attempting to fairly evaluate the subject.

10.7e Evaluating a Campus Resource

Shorter: Write a paragraph about a campus resource you have used productively (writing center, math lab, student health center, financial planning office, career services website, and so on), or one you believe would help you become a more successful student.

Longer: Add to your first paragraph by doing some research on the source. Where is it located? How often is it open? Who staffs it? Which students seem most likely to take advantage of the resource? Based on some quick Internet research, how does the resource on your campus compare with that of other colleges and universities?

Then schedule a visit to or a video call with the campus resource. Try to set up an interview with a person in charge. Make a list of questions you'd like answered, and be prepared to take notes, or to record the conversation on your phone or within the video app. When you connect with your host, ask for further information about the resource. After the conversation, look through the new material and incorporate it into an evaluation that compares what you expected to find and what was actually there.

If you decide to turn your evaluation into an essay, review this chapter and make sure you address each major criterion for a successful evaluation essay.

Open-Topic Essay Ideas If your instructor has given you an open-ended assignment, and you've decided not to write about the thing you chose at the beginning of this chapter, consider some of the most commonly evaluated items:

- *Something you can watch, listen to, or read*: a streaming show, a movie, a play, a video, a song, a podcast, a concert, a book

- *Something you can eat or drink*: a meal at a restaurant, a new energy drink, a gluten-free version of a popular pizza brand
- *Something you can play*: a sport, a video game, a musical instrument
- *Something you use frequently*: a smartphone app, a laptop, a ride-sharing service

Again, the more *specific* the item you choose to evaluate, the easier it will be to focus your evaluation.

11

Arguing a Position

11.1　Seeing Argument as an Academic Habit

Most of us think of an "argument" as two people shouting angrily at one another, both eager to make their point and neither particularly interested in hearing the other's. In the world of your college classroom, however, an argument is actually closer to a conversation. Making a good argument involves listening to others and seeking common ground in a legitimate give-and-take exchange. Only after you've studied multiple perspectives and tried your best to impartially decide on the strongest argument should you attempt to convince your readers of the merits of your point of view by making a well-defined *claim* and then offering sound *reasons* supported by concrete and persuasive *evidence*. Indeed, in most academic settings, "arguing" with logic and evidence is considered one of the most effective ways to communicate. One of the ways teachers encourage the habit, as you may recall from times when you've raised your hand in class, is to expect you to present evidence in support of an opinion.

Another way in which a classroom discussion mirrors argumentative writing is in the role emotion plays. Initially, that might sound like a contradiction: if logic and reason are the mainstays of a strong academic argument, what role do *feelings* play in the equation? Once you think about it, though, you realize that you are most likely to raise your (real or virtual) hand when you truly care about what's being discussed. Often, that passion arises because you feel something isn't right, and you believe it's possible to make that something better. When you're assigned to write an argument essay, and if you are free to choose your subject matter, choose a topic that matters to you personally—some issue that makes you want to convince other people that your way of looking at things makes sense. Even if your topic is assigned by your instructor, look for a way in that allows you to speak for values and ideas that you hold dear.

This chapter emphasizes classic academic argument, which is especially focused on claims, reasons, and evidence. Granted, in what can sometimes feel like a post-truth world, you might ask, *What difference does it make whether or not I'm able to make a convincing argument?* Fortunately, in your first-year composition course, logic and reason, good sense, and good manners still rule the day. Good writers of argument are critical thinkers who question the purpose, audience, and context of any piece of evidence they consider and who think through the assumptions behind a position. This chapter helps you strengthen these skills so that you can effectively argue a position in any college course.

UP FRONT: Deciding on an Argument

The Assignment

Write an essay in which you take a position and make an argument. The chapter guidance, examples, and DIY prompts will help you complete the assignment. Follow your instructor's notes about length and formatting. Keep these guidelines in mind as you choose a text to study.

Select a topic that you care about. The more important it is for you to convince others of your argument, the more effort you will put into making your case. If you care about something passionately, chances are that you can make others care about your topic, too.

Narrow your topic so that it can be reasonably covered in a short academic essay. While we may urgently need to combat climate change as a whole, the scope of your essay should be restricted to something limited like the need to reduce our air travel or the benefits of exchanging a car for a bike.

Do some exploration; identify multiple positions in the debate. Do a little initial reading to make sure that you are pursuing a debatable topic and that you understand the range of arguments that have been made about it.

Make sure you can defend your position. You'll need specific reasons for believing the way you do. Early in the writing process, even making a quick list of the three or four reasons you most strongly believe in your position can be extremely helpful.

Be certain to seek out concrete evidence to support your position. Each part of your argument will need to be supported by specific evidence from credible sources.

DIY 11.1 Summarize Your Potential Argument

Write a paragraph in which you summarize the argument you imagine using for this assignment. Either respond to your instructor's prompt, which you should read very carefully, or use the guidelines described earlier to argue a position of your own. Chances are that your ideas about your argument will be modified as you work through the chapter and read about your topic. That's fine. Don't cling to an argument if you no longer hold the beliefs you had when you began the composing process.

An Invitation to Read: An Argument Essay

Institute for Humane Studies at George Mason University

Lately, it seems harder to talk to people who don't hold the same opinions and beliefs that we have. It's a problem not just on campus and in the United States, but also around the world, and many people have come to believe that the problem starts with a lack of listening. In "The Presumption of Good Faith in Campus Conversation," Emily Chamlee-Wright—president of the Institute for Humane Studies and a former professor at Beloit College—argues that what's missing from campus and national dialogue is the assumption that "we expect that our conversation partner is interested in learning from us and is seeking to understand our point of view." Listening with "good faith," she believes, can be the beginning of lively and possibly life-changing conversations. Chamlee-Wright's work originally appeared in the opinion section of a publication read by college faculty and administrators.

Critical Reading Tip

In "The Presumption of Good Faith in Campus Conversation," Emily Chamlee-Wright spends the first part of the essay establishing herself as a credible writer on her topic. As you read, think about why that credibility is so important to her overall argument.

The Presumption of Good Faith in Campus Conversation

EMILY CHAMLEE-WRIGHT

1   I recently returned to Beloit College, where I taught for nearly 20 years before moving on to Washington College and the Institute for Humane Studies. Slated to speak on the topic of campus speech at an institution still wrestling with its own speech-related controversy, I was somewhat nervous.[1]

---

[1] Earlier in the year, Beloit students had shut down a planned talk by conservative icon Erik Prince by banging on drums and building a barricade of chairs in front of the stage where he was scheduled to speak.

fizkes/Shutterstock

2   I needn't have been. Perhaps it was the bookish title of my talk—"Conversational Ethics: What Would Adam Smith Have Us Do?" Perhaps I still had some street cred on campus. Or perhaps folks were simply worn out. But no one came loaded for bear.

3   Smith has a lot to teach us about the ethics of conversation, particularly when public discourse becomes acrimonious. In *The Theory of Moral Sentiments*, he observed that the "violence and injustice of faction" tests us in ways that the ordinary "bustle of business in the world" does not. He writes, "The violence and loudness with which blame is sometimes poured out upon us seems to stupefy and benumb our natural sense of praise-worthiness and blame-worthiness." In other words, the clamor of the crowd can make it hard to tell right from wrong.

4   Smith counsels that to prepare ourselves for the prospect of unjust condemnation, we must gain practice at viewing our beliefs and conduct not from the vantage point of the crowd but from the perspective of a well-informed impartial judge. If this imagined "impartial spectator" approves of our stance, then we are justified in ignoring the clamor. With practice, we become wiser and more accustomed to summoning the "self-command" we need to stand tall in the face of injustice.

5   But a sophomore in the audience recognized that this advice only helps the speaker. It doesn't stop us from being part of the unjust crowd. He asked, "What can we do, in practical terms, to keep the conversation positive?" It was one of those moments when a dozen possible answers come to mind, but the voice in your head says, "Pick one!" The words that came out

of my mouth were, "We could all do a better job of assuming good faith."
Then the voice said, "Why did you pick that one?"

6   As soon as I said it, I realized that the 19-year-old asking the question
might not know what I meant by such an old-fashioned phrase. I realized
too late that though I use the phrase frequently, I had not thought through
a full explanation of its meaning. As I started to unpack it in the moment,
I realized what a potent concept it is and how far we have drifted from it.

7   Assuming good faith means that we expect that our conversation
partner is interested in learning from us and is seeking to understand
our point of view. It means that we should assume, unless we have good
evidence to the contrary, that their intent is not to deceive or offend. We can
certainly point out when an error has been made or why offense has been
taken, but it should be with the intent of making the conversation better, not
closing it down.

8   A presumption of good faith demands a lot from us. It requires that we
suspend judgment long enough to ask questions in a spirit of openness and
curiosity. If the student in the audience and I disagree, I should focus first on
figuring out why it is that he and I draw different conclusions even though
we are looking at the same world. Perhaps there's something in his history,
or mine, that led us to different places.

9   Good faith means that I should take my time to thoughtfully consider
his perspective before I decide to praise it or condemn it. But time for
thoughtful consideration seems to have fallen out of fashion. As we saw in
the Covington Catholic story—in which a viral video clip inspired many to
signal their disgust for a group of teenage boys accused of racism and disrespect, only to learn later that the story was far more complicated—we feel
pressure to be the first to signal our moral commitments to the world.[2] We
fear that if we take our time we will be seen as being complicit with wrongdoing. So, we take shortcuts. We bypass the hard work of moral reasoning,
and instead praise or condemn based on factional affiliation.

10   But through the cracks of the political divide we are also seeing positive
examples emerge. University of Michigan students Kate Westa and Brett
Zaslavsky, for example, lead WeListen, a bipartisan club dedicated to civil
cross-ideological debate. At the national level, StoryCorps' One Small Step
is facilitating one-on-one conversations in which people who disagree listen
and respond to one another with respect. This is good faith in practice.

---

[2] While accounts of what actually happened vary, a short version is that a group of students
from Covington Catholic High School in Kentucky were visiting the Lincoln Memorial in
January of 2019. Several of the students were wearing "Make America Great Again" hats, and
a video appeared to show them mocking a Native American activist. The students were widely
reviled as bigots. However, subsequent video showed that—just prior to the viral video—the
students, as well as a number of passersby, were being taunted by another group, and the
activist intervened. Viewers of the original shorter video made assumptions without having a
full understanding of the events.

11   Arguably, there are exceptions to when we are expected to assume good faith. If we extend this and other conversational courtesies to incendiary speakers who gain prominence by violating those same courtesies, it is out of grace, not entitlement. We are obliged to respect their First Amendment rights but nothing more. Incendiary speakers, however, are the exception. And we shouldn't base our ethical standards on the exception. Our default should be the presumption of good faith.

12   The practice of good faith is not an obvious remedy. It's a difficult discipline. It offers none of the psychic rewards that moral outrage delivers. But it's a practice that keeps the conversation going. And it's a practice that allows everyone in the conversation to teach and to learn.

Reading Questions

1. Begin by identifying Chamlee-Wright's argument. What are the main points she is trying to convince her readers to believe?

2. How persuasive do you find "The Presumption of Good Faith in Campus Conversation"? Point to specific passages and examples in the essay and explain why you believe they do, or don't, serve to further the author's argument.

3. Reread the essay and underline any unfamiliar references. Who, for instance, is Adam Smith? What is his book *The Theory of Moral Sentiments* about? Do some digging on your phone or computer. (If you want to dive more deeply into the subject, check out the entry in the *Stanford Encyclopedia of Philosophy* at plato.stanford.edu.) When you have found the answers to all your questions, reconvene as a class, and make sure that every student understands every reference in the article.

4. Using Emily Chamlee-Wright's essay as your model, make a list of the main features of an essay that argues a position. Note: The paragraphs in opinion pieces such as this one are typically shorter and more numerous than those in an academic essay of the same length.

11.2 Supporting a Claim with Reasons and Evidence

A strong academic argument is based on logic and reason, so it's not surprising that the structure for an argumentative essay is itself logical and reasonable. When you're arguing a position, you begin by making an arguable claim. You then provide reasons for the validity of that claim, each of which is supported by one or more pieces of evidence.

Make a Claim

A claim is a statement you make that other people may disagree with. Your position in a particular debate rests on your arguable claim.

Of course, while it's easy to make claims—we do it all the time—making a worthwhile claim, one that will sustain an academic essay, takes a little more thought and planning. As you begin thinking about the claim for your essay, consider the following advice:

- **Your claim should be worth making.** You may remember a toy called the "fidget spinner" that was all the rage among elementary school kids (and others!) a few years ago. Although a claim such as "Fidget spinners are fun" is certainly one about which rational people might disagree, writing an entire paper on such a topic is hardly worth your time—or your readers'. Instead, look for ways to move the discussion about something small and trivial into the larger world. A much more substantial claim on this topic would be: "Fidget spinners are one of the clearest examples of the ways that toy manufacturers manipulate children and their parents."

- **Your claim should be debatable.** Rational people aren't going to argue with basic facts like, "Trees absorb carbon dioxide," or, "George Washington was the first president of the United States." However, it doesn't take much effort to transform those statements of fact into arguable claims. "Trees planted too densely can make global warming worse" is a worthwhile revision of the first statement, just as "George Washington was the most influential president in the history of the United States" changes the second factual statement into a claim worth debating.

- **Your claim should not be too personal.** If your claim is "Drake is my favorite musical artist," then no reasonable person can argue with you because your private opinion about Drake offers no grounds for argument. There is no debate here. A strong, arguable claim might be something along the lines of "Drake's music represents the most skillful balance of singing and rapping in popular music in the twenty-first century."

As you can see, the best claims for an argumentative essay tend to focus on larger social questions and require thought, creativity, and often research to support them.

In an argumentative essay, a claim is usually expressed most succinctly in the thesis statement. In academic writing, a writer can usually form a thesis by asking and answering a question. In the case of "The Presumption of Good Faith in Campus Conversation," for instance, Chamlee-Wright answers her implied question, "What is required to make campus conversations more productive and civil?" with her title.

Incidentally, while you will probably place your thesis at the end of your opening paragraph, which is in line with a common convention for college essays, editorial writers tend to have a bit more freedom. What looks most like a thesis statement in "The Presumption of Good Faith in Campus Conversation" is actually located in the middle of the essay, when Chamlee-Wright tells the student that the solution to keeping campus conversations positive is to "do a better job of assuming good faith." When you write, you may have some flexibility with where you state your position.

The advantage of placing your thesis statement at the end of your introductory paragraph, of course, is that that's where your reader might expect to find it. Wherever you decide to locate your thesis, be sure it meets the guidelines described in Section 5.4

Generate Reasons to Support a Claim

No claim is made in a vacuum. You believe something because you have reasons—however solid or dubious they might be. Fortunately, the logical nature of an academic argument means that the very act of listing the reasons for your claim will provide you with a pretty good idea of how strong your argument is. Inevitably, the reasons for your claim will create the foundations of your body paragraphs, and clearly stated reasons will become the basis for the topic sentences of those paragraphs.

As with forming a thesis, a question-and-answer strategy will serve you well as you generate reasons for your claim. Looking once more at "The Presumption of Good Faith in Campus Conversation," we can break the authors' claim down into reasons by asking *why* the claim is made. Each answer becomes the potential basis for a main point in the essay.

Here, for instance, is the claim made by Emily Chamlee-Wright:

> **Claim** The best way to keep conversations positive on campus is to assume the "good faith" of one's listener.

Here are some of the reasons in support of that claim:

> **Why?**
> . . . because "the clamor of the crowd can make it hard to tell right from wrong."
> . . . because assuming good faith better helps one see an issue "from the perspective of a well-informed impartial judge."
> . . . because assuming good faith will help us "become wiser and more accustomed to summoning the 'self-command' we need to stand tall in the face of injustice."

. . . because assuming good faith encourages us to "suspend judgment long enough to ask questions in a spirit of openness and curiosity."

. . . because assuming good faith forces us to address "the hard work of moral reasoning."

. . . because assuming good faith allows "positive examples" to emerge.

. . . because assuming good faith is a practice that "keeps the conversation going."

. . . because assuming good faith "allows everyone in the conversation to teach and to learn."

As you read through the answers explaining *why* good faith is so crucial to productive campus conversations, you'll notice that each one begins with "because." That's a helpful planning word to use as you come up with your reasons, but of course you wouldn't necessarily want to repeat it over and over in your essay.

Examine Underlying Assumptions

Most arguments rest on one or more assumptions, something accepted as true. Take another look at the list of reasons in the previous section. A commonality among the reasons is that they assume readers agree that one type of society is better than another. Emily Chamlee-Wright clearly believes that the best type of society is one is one that values thoughtfulness, reason, and courtesy. This is the *underlying assumption* on which the entire essay rests. It may be a largely unspoken idea, but the very fact that the assumption is silent can make it more powerful.

Here is another example that may help explain underlying assumptions:

Claim: States must pass laws to expand vote-at-home options.

> *Why?* Having more vote-at-home options would increase voter turnout.
> *Why?* Having more vote-at-home options would increase access to the voting process by traditionally underrepresented populations.
> *Why?* Having more vote-at-home options would decrease intimidation of voters at polling locations.

Underlying assumption(s): It is the states' obligation to protect voters' rights and encourage participation in the democratic process. Government by the people and for the people works better when more people vote.

When you're analyzing someone else's claim, you'll want to figure out what sort of worldview the writer's underlying assumptions support. Knowing the reasons *behind* the stated reasons for a claim provides you with a much stronger understanding of the arguments you encounter. When you construct your own set of reasons in support of a claim, you will want to examine your own underlying assumptions (or seek help from an outside reader to do so) as you decide whether to openly state them in your essay or not. Do your reasons reflect a worldview and a set of values that most people embrace? Or only some people?

Provide Evidence to Support Reasons

If you've ever studied the architecture of cathedrals, you'll be familiar with the term "flying buttress." If not, all you need to know is that a flying buttress is a slanting structure, often made of brick or stone, which usually takes the form of an arch and supports the main walls of some Gothic cathedrals.

The nave of France's Notre Dame cathedral is supported by a series of flying buttresses.

If you're having trouble creating a visual equivalent of how your evidence supports your reasons, you might look at the flying buttress image in this section. Think of the flying buttresses as your evidence (after all, "buttress" does mean "support") and the main part of the cathedral (called the nave) as the reasons that evidence is holding up.

Although it is just over nine hundred words long, Chamlee-Wright's essay includes quite a few "flying buttresses" to support her claim that good faith is a requirement for positive campus conversation. She employs several types of evidence that are commonly found in argumentative essays.

> Knowing the reasons *behind* the stated reasons for a claim provides you with a much stronger understanding of the arguments you encounter.

Types of Evidence

- **Quotations.** Pithy short quotes have been a feature of essays since at least the heyday of Michel de Montaigne and Francis Bacon in the sixteenth and seventeenth centuries, and they are no less effective when used by essayists writing today. "The Presumption of Good Faith in Campus Conversation" (11.1) features several quotations, including five from Chamlee's Wright's main source—Adam Smith's *The Theory of Moral Sentiments*—as well one from the student whose question inspired her essay.

- **Personal examples.** Firsthand evidence can be very powerful, and a personal example from the writer's own life *that is relevant to the issue* can be quite persuasive. That is certainly the case in "The Presumption of Good Faith in Campus Conversation," where the author's experience speaking on a controversial topic at the school where she used to teach forms the spine of her entire essay. Not all assignments ask for personal experience, but as a first-semester composition student, you will sometimes be asked to discuss your own interactions with your assigned topic.

- **Examples from the larger world.** Chamlee-Wright includes examples of good faith not working *and* working well. She discusses the unfair treatment of the Covington Catholic High School students at the National Mall then in the next paragraph shifts to positive examples of good faith in action: the University of Michigan's WeListen club and the StoryCorps's One Small Step program. References to all three examples are linked in the original online article, which is often a smart move when your work is being published online.

- **Contemporary and historical references.** The more you can demonstrate your authority as a scholar or a budding scholar, the more likely it is that readers will believe your thinking is broad and inclusive. Chamlee-Wright, for instance, establishes her scholarly credentials early in her essay by demonstrating—especially in paragraphs 3 and 4—her perceptive understanding of *The Theory of Moral Sentiments*, a complex work originally published in 1759.

In addition to the types of evidence listed earlier, authors of argumentative essays also frequently use the following as evidence:

- **Verifiable data and references to published studies.** In our number-loving culture, poll results and statistics, research findings, and, of course *facts*, remain persuasive to a large segment of readers. Had she chosen a different strategy for reaching readers, Chamlee-Wright could have easily cited data showing how far apart Americans of different political persuasions have grown from one another—or scholarly studies about society's growing polarization.

- **Analogies.** Human beings love comparing one thing to another, especially when a known concept helps to explain something unknown. Analogies—including similes and metaphors—show a similarity between two different things and can make effective evidence, even if, by definition, they are more creative than exact. Good faith, Chamlee-Wright might have said, is like rain falling on a parched land after a long drought.

- **Stories by other people.** You know the feeling: you're reading through a long boring document when suddenly the author starts telling you a story. Suddenly, your interest perks up. There are characters and description, a bit of plot, and maybe even some dialogue. Ideally, the story or anecdote relates directly to the topic under discussion, but even when the connection is only tangential, a little narrative can go a long way in recapturing your readers' interest. One reminder: unlike personal examples, stories by and about other people are often drawn from sources or from your own ethnographic or field research, so even if you are just paraphrasing or summarizing someone else's anecdote, the original version should be cited.

- **Visuals.** Most news or feature writing published today—especially if it is online—includes at least one visual, often at the beginning of the essay. Visuals can include photos, data charts, infographics, maps, and more. You can read more about using visuals in Chapters 14 and 15.

Integrate Evidence

Strong writers are able to shift from their ideas to the ideas of others and back again skillfully within a paragraph (see Section 6.3). When you write with sources, you don't want to simply drop in facts and quotations without explaining why they are important. Your opinions about and analysis of your paraphrased and quoted material make a difference.

To see how well evidence can carry a paragraph, here's an example from paragraph 9 of "The Presumption of Good Faith in Campus Conversation." The paragraph progresses from a topic sentence (in this case, it's two sentences) to the evidence to the author's commentary.

Good faith means that I should take my time to thoughtfully consider his perspective before I decide to praise it or condemn it. But time for thoughtful consideration seems to have fallen out of fashion. As we saw in the Covington Catholic story—in which a viral video clip inspired many to signal their disgust for a group of teenage boys accused of racism and disrespect, only to learn later that the story was far more complicated—we feel pressure to be the first to signal our moral commitments to the world. We fear that if we take our time we will be seen as being complicit with wrongdoing. So, we take shortcuts. We bypass the hard work of moral reasoning, and instead praise or condemn based on factional affiliation.

Topic sentence

Evidence

Commentary

As indicated earlier, the paragraphs in an academic essay are likely to be longer than those in a newspaper editorial. That means in your essay you'll have more room for your own ideas and observations. Nevertheless, you'll find the same basic principle is at work: your chosen facts, quotations, anecdotes, statistics, and so on will do some of the heavy lifting of your argument, while the main job of your commentary will be connecting the evidence to your main argument and pointing out its importance.

One final word on locating and evaluating evidence: as you'll see in the student essay at the end of this chapter, research may end up being an integral part of your composition process. When you're online or in the library, try to apply the FACTS Checklist (see Section 16.2) against each of the sources you are considering, ensuring that they are Fair, Accurate, Current, Trustworthy, and Suitable for your essay.

DIY 11.2 State Your Claim and Your Support for It

State the claim you intend to make in your essay. Then list the main reasons for your claim. For each reason, ask, *Why is this reason important?* Then begin your answer with *Because. . . .* After each reason, provide one or two pieces of concrete and persuasive evidence. Finally, describe the underlying assumption on which your claim is built.

11.3 Appealing to Your Audience

In an argumentative essay, your ultimate goal is to persuade readers that your way of looking at a particular topic is the most reasonable one. So far in this chapter, the importance of logic is emphasized, but of course reason isn't the only method of appealing to an audience, which is why in this section we'll take a look at Aristotle's three appeals: *logos*, *ethos*, and *pathos*.

Understand Aristotle's Three Appeals

The Three Appeals are modes of persuasion originally intended by the philosopher Aristotle as guidelines for public speaking in ancient Athens. *Logos* is an appeal to reason. *Ethos*, which you will also want to braid into your essay, is an appeal to the speaker's credibility; the more credible you are, Aristotle argued, the more likely your audience will believe you. Finally, *pathos* is an appeal to emotion. If you feel strongly about your topic, or if you know your audience feels strongly about the topic, you may well employ this mode of persuasion, but try to do so in combination with other appeals and without placing feeling and sentiment at the center of your argument.

Logos

Historian Paul Anthony Rahe defines *logos*, or logical appeal, by paraphrasing Aristotle in his book *Republics Ancient and Modern*: logos "makes it possible" for humans to use reason "to perceive and make clear to others . . . the difference between what is advantageous and what is harmful [and] between what is just and what is unjust."

Clearly, Emily Chamlee-Wright believes that the use of reason will move people to do the right thing—reestablishing "the hard work of moral reasoning." The final paragraph of her essay neatly summarizes her argument: although good faith requires "difficult discipline" and doesn't provide us with "the psychic rewards that moral outrage delivers," it is nevertheless a practice that keeps people talking and "allows everyone in the conversation to teach and to learn."

Logos depends on evidence, and while Chamlee-Wright's evidence is selective, she never makes a claim without backing it up. As you compose your essay, make sure that every single reason you propose in support of your claim is buttressed by at least one piece of concrete and persuasive evidence—evidence that can come in the form of data, precedents, cause and effect analysis, expert testimony, and more.

Ethos

Probably the single most notable aspect of "The Presumption of Good Faith in Campus Conversation" is Chamlee-Wright's demonstration of her credibility as an educator and college administrator. Ethical appeals, or appeals to *ethos*, ask readers to see a writer as trustworthy.

At the beginning of the essay, Chamlee-Wright modestly tells readers that she was "somewhat nervous" to speak at her former college, even though she is an established scholar and former Dean at the school, who may still have "some street cred on campus." In fact, the very title of her presentation at the college is "Conversational Ethics." She discusses Adam Smith's *Theory of Moral Sentiments* calmly and rationally, and explains how, after being questioned by a student, she came to see Smith's concept of "good faith" as a way to conduct principled and respectful conversations. Appropriately, throughout her essay, she herself adopts the tone of someone who is decent and trustworthy.

As you position yourself in your essay, think about how you can persuade your readers that you are a person of good character who deserves to be listened to. One way to do that, like Chamlee-Wright, is to establish common ground with your audience. Another is to communicate that you are knowledgeable about your topic. Let your readers know that you are informed and that your opinion is considered and thoughtful.

Pathos

Think of the difference between the words "nosy" and "curious." A person you would describe with these words wants to know more about people or situations. But who would you want as a friend or coworker? The nosy one or the curious one? Words can be neutral, or they can have emotional associations. Where "curious" is fairly neutral, "nosy" has a negative *connotation* and suggests behavior that most people find quite negative. "Nosy" goes beyond knowing; nosy sneaks and peeks and pries about. Because words can carry different connotations, or emotional associations, word choice is often a key consideration in any argument.

Chamlee-Wright's language choices generally avoid drama, instead echoing her call for fairness and rationality. She explicitly and implicitly praises "the perspective of a well-informed impartial judge," "self-command," "openness and curiosity," "conversational courtesies," and "grace." However, she is not above using words with emotional associations, as when she tells us that the Covington Catholic story inspired many people to feel "disgust" for the teenage boys involved. Chamlee-Wright also uses emotionally charged words when quoting Adam Smith, who laments how "'violence and loudness'" can "stupefy and benumb" our normal good natures.

Of course, it's not just the language you use, but also the examples you provide. The best writers of argument know when to use appeals to emotion to stir a reader's pride, fear, confidence, or insecurity. Chamlee-Wright dials into her reader's experience with regret when she warns us against jumping to conclusions, as in the controversy over the Covington Catholic students. And she stirs hope in readers with stories about the positive work that can be done when people adopt good faith policies, as in the cases of the University of Michigan's WeListen club and StoryCorps' One Small Step project.

As you can see, while *pathos* may not be at the center of your argument, it still has the potential to move readers. Use the language of pathos subtly and examples of it sparingly. However, when you feel you need to drive home a point, don't hesitate to call on this effective mode of persuasion.

DIY 11.3 List Your Appeals to *Logos, Ethos, and Pathos*

Start a document and make three columns labeled *Logos, Ethos,* and *Pathos.* In each column, give examples of how you plan to appeal to your readers' logic, desire for credibility, and emotions. Your *Logos* column should have the most entries; be sure to include at least one example or idea that can work for the other two modes of persuasion.

11.4 Considering Other Opinions

When you're in the midst of an actual conversation with someone who disagrees with a point you're making, you know it right away. That person is likely to hold up their hands and interject "Now wait a minute!" or ask a direct question that you can answer then and there. Unfortunately, when you're writing, you need to *imagine* the responses of people who might not agree with your argument. Perhaps the best way to do this is by attempting to see the world from the point of view of the people you disagree with—which is nearly always a worthwhile exercise.

You can also predict what opposing arguments might be by thoroughly researching your issue. Take note of the most frequent and convincing counterarguments, knowing that if you tend to favor one side of an argument, you can be pretty sure that some of your readers will lean in the other direction.

Respond to Objections

As an example of how to anticipate counterarguments—positions that represent an objection to your own—look again at the claim and informal outline from Section 11.2. If we look at these arguments from the perspective of a skeptic, it doesn't take long to anticipate some possible counterarguments:

Claim: States must pass laws to expand vote-at-home options.

> *Why?* Having more vote-at-home options would increase voter turnout.

> *Why?* Having more vote-at-home options would increase access to the voting process by traditionally underrepresented populations.

> *Why?* Having more vote-at-home options would decrease intimidation of voters at polling locations.

aren't secure, could lead to fraud

but might unnecessarily drag out ballot counting

disadvantages young voters

Whether or not you find these arguments believable or baseless doesn't really matter, at least in the early stages of assembling potential counterarguments. In fact, if you want to argue convincingly against your opponent's position, it's crucial that you completely let go of your own way of thinking for a while and fully enter your opponent's mindset. Then you can start to plan your response to any objections.

When you're drafting, it's always good to push against your own position. If it's not strong enough, then consider adjusting your thesis, or at least finding more evidence to support your position. Developing an argument is all about testing its strengths, identifying its weaknesses, and ultimately buttressing your central claim. Here are a few more tips for addressing a range of audience responses to your claim:

Tips for Addressing Audience Response

Here are a few more tips for addressing a range of audience responses to your claim:

- **Look for common ground.** Chamlee-Wright spends her first two paragraphs demonstrating that she is an established part of the college community. That makes sense, given that her essay was first published on a website called *Inside Higher Ed*. Her argument is further based on the underlying assumption that most college students (and professors) would prefer to have a polite and reasoned conversation about controversial matters. Chamlee-Wright seems to believe that she is in harmony with most of her audience, but even when you are strongly opposed to your opponent's position, try to reach out to as many readers as possible.

- **Concede when it is appropriate do so.** Acknowledge when the other side has a valid claim. We see this acknowledgment in paragraph 11 of the "The Presumption of Good Faith in Campus Conversation," when Chamlee-Wright allows that "there are exceptions to when we are expected to assume good faith." Admitting that those who don't share your beliefs may have a sensible counterargument shows that you are a reasonable person, someone whose opinion is worth considering.

- **Pivot toward your own argument as soon as possible.** Be fair, but don't give any undue weight to potentially damaging counterarguments; you don't want them to overwhelm your own opinions. Immediately after the sentence quoted in the previous bullet point, for instance, Chamlee-Wright returns to her argument for good faith, contending that even when we disagree with an unruly speaker, it is still possible to be a courteous listener, although "out of grace, not entitlement."

- **When possible, refute opposing opinions politely.** When addressing a specific counterargument, use concrete and specific evidence whenever possible to rebut your opponent's position. Be reasonable, even if the other side isn't. When appropriate, acknowledge *why* they might hold the beliefs they have before demonstrating the flaws in their arguments. After considering the case of "incendiary speakers" in paragraph 11, Chamlee-Wright concludes with a civil but crisp rebuttal: "we shouldn't base our ethical standards on the exception."

- **Get tough when you have to.** While the old saying that you catch more flies with honey than with vinegar has some merit, in an argumentative essay, it's sometimes best to tackle an opposing argument head-on.

A question-and-answer strategy may come in especially handy when addressing counterarguments. Imagine the questions your opponents might ask of your claim or your evidence and frame your response as answers to those questions. Such a move shows that you are aware of a larger audience—those who are likely to agree with you, those who are neutral, and those who are likely to disagree with you—and that awareness in itself can make readers more open to your ideas.

That's not to say, of course, that you should ask only easy questions. Ignoring the most pressing inquiries of those who don't agree with you will make you seem as though you're afraid of their positions. However, you can *shape* your questions in ways that will allow you to answer your readers' concerns with force and elegance.

Consider Where to Respond to Objections

Finally, you might be wondering where in your essay you should address counterarguments. Ultimately, that decision depends on the organization of the specific essay you happen to be writing. However, there are three main strategies for addressing counterarguments in an academic essay:

- **Early on.** From this perspective, the best way to attend to counterarguments is to bring them up right away so that they don't have a chance to undermine your own arguments. As early as the opening paragraph or the first body paragraph, you might introduce the strongest arguments against your own way of thinking and then spend the remainder of the essay explaining why readers should find your own ideas more persuasive.

- **Throughout the essay.** Using this tactic, you would preface each of your own main points by acknowledging how others might view the situation differently. Then you would proceed through the essay by refuting those counterarguments, point by point, paragraph by paragraph.

- **Toward the end.** Perhaps the most common tactic in a short academic essay is to spend your first two to four paragraphs arguing for your point of view. You then pause and acknowledge the validity of other ideas before concluding with one more paragraph of your own, which generally highlights your strongest argument. You can see an example of what this strategy looks like in the graphic organizer in DIY 11.4b.

DIY 11.4a Outline and Refute Counterarguments to Your Position

Write a sentence or two describing *each* of the strongest counterarguments to your own position. Then go back and try and refute each of those counterarguments with a short paragraph in support of your own argument.

DIY 11.4b Plan Your Argument with a Graphic Organizer

Most writers benefit from (1) the process of writing something out and (2) being able to see what their thoughts look like on the page. See where you are with your argument by organizing your points graphically, making sure to include evidence for each of the reasons that supports your claim. Note that there is no best place for responding to counterarguments.

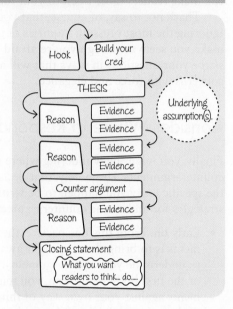

11.5 Recognizing Logical Fallacies

If you can make your opponent's argument seem irrational while your position appears reasonable, you will maintain a clear advantage in the eyes of most academic readers. Therefore, one of the most effective ways of countering an argument you don't embrace is to demonstrate that it has a fundamental flaw in its logic. There are hundreds of logical fallacies—more than can be covered here—but most of them result from a claim that is unproven or unprovable.

One of the most common forms of logical fallacy is the **False or Faulty Syllogism**. A syllogism draws a conclusion from two given propositions or premises. As its name suggests, a false syllogism begins from a false premise. For example:

- Irma is blinking rapidly while she talks to me. (premise)

- People who lie often blink rapidly. (premise)

- Therefore, Irma is lying to me. (conclusion)

As you can see, this faulty syllogism relies on the false assumption that everyone who blinks rapidly is also lying. While Irma *might* be lying to the speaker, she could also be blinking because she has an eye infection or has something in her eye. Relying on a "false inference" results in a conclusion that can't be trusted.

You can often sense that an argument is fallacious, even if you can't quite name what's wrong with it. Indeed, while it's good to be able to identify logical fallacies by name—like those listed below—it's even more important to simply keep your "b.s. detector" in the *On* position whenever you are making or responding to an argument.

Ad Hominem **Attack.** *Ad hominem* is Latin for "to the man" and refers to an attack against the character of a person rather than a critique of that person's argument. For example, if I say, "Larry can't be an advocate for equal rights because he cheats on his wife," I am shifting away from the main focus of the debate and centering it instead on Larry's moral failings.

Bandwagon Appeal. A bandwagon is, as its name suggest, a wagon with a band playing on it. Back in the nineteenth century, politicians would drive horse-drawn wagons through town, hoping people would literally jump on board and support the politician. In today's terms, a bandwagon appeal refers to the idea that because everyone else is going along with something you should, too—even if you know you shouldn't.

Begging the Question. Nowadays, people often use the phrase "That *begs* the question" to mean "That *raises* the question." Actually, in the world of logical fallacies, begging the question is a circular argument in which the arguer assumes that what they are trying to prove is already true, usually by verbal trickery. For instance: "Everyone knows the free press cannot be trusted." There is no argument here, only an assertion that is supported by the assertion itself.

Either-Or **Reasoning.** This fallacy asserts that there are only two possible and completely opposite options for responding to an issue, when, in fact, there are plenty of options somewhere in the middle. "Unless everyone adopts a presumption of good faith in conversation, college campuses will lapse into violent anarchy" is an example of *either-or* reasoning.

False Analogy. This fallacy occurs when comparing two ideas or objects that seem to be the same, but are, in fact, significantly different. You might, for instance, say, "Because Twitter puts restrictions on what its users post, the government should place similar restrictions on the free press." However, while both Twitter and the free press are instruments of communication, Twitter is a single, private corporation, and the free press is a vast complex of organizations that have long been protected by the Constitution's First Amendment.

Hasty Generalization. As you might guess from its name, this fallacy involves jumping to a conclusion that is based on faulty evidence. If, for example, you were having a picnic at the beach and a seagull swooped down and pecked you on the head, you would not—as traumatic as the incident might have been—be able to conclude that all seagulls attack humans.

Oversimplifying. As the word implies, oversimplification is the fallacy of boiling a complex set of factors down to a single easy answer. Claiming, for example, that the cause of homelessness is a lack of motivation on the part of people experiencing homelessness would be to ignore other factors such as substance abuse, unemployment, systemic poverty, lack of affordable housing, domestic violence, and many others. When an issue is complicated, it's best to talk about a single cause as, at most, "contributing to" or being "part of" the overall problem.

Post hoc ergo propter hoc. This Latin phrase translates as "after this, therefore because of this." The fallacy here is that just because one thing happened after another one did, the first thing *caused* the second. Returning to the scene at the beach described earlier, suppose on the morning before you were attacked by the seagull, you wrote an angry letter to your local newspaper condemning seagulls as "dirty scavengers." As much as the subsequent attack might seem "poetic justice"—that is, you got what you deserved—writing the nasty letter about seagulls had nothing to do with your being bitten by one.

Red Herring. The idea of a red herring goes back several hundred years to the practice of dragging a red herring (a salted, smoked fish) in front of a pack of bloodhounds to lead them off the track of the person they were pursuing. Consequently, a red herring is any tactic a writer uses to divert readers from a more important issue.

Slippery Slope. This argument suggests that one event will inevitably lead to another event that is much worse. For instance: "If one instructor allows a student to turn in a late essay, pretty soon all students will expect the same treatment from all instructors and no student will ever turn in an essay on time again." Allowing one student to turn in a late paper one time might mean others would ask for the same consideration; that doesn't mean no essays would ever again be turned in on time.

Straw Man. Like a scarecrow in a cornfield, a straw man isn't a real person. A straw man argument is a claim—often through extreme exaggeration—that someone else is making an argument that the person has not actually made. Suppose, for instance, after a school shooting, a proponent of gun control says, "We need to have stricter background checks to keep guns out of the hands of mentally unstable individuals." If someone were to reply, "So, you want to take away all our guns and overturn the Second Amendment," that second person would be engaging in a straw man argument by grossly misrepresenting what the first person really said.

To learn more about logical fallacies and how some writers try to cheat the dictates of logic, search online using the keywords "logical fallacies" and "site:.edu."

DIY 11.5 Identify Logical Fallacies

If you have completed a draft of your essay, reread it and see if you can spot any logical fallacies. Eliminate those you find. If you're still working on your essay, take another look at "The Presumption of Good Faith in Campus Conversation" (11.1) and try to locate one or more logical fallacies.

An Invitation to Read: An Argument Essay

Long before she was an award-winning investigative reporter for *The New York Times*, Nikole Hannah-Jones was a high school writer who wrote convincingly about her own experiences with desegregation in her Iowa town. Today, Hannah-Jones covers civil rights and racial justice issues and is the recipient of a 2020 Pulitzer Prize for Commentary and a 2020 National Magazine Award for podcasting. In the following except of her essay, "The Idea of America," she argues that the year 1619, which marked the first arrival of enslaved Africans to the American colonies, should be considered every bit as "important to the American story" as the year 1776.

The Idea of America (excerpt)

NIKOLE HANNAH-JONES

1   My dad always flew an American flag in our front yard. The blue paint on our two-story house was perennially chipping; the fence, or the rail by the stairs, or the front door, existed in a perpetual state of disrepair, but that flag always flew pristine. Our corner lot, which had been redlined by the federal government, was along the river that divided the black side from the white side of our Iowa town. At the edge of our lawn, high on an aluminum pole, soared the flag, which my dad would replace as soon as it showed the slightest tatter.

2   So when I was young, that flag outside our home never made sense to me. How could this black man, having seen firsthand the way his country abused black Americans, how it refused to treat us as full citizens, proudly fly its banner? I didn't understand his patriotism. It deeply embarrassed me.

3   I had been taught, in school, through cultural osmosis, that the flag wasn't really ours, that our history as a people began with enslavement and that we had contributed little to this great nation. It seemed that the closest thing black Americans could have to cultural pride was to be found in our vague connection to Africa, a place we had never been. That my dad felt so much honor in being an American felt like a marker of his degradation, his acceptance of our subordination.

4   Like most young people, I thought I understood so much, when in fact I understood so little. My father knew exactly what he was doing when he raised that flag. He knew that our people's contributions to building the richest and most powerful nation in the world were indelible, that the United States simply would not exist without us.

Brent N. Clarke/Getty Images

5   In August 1619, just 12 years after the English settled Jamestown, Va., one year before the Puritans landed at Plymouth Rock and some 157 years before the English colonists even decided they wanted to form their own country, the Jamestown colonists bought 20 to 30 enslaved Africans from English pirates. The pirates had stolen them from a Portuguese slave ship that had forcibly taken them from what is now the country of Angola. Those men and women who came ashore on that August day were the beginning of American slavery. They were among the 12.5 million Africans who would be kidnapped from their homes and brought in chains across the Atlantic Ocean in the largest forced migration in human history until the Second World War. Almost two million did not survive the grueling journey, known as the Middle Passage.

6   Before the abolishment of the international slave trade, 400,000 enslaved Africans would be sold into America. Those individuals and their descendants transformed the lands to which they'd been brought into some of the most successful colonies in the British Empire. Through back-breaking labor, they cleared the land across the Southeast. They taught the colonists to grow rice. They grew and picked the cotton that at the height of slavery was the nation's most valuable commodity, accounting for half of all American exports and 66 percent of the world's supply. They built the plantations of George Washington, Thomas Jefferson and James Madison, sprawling properties that today attract thousands of visitors from across the globe captivated by the history of the world's greatest democracy. They laid the foundations of the White House and the Capitol, even placing with their unfree hands the Statue of Freedom atop the Capitol dome. They lugged the heavy wooden tracks of the railroads that crisscrossed the South and that helped take the cotton they picked to the Northern textile mills, fueling the Industrial Revolution. They built vast fortunes for white people North and South—at one time, the second-richest man in the nation was a Rhode Island "slave trader." Profits from black people's stolen labor helped the young nation pay off its war debts and financed some of our most prestigious universities. It was the relentless buying, selling, insuring and financing of their bodies and the products of their labor that made Wall Street a thriving banking, insurance and trading sector and New York City the financial capital of the world.

7   But it would be historically inaccurate to reduce the contributions of black people to the vast material wealth created by our bondage. Black Americans have also been, and continue to be, foundational to the idea of American freedom. More than any other group in this country's history, we have served, generation after generation, in an overlooked but vital role: It is we who have been the perfecters of this democracy.

8   The United States is a nation founded on both an ideal and a lie. Our Declaration of Independence, signed on July 4, 1776, proclaims that "all men are created equal" and "endowed by their Creator with certain unalienable rights." But the white men who drafted those words did not believe them to be true for the hundreds of thousands of black people in their

midst. "Life, Liberty and the pursuit of Happiness" did not apply to fully one-fifth of the country. Yet despite being violently denied the freedom and justice promised to all, black Americans believed fervently in the American creed. Through centuries of black resistance and protest, we have helped the country live up to its founding ideals. And not only for ourselves—black rights struggles paved the way for every other rights struggle, including women's and gay rights, immigrant and disability rights.

9 Without the idealistic, strenuous and patriotic efforts of black Americans, our democracy today would most likely look very different—it might not be a democracy at all.

10 My father . . . knew what it would take me years to understand: that the year 1619 is as important to the American story as 1776. That black Americans, as much as those men cast in alabaster in the nation's capital, are this nation's true "founding fathers." And that no people has a greater claim to that flag than us.

Reading Questions

1. The American flag is a potent symbol in "The Idea of America." What does the flag mean to the writer's father? What does it symbolize to Hannah-Jones as a child, and, much later, as the adult woman who writes this essay?

2. In paragraph 6, Hannah-Jones lists the many contributions of enslaved Africans and their descendants to the success of the colonies. Which of those do you find to be the strongest reasoning for her statement in her last sentence that "no people has a greater claim to that flag than [black Americans]"?

3. Identify the writer's use of *logos, ethos,* and *pathos*—one instance of each. Which type of appeal do you find is most successful in this essay?

An Invitation to Read: A Student Argument Essay

"The Crown Juul of Addiction" is student Ethan Fischer's response to the rise in popularity of the electronic cigarettes known as Juuls. The essay began as a response to Ethan's interaction with his "Juuling" roommate and quickly became a well-reasoned and well-researched argumentative essay. According to Ethan, "I knew, more or less, my personal opinion, but I wanted to see a bigger picture with statistics and research. One thing that was really helpful was I started a Works Cited page right away, and each time I quoted a source, I immediately looked up how to do the MLA citation for it. When I finished drafting, I didn't have to go back and do all the citations at once, which normally takes me a long time."

Fischer 1

Ethan Fischer

Professor Starkey

Engl 110

20 March 2020

The Crown Juul of Addiction

One Saturday morning at the beginning of first semester, I walked into the kitchen of my apartment to see my new roommate, Jacob Wheeler, sitting at the table with his laptop open, puffing on what looked like a USB drive. "Dude," I told him. "No smoking, remember? It's in the lease." "I'm not smoking," he replied. "It's a Juul." And with that, we had a long conversation about whether or not vaping on a Juul was the same thing as smoking. Jacob argued that it was better; I argued that it was worse. You might wonder why I care. Well, two of my grandparents, people I was very close to as a child, died of lung cancer, and I don't want to see the same kind of addiction taking over my generation. Addiction to opioid drugs has taken center stage in the US, and with good reason, but any kind of addiction can be dangerous and destructive, especially for young people. Sales of Juul vaporizers should be immediately halted because this type of e-cigarette gets people addicted to nicotine, starts young e-smokers on the path to traditional tobacco cigarettes, and keeps people from taking the final, healthy step of quitting smoking altogether.

E-cigarettes are a delivery method for high-concentration nicotine, which should be more concerning than it appears to be. Writing in *Medical News Today*, editor Adam Felman says that while "not cancer-causing or excessively harmful on its own, nicotine is heavily addictive and exposes people to the extremely harmful effects of tobacco dependency." According to *WebMD*, nicotine withdrawal symptoms "may include headaches, anxiety, nausea, and tobacco cravings." Other than a giving you a buzz, which my roommate Jacob describes as "not

Opening dialogue engages readers.

Thesis statement presents the writer's position.

Topic sentences focuses the paragraph.

Specific evidence supports the writer's line of reasoning.

Fischer 2

lasting very long, especially when you get used to it," nicotine doesn't serve much of a purpose. And yet, journalist Ben Tobin reports that "Juuls use nicotine salts, which exist in tobacco and contain a higher concentration of nicotine than many liquids in other e-cigarette brands." In fact, this hyper-dose of nicotine recently led Israel to ban the import and sale of Juul e-cigarettes because, according to the Israeli Health Ministry, the Juul pods contain "nicotine at a concentration higher than 20 milligrams per milliliter" and therefore pose "a grave risk to public health" ("Israel"). Not surprisingly, Juul representatives fired back, saying Juul was "incredibly disappointed" because Juul is "a true alternative to combustible cigarettes" ("Israel"). The question, though, is *why* do we need an alternative to tobacco cigarettes that is basically a nicotine delivery machine?

Even if addiction to nicotine might seem basically harmless, there is plenty to worry about when we think of vaping as a gateway habit. A team of researchers from the University of Pittsburgh published a study in the *Journal of the American Medical Association* that found "Young adults who use electronic cigarettes are more than four times as likely to begin smoking tobacco cigarettes within 18 months as their peers who do not vape. . . . The findings demonstrate that e-cigarettes are serving as a gateway to traditional smoking, contrary to their purported value as a smoking cessation tool" ("E-Cig Use"). Even Jacob admits that although he knows traditional cigarettes can cause cancer, vapers "get to a point where the buzz from a Juul just isn't strong enough, and you really want a cigarette. So I've been smoking cigarettes a lot more, especially when I'm partying." The trend is worrisome.

Unfortunately, young people do not seem worried at all, and vaping is popular in school and social settings. My younger sister is a high school junior in San Diego. I emailed her for a reaction to Tobin's findings about high school students in Connecticut,

Includes a quotation from an unpaginated web source.

A short form of the title is given in parentheses for a source with no author listed.

Addresses a counterargument.

Quotations from experts and from a personal contact support the thesis.

The writer uses an emotional appeal.

Fischer 3

who, according to a teacher Tobin interviewed, spend "copious amounts of time in the bathroom." These kids were Juuling, and the "bathrooms would become 'little tent cities'…with kids bringing blankets and sitting on the sinks." My sister said she hasn't seen any "tent cities" in the bathrooms of our high school, but she did say, "Juuling is everywhere. Most people don't even bother to go to the bathroom, they just do it between classes, or at lunch. Sometimes you see people Juuling in the back of the classroom when the teacher's back is turned" (Fischer). More research is necessary, but based on two observations, it seems as though the concerns about how widespread vaping is among young people may have some foundation in reality.

But what does the company itself have to say about all the controversy? Here's the mission statement from Juul Labs (which refers to the product as JUUL but the company as Juul): "Juul was founded by former smokers, James and Adam, with the goal of improving the lives of the one billion adult smokers. We envision a world where fewer people use cigarettes, and where people who smoke cigarettes have the tools to reduce or eliminate their consumption entirely, should they so desire." Vaping is seen by the founders and some others as a means to decrease smoking, certainly a positive goal given the number of deaths related to smoking habits. While Juul Labs's mission statement sounds like a generous and worthwhile goal, research shows that a much better alternative to vaping on e-cigarettes and *hoping* to end addiction to smoking is just to stop smoking, period. Dr. Nicola Lindson-Hawley of Oxford University says, "With addictions other than smoking, we aim to get people to cut down gradually rather than stop abruptly. But with smoking, the norm is to advise people to stop all at once" (qtd. in Costa). Dr. Lindson-Hawley's recommendations are based in part on a study published in the *Annals of Internal Medicine* that showed that while 39.2 percent of

The writer engages with the source and pushes back.

Fischer 4

study participants in the gradual group remained smoke-free, 49 percent who abruptly quit remained smoke-free (Costa). In other words, the longer you take to quit smoking, the less likely you are going to be able to do it, which undercuts the whole supposed purpose of Juuling.

Finally, you have to wonder if the founders of JUUL are really just innovating out of the kindness of their hearts. Ben Tobin speaks to the financial motive:

> Juul Labs raked in over $1.1 billion in retail sales for its e-cigarettes over the 52-week period ending July 14, according to a Wells Fargo Securities analysis of Nielsen data. In July, the company had more than 70 percent of all e-cigarette revenue, excluding online sales and sales at specialty shops, according to Nielsen.

The sizeable financial return is a really good reason why Juul Labs isn't going to stop manufacturing its product unless the government shuts the company down. I realize that will be extremely difficult and will involve hearings and legislation, but I strongly think it's worth making the effort. Legislation will help high school and college kids who don't know what they're getting into when they buy their first Juul mango pods. As Jacob said to me the other day, "Juuling is really starting to bring me down."

Not only is the habit bringing young people down, but it's destroying their lungs as well. The CDC confirmed that as of February 2020, there were nearly three thousand hospitalizations or deaths connected to E-cigarette- or Vaping-Associated Lung Injury (EVALI). The CDC further recommends that vaping products such as e-cigarettes "should never be used by youths [or] young adults." Legislation banning the sale of vaping products would be a step in the right direction from a public health perspective—especially in a year when we have more than enough public health battles to fight.

Data points provide strong evidence and a logical appeal.

Conclusion reiterates the writer's thesis and ends with a successful emotional appeal.

Fischer 5

Works Cited

Centers for Disease Control and Prevention. "Outbreak of Lung
Injury Associated with the Use of E-cigarette, or Vaping,
Products." *Smoking and Tobacco Use*, 25 Feb. 2020, www
.cdc.gov/tobacco/basic_information/e-cigarettes/severe
-lung-disease.html.

Costa, Samantha. "Health Buzz: Cold Turkey Best Way to
Quit Smoking." *U.S. News & World Report*, 15 Mar. 2016,
health.usnews.com/wellness/articles/2016-03-15/cold
-turkey-best-way-to-quit-smoking.

"E-Cig Use Increases Risk of Beginning Tobacco Cigarette Use
in Young Adults." *Pitt Health Sciences*, U of Pittsburgh
Medical Center, 11 Dec. 2017, www.upmc.com
/media/NewsReleases/2017/Pages/ecig-to-cigarette.aspx.

Feldman, Adam. "Everything You Need to Know About
Nicotine." *Medical News Today*, 11 Jan. 2018, www
.medicalnewstoday.com/articles/240820.php.

Fischer, Mia. E-mail to the author. 4 Mar. 2020.

"Israel Bans Juul Cigarettes Citing 'Grave' Public Health Risk."
Reuters, 21 Aug. 2018, www.reuters.com/article/us
-ecigarettes-israel/israel-bans-juul-e-cigarettes-citing
-grave-public-health-risk-idUSKCN1L61YW.

Juul Labs. "Our Mission." *JUUL*, 2020, www.juul.com
/mission-values.

"Nicotine Withdrawal Directory." *WebMD*, 2018, www.webmd
.com/smoking-cessation/nicotine-withdrawal-directory.

Tobin, Ben. "Back-to-School Smoking: Juul Labs E-cigarette
Sales Growth Vexes Teachers." *USA Today*, 16 Aug. 2018,
www.usatoday.com/story/money/2018/08/16/juul-labs
-back-school-teachers-e-cigarettes/917531002/.

Wheeler, Jacob. Interview with the author. 2 Mar. 2020.

Reading Questions

1. What are the main reasons the writer gives for arguing that "sales of JUUL should be immediately halted"? What evidence does he provide to support each reason?

2. Based on "The Crown Juul of Addiction," what sort of *values* do you think Ethan Fischer has? What are his underlying assumptions? What do you think his perfect world would look like?

3. Assess the writer's sources. In your opinion, which are the most, and least, effective? Explain why.

Chapter 11 Checklist
Arguing a Position

☐ **Have you found a way into your argument that allows you to write with both passion and logic?**

The best argumentative essays are usually those that grow from a writer's deep level of caring about the issue *and* a clear, compelling set of reasons and evidence for making a particular claim.

☐ **Does your essay have a clear, focused, and arguable claim?**

Crafting the central assertion of your essay so that it is persuasive, memorable, and easy to argue will help ensure that you stay on track from the first sentence to the last.

☐ **Do you have sufficient and specific reasons for your claim?**

A claim without defensible reasons is like a bird without feathers—it won't fly. Ideally, you will generate more reasons than you actually use in your essay, employing only those that are the most effective.

☐ **Is each of your reasons supported by one or more pieces of credible and convincing evidence?**

Your claim is only as compelling as the reasons for it, and your reasons are only as strong as their supporting evidence. Don't include a reason for your claim if you don't have the evidence to back it up.

☐ **Does your essay make skillful use of Aristotle's three modes of persuasion: *logos*, *ethos*, and *pathos*?**

Logic is the horsepower that will keep your argumentative essay running, but it also helps to establish yourself as a credible speaker on your topic and to include a few well-timed moments of *pathos*.

☐ **Have you carefully considered—and conceded, qualified, or refuted—each of the most persuasive counterarguments to your claim?**

A big part of writing a strong argument is knowing its flaws and anticipating where readers will be most skeptical. Rather than ignoring potential counterarguments, identify and directly respond to those that are most likely to undercut your claim.

☐ **Have you looked for and eliminated logical fallacies from your essay?**

Remember that while it's helpful to be able to name a flaw in your, or your opponent's, argument, it's even more important to know a logical fallacy when you see it and to be able to explain why it is a problem.

11.6 Making It Stick

How will you argue a position with reason and evidence?

Working Together

11.6a Reviewing a Draft Argument   In a small group, take turns sharing (1) the **claim** you are making in your draft, (2) the **reasons** you are making the claim, and (3) the **evidence** you have to support your reasons. If your instructor has given you draft goals, keep those in mind during the review.

Listen carefully when peers discuss their drafts. If you are critiquing the argument, be kind and respectful — say what you think is going well, but don't let the author off easily if the claim, reasons, or evidence seem less than persuasive. Your goals are to ask questions, identify holes in the writer's argument, and suggest ways of strengthening the claim or the reasons.

When your draft is up for discussion, take careful notes, and don't be upset if the people in your group find weak spots in your argument. People with a growth mindset (see Section 3.2) see such discussions as opportunities to improve.

Applying What You Know

11.6b The Doubter and the Believer   Find two people with whom you are willing to share a draft. They could be family members, peers, or classmates. Assign one person to be "the Doubter," someone who is skeptical of every claim; assign the second to be "the Believer," someone who looks for reasons to believe any claim, no matter how far-fetched.

After you share your draft, ask the Doubter and the Believer to go to work. The Doubter looks for holes in the essay's argument and gaps in its logic, while the Believer finds moments in the essay that inspire trust and confidence.

Ask the two to switch roles and see if anything else comes up. Take notes on the conversation with the goal of identifying the essay's weakest and strongest moments.

11.6c Bolstering Your Argument with Further Evidence   Review each of the main points of your essay. Do you have the kinds of evidence you want? Continue to search for one more piece of evidence to support each of the main parts of your argument. Look at gaps in your evidence. Do you have enough data? Is there an opportunity for a visual? Are there perspectives you might still need to represent? (For example, if you are writing about voter suppression in poor immigrant communities, do you need to add the voices of those community members in your essay?)

Compare your new evidence with what you currently have in the essay. Are the new pieces of evidence strong enough to *add* to your essay? Could they replace one or more pieces of evidence that you are currently using?

11.6d En-Titled   On your own or with a peer, describe in three to four sentences your topic and your argument. Then brainstorm titles for the essay — keeping in mind what you want your audience to think, feel, or do after they finish reading. Take another look at Section 7.4 and try to come up with something that's catchy without being silly or sensational — the sort of title that would make a reader want to dive right into the essay.

Invitations to Write

11.6e It Could Be Better

Shorter: Make a list of five aspects of life that you think could be better. These could be big things, like eliminating the widespread emission of greenhouse gasses, or small things, such as changing the unfair work schedule at your job. Then look at your list and choose the one that's

the most important to you personally. Write a couple of paragraphs about *why* the thing you chose could be better.

Longer: Transform your initial ideas into an essay that argues for the importance of your chosen issue. Your claim should be supported by clear and compelling reasons, each of which should be reinforced by persuasive evidence.

11.6f Against the Truth

Shorter: Make a list of five things that you *don't* believe in or that you have serious reservations about. Choose the one you find the most offensive and explain why it goes so deeply against your way of thinking.

Longer: Then write a piece arguing *in favor of* the very issue you disbelieve. Do your best to identify the most compelling reasons and evidence in support of the issue and write your essay in such a way that it sounds as though you are, indeed, a true advocate.

Open-Topic Essay Ideas   If your instructor has given you an open-ended assignment, and you're still search for something to write about, do an online search for "401 Prompts for Argumentative Writing," a list that is periodically updated by the staff of *The New York Times* Learning Network. The prompts cover issues from social media and video games to gender and politics and are deliberately phrased to allow for a wide range of opinions — from very progressive to very conservative.

12
Proposing a Solution

REFLECT

Write Before You Read | Activity to connect what's new with what you already know 275

READ & WRITE

DIY (Do-it-yourself) activities offer just-in-time support for all the skills in this book.

REFLECT

Write Before You Read   Think about a few problems you've had in your life outside of school — maybe you've had a boss that treated you unfairly, you wanted to buy something that you couldn't afford, or your best friend moved to a different town. Most likely you've had to come up with one or more ways to solve a real-world problem. With a recent experience in mind, describe your process for finding a solution to a problem.

12.1 Solving Problems

It tough when you don't get enough Likes on your Instagram post. Fortunately, that's a problem about which the Internet has lots of advice: use more popular hashtags, take better photos, partner with a brand, tag the accounts of powerful people, and on, and on. So, there's the problem and the set of solutions for your next essay, right? You're practically finished right now.

Actually, no. If you take a step back and ask yourself if increasing the popularity of your personal Instagram account is a problem worthy of an academic essay, you'll probably have to admit that it's not. All right, you might be thinking, *if Instagram is too trivial, I'll go for something extremely serious, like "World Hunger and How to End It."* Unfortunately, that's a problem that has been around about as long as people have lived on the planet, and no one has solved it yet. Granted, people do have ideas, but just describing the problem would require far more words than your instructor has allotted for this essay, and it would take even longer to explain how any solutions might address such a long-entrenched problem.

In short, while boosting the profile of your Instagram account and ending world hunger are problems for which solutions could be proposed, neither topic fits the scope of a typical brief academic essay. Not to worry: There is still a range of issues out there worth both your (and your reader's!) time, energy, and attention.

As you begin to imagine a topic for this essay, try to think of problems that

- matter to you personally *and* to people you don't know
- are significant, yet limited in scope
- might be solved on a local level

Of course, your instructor may have already assigned you a very specific problem for this assignment. If that's the case, you'll still need to work on breaking the problem down into its separate parts, searching for the best possible solutions and considering alternatives.

DIY 12.1 Choose a Problem to Solve

Write a paragraph in which you summarize the problem you hope to solve and the most logical solution(s) you have. If you have been assigned a prompt, your response should focus on what your instructor has asked you to do. If you've been given some leeway to choose an issue, use the guidelines in 12.1 to sketch out a problem and its possible solution(s).

UP FRONT: Identifying a Problem and Proposing a Solution

The Assignment

Write an essay in which you identify a problem and propose a solution. The chapter guidance, examples, and DIY prompts will help you complete the assignment. Follow your instructor's notes about length and formatting. Keep these guidelines in mind as you choose a problem to solve.

Identify a problem that you want to see solved. Think about the things that upset you the most. If you could solve any problem in the world today, what would it be? As always, when you're writing about something that really matters to you, you are more likely to make it matter to your readers.

Narrow the problem so that it can be reasonably covered in a short academic essay. Eliminating gun violence in America is a pressing national problem, but you're not going to be able to present the problem and solve it in a short academic essay. Instead, try to zero in on one particular aspect of the issue, like trying to broaden background checks in your state to restrict gun sales to people with mental illness.

Propose a realistic solution. Writing about a problem that has no credible solution will only cause you frustration for this assignment. Even if your solution won't be easy to achieve, it should still be *possible*.

An Invitation to Read: A Proposal Essay

Bethany Brookshire has a BS in biology and a BA in philosophy from the College of William and Mary, and a PhD in physiology and pharmacology from Wake Forest University School of Medicine. She is the guest editor of *The Open Laboratory Anthology of Science Blogging*, 2009, and the winner of the Society for Neuroscience Next Generation Award and the Three Quarks Daily Science Writing Award, among others. "Why People Don't Vote, and What to Do About It" was published in *Science News* on November 4, 2016, just four days before the presidential election. Interestingly, while Brookshire briefly mentions the 2016 candidates in her introduction, her focus is on solving the larger problem of getting Americans to vote, still a challenge in smaller elections. Note that in 2020, voter turnout for the presidential election was more than 66%.

Why People Don't Vote, and What to Do about It

BETHANY BROOKSHIRE

adamkaz/Getty Images

Critical Reading Tip

In order to evaluate how effective a writer's solutions are for a given problem, it's important to identify each problem and proposed solution. One way to make sure you have all the evidence in front of you is to put it in a single document. You can practice with this article by creating a document with two columns. On one side, list all the problems Brookshire identifies; on the other side, list her solutions. Then, below the columns, assess whether you think the solutions will solve the problems.

1   On November 8 [2016], millions of voters will turn out to decide whether Hillary Clinton or Donald Trump will be the next president of the United States. And millions of eligible voters will just stay home.

2   Voter turnout in the United States is incredibly low compared to other modern democracies. In the 2012 presidential election, 53.6 percent of the voting-age population turned out to vote [and in 2016, the turnout was 58.1 percent].

This puts the United States well behind countries such as Turkey (84.3 percent turnout in 2015) and Belgium (87.2 percent in 2014), where voting is compulsory. But the U.S. also lags behind other countries with voluntary voting, such as Sweden (82.6 percent turnout in 2014), France (71.6 percent in 2012) and many others. In fact, the U.S. ranks 31st out of 35 developed countries in voter turnout, according to a recent Pew Research Center study.

3   It's a little surprising that Americans are such unenthusiastic voters because they are fairly interested in politics, notes Mert Moral, a political scientist at the State University of New York at Binghamton. "If you look at survey data you find more Americans are equally if not more engaged than their counterparts [in other countries]," he says. "They have bumper stickers, they talk about politics [and] they are interested in political topics at the local level."

4   Why don't people vote? Below are four well-studied reasons why people may not head to the polls on November 8, followed by four tactics to get more people to go to the ballot box.

Voter registration takes work.

5   In many countries, people are automatically registered to vote. Not so in the United States. "The U.S. system puts the burden on the voter," says Barry Burden, a political scientist at the University of Wisconsin–Madison. A 2012 Pew Research Center study reported that 51 million eligible citizens aren't registered to vote. Easier registration could bring that number down and, hopefully, boost the number of people who vote. In a 2013 study in the *American Journal of Political Science*, Burden and his colleagues showed that over the 2004 and 2008 presidential elections, allowing people to register to vote at the polls on Election Day increased voter turnout.

Lack of a college education—and all that comes with it.

6   The single biggest predictor of whether or not people will vote, Burden says, is education level, which has direct and indirect effects on voting. "People are more likely to vote if they have information about the candidates and the process of voting, higher levels of income and education, find themselves living and working in networks of other people who vote," he says. "Other people who are disadvantaged in those ways are much less likely."

Two parties may not be enough.

7   In a two-party system, people might not be able to find someone who represents their views. And if they don't, Moral says, they might just stay home. "A third-party candidate can't win an election here," he says. "This makes people vote for major party candidates or they don't turn out at all."

People get burned out, and sometimes just don't care.

8   There are some people who just don't care about politics. Some people who don't vote are people "in social groups [that don't] really regard politics as an important issue," explains Eyal Winter, an economist at the University of Leicester in England and the Hebrew University of Jerusalem in Israel. And strictly rationally, he notes, "it makes no sense to vote." It's very rare for a single vote to change the outcome of an election, and most cases are limited to small, local races. Most of the time, your personal vote just isn't going to make a difference. Why bother?

9   And too many elections might make voters face burnout. "One of the things that makes the U.S. strange is that there [are] a lot of elections," says Burden. "We ask voters to make a lot of decisions." Getting out to the polls can be a hassle, and learning about every single issue takes time. "We have a complicated system and I think that produces fatigue."

What works in getting people to the polls?

10   No matter what the party, politicians and many citizens want to see their side turn out as much as possible. Facebook users plead with their friends. Politicians hire phone banks to call thousands of people in battle-ground states. Celebrities beg over YouTube. But four main methods seem to stand out.

Educate early and often, and make voting mandatory.

11   The messages people receive early in life have a strong impact on whether people vote, says Donald Green, a political scientist at Columbia University in New York City. It helps if parents and teachers let kids know "voting is important—it's what makes you a functioning adult." This message may come through in civics and government classes.

12   More education increases the likelihood of voter turnout. But one does not simply send everyone to college to boost voting. Another way to increase turnout is to make it required. Using data from 28 advanced countries, Aina Gallego, a political scientist at the Institute of Public Goods and Policies at the University of Barcelona in Spain, showed in a 2010 study that compulsory voting reduced inequalities in education and voter turnout—simply because everyone had to go do it.

13   Unfortunately, you can lead voters to the polls, but you can't make them have an opinion on the candidates. Moral examined 18 European party systems and found that compulsory voting goes hand in hand with increased numbers of spoiled and invalid ballots—slashing through them,

turning them in blank, or writing in a candidate like "Mickey Mouse." Not voting may result in a fine, but it's also costly to get informed on the issues, he says. The net result is that politically uninformed people may "go out to vote, they don't know who to vote for and they spoil their ballot." Moral published his results August 9 in *Political Research Quarterly*.

Peer pressure people to the polls.

14 A healthy dose of name-and-shame can have a big effect on Election Day. In a 2008 study in *American Political Science Review*, Green and his colleagues applied a little social pressure to voters. They sent 180,000 people in Michigan (where voting records are publicly available) a series of mailings before the August 2006 Republican primary for the state elections.

15 Simply asking people to vote resulted in a 1.8 percentage point increase in turnout. Asking people to vote and notifying them that they were being studied—and that their votes were a matter of public record—increased turnout by 2.5 percentage points. But when the mailings also displayed the voter's previous voting behavior to the voter and other people in their household, there was a 4.9 percentage point increase in voter turnout compared with people who didn't get a mailing. If the voters were then also shown their neighbors' voting records, there was an 8.1 percentage point bump in voter turnout.

16 But while shame may get out the vote, Green cautions that it probably also burns bridges. "I think it produces backlash," he says, the most heavy-handed naming and shaming especially. In their study, Green and his colleagues noticed that people who received the most shame-heavy mailings also tended to call the number on the mailings—and demand to be left alone.

17 More positive peer pressure might prove effective without the dose of shame, Green notes. Get people to pledge that they'll show up, and remind them that voting is a matter of public record. "Maybe the most effective is a close friend or coworker who says 'let's walk to the polls together,'" he says.

A little healthy competition never hurt.

18 They don't call elections "races" for nothing. In a 2006 study looking at U.S. gubernatorial races from 1990 to 2005, Winter and his colleague Esteban Klor at the Hebrew University of Jerusalem looked at differences between who was leading in the polls prior to elections and the voting results for those races. They found that when polling numbers are close, voter turnout increases, especially for the side with the slight majority in the poll. "It's nicer to support your team when you're expected to win," Winter

explains. Close races, while nail-biting for candidates and voters alike, might make people turn out in higher numbers.

19 But of course, if you want to have healthy competition, it's best to have likeable candidates. When it comes to the upcoming presidential race, Burden says he would not be surprised if turnout is even lower than usual. "That's where things are pushing," he says. "We know surveys have shown these two nominees have lower favorability ratings than any two other nominees in the history of polling." Those low favorability ratings may keep people away on Election Day.

The personal touch is best.

20 Hundreds of nonpartisan, bipartisan and partisan studies have been done on how to win campaigns and influence people, looking at everything from the cost per vote of robo-calls to how to craft the perfect email subject line. But the most effective message is face-to-face and one-on-one, says Green, who, along with colleague Alan Gerber of Yale University, wrote the book, *Get Out the Vote: How to Increase Voter Turnout.*

21 For politicians, this means getting out and canvassing the streets. But maybe someone just wants to get their sister, friend or spouse to vote. In that case, he says "the most effective message would be to express your own interest in the election, your own desire to vote and your own desire to see them vote." Getting them to vote the way you want them to, however? That's a different matter.

Reading Questions

1. Take another look at "Why People Don't Vote, and What to Do About It" and rank the four problems and the four solutions from 1 (Most Important) to 4 (Least Important). Then discuss why you ranked the problems and solutions as you did. Refer to specific evidence in the appropriate sections to support your conclusions.

2. Identify each piece of concrete evidence Brookshire offers to make her point (use e-book tools or digital markup tools if you're reading the article in an e-book). How much does Brookshire rely on her sources to discuss the problems and solutions of voter turnout? How much of the essay is composed of her own opinion?

3. Think of one additional problem that causes a lack of voter turnout and one more solution for that problem. How do your alternative problem and solution stack up against Brookshire's? What evidence would you use to argue that your problem and solution are more significant than the ones she names?

12.2 Identifying and Investigating a Problem

The basis for many argumentative essays is the idea that something is wrong and it needs to be made right. When you're arguing a position, your focus is on calling out the problem and explaining why it needs to be solved. When you're proposing a solution, however, your emphasis is at least as much on the solution as on the problem.

Therefore, as you begin to think about the problem you want to discuss solving, you'll also want to be aware of whether or not there's a reasonable chance of being able to fix it. Indeed, the ideal problem for this essay is one that you can see clearly and—in part because you have substantial interest—one that you believe you know how to solve.

Choosing a problem you know well and which you have a strong idea of how to solve is like riding a bicycle downhill. Sure, you have to steer and brake, but much of the work is being done for you by the force of gravity. If, on the other hand, you choose a problem that you don't know much about and that's hard to solve, you're like a bicyclist laboring up a steep hill. A great deal of your energy is going to be expended just making sure that you move forward, and in the time it takes a downhill cyclist to zoom from top to bottom, you'll still be creeping up the hill's lower reaches.

Questions for Identifying a Suitable Problem to Write About

To make sure yours is a problem that will make a suitable topic for an essay, here are a few questions worth asking:

1. **Is the problem worth solving?** Trivial problems, like getting the best price on your next pair of shoes, can be solvable, but they don't normally deserve the focus of an entire college-level essay. Write about something that has real-world implications for the people affected by it.

2. **Can you write confidently about the problem?** You don't have to be an expert in regard to your problem, but you should be able to discuss it with some authority—and sometimes lived experience will provide a meaningful perspective. The more thoroughly you know your problem, the more confidence your reader will have in you as a potential problem solver. If you want, for instance, to write about how to more fairly allocate hours and wages to workers in the fast-food industry, having worked for three years at Burger King makes you especially credible on the topic.

3. **Can you clearly envision at least one workable solution?** While the solutions to a problem are often discovered during the research process, it's risky to choose a problem that you don't see any way of solving at the outset. That doesn't mean you shouldn't investigate an issue that you feel passionately about, but you should be able to foresee a reasonable way of dealing with the problem. If you want to solve the bicycle traffic jams that occur on campus between classes, for example, it would be helpful to begin with, say, the idea of a bike-sharing program, even if that doesn't turn out to be one of solutions you ultimately suggest in your final draft.

4. **Can you write about a local version of the problem?** Bethany Brookshire's essay takes on the national problem of voter apathy in the United States. If you feel that a national or international version of your problem is too big to handle in a short college essay, consider focusing on a similar problem closer to home. You could, for instance, address the lack of voter engagement in your own community or even on your own campus. Local problems are sometimes easier to fix than national or global problems, and your local readers—including your instructor—may find themselves more engaged by your topic.

DIY 12.2 Research the Problem

Take a look at the list you made earlier of at least five problems you think need to be solved. Ask the four questions identified in Section 12.2, then choose the problem that seems most suitable as a topic for this essay. Do 20 to 30 minutes of quick online research on the problem, taking notes on your findings, and thinking about how your findings line up with your own ideas. Does your problem appear to have one or more reasonable solutions? Can you find or think of a *local* version of the problem to solve? If the first problem you select doesn't seem like a good fit for this assignment, research a different problem until you find one you think will work.

12.3 Breaking Down and Narrowing the Problem

Even relatively simple problems can usually be broken down into smaller parts, and complex problems inevitably have complex causes. Separating the elements that make up your problem is often the first step toward discovering your essay's structure.

Bethany Brookshire, for example, isolates four smaller aspects of the larger problem of people staying away from the voting booth:

1. Voter registration takes work.

2. People without a college education are less likely to vote.

3. Two parties may not be enough.

4. People get burned out and sometimes just don't care.

These four parts of the problem of voter turnout not only become the first four sections of "Why People Don't Vote, and What to Do About It"; they also guide the writer toward the four solutions that she offers in the second half of her essay.

In addition to assisting you in envisioning the structure of your essay, breaking the problem down into smaller parts may also lead you to the insight that you want to focus on only *one* aspect of the problem. Writing about a local version of a national problem can provide you with a much more manageable topic—and so can concentrating on a single side of a multifaceted problem.

Suppose, for instance, that you—with good reason—feel climate change is the most severe and pressing problem facing all living things. You would be right to want to address the issue head on, but climate change is a *big* problem with many different facets. Instead of trying to solve the problem of climate change, you would do better to progressively narrow your topic down to a manageable angle. Here's an example of that process:

> Climate change ⇒ Extreme storms ⇒ Hurricane Harvey ⇒ Lack of hurricane preparation for Hurricane Harvey

Writing about the lack of hurricane preparation in metropolitan areas and how to solve the problem before the arrival of the next hurricane could make a strong essay. However, as the example above suggests, you could keep narrowing the topic. If you lived in an area affected by the storm, you might make the scope of your essay very local.

DIY 12.3a
Narrow the Problem

Follow the example in 12.3 (climate change to hurricane prep) and look for ways to limit the scope of the problem you have chosen to write about. Keep narrowing it down until you can envision a specific and realistic solution for the problem.

Take an Even Closer Look

Once you have a problem that (1) interests you, (2) seems solvable, and (3) is about the right scope for your essay assignment, you'll want to dig deeper into its background and causes. The more you know about your problem, the more you'll be able to describe its key elements and disregard aspects that are irrelevant to your essay—both of which will help you to present more convincing solutions. Therefore, it's worth asking the following questions:

1. **How long has the problem been around?** Frequently, problems arise because something that had previously been stable changes. Being able to pinpoint when school shootings became so much deadlier, for instance, might help you locate at least one of the sources of our current catastrophic situation.

2. **Who or what is causing the problem?** Once you've found out when a problem began or intensified, you'll want to know its cause. While complex problems have complex foundations, if you dig deep enough, you can usually find a person or idea or policy or phenomenon that not only initiated the problem but keeps it alive and well. You are on your way to satisfactorily answering the *Who?* and *What?* of your problem if you can identify its *major* source in a single sentence.

3. **How bad is the problem?** You know that an inconsequential problem isn't worth writing about, and an intractable problem *can't* be written about. Gauging the severity of your problem can help you decide whether or not it's right as a topic for your essay. Again, focusing on a single aspect of a larger problem—such as how to respond to extreme storms rather than how to eliminate climate change—will often help you find a topic appropriate for this assignment.

4. **Why hasn't the problem been solved yet?** Human beings are ingenious creatures, and it's the rare problem we don't attempt to solve. If your problem is bad enough for you to write about it, other people have probably taken a crack at trying to figure out a solution. If you've narrowed your problem down to a local issue—like increasing voter turnout on campus—look for solutions in response to similar problems in another location, or on a larger scale, to assess the extent to which they might succeed or fail in your area.

Identify Your Audience

Imagine that you are making your most passionate speech ever. Let's say you're from Boston, and the speech you're making is about how great your hometown baseball team is and how pitiful their archrivals are. You're in a large auditorium, but you're nervous, so your eyes have been closed the entire time you've been on stage. Finally, you finish speaking, certain that you've nailed it, you take a bow, open your eyes—and rather than a hall full of Red Sox caps, you see nothing but seething fans dressed in New York Yankees apparel. Suddenly it hits you. You never got around to specifying an audience for your speech, and the wrong one showed up.

That scenario reminds us of the risks of writing a problem-solution essay without addressing a specific audience. You may make a strong case, but if you've made it to the wrong audience, it may fail.

As you compose your essay, think about who you imagine reading it. There are three likely audiences for a typical problem-solution essay, and it's useful to keep all of them in mind:

the people most affected by the *problem*	the people most affected by the *solution*	the people who can *make the change* you want to see take place

Sometimes those groups overlap, but sometimes they don't, so let's take a look at each one separately:

- **The people most affected by your problem.** Let's say the problem you are tackling is the high incidence of unhoused families in the downtown area of your city. The people most directly affected by the problem are, of course, the families themselves, some of whose members who may also suffer from extreme poverty, mental and physical health issues, a susceptibility to street violence, and a host of other ills. But it's not just the unhoused families who are affected, it's also the people they interact with, especially those who live and work downtown. Already, that's a diverse audience with potentially very different goals and expectations for how to "solve" these families' housing problems.

- **The people most affected by your solution.** Now, let's imagine that your primary solution is to build affordable family housing on a tract of empty land between two middle-class suburban developments and to set aside the majority of the new units for unhoused families. Once again, the unhoused families will be profoundly affected by this change, but so will their new neighbors, who may worry about how the influx of additional students will affect a school system that is perhaps already too budget-strapped to hire more teachers. As you can see, each time we add a new interest group into the mix, the potential solution becomes even more complicated.

- **The people who can make the change you want to see take place.** Finally, let's suppose that the only way you can get your proposal through is if a countywide ordinance is passed. Suddenly, your audience—while still complex—comes into much clearer focus. The people you are writing to are those who (1) live in the county and (2) are likely to vote. Data tells us that the unhoused—those most affected by your proposal—rarely vote, so they are a less immediate audience than the homeowners in the suburbs, the people who live and work downtown, and anyone in the county—which might also include rural residents—who may head to the ballot box to decide the fate of your solution.

As this brief example shows, "gaming out" the possible responses of your audience—that is, running through a number of potential situations and outcomes—can be a complicated process. Nevertheless, it's a worthwhile activity, nearly always helping you to get a better handle on your topic.

Here are a few takeaways from the previous scenario that you can apply when deciding how to reach your audience:

- **You can't please everyone.** You are bound to disappoint, if not anger, certain members of your audience; not everyone is going to be won over, no matter what you say. Don't fret. As TV psychologist Dr. Phil says: "Get over it."

- **Address your primary arguments to those who can make a difference.** In the situation described above, your main audience is people who are likely to vote on county ordinances. The more research you did to identify those people and their preferences, the more likely you could gauge your pitch to appeal directly to them.

- **Try to get movers and shakers on your side.** One way to reach your audience is to demonstrate that those who matter in your community agree with you. In a situation like this one, which requires new legislation, getting area politicians, and possibly local celebrities, to endorse your position could result in sufficient popular support to pass the ordinance.

DIY 12.3b Identify Your Primary Audience

Write a short paragraph describing each of the following segments of your audience:

1. The people most affected by the *problem*
2. The people most affected by the *solution*
3. The people who can *make the change* you want to see take place

Once you identify all the stakeholders, zero in on those who can most help you accomplish your purpose and consider them the primary audience for your proposal.

12.4 Envisioning Concrete and Realistic Solutions

One advantage to writing about a problem that you feel strongly about and feel deeply invested in solving is that you are more likely to seek specific and achievable solutions. However, even if the problem you're writing about isn't one in which you have a strong personal stake, you should still look for ways to solve it that have a real chance of succeeding. Be flexible in envisioning different approaches to problem solving.

See Ways to Implement Solutions

Here are a few common ways that solutions are implemented.

- **Change or enforce existing laws.** It can be hard to pass new laws, especially if they don't have broad and enthusiastic support. Brookshire (see Section 12.1) recommends changing the law to make voting mandatory—an idea that does have merit—but she carefully avoids explaining how that might be done during our era of fractured politics. A more practical alternative might be advocating for the stricter enforcement of existing, but loosely enforced, laws.

- **Educate.** It can be difficult to change people's minds, but education is often the starting point. Brookshire recommends that parents and teachers "let kids know 'voting is important—it's what makes you a functioning adult.'" She suggests that the "message may come through in civics and government classes," although more specificity about how to incorporate this message into the curriculum would have made this a stronger solution. Whenever possible, spell out just what form the education needs to take.

- **Borrow or modify another solution.** Employing a variation on a solution for a similar problem is one of the most frequent ways of putting a new solution into practice. Brookshire, for instance, borrows the idea of mandatory voting from European countries where it is already in place. She also suggests that there is some value in a wider adoption of Michigan's policy of making voting records public.

- **Compromise.** Lately, "compromise" has become something of a dirty word, but finding an acceptable middle ground is one of the oldest human strategies for getting things done. If you gain more than you give up, compromise can be a winning strategy.

If the solution to your problem will require several steps that must take place in chronological order, you'll want to cover the *parts* of the solution *in the order* in which they must be achieved. For instance, if you believe that solving the problem of homelessness first involves (1) providing unhoused people with food and temporary shelter, then (2) offering them counseling, and (3) lastly—only after they are off the streets and talking with professionals—supplying them with permanent housing, your essay should discuss the steps in that order.

If, on the other hand, the parts of your solution are like Brookshire's and don't need to be implemented in any particular order, you'll probably want to begin with your *second-most* persuasive solution and end the essay with your *strongest* idea.

Finally, be careful to avoid the *either-or* reasoning discussed in Section 11.5. You'll recall the *either-or* fallacy asserts that there are only two possible options completely opposed to one another, when, in fact, there are often lots of options between the two extremes. While a statement like, "*Either* we get every eligible voter to the polls, *or* our democracy will collapse" may *feel* true, it ignores not just the many alternatives to 100% participation, but also the fact that our democracy has continued uninterrupted for more than 250 years even though people have often chosen to avoid or have been prevented from engaging in their civic duty to vote.

Research to Find Evidence

By now, engaging in research is probably embedded in your composition process. You realize that research is useful before, during, and even after the drafting of an essay. If you need a piece of information, you go out and find it. Consequently, you've probably been doing some sort research since the moment you were given your assignment. That's as it should be. Granted, you will be able to come up with some solutions to your problem simply by sitting there and thinking, but drawing on the work of those who have thought about the problem before is useful and logical.

Bethany Brookshire has a PhD in physiology and pharmacology; what's more, she's writing for a website called *Science News*, so it's not surprising that her research is strong. Indeed, she doesn't discuss a single problem or solution without drawing on evidence from an expert in the field or a legitimate statistical study—an example worth following.

Brookshire is especially skilled in the art of using quotations. Hers are concise, contextualized and clearly attributed to their source. In paragraph 5, for example, she states one of the problems connected to low voter turnout, offers a succinct and relevant quotation, and concludes by attributing the quote its source while citing the source's authority:

> In many countries, people are automatically registered to vote. Not so in the United States. "The U.S. system puts the burden on the voter," says Barry Burden, a political scientist at the University of Wisconsin–Madison.

This variation on the "quotation sandwich" (see Chapter 6) is done with such seeming ease that we may not register how much information Brookshire has managed to pack into just three sentences and thirty-seven words. And while the choice of quotations in her essay is smart, Brookshire also does an excellent job of using paraphrase and summary to convey her sources' main points.

Another strength of Brookshire's research is the *range* of experts from whom she quotes: published scholars from reputable US institutions, international professors and researchers, and graduate students.

Brookshire also quotes from a variety of *types* of sources, referencing everything from scholarly journals like *Political Research Quarterly* and *American Political Science Review* to Alan Gerber's book *Get Out the Vote* to a Pew Research Study to personal interviews with some of her authorities. However long it actually took Brookshire to conduct her research, it *feels* as though she has studied her topic thoroughly and has now become something of an expert herself.

As you compose your problem-solution essay, consider following Brookshire's lead and including at least one survey and one interview. Again, if at all possible, think local. Yes, a national issue, like the one covered in "Why People Don't Vote, and What to Do About It," requires national polls to collect information on people's voting habits. However, if you're attempting to solve a community or campus problem, a survey of your classmates, featuring both direct questions and open-ended responses, can produce useful results. Similarly, interviews with local experts will be easier to set up than interviews with world-renowned authorities; in addition, the specialists in your own community will have a much more detailed picture of the problem you are trying to solve.

One word of caution—as you begin incorporating research into your essay, don't grow overly attached to a single strong source. While it can be tempting to quote from that source over and over, the person may end up sounding like the coauthor of your essay. Instead, use Brookshire as a model and try to employ a variety of credible sources throughout your essay.

DIY 12.4 Gather Evidence to Support Your Solutions

Take out your notebook or start a document. Write out *each* solution to your problem at the top of its own page, and then devote the rest of the page to gathering evidence in support of that solution. Online and library research should be a part of that evidence, but you should write ideas for other ways to buttress your argument, whether it's an interview with a professor, an in-class survey, or another idea that's just occurred to you.

12.5 Anticipating Counterarguments and Alternative Solutions

Once you come up with a list of possible solutions, you'll want to test them against the counterarguments or objections they are sure to inspire. This is a good time to adopt the role of the skeptic, someone who doesn't take anything on faith.

Basically, a lousy solution is anything that isn't going to work, so imagine your skeptic constantly looking for reasons why your solutions are flawed and envisioning better solutions than the ones you've come up with. Be tough on your own ideas: subject *each* solution to as many questions as you can think of, including these:

- **Is it cost effective?** One of the biggest objections to any new proposal is expense. At the very least, you should try to offer solutions that are less expensive than the problem itself. A solution that is inexpensive or, better yet, *free* will be hard for your readers to resist.

- **Is it easy to implement?** The more "moving parts" a solution has, the harder it can be to make it work. Avoid the unnecessarily complex, and whenever possible embrace the simple and straightforward.

- **Will it cause more problems than it solves?** Physicians assessing how to treat a patient will often use the Latin phrase *Primum non nocere* as their guiding principle: "First, do no harm." You should take a similar attitude when formulating your solutions and be thoughtful about any solution that has the potential to harm more people than it helps.

- **Has it, or some variation, been tried before and failed?** Borrowing or modifying existing solutions is one of the most common ways of putting a new one into practice. Before you take that step, though, you should be able to explain why your new approach to an old solution will work better than the one on which it is based, especially if the previous solution was ultimately unsuccessful.

- **Is there a better solution than the one you are offering?** This may be the most important question to address. If there is a popular alternative solution that you believe is faulty, be sure to describe its shortcomings and explain why your less popular idea is, in fact, preferable.

Assess Problems and Solutions Using a Template

One way to assess whether or not your solutions are concrete and realistic is to evaluate each part of the problem, using a template like this:

Aspect of problem	
Solution	
Evaluation of solution	

Let's use one of the problems and solutions in "Why People Don't Vote, and How to Change It" as an example:

Aspect of problem	People get burned out and don't care about voting
Solution	Use peer pressure to get people to the polls
Evaluation of solution	Brookshire references a 2008 study in the <u>American Political Science Review</u> that shows voter turnout in Michigan increased when people had their voting habits publicly compared to their neighbors'. She does admit, however, that the policy has its limits. When voters receive too many "shame-heavy mailings," they "demand to be left alone." Overall, this particular solution has the potential to be effective, but only up to a point.

DIY 12.5a Assess Your Solutions to a Problem

Create a document that uses the template you see in Section 12.5. Within your proposal, you are most likely dealing with three or four aspects of a larger problem. For each aspect, list your solution and then evaluate, or *judge*, that solution, keeping in mind probable objections.

On the next page of your document, or even in a comments field, write a short paragraph explaining why each of your solutions is ultimately better than other options.

DIY 12.5b Plan Your Proposal with a Graphic Organizer

Most writers benefit from (1) the process of writing something out and (2) being able to see what their thoughts look like on the page. See where you are with your proposal by organizing your points graphically, making sure to include evidence for each of the solutions you propose. Note that there is no best place for responding to counterarguments.

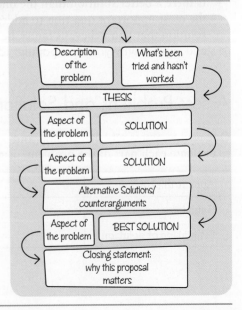

12.6 | Using Visuals

Just as you now employ research as an integral part of your composing process, you probably also, almost automatically, think about how your essay will look on the page or the screen—wherever your most important readers will see it.

Use Visuals to Emphasize Your Strongest Points.

Consider emphasizing elements of your proposal with photos, tables, infographics, or other graphic elements. Even if your visual simply echoes a point you've been making, your readers are more likely to remember that particular point than one without a visual emphasis. And of course, a visual that expands the ideas in the text itself is generally even more powerful.

If your problem is a local one, you may want to include pictures that you have taken yourself. Spend some time thinking about what you would want to emphasize in the photos and what that emphasis might require of you as the photographer. Do you want a close-up shot? Would a high or low angle invite the viewer to see something differently?

Sometimes visuals such as photographs can add interest and evidence to an essay. This photo could help a writer describe California's problem with annual wildfires. Shown here is smoke from the Jesusita Fire, Santa Barbara, California, May 6, 2009.
David Starkey

I took the photograph in this section from my backyard the day after the start of the Jesusita Fire, which destroyed 80 homes and burned more than 8,700 acres in and around Santa Barbara. I tried to capture the size of the fire relative to the sizes of individual homes near me. If I were writing an essay proposing solutions for how to reduce wildfires in California, a thoughtful presentation of the image could be a stark reminder of the widespread damage fires can do.

Keep the Design Simple and Clean

While one or two well-chosen visuals can noticeably enhance your essay, steer away from clutter. Perhaps the most useful design element in a problem-solution paper, or in most academic essays, is a series of headings. These handy devices clearly mark the different parts of your essay while identifying the content of each section. Visually indicating the length of each passage in an essay enables you, the author, to shape your readers' experience of the material.

Take Advantage of Software Programs

While the design features on Google Docs tend to be fairly basic, Apple Pages now has improved features for incorporating charts, tables, and media into documents, and Microsoft Word has a wide range of design and visual elements to engage your readers, present a range of content, and sharpen the look of your essay. ("SmartArt" and "Chart" in the Insert tab are good places to begin.)

DIY 12.6 Identify Key Places to Insert Visuals

Reread your essay and locate one or two places where a striking visual — whether it's your own photograph, or a graph or chart borrowed (and cited) from one of your sources — will emphasize a point you are eager to make.

An Invitation to View: A Proposal

A lively and popular TED Talk by New Jersey judge Victoria Pratt effectively shows the process of identifying compelling problems and clear solutions. In her Talk, viewed more than 1.2 million times, Pratt spells out how she practiced criminal justice reform every day in her courtroom, guided by a single, simple overarching solution: respect. Today Pratt is a professor of criminal justice at Rutgers University.

How Judges Can Show Respect

VICTORIA PRATT

Michael Appleton

To watch "How Judges Can Show Respect," simply search online for **"Victoria Pratt" and "TED Talk."** Watch "How Judges Can Show Respect." In an engaging presentation, Pratt may convince you, as she has so many others, that her call for change in the U.S. criminal justice system is both reasonable and achievable.

Reading Questions

1. In your own words, how would you describe "procedural justice"? If procedural justice is Pratt's solution, what problem is it solving?

2. According to Pratt, what are the four main principles of procedural justice? Based on your own observations and the stories Pratt tells in her TED Talk, which principle do you think is the most important, and why?

3. The effectiveness of a video presentation depends in large measure on the speaker's voice and mannerisms, and on the overall impression they make. Describe Pratt's presentation style and explain why you think she is an effective or ineffective public speaker.

An Invitation to Read: Student Essay

Zoe Rojas notes that although she knew she wanted to write on this difficult topic, sex trafficking, "as soon as [she] learned about it," one of her biggest problems was "finding data that described how big the problem was. Obviously, the people involved try to keep it as secretive as possible." Nevertheless, she persisted, and even though she found it impossible to judge the size of the problem, she was able to find information about the problem through local media — enough information to propose a few solutions to be considered.

Rojas 1

Zoe Rojas

Professor Starkey

Engl 110

30 September 2018

Sex Trafficking in Santa Barbara

When most people hear "Santa Barbara," they picture an idyllic beach paradise, populated by movie stars and surfers. They might never associate this glamorous town with sex trafficking; it seems like the kind of crime that happens somewhere else. In reality, sex trafficking is alive and well in our own country, and Santa Barbara, our perfect- seeming town, is actually a popular hub for this criminal activity. According to local investigative journalist Leah Bartos, twenty-five percent of locally incarcerated girls and young women have been identified as sex trafficking victims or, as she calls them, "victims of commercial sexual exploitation." Lisa Conn, a Santa Barbara mental health provider for juvenile justice, says that incarceration is "just the tip of the iceberg"; victims of sex trafficking "display symptoms of complex trauma and in particular, sex trauma," says Conn (qtd. in Bartos). This trauma is both physical and emotional. According to gynecologists Neha Deshpande and Nawal M. Nour, "[s]ex trafficking victims are particularly susceptible to sexually transmitted infections such as gonorrhea, syphilis, urinary tract infections, and pubic lice." Deshpande and Nour also note that the emotional impacts can be severe; the victims "may face moderate to severe psychological trauma from daily mental, emotional, and psychological abuse and torture." Many turn to drugs or self-harm to escape their pain, the authors point out. Because sex trafficking is so devastating for its young victims, we must root out the causes of this problem and find some solutions that work. Among the solutions that seem most worthwhile are educating the general public by bringing the problem out into

Writer describes the problem in vivid detail.

Thesis states an overall proposal.

Rojas 2

the open, treating the girls as victims and their male exploiters as criminals, and doing everything possible to provide therapy and rehabilitation for those who have suffered horrible crimes.

One big contributor to the problem is society's ignorance of it. People don't normally make laws or change things until they realize a problem exists. There needs to be recognition that this problem is occurring right here under our noses. The California Health Report notes that almost all of the victims that have been discovered in Santa Barbara are in fact residents. This is a global problem, but it's a local one too, and it's important to understand this. To find out more about people's awareness of this problem, I handed out a survey in all of my classes. Eighty total students participated. To my surprise and disappointment, not a single student reported knowing that sex trafficking is happening in Santa Barbara. Both residents of and visitors to Santa Barbara need to be educated.

In a TED Talk called "The Face of Human Trafficking," district attorney Megan Rheinschild discusses how overwhelming the issue is, arguing that "humanity is the casualty of human trafficking." Nevertheless, the fact that she has put the problem out there online, where you can watch it on *YouTube*, helps to bring the issue into the light. Rheinschild is not alone in her efforts. Sharon Byrne reports in the *Santa Barbara Independent* that the "United Nations Association of Santa Barbara and Tri Counties took great interest in this issue, and produced a forum on the topic last year to educate the community." It's excellent news that things are starting to happen in Santa Barbara, but more needs to be done. Perhaps the DA or even victims could come to the local schools and explain the problem to students and parents. Until this problem is fully out in the open, the community won't be able to solve it.

Another cause of this problem is, because of the stigma associated with sex trafficking, the difficulty of getting young women to testify against their traffickers. Often, the

Introduction of the first aspect of the problem: peoples' lack of awareness.

Credible evidence bolsters the writer's discussion of the problem.

Writer discusses a second aspect of the problem.

Rojas 3

women develop an attachment to these men. Mental health expert Conn notes that the young women she worked with "had an intense loyalty to the men" who were abusing them, describing the girls as "almost brainwashed" (qtd. in Bartos). Sometimes the women are afraid to testify because their traffickers threaten them or their families. And since prostitution is a crime, many women are imprisoned, even though they should be considered victims, not criminals.

Unfortunately, traffickers can be shifty and hard to catch. However, it's fairly easy to catch the customers, who may or may not realize that the women they hire for sex are underage and being held hostage. One important way to help the young women is to treat them as the victims and the customers as the criminals. In January 2017, Santa Barbara Police conducted a sting operation at a local motel and caught six men who were arrested and charged with "solicitation of prostitution" (see fig. 1). The local news outed these men, putting their names, ages, and pictures into their news story. The men were caught in January because it is known as Human Trafficking

Writer introduces one possible solution.

Fig. 1. A motel in Santa Barbara, CA. Photograph by the author.

Rojas 4

Awareness Month—another good sign that publicity about the problem is increasing ("Six Local Men"). The shame of being exposed in this way might create a deterrent for those hoping to purchase sex. Though the effect isn't yet known, it makes sense that if traffickers have no customers, their "business" will fold.

Because the victims of sex trafficking face a mountain of physical and psychological problems, they desperately need all the help they can get. Though much more needs to be done, a local charity in Santa Barbara has just opened a safe house for young victims. According to an article in KEYT news, the Junior League of Santa Barbara "has a new resource in the battle against human sex trafficking": S.A.F.E. House is "the county's first therapeutic and rehabilitative shelter for victims of sex trafficking and exploitation" (Farnsworth). The house is intended for girls between 12 and 17 years old. S.A.F.E. House's residents report that their stay is "the longest stretch of normalcy they've ever experienced." One young woman quoted in the article tells the author, "I want to plan on going to college. I want to get my PhD" (Farnsworth). This is impressive, but it's worth noting that S.A.F.E. House is just one four-bedroom house. The community needs more facilities like this if we want to help all of the victims of these horrific crimes.

Many residents of Santa Barbara may call the town a paradise, but it's not that way for everyone. For those who want to help these threatened young women, there are a few simple things to do. Spread the word to people you know. If you have a chance, volunteer where you can help make a difference. And call the police if you see suspicious activity around hotels or motels. As much as the community might want to look the other way, we need to acknowledge the truth: Santa Barbara, with its ocean views and tourists, is a target for sex traffickers. And what's needed are practical solutions to educate people, reform the justice system, and treat—not shame—the victims.

Discussion of why solutions matter for this issue.

The conclusion calls for action.

Rojas 5

Works Cited

Bartos, Leah. "Confronting Child Sex Trafficking on the Central Coast." *California Health Report*, 23 Aug. 2016, www .calhealthreport.org/2016/08/23/confronting-child-sex -trafficking-on-the-central-coast.

Byrne, Sharon. "Human Trafficking: It's Happening in Front of You." *Santa Barbara Independent*, 21 Sept. 2018, www.independent.com/news/2018/apr/21/human -trafficking-its-happening-front-you.

Deshpande, Neha, and Nawal M. Nour. "Sex Trafficking of Women and Girls." *Reviews in Obstetrics & Gynecology*, vol. 6, no. 1, 2013, pp. e22-e27, www.ncbi.nlm.nih.gov /pmc/articles/PMC3651545.

Farnsworth, Beth. "Junior League of Santa Barbara Helps Empower Human Sex Trafficking Victims." *KEYT News*, 26 June 2018, www.keyt.com/news/safety/junior-league -of-santa-barbara-helps-empower-human-sex-trafficking -victims/759215178.

Rheinschild, Megan. "The Face of Human Trafficking." *TEDxSantaBarbara*, uploaded by Mark Sylvester, 2 Oct. 2017, tedxsantabarbara.com/2017/megan-rheinschild.

Rojas, Zoe. Photograph of a Santa Barbara Motel. 27 Sept. 2018. Author's personal collection.

"Six Local Men Among 474 Arrested in Statewide Human Trafficking Case." *KSBY News*, 31 Jan. 2017, www.ksby .com/story/34395365/6-local-men-among-474-arrested-in -statewide-human-trafficking-case.

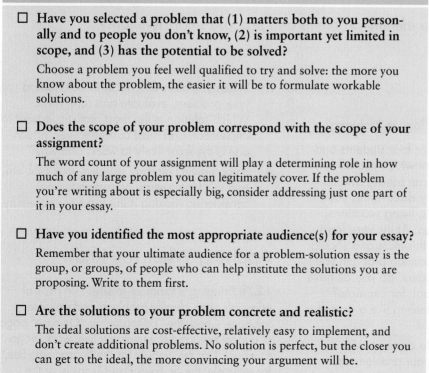
Reading Questions

1. Where do you find yourself most, and least, engaged in "Sex Trafficking in Santa Barbara"? Point to specific passages in the essay to justify your response.

2. Although it isn't very long, Zoe's essay employs quite a bit of research (she cites six sources in about 1,000 words). Make an argument for or against the use of research in a short problem-solution essay. Refer to "Sex Trafficking in Santa Barbara" to support your position.

3. If Zoe were your classmate, what advice would you give her to make a strong essay even stronger?

Chapter 12 Checklist
Proposing a Solution

☐ **Have you selected a problem that (1) matters both to you personally and to people you don't know, (2) is important yet limited in scope, and (3) has the potential to be solved?**

Choose a problem you feel well qualified to try and solve: the more you know about the problem, the easier it will be to formulate workable solutions.

☐ **Does the scope of your problem correspond with the scope of your assignment?**

The word count of your assignment will play a determining role in how much of any large problem you can legitimately cover. If the problem you're writing about is especially big, consider addressing just one part of it in your essay.

☐ **Have you identified the most appropriate audience(s) for your essay?**

Remember that your ultimate audience for a problem-solution essay is the group, or groups, of people who can help institute the solutions you are proposing. Write to them first.

☐ **Are the solutions to your problem concrete and realistic?**

The ideal solutions are cost-effective, relatively easy to implement, and don't create additional problems. No solution is perfect, but the closer you can get to the ideal, the more convincing your argument will be.

☐ **Have you addressed potential counterarguments and considered alternative solutions?**

Imagining what skeptics might say about your solutions will allow you to anticipate and address those objections in your essay. Don't shy away from counterarguments; instead, politely but firmly explain why they don't measure up to your own solutions.

☐ **Does your research draw on a range of sources?**

The broader and deeper your research is, the easier it will be for you to show that your solutions have been tested and found worthy.

☐ **Have you selected appropriate visuals?**

Punctuate important points with intelligent, high-impact visuals, being sure to caption and place them according to the citation style you are using.

12.7 Making It Stick

How will you identify problems and propose smart solutions?

Working Together

12.7a Brainstorming Solutions to Problems

1. Form a group of three or four students and decide on a problem for which you *all* can suggest solutions. You can usually find an appropriate problem by discovering your group's shared interests, living situations, backgrounds, and so on. At the very least, you are all enrolled in this class and should be able to identify a common problem you face in as a college student: do you all have trouble paying for school, for example? managing your time? feeling like a part of a school community?

2. Working together, try to come up with as many solutions for your problem as possible.

3. When you have at least three solutions to your problem, evaluate and rank them. Which solution is the most realistic, easiest to implement, and most cost-effective? Which one is the *least* likely to work, and why?

4. If you haven't already selected your problem, and this topic seems interesting to you, considering making it the focus of your essay.

Applying What You Know

12.7b Bringing a Problem to Life   Writers of editorials often identify problems and propose solutions. Check the "Editorials" or "Opinion" page of a local news outlet where you live, work, or go to school. (Try the website for the *Sacramento Bee*, for example, the *St. Louis Post-Dispatch*, or the

Tampa Bay Times.) Choose and read an opinion piece, focusing on how that writer has described a problem to be solved. How might you make the problem more vivid by suggesting descriptions that reference the five senses? How would you try to get the reader to see, hear, smell, taste and/or touch it? In short, how would you bring the problem to life?

12.7c Strengthening Solutions
Identify an opinion piece in your campus newspaper or news site. Read the piece and identify two solutions the writer is suggesting. How would you make those solutions *stronger*, not different? If necessary, do a little research on the writer's behalf to suggest a source or two that might make one or more of the writer's solutions more robust and convincing.

Invitations to Write

12.7d Structuring Your Proposal Essay

Shorter: Define your problem in a single sentence. Then describe your proposed solutions: one or two sentences for each solution.

Longer: Write an outline for your essay in which you respond in a sentence or two to each of the numbered instructions below.

Introduction
1. Describe your problem vividly, so that readers can picture it for themselves.
2. State your thesis.

Body Paragraphs *(Repeat 3–5 for each body paragraph.)*
3. Describe the major *part* or *aspect* of the problem covered by this paragraph.
4. Describe the solution to the problem.

5. Summarize your research and other evidence to support the solution's effectiveness.
6. Address and refute any significant counterarguments.

Conclusion
7. Describe how the community/state/nation/world will be a better place, thanks to your solution(s).

When you're finished, continue fleshing out this detailed outline until it becomes a full-fledged essay.

Note: This outline is just *one* of many possible ways to structure your essay, although it's a structure that has worked for many students. If your proposal seems to require a different organization, try what seems to work best for your particular essay.

12.7e Solving an Argument

Shorter: Take another look at the arguments you considered writing about in the previous chapter but which you didn't end up pursuing. Try to identify at least one of these potential argument essay topics that would have been stronger if the ultimate focus had been on the *solution* to the problem you were arguing.

Longer: Turn your argument essay idea into a problem-solution essay by following the guidance offered in this chapter.

Open-Topic Essay Ideas
If you are still looking for an essay topic, browse this list of issues my students have successfully addressed in problem-solution essays. Most of the following are broad topics that students found had to be further narrowed:

Addiction to . . .
alcohol and drugs, gambling, nicotine, social media, video games

Bias against . . .
  people from certain race backgrounds, people
  with disabilities, transgender people, women
College education costs
Cyberbullying
Economic inequality on campus
Environmental issues:
  climate change disbelievers
  extreme storms
  hydrofracking
  recycling on campus
  urban encroachment
  wildfires

Family violence
Free speech on campus
Food insecurity
Gun violence
Paying college athletes
Local traffic issues
Microaggressions
Police brutality
Resolving workplace conflicts
Suicide prevention

13

Analyzing a Text

Write Before You Read   Do a quick web search to find the lyrics to one of your favorite songs. Look closely at the words, then write a short paragraph describing *what* the song says and a second paragraph analyzing *how* the songwriter uses language to convey meaning and emotion.

13.1   Showcasing Your Reading Skills

Throughout the semester, you've been learning to read more carefully and consciously. You're becoming, in short, a college reader. The skills you've been developing will serve you well in this particular assignment, where you will be writing an essay in which you analyze a text. This type of analysis is often called *rhetorical analysis*—that is, it examines the art of effective writing or speaking.

Often, when students do a close reading of a literary text like poem or story, they are looking for "hidden meanings." That can seem like a pretty daunting undertaking. After all, how are you supposed to uncover those meanings when they're hidden? A rhetorical analysis asks you to determine whether a text is successful and to examine the author's choices, asking how the text was composed and why.

Fortunately, the more experienced you become as a reader, the more aware you will be of why and how writers use language, structure, and design in certain ways. When you truly scrutinize a written text, you will begin noticing every element on the page, from word choice to repetition to the various connotations of important words. You'll be aware of the text's pacing, typography, use of other sources, its appeals, and so on. Moreover, when you take a step back and look at the context in which a work was written, you'll often notice elements of a text that weren't immediately apparent. You'll want to know why it was written and for whom. You'll ask how other readers have responded to the text and how their opinions influence your own.

While analyzing a text does require an intense focus, when you do it well, you'll find that you have an understanding and appreciation of another writer's work that is impossible to achieve any other way. The bonus? You'll expand your own repertoire as a writer by studying what other writers do well to achieve a particular effect on their readers.

> A rhetorical analysis asks you to determine whether a text is successful and to examine the author's choices, asking how the text was composed and why.

UP FRONT: Choosing a Text for Close Reading

The Assignment

Write an essay in which you analyze a text of your choice. The chapter guidance, examples, and DIY prompts will help you complete the assignment. Follow your instructor's notes about length and formatting. Keep these guidelines in mind as you choose a text to study.

The text should fit within the parameters of your assignment. Pay careful attention to the prompt. While you might think the lyrics of your favorite song will be the perfect text for your assignment, your instructor may have included guidelines that specify the types of texts you may choose. If you have any doubts about a text's suitability, check with your instructor before you begin writing.

It should be fairly short. This is not the time to analyze your favorite book. Instead, seek out a text that you can comfortably read, view, or listen to over and over. Speeches are popular, not only because of their relative brevity, but also because their purpose and audience tend to be fairly clear. If you are given the option of choosing a multimedia text for analysis, consider doing a close reading of a commercial or public service advertisement, or a limited section, possibly even a single page, of a website.

It should be worthy of analysis. If your text is so simple or straightforward that it needs no explanation, then it's not going to give you much to talk about in your essay. Look for a work that is complex enough to require the careful attention you will be paying to it.

DIY 13.1 Get to Know the Text

If you've already been given a text for this assignment, get to know it well. *Really well.* Read it and mark it and read it again and again until it becomes like an old friend whose words and thoughts you can predict. If you haven't yet chosen a text, and your instructor has given you some flexibility to select your own, consider the tips from 13.1 as you search for a text that is a good fit for a close reading.

An Invitation to Read: A Historical Speech and a Contemporary Response

The Gettysburg Address, Abraham Lincoln's most famous speech, is also one of his shortest. Delivered on the Civil War battlefield at Gettysburg, Pennsylvania, on November 19, 1863 — four and a half months after the Battle of Gettysburg — the speech has become a touchstone to which Americans return in times of national trauma.

William Safire's "A Spirit Reborn" was published in *The New York Times* on September 11th, 2002, the first anniversary of 9/11. While the essay provides a careful analysis of Lincoln's Gettysburg Address, it's clear that for Safire the speech is much more than an interesting historical document. The Gettysburg Address is a way to help understand the tragedy of September 11th, serving as a "reminder that our government's legitimacy springs from America's citizens; the people, not the rulers, are sovereign." Safire, a self-proclaimed "libertarian conservative," was a speechwriter for Richard Nixon and for thirty years wrote a column called "On Language" for *The New York Times Magazine*.

The Gettysburg Address

ABRAHAM LINCOLN

Critical Reading Tip

Lincoln's speech was composed more than 150 years ago, so the language is different than what we are used to do today. Nevertheless, Lincoln's words are justifiably famous and memorable. During your first reading of the text, do your best to understand *what* he is saying. Then reread "The Gettysburg Address" and begin thinking about *how* Lincoln uses language to make his main points.

1   Four score and seven years ago our fathers brought forth on this continent, a new nation, conceived in Liberty, and dedicated to the proposition that all men are created equal. Now we are engaged in a great civil war, testing whether that nation, or any nation so conceived and so dedicated, can long endure. We are met on a great battle-field of that war. We have come to dedicate a portion of that field, as a final resting place for those who here gave their lives that that nation might live. It is altogether fitting and proper that we should do this. But, in a larger sense, we can not dedicate—we can not consecrate—we can not hallow—this ground. The brave men, living and dead, who struggled here, have consecrated it, far above our poor power to add or detract. The world will little note, nor long remember what we say here, but it can never forget what they did here. It is for us the living, rather, to be dedicated here to the unfinished work which they who fought here have thus far so nobly advanced. It is rather for us to be here dedicated to the great task remaining before us—that from these honored dead we take increased devotion to that cause for which they gave the last full measure of devotion—that we here highly resolve that these dead shall not have died in vain—that this nation, under God, shall have a new birth of freedom—and that government of the people, by the people, for the people, shall not perish from the earth.

A Spirit Reborn

WILLIAM SAFIRE

1   Abraham Lincoln's words at the dedication of the Gettysburg cemetery will be the speech repeated at the commemoration of Sept. 11 by the governor of New York and by countless other speakers across the nation.

Stacy Walsh Rosenstock / Alamy Stock Photo

> **Critical Reading Tip**
> William Safire focuses his analysis of "The Gettysburg Address" on the word "dedicate," which he tells us occurs five times in 266 words. Before you begin reading, look up the word "dedicate" and read through its various meanings. Then, as you proceed through "A Spirit Reborn," think about why Safire focuses on certain definitions of "dedicate" and how those meanings bolster his overall interpretation of Lincoln's speech.

2   The lips of many listeners will silently form many of the famous phrases. "Four score and seven years ago"—a sonorous way of recalling the founding of the nation 87 years before he spoke—is a phrase many now recite by rote, as is "the last full measure of devotion."

3   But the selection of this poetic political sermon as the oratorical center-piece of our observance need not be only an exercise in historical evocation, nonpolitical correctness and patriotic solemnity. What makes this particular speech so relevant for repetition on this first anniversary of the worst blood-bath on our territory since Antietam Creek's waters ran red is this: Now, as then, a national spirit rose from the ashes of destruction.

4   Here is how to listen to Lincoln's all-too-familiar speech with new ears.

5   In those 266 words, you will hear the word *dedicate* five times. The first two times refer to the nation's dedication to two ideals mentioned in the Declaration of Independence, the original ideal of "liberty" and the ideal that became central to the Civil War: "that all men are created equal."

6   The third, or middle, *dedication* is directed to the specific consecration of the site of the battle of Gettysburg: "to dedicate a portion of that field as a final resting place." The fourth and fifth times Lincoln repeated *dedicate* reaffirmed those dual ideals for which the dead being honored fought: "to the unfinished work" and then "to the great tasks remaining before us" of securing freedom and equality.

7   Those five pillars of dedication rested on a fundament of religious metaphor. From a president not known for his piety—indeed, often criticized for his supposed lack of faith—came a speech rooted in the theme of national resurrection. The speech is grounded in conception, birth, death and rebirth.

8   Consider the barrage of images of birth in the opening sentence. The nation was "conceived in liberty," and "brought forth"—that is, delivered into life—by "our fathers" with all "created" equal. (In the 19th century, both "men" and "fathers" were taken to embrace women and mothers.) The nation was born.

9   Then, in the middle dedication to those who sacrificed themselves, come images of death: "final resting place" and "brave men, living and dead."

10   Finally, the nation's spirit rises from this scene of death: "that this nation, under God, shall have a new birth of freedom." Conception, birth, death, rebirth. The nation, purified in this fiery trial of war, is resurrected. Through the sacrifice of its sons, the sundered nation would be reborn as one.

11   An irreverent aside: All speechwriters stand on the shoulders of orators past. Lincoln's memorable conclusion was taken from a fine oration by the Rev. Theodore Parker at an 1850 Boston antislavery convention. That social reformer defined the transcendental "idea of freedom" to be "a government of all the people, by all the people, for all the people."

12   Lincoln, 13 years later, dropped the "alls" and made the phrase his own. (A little judicious borrowing by presidents from previous orators shall not perish from the earth.) In delivering that final note, the Union's defender is said to have thrice stressed the noun "people" rather than the prepositions "of," "by" and "for." What is to be emphasized is not rhetorical rhythm but the reminder that our government's legitimacy springs from America's citizens; the people, not the rulers, are sovereign. Not all nations have yet grasped that.

13   Do not listen on Sept. 11 only to Lincoln's famous words and comforting cadences. Think about how Lincoln's message encompasses but goes beyond paying "fitting and proper" respect to the dead and the bereaved. His sermon at Gettysburg reminds "us the living" of our "unfinished work" and "the great task remaining before us"—to resolve that this generation's response to the deaths of thousands of our people leads to "a new birth of freedom."

Reading Questions

1. What did Safire's analysis of the Gettysburg Address tell you about Lincoln's speech that you didn't know prior to reading his essay? (As always, you should look up references you didn't understand.)

2. In paragraphs 5–7, Safire analyzes how Lincoln uses the word "dedication." In paragraphs 7–10 he examines the theme of "conception, birth, death and rebirth." Reread those passages and explain how Safire's focus on individual words and phrases helps him make sense of the speech as a whole.

3. What do you think of the inclusion of the "irreverent aside" in paragraph 11 and the beginning of paragraph 12? Does it expand the historical context of the Gettysburg Address, or does it sap Safire's own essay of some of its energy and momentum?

13.2 Reading the Text Actively and Critically

The active and critical reading strategies that you've been developing are especially important when the subject of your essay is another text. Once you know the text you'll be analyzing, it's time to become an active participant in the conversation with your text. You can begin this process by taking a few important first steps:

Steps for Reading Actively

- **Read and reread your assignment.** Take a careful look at the assignment guidelines your instructor has provided. Is there any specific type of analysis your instructor wants you to perform? If so, will you need further instruction in how to do what you need to do? If you're being asked to use outside sources to help with your interpretation of the text, what sort of material does your instructor want you to draw on, and how many sources are required? How long should the essay be, and when is it due?

- **Find a way to slow down your reading process.** Deliberately try read more slowly, pausing after each sentence or paragraph. Some readers read out loud; others read collaboratively. Still others retype the entire text they're studying to force themselves to slow down. You may be surprised how the simple act of entering the words of the text into your computer—letting your brain and fingertips connect with the original work—provides you with fresh perspectives on the writer's composition process.

- **If you can, take the text out of the environment in which you found it.** If you're analyzing a written text, consider printing it. If you're analyzing a visual or multimedia text, isolate it by copying and pasting it to a blank slide or page. By separating the text in this way, you may notice aspects of the text that would otherwise have slipped past your attention. On a hard copy, you can use a pen or pencil to annotate, which may lead you to insights you wouldn't have had if you weren't physically marking the page. On digital copy, use a comment feature to mark up the work.

Engage with the Text

The following strategies will help you engage actively with a text:

- **Preview before you read.** Read the title, any introductory material and the first paragraph, then skim the text, slowing down periodically to fully read any sentence that catches your interest. Pay special attention to the concluding paragraph or paragraphs, where authors frequently sum up the text's main points, and be aware of any headings or visuals.

- **Read the text aloud.** Especially if the text is unfamiliar to you, it's worth reading it aloud—to yourself or a friend—pausing to talk about any thoughts that occur to you in the reading process. If you're studying a speech, look for a transcript.

- **Annotate.** This is where your conversation with the text really begins. Mark as you read, underlining important or unusual words, commenting on important passages, or noting design features and strategies. Ask questions. Lots of them. Your margins should be filled with queries about the text you want answered—everything from the meaning of a word to the context of a big idea.

- **Challenge the text.** Asking questions of the text will inevitably result in challenging it. Just because a text is "published" doesn't mean you can't disagree with the writer's or speaker's ideas. Even if your overall analysis turns out to be favorable, you will still want to note those moments when the text doesn't quite seem to get it right.

- **Make connections.** Make notes of where the text reminds you of something else you've read or heard. Point out what it has in common with similar texts you've encountered. How is it different?

- **Try to visualize what you're reading.** Not all nonfiction texts make use of the mental pictures, or images, that creative writers love so well, but even when the author is only using abstractions, you can still *try* and imagine the speaker and the audience, and their interaction with one another.

- **Summarize as you go.** Every few paragraphs, or few hundred words—wherever there's a clear stopping point in the text—pause long enough to summarize for yourself what you've been reading. For an assignment like this one, it's often most helpful to do that summary in writing, but at the very least you should periodically take a quick breather to make sure you're confident that you understand what you've just read.

> **DIY 13.2a** Read the Text Actively and Critically
>
> Follow the guidelines in this section to read and annotate your text actively and critically. If your first round of annotations feels unsatisfying, re-engage with the text either in print or on your computer screen — whichever version you did not read the first time around. Write notes about one writing technique or one sentence you're surprised by.

Identify the Writer's Claims, Goals, and Values

Once you've read, reread, and annotated your text, you should be prepared to identify the major claims, goals, and values presented in the text. As you begin writing, you should be able to answer the following questions:

1. **What is the writer's main point?** Ideally, you should be able to summarize the main point of the text you are studying in a single sentence. Often, the writer will explicitly state the text's major focus, typically either at the beginning and/or end of the text. In "A Spirit Reborn," William Safire's main point seems to come in the final paragraph (see Section 13.1), and it might be summarized like this: "The living must carry on the 'unfinished work' of the dead in order to create 'a new birth of freedom.'"

2. **What does the writer want to happen?** In some instances, as in Safire's essay, the author's main point will indicate what readers should do after finishing the text. In the case of "A Spirit Reborn," readers are urged to continue fighting for the freedoms that can no longer be fought for by those who died in the 9/11 attacks. Your text may not make the author's wishes so explicit, but most writers do make requests or demands of their readers, even if those appeals are subtle. If you study a commercial ad or a public service ad, you'll find that the creators of those ads often have more explicit calls to action.

3. **What are the writer's values, both stated and unstated?** Chapter 11 discusses how authors argue a position depending on their values and their underlying assumptions about the world. When you're analyzing

a text, you'll want to know as much about the author (or creator or speaker) as possible. That information may be found in your research, or it may become evident simply through your close reading of the text.

4. **Why does the writer claim, or imply, that the text matters?** A text worth analyzing is one that the writer believes matters in some significant way. Again, you should probably be able to summarize why the writer believes the text matters in a single sentence. We might, for instance, say of Safire's "A Spirt Reborn" that the author believes his essay matters because "It demonstrates how Lincoln's Gettysburg address can continue to inspire Americans when they seem to be at their lowest."

DIY 13.2b Answer Questions about the Text

Answer each of these four questions as it applies to the text you are analyzing: What is the writer's main point? What does the writer want to happen? What are the writer's values, both stated and unstated? Why does the writer claim, or imply, that the text matters?

Put the Text in Context

To analyze a text well, you not only have to know what it is saying, you should also know the context in which it was created. The Gettysburg Address, for instance, was spoken by Abraham Lincoln on November 19, 1863, on one of the bloodiest battlefields of the Civil War, only four and a half months after that battle had been fought. While the tide had turned in the Union's favor, the Civil War was still raging, and the ultimate outcome was far from determined. Thus, Lincoln's speech was both a solemn reminder of all the lives that had been lost as well as a call to the Union Army to recommit itself to finishing the difficult job ahead.

William Safire's "A Spirit Reborn" was composed under loosely comparable circumstances. Like Lincoln, Safire was somewhat removed in time from the violence he was discussing, but the 9/11 attacks were close enough that the feelings of most readers would still have been incredibly raw. Of course, there is an additional layer to "A Spirit Reborn," as Safire uses' Lincoln's words to comment—both explicitly and implicitly—on the contemporary tragedy.

Not knowing this information doesn't keep you from gaining a general understanding of either Lincoln's or Safire's texts, but it does keep you from fully appreciating the power of each text. And as the critic analyzing the text, it's your job to identify and research key references and then summarize them for your readers.

We know that audience is a key factor in the shaping of any piece of writing, so a big part of determining historical context is knowing for whom the author was writing. While Abraham Lincoln's immediate audience was the people gathered to remember the dead at Gettysburg, the press was incredibly active during the Civil War, so Lincoln knew his words would receive a wide hearing, both in the Union and the Confederacy. Therefore, while his primary audience was the people gathered at the Gettysburg battlefield, his ultimate audience was, quite literally, the larger country and the entire world.

Safire's initial audience wasn't quite as large, but he was writing in the *New York Times*, one of the country's major newspapers, headquartered in the city that suffered the most from the 9/11 attacks. Safire's columns typically focused on how people use language, and his customary, or primary audience, would not have been disappointed by his careful linguistic analysis of Lincoln's speech. However, Safire, writing on the first anniversary of 9/11, must have known that the audience for this particular column was going to be much wider than his usual readership.

As you work to put your own text in context, try to answer these questions:

1. **When was the text written and presented or published?** The more recent the text, the more detailed you can be about what current events were taking place at the time of the text's publication. Not everything going on will be relevant to your textual analysis, but significant events—like the fact that the Gettysburg Address was delivered in the middle of the Civil War—should be acknowledged and explored. Similarly, the appearance of "A Spirit Reborn" on the first anniversary of 9/11 adds significantly to its power.

2. **Where was it first presented or published?** Just as relevant as *when* the text was created is *where* it first appeared. The Gettysburg Address was delivered at the site of the Battle of Gettysburg, and "A Spirit Reborn" was published in the *New York Times*: both of these facts help provide a frame of reference that deepens our understanding of the two texts.

3. **What was the occasion for which it was composed?** Even more important than when and where the text was composed is the reason *why* it was written. Here is where your research can play an especially helpful role, as you investigate both the writer's background and the historical circumstances that prompted the author to compose the text.

4. **Who is the writer's primary audience?** Whatever the secondary audiences, it's important to begin by pinpointing just whom the author *first* pictured reading or hearing the text. As noted above, Lincoln's primary audience was the people listening to his speech, while Safire's normal audience consisted of the regular readers of his column, "On Language."

5. **What other audiences are important to the text?** A thorough analysis of context always involves thinking about the writer's *complete* audience. Both Lincoln and Safire knew their texts would have wider than normal readerships, and it's interesting to consider what changes they might have made to connect with their much larger secondary audiences.

DIY 13.2c Explain the Origin of the Text

Write a paragraph or two about the origins of the text you are analyzing. You may have to dig a little. Explain where and why it was composed and when and where it was first presented to the public. Provide any other compelling and relevant social or historical facts that you learned about the text.

13.3 Analyzing the Writer's Craft

As a beginning college writer, you may feel, at first, as though you don't have a lot to say about how another, more experienced writer approaches their craft. That's true to an extent; however, while you may not have a lot of technical terms at your fingertips, you are perfectly capable of talking about what you see on the page. You don't have to be a professional writer or rhetorician to recognize when a writer makes a strong point or fails to do so.

Keep in mind that while an effective analysis will involve some summarizing—reporting *what* the text says—the best analytical writing explains *how* the text does its work. Instead of simply repeating, point by point, the text's main ideas, add to the reader's understanding of the text by noting the writer's choices and strategies.

Take a Closer Look at Structure

One task you have as an analytical writer who is studying a text is to take inventory of the larger structure of the work. What do you notice about the way it is organized? Is its structure predictable or unexpected? Obvious or subtle? Does the writer make use of headings or questions to help the reader along? If you were studying Barack Obama's 2018 eulogy for Senator John McCain, for example, you might notice this structure: humor, biography, tribute. And after thinking about the oddity, you may take notes about why a speaker would want to begin with humor on such a somber occasion—a funeral for a well-respected public servant—and what effect the speaker's choice has on the audience.

Take a Closer Look at Words and Sentences

Another way to begin a careful analysis of a text is to look closely at the words the writer chooses and how those words are put together in sentences. As you read through your text one more time, ask yourself:

1. **Does the text employ ordinary or unusual words?** If your text was written long ago, words that seem unusual to you may have been quite normal at the time. Therefore, the older the text, the more effort you might have to put into differentiating between everyday and atypical word choices. However, if your text is contemporary, you should be able to detect when the writer is employing words you are used to hearing and when the text seems to be striving for something extra. Especially when the text is mostly composed of ordinary language, pay special attention to those moments when it rises above the commonplace.

2. **What mood or tone do the words suggest?** The type of words a writer chooses creates the mood or tone of the text. Some of the key words

in Lincoln's speech, for instance, like "consecrate" ("declare something sacred") and "hallow" ("to honor as holy"), evoke what Safire calls "a fundament of religious metaphor." Again, zero in on words you are unfamiliar with or that stand out for some reason, and identify both their denotations, what they literally mean, as well as their connotations, the feelings or ideas evoked by or associated with the words.

3. **Are the sentences *mostly* long and complex, or short and simple?** The longer and more complex the sentence, the more you may feel as though the writer is trying to impress you with a mastery of language. While this mastery may be impressive, it may also obscure the writer's message. On the other hand, texts made up mostly of short and simple sentences—especially if they were written by a professional writer—generally suggest that the writer's primary goal is to connect with readers and plainly state the text's main points. An exception to this rule can be seen in Martin Luther King Jr.'s "Letter from Birmingham Jail," where he uses a 316-word sentence to communicate what it is like to *wait* for racial justice. If you come upon extraordinarily long or short sentences, question what the intended effect is.

4. **What words, phrases, sentences, or ideas are repeated?** Repetition, especially in a short text, is noticeable, and for that reason, writers use it to emphasize their most important points. Safire, for instance, notes that in Lincoln's very short speech, "you will hear the word *dedicate* five times," an observation that he spends three paragraphs exploring. Discussing why you think a writer makes use of repetition often leads to valuable insights about the text as a whole, with patterns of language helping to create the text's themes.

5. **What, if any, imagery does the writer use?** "Imagery" in writing refers to any evocation of one of the five senses. As you imagine the text in your mind, identify those moments when you can almost see, hear, smell, taste, or touch what the writer is referring to, and examine how the imagery helps convey the writer's points. In "A Spirit Reborn," for example, Safire is particularly interested in imagery suggesting "conception, birth, death and rebirth."

6. **Are there places where you become confused?** Sometimes an author does a poor job of communicating, but if the text you are analyzing is by a professional writer or speaker, those moments when you feel lost or confused might actually be the places that deserve your fullest attention. Mark the difficult passages, then spend some time analyzing why and how they are different from the rest of the text.

> **DIY 13.3a** Analyze Words and Sentences in the Text
>
> Carefully reread your text, looking at how it works, sentence by sentence and word by word. Make notes in response to these questions: Are any of the words ordinary or unusual? What mood or tone do the words suggest? Are the sentences long and complex, short or simple? Are ideas, words, or phrases repeated? Does the writer use imagery? Is anything confusing?

Understand Aristotle's Three Appeals

Examining how a writer employs Aristotle's appeals to *logos*, *ethos*, and *pathos* (see Section 11.3) can reveal a great deal about what strategies that author believes will have the strongest effect on their audience. Take another look at the text you are analyzing and examine it through the lens of each appeal:

Logos: **What evidence does the writer provide to support the text's claims?** While your text may operate primarily in a nonlogical way, sound reasoning and supporting evidence should continue to be a criterion by which you evaluate how well the text achieves the author's goals. If the text you are studying includes little or no appeal to logic, question why and what the writer's intended effect might be.

Ethos: **In what ways does the writer come across as credible and trustworthy?** Because we want to trust the people writing or speaking to us, you'll want to assess whether or not your author comes across as a believable speaker, someone in whom you can place confidence. If there are moments when you lose that confidence, investigate why that happens.

Pathos: **How does the writer trigger the audience's emotions?** If you were particularly moved by a passage in the text, explore why it moved you. How did the writer use specific words or sentences to evoke or manipulate, your feelings about the topic? Do you think the writer intended to rouse fear, anger, pride, embarrassment, hope, or something else in the audience?

DIY 13.3b Identify Appeals in the Text

Look for examples of *logos*, *ethos*, and *pathos* in the text you are studying and write about how each appeal attempts to persuade the audience to accept the author's or creator's view of the world. Don't generalize. Find and discuss specific words, sentences, and passages where each appeal is on display.

Refer to Your Text

Because the words in the text you are analyzing are the focus of your own essay, you'll be referring to your text a lot. When doing so, make effective use of the tools that writers use to discuss another writer's work: summary, paraphrase, and quotation.

- **Summary.** At some point early on in your essay, you will want to summarize the entire text for your readers in a few brief sentences. Summary is especially important when readers are unfamiliar with the work you are analyzing. Don't, however, confuse summary for analysis. Remember that the focus of your essay is on *how* the writer uses language, and less on *what* the language says.

- **Paraphrase.** Although short direct quotations will provide you with your most potent evidence, periodically you may want to paraphrase from the text (see Section 6.3 for more details). Paraphrasing is also a useful way of ensuring that you understand what you're reading. If the text is short enough—like Lincoln's Gettysburg Address—you might want to write a paraphrase of every sentence.

- **Quotation.** Because you may be quoting frequently from your text, you'll want to do it correctly. Review 6.3 to make sure you know how to handle various types of quotations. If you're working from a printed text, don't forget to include parenthetical citations with the page numbers (or, if the text is very short, line numbers).

Analyze a Visual or Multimodal Work

In Chapter 14, you will learn a number of strategies for reading visual and multimodal works. For the moment, though, we'll highlight just a few important elements to consider when writing about objects in which text plays only a limited role or no role at all. Remember that while you may be "reading" an advertisement, or a song on YouTube or, in this case, a photograph, you should apply the same close attention to the work's context and purpose, its structure and detail, and its appeals to *logos*, *ethos*, and *pathos*.

- **Describe the work.** Even if you include a representation of the work in your essay, it's still important for you to describe it. Description not only makes the work more vivid for your reader—and yourself—it also allows you to shape what will we be discussed, and what will be left out. Your description may include both your own words as well as quotations from source texts. When describing the photo in this section, for instance, you might quote from the website of the Jewish Museum of Berlin, where Menashe Kadishman's *Shalekhet (Fallen Leaves)* can be found. The museum's description provides the important factual information that the work consists of "more than 10,000 faces with open mouths, cut from heavy round iron plates," which cover the floor of a long, high concrete gallery.

- **Provide context.** The work you plan to analyze didn't just appear out of nowhere. People create things to accomplish certain purposes, even if those purposes aren't immediately apparent. In the case of *Fallen Leaves*, it's important to know that the installation is housed in a German museum dedicated to remembering victims of the Holocaust. Some background information on Menashe Kadishman, the Israeli

Shalekhet (Fallen Leaves) by Menashe Kadishman.

sculptor who created the work, would also help a viewer understand the intent of *Fallen Leaves*.

- **Focus on key features.** Just as you would look for the main points in a piece of writing, try to identify the most important aspects of the non-textual work you plan to analyze. In the previous photo, the faces are quite similar, with rough ovals suggesting mouths and a slash through the iron circles representing eyes and noses. However, as you look closer, you notice that no face is exactly the same—as is the case with actual human beings—and some of the iron plates appear to be newer and more polished, while others are already rusted.

- **Acknowledge the ways the work is different than a written text.** Before you begin writing, take some time to assess those elements in your work that are markedly dissimilar from a written text. Your task as a writer becomes more complex when the object of your analysis exists in time as well as space. For instance, if you were analyzing the *performance* of a speech, rather than just the text itself, you would likely discuss aspects of the presentation such as the speaker's physical stance, body movements and tone of voice. Similarly, if your essay focused on a video of *Fallen Leaves*, or an actual visit to the installation, you would likely discuss several key features of the work not seen in the photograph. First, there is the space itself. Sunlight leaks down from a skylight three stories above the otherwise unlit room. Visitors are invited to walk to the end of the hall, which grows smaller and darker. As they do, they feel the unmistakable presence of the iron discs beneath the soles of their shoes. Then there is the element of sound. Footsteps on the metal faces make an ominous clanking noise that seems to evoke the industrialized murder committed in the Nazi death camps.

- **Determine the work's appeal to *logos*, *ethos*, and *pathos*.** Not every work will connect fully, or at all, with each of the three appeals, but it's worth investigating whether the work's creator is making use of logical proof, demonstrating their own ethical credibility, or playing to the audience's emotions. While *Fallen Leaves* doesn't overtly appeal to logos, it does very clearly try to connect with viewers' feelings. And the sheer size, ambition, and physicality of the installation seem to speak to Menashe Kadishman as a person with the credibility to comment on his subject.

13.4 Organizing Your Essay

While the structure of your textual analysis essay—like any essay you write—should be dictated by what you are writing about and how you are approaching your topic, it's always helpful to have a model in mind, particularly if you're having trouble organizing your thoughts. Therefore, the following suggestions for structuring your essay are meant to help generate ideas rather than box you in:

- Hook your reader with an interesting and relevant anecdote or a mention of a big idea that the text seems to be addressing.

- Briefly summarize or describe the text you will be analyzing. Mention the author's (or speaker's or creator's) name and the title of the text. Say what you think the point of the text is.

- Write a thesis that specifically states your judgment about whether the text, or an aspect of the text, is effective and why.

- Begin each body paragraph with a topic sentence that clearly relates back to the corresponding part of your thesis statement.

- Within each body paragraph, focus on *analyzing* the particular element or aspect of the text referenced in your topic sentence; do not simply summarize what the text says. If you are writing about multiple aspects of a text, use a body paragraph for each aspect. If you're analyzing a TED Talk, for example, you might focus on three separate aspects of the speech: the speaker's choice to start off with a personal story, the speaker's use of statistics and data points, and the speaker's repetition of a key question throughout the talk.

- Use the text itself as your primary evidence, with short quotations or design or delivery features as the main source of that evidence.

- Use outside sources only when they are necessary to substantiate a claim you've made or when they help provide a richer understanding of your text.

- Conclude with an overall judgment of your text, indicating its cultural, social, or historical significance.

DIY 13.4 Plan Your Analysis with a Graphic Organizer

Most writers benefit from (1) the process of writing something out and (2) being able to see what their thoughts look like on the page. See where you are with your analysis by organizing your points graphically, making sure evidence for your analysis is in place. (For more on outlining, see Section 5.5.)

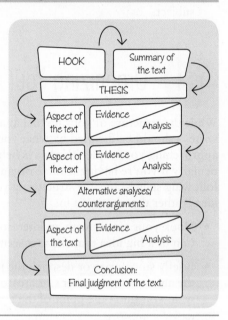

An Invitation to Read: An Analysis of an Advertisement

Gillette's 2019 "Toxic Masculinity" ad, the company's response to the #MeToo movement, invited a conversation and divided its viewing audience. (If you haven't already seen the commercial, it's just a YouTube search away.) University of Southern California marketing professor Marlene Towns jumps into the debate with an analysis that takes on the company's purpose, message, multiple audiences, and strong (some have argued too strong) appeals to *pathos*, or emotion.

The New Gillette Commercial: The Best an Ad Can Get

Marlene Towns

1   The recent commercial from Gillette, titled "Toxic Masculinity," has sparked a great deal of discussion and controversy. Unlike many debates over the merits of particular ad messaging or brand communication decision, there aren't simply two sides or easy love it/hate it reactions. This one seems to be a bit more complex and people's reactions more emotional and nuanced. On its face, the ad, which is ostensibly targeted at the typical male Gillette user, is quite simply beseeching men to be "better" and to work toward the goal of being their best. This is similar in spirit to, say, Dove's long-running "Campaign for Real Beauty" campaign, which points out the many ways in which women can be their own worst enemy when it comes to their self-image. But while we are used to this type of prescriptive ad messaging targeting women and their emotions, men are more often appealed to with humor and lighthearted quips or sex-based appeals. So, Gillette's approach has really struck a nerve for some and a chord for others.

2   Those who have expressed negative reactions to the spot seem to feel that the brand is pointing to the most negative stereotypes of men in an accusatory fashion, which seems at odds with the goal of winning them over as customers. Many of these negative reactions reference recent social and political debates played out in the media, such as the #MeToo movement, Supreme Court nominee accusations and celebrity figures who have been accused of various forms of sexual misconduct. To the extent that anything these days that can be viewed as remotely political is likely to evoke strong visceral reactions, controversy is inevitable. On the other hand, one might argue that there is nothing inherently political about being a decent human being and, in this case, raising decent men.

3   Much like positive body image and self-confidence do not directly emerge from the use of Dove products, there is a relevant connection, albeit counterfactual in nature, between the beauty industry and women's feelings toward beauty and particularly the acknowledgement and embrace of their own beauty. Likewise, a brand like Gillette has long had the slogan "The Best a Man Can Get," which has subtly emphasized the importance of living one's best life and being one's best—a goal that goes beyond razors and shaving to appeal to higher-order needs. It seems fully within that vein that Gillette would encourage men to be their best in other ways as well.

4   In line with their other recent concurrent campaign, which profiles the coming of age of Shaquem Griffin (an NFL linebacker player who succeeded despite being born with amniotic band syndrome resulting in his left hand being amputated when he was a child), Gillette proposes that "your best never comes easy" and portrays Griffin being raised to work hard and

succeed despite his particular physical challenges. Both ads include Gillette products as part of the journey to manhood, which is a perfect parallel. Shaving is often seen as a rite of passage from boyhood to manhood and a shared teaching experience from father-figure to son along with many other life lessons on becoming a man and being one's best. For Gillette, "grooming" goes far beyond the literal act but embraces grooming future selves and future generations of men. In this vein, their messaging in the current campaign is incredibly topical and timely.

5   Another argument that could be made as to why the current ad message is so on point is the reality of who the target audience really consists of. While men are clearly the target audience for the messaging and the protagonist in the ad, women are often the household purchasers and decision-makers for many household and grooming products. Many men do hold specific preferences for brands of grooming products — particularly razors — but women make many such decisions for the household and serve as the purchaser of the products, so their reaction matters as well.

6   An unscientific analysis of online reactions seems to show women's reactions to the spot are overwhelmingly positive, which Gillette's brand team no doubt predicted. One issue that I do take with the spot is the title of the ad, which may work to undermine the incredible potential of the spot to be received as positively as it could be and that is the title: "Toxic Masculinity." While it is not aired with the title, even the references to it in coverage, online and in discussion emphasizes the negative and perhaps contributes to some people's defensive stance. The term "toxic masculinity" is a bit jarring and frames the spot as an accusation aimed at men and manhood in general rather than the learning opportunity that it is meant to be.

7   For all men, including those who are totally innocent of any bad behavior as well as those who may reflect on words or actions both intentional and not, the ad ideally can serve as an answer to the questions: "What can I do?" and "How can I make a difference?" It provides illustrations of how words or actions can be destructive and what can be said and done in such situations and also serves as a reminder that young generations of boys and men are looking to these examples as opportunities to learn and grow.

8   What makes the ad so successful, though, is the fact that it has sparked sharing, conversation, debate, discomfort, introspection, thought, articles, press and discussion. It has made us feel, which is an often elusive goal for brands, and it has made us think. It has made men think of Gillette as more than just another manufacturer of razors but as a brand with meaning and with values and, perhaps, part of their journey to manhood.

9   Interestingly enough, despite the controversy (or, in fact, because of it) one's reaction to the Gillette spot has itself become a barometer by which to gauge the very existence of toxic masculinity. Per one social media meme, "Your response to the Gillette commercial tells me all I need to know about you as a person." For this and for their contribution to the dialog and movement toward creating change, bravo Gillette.

Reading Questions

1. In your own words, define "toxic masculinity." Can you name some specific examples of toxic masculinity not discussed in Towns's essay?

2. Do you think that an advertisement for products like razors and shaving cream can actually make a difference in the way that people behave? What reasons do you have for your opinion?

3. Do a YouTube search for Gillette's "Toxic Masculinity" commercial (also known as "The Best Men Can Be") and watch it. How accurately do you think Towns has represented the ad? What elements would you emphasize that she has downplayed or not mentioned at all?

An Invitation to Read: A Student Analysis of a Speech

In 2018, Oprah Winfrey received the Golden Globes' Cecil B. DeMille Award, given annually by the Hollywood Foreign Press "to a talented individual for outstanding contributions to the world of entertainment." Oprah's speech was so powerful that almost immediately her name was mentioned as a 2020 presidential candidate. While student Curran McCrory found "the push for Winfrey to run for president slightly outrageous," he nevertheless acknowledges, "there is no denying that her speech was effective." Curran wrote the following essay in part because he thought Oprah's message "is something everyone should hear in an era where the idea of 'truth' is so controversial." You can read a transcript of Oprah's speech on the websites of several established news organizations (CNN, Los Angeles Times), and you can watch the complete speech on YouTube.

McCrory 1

Curran McCrory

Professor Starkey

English 110

13 October 2018

Analysis of Oprah Winfrey's Speech at the
75th Golden Globes

2018 is quite a complicated time to be an American. Political tensions are on the rise, and many insist that our country has never been more divided. At the same time, we're

The writer uses political context as a hook.

McCrory 2

breaking historical records for political activism. Since January of 2017, activist groups have held the four largest organized marches in American history, all in Washington DC, with the 2017 and 2018 Women's Marches taking first and second place. Women across the United States are coming together to tell their stories and to be heard like never before. The nation is finally having a discussion that has been kept quiet for decades, and that discussion once again exploded across the national stage on January 7, 2018, when Oprah Winfrey accepted the Cecil B. DeMille award at the 75th Golden Globe Awards (see fig. 1). Because she was the first Black woman to receive the award, and because she is one of our generation's most eloquent storytellers, her speech was, of course, moving and incredibly timely. Winfrey's speech succeeds because she connects to her audience through three distinct strategies: telling vivid stories, reminding us of how historical events

Thesis communicates the writer's position and introduces the three specific aspects of the text for analysis.

Handout, Paul Drinkwater/NBCUniversal via Getty Images

Fig. 1. Oprah Winfrey delivers a speech in January 2018. Paul Drinkwater. *75th Annual Golden Globe Awards Show*. 7 Jan. 2018. *Getty Images*, www.gettyimages.com/detail/ news-photo/in-this-handout-photo-provided-by-nbcuniversaloprah-news-photo/902753412.

McCrory 3

continue to resonate to the present day, and showing how sexual violence in the world of Hollywood reflects what happens in the rest of America.

Winfrey's gifts as a storyteller were on display for decades in her TV show *Oprah*, and she demonstrates the power of those gifts at the start of her speech. Winfrey begins with a vivid memory from her childhood, watching Sidney Poitier win the Academy Award for best actor in 1964. Details are the heart of a good story, and Winfrey uses them well. She tells us that while watching the Oscars, she was "a little girl sitting on the linoleum floor of my mother's house in Milwaukee." That's a vivid image, and it becomes even more vivid when she describes her mother coming "through the door bone tired from cleaning other people's houses." We also see the awards show through young Oprah's eyes, as she subtly registers the overwhelming force of race in the United States by stating that Poitier's "tie was white, and of course his skin was black." With a few well-chosen images, Winfrey expertly evokes the working-class life of the young girl who would go on to become one of the most famous, and richest, women in the world (Mejia).

Winfrey continues to use storytelling as she transitions to the most powerful strategy in her speech: the use of an extended and poignant historical reference. About halfway through the speech, she tells the horrific story of Recy Taylor, a Black woman who in 1944, was "abducted by six armed white men, raped, and left blindfolded by the side of the road coming home from church." Winfrey notes that Rosa Parks, one of the most celebrated women in America for her activism in the Civil Rights Movement, was assigned to Taylor's case. Unfortunately, even Parks was unable to bring justice to Taylor under the twisted judicial system of the Jim

Topic sentence previews discussion of the first aspect of analysis.

Thesis communicates the writer's position and introduces the three specific aspects of the text for analysis.

Analysis is strengthened with specific examples from the speech and from the writer's research.

Crow South. In an obituary in *The New York Times*, Sewell Chan compares Taylor's story to another tragic historical moment. He writes, "Mindful of the outrage surrounding the case of the Scottsboro Boys—nine black teenagers who had been wrongly accused of raping two white women in 1931—the county prosecutor took care to provide a semblance of equal justice. But it was an empty gesture." Because she was a woman of color, Taylor's case was not given the same attention and her case was dismissed. However, Winfrey's recounting of this almost forgotten historical moment makes it more relevant than ever. At least for a couple of days, Winfrey is able to put Recy Taylor's life in the center of the national dialogue.

> Writer comments on the importance of the speaker's strategy.

After sharing Taylor's story, Winfrey concludes her speech by showing how the current state of female inequality in the United States is everywhere, not just in Hollywood. She talks about the significance of the #MeToo movement without naming specific names, and she doesn't have to. Most in the room are familiar with the sexual misconduct allegations made against legendary Hollywood titans such as Harvey Weinstein, Kevin Spacey, Bill Cosby, and many more. The controversial movement erupted from the core of Hollywood, but she makes sure to remind everyone that these issues do not just plague the entertainment industry. Referring to all the women across the country who experience the same injustices on a daily basis, Winfrey says:

> They are domestic workers and farm workers. They
> are working in factories and they work in restaurants
> and they're in academia, engineering, medicine, and
> science. They're part of the world of tech and politics

McCrory 5

and business. They're our athletes in the Olympics and they're our soldiers in the military.

Winfrey's naming of so many specific fields outside of show business emphasizes that celebrities make up only a tiny fraction of the population of women who experience sexual violence. This point is echoed on the #MeToo website, where organizers explain that their focus is to provide support for "a global community of survivors from all walks of life." As she does in her opening story about watching Sidney Poitier receiving his Oscar, Winfrey shows that there is a powerful connection between all suffering people, whether they are famous or not.

Winfrey wraps up her speech by suggesting that there is great hope for the future. She believes in the process that has gotten us to where we are today, and has faith that it will take us to a day where this conversation will only be in the past. She enthusiastically cries out, "I want all the girls watching here, now, to know that a new day is on the horizon!" People who watch or read this speech fifty years from now may have forgotten how hopeless many Americans felt in early 2018, but the speech's historical context is key to its power. Winfrey concludes with more words of encouragement: "And when that new day finally dawns, it will be because of a lot of magnificent women, many of whom are right here in this room tonight, and some pretty phenomenal men, fighting hard to make sure that they become the leaders who take us to the time when nobody ever has to say 'Me too' again." Winfrey succeeds in making a connection because she invites her audience to be hopeful, too.

Conclusion comments on the speaker's call to action.

McCrory 6

Works Cited

Chan, Sewell. "Recy Taylor, Who Fought for Justice After a
    1944 Rape, Dies at 97." *The New York Times*, 29 Dec. 2017,
    ww.nytimes.com/2017/12/29/obituaries/Recy-taylor
    -alabama-rape-victim-dead.html.

Mejia, Zamenna. "Oprah Winfrey, Worth a Record $4 Billion,
    Becomes One of the World's 500 Richest People." *CNBC*,
    21 June 2018, www.cnbc.com/2018/06/20/oprah-winfrey
    -worth-4-billion-now-one-of-the-worlds-richest-people.
    html.

Me Too. metoomvmt.org. Accessed 20 Sept. 2018.

Winfrey, Oprah. "Read Oprah Winfrey's Rousing Golden Globes
    Speech." *CNN*, 10 Jan. 2018, www.cnn.com/2018/01/08
    /entertainment/oprah-globes-speech-transcript/index.
    html. Transcript.

Reading Questions

1. Watch or read Oprah's Golden Globes speech, then make a list of aspects of the speech you noticed that Curran did not discuss in his essay.

2. In your opinion, what are the most effective elements of Curran's essay? Where can he still improve?

3. Compare Oprah's 2018 speech to a more recent powerful speech by a public figure. What do they have in common? How are they different? Which is more effective and why?

Chapter 13 Checklist
Analyzing a Text

☐ **If a text was not assigned to your class, have you chosen an appropriate text for this assignment?**

Your text, whether it is written, visual, or multimodal, should fit within the guidelines of your assignment, be fairly short yet worthy of analysis, and inspire confidence that you can thoroughly understand and analyze it.

☐ **Have you actively read or viewed the text a number of times?**

Your engagement with the text should be complete. Read the text aloud and annotate it; summarize and challenge it; identify the writer's claims and place the text in context. If the text includes sound or visuals, make a note of those, too. In short, by the time you finish writing your essay, the text should feel like an old friend.

☐ **Have you carefully analyzed the writer's craft?**

In a textual analysis, *how* the writer uses language is at least as important as what the writer says. Look carefully at the structure, at words and sentences, and at images and appeals to the writer's (or speaker's) audience. Notice how language is used to create patterns and themes.

☐ **Is the structure of your essay clear yet flexible?**

Early on, your essay should state which elements of the text you will be analyzing and why they are important. Each body paragraph should have a particular focus, although you will want to allow for some flexibility in how you approach the different textual elements you are examining.

13.5 Making It Stick

How will you break a text down and analyze the writer's strategies?

Working Together

13.5a Reading Texts Collaboratively Form a group of three or four students for the purpose of taking a fresh look at the text you are writing about. If your instructor has assigned a common text, or you and your partners just happen to be writing on the same text, explain your own analysis to your partners and find out what they saw and learned from the common text that you missed. Compare the specific aspects of the text that you decided to analyze with group members' choices.

If individuals in the class are writing on different texts, share your text with your partners until everyone has read everyone else's text. Then spend some time discussing each person's text. Talk about what stood out to you and why. Point to specific words, formatting, sentences, and passages when explaining your response to the text.

Take notes on what your partners say and try your best to provide them with new insights for their essays.

Applying What You Know

13.5b Thesis Check   Review your working thesis statement using this checklist.

Thesis Checklist

A successful thesis statement should

☐ be focused and specific

☐ not be a statement of fact

☐ include a topic and a claim

☐ answer a question, whether specifically asked or implied

☐ be arguable and worth arguing

☐ provide a plan for the essay

☐ be a statement, not an "announcement"

Revise your thesis statement if needed — and if you are working with a partner, help your partner to revise. Take another look at Section 5.4 if you need to review the elements of a strong thesis statement.

13.5c Organization Check   Review the organization of your essay using this checklist.

Organization Checklist

A successful textual analysis essay should do the following:

☐ hook the reader with an interesting and relevant anecdote or line of questioning and briefly describe or summarize the text that will be analyzed

☐ have a thesis that specifically states your judgment about whether the text, or an aspect of the text, is effective and why

☐ feature body paragraphs that (1) begin with a topic sentence that clearly relates to the thesis statement and (2) focus on analysis of the particular element of the text referenced in the topic sentence

☐ use the text itself as primary evidence, with short quotations or design or delivery elements as the main source of that evidence

☐ use outside sources only when they are necessary to substantiate a claim or when they help provide a richer understanding of the text

☐ conclude with an overall appreciation of and judgment of the text, indicating its cultural, social, or historical significance

Invitations to Write

13.5d Analyzing Contemporary Speeches

Shorter: In the search engine of your choice, find a speech by typing "speech" + "transcript" + the name of someone whom you feel is currently making interesting speeches. Write a one paragraph quick take on the speech, using one or two of the sections in this chapter as strategies for focusing your analysis.

Longer: Follow all the relevant steps described in this chapter and turn your brief analysis of a speech into a full essay.

13.5e Analyzing Editorials and Opinion Pieces

Editorial and opinion pieces, or "op-eds" as they as sometimes called — for "opinion-editorial" — usually feature good writing on a controversial and current topic. Find an intriguing op-ed, and in a couple of paragraphs, examine the moves the writer makes to interest you in the text and persuade you of the strength of their position. (You can find appropriate editorials in magazines like *Newsweek, Ebony,* and *Time,* and in newspapers such as the *New York Times,* the *Wall Street Journal,* and the *Washington Post.*)

Longer: Use your early notes as the basis for an essay-length analysis of an effective "op-ed." Pay at least as much attention to *how* the author makes a point as you do to analyzing the content of the author's argument.

13.5f Analyzing Reviews

Shorter: Visit a site that publishes film, music, book, or video game reviews. Then choose a particularly well-written review and write a couple of paragraphs of analysis, taking particular note of how the writer uses language to persuade you of the validity of his or her evaluation.

Longer: Write a full essay analyzing an evaluative text. Remember that your essay is analyzing the evaluator's (the writer's) strategies, not the particular film or album being evaluated. If you are analyzing a review of a movie you really love, for example, your focus should remain on the *text* of the review; your own opinion of the movie should not be an important part of the discussion.

13.5g Analyzing Multimodal Works

Shorter: Select a work that contains little or no text. Describe the work in such clear and precise detail that someone who has never seen it, or has no idea what you are talking about, will be able to form a clear mental picture of the work.

Longer: Develop your opening description into a full essay using the suggestions offered in "Analyzing a Visual or Multimodal Work" (see Section 13.3). Provide context for the work's creation and reception; focus on key features of the work; judge the creator's strategies and intentions; explain why you think the work is successful or unsuccessful.

14

Reading and Writing Multimodal Texts

REFLECT

Write Before You Read | Activity to connect what's new with what you already know 335

READ & WRITE

DIY (Do-it-yourself) activities offer just-in-time support for all the skills in this book.

MAKING IT STICK

Write Before You Read Think about the text messages you write every day. It's likely some of them include a combination of text and one or more visuals — in the form of emojis, gifs, or photos. Write a short paragraph exploring *why* you text with visuals, what purposes those visuals serve, and how text messages might be different if you had no capability to include visuals.

14.1 Understanding Multimodal Texts

When you were in high school, you might have had to compose a poster for a biology project. Such a project might have included words, images, and data charts explaining your research on how vegetable gardens respond differently to different soil types. If you've ever completed a project like this, then you've already written multimodally. In the past, you may have seen a video ad for a political campaign—words and images combined on screen with a running voice narrative in the background. Again, this is a multimodal work. In college, your coursework may ask you to read or write in multiple modes. But what does this mean?

Communicators use different methods, or modes, for reaching audiences: words, still images, moving images, and sounds. When a communicator uses a combination of modes, the "text" becomes multimodal rather than monomodal. While multimodal texts may *look* different than traditional essays, they rely on the same principles of logic, evidence, and clarity. Indeed, contemporary readers, who tend to be digitally and visually savvy, may be even more skeptical of a shabbily constructed multimodal text than they are of one made only of words and letters.

This chapter covers a few of the realms of college composition that lie beyond the more traditional modes of communication. We begin by discussing how professional writers employ visuals to strengthen an argument (returning to David Leonhardt's "Is College Worth It?" in Section 2.1). Then we'll examine several ways you can use multiple modes in your writing before expanding the focus to writing meant to be read primarily in a digital version. Next, we'll look at a particular type of multimodal writing: classroom presentations. The chapter closes with a student's multimodal composition.

14.2 "Reading" Visuals

If you're like most people, when you hear the word "read," you assume the thing to be read will be what is called "alphabetic text"—that is, words in a sentence like this one. However, "reading"—the act of decoding and understanding—can also be applied to just about anything, including photographs, drawings, paintings, ads, videos, and movies.

In order to read a visual, you have to look at it as carefully as you would at a written text, "rereading" it over and over, until you have a clear idea of what is actually there in front of you. Let's begin by thinking about how visuals can be analyzed in conjunction with an accompanying text.

Use the "Noun + 1" Strategy

One strategy for looking closely at visuals draws on the definition of a "noun" that you may remember from elementary school: a person, place, or thing. Those three elements turn out to be an effective way of describing most visuals, particularly images, photographs, and paintings. You need add only one more important element for analysis: the point of view from which the image is seen.

Obviously, not every aspect of every visual needs to be discussed in every context, but when you're focusing on the details of an especially important image, ask yourself the following questions, using the Noun +1 strategy:

- **People:** Who, if anyone, is in the image? If there are no people, is their absence significant in any way? If there are people, what are they doing? What are they wearing? What are the expressions on their faces?

- **Place:** Where is the image set? Is it inside or outside? Is the setting urban, suburban, or rural? What's the weather like and what time of day is it?

- **Things:** Other than people and a place, what else does the image show? Typically, one or two objects will stand out: the AK-47 being carried by a soldier, for instance, or the glass of whiskey in the hand of a woman at a bar.

- **Point of View:** Where is the camera, or the artist's point of view, in relation to the subject of the image? Is it an aerial view or at ground level? Is the subject shown at eye-level, or from slightly above or below the spectator's viewpoint? And how far is the camera or artist from the subject? Is it a close-up, or is the subject seen from a great distance?

Jill Scott at Temple University.
AP Photo/The Philadelphia Inquirer, David Swanson

Take another look at the photograph from David Leonhardt's essay, "Is College Worth It?" The photograph is reprinted in this section so that we can "read" it using the Noun +1 categories.

People: The people in the far background are nothing but blurry dots. To the left, and in the middle of the photo, you can see the out-of-focus backs of two recent graduates. The center of attention is clearly the young woman on the left—Jill Scott, according to the caption—and a man next to her, who appears to be slightly older. The man, also a graduate, is obviously star-struck to be in the presence of the singer of hits like "So in Love" and "Hate on Me." In the selfie he is taking of the two of them, Scott smiles pleasantly, but the man's expression is one of complete delight.

Place: The photo appears to be taken inside a large indoor arena. You know from the caption that the graduation is taking place at Temple University, so this could be the home of the university's renowned basketball team. No visible daylight enters the space, but it is well lit, with one especially bright light shining down from the rafters in the area behind the man's head.

Things: The first objects you are likely to notice are the caps and gowns worn by the woman and man. The man also wears some kind of medal. The other noticeable *thing* in the picture is the man's phone, which he will use to capture his own image of graduation—highlighted by the appearance of a famous R&B singer.

Point of View: The photo is shot from below, almost as though the photographer's camera were an extension of the man's outstretched hand. Neither Jill Scott nor her admiring fan are looking toward David Swanson's camera, so the picture also feels as though we are getting a secret glimpse of their interaction.

Overall, the picture exudes happiness and celebration, and you can easily see why Leonhardt (or his editor) chose this photograph to illustrate an article arguing for the value of a college education. However, the photo displays nothing of the years of hard work leading up to the graduation ceremony; it shows only the pure joy of receiving a college degree.

The second visual that appears with Leonhardt's article is a line graph entitled "Median Weekly Earnings by Education Level." A graph shows the relation between two sets of data. The vertical set of information on the left is called the "y-axis," while the horizontal information on the bottom is referred to as the "x-axis." To read a graph, you look for the place where the y- and x-axes intersect. In the graph shown here, for instance, we can see that in 2000, college graduates—represented by the purple line on the top—made, on average, between $800 and $900 per week; by contrast, high school graduates—represented by the gray line—made, on average, $500 per week. The disparity grows significantly as we look at the lines as they reach the year 2020. That year, college graduates made nearly $1,400 per week compared with roughly $775 per week for high school graduates.

The image itself is rather plain, but the point is clear: you will regret not getting a college degree.

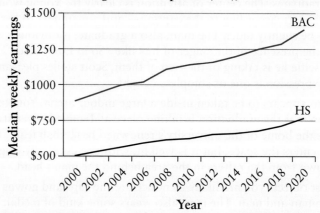

Median weekly earnings by education level, bachelor's degree (BAC) vs. high school diploma (HS), 2000–2020

A graph comparing median weekly earnings among people with a bachelor's degree and those with a high school diploma.

Data from Bureau of Labor Statistics 2020.

In an article like Leonhardt's, which is mostly alphabetic, visuals tend to be placed early on, to capture the reader's attention, and that's the case here. It is, however, unusual in an article with just two visuals to find them placed back to back. One explanation might be that because Leonhardt's article is fairly short, these dual illustrations serve as a kind of double whammy to drive home his point about both the emotional and the economic benefits of earning a college degree. The visuals boost both the *pathos* and the *logos* in his argument.

DIY 14.2 Use the Noun +1 Strategy to Analyze an Image

Choose an online image that is part of a longer alphabetic text and provide your own analysis of the image and how it functions in relation to the words around it. Use the Noun +1 strategy — asking questions about *People*, *Place*, *Things*, and *Point of View* — to guide your reading of the image.

Explore Modal Combinations

When you "read" works in which alphabetic text is not the dominant mode, it helps to ask questions about how and why the modes are combined. Many public service ads, for example, are produced as videos and include text, moving images, and sound (often with both narration and music). Public service ads—ads designed to sell an idea rather than a product—often address social issues such as bullying, gun safety, racism, autism awareness, disaster preparedness, campus sexual violence, and more. The Ad Council (adcouncil.org) includes plenty of PSAs on its website for study.

If you are assigned to study or choose to study a multimodal text, first take note of what happens in each of the modes. Setting up a grid might help.

Words	Images	Sounds (narration, music, sound effects)

Pay attention to the styling of words, images, and sounds, too. Are the words in all caps? Small or large? Why? Are the images in color or in black and white? Why? Is there a sound motif such as laughter, gunshots, or footsteps? Why?

Finally, ask yourself questions about how the modes work together and what effect the composer may wish to create. Just as you do when analyzing a traditional print text (see Section 13.2), identify the composer's purpose or reason for the work, the target audience, and the larger context for the work.

14.3 Writing with Visuals

Once you start looking for visuals in other people's writing, it's hard not to notice how prevalent they are. Even Old School media like the *New York Times* and the *Wall Street Journal* make visuals a significant part of almost all the writing they publish, so you can be sure that more cutting-edge publications—especially those that appear mostly or entirely online—consider visuals as important, if not *more* important, than the written text itself.

When you write for a college assignment, your instructor may encourage or expect you to incorporate relevant images. A well-chosen visual can provide an opportunity to emphasize, extend, or elaborate on what you have to say with words.

The images you incorporate into your essay may work on the level of *pathos* (emotion), *logos* (reason), or *ethos* (the speaker's credibility)—or a combination of two or three of those appeals. Indeed, because most academic essays are composed primarily of words, images have a power they might not have in another, image-rich context, like a website. Therefore, be selective: the more images you include, the less impact each one will make.

The fact is, of course, that you probably already have a great deal of experience matching images with texts on social media. Nevertheless, knowing what to highlight and what to leave out can be a challenging aspect of visual communication, so it's worth remembering a few general pieces of advice:

Tips for Using Visuals in Your Writing

- **Choose visuals that are relevant to your purpose.** Even more than an irrelevant sentence, an inappropriate or unrelated image truly stands out. Don't use a visual if it doesn't help you achieve your purpose—to report, persuade, instruct, compare, inspire, and so on.

- **Choose visuals that address your audience's needs.** Deciding what sort of visuals will be most effective should include identifying who will be reading or viewing your work and what they might need or expect to see.

- **Place your visuals where they have the most impact.** It's especially important that infographics like charts and graphs are close to the text in which they are discussed, but every visual should be placed logically and where it will have the most impact.

- **Make good use of empty space.** When you begin composing with visuals, be deliberate about placement and spacing. Adding space around a visual can make it more noticeable. While you may not have flexibility in a traditional essay (because MLA and APA dictate how to place visuals, see Chapters 18 and 19), more visual genres such as slide presentations and posters will challenge you to think more about space.

- **Don't overuse visuals.** Just as a little color goes a long way, so will a few well-chosen visuals make a better impression than if your essay looks like someone's photo book.

- **Don't leave an image unexplained.** You will want to make a direct connection between the visual and the text of your essay so that readers will not be confused about your meaning.

- **Use captions, when appropriate.** If you are using pictures that you have taken yourself, and the pictures are self-explanatory, you may not need to caption your visuals. However, if you're drawing on outside sources, readers should be able to quickly and easily tell what they're seeing.

- **Cite your sources.** The caption is important, but your citation isn't complete until you've given full information about the visual in your Works Cited or References page. See Chapters 18 (MLA) and 19 (APA) for guidelines.

Understand Visual Arguments

One of the most powerful uses of visuals is as evidence for an argument. If your purpose is to persuade and if your audience is persuadable, a picture may not be worth *quite* a thousand words, but it does serve to nudge the viewer. Turn back to the reading in Section 3.4 of this book—a *Los Angeles Times* article about a young man who found success at a prestigious university despite great odds. The smiling image of Kashawn Campbell radiates a sense of hope and purpose. Kurt Streeter spends quite a few words in his article describing Campbell's optimism, but Bethany Mollenkof's photograph *shows* it to you in an instant. Moreover, when you are referencing historical events that may be unfamiliar to your readers, a well-selected photograph or map may go a long way toward convincing skeptics that something important did actually occur in the way you describe it.

Finally, visuals can sometimes make an argument on their own, or with the help of just a few words. Indeed, the visual component of an advertisement is often its most important element. For example, take a look at this 1959 advertisement for the Volkswagen Beetle.

Think Small. Source: DDB Worldwide Communications Group LLC.

JUNE 25 | **PRIDE**

Made with crème colors that do not exist

"Pride." Source: Oreo

At the time, the majority of new cars in the United States were enormous gas guzzlers. Advertising genius Bill Bernbach promoted the Beetle by deliberately emphasizing the very thing that American buyers would presumably shun: a car so tiny that it is barely visible in a huge field of white. The upending of traditional expectations worked. While there is text below the tag line "Think small"—notes about fuel economy and affordability—what most viewers will remember is the lone little car that turned out to inspire a revolution in transportation, advertising, and pop culture.

Fast forward to 2012, when Oreo—yes, *Oreo*—made an argument with a few words and a single, surprising image. The image had nothing to do with cookies. Oreo's "Pride" campaign made the arguments that LGBTQ+ pride is worth celebrating and, coupled with the company's #ProudParent campaign, that acceptance of people of all gender and sexual identities is important.

With the rhetorical considerations of purpose and audience in mind, think carefully about which visuals you select for your essay, and why and how you plan to use them.

Use Charts and Graphs

Not every academic essay will benefit from charts and graphs, but if you have striking (and, of course, reliable) statistical information, a visual representation of that data can make a big impression on your readers.

One of the easiest charts to use is the pie chart, which, as its name suggests, looks something like a pie and, through the imagery of "slices," shows how a whole is divided into two or more parts. (You can make basic pie charts in Word or in Google Docs simply by selecting Insert > Chart > Pie.)

The pie chart to the left draws on information from a 2017 United States Census report indicating that 33.4% of American adults have a college degree. That fact allows us to deduce that almost 67% of American adults do *not* possess a college degree. Entering that information in the appropriate chart results in the following graphic representation of the large difference between the number of Americans with college degrees and those without.

Percentage of American Adults with a College Degree in 2017

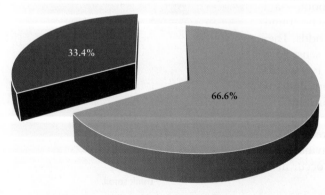

- College Degree   - No College Degree

Pie charts help readers visualize data.

In his article "Is College Worth It?" (see Section 2.1), author David Leonhardt uses data to reinforce his thesis that a college degree is worth the investment. For instance, he cites statistics from a report by the Economic Policy Institute indicating that the average hourly wage for college graduates is $32.60, while the average wage for nondegree holders is $16.50. A difference in earning power that substantial can be emphasized in a pie chart, or, better yet, in a 3D cylindrical graph like the one here.

The more complicated the data, the more useful charts and graphs become. (Accurate titles, labels, and captions are especially important when the information is complex.) Whenever you feel you may be losing your reader with your numbers, turn those numbers into visual representations that your audience can more easily understand.

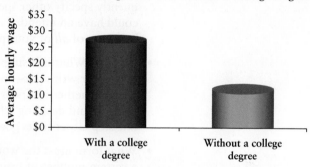

Differences in Earnings with and without a College Degree

Bar graphs can show relationships between data points.

DIY 14.3b Create a Chart or Graph

Locate a place in an essay you are currently writing (or one you have already written) where a chart or graph would enhance your argument, then create the appropriate graphic. Be sure to title, label, and provide a caption for your graphic. Then write a short paragraph — some or all of which you might use in your essay — explaining the importance of the chart or graph.

14.4 Writing Multimodally

As you've already seen, multimodal writing at its core means writing in more than one mode. It can also mean writing for a digital environment, in which case you've probably been doing it all day long. Every time you send a text message with an emoji, a photo, or a video attached, you are communicating in at least two modes: words plus still or moving images—or even sound. In fact, if you look through the text messages on your phone, you'll probably feel that if there's a long string of exchanges only in "alphabetic" text, that is, words on a page or screen, the exchange may have become a bit boring. We're so used to seeing images everywhere we go—on TV and in movie theaters and on billboards, on computer and mobile phone screens—it makes sense that visuals should play an increasingly important role in academic essays. And with the rise of podcasting, sound, too, may take on new roles in college writing.

Whatever form your essay takes, you'll want to know the answers to these questions about your writing situation:

- **Audience: Who is reading the work?** Audience always matters. Yes, your instructor is one audience for your work, but writing prompts frequently specify other specific audiences. Work that is published online could have an intended audience (specific) or a very general one. Always be aware of *all* of your potential readers.

- **Purpose: What is it supposed to do?** The purpose of an essay—your reason for writing it—provides its focus. Every move you make as a writer, whether it's incorporating a secondary source or choosing a photograph and deciding where to place it, should serve to get your essay one step closer to its goals.

- **What form must the work take?** Just as a research paper might require a certain number of primary and secondary sources, a multimodal essay may need to include an infographic, a photograph, and a video. As always, write from the specific prompt you are given.

- **Where and how will it be read?** Writing online means reading online, and we know that can happen on our phones, on tablets, and on computers. Make sure that your multimodal essay is as easy to read across platforms as its hard copy equivalent.

Note: Composition instructors' familiarity with technology varies. While you may be able to ask a few questions as you work on a project, do not expect your instructor to perform tech support for you as you work on your project. Often you can ask a peer or someone at your school's Help Desk to help you solve a problem.

Use Color

Color, as you may have noticed while reading this book, can be an effective way of connecting similar sections and distinguishing between different parts of a text. Headings stand out when they're in color. Color charts and graphs are more likely to be read and examined than those in black and white. And while a photograph that was made, and intended to be reproduced, in black and white can be a work of art, the average photograph is more likely to catch a reader's eye if it is in color.

Color can be used in print just as easily as it can in a digital environment. It is discussed in the context of multimodal writing for several reasons. First, color is much more of an integral part of composing an online document; we expect color when we open up a webpage in a way that we aren't necessarily looking for it when we open up a book. Second, color onscreen is usually more vivid than color on a piece of paper. Finally, some students don't have access to color printers, so the only way they can realistically use color is when composing work that will be viewed on a screen.

The most striking contrasts are between colors that are complementary. Complementary colors are so different from each other that when the two colors are combined, they essentially cancel each other out, producing black, white, or gray.

You'll notice the strong effect complementary colors have on the eye when you look at a Red Green Blue color model. In the graphic in this section, the complementary colors red and cyan, green and magenta, and blue and yellow practically vibrate when they are placed next to each other. It's a striking effect, but many readers will find it distracting, if not downright unpleasant.

You can see another version of how colors work by looking at a "color wheel." The colors at the top of the wheel—red, orange, and yellow—are called warm colors, while violet (or purple), blue, and green are considered cool. You'll notice that colors close to each other on the color wheel seem compatible; they certainly don't make for the jarring contrast of complementary colors.

If you're a visual artist or a designer, you may have your own ideas about which colors work best together. If you're simply hoping to make the best use of color in an academic assignment, here are a few guidelines to consider.

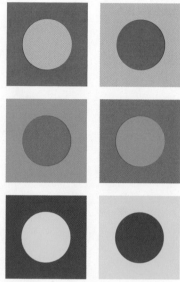

Complementary colors in the RGB color model.
Fouad A. Saad/Shutterstock

Monochromatic Color Wheel

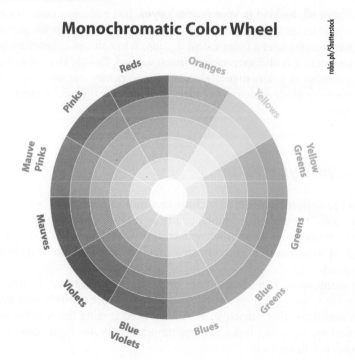

robin.ph/Shutterstock

Guidelines for Using Color

1. **Think about how the colors will work in conjunction with everything around them.** Unlike black print on a white page, which basically becomes "invisible" after a few moments, colors leave an impression, and they play off one another whether you want them to or not. Look at the *entire* area where your colors appear to see if they function as you intend them to, whether the area is a hard copy page, a slide, or other work.

2. **Be consistent.** Consistency is particularly important when using color for type. If for instance, your first main heading is violet, then all subsequent main headings should be violet; if your first subheading is blue, all subheadings should be blue; and so forth. Consistency keeps your reader from being confused.

3. **Be aware when you use color.** In both hard copy traditional essays and digital presentations, keep in mind that the *less* color you use, the more noticeable it will be. An assignment that looks like a Skittles ad may be appealing at first, but the novelty will quickly wear off. Moreover, you may need to think about accessibility issues; not everybody sees color the same way you do; in fact, some people (4–8% of all adults!) don't see color at all.

4. **Above all, be kind to your reader's eyes.** Just because a color is easily available, that doesn't mean you should use it. Microsoft Word, for instance, features a color called Spring. While this is a cheery variation on green, it is also extremely difficult to read. Google Docs also features a number of colors that might seem fun in theory, but which in reality are more likely to distract readers than increase their enjoyment of your essay.

Consider Hypertext

One of the easiest elements to include in a multimodal essay is a hyperlink, or just "link," an embedded word or phrase that allows a reader to move from the anchor text to another text with just a tap or click. Compared to finding information in books, clicking on a link can feel like traveling at warp speed.

In many ways, hyperlinks are essential to online reading. If they weren't, we wouldn't find ourselves sitting down for what we thought was going to be five minutes only to discover that we'd been surfing the web for hours. Nevertheless, including links in a multimodal essay has both opportunities and potential drawbacks.

Advantages to Including Hyperlinks in Essays

- **Your essay will be expansive.** There's a big online world out there with more than two billion live websites. While many people now take the Internet for granted, it still provides a magic carpet ride to an almost endless array of places and ideas.

- **Your links will demonstrate that you know what else is out there.** Linking to intelligent sources on your topic shows that you've done good research and discovered some worthwhile primary and secondary sources.

- **Links take your reader directly to the source material.** Hyperlinks take your readers straight to the places where you found your information. *Don't believe me?*, a link seems to ask. *Here, see for yourself.*

- **Links connect readers to professional multimedia.** While students who are technologically savvy may prefer to create their own audiovisual material, for the rest of us, links can send readers to powerful multimedia experiences that would be too costly and time-consuming for the average person to make.

Disadvantages of Including Hyperlinks in Essays

- **The reader will leave your essay.** That's the point of a hyperlink, of course, but the moment readers stop reading your work, they are reading someone else's.

- **The reader may become distracted.** Because a link takes readers away from your essay, it keeps them from focusing on your own writing and ideas. In a blog post entitled "Experiments in Delinkification," Nicholas Carr calls hyperlinks "a more violent form of a footnote. Where a footnote gives your brain a gentle nudge, the link gives it a yank."

- **The reader may feel you are less capable of making an argument on your own.** You might use linking to support your own lines of argument. However, relying on links to do your work for you might make your work less powerful and less appealing to the reader who wants to know what *you* think and why.

Linking is certainly convenient for both the writer and the reader. However, think about whether you need your reader to experience a source fully or whether it might be better to just paraphrase, summarize, or quote (see Section 6.3) from the source.

Make Slide Presentations

Significant use of color and linking are often notable features in one of the most commonly assigned multimodal compositions: a slide presentation. Obviously, the specifics of each presentation vary depending on the course and instructor, but there are a handful of presentation software packages that students turn to again and again.

Presentation Software Options

- **Google Slides.** While the themes are fairly plain, Google Slides has the advantage of being a free, easy to learn, and convenient platform for collaboration and instructor grading.

- **PowerPoint.** PowerPoint offers much greater visual and technical variety than Google Slides, but this program is part of the Microsoft Office package and is not free. To collaborate with classmates, everyone will need to have PowerPoint; it will need to be loaded onto the computer on which the presentation is being made; and your instructor will need to have it if you are submitting the presentation for a grade.

- **Prezi.** Although collaboration with other authors isn't as seamless as it is on Google Slides, a Prezi presentation is much more dynamic. You zoom back and forth and in and out of the various slides, and there's a fluidity that's definitely lacking in Google. However, at the time of this writing, Prezi was no longer a free software.

- **Canva.** Canva offers many options for fonts and images. It's far more sophisticated-looking than Google Slides, although it doesn't move from slide to slide as smoothly as Prezi. Like Prezi, it will require you to take out your credit card if you want to use it beyond a short trial period.

Whatever software you end up using, you'll want to follow a few basic guidelines when you create your presentation:

Guidelines for Creating Presentations

1. **Follow the prompt.** As always, do what you've been asked to do. Be creative, but don't forget to cover the material required by your assignment.

2. **Limit the amount of text on each slide.** One idea per slide is a good rule of thumb. If you squeeze a bunch of text into a single slide, your

audience is either going to stop paying attention to you and start reading the text or stop paying attention altogether.

3. **Use large, readable fonts.** The less text you include on a slide, the larger
you can make the font size. The general rule of thumb is 24-point type
or larger. Whether your audience is in the class with you or on a Zoom
call, make it easy for the viewer to see your slides.

4. **Think visually.** Include a high-resolution image when you can and try to
make the text and image seem as though they were made for each other.

5. **Cite your sources.** This might mean a citation at the bottom of the slide,
or if that looks too clunky, a Works Cited page at the end of the presentation. In either case, don't claim that you created material that you
borrowed from someone else.

6. **Make use of the speaker/presenter notes.** These notes to yourself are
features of all four of the software programs mentioned earlier. You
can see the notes on your computer, but they aren't projected to a live
audience. If you are presenting online by sharing your screen, come up
with another way to have your notes in front of you.

7. **Collaborate equally.** If you're presenting with a group, as is often the
case, make sure that one person doesn't do all the work and that another person doesn't do all the public speaking. Set out group responsibilities early on and check in frequently with one another to ensure that
everyone is doing the work they're supposed to do.

**DIY 14.4 Create a
Simple Presentation**

Practice making a
slide presentation.
Choose a very simple
subject — how to replace
a light bulb or create
a guide to the best
snack machines on
campus — and make an
introductory page and
three or four supporting
slides. Make effective use
of color and, if neces-
sary, links. Google Slides
is generally the most
convenient and easily
accessible program, but
if you are more familiar
with another presentation
tool, use what works best
for you.

14.5   Following Your Writing Wherever It Needs to Go

Professors have plenty of good reasons for assigning the writing strategies
that have been discussed in Chapters 10–13 of this book. You wouldn't get
very far in an art history class, for instance, if you weren't able to make
intelligent evaluations and justify them with concrete evidence. What's more,
as we've seen throughout *Hello, Writer*, knowing how to make an argument
is at the heart of much of the writing you will be doing in college, as is being
able to propose smart, practical solutions to the problems you encounter in
the various disciplines you will study, such as nursing and engineering. And
the careful analysis of other people's writing is central to many majors, from
English literature to history to political science.

However, when you're not being asked to follow the "rules" of a specific genre, you may want to take advantage of whatever strategy best solves the problem in front of you. If in one sentence you make an evaluation and in the next you're focused on making an argument, that's perfectly fine. In fact, as long you address the purpose and audience of your essay, you probably won't even notice as you move from one strategy to the next. Like most professional writers, you'll be too caught up in the act of writing to register when you move from arguing a position to proposing a solution, or when you shift from evaluation to analysis. The writing happens and you follow it where it leads, unconcerned about classifications.

This type of writing is sometimes called "creative nonfiction." In "Suddenly Sexy: Creative Nonfiction Rear-ends Composition," Wendy Bishop sympathizes with students' desire to write "scholarly essays of personal voice, essays that demonstrate 'presence,' and even essays of personal disclosure." Indeed, creative nonfiction, which tells the truth but does so in a way that highlights the writer's style and freedom of thought, may be the ultimate example of mixing and matching writing strategies.

Ylonda Gault Caviness uses creative nonfiction in "We Go Way Back," an essay in which she reflects on her respect for Michelle Obama. In this excerpt, the relationship feels real and feels personal—despite the fact that Caviness does not actually know Obama—a feat the author accomplishes with her "translations."

> My girl does not suffer foolishness. She will graciously oblige but, with a knowing look, I can tell she is not here for simple-minded queries into her intrinsic strength, her mother wit, or her straight-up truth.
>
> I saw it back in 2007, when 60 Minutes' Steve Kroft asked if she feared for her husband's safety as a presidential candidate, Michelle Obama looked dead in the camera: "The reality is that as a Black man, Barack can get shot at the gas station."
>
> *Translation: "Please. We all know what time it is."*
>
> Months later, she gave me and other women an insider wink with CNN's Larry King. In an attempt to contrast the Bush administration's stubborn stance on warring with Iraq, King wanted to know if the then-presumptive presidential nominee had a mind that could be changed. "I change it every day," she deadpanned.
>
> *In other words: "You better recognize."*
>
> The white media establishment was not ready.
>
> —Ylonda Gault Caviness

While a creative nonfiction essay may not be right for every class, if your instructor assigns one, be open to the happy surprises that can come into your writing when you are given the freedom to compose in different ways. As always, your audience and writing situation will dictate what and how your write, but the more confident you become as a writer, the more you will want to stretch your writing muscles and see where they will take you.

An Invitation to Read: A Multimodal Student Essay

Angela Edwards's assignment was to write a reflective essay on the broad topic of making the transition from high school to college. Angela zeroed in on college writing as her topic, and she used visuals and links to help bring her ideas about racial justice and writing to life for her readers. She called the essay "fun to write," although before the class, she had never heard of multimodal composition, and she admits that she had done very little reflective writing.

Edwards 1

Angela Edwards

Professor Starkey

English 110

15 November 2020

How to Become a College Writer:

Persistence and Passion

College writing sometimes gets a bad rap. Some students anticipate boring term papers and then write boring term papers in a bizarre self-fulfilling prophecy. Others anticipate total freedom and then are surprised to hear about purpose and audience and rules. I wasn't sure what to expect. I knew I liked to write, but I always struggled with having something to say. A lot of times in high school, I just gave up and turned in something I wasn't even three-quarters happy with. College writers have to go to battle sometimes, fighting boredom and frustration, writer's block, a deadline, and the urge to say nothing. College writers must have something to write about, must have something to say, and must keep writing.

Senior year in high school, I liked it when my English teacher used the word "invention" for prewriting, and it made me think of all of the famous inventors that I had learned about. Thomas Edison and the light bulb, Alexander Graham Bell and the telephone, Albert Einstein and the theory of relativity—all of these people became inspiration for me.

The writer reflects on previous experiences with writing before giving her advice for college writers.

Edwards 2

(Hm. Why didn't I ever learn about *women inventors*?) If I could invent something good on paper, I'd be like a genius. If I could have a "light bulb" moment, everything would be ok. What I came to understand was that inventions are usually not instant and unexpected. Most of the time, they are the result of years of trial and error, practice, and failure. Edison's light bulb invention was the product of his team's work on "at least three thousand different theories" in the span of two years, according to The Franklin Institute ("Edison's Lightbulb").

Over the course of my senior year in high school and my first semester in college, I learned that writing is like invention. Even if you feel blocked and stumped, you have to do it. Even if all that comes out for an hour is crap, you have to keep hitting the keys. You have to experiment. You have to believe that somewhere in the space between your fingertips and the keys is a spark. In my experience, ideas are not going to come to you unless you go looking for them. A writer can't just sit there and wait. A writer has to write. I learned how to be patient and persistent.

I also learned that identifying a passion is helpful. Edison's passions were chemistry and engineering. I discovered mine in the summer of 2020, a horrible summer of public health worries, environmental catastrophes, and horrifying police brutality against Black people. My two best friends and I are active on social media and had followed the Black Lives Matter movement for a few years. Then we heard about the killing of George Floyd by Minneapolis police. For us, it was an electric moment—a light bulb moment. We were stunned and angry. Those charged with serving and protecting the American people willfully took the life of a Black man with excessive use of force, prompting a national rallying cry: "I can't breathe." (See fig. 1.)

Both Word and Google Docs allow writers to include live hyperlinks (shown here in blue) for online or digital delivery.

Recalling an earlier image in a new way can unify an essay.

Edwards 3

Fig. 1. Racism protest poster. Nicolas Tucat. *Racism-Protest*.
9 June 2020. *Getty Images*, https://www.gettyimages.com
/detail/news-photo/woman-holds-a-placard-depicting-george
-floyds-face-and-news-photo/1218896623.

When my 18th birthday came, just a few days after
Floyd's killing, I registered to vote and decided that a life
of activism was important to me and that racial justice,
specifically, was worth fighting for. I discovered that having
a passion gave me something to say and something to write
about—in English classes, psychology classes, on social
media, and elsewhere. I started researching use-of-force laws
and the proposed "8 Can't Wait" police reforms (see fig. 2)
that President Obama talked about in his Town Hall on Racial
Justice and Police Reform in early June. I began talking to
everyone in my family and in my multicultural neighborhood
about their interactions with law enforcement and going to
public forums whenever I could.

Becoming a college writer is just part of who I am as a
person, but I like that I can combine who I am as a person
with who I am as a writer. Just before the June 7 protest

Adding images can lend
emotional or logical appeal to
an essay — or communicate
the writer's credibility
and trustworthiness.

The writer includes images
by using figure numbers
and captions, following
MLA guidelines.

Edwards 4

Fig. 2. 8cantwait Campaign Poster. 5 Oct. 2020. *Campaign Zero*, www.joincampaignzero.org.

Reflective writing calls for first person, the use of "I."

march in Hollywood, my friends and I made "I Can't Breathe" masks and planned to wear them proudly as we marched. I felt strong that day, and even though my mouth was covered, I felt like I had a voice. I felt unified with fifty thousand other marchers—all of us calling for a really important and necessary change, and all of us calling out the names of Jacob Blake, Breonna Taylor, Ahmaud Arbery, and others. I keep the mask that I made for the march at my desk for inspiration. Sometimes I still don't know what I'm going to write, exactly, but I don't just sit around and wait. I usually find myself freewriting about something I've seen or read. My mind wanders to the cause of racial justice and I keep at it, figuring out how I can shape my passion to the paper I'm writing and use my writing to call others to action.

Edwards 5

Becoming a college writer is a process of inventing yourself, when it comes right down to it. And it can be frustrating because invention takes time and patience. There is such great power in having something to care about and something to say about it. There is even power in the simple act of persisting—of going to battle for something important.

Edwards 6

Works Cited

8cantwait Campaign Poster. 5 Oct. 2020. *Campaign Zero*, www.joincampaignzero.org.

"Edison's Lightbulb." *The Franklin Institute,* 2020, www .fi.edu/history-resources/edisons-lightbulb.

Tucat, Nicolas. *Racism-Protest.* 9 June 2020. *Getty Images*, https://www.gettyimages.com/detail/news-photo/woman -holds-a-placard-depicting-george-floyds-face-and-news -photo/1218896623.

Reading Questions

1. What is your first impression of "How to Become a College Writer"? Be specific when you point to moments that you thought were effective or ineffective.

2. Reflecting on your own transition from high school to college or from work to college, what advice would you give if you were asked how a person can become a good college writer?

3. How do you think Angela's uses of visuals and links strengthen her essay? What is the impact on readers?

Chapter 14 Checklist
Reading and Writing Multimodal Texts

☐ **Do you understand the basics of reading and writing with visuals?**

Recognizing how professional writers employ visuals is one of the best ways to learn how to use them in your own work. As you encounter different types of texts, be aware of how visuals, graphics, typography, and color affect your reading experience.

☐ **Have you reread at least one of your previous essays with an eye to improving its design or creating multimodality?**

Even when your essay is meant to be primarily alphabetic, it's always a good idea to remain open to opportunities to increase its readability and to add visual evidence or impact.

☐ **For your multimodal composition, have you made sure to start with basic rhetorical questions?**

Starting out by identifying your overall purpose and message, your target audience, the genre in which you will be writing, and your method of delivery (print, digital, a combination) will focus your efforts and increase the chances that your work will be effective.

14.6 Making It Stick

How will you read and write multimodal texts?

Working Together

14.6a Reimagining Your Work   Bring in a copy of an essay you have already written this semester, one without any comments on it. Share your copy with a partner and suggest ways that the current version can be improved using the elements discussed in this chapter. As a reminder, those elements include integrating visuals or sound, using color, building in links, and thinking more flexibly and creatively about your purpose and voice. Write down your suggestions for your partner and ask questions about the suggestions that you receive for your own essay.

Applying What You Know

14.6b Looking at the News   Find an article online by searching for "News" or searching the website of your local online newspaper. Study the article to discover how multimodal it is. Take notes on what's happening in each mode using the following grid. Then write a paragraph about how the modes work together to inform the reader about the news subject.

Words	Images	Sounds (narration, music, sound effects)

14.6c Studying Your College Website Visit the home page for your college and answer the following questions:

1. What are the purposes of your college's website? Can you identify a primary purpose?
2. What are the audiences for your college's website. Can you identify a primary audience?
3. How does the college use words, images, sound, and video to fulfill its purpose and meet the needs of its audience?
4. If someone asked you, what two changes would you suggest the school make to the website, and why?

Invitations to Write

14.6d Writing about What You Love

Shorter: Write a single paragraph about the thing you love most in the world — listening to hip hop or EDM, taking photos, skateboarding, posting on social media, baking pies, strategizing in your fantasy sports league, or whatever.

Longer: Use that paragraph and image as the basis for a full essay, one that tells stories and

provides rich details to help explain why your subject means so much to you.

14.6e Writing with Your Own Photographs

Shorter: Cut and paste a photograph of your own into a word processing document, then write two or three paragraphs inspired by the photo. Your text doesn't have to directly describe the image, but the words and picture should be related in some important way.

Longer: Write a creative nonfiction essay that incorporates multiple photographs you have taken yourself. Use the photographs as a unifying device or allow the text to link the photographs. In either case, both the visual and the alphabetic elements of the essay should be connected and equally essential to its overall goals.

14.6f Writing a Multimodal Essay

Shorter: Compose what you consider to be the equivalent of one-page of multimodal writing.

You might do this in a Google or Word document that your readers will view online or while using a presentation software like Google Slides or Prezi. Choose whatever subject interests you, but it should be appropriate for the format in which it appears.

Longer: Turn your one page of multimodal writing into a full essay. Make good use of design elements, including color and photographs, and employ links where necessary. If you feel inspired, consider incorporating video or audio into the piece.

Writing with Research

15

Establishing Your Research and Writing Goals

Write Before You Read Think back to three times in your life when you have done research that was not for a school assignment. What were your goals? Who was your audience? Write a brief paragraph in which you talk about what those experiences had in common. How were the experiences similar to or different from a school research assignment that you remember?

15.1   Getting Comfortable with Research

Your attitude toward research might have a lot to do with how you interpret the word "research." If you use that word to describe looking for a music video on YouTube, trying to find the best price for a textbook on Amazon, or searching for a new roommate on Craigslist, then academic research may sound like an extension of skills you already have. The truth is, almost everyone in the wired world is conducting research from morning until night. In fact, we're so used to checking restaurant reviews on Yelp! or movie reviews on Rotten Tomatoes or the price of a concert ticket on StubHub that we forget that we had to learn, at one point, how to conduct even these everyday types of research.

Part 3 of *Hello, Writer* teaches you how to find and use information—and how to use what you know about everyday research to become a better academic researcher.

> In fact, we're so used to checking restaurant reviews on Yelp! or movie reviews on Rotten Tomatoes or the price of a concert ticket on StubHub that we forget that we had to learn, at one point, how to conduct even these everyday types of research.

How Academic Research Differs from Everyday Research

- **You'll be doing more, and more sophisticated, research.** You're already an experienced researcher when it comes to navigating the tasks of daily life. Now you'll build on those skills to begin sustained inquiry into a topic; your inquiry will require you to look at multiple sources from a variety of perspectives and evaluate which are worth citing and which are better ignored.

$\rightarrow$

- **Your research will be under greater scrutiny.** Even when you're just researching the best place to eat or which movie to see, you and your friends will gravitate toward sources that have been reliable in the past. However, college instructors will expect you to evaluate each source critically and carefully using some version of the FACTS checklist, which ensures that the material is Fair, Accurate, Current, Trustworthy, and Suitable for your essay (see section 16.2).

- **You'll be incorporating your research into a written document.** When you're doing research about which pair of jeans or high-top sneakers to buy, you probably wouldn't do much more than briefly quote a review in a text message to a friend. In a researched essay or presentation, however, the fluent use of quotation, paraphrase, summary, and data will be important to your success.

As I have stressed throughout this book, the more you practice a skill, the easier it becomes. If you're lucky, you won't become just comfortable doing research, you'll actually grow to love it. However, because there is so much information out there, it's easy to get distracted. We've all begun a Google search that ended a half hour and a dozen topic shifts away from where we started. While a healthy sense of curiosity will serve you well in your research writing, you'll want to be aware of those times when your research is taking you further and further away from the topic you are writing about.

Above all, don't be intimidated by the assignment. Think of your research essay as an opportunity to use your natural curiosity in service of your academic goals. And if the research process does occasionally become a grind, remember the advice that Anne Lamott's father gave to her brother as he struggled to complete a report on the birds of North America the night before it was due: "Take it bird by bird, buddy. Bird by bird."

15.2 Understanding and Planning for Your Assignment

In many ways, understanding and planning your research paper is similar to the preparation you've done for other assignments in this book. As always, you'll want to do the following:

- **Know the prompt.** Reading and rereading your assignment should always be a first step for you. Be aware of *all* the requirements.

- **Allow sufficient time to do the work.** In some ways, your research essay is just a longer and more complex version of previous essays for this class. The length requirement will make a big difference in how you approach the assignment, as will the depth of research your instructor requires. By now, you should have a sense of the amount of time it takes for you to compose, revise, edit, and proofread a typical page in an academic essay. If possible, *double* that time when approaching a research essay. It's not just that the research you'll be doing will require more time, it's also going to take longer to effectively incorporate that research into your essay.

- **Write to explore.** Thinking and talking about your essay are great ways to get started, but you never really know how much you have to say about a topic—or how interesting it really is to you—until you actually begin writing. As you research, keep a document in which you write about what you've read and what questions you still want answered. This file may become your rough draft, or it may only be a place to sort through your thoughts, but whatever you do with the writing, the act of composing will almost certainly help clarify your thinking.

Understand Assigned vs. Open-Ended Topics

One of the most significant factors in determining how you approach your research essay is whether or not you are allowed to choose your own topic and frame your own question for research. Some instructors ask their students to focus on a fairly narrow range of possible research areas. Other teachers encourage students to follow whatever interests them. And many instructors offer a range of topics but limit the scope of the paper in some way. As with any assignment, you'll want to get a clear picture of the assignment's guidelines before committing yourself to a particular approach.

Assigned Topics

Some composition classes focus on a single broad topic or theme throughout the semester. If that's the case for your class, you'll already be something of an expert on your subject. For instance, if your class theme has been *bias*, you'll probably be aware of issues like implicit versus explicit bias, structural racialization, and microaggressions. Ideally, some aspect of the class will have fired your imagination, and you'll be looking forward to exploring it in more detail.

However, even if all semester long you've been jumping among a few different themes, try to see the research assignment as an opportunity.

Here are some ways to help you embrace an assigned topic and make it your own:

> ## Ways to Approach an Assigned Topic
>
> - **Look for a personal connection.** Even in an assignment with strict boundaries, you should be able to find *some* link between you and your topic. Remember that your instructor has chosen a particular subject believing that all, or at least most, of the students in class would find it interesting. Take another look: Isn't there something that makes you think, "Ah, I'd like to know more about *that*"?
>
> - **Leverage any readings and assignments you've already been given on the topic.** Especially if your research project is the culmination of a semester-long theme, you should have a sense of the type of research your instructor values. Indeed, they may have provided some of that research for you. Before you begin further research, take stock of what you already know and have in hand.
>
> - **If you don't like your assigned topic, try to "re-vision" it.** If you feel you could engage more effectively with the topic by writing just *a little* outside the assignment, talk with your instructor and see if you can negotiate a compromise. If your instructor insists that you stay within the assignment's boundaries, consider writing in opposition to conventional wisdom about the topic—making sure, of course, that you have sufficient valid concrete evidence to support your counterargument.

Open-Ended Assignments

While some instructors believe students benefit from a semester-long theme, others prefer to allow maximum flexibility when it comes to researched writing. You might find that freedom initially intoxicating, but the trick is to identify a topic you're really interested in *and* one in which you have at least some expertise. Sometimes it helps to look at topics that have worked for previous students. Here are a few subjects that my students have successfully researched:

- the environment and climate change
- ethics and morality
- feminism
- food
- free speech
- generation selfie

- gun control
- happiness
- immigration
- mental health
- music
- prejudice
- sports
- racial identity
- social media

You can find these topics—along with two essay prompts—in the Invitations to Write at the end of this chapter (15.7).

If the lists in this chapter don't ignite your interest, here are two tips to consider as you're searching for a research subject:

- **Don't necessarily choose the first topic that comes to mind.** Granted, you may be passionate about exploring a particular subject and your research writing could provide the perfect opportunity to do so. If that's the case, lucky you! However, if you're not really sure what you want to write about, spend a day or two checking out different areas of interest. Even if you're working in a compressed time frame, don't select a topic until you're sure you care enough about it to actually want to do the necessary research and writing on it.

- **Make sure you can comfortably research the topic in the time frame you've been given.** Once you've selected a topic, you'll need to assess whether or not you have the time to do it justice. Ideally, your passion for the topic will align with the number of weeks you've been given to research it, but sometimes you'll find that a topic you care about deeply is just too big for this particular assignment.

Start with Purpose and Audience

As you begin to think about your assignment, it is important to consider your purpose, or *reason*, for writing—and the audience, or *readers*, of your writing.

Purpose

Writers compose to meet a variety of purposes; people write to persuade, to propose, to inform, to evaluate, to analyze, to entertain, to reflect, to share a story. Sometimes you'll find that a writer writes for more than one reason—that a story, for example, works in the service of an argument or that, in the course of proposing a solution, a writer also informs a reader. When you're writing an essay responding to an assigned topic, you already have a clear set of boundaries and a built-in focus; your main task related to purpose is simply to adhere to the goals that have already been set for you. If your assignment is more open-ended, you'll want to begin the research process by working from a clear understanding about what it is you are supposed to do in your writing. Think about possible research questions you may be asking:

- *Why* questions sometimes lead you to argue or to analyze: Why are rising COVID-19 cases prompting a redefinition of higher education?

- *What* questions sometimes lead you to inform or to propose a solution: What are the best solutions for supporting at-risk student populations during remote learning?

- *How* questions sometimes lead you to evaluate or to reflect: How can high school seniors choose among colleges they have never visited in person?

Knowing why you are writing is an important first step in the research writing process. For more on asking research questions, see section 15.5.

Audience

If your instructor has assigned your topic, the prompt will sometimes specify your audience. If your audience is determined for you, then, once again, it's all a matter of focus. As you cycle through the composing process—prewriting, researching, writing, revising, and doing it all over again—you'll want to continually think about how your words, ideas, and evidence are likely to affect the readers, real or imagined, for whom you are writing.

Knowing your audience is equally critical when you're working with an open-ended prompt. Early in the research process, you should begin imagining your ideal readers. Say, for instance, that you are researching whether or not athletes in high-profile Division 1 college sports should be paid. The NCAA Board of Governors would make for a very different audience than the college athletes themselves or even college students in general.

Purpose and audience are intertwined, and both those considerations will affect what information you include in your essay. A research essay in which the writer tries to convince the Board of Governors to pay student athletes would likely be formal in tone and data driven for logical appeal, whereas an essay attempting to persuade college students that certain athletes should be paid might have a slightly less formal tone and more emotional appeal.

DIY 15.2a Identify Your Purpose and Audience

If your instructor has already provided you with a prompt, briefly identify the specific purpose and audience for your research paper. If you're working from an assigned topic, all you need to do is scan your prompt until you locate the information. If you'll be writing from an open-ended assignment — or you don't yet have a prompt — write down two or three topics or questions you think you'd like to research, then do your best to imagine the most likely purpose and audience for a paper investigating those issues.

Consider Length, Genre, and Delivery

In addition to purpose and audience, it will be important for your planning purposes to know the expected length, genre, and method of delivery.

Length

Some instructors specify length for an essay; others don't. A research essay of 2,500 to 3,000 words using Times New Roman Font is about ten to twelve pages double-spaced. By contrast, a research assignment that asks for 1,000 words is more like four pages. One will be more complex and detailed than the other. One may require a dozen or more sources, the other just a few. If your research is not a traditional essay, "length" may refer to a time or to something else—a five-to-ten-minute presentation, a twelve-panel comic, or a six-installment series of blog posts. Length will affect your planning, your thinking, and your search for sources.

Genre

Genre refers to the type of writing you are being asked to deliver. An essay is a pretty traditional genre for research. Most college research essays are multimodal—that is, they rely on both words and images (or sound, or video) to achieve their purpose (see Chapter 14). Your instructor may give you the option of alternate genres in which to present your research: a speech, a slide presentation, a poster presentation, a video essay, a podcast, a newsletter, a report, or something else.

Delivery

Most college students deliver their work in digital form, although some instructors still accept or require hard copy printouts. If you are delivering your work online or in another digital method, be sure that your intended audience can open any files, view any visual media, or load sound files as needed. Be sure to include alt text if you believe your audience may include readers who are visually impaired. Design documents and slide shows with accessibility in mind (see section 14.4).

Manage Stress

It's easy to get overwhelmed with a longer, more demanding research assignment—especially one that comes at the end of the semester and has deadlines that compete with major tests or projects in your other classes. Take a breath. A research essay, like all the other assignments in this book, can be broken down into manageable steps that you take one at a time. Instead of picturing a monolith, a giant imposing stone structure, think of your research paper as a three-foot brick wall. A brick wall is still a challenge to make, particularly for people who have never built one, but it can be constructed in a reasonable amount of time, if—to use a variation on Anne Lamott's theme—you take it brick by brick.

As a way to keep calm and carry on, consider keeping a calendar or making a timeline for your research essay or project (see section 15.6).

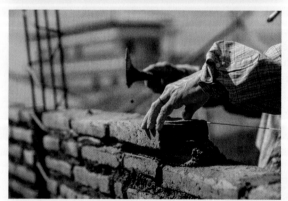

View Pictures/Getty Images

Research writing, like any long-term goal, can seem overwhelming until you break it down and imagine the smaller steps for success.

Jung Getty/Getty Images

Consider Analogies for Writing

Analogies about writing are necessarily inexact. When you're writing a research essay, you're not really building either a monolith *or* a wall—you're composing an essay. Yes, you'll want to construct an argument that is as strong as a brick wall, something solid that won't collapse the first time someone gives it a shove. However, writing a research essay might more closely resemble the process an artist goes through when making a work of art.

People have been comparing writers to visual artists for a long time—to painters, watercolorists, sculptors, photographers, filmmakers, and the list goes on. For me, the writer of a research paper most closely resembles an assemblage artist. Assemblage artists are essentially three-dimensional collage artists. They find interesting objects then juxtapose them in ways that make, to quote artist Pablo von Lichtenberg, "an organized and aesthetically pleasing combination."

Think of the research you'll be working with as the found objects making up an assemblage and the writing strategies you learned in Part 2 as the various approaches you might take to assemble those pieces into an intriguing, yet coherent work of art. Granted, that might sound a little far-fetched, and your research paper will almost certainly look more formal, and conventional, than Pablo von Lichtenberg's assemblage art. However, as we emphasized throughout Part 2, when writers are composing outside the classroom, they often become quite creative as they mix and match materials and writing strategies in the course of a single document.

Indeed, as you compose your research paper, you will probably use most, if not all, of the approaches covered earlier in this book. Because research papers often begin by investigating a problem, your essay may well propose a solution to that problem. Research papers also report information and evaluate it. Analysis will be required to make evaluations and propose solutions, and, of course, persuasion is part of the DNA of most academic essays.

If your assignment is to compose a multimodal research project, you may fulfill multiple purposes, but you'll be doing so across different media. You will likely include photographs and charts, as well as video and audio clips. In doing so, your research project may more and more come to resemble an assemblage—"the expression or application of human creative skill and imagination"; in other words, a work of art.

Assemblage art by Pablo von Lichtenberg

DIY 15.2b Create an Analogy for Your Research Paper

This section explains that a research paper is *not* like a monolith but *is* somewhat like a brick wall and a work of assemblage art. While no analogy can ever be precise, thinking in metaphorical terms can often lead to surprising insights. Whether or not you've ever written a research essay before, come up with your own analogy comparing the writing of a research paper to an activity you think it resembles.

15.3 A Sample Topic: Student Success

As a college student, you may feel that few issues matter as much as your success in school. Completing your college education will allow you to follow your chosen career path, and, ideally, lead you to become your best self. It makes sense, therefore, that the sample research paper topic to be investigated in Part 3 of *Hello, Writer* is college success.

If you ask yourself, "What makes a successful college student?" a number of ideas are likely to spring to mind. You might, for instance, focus on practicalities. From this perspective, you could say that a successful college student is someone who

- sets priorities
- manages time well

- takes effective notes

- lives on a budget

Or maybe you see college as primarily an opportunity to improve your intellect. In that case, you might define a successful college student as someone who

- develops critical thinking skills

- improves as a critical reader

- wrestles with challenging concepts

- masters the research process

For some students, college success might translate directly into employment. From that point of view, a successful college student is someone who

- majors in a field with strong career prospects

- acquires useful job skills

- interns with a vibrant company

- translates college connections into an interesting, well-paying job

Then again, you might believe sociability is the primary criterion for judging success in college. In that case, you could say a successful college student is someone who

- bonds with roommates

- develops a group of true and lasting friends

- enters into romantic relationships

- has the best time of their life

Of course, you're likely to judge college success by a combination of these, and other, factors. The important thing—with this subject or any other you might explore—is to begin breaking it down into its separate parts—the bricks—as soon as possible.

Read a Sample Research Essay Prompt

As you well know, the possible responses to a topic are determined by the writing prompt, so let's take a look at one designed for this subject. Because we'll return to this assignment throughout this part of the book, read the following prompt carefully. A full student essay written in response to this prompt, and formatted in MLA style, appears in section 18.5.

Research essay prompt

In a research essay of 2,000–2,500 words (8–10 pages *plus* a Works Cited page) answer the following question: **What does it take to be a successful college student?**

Use your essay to present a researched argument directed at other students hoping to attend and succeed in college. Discuss three to five attributes of a successful student in some depth. You should also consider the essay an opportunity to explore *realistic* success strategies that will help guide you, personally, through your college journey. It may be useful to include typical barriers to success in the context of your discussion.

You should incorporate at least ten, but no more than fifteen, relevant and credible primary and secondary sources in your research essay. Sources can be drawn from digital or print resources and can be textual, visual, or multimedia. Format your work and cite your sources in MLA style. Include a separate Works Cited page.

15.4 Discovering Your Focus

The research you do for your paper will very often dictate its form and tone. However, it may take a while for you to discover the focus of your essay. That's okay. "You are not looking for a single source that gives you the 'truth' about your topic," Lisa Ede points out in *The Academic Writer*. You will narrow your focus and construct your argument after examining the ideas of "a community of thinkers" who are also focusing on your topic.

Understand Conversation as a Research Metaphor

When you become a researcher, essentially, you join an ongoing conversation about your topic. This idea is one you may have heard before; it was perhaps most famously summarized by Kenneth Burke in *The Philosophy of Literary Form*:

> Imagine that you enter a parlor. You come late. When you arrive, others have long preceded you, and they are engaged in a heated discussion, a discussion too heated for them to pause and tell you exactly what it is about. In fact, the discussion had already begun long before any of them got there, so that no one present is qualified to retrace for you all the steps that had gone before. You listen for a while, until you decide that you have caught the tenor of the argument; then you put in your oar. Someone answers; you answer him; another comes to your defense; another aligns himself against you, to either the embarrassment or gratification of your

opponent, depending upon the quality of your ally's assistance. However, the discussion is interminable. The hour grows late, you must depart. And you do depart, with the discussion still vigorously in progress.

Fast forward to today, and to a setting that's a party, not a parlor. A contemporary and nonsexist version of Burke might read something like this:

> Imagine you enter a friend's house party. You're late and everyone is amped up on some subject you've never heard of. After a while, though, you start to get the gist of what they're saying, and you decide to put your two cents in. Suddenly, you have everyone's attention. One of your friends agrees with you. Someone you don't know thinks you're dead wrong. Pretty soon, you're as much a part of the argument as anyone there. Finally, though, you get tired and have to leave. As you look over your shoulder, you realize that new people have arrived, and others who were there when you showed up have already left. The guests are different, but the conversation is obviously going to go on and on.

Finding your focus for an academic essay often means starting by listening to the conversation—all that's being said about a particular issue from a wide range of perspectives—then taking part in that conversation and bringing something new to it.

Conduct a Quick Search

To enter the ongoing conversation about your topic, you will need to know what other people have been saying about it. Going to a parlor, or a house party, where everyone is discussing the subject would make things easy for you, but let's face it, that may not happen.

Instead, you'll most likely head to the conversation that's happening online. While your later research will be much more thorough, it's worth doing a quick search to get a sense of the major issues preoccupying people who have thought a great deal about your topic. Going online will give you the chance to "overhear" both experts and amateurs who care enough—like the people in the party—to put their oar, or their two cents, in.

Here are a few suggestions for quick-searching a potential topic; each of these strategies, and many more, will be discussed in some detail in the next chapter:

Strategies for Quick-Searching a Topic

1. **Google News** Google News returns results only from news sources; usually, though not always, these sources are trustworthy, if not particularly thorough.

2. **Google Scholar** Rather than searching Google, which often returns thousands (and sometimes millions) of results on a topic, Google Scholar narrows a search to return only scholarly sources—those written by scientists, researchers, and academics and published in peer-reviewed journals.

3. **Wikipedia** Although you may find that instructors discourage the use of Wikipedia articles as sources for an academic essay, browsing these articles to gather basic facts, read definitions, or get a working timeline related to your topic is often worth the effort. Authorship is not listed on Wikipedia, but often a quick search can indicate where or what you might explore next.

4. **Your college's online databases** There will be a discussion in the next chapter about how to make the best use of your college's databases, but even early on, you can get a decent sense of what people are talking about by logging into your school's main database portal and typing your search term.

DIY 15.4 As You Search, Make a List of Recurring Themes

Do a quick search of the research essay topic you've been assigned, or the one you have chosen to write about. Then make a list of five to seven relevant themes or subtopics that occur *at least twice* in your searches. Some or all of these recurrent themes might be key elements in your initial draft.

15.5 Generating a Research Question

As you continue searching online and your thinking moves from the very general to the more specific, you'll start noticing recurring issues and key terms. The more you research, the more likely you'll begin to see a path forward. Those elements of the topic that speak most to you personally, and which you would most like to spend time writing about, will gradually help you bring your topic into focus.

Once you've discovered a possible focus for your research paper, the next step is to further narrow that focus with a research question. We've talked in previous chapters about how a thesis answers a question, whether specifically asked or implied. A research question also performs that function: it asks the question that you will answer in your essay.

The sample prompt on college success begins as a research question: "What does it take to be a successful college student?" However, there are a few different ways you might take that topic based on how you define "college success." If you decided to focus on a single area of college success, you could refine the research question in the prompt by asking, "What steps can students take to successfully develop their intellect?" or, "How can a student successfully move from college directly into a rewarding, high-paying job after graduation?"

Big and broad subjects such as food, sports, music, and the environment might be narrowed to manageable topics by asking very specific questions:

Food: Are the foods served on campus sustainable over the long term?

Sports: Why should Division I football and basketball athletes be paid to play while they are still in school?

Music: How are music industry labels such as "pop" and "urban" racist?

The Environment: Why is carbon-capture technology worth financing?

It may sound like circular reasoning to say that a good research question is any question that produces a good research paper, but it's important to remain flexible when generating your question. Nevertheless, there are a few specific queries you can address to yourself when you think you have the question that will focus your paper:

Questions to Ask about Your Research Question

- **Does the research question address the prompt?** Writing from a research question that doesn't apply to the prompt you've been given may make for an interesting essay, but instructors can be tough graders when students don't follow the assignment they've been given. If you think you might be going outside the boundaries of the assignment, schedule a quick chat with your instructor.

- **Do you really want to know the answer to the question?** If you don't have a lot of latitude with the assignment, you might be tempted to answer, "Not really." However, if that's the case, see if you can approach the assignment from a different angle. You want to ask a question to which you don't know but *want to know* the answer.

- **Can you reasonably expect to locate the research necessary to answer the question?** While you may be deeply interested in a topic—you may even want to devote your life to its study—you only have a set number of weeks to research and write your paper. If the topic is too obscure, or if it relies on information you don't have access to, consider moving on to your second-favorite subject.

- **Is the question narrow enough for your assignment?** If you're genuinely excited about your topic, you may want to find out everything about it. That's not possible, of course, and trying to cover too much ground means that your essay will stay at the level of broad observations and generalities. Remember that you're writing a brief essay.

- **Is the question broad enough to generate the number of pages you've been assigned to write?** You'll recall from the stacked Venn diagram in section 5.3 that it's possible to narrow your topic down *too much*. A research question that you can comfortably answer in a 500-word essay might turn a 2,000-word essay into a bundle of repetitions and redundancies.

A strong research question is like the lighthouse that helps keep a ship off the rocks and brings it safely back to port. If you ever feel you're going off-track, all you have to do is return to your research question. Does the paragraph you are currently writing help to answer the question? If so, great. If not, that paragraph either needs to be deleted or revised so that it is responding directly to your question.

DIY 15.5 Freewrite on Your Research Question

If you are already working with a prompt that has a built-in research question, such as "What does it take to be a successful college student?" begin answering that question in a ten-minute freewrite. If you've been given permission to investigate a topic of your choice, or you don't yet have a prompt, write down a list of possible questions that could sustain a focused research paper. Use the advice in section 15.5 to guide the composition of your own research question, then freewrite in response to that question.

15.6 Drafting a Timeline

The biggest challenges students face when working on a longer assignment are starting early and allowing enough time to complete the work. Writing a good essay takes time—almost always more time than you're hoping it will take. Therefore, any buffers you can build into your schedule—an extra hour for research here, two hours for revision there—will reward you with a stronger final draft.

In some first-year writing courses, research essays are assigned toward the end of the semester, which may mean working on other semester-end projects and preparing for final exams at the same time. It can be a lot to juggle, and you may want to revisit the discussion of time management in section 1.2. Deal with the inevitable stress in as healthy a fashion as you can and remember that there's no substitute for beginning work on your research paper as soon as it is assigned.

Being able to lavish lots of time on your research essay will most likely make it better. However, it's the rare student who doesn't have plenty of other activities, obligations, and people competing for their time. That's all the more reason to think ahead and plan a realistic schedule.

The amount of time you'll be allotted to write your research paper will vary from class to class and instructor to instructor; however, four weeks is a fairly common time frame. If you have a month to complete your assignment, use the following timeline as a point of reference. Keep in mind that although this timeline is presented as fairly linear (plan, research, write, revise), you will almost certainly be moving fluidly through all of these stages multiple times over the course of four weeks.

Sample Schedule for Writing a Research Paper

Week 1	• Enter the ongoing conversation related to your topic; do some quick searching, find a potential focus for your essay, generate a research question, and begin researching.
	• Talk about your topic with your tutor, your instructor, your friends, and your family. Meet with a librarian if you have questions.
	• Take notes and be open to changing your mind.
Week 2	• Dive into your research, making sure you have access to the material you'll need to complete your assignment.
	• Identify relevant primary and secondary sources; take notes and keep track of information to use in your essay.
	• Draft a working thesis and an informal outline.
	• Change your approach or your topic if you sense you are not on the right track.
Week 3	• Research and write; write and research. By midweek, you should have a rough draft.
	• Seek feedback from a writing center tutor, your instructor, a peer, or some combination.
	• Start revising. Close up gaps in your research and gaps in your argument. Place visual evidence where it will be most effective.
	• Draft a Works Cited page for an MLA-style essay (this is called a list of References in APA style).

Week 4	• Continue filling in any holes in your research.
	• Exchange drafts with a classmate whose opinion you value.
	• Step back from the essay for a full day, so that you can see it with fresh eyes. Then start your final draft.
	• If you have visuals such as photos, tables, and graphs, be sure to place them, caption them, and cite them in the style required by the assignment.
	• Make sure you carefully edit and proofread your final draft, double- and triple-checking your in-text and end citations to confirm that they follow the appropriate guidelines.

Make Adjustments to fit Your Deadline

If you have more than four weeks to write your research paper, spend extra time on your initial exploration and investigation. Dig deeper into the research. Allow plenty of time to craft the essay itself. Rather than taking a single week to revise, edit, and proofread your draft, for instance, spend two. Warning: don't let that extra time lull you into thinking you can squeeze the entire process into a couple of weeks. Use those extra days to good advantage.

If you have less than four weeks from start to finish, compress the process somewhat, but don't skip any steps. It's still important that you take the first few days to get to know your topic, to do some initial research, and to talk about it with a librarian and with your friends, classmates, or a tutor. That said, get to work as quickly as possible. Remember that you want to spend as much time on the writing of the paper as you do on the research, so begin composing early, and try to complete a rough draft at least a week before the final draft is due.

DIY 15.6 Make a Research Project Timeline

Make a week-by-week timeline for the completion of your research essay *now*, while you have all the time ahead of you. Leave plenty of space after each week in the timeline, and when you've completed your research and writing plan, add all your additional obligations for that week — other classes, work, social plans — anything that will compete with your research paper. Use the Sample Schedule in this section to remind you of tasks typically associated with a research assignment.

Chapter 15 Checklist
Establishing Your Research and Writing Goals

☐ **Have you carefully read the prompt for your research paper?**

Doing so will ensure that you know how long an essay is expected to be, when it is due, how many sources are required, who your audience is, which documentation style will be used, and whether your topic is open-ended or has been assigned by your instructor.

☐ **Have you performed a quick online search to find out what people are saying about your topic?**

Take notes and save web addresses when you come across a particularly good source, but mostly spend this time getting a feel for the major issues currently associated with your topic.

☐ **Have you written a focused research question that can be answered in the time you have allotted for the assignment?**

Your question should genuinely spark your interest, and be narrow enough to focus your paper, while broad enough to generate sufficient material to comfortably hit your word count.

☐ **Have you made a timeline for the completion of your research paper?**

Writing out a week-by-week schedule will provide you with focus across the entire assignment, while giving you some flexibility for managing work, your social calendar, and assignments in your other classes. As you get closer to your deadline, you may also want to make a day-by-day calendar.

15.7 Making It Stick

How will you establish your research goals and focus your research writing efforts?

Working Together

15.7a Examining Research Questions In groups of three or four students, talk about your topic and research question. Ask group members if they think your research question is focused enough. Ask if they have any angles or sources to suggest. Do they have interesting ideas about your topic that you haven't thought about? When another writer is talking, tell them what you find most attention-grabbing about their topic. What would you like to learn more about?

Make suggestions for possible sources the writer might consult.

Applying What You Know

15.7b Questions and Answers for Your Research Topic

Write down the answers to the following questions about your research topic:

- What is the most interesting aspect of your topic? How can you maximize that aspect of your research paper?

- What is the least interesting aspect of your topic? Can you eliminate that aspect altogether? If not, how can you minimize it in your research paper?

- What is the most confusing aspect of your topic? Who can you turn to — your instructor, a tutor, an expert in the field — to help you work through your confusion?

If it's possible to do so, share your responses with a partner, a small group, or the entire class. As you do so, look for ways to help your classmates transform their essays into work that will generate enthusiasm and excitement — for both the writers and the readers.

15.7c Organizing with Notecards

Buy a pack of old-fashioned 3-by-5-inch notecards. (If you can't find notecards, you can always fold a few pieces of printer paper into fourths and use scissors to make your own cards.)

Write down one important piece of information on each card. It could be a quotation or a fact you uncovered in one of your quick searches, an idea you want to pursue, a point you think is worth making, or a possible topic sentence. Try to complete 10–12 cards.

Then find some open space — a kitchen table, or the floor of your room, and organize the cards

in a way that may make sense for your essay. Once you have a working order, number the cards in pencil, knowing that this is still a very early organizational sketch for your research essay.

Invitations to Write

15.7d Prewriting for Research

Shorter: Make a list of all the areas of your topic that you think you will need to cover in your research paper. If you don't know what you want to investigate, make a list of (1) why you chose this topic in the first place or (2) other topics that might work better for your research paper.

Longer: Look back through the various prewriting strategies discussed in Chapter 4 and try at least three of them. In addition to listing, the following strategies are covered:

- Freewriting
- Questioning
- Quick searching
- Curating quotations
- Mapping
- Letter writing

15.7e Making a Case

Shorter: Write a paragraph or two about a topic that you are truly passionate about, but which you think is inappropriate for a college research paper. Explain both what you love about the topic and why it doesn't really count as the subject for an academic essay.

Longer: Now, whether or not you think your instructor would ever allow you to write about the topic, write two or three paragraphs attempting to persuade your professor that you *should* make this topic the subject of your research paper. Proofread your work carefully, then show it to your instructor. Maybe this will end up being your topic. Even if you don't write about this subject for this class, hold on to what you've written. It may come in handy someday.

15.7f Remembering Why You're Here

Shorter: Writing a research paper can be a big, demanding job. At this point in the semester, some students may wonder: *Why bother?* Write a paragraph or two answering that question. Remind yourself why you're in college, and what you hope to achieve after graduation.

Longer: Take the process one step further and write about how the research skills you are developing as you draft your paper will be useful to you (1) in other classes and (2) in the career you hope to pursue when you graduate from college.

Research Paper Topics

Some or all of the topics below may be assigned by your instructor, or — if you have an open-ended assignment — you may want to choose one of them for your research paper. Your instructor may also be open to alternative prompts for each topic.

Climate Change/The Environment

Essay Prompt 1: Is it too late for our planet to recover from human-caused harm? Defend your response with three to five compelling arguments for, or against, the inevitability of climate catastrophe. If you have some ideas about how to save Earth, focus on strategies that are likely to find the widest buy-in from citizens around the globe.

Essay Prompt 2: Evaluate the health of your local environment: the place where you live, go to school and/or work. What are the key elements of the environment? How do they all fit together? What aspects of your environment are strong and thriving? Which are fragile and in danger of failure?

Feminism

Essay Prompt 1: "Feminism" means very different things to different people. Find out what significant thinkers have said, and are saying, about feminism, then come up with your own definition of the word, providing concrete and specific examples to illustrate each of the main parts of your definition.

Essay Prompt 2: Examine a film or television or series you've seen that has been labeled a feminist work. Make a claim about how the work embodies feminist goals and ideas. Include specific examples from the work as well as research to support your claims.

Food

Essay Prompt 1: Choose one meal you've eaten in the past week — it could be a plate of spaghetti, or a taco, or a veggie burger — and find out where the ingredients come from. Who grew or manufactured the ingredients? What corporations are involved in sourcing and marketing them? Who benefits, and who is hurt, getting your meal to you? (Listen to *Planet Money*'s "T-shirt Project" on National Public Radio — npr.org — to get an idea of how you might pursue this project.)

Essay Prompt 2: Explore the world of "foodie culture." How has the emerging preference for "food as art" and farm-to-fork meat and produce changed how farmers grow, and eaters consume, food?

Free Speech

Essay Prompt 1: What are your rights as an American citizen when it comes to free speech? What can you legally say or write? What sort of speech or writing is forbidden? Discuss the current state of free speech, including the rights you wish you had that you don't, and vice versa.

Essay Prompt 2: Search Google News for "free speech" + "campus" and see what controversies are currently happening in North America. Choose two or three related incidents and explore what they have in common and how they differ from campus to campus. Then evaluate the motivations of the various players in the debate. Are most college students "snowflakes" who can't take the heat of the real world, or are right-wing groups unfairly targeting students who refuse to have racist ideology disseminated on their campuses?

Generation Selfie

Essay Prompt 1: Explain why you think "Generation Selfie" is, or isn't, an accurate name for people born from the mid-1990s to the mid-2000s. (This demographic is also referred to as Gen Z, Centennials, and Post-Millennials.) You might talk about how other generations better fit the description of "Generation Selfie" — after all, Millennials and even Baby Boomers seem to take a lot of pictures of themselves. Consider why self-representation might be so important to the group you study.

Essay Prompt 2: Choose one social media platform that features lots of photographic self-portraits — Instagram, Snapchat, Facebook, etc. — and investigate the culture and economy of that platform. What causes up- and downswings in the platform's popularity? What

tactics do the heads of the various social media employ to keep their users coming back for more?

Gun Control

Essay Prompt 1: For many citizens, gun violence in the United States seems an unsolvable problem. If you agree there seems to be no solution, explain what forces are at work that keep America from passing policies on which *most* reasonable people might agree. If, on the other hand, you believe there is still hope, propose one or more solutions to gun violence that have received significant public support in the past.

Essay Prompt 2: Write profiles of two people: a person who owns a gun, and someone who doesn't. (Keep the focus on others: don't write about yourself.) How are these people different? What do they have in common? If there are areas on which they agree, how might those areas be the basis for a coming-together on public policy? Use your research to place the people you are profiling in a larger context, and to speculate on the future of gun control in America.

Happiness

Essay Prompt 1: Happiness appears to be a fleeting thing. Almost the moment most people feel happy, the emotion begins to ebb away. Explore the phenomena of why the majority of human beings have such a hard time achieving and maintaining happiness. What lasting solutions, if any, do you see for our happiness deficit?

Essay Prompt 2: Should happiness be a person's ultimate goal? If so, explain why happiness is more important than, say, doing good works, saving the planet, providing for one's family, and so on. Similarly, if you think happiness is overrated, explain why other areas of life deserve more attention.

Racial Justice/Social Justice

Essay Prompt 1: Discuss *The New York Times Magazine's* 1619 Project, which seeks to redefine the American narrative. Do you think it's advantageous or foolish (or something else) to trace our country's history back to the time when enslaved Africans first landed in North America? Explain your reasoning.

Essay Prompt 2: 2020 brought police brutality, systemic racism, and the Black Lives Matter movement to the daily news with a new energy. Calls for law enforcement policy reform were met with mixed reactions. Take a look at the eight Can't Wait website (8cantwait.org) and research whether your local police departments have adopted some or all of the eight recommended policing policies. Take a position on whether we should or should not change policing in the United States.

Immigration

Essay Prompt 1: Overall, do you think immigration hurts our country or makes it better? Consider culture, the economy, and other factors. As much as possible, base your response on data, credible expert testimony, and relevant lived experience — either your own or others'.

Essay Prompt 2: Compare the immigration policies of the United States and Canada (or the United States and another country of your choice). In your opinion, which country has a more reasonable policy and why? If you were in charge, how would you change U.S. policy?

Mental Health

Essay Prompt 1: Compare and contrast medical and public attitudes toward mental health 100, or 50, or 25 years ago to attitudes today. Are there any stigmas attached to mental health issues that seem to linger from an earlier time? What work still needs to be done?

Essay Prompt 2: Explore a single mental health issue that affects you or someone close to you. It could be ADHD, anxiety, depression, an eating disorder, OCD, PTSD — anything you want to write about. Use your research to place you or the person you know in a larger context. Use your personal connection to put a real-life face on the research.

Music

Essay Prompt 1: Some people identify themselves primarily through music. What do these people gain by doing so? What do they lose? Combine academic research with the experiences of people you know who are defined by music to explore how music shapes certain people's values and life choices.

Essay Prompt 2: Choose a type of music that — for the moment, at least — you emphatically do *not* like. Then investigate what it is about the music that appeals to its fans. Age, race, gender, social class — all these factors may play a role in explaining the music's attraction. Even if, for instance, you can never see yourself attending a Screamo concert, why does such an event speak to a certain segment of the population?

Sports

Essay Prompt 1: Professional football is America's most popular sport, despite the fact that its players routinely suffer injuries that are found in no other occupation. In fact, due to the toll the sport takes on their bodies, former players experience a sharp decline in quality of life after they retire. Explore the issue and explain why you think either (1) the sport should be terminated, or (2) play should go on as it currently is, or (3) specific major changes should be implemented.

Essay Prompt 2: Compare and contrast the lifestyles of male and female athletes in one particular college sport. For example, what, if any, benefits do Division 1 male basketball players receive that are not awarded to their female counterparts? Do they receive the same housing facilities, academic support, counseling, scholarships, medical care, and so on? If you find a disparity between the lives of male and female college athletes, what do you think should be done to improve the situation? How effective has Title IX been in addressing past inequities?

16

Locating and Evaluating Sources

REFLECT

Write Before You Read | Activity to connect what's new with what you already know 385

READ & WRITE

DIY (Do-it-yourself) activities offer just-in-time support for all the skills in this book.

Working Together | Collaborative and community-building activities 406
Applying What You Know | Activities to reinforce and extend chapter content 406
Invitations to Write | Brief writing prompts 406

REFLECT

Write Before You Read   When you're thinking of buying something, where do you look and whose opinions do you trust? When you hear about a current event or a term you're not quite sure of, which websites do you feel confident will provide you with dependable information? And if there are certain places you rely on, are there others you avoid because you feel they are biased? Write a few paragraphs explaining what makes you believe certain sources and doubt others.

16.1   Thinking Like a Researcher

It's likely that you have your own ideas about what "research" is and who "researchers" are—and it may be that you see yourselves in those words or you don't. If you are in a college course right now, the fact is that you will be asked to be a researcher and a research writer. So: Hello, research writer.

Wendy Bishop, coeditor of *The Subject Is Research*, describes how her passion for research was transformed from something she was "told to do" to something she "wanted to do." She talks about her realization that research is a part of everything she does in life. "Each experience," she says, "sent me to books, to experts, to the Internet, where I would put my developing knowledge in dialogue with others . . . not in [any] order but all at once." You may have experienced this same research frenzy when you are trying to solve a specific problem with research. You need a new apartment, for example, so you talk to friends, search online, look at ratings and posts—hopping among sources, and disregarding some, to help you draw your own conclusions about the best place to live.

Granted, some researchers—both professors and students—work best if they proceed methodically from one step to the next, but just as often researchers bounce from one source or idea to the next, reading, writing a bit, searching, reading some more, making their way toward their goal in stops and starts.

However you conduct your research, the important thing is to think like a researcher. The qualities of a good researcher are many, but the following guidelines are particularly useful for an undergraduate doing research for a class.

Qualities of a Good Researcher

- **Be curious.** Start by choosing a topic or approach to your research that truly interests you, then let your curiosity run wild. Think of your research paper as an opportunity to foster your spirit of inquiry.

  - **Be patient.** Research is full of dead ends; don't give up the first time you hit one. Instead, keep looking, ask for help, talk to a friend, classmate, tutor, or your instructor about where you're getting stuck. And when your research is going well, you'll want to take time to keep track of your sources, so they don't disappear in the whirlwind process of discovery.

  - **Go where your research takes you.** Part of the fun of thoroughly researching a subject is going to surprising places and hearing from new voices. It's the rare researcher who doesn't come across a startling claim or a contrarian point of view that shifts the paper's original focus. Embrace the unexpected. Like a good detective, follow your leads.

  - **Be willing to change your mind.** If your research causes you to realize that the answer to the research question you posed in the previous chapter will not work or that your working thesis is missing the mark, be open to changing your approach to your topic.

American writer Zora Neale Hurston has defined research as "formalized curiosity. It is poking and prying with a purpose."
State Archives of Florida/Florida Memory/Alamy

While curiosity, patience, and openness to new ideas and approaches are necessary qualities for a good undergraduate researcher, you'll also benefit from having a friend on the inside, someone who is a professional researcher and a consistent source of good advice. That person is your reference librarian—someone who has a real passion for helping students locate relevant, vetted information. Reference librarians are wired and ready to connect you to a host of resources you had no idea were out there.

DIY 16.1 Find Out How to Contact Reference Librarians

Log on to your library's website and find out how to contact the reference librarians at your school. Then, if you have a question about your research paper topic, send the librarian a message asking for information about your project. If you don't yet have an assignment, respond to the DIY prompts in this chapter with the prompt in 15.3: "What does it take to be a successful college student?"

16.2 Getting at the Truth

With so much distortion and dishonesty in online materials, it can be hard to know who to believe. Even the terminology used to describe misinformation is open to debate. To take just one example, the term "fake news" is used to mean everything from a deliberately false or misleading statement to a media story reporting news that is factually accurate but distasteful to the person hearing it.

In fact, there is so much false information posing as truth that entire websites are devoted to disproving false information. Snopes.com does a good job of debunking urban legends, which are often started as Internet rumors. And FactCheck.org is a nonprofit, nonpartisan website run by the University of Pennsylvania's Annenberg Public Policy Center. Search "online fact checkers" to find other sites.

Of course, outside of the classroom, in "real life," people can choose to ignore any facts that conflict with their own way of seeing the world. Sometimes that attitude doesn't hurt anyone, but sometimes it does. In the past fifty years alone, tribalism, resentment, and willful ignorance have resulted in genocides in Cambodia, Rwanda, Darfur, and Bosnia. More recently, a willful denial of facts led to higher instances of sickness and death in the United States as the COVID-19 pandemic changed life as we knew it.

Talking about your research paper as part of a continuum that includes historical atrocities and public health crises may sound as though it's exaggerating the importance of what you do in this class, but the connection is worth pondering. The next time you decide whether or not to use a source, don't just think about how it will affect your grade, think of what your decision says about you as a person who demands to know the truth.

Use the FACTS Checklist

But what *is* the truth? For your instructor, it likely means information that can be verified by multiple credible sources. The FACTS checklist can be used to evaluate, or judge, the credibility of potential sources for your work. **FACTS** stands for Fair, Accurate, Current, Trustworthy, Suitable. The FACTS checklist is a series of questions that you ask about a source, particularly one you find through a general Internet search. You can refer to the FACTS checklist throughout the writing process, and while it is primarily meant for online research, it applies equally well to print sources.

FAIR	ACCURATE	CURRENT	TRUSTWORTHY	SUITABLE

FACTS Checklist

FAIR	• **Is the source fair and objective?** Reasonable sources value their reputations for making fairly considered, objective judgments, and they work hard to maintain those reputations. • **Is the source prone to making inflated, one-sided claims?** Be wary of authors who seem to be exaggerating, especially when the subject would be best approached from a neutral position. Imagine talking to your source in person. Would the conversation be rational and calm, or do you picture the source shouting in your face? • **If the source seems biased, does that bias appear to be interfering with the truth?** No source is entirely bias free, but some news organizations—MSNBC on the left, for example and FoxNews on the right—clearly favor a particular ideological point of view, which may affect which news they focus on and how they report it. In contrast, middle-of-the-road news organizations, like those sponsored by NPR and the BBC, try very hard to report both sides of an issue.
	Fairness Check: A source that attempts to transcend bias and present all sides of an argument is generally one that can be trusted.
ACCURATE	• **Is the information supported by evidence?** Look for sources that showcase detailed supporting information; avoid the general, the ambiguous, and the incomplete. • **Is the source in a particular domain?** If a website wants to sell you something, the information it provides may be skewed. Though domain names are no guarantee of a source's accuracy, those ending in *.org*, *.gov*, and *.edu* tend, overall, to be more credible than those ending in *.com* or *.net*. • **Is text in the source well written?** Don't trust a poorly written source. If the author didn't take the time to proofread and correct grammar, spelling, and typographical mistakes, chances are content of the source is poor quality, too.
	Accuracy Check: The sources you cite should be evidence based, truthful, and well written.
CURRENT	• **When was the source last updated?** For some projects, currency, or how up to date a source is, will be very important; for others, not as much. For an essay on voter turnout in the United States, you are going to want to include sources from 2020 or later. For an essay on women's right to vote and the 19th Amendment, you may be OK with a wider range of dates.

	• **If there is no date on the source, would a lack of timeliness affect the validity of its information?** A website hosting historical documents—the transcript of Frederick Douglass's *Narrative*, for example—wouldn't need to be updated as frequently as a website devoted to artificial intelligence. Nevertheless, interpretations of history change, even if the documents they are based on stay the same. If a website has not been updated in years, consider looking elsewhere for your information.
	Currency Check: With certain exceptions for historical documents, the more recent your source, the more likely it will be useful evidence for your argument.
TRUSTWORTHY	• **Can the evidence provided by the source be corroborated by another source?** Authors who feel confident in their own sources will let readers know who authored the information and where it was originally published, either through citations or hyperlinks. The more frequently a source is substantiated and appears in print or on credible websites, the more trustworthy it is. If an unsubstantiated claim appears on only one website, or if the same claim appears elsewhere, but never with any evidence to back it up, be wary.
	• **Does the source list an author or authors?** When conducting research for an essay, being able to list an author is important. Thoughtful journalism, peer-reviewed research, and data sharing are hard work, and the people and organizations who do that work want to be acknowledged. If it's impossible to tell who wrote what you are reading, find another source.
	• **If the author is named, are credentials listed?** You will want to know whether your source has the authority to speak on the subject you're researching. If your author is a person, are they a longtime professor or researcher, a journalist who specializes in an area of investigation, a person whose lived experience is relevant to the issue? If the author is an organization, what are the mission and values of the group?
	Trustworthiness Check: If credentials are missing, a source's reliability cannot be verified.
SUITABLE	• **Is the source appropriate for your particular essay?** While the source might not meet the FACT test, it may be useful (or S, Suitable) for your essay after all. For example, even though a teen who is hospitalized with COVID-19 is not an "expert" in infectious diseases or public health policy, you may need their perspective and experience in an essay on how the disease affects young people in surprising ways.
	• **Are your sources all in the same "lane"?** Each source should support, extend, challenge, or provide context for other sources you're using. A source that just repeats what another source offers may not be suitable. Similarly, if your Works Cited list is full of personal stories, might it help to supplement the stories with data or a few research findings to give the stories context?
	• **Does the source meet the requirements of your assignment?** A Wikipedia article, for instance, may be entirely trustworthy, but most professors want students to look beyond this source to the more credible sources on which it is usually based. If your instructor tells you a source isn't suitable, don't use it.
	Suitability Check: Not every source is right for every writing project. Even if you trust the source's accuracy and fairness, you still need to assess whether or it will be useful for your argument.

DIY 16.2 Use the FACTS Checklist to Evaluate Sources

Locate two sources that address your research paper assignment or, if you don't yet have an assignment, that address the student success prompt in section 15.3. Use the FACTS checklist to evaluate each of the sources you are planning to use. Write brief notes for each source, and make sure each source genuinely meets the test of fairness, accuracy, currency, trustworthiness, and suitability.

16.3 Understanding Primary and Secondary Sources

As you conduct your research, your instructor and the librarian may refer to "primary" and "secondary" sources. Primary sources are the original, or first, sources of information. A secondary source is a work analyzing, evaluating, or commenting on the original source. While secondary sources often contain *some* of the same information as the primary sources, a secondary source's main purpose is analysis or interpretation of the original source.

For example, Beyoncé's album *Lemonade* is a primary source, as it is an original work of art. Carrie Battan's article in *The New Yorker*, "Beyoncé's *Lemonade* Is a Revelation of Spirit," is a secondary source; its purpose is to analyze and evaluate *Lemonade*. Even though Battan's essay contains quotations from and descriptions of the songs on *Lemonade*, you would never mistake her piece of writing about the album for the album itself. The following table presents a few more examples of the difference between primary and secondary sources.

Primary Sources	Secondary Sources
Autobiography *Crazy Brave*, a memoir by Joy Harjo	**Critical commentary** "Standing between the Doorway of Panic and Love," a critical study of the Harjo memoir by Shelby Settles Harper
Film *Get Out*, a film written and directed by Jordan Peele	**Film review** "A Review of *Get Out*: On White Terror and The Black Body," a review by Kevin Lawrence Henry, Jr.

Primary Sources	Secondary Sources
Research study "Associations Between Time Spent Using Social Media and Internalizing and Externalizing Problems Among US Youth," a scholarly article written by Kira E. Riehm et al., the team of researchers who conducted the 2019 study. The article presents findings associated with the authors' study of more than 6,500 adolescents.	**Summary of research findings** "Time Spent on Social Media Linked to Mental Health Challenges in Adolescents," a summary of Riehm et al.'s study findings, written by Emily Pond, a journalist specializing in health research, and published on a website called *Psychiatry Advisor*.

Whether or not your research paper will draw on primary or secondary sources depends a great deal on your instructor and the assignment you've been given. Some instructors prefer that students use primary sources so that students can be the main interpreter and evaluator of the original evidence. Other instructors are more interested in having their students determine the validity of the analysis made by secondary sources.

16.4 Using Online Databases

Your college or university library subscribes to at least one general database covering a wide range of academic disciplines. Among the most popular databases are Academic Search Premier (compiled by EBSCO Information Services), OneSearch, ProQuest, JSTOR, and Nexis Uni. Many schools also subscribe to more specialized databases, such as MEDLINE for the medical sciences, Project MUSE for the humanities, and PsychINFO for Psychology.

Unless you already see a very clear path for your research, it's normally best to begin searching a general database. Don't feel obliged to check out every single article—there are often thousands of them. Instead, skim through the listings, take notes and jot down keywords. If you do find an article that looks especially promising, most databases will allow you to save it to a folder, print it, or email it to yourself.

Understand Common Types of Searches

As you explore your library's database, you'll find that the three most common types of searches are keyword, subject, and field (or advanced).

- **Keyword Search** Databases usually open in "keyword" or "basic mode." You type a word or phrase associated with your topic into a search box, and the search engine matches the word or phrase against the entire database. You will receive many results that don't apply to your essay's focus; in that case you can limit by the type of source, the date of publication, and whether your library has access to the full-text article.

- **Subject Search** As the name implies, a subject search shows results only when the word or phrase you've entered actually appears in the database's subject field. A subject search can be trickier because search terms are matched against a predetermined list of subjects. Most librarians advise that students conduct both keyword and subject searches for best results.

- **Field or Advanced Search** The field search is often accessed through an "Advanced Search" link and allows you to look for material using a number of very specific search criteria: title, date, author, type of publication, subject terms, geographic terms, document type, and more.

You can often use what are called "Boolean operators" to refine your search. Using AND will narrow a search and return only results that include

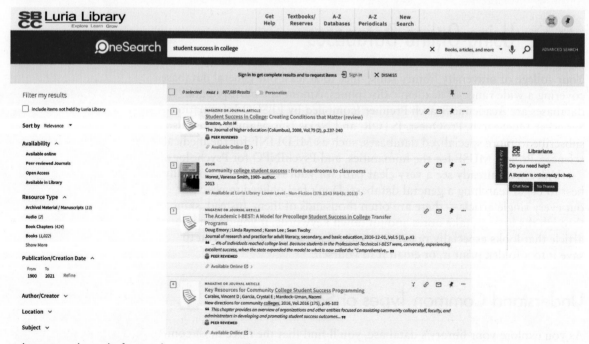

Subject Search results for "student success in college" in the OneSearch database

both words or phrases: *college success* AND *study skills*. Using OR will expand a search: *college success* OR *study skills*. Using NOT will filter out a specific result that keeps showing up but that is not helpful: *college success* NOT *textbooks*.

DIY 16.4a Practice Different Search Strategies

Begin searching your library's online database for your topic using keyword, subject, and advanced searches. Use Boolean operators to narrow or expand your search and take careful note of search terms suggested by the database itself. (Again, if you don't have a research paper prompt, you can look for material answering the question in section 15.3, "What does it take to be a successful college student?")

Search Newspapers and Magazines

One option for a database search is to focus on newspapers and magazines (also called "periodicals" because they are published on a regular, or "periodic," basis). You can click on the appropriate search button—Newspapers or Magazines in Academic Search Premier and ProQuest—or you can search newspaper-only databases such as US Newsstream.

Starting your database search looking through newspapers and periodicals, rather than scholarly journals, has the following advantages:

- **The material is current at the time of publication.** What's more, online databases allow you to change the search parameters so that you only find the very latest information.

- **The material is newsworthy to more than just scholars in the field.** Often newspapers pick up reports that appear in specialist scholarly journals because the editors realize that the research findings will be of interest to a wider audience.

- **The articles are written for a general audience.** Reporters and columnists for newspapers and periodicals write to be understood, which makes them excellent sources to learn from and quote. When good journalists talk to experts, they translate the language of scholars into language that's clear to most people.

Exploring the newspapers and magazines in your database is especially helpful in the early stages of the research process. Searching "student success strategies" in newspapers and magazines in Academic Search Premier, for example, returns an article in *The Chicago Tribune* about managing student debt written by Indiana University president Michael McRobbie. If you were still deciding what qualities make a successful student, you might well be struck by how important it is to seek value for your investment. That insight could result in an entire section of your research paper focusing on financial considerations for students.

Search Scholarly Journals

Articles in scholarly or academic journals can provide you with some of the most convincing evidence you will use in your research paper. Articles in these journals are "peer reviewed" by other scholars, which keeps the quality high, and conclusions are typically based on evidence and data and meticulously sourced.

Because scholarly journals are primarily for academics in the same field, the reading can be a challenge for someone who is not already an expert. Here are a few tips for navigating scholarly journals.

How to Navigate Scholarly Journals

- **Follow normal previewing strategies before you begin reading.** Read the title, any preliminary text and the first paragraph. Skim the text, looking for headings and visuals—writers of scholarly articles frequently highlight their findings in graphs and charts. Finally, read the conclusion, which often neatly summarizes the entire article.

- **Read the abstract carefully (but don't quote from it).** When you click on the search results in a database, other than the title of the article itself, the thing most likely to jump out at you is a paragraph-length summary of the article, which is called the abstract. Read it closely, but don't quote from it in your essay. (An abstract may be written by the journal's editors rather than the author.) Instead, think of the abstract as a kind of first look at the article itself.

- **Don't worry if you don't understand everything.** Scholarly articles are written for other scholars, so the authors often employ the specialized speech of that academic field. If you're not sure whether the article is useful, read it quickly. If you hit a particularly dense passage of jargon or citations, skim to the next passage that you're comfortable reading. In the initial phase of your research, you're mostly looking to get a sense of an article's overall argument. If it turns out to be one you rely on in your paper, you can go back and read the piece more carefully.

- **Look for information or data that support your thesis, extends your thesis, or offers a counterargument.** Save the information in a format that will allow you to include the information easily in your essay. Take notes that include any quotations, the article's title and author(s), any additional publication information required by MLA (p. 437) or APA (p. 475), and a note about how the passage or data connects to your argument or counterargument.

If you find a quotation or other information that looks relevant, you can save time if you "curate" the information, drafting a few sentences that might actually appear in your research paper. To do this, you'll often—though not always—want to include (1) the title of the journal, (2) the title of the article, (3) the author's name and credentials or area of expertise, and (4) the quotation or information itself.

Sample Student Note

Writing in the journal *Education*, East Carolina University professor Meghan Millea and three of her colleagues argue that data from their study suggest that "universities should invest in smaller class sizes and focus on students' financial constraints to improve student success." Interestingly, the team concedes in their article "What Matters in College Success? Determinants of College Retention and Graduation Rates" that "two factors typically considered important for retention and eventual graduation, absenteeism and on-campus residence" do *not* play a significant role in graduation rates at ECU (320).

Journal title

Author's name(s) and credentials

Article title

Material from the source

Search Online Encyclopedias

While hardcover encyclopedias, like the *Encyclopedia Britannica*, are mostly gathering dust on the bookshelves of libraries and your grandparents' homes, digital encyclopedias such as Wikipedia are thriving and used by millions of people every day. In fact, many of us—professors and students alike—may be so used to turning to Wikipedia for our first overview of a subject that we forget about the online encyclopedias available through our library databases.

Companies such as Elsevier, Gale, Oxford, Sage, and Wiley-Blackwell produce encyclopedias that cover topics ranging from anthropology to zoology—and everything in between. The entries are often written by experts in the field, and, in general, the articles are more thorough, and more thoroughly peer reviewed than the material you would find in Wikipedia.

DIY 16.4b Curate Quotations

Choose quotations from *two* of the most promising articles from your database search and curate them in a format that will make their later inclusion in your essay much easier. Again, you'll want to include the following information: the title of the journal, the title of the article, the author's name/credentials, a brief introduction to the article, and a quotation from the article.

16.5 Using Books

Some students find that books, book chapters, or a book's frontmatter (the introduction, for example) can provide useful and in-depth evidence for their essay. If you attend a large university, you may have access to hundreds if not thousands of print books. If you attend a small college, the collection may be nearly as impressive; if not, you can often borrow a book through interlibrary loan.

Students can often find e-books and digital books through their college library for free download. An online chat session with or email to a reference librarian at your school is a smart first step to accessing book content if your topic warrants reading longer sources.

16.6 Using the Internet

The Internet is both the wonder of the modern age and the black hole into which many a student researcher is sucked, never to return. That last statement may be an exaggeration, but a student working on a research essay can sometimes feel as though they are spiraling down a void from which no escape is possible.

In fact, if this book seems to be continually nudging you back to the library and your librarian for help with your research, that's because it is. In an article published in *American Libraries,* "Ten Reasons Libraries Are Still Better Than the Internet," Marcus Banks notes that "libraries are safer spaces," "librarians do not track your reading or search history to sell you things," "librarians do not censor," and "librarians guide you to exactly what you need."

Still, researchers love the convenience of the Internet, so it's worth discussing some cautions when searching the Internet and pointing out several sometimes-overlooked Internet resources. To begin with, of course, you'll want to test any Internet source you're considering against the FACTS checklist (see section 16.2). Is the source fair? Accurate? Current? Trustworthy? Suitable to your assignment? If your source meets each of these criteria, you've probably located material that can be useful in your research writing.

Guidelines for Online Searches

As you search online, use the following guidelines to return results most likely to pass the FACTS test (see section 16.2).

- **Vary the use of quotation marks around your search terms.** You can narrow your search by using quotation marks around a search term and expand it greatly by eliminating them.

- **Pay attention to the domain.** Sites that end in .org., .edu., and .gov are *generally* more accurate suppliers of legitimate information than .com, .net., and .tv. At the very least, be aware of a website's underlying goals. Note that websites published in other countries may have a country code as the domain: .ca for Canada, .jp for Japan, and so forth.

- **Demand credibility from your sources.** As you know, anyone can say anything on the Internet. Therefore, the source you are citing should present some credentials—either in an author's note or in the body of the piece of writing—that causes you to trust them. And you should be able to verify these qualifications against multiple other sources.

- **Be wary of anonymous sources.** Unless the website is from a genuine and long-established nonprofit—the United Nations Children's Fund, for example, or the Audubon Society—ask yourself why an article on a legitimate website doesn't list an author.

- **Demand quality from the website.** A site with grammatical and spelling errors or with an unprofessional presentation is not worth investigating or using. Keep in mind that building your own *ethos* (credibility) as a researcher requires that you insist on high-quality sources.

- **Stay away from "paper mills."** Companies that sell essays written by someone else will not help you to be a successful college student or develop the writing skills you need to succeed after college. Avoid these sites.

- **Use Wikipedia as a jumping-off point.** Although Wikipedia articles are crowd-sourced, they are increasingly reliable, especially those that list sources at the end. Noam Cohen, a technology columnist for *The New York Times*, calls Wikipedia "the Good Cop of the Internet." However, for academic projects, it's best to explore the citations or use insights gathered from Wikipedia pages to launch new searches.

- **Try Google Scholar.** Google Scholar focuses on scholarly, peer-reviewed articles. While you may encounter sites with paywalls, a typical search also returns credible sources that you might not find elsewhere.

DIY 16.6a "FACTS-Check" Online Sources

Use the Internet to search for sources for your research paper. Follow the search tips in section 16.6 and test any sources you're considering against the FACTS checklist. Be sure to keep a record of each potentially strong source so that you easily find it again.

DIY 16.6b Use Wikipedia as a Jumping-off Point

Search for your topic on Wikipedia, following any interesting internal links in the article. However, when you think you've found material for your paper, go directly to the *original sources* of the entry via the Notes/References or External Links listed at the bottom of the page. Write brief notes for one of the sources you find using this method.

Search Blogs and Other Social Media

Blog posts and other social media posts can lend flavor and focus—and sometimes even fight—to a research essay. Many of the issues we debate today are discussed in social atmospheres as well as in traditional publications: immigration, criminal justice reform, public health, education, the economy, the nature of democracy, and more. People posting on social media range from experts to public officials to everyday people. Some of the discourse is even-tempered, respectful, and factual. And some of it is, well, not.

Before you use posts as evidence, consider your purpose for writing, your audience, your topic, and your research question. Is the post you are considering suitable for the discussion and for the purpose you want to achieve? Will the post appeal logically or emotionally to your target audience? Does the post provide a useful perspective on your research question? Does the post point you in the direction of other sources or voices that could be useful?

Just as with any source, you want to be able to determine the credibility and credentials of those posting, identify their biases, and follow patterns in their posts.

16.7 Seeking Out Professional and Personal Interviews

Interviews involve the back-and-forth of conversation, so they tend reveal the actual speaking voice of an expert rather than the more formal expressions found in scholarly journals. Moreover, because they are usually less structured than written work, interviews often go to unexpected places, providing you with new avenues of investigation and discovery.

Search for Professional Interviews

While it would be nice to personally interview the most renowned experts on your topic, doing so is probably not realistic—unless that expert happens to be a professor at your school. Fortunately, you may find that a journalist has already done the work for you. However, before you refer to a published interview in your research paper, make sure the site on which it is published is trustworthy. You'll find credible interviews on the websites of newspapers like *The New York Times*, *The Washington Post*, and *The Guardian* and magazines such as *Time* and *Newsweek*, as well as in numerous publications focusing on particular fields like music, politics, science, and so on.

> **DIY 16.7a** Search for Relevant Professional (Published) Interviews
>
> Search online for interviews on your topic. Skim each potential interview looking for mentions of material relevant to your research question or use the Find function on your computer to search for relevant keywords in an interview transcript. Write brief notes about what these kinds of sources offer that the written sources you've found so far don't.

Conduct Personal Interviews

Unlike the formal, sometimes dry voices of professional scholars in their academic articles, interviews allow these experts to speak in a voice that's closer to the one they use in real life. Unfortunately, there won't always be a published interview that addresses your specific topic. And even if you do locate one, the interviewer may not ask the questions that elicit the answers you're looking for. One way around this is to conduct your own interview with an authority in the field you are studying or with someone whose lived experience is relevant to your research question.

Whether the person you are interviewing is a professor on your campus, a professional in the community, a peer, a family member, or someone you contact online, be respectful of the person's time and grateful for the opportunity to talk.

Tips for Successful Interviewing

Some people are natural interviewers. They are good listeners and know how to draw others out. But everyone *can* conduct a satisfactory interview with the right preparation. Here are some suggestions for making the best use of the time you have with your interviewee.

- **Write out a list of questions before you conduct your interview.** As every professional interviewer knows, it's better to have too many questions

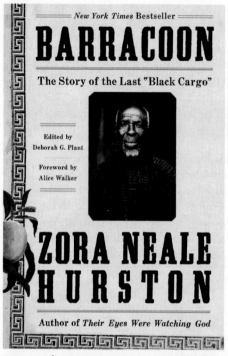

Zora Neale Hurston wrote *Barracoon: The Story of the Last "Black Cargo"* based on the three months she spent interviewing Cudjo Lewis, who traveled as an enslaved man on the *Clotilda,* the last recorded slave ship to arrive in the United States from Africa.

than too few. Some interviewees are surprisingly nervous, so they begin by answering with short or one-word replies.

- **Be open to leaving your set questions and following up on interesting comments made by your subject.** Yes, you want to have your most pressing questions answered, but the person you are interviewing is the expert on the subject, not you. If they go off in a direction you hadn't anticipated, but which may deepen and expand your research, listen carefully.

- **Focus on the person's expertise and make the most of the time.** While a few friendly, nonintrusive personal questions are appropriate at the beginning and end of the interview, once the interview has begun, keep your focus on the topic you want covered.

- **If you can, take notes *and* record the interview.** You will want to be able to access a recording for exact quotations, and the notes you write may be able to capture the speaker's emphasis or enthusiasm, especially if the interview was in person or on a video call.

- **Ask the interviewee if they want to add anything else before you close.** Give the person time to think over what they have said. Often this final question results in a cogent summation of what the person has been trying to tell you or a surprise disclosure that they've been (perhaps subconsciously) wanting to make throughout the interview.

Prepare a List of Questions in Advance

Prepare a mixture of direct and open-ended questions before meeting with your interviewee. If, for example, you were interviewing an academic counselor about ways students can become more successful, you might ask the following questions:

Direct

- What grants can college students tap into to pay for their textbooks?

- What help is there on our campus for students with learning disabilities?

- I noticed the counseling center offers "student success workshops." What takes place in those workshops?

Open-Ended

- What advice would you give to a student who is struggling to succeed in college?

- What relationships does a student need to develop in college to succeed?

- What qualities do you see in the most successful students?

Both types of questions can produce useful material for your research paper. Your academic counselor's response to the direct questions about resources for students with learning disabilities, for instance, might work well in a paragraph about how successful students are reliable users of campus resources. The answers to the open-ended questions about what advice the counselor would give to a struggling student might be as obvious, "Spend more time studying." Or it might turn out to be something you didn't expect to hear, such as, "Practice yoga." Even if general questions tend to elicit general answers, the possibility that you might receive one remarkable answer makes them worth asking.

DIY 16.7b Prepare to Interview an Expert

Identify the sort of expert who can help answer some of the questions triggered by your research paper topic. (If you don't have an assignment yet, respond to the prompt we've been working with in Part 3: "What does it take to be a successful college student?") Then, using the tips above, write out a list of both direct and open-ended questions for your expert. Now, locate a specific expert whom you can interview. Ideally, this will be someone on campus you can speak with personally or on a video call. Finally, contact that person to set up an interview.

16.8 Varying Your Sources and Including Visuals

Typically, a research essay prompt will not only require a certain *number* of sources, but it will also ask for a *variety* of sources. Your instructor will be looking for a selection of different types of sources not just to make sure you know how to do different types of research—although that is certainly an important reason—but also to ensure that you look at your topic from multiple perspectives.

When you locate a particularly good source, you may be tempted to overquote from it. If you do, however, your essay may end up sounding like a report on that author's research. Put your sources to work for you: decide which roles or jobs you need the sources to fill and use them accordingly. You will need a variety of sources to play a number of roles:

- Sources can define terms.

- Sources can summarize a debate.

- Sources can provide support for your thesis.

- Sources can provide counterarguments to your thesis.

- Sources can present the most current research studies related to your topic.

- Sources can tell stories that humanize your topic.

- Sources can offer data that can help you state the size of a problem.

- Sources can represent ideas in visual ways.

If your instructor insists that you have a certain number and type of sources—for example, four scholarly journals, two news articles, one interview—you'll want to follow those guidelines. However, even if the parameters for your sources are left intentionally open, be smart and use ideas, quotations, and visuals from a combination of sources: books and magazines, scholarly journals and newspapers, interviews and blogs, surveys and encyclopedias, and podcasts and infographics. A range of sources will demonstrate not only that you've done extensive research, but it will also make it possible for your sources to have a lively "conversation" among themselves.

If you use visual or multimedia content, be sure that it is unaltered and from credible sources. Use these materials ethically and purposefully—not just to decorate your essay. Follow MLA (Chapter 18) or APA (Chapter 19) guidelines for placing, citing, and captioning visuals in your work.

DIY 16.8 Review Your Sources

Review the sources you are currently planning to use in your research paper. Do you have an abundance of one particular type of source? Personal blog posts, say? Or do the majority of your quotations come from a single article or website? If so, choose a couple of the sources that are *most* relevant to your paper, and put the others aside for the moment so you can continue your research. Very often, you'll find that pushing yourself to go beyond the first sources you locate results in a much richer array of research to draw on when you sit down to compose your paper. Write brief notes about your review, being specific about which sources are worth keeping and why.

16.9 Keeping Track of Your Sources

The most important strategy for keeping track of your sources is to store everything in one place. If you normally work on a single computer, create a folder on your desktop. If you move from place to place, make a folder on your Google Drive, or email links to yourself that you save in a research paper folder. Whatever you do, try not to have your material out of reach when you need it.

Another important reason for keeping a handle on your sources is to avoid unintentional plagiarism. If you write something down but don't record who originally said it, you may accidentally slip a passage into your paper, forgetting that it was written by someone else. Instructors can easily find instances of plagiarism by using a similarity checker tool or copying and pasting questionable material into a search bar. And plagiarism, as your instructor may tell you, is one of the most serious breaches of trust in a writing class. Don't do it.

Setting up a basic research log is a good idea and is as simple as opening a new Word or Google document. A research log allows you to keep track of your sources and tag them to the appropriate parts of your project. As your research paper will likely have several distinct sections, it's helpful to keep the sources for each section separated. If you were writing about student success, for instance, you might group sources for each main subtopic together under a heading: Time Management, Study Habits, Financial Responsibility, and so on.

DIY 16.9 Catalog Your Sources

If you have free access to a citation management program, open an account and begin using the program to keep track of and comment on your sources. If you prefer to go low-tech, open a new document and start a simple research log, making sure to group related sources together.

16.10 Writing an Annotated Bibliography

Writing an annotated bibliography can be an important step in analyzing and evaluating a group of sources and in making certain you have a range of trustworthy sources that will play useful roles in helping you to answer your research question.

An annotated bibliography is a list of sources that includes a summary for each source. If you have six sources, you will have six entries in your annotated bibliography. Each entry includes a correctly formatted citation and a summary, known as the "annotation." Typically, the annotations in an annotated bibliography do the following:

- summarize the content and focus of the source

- suggest the source's usefulness to your research

- evaluate its method, conclusions, and reliability

Preparing an annotated bibliography can offer a handy tool when you begin drafting your paper. The basics of what you need to know about each source are right there at your fingertips, contextualized and already cited.

Full citation in MLA style

Summary presents focus and
organization of source

Evaluation points to the
authors' methods and the
accessibility of the text

Mentions specific usefulness of
the source

Sample Annotated Bibliography Entry (MLA Style)

Doyle, Terry, and Todd Zakrajsek. *The New Science of Learning: How to Learn in Harmony with Your Brain.* 2nd ed., Stylus, 2018.

Doyle and Zakrajsek, teaching and learning experts at major U.S. universities, base their book on neuroscience research and discuss the measurable physical changes in the brain when learning is happening. The authors emphasize that "learning anything new takes more time, practice, and skill than people think" (113). Each chapter offers concrete examples of how students can change their behavior to perform better both inside and outside of the classroom. The authors discuss everything from using patterns to better analyze and remember material to making effective use of sleep and breaks to improve the quality of studying. Doyle and Zakrajsek rely on published scientific research to support their suggestions. Each chapter ends with References, which lends authority to their overall approach. As the book's title suggests, its focus is on the science of learning, but it is written in language that speaks directly to the average college student. I will be able to use Doyle and Zakrajsek's strategies to make the argument that learning skills can be acquired and practiced.

The entries in an annotated bibliography should be arranged in alphabetical order, just as in a Works Cited list (see MLA style, p. 437) or in a list of References (see APA style, p. 475).

DIY 16.10 Create an Annotated Bibliography

Write an annotated bibliography for some or all of the sources you currently plan to use in your research paper. If you begin annotating a source and realize that you can't summarize the source's usefulness to your research, or if you can't evaluate and identify the source's reliability, it may be an indication that you need to find a different source.

Chapter 16 Checklist
Locating and Evaluating Your Sources

☐ **Have you identified and possibly contacted your reference librarian?**

As an apprentice researcher, you'll want a partner by your side. Your college's reference librarians are among your strongest advocates and allies, and you should get in touch with them as soon as you have questions about your research.

☐ **Are you using the FACTS checklist to evaluate your sources?**

Each source you use in your research paper should meet the FACTS test – that is, it should be Fair, Accurate, Current, Trustworthy, and Suitable to your assignment.

☐ **Did you begin your research by using your college's online database?**

As you begin researching, your first impulse may be to turn to Google. Instead, start your research process by investigating sources that have already been evaluated by editors and experts.

☐ **Have you searched for relevant books, articles from websites, and other credible sources?**

Books, articles, news sites, government sites, fact sheets, and some social media sites can provide trusted and authoritative information. It is possible to find some scholarly work on the open web.

☐ **Have you considered conducting an interview?**

If you feel the personal touch is missing from your paper, think about conducting your own interview. Especially when your topic is close to home, the people around you will often have some surprisingly insightful comments to contribute to your research.

☐ **Are you keeping track of and varying the sources you plan to use in your research paper, including visuals?**

Try to keep all your sources in one place, whether that means creating a basic research log in a Word document or using a citation management program. Vary the types of sources you use, keeping in mind the "work" you want your sources to do.

16.11 Making It Stick

How will you find and evaluate sources for your research project?

Working Together

16.11a Throwing a "Source Party"   Have a "source party" by inviting two classmates to read and evaluate all the sources you have collected so far for your research paper. You'll do the same for them. Use the FACTS checklist (Fair, Accurate, Current, Trustworthy, and Suitable for your paper) as well as the other guidelines in this chapter to assess each other's sources. If your classmates' have any sources that you find questionable, explain why and suggest alternatives.

Applying What You Learn

16.11b News Check   Think of a topic that's been on your mind lately. It doesn't have to be a school topic, but something, perhaps, that you've been hearing in the news — the latest debate about x, y, or z. Go online and find two sources of information about the topic. Use the FACTS checklist in section 16.2 to evaluate the two sources. Write notes about what you find.

16.11c How Do Sources Use Sources?
Using any topic that's on your mind, look for two sources that offer information about or discussion of the topic. Check to see if the sources you've found refer to other sources. (Keep looking until you have found two sources

that refer to other sources.) Do they mention studies or data, including visuals or links? Write a paragraph about how each source is using other sources and what effect those sources have on the source itself.

Invitations to Write
Use the following prompts to help steer your research in productive directions.

16.11d Completing Your Research

Shorter: Make a list of all the research you still need to do before you feel comfortable drafting your research paper.

Longer: For each item on your list, write a sentence or two that (1) describes *where* you plan to search for the material you still need, and (2) *how* you plan to use that material in your research paper.

16.11e Annotated Bibliography

Shorter: Write an annotation for each of the *two* sources you are most likely to use in your research paper.

Longer: Write entries for all of the sources you plan to use in your research paper. If your instructor wants you to include your annotated bibliography with your research paper — or is asking you to submit it as a separate assignment — make sure you carefully revise, edit, and proofread each entry before turning it in.

16.11f Thinking about Plagiarism

Shorter: Without consulting any sources, write a short definition of plagiarism. Give at least one or two examples of plagiarism.

Longer: Now, go online and locate your school's plagiarism policy. After you have read through it carefully, compare your initial description of plagiarism with how it is described at your college or university. Write a short response to these questions: What is considered plagiarism that hadn't occurred to you? What are the penalties for plagiarizing at your school? What advice would you give other students to avoid plagiarism?

17

Drafting and Revising Your Research Essay

REFLECT

READ & WRITE

DIY (Do-it-yourself) activities offer just-in-time support for all the skills in this book.

MAKING IT STICK

REFLECT

Write Before You Read   What do you know about your research essay topic now that you didn't know when you began your research? What's been most surprising? Discuss any evidence or outcomes you weren't aware of when you started the research process.

17.1   Building on What You Already Know

You might be wondering how drafting and revising a research essay is different from the writing you've been doing with the help of other chapters in this book. The truth is, much of what you've already learned you can apply to research writing. From reading strategies (Chapter 2) and revising strategies (Chapter 8) to taking positions (Chapter 11) and making evaluations (Chapter 10), you can draw on just about everything in *Hello, Writer* to make your research essay stronger.

Indeed, this chapter's primary purpose is to remind you of the elements of the composition process that are particularly important to research essays and to steer you away from common mistakes writers make when they compose research-based essays.

Complete student-written research essays appear in sections 18.5 (MLA) and 19.5 (APA).

17.2 Beginning with Focused Prewriting

When you begin writing a shorter essay, you generally haven't thought about the topic as deeply as you have after doing the research for a longer essay. Because of that extensive study and exploration, prewriting for your research essay is likely to be richer and more complex. Also, since you already have ideas and material to work with, you'll want to focus your prewriting on each of your subtopics, rather than on the main overall topic.

Let's say you're writing about the need for mental health resources for students at your college. It may be more fruitful to write about your subtopics separately—a focused, ten-minute prewrite on each of the following ideas: causes for declining mental health among teens and young adults, current resources, gaps in resources, peer-to-peer outreach initiatives, and teletherapy.

As a reminder, here are some of the most common prewriting strategies (see also section 4.3):

DIY 17.2 Generate Ideas for Your Subtopics

For the research essay you are currently writing (or using the student success prompt in section 15.3, if you don't have an assignment), list each of the *main* subtopics of your research paper and use one *different* method of prewriting for each area to generate ideas and text for your essay. Chapter 4 covers prewriting in great detail, so if you're having trouble getting started, it's worth revisiting.

- Freewriting
- Questioning
- Listing
- Quick searching
- Curating quotations
- Mapping
- Letter writing
- Talking and listening

Keep track of the prewriting you do on each of your subtopics; when you're finished, read through it all to see what it tells you about your topic overall. What do you already know a lot about? Which areas of your topic need further research and thinking?

17.3 Crafting a Working Thesis

As with any academic essay, it helps to have a focus when you begin writing, even if you know that focus may change during the composition process. Ideally, your research and focused prewriting will have brought you to a place where you can envision a specific way to approach your topic. It's that critical time in the composition of any essay when you begin to think about your thesis statement. As a quick reminder from section 5.4, a strong thesis statement

- is focused and specific

- is not a statement of fact

- includes a topic and a claim

- answers a question, whether asked or implied

- is arguable and worth arguing

- is often longer than a single sentence

- provides a plan for the essay

- is a statement, not an announcement

Your thesis statement for this assignment will normally begin as an answer to your research question. As an example, let's return once more to the sample prompt we've been working with over the past two chapters: "What does it take to be a successful college student?" (from section 15.3). In response, you might—using one of the other clusters of ideas developed in Chapter 16—write the following thesis statement, which acts as a game plan.

Sample Thesis Statement: Game Plan

The most successful college students are those who set priorities, manage time well, take effective notes, and live on a budget.

That sentence is just twenty words long, but it offers a clear multipart plan for the research paper ahead. Rather than floundering around trying to come up with areas for research, a student working with this thesis statement knows exactly what to write about. In fact, you can imagine the sections of the essay just from reading the sentence:

setting priorities

managing time well

taking effective notes

setting and sticking to a budget

Sure, those subtopics might expand or contract during the writing of the paper. Maybe more areas of focus will be needed. You never know what your essay will look like until you begin writing it, but with this working thesis, you have a well-defined path forward.

Not all thesis statements have to function like a map or blueprint. And keep in mind that not all thesis statements are a single sentence. The following thesis responds to the question "What does it take to be a successful college student?" by suggesting an overall theme or controlling idea for the essay. The writer's position, expressed in two sentences, is less specific than a game plan thesis, but no less useful.

Sample Thesis Statement: Controlling Idea

There is no single defining college student experience; millions of students attend thousands of colleges in America each year. But the most common attribute of a successful college student is a general openness, an attitude that welcomes new experiences.

As you craft your working thesis, here are a few reminders about how to make it suitable for your research paper.

Developing a Working Thesis Statement

- **Consider building a plan into your thesis.** Yes, this is still a working thesis, likely to be modified during drafting and revision. Nevertheless, it will save you time and frustration if your thesis serves as a guidepost for the rest of your essay.

- **Remain flexible.** Resist the temptation to stay with a bad idea just because you've put a lot of work into it. Instead, save the material you've already written in another document—it may still come in handy—and go back to the drawing board.

- **Remember your audience.** Think about your audience's background, interests, life experiences, and potential biases. If you have a particularly strong position on a topic, consider how it will be received by your likely readers (including your instructor and classmates) and what appeals you will need to make to be most persuasive.

DIY 17.3 Craft a Working Thesis

Write a working thesis that answers the research question you have formed for your current assignment (or the student success prompt in section 15.3). Follow the guidelines above as you craft a focused yet flexible thesis that is directed at your paper's specific audience.

17.4 Arranging Ideas; Selecting and Organizing Evidence

Once you have an idea what your overall claim will be, you can plan the sections of your essay. Arrange your ideas in a way that will both meet your audience's needs and serve your purpose(s). Consider how much background information you will need to give. Consider whether you will want to start with your strongest point or end with it. Determine whether you will need to define any terminology or put the discussion into a specific context. Keep in mind as you organize your ideas that you will want to acknowledge perspectives or positions other than your own (because doing so presents you as fair-minded and knowledgeable). There is no right or wrong place for any of these parts of your essay.

Write an Outline

Some writers formalize the arrangement of their ideas in an outline. A sketch outline is more like an informal list; a sentence outline is a full-blown formal, detailed plan written in complete sentences (Chapter 5). In terms of depth and detail, a topic outline is somewhere in between the two, which makes the topic outline a good tool for organizing the early draft of your research essay. Remember that both outline and thesis are in "working" mode, so you should anticipate that they will continue to change and to modify one another throughout the composition process.

Here's one of the thesis statements from earlier in the chapter: "The most successful college students are those who set priorities, manage time well, take effective notes, and live on a budget." Suppose you want to focus on the subtopic of how managing time well contributes to college success. That section, which would likely span multiple paragraphs, might be outlined like this:

I. College success requires excellent time management skills. A successful student . . . *(section topic)*
   A. Balances school, work, and social life *(Subtopic: Skill One)*
      1. Ensures that school and work schedules never overlap *(Supporting evidence: example of skill)*
      2. Builds in time for socializing *(Supporting evidence: example of skill)*
      3. Sets aside sufficient time for studying *(Supporting evidence: example of skill)*

B. Avoids procrastination *(Subtopic: Skill Two)*
  1. Divides large tasks into small parts *(Supporting evidence: example of skill)*
  2. Disconnects from social media, games, phone, etc. *(Supporting evidence: example of skill)*
  3. Draws on the support of friends and family to stay on task *(Supporting evidence: example of skill)*
C. Employs time management tools *(Subtopic: Skill Three)*
  1. Follows daily planner *(Supporting evidence: example of skill)*
  2. Makes and follows to-do lists *(Supporting evidence: example of skill)*

While this portion of a sample topic outline *is* rather detailed, it's the result of some fairly basic research on the topic. Moreover, as you can see, it provides a very clear plan for how to approach the subject matter. In conjunction with a strong working thesis, a topic outline like this one would eliminate much of the uncertainty involved in composing a draft.

Is this plan *too* detailed? Possibly. By this time in the semester, you are beginning to know yourself as a writer. If you're someone who experiences writer's block whenever you don't know your next step in the writing process, then the more planning and organizing you do in advance, the more comfortable you are when you sit down to write. On the other hand, if knowing just what you're supposed to do takes all the fun out of writing, then an outline like the one in this section might be too directive. It might not give you the freedom to explore aspects of the topic that will come to you only during the actual writing of the paper.

DIY 17.4a Draft a Topic Outline

Using your working thesis and the arrangement of your sources as a guide, write a topic outline for your research paper. (As with all the DIYs in this chapter, use the student success prompt in section 15.3 if you don't yet have an assignment.) Your own thesis and outline may not be as formal or as detailed as the example above, but they should provide you with a clear plan for the first draft of your essay.

Organize Your Evidence

During the process of finding and evaluating sources, you might have taken notes and curated quotations that you thought you might use in your essay. It's time now for your notes to meet your outline! Look through your sources—and specific passages and data points—with the plan for your essay in front of you. Which pieces of evidence do you need for each idea? What roles do you need your sources to play in the service of helping you to answer your research question?

In the following example, you can view a small bit of the outline we saw earlier in this section, along with notes that the student took on a source.

B. Avoids procrastination
   1. Divides large tasks into small parts
   2. Disconnects from social media, games, phone, etc.
   3. Draws on the support of friends and family to stay on task

> Source: Art Markman, "To Achieve a Major Goal, First Tackle a Few Small Ones." *Harvard Business Review*, 24 Feb. 2017, www.hbr.org/amp/2017/02
>
> "To achieve a large-scale goal for the first time, it is best to work your way up through more manageable projects. The idea is to shorten the learning cycle by tackling a smaller project, so that you can get early feedback and hone your approach before taking on the complex tasks associated with the bigger project."

After fitting the source to a specific part of the outline, the student can then begin to draft a paragraph that weaves their own ideas and the ideas from the source (underlined) in a way that supports their thesis:

Successful students also avoid procrastination and stalling. Sometimes procrastination is a by-product of feeling overwhelmed, and since so much of college can be overwhelming, especially for first-year students, most students tend to put off anything that doesn't have to be done immediately. Psychology professor <u>Art Markman encourages people to "work [their] way up through manageable projects"</u> instead of trying to <u>"achieve a large-scale goal"</u> all at once. For example, breaking a major assignment down into smaller, more easily achievable tasks is one way to boost productivity and avoid procrastination. <u>An added bonus, according to Markman, is that those who move steadily on smaller pieces of a project "can get early feedback"</u> on their work, which may make later stages of the project go even more smoothly.

    Another way to avoid procrastination is . . .

Transition from student's previous idea

Student

Source

Student

Source

Transition to the student's next idea

Putting your sources to work to help you achieve your goals will be an important step in your drafting process. Consider the following tips as you draft and develop your essay.

Tips for Selecting and Organizing Your Sources

- **Arrange sources so that they reinforce one another.** If you really want to make your point, introduce a strong piece of evidence to support your argument and then follow it up with an even more persuasive source—perhaps one that extends the thinking of the first.

- **Don't overdo the data.** Yes, introducing and discussing two or three strong sources in the same paragraph or two can considerably strengthen your argument. When you feel passionate about your topic, you may want to employ your sources one after another, like an invading army of White Walkers in *Game of Thrones*. But don't go overboard. Readers are reading primarily for your ideas.

- **Avoid obvious contradictions between sources.** Sometimes two really useful sources cancel each other out. You can avoid this problem by acknowledging the difference of opinion and positioning one source as a counterargument to the other. Make sure, though, that you reconcile the differences, which typically means conceding that one source is more persuasive than the other.

- **Use balance for stylistic and rhetorical effect.** Instead of crushing your reader with pages and pages of numbers or with sad story after sad story, try to achieve harmony among your sources and balance logical appeals with emotional and ethical ones (see section 11.3).

- **Use your most intriguing or provocative source in your introduction.** section 7.2 covers a number of strategies for introducing your essay, many of which rely on a thought-provoking, if not outright challenging, quotation. As you research your paper, keep an eye out for quotations that are likely to stimulate your readers' interest in your topic.

- **Save your most eloquent source for the end.** Think about what you want readers to think, feel, or do at the end of your essay. Now think about which source is most likely to inspire that feeling or action. Save that source for your conclusion.

- **Avoid "quotation factories" like Bartleby, Goodreads, and Brainy Quote.** The quotations and other source materials you use should be drawn from *relevant sources*, people and organizations engaged in the debate with you, not plucked out of context from online quotation collections.

DIY 17.4b Organize Your Sources Effectively

Using the advice in section 17.4, organize the sources you are planning to use in what you believe is their most effective arrangement. For each part of your outline or plan, think about what roles you need your sources to play, and then add your sources to your outline or plan.

17.5 Balancing Synthesis and Discovery

In Chapter 15, the writer of a research essay was compared to an *assemblage* artist, someone who takes various objects and fashions them into a work that didn't exist before. As you draft your research project, you will be performing a similar type of synthesis, using your intelligence and creativity to combine your sources into something new. Once you add *your* voice to the research conversation, that conversation changes and becomes something that didn't exist before.

While in some ways your sources will shape your essay, ultimately, it's up to you to take control of those sources and put them in service of the main points you want to make. In that sense, you might be less like an artist and more like the coach of a talented team. You've got the players to win, but they can't win by themselves—not without your guidance and not unless they're working together. That's your job: to get the best out of each player (or source) and to use them in the position and at the time they are most likely to contribute to a winning effort.

When you synthesize, you put sources side by side and in conversation with one another—and then you come in with your commentary or analysis. Sometimes in examining sources side by side, you discover a gap. Synthesis can sound a little like this:

> The road to solving the X problem will be bumpy, according to Source 1, who says, "_____." Source 2 argues that the solution is in reach but might "force us to _____." Both approaches work, but they point to the need for more _____.

This is just a template, of course, but it represents a writer who is being thoughtful about a debate, issue, or problem and using the sources they've gathered to spark and drive the thinking.

As you write, pay attention not only to your ideas but also to your voice. Research writing for a school assignment is usually more formal than everyday speech, but it doesn't have to be stiff or overly academic. Instead, let your readers hear something of who you really are. Your writing shouldn't be careless and slangy, but you will want to sound like a real human being with an informed and valid opinion about your topic—a person in conversation with others about a topic that matters to all of you.

Using your own authorial voice and keeping the "game" moving will also help you address the *So what?* question. Acknowledging that you have some enthusiasm for your subject, as you intelligently combine and comment on your sources, will satisfy your readers' natural desire to know why they should be investing time and mental energy in your essay.

As you know from previous essays that you have written, whatever planning you put into place when you begin writing, you'll still be making discoveries along the way. You know, too, that the first draft is not the time to be overly concerned about what others will think of your work. Instead, you'll want to just jump in and *write*.

DIY 17.5 Write a First Draft of Your Research Essay

Clear some time from your calendar — three or four hours, at least — then write a draft of your research paper. Use your thesis and outline and whatever other planning tools you have at your disposal, but don't worry too much about the quality of the writing. Instead, discuss each of the major subtopics of your essay in as much detail as you can, knowing that this draft is simply the first version of what will ultimately become your finished research essay. Choose a preliminary placement for each of your sources.

17.6 Integrating Sources Effectively

Successful research essays weave together a writer's ideas with the ideas of others in the service of answering a research question. Integrating the two so that the ideas flow smoothly can be a challenge. When you write your research essay, you will represent others' ideas by quoting their words or by summarizing or paraphrasing their ideas. You'll show that you have done the research and the thinking. This section presents strategies for presenting the ideas of others within your own writing.

As always, whenever you are borrowing the words or ideas of someone else, make sure to give appropriate credit. Direct quotations should be placed within quotation marks, and the original source of ideas conveyed through paraphrase or summary must be clearly acknowledged.

Often short direct quotations can liven up your essay with the voices of the scholars and thinkers you've been learning from; they can also demonstrate that you've really done the reading and, like a gold miner sifting through tons of gravel and sand and mud, have unearthed some nuggets along the way. Paraphrases and summaries can add critical source information when the exact language of an author isn't necessary.

Integrate Quotations

One of the skills you will develop when writing a research essay is using quotations in more complex ways. This means integrating quotations, the exact language of other writers, both correctly and well. You want to aim for both accuracy and eloquence.

Block Quotations

Quotations of more than four lines should be indented in a block quote and introduced by a sentence ending with a colon. Quotation marks aren't needed; the indented format lets readers know the entire block is taken from the source. The citation follows the last period.

> In *Make It Stick: The Science of Successful Learning,* authors Brown, Roediger, and McDaniel offer learning tips for students. They write:
>
> > Embrace the fact that significant learning is often, or even usually, somewhat difficult. You will experience setbacks. These are signs of effort, not of failure. Setbacks come with striving, and striving builds expertise. Effortful learning changes your brain, making new connections, building mental models, increasing your capability. The implication of this is powerful: Your intellectual abilities lie to a large degree within your own control. (201)

Remember, the longer the quotation, the more responsibility you have for discussing it in your article. A long quotation dropped into a paragraph without any analysis or explanation may look like a transparent attempt to run up the essay's word count. If you use a longer passage from a work you want to showcase, spend some time connecting the ideas to the point you are making.

Sentence-Length Quotations

When writing a sentence-long introduction for a quotation that is itself one sentence or longer, you can introduce the quotation with a colon or use a signal phrase and use brackets to change the capitalization.

> In *Mindset: The New Psychology of Success*, psychologist Carol Dweck concludes that familiarity with a concept often triggers a positive response to that concept: "Just learning about growth mindset can cause a big shift in the way people think about themselves" (226).

> In *Mindset: The New Psychology of Success*, psychologist Carol Dweck concludes that familiarity with a concept often triggers a positive response to that concept. According to Dweck, "[j]ust learning about growth mindset can cause a big shift in the way people think about themselves" (226).

Quoted Words or Phrases

Sometimes you don't need to quote an entire passage or even an entire sentence. Borrowing another author's wording or phrasing and tucking it into your own idea is often effective; just remember to use quotation marks around the exact language and cite the source at the end of the sentence.

> Often, "just learning about growth mindset" can be enough to spark a change in the way someone thinks about their own failures and successes (Dweck 226).

Note that when the author is not mentioned in the body of the sentence, the in-text citation should include the author's name in parentheses.

A Quotation within a Quotation

When you quote an author who is quoting someone else, place double quotation marks on the outside ("/") of the quotation, then single quotation marks ('/') inside to show where the second quotation begins and ends. In the following example, a student is quoting Elaine Fox. In Fox's quotation, she quotes William James.

> Elaine Fox writes that psychologist William James "preempted the contemporary notion of brain plasticity back in 1890, when he wrote that the brain is 'endowed with a very extraordinary degree of plasticity'" (131).

Using an Ellipsis

An ellipsis is a series of three spaced dots (. . .) used to indicate that some words have been omitted from the material being quoted. You use an ellipsis (plural: ellipses) when parts of a quotation are irrelevant to your essay. Below is an example of ellipsis use, based on a quotation from Elaine Fox's book *Rainy Day, Sunny Brain*:

> **Original Quotation**
>
> Ironically, William James, the founder of experimental psychology in the United States, preempted the contemporary notion of brain plasticity back in 1890, when he wrote that the brain is "endowed with a very extraordinary degree of plasticity."

Use an ellipsis when you're leaving out material in the middle of a sentence. If, for instance, you assumed your readers knew who William James was, and you wanted to eliminate the clause describing his qualifications, you might make the following edit:

> **Quotation with Words Omitted**
>
> "Ironically, William James . . . preempted the contemporary notion of brain plasticity back in 1890, when he wrote that the brain is 'endowed with a very extraordinary degree of plasticity.'"

Take care not to use ellipses to misrepresent a source or to remove the parts of a quotation that don't support your claim. If you do quote from a source whom you don't agree with, acknowledge that fact.

Modifying a Quotation with Brackets

Brackets ([ ]) are used to insert a clarifying word or phrase in a quotation when the absence of that word or phrase would make the sentence unclear or to make a change in capitalization or grammar to make sure a sentence flows smoothly.

> Angela Duckworth argues that "It's also in school [that grit matters], especially for kids at risk of dropping out."

The fuller Duckworth passage is this: "So it's not just at West Point or the National Spelling Bee that grit matters. It's also in school, especially for kids at risk for dropping out." The writer wanted to capture just the last sentence, but the last sentence by itself doesn't say clearly what the "it" is. As with all methods of quotation, brackets should not be used to change the meaning of the quotation in a significant or deceitful way.

Use Signal Phrases to Introduce Quotations and Other Borrowed Material

When you use quotations (and summaries and paraphrases) in your writing, take care to introduce them or set them up. This way, your reader won't become confused about which ideas are yours or how the sources you use contribute to the points you are making. You can use language to *signal* to your readers that you are transitioning from one voice to another.

Angela Duckworth argues _____.

_____, according to Dweck.

Brookshire disagrees and instead explains that _____.

Choosing an appropriate verb can often help signal a source's position in relation to your own or to that of another source. The following are common signal verbs in academic writing:

admits	explains
agrees	insists
argues	notes
believes	observes
claims	points out
confirms	rejects
denies	reports
emphasizes	suggests

The effective use of relevant quotations may be the difference between a good research paper and an outstanding one, but effectively integrating quotations into your essay can be challenging. Here are a few more tips to help you work quotations into your essay as smoothly as possible.

Tips for Integrating Quotations

- **Avoid "dropped" quotations.** This is just another way of saying always introduce quotations. Most readers would probably agree that a sentence in quotation marks in the middle of a paragraph—with no explanation of who said it or why it's there—is worse than no quotation at all.

- **Give each quotation its proper due.** If it's worth quoting, it's worth discussing, even if that discussion takes the form of only a sentence or two of commentary. Your reader wants to know how the evidence supports your ideas.

- **Avoid quotation traffic jams.** In this scenario, the student is simply trying to squeeze as many of the required sources together in as tight a space as possible, so one quotation follows another with little or no explanation between the quotations. Rather than serving to move the essay forward, the quotations pile up and stall the essay's momentum.

- **Use block quotations sparingly.** A block quotation is a quotation of more than four lines that is indented and has no quotation marks around it. Some passages are so convincing, and so essential to your argument, that you want to include the entire thing. However, lots of long quotations can drown out your voice and your ideas—and, worse, they can give the impression that you are primarily trying to pad your word count.

Integrate Summaries and Paraphrases

Let's use yet another analogy for your research paper. Imagine that writing it is like making a movie—a complicated endeavor that takes a lot of backstage help. If strong quotations are like the movie stars of your paper, and you, the author, are like the director, then summary and paraphrase might be like the supporting cast or the extras—necessary, of course, but perhaps not as flashy.

Summary

When you summarize, you use your own words to represent the ideas of a source in a briefer format than the original. You communicate only the most important points. You can summarize an article, a film, a speech, or another work often in a couple of sentences by capturing the main point and most critical supporting points.

Here are a few reminders about how to use summary effectively:

- **Summarize to convey important points that are too long to quote or paraphrase.** Not every source can be squeezed into a single quotation. Fortunately, you can recap an entire article, or even a book, in a sentence or two.

- **Be accurate and objective.** To the best of your ability, sum up what your source has *actually* said—not what you wish they'd said or how you feel about what they've said. Be especially vigilant and truthful when summarizing sources with whom you disagree.

- **Use your own words whenever possible.** In a longer summary, you might quote a crucial word or phrase from your source, but in general you'll want to use your own language, not that of the source.

- **Indicate and cite your source.** Just as you would a quotation, introduce your summary with a signal phrase, and be sure to use appropriate MLA or APA documentation to cite it. In summarizing a source that covers two or more pages, that internal citation might look like this in MLA: (Bishop 25–58) or like this in APA: (Bishop, 2001, pp. 25–58).

Paraphrase

When you paraphrase, you use your own words to represent the ideas of a source, but in roughly the same length as the original. A paraphrase presents your understanding of a source's idea. In the following example, an original passage appears first, and a paraphrased version follows.

Original

Some of my strongest performers did not have stratospheric IQ scores. Some of my smartest kids weren't doing so well. And that got me thinking.

—Angela Duckworth

Paraphrase

Angela Duckworth noticed that success among her students wasn't tied to traditional intelligence scores. That observation piqued her curiosity.

Note that the student includes the source's name in the sentence. Since the source is an unpaginated online video, there is no page number to put in parentheses. The author's name in your sentence is a clue to your reader to check your Works Cited page to locate publication information for the source.

DIY 17.6 Improve Your Use of Quotation, Summary, and Paraphrase

Open the file for your research essay draft, then highlight all of the quotations, summaries, and paraphrases you have used, using a specific color for each of the three ways of reporting another person's ideas. Look back over section 17.6, and make sure you are following the suggestions for effectively integrating sources into your research essay. Revise as needed to make sure your use of sources is accurate and effective.

Here are three reminders about what it takes to paraphrase well:

- **Use your own words.** Just as you would when summarizing, make sure the paraphrase is in your own words, not your source's. It's always worth double- and triple-checking paraphrases to ensure that you haven't inadvertently plagiarized a source.

- **Paraphrase when your words are clearer than your source.** Sometimes your source has an important idea but stumbles when expressing it. If you can say the same thing better than your source, then use paraphrase.

- **Cite your paraphrases, just as you would a quotation.** Even if the words are your own, the ideas expressed in a paraphrase are not. Introduce the paraphrase with a suitable signal phrase and be sure to include an internal and end citation for the source.

17.7 Documenting Sources and Avoiding Plagiarism

How do you let your readers know *exactly* where you found each of the sources you used in your essay? You've been advised throughout the book to turn to Chapters 18 (MLA) and 19 (APA) to get details on the two most common documentation styles (sometimes referred to as citation styles). While it may feel tedious to cite every idea and phrase you borrow from your sources, ultimately, documentation is more than just mere record-keeping.

Understand Why Writers Document Sources

Documentation is, in the words of Professor Howard Tinberg, "a product of conversations among knowledgeable communities." Now that you've entered the scholarly conversation, it's part of your responsibility to identify your sources so that other thinkers might follow your trail. Also, accurate documentation gives credit to others in the conversation and demonstrates the care that you take as a peer researcher. In short, it shows you've done your homework.

One word of caution that will save you from many potential citation problems: when in doubt, cite your source. It's much better to err on the side of being too careful than to accidentally use someone's words without attribution and, therefore, plagiarize.

As you scroll through the models in Chapters 18 and 19, you may think, *There are so many rules and regulations. Who could possibly keep track of them all?* The answer? Practically no one, but that's okay. You have this book, which will allow you to look up documentation rules and models when you need to. You will be expected to cite your sources both in the body of your essay and in a list of works cited (MLA) or references (APA) at the end of your essay. Paying attention to these requirements as you draft and revise will save you from having to scramble right before the essay is due.

> **DIY 17.7a** Check the Accuracy of In-Text and End Citations
>
> Reread the quotations, summaries, and paraphrases that you highlighted for DIY 17.6. Now check each one to make sure it has an accurate internal citation (MLA 18.2; APA, 19.1) and a corresponding end citation in the Works Cited or Reference list (MLA, 18.3; APA 19.2).

Avoid Plagiarism

Plagiarism is the intentional or unintentional use of someone else's words or ideas as though they were your own. Among academics, plagiarism is considered a serious offense. It breaks every school's stated rules, but it also substitutes for learning. Writers who plagiarize aren't making any progress in their development as writers.

Often the research essay is positioned as a high-stakes assignment—sometimes worth a quarter of the grade for the semester—and the temptation to plagiarize is strong. Resist. The long-term consequences of being discovered cheating will not only affect your grade for this essay, and consequently the class itself, but you are also likely to find your name on a plagiarism list kept by your institution's academic dean—you may even risk your eligibility for certain internships and co-ops. It's just not worth it.

Tips for Avoiding Plagiarism

1. **Start your research early.** The more of your own research you have in hand early in the composing process, the less tempted you will be to steal someone else's work.

2. **Keep track of your sources.** If you have been careless about curating and storing your sources, you might accidentally use someone else's words. While you might claim that accidental plagiarism is unintentional, it's plagiarism, nevertheless.

→

3. Use quotation marks around all borrowed language. If somebody else said it, give them proper credit by indicating which words are theirs.

4. Make sure paraphrases and summaries are in your own words. Occasionally, you'll want to use a word or phrase from the original source. If you do so, make sure you acknowledge that direct borrowing with quotation marks.

5. When in doubt, cite your source. One more time, especially if it's getting close to your due date and you can't consult your instructor or librarian, if you have any doubts, err on the side of caution and include a citation.

Remember that when you're writing a research paper, your instructor has *asked* you to find sources. Just make sure you acknowledge them. If you're unclear about what to cite, you should, as noted earlier, err on the side of citing too much rather than too little. However, it's possible to get so worried that you begin to think you should cite *everything*, which is not the case.

You *Don't* Need to Cite the Following:

- **Common knowledge.** Not every single source needs to be acknowledged with a citation. That would make writing itself almost impossible. If you were to write, for instance, that the United States suffered a serious attack on September 11, 2001, you wouldn't need to cite a source for that. That's an event and a day with which most Americans are familiar.

- **Information from well-known documents.** The Declaration of Independence, for instance, wouldn't need to be cited, as it is a well-known historical document that can be accessed on numerous sites.

You *Do* Need to Cite the Following:

- **Quotations, paraphrases, and summaries.** When someone else speaks, the reader wants to know who they are and where they said what they said. While paraphrases and summaries employ your own words, you *are* borrowing someone else's ideas, and you need to acknowledge that borrowing with a citation.

- **Provocative or debated information.** If the information isn't accepted by *most* reasonable persons, you'll want to indicate where you found it. You wouldn't have to cite your claim that Earth is round, for instance, but you would need to cite your source claiming that a certain policy is the only possible solution for immigration reform.

- **Information that is NOT common knowledge.** We all know Earth is round, but not everyone knows the temperature at Earth's core is approximately 10,800 degrees Fahrenheit. The former information doesn't need to be cited; the latter does.

- **Statistics.** "Lies, damned lies, and statistics," Mark Twain famously said, suggesting that statistics are even worse than lies *and* damned lies. Statistics are very frequently in dispute, so make sure you cite them, no matter how certain you are that everyone should agree on the accuracy of your source.

DIY 17.7b Check for Plagiarism

Using the guidelines in section 17.7, check your research paper for possible instances of plagiarism. If you need help doing so, make an appointment with a tutor in your school's writing center, who will be able to offer additional guidance.

17.8   Designing and Presenting Your Research

After weeks of research, and all the effort that goes into composing a solid first draft, you may forget to attend to how your research essay *looks*. Nevertheless, it's worth presenting your research in a format that your reader expects but that is also elegant and readable. Taking just a little additional thought and time can make a significant difference in how your essay or digital presentation is received.

Consider Using Headings and Subheadings

A longer research work may benefit appreciably from headings and subheadings—short titles announcing what will be covered in a section—like those you find throughout this book. In *Stylish Academic Writing*, Helen Sword compares well-placed headings to "neatly labeled doorways that lead us from one well-proportioned room to the next." As a research writer, you are an architect of sorts, designing your reader's experience through your ideas.

A heading announces a major topic, with subheadings indicating important parts within that topic. If you're writing from a topic outline, you can often pull the headings and subheadings directly from your outline. Headings may change in size and position as you move from a heading to a level-one subheading and so forth. It's worth thinking about the

> As a research writer, you are an architect of sorts, designing your reader's experience through your ideas

documentation style in which you are writing. See 18.4 (MLA) and 19.3 (APA) for formatting guidelines.

Headings and subheadings should use parallel structure; that is, there should be a similarity between the phrasing of the titles. For instance, if you have a group of section headings that begins with "Playing Fair," "Writing Well," and "Learning More," it would throw the balance and readability off if you suddenly abandoned the "-ing" pattern and used "Read Carefully" instead of the parallel "Read*ing* Carefully."

Consider Using Lists

As you can see, this book contains numerous lists. Whether lists take the form of numbers, letters, bullet points, or other shapes, they cut through the clutter and announce, "*This* is what's really important: pay attention." One reason lists are so effective is that we are used to seeing—and often making—them in our own lives. A research writer may want to use a list instead of a paragraph to display certain grouped ideas: causes, effects, problems, solutions, steps, areas affected by an issue, populations affected by an issue, and so on.

Use Colors and Fonts Wisely

When you're designing a web page or a slide presentation, color is one of your first and most important concerns. If you are presenting your research in one of those genres, see section 14.4 for guidance. In a first-year college research essay, however, content will be your primary emphasis. For this reason, you should use color sparingly and consistently in an essay.

In general, your font should stay uniform throughout the body of the paper. When selecting your main font, err on the side of tradition. Times New Roman is so common that it will be almost invisible to your reader's eye. Other common fonts include Arial, Garamond, Calibri, and Georgia. Use MLA and APA guidelines to help you style your type; there are rules for which kinds of words should be set in italics or in boldface type.

Include Effective Visuals and Multimedia

The use of visuals and multimedia is covered in Chapter 14, but it's worth revisiting a few important points that may be relevant to your research writing. Whether your final draft is delivered online or as hard copy, remember the simpler-is-better motto. Use white space where appropriate. Keep your design uncluttered, elegant, and easy to read. And follow MLA or APA formatting guidelines for placing and captioning visual elements.

Tips for Using Visuals and Multimedia

Here are a few reminders about the best ways to use images, graphs, charts, and multimedia:

- **Tell your readers what you want them to see.** If you want your reader to examine certain aspects of a visual or sound clip, you need to be explicit in explaining why it is important.

- **Keep the visual close to where it is being discussed.** Your reader shouldn't have to go searching through your paper looking for the visual you are talking about. It is good practice to place visual elements within or immediately after the paragraph in which you discuss them. Wrapping the text around the visual is one way to ensure that the discussion and image are right next to each other.

- **Be honest.** Don't use visuals or sounds in ways that are deliberately misleading. If you crop or change an image, alert your reader.

- **If your essay will be delivered online, don't overlink.** We're so used to reading hyperlinks in webpages that the absence of links in any online document would be startling. If you're writing online, be thoughtful, though: it's easy to overlink. Each time you link, you're inviting your reader to move away from your own work and into someone else's.

- **Use video and sound judiciously.** When you ask your reader to watch a video or listen to a sound clip, you're taking time they could be using to read your essay. Edit carefully—even a one-minute clip should be well worth your reader's time and focus.

- **Use captions.** Let your readers know what they're seeing or hearing and where it comes from.

- **Cite your sources.** Just as you would cite a quotation from a written source at the end of your paper, so should you accurately and correctly document any visual or multimedia sources you use in your essay. See Chapters 18 (MLA) or 19 (APA) for models.

DIY 17.8 Integrate Visuals and Multimedia Effectively

If your research essay includes visuals and multimedia, make sure you adhere to the guidelines in this section, as well as those discussed in Chapter 14. Write out a plan indicating where you will place, caption, and cite each visual or multimedia element.

Revising Your Research Essay

The moment you've finished your first draft, you may breathe a sigh of relief, and you should! You may also immediately have ideas for how to strengthen and improve your work. Depending on your timetable, you'll want to begin, fairly soon, that stage of revision that many writers refer to as "redrafting." Think of redrafting or revising as that part of the composition process after your initial draft but before editing and proofreading.

When you're taking a second or third pass through your draft, you should still feel comfortable making significant changes to the essay, in particular, filling in gaps in your research. However, you should also begin thinking, *Ah, yes, what I'm doing here works—this is the right way to go.* At this point, you should also seek help from additional readers. Make an appointment to see a writing center tutor either face-to-face or online, visit your instructor during office hours, or ask a friend or family member to read an initial draft.

Make Time to Revise

Often, the difference between a weak paper and a strong one, or a good essay and one that is truly outstanding, comes down to the thought, time and effort you put into this stage of the writing process. Even if you write quickly and fluently, allowing plenty of time to go back and look at your paper again and again will nearly always make it better.

Tips for Revising Your Research Essay

Here are a few tips for putting your initial revision, or "redrafting," time to good use:

- **Ask the big questions.** When you're reading over an early draft, have your assignment close by. Have you achieved the purpose you set out to achieve (argue a position, explain a concept, apply a theory)? Is your thesis strong, clear, and focused? Have you made every effort to appeal to your readers and take their needs into account? Is the essay organized in a way that fits your thesis and meets your readers' needs? If you must make big changes, don't overwrite your early work; make a separate file or use a track changes (Word) or suggestion (Google Docs) feature as you work.

- **Create a reverse outline.** Write a reverse outline (see section 8.2) for the current draft of your research paper. Be sure to record only what is on the page, not what you wish was there. Ask yourself if you've spent too much or too little time on a particular subtopic. Have you left out something that is important to your argument? Have you included and addressed counterarguments? Does your essay—in outline form—look like something that you would want to read?

- **Consider reviewers' feedback.** If you had a writing center session or asked anyone else to review and comment on your draft, evaluate the feedback you received with your writing goals and the assignment in mind. You don't have to incorporate every suggestion you receive; use the feedback to drive your own thinking about which parts of the essay are off-target or confusing—and which parts are strong and need just polish.

- **Fill research gaps.** If you need additional material to support or strengthen a point you're making or to define a term or a concept, find and add the material, being sure to add an entry in your Works Cited or Reference list.

- **If you see a change that needs to be made, make it now.** "I'll deal with that later" is not a productive response when you have a deadline on the calendar. If you must put off a larger overhaul of one part of the essay (maybe because you have an upcoming shift at work), make notes to yourself about where to start when you come back to the essay.

- **Begin where you ended your previous revision session.** If you begin your redrafting at the beginning of your essay every single time, you'll lose focus and energy by the time you read your way back to the last changes you made. Instead, mark where you've finished your last revision then start fresh next time exactly where your work needs the most attention.

Some successful writers take the time to make a revision plan for themselves. If your instructor has assigned Achieve, software that may accompany your book, you may be familiar with the revision plan feature that is built into the writing tools.

Double-Check Your Sources

Sometimes when you're in a rush, you use a source that, on reflection, you realize doesn't really meet the standards described in Chapter 16. Maybe you're quoting from a paper another undergraduate student posted for a class like this one. Perhaps you've summarized an abstract instead of a full article. Or possibly you discover that one of your sources is more opinionated than informed.

You may be thinking: *What's the harm? My instructor can't possibly check* every *single source I use.* You'd be surprised. And even if your instructor doesn't check every source, they can easily spot URLs that are questionable and can tell when quotations all seem to come from the first page of an article. Keep in mind that the sources you choose and use reflect on you as a writer just as much as your actual writing. You can build your own ethos, or credibility, by presenting sources that are fair, accurate, trustworthy, current, and suitable. Your reputation is on the line. Take the time now to eliminate sketchier sources and find more suitable ones. Revisit the school's database or meet with a librarian. You want to be able to stand behind every source you've cited.

DIY 17.9a Ensure that You Use Strong, Trustworthy Sources

Take a careful look at each source you plan to use in your research essay and make sure it stands up to the criteria on the FACTS checklist in section 16.2. Identify those sources that don't pass the test and find stronger alternatives.

DIY 17.9b Seek Feedback on Your Draft

Meet with one or more readers for a conference on your research paper. Listen carefully to what they have to say, and if possible, have each reader address the questions above. Take notes after each feedback session, and make sure to write the name of the reviewer at the top of the session notes.

Seek Feedback

It's crucial that you receive as much feedback as possible throughout the research and writing process. This feedback is likely to begin with a meeting with your reference librarian and include visits with a tutor and your instructor. You may also have informal discussions with your classmates and friends and family. In fact, the more you talk about your research paper, the clearer its strengths and weaknesses are likely to come into view.

As you conference with various people, ask them to comment on what they see as the most important problems you still need to solve. It's also worth having your readers address the following important questions:

- Does the thesis address what's actually covered in the research paper?
- Is there too little research? Too much?
- Is the research clearly and accurately documented?
- Is the research seamlessly integrated with the writing?
- Has the *writing* of the paper been given as much attention as the research?

17.10 Editing and Proofreading Your Research Essay

Following the strategies covered in Chapter 9 is a good way to start the process of editing and proofreading your research writing.

Here are a few more ideas for ensuring your writing is as strong as it can be.

1. **Write complete sentences.** As you look back over your writing, pay attention to sentence boundaries. That means being especially aware of common errors like comma splices, run-on sentences, and sentence fragments.

2. **Use active voice.** Your sentences will usually be more compact and have more energy if you write in the active voice—*State police departments adopted the new practices in January 2021*—rather than in the passive voice—*The new practices were adopted by state police departments in January 2021.*

3. **Prefer the clear to the complicated.** When you have a choice, select the concrete word over the abstract, the familiar word over the contrived. Don't try and impress your readers with language that's not entirely under your control.

4. **Be accurate.** Although they are not the same thing, clarity and accuracy are closely related. Accuracy requires exactitude, a refusal to say anything other than precisely what you mean.

5. **Mix it up.** A research paper composed entirely of short simple sentences is just as dreary as one that's made up of only long, compound-complex constructions. Just as most people prefer a little variety in the music they listen to, most readers appreciate a range of sentence types in an extended piece of writing.

6. **Avoid biased language.** Take care that your language respects all potential readers and that you don't make assumptions related to race, ethnicity, class, language, sexual orientation, or other important identity markers.

7. **Know your own errors.** By this time in the semester, you should have a pretty good sense of the *types* of errors you tend to make, which, ideally, you have been recording in your personal grammar log. Be hyperaware of those errors, deliberately seeking them out as you make your final edits.

8. **Ask if you don't understand.** This may be the most important lesson you take away from the entire book. If you don't know the answer to a question about your research and writing, someone else almost certainly does. Find out who and ask them.

DIY 17.10 Edit for Grammar, Punctuation, and Style

Skim Chapter 9, and then reread your own essay, keeping a careful eye out for errors in grammar, punctuation, and style. Edit where necessary. If you are unsure what change or correction to make, mark the area of your essay and ask your instructor or a writing center tutor.

Proofread Your Research Writing

You're close now. Very close. Weeks of work are about to pay off. Now make one final, focused push to ensure what you turn in represents your *best* work.

- **Reread the prompt and grading rubric—again.** Carefully read the prompt once more to make sure you haven't left out anything that's required. If you've been given a grading rubric, look closely at the expectations for each aspect of your essay. Does your paper have what it takes to receive the highest grade?

- **Read your paper aloud one final time.** As you do so, ask yourself: Are the thesis and topic sentences exceptionally clear and focused? Is the supporting evidence plentiful and purposefully selected? Does the paper read smoothly? Do you like what you hear?

- **Now go back silently and read *every* sentence carefully.** Poets and song-writers scrutinize every *syllable* of their writing before they feel the work is final. Consider bringing that level of scrutiny to your research paper. Pay attention to every word, and certainly to every sentence. Be particularly conscious of the types of errors that you know you tend to make.

- *Triple*-**check your in-text and end citations.** This may be your first extensively researched and documented essay as a college student. If so, check your citations against the advice in Chapter 18 (MLA) or Chapter 19 (APA) of this book.

- **If your research paper is multimodal and/or digital, have you checked that everything is working?** Are the images properly uploaded? Do the video and audio links function as you want them to? Do the links click through? Try viewing your paper on different browsers to confirm there are no major glitches.

Chapter 17 Checklist
Drafting and Revising a Research Paper

☐ **Have you modified your working thesis to reflect the actual content of your research paper?**

A working thesis guides the drafting of an essay, but the thesis usually changes during the composition process. Make sure the thesis in your final draft corresponds with the content of your essay.

☐ **Have you selected the best sources for your paper and arranged them in the most persuasive order?**

Don't settle for less than the best sources for your paper, the ones that are the most fair, accurate, current, trustworthy, and suitable; and make sure they appear in an order that maximizes their effectiveness.

☐ **Are your sources effectively integrated into your paper?**

In a paper with well-integrated sources, the movement back and forth from your own commentary to that of your sources is clearly marked, yet unforced and easy to follow.

☐ **Have you checked, re-checked, and checked again that each in-text and end citation correctly follows the guidelines of your assigned documentation style?**

The citation system you are using is likely to be unfamiliar to you, which is all the more reason to follow it carefully. However, even if you've used MLA or APA before, assume you're doing it wrong until you check your in-text and end citations against the appropriate style guide.

☐ **Have you employed design features that make your research paper easier and more inviting to read?**

Use images, as well as variations in color and font, discerningly. Make your paper appealing without overwhelming your reader with unnecessary glitter and flash. Follow formatting guidelines for the style in which you are writing.

☐ **Have you carefully revised, edited, and proofread your paper?**

Remember that even if your research is superb, unless your writing is equally good, your paper won't get the grade you are hoping for. Give yourself plenty of time to draft and redraft, and don't rush through the important process of editing and proofreading.

☐ **Have you read through your essay one final time to ensure that there are no instances of plagiarism?**

For many instructors, even one case of plagiarism in a research paper will result in a failing grade for the entire paper, which may result in your failing the entire course. Don't cheat, and don't omit proper acknowledgment of *any* material you have borrowed from others. When in doubt, cite your source.

17.11 Making It Stick

How will you draft and revise your research essay?

Working Together

17.11a Balancing Act   In class or online, exchange your draft with another student. You'll be checking to see if there is a balance in your classmate's research paper between their own ideas and commentary and the material from outside sources:

1. Use one color or font to highlight everything that is clearly the student writer's writing, thinking, and commentary.
2. Use a second color or font to highlight everything that you believe comes from a source; it could be direct quotations, summaries, or paraphrases of other writers' ideas.
3. Use a third color or font to highlight anything you can't determine to be the writer's ideas/ words or a source's ideas/words.
4. Use the commenting function to show which uses of sources are not introduced by signal phrases.

When you're finished, return the marked draft to your classmate, and offer whatever advice you have for how to address any issues of imbalance or failure to properly introduce sources.

Applying What You Know

17.11b Reflecting on Research Skills   Write a two-page letter to yourself reflecting on what you did well in this assignment that you can do again the next time you are assigned a research essay — in any class. Deepen your reflection by considering what you *didn't* do well this time that you can improve on in your next research paper. What specific steps would you take to strengthen your research writing skills or habits?

Invitations to Write

17.11c Improving Your Paragraphs

Shorter: Choose what you think is the *weakest* paragraph in your research essay. Make a list of all the things in the paragraph that don't quite work: there is no topic sentence, several sentences are confusing, it contains no supporting evidence, and so on.

Longer: Revise the paragraph based on your own diagnoses of its problems: write a topic sentence, rephrase the confusing sentences, and locate and incorporate a relevant source into the paragraph. If you have time before the paper is due, identify and revise the problems in your next weakest paragraph, and the one after that.

17.11d What You Learned

Shorter: Write several paragraphs describing what you learned about your topic while writing and revising your research essay.

Longer: If you had time to continue working on this topic, how could you see your work evolving? Think about other genres: What kind of speech or factsheet or public service campaign would you develop with what you've learned by completing this research project? Write a plan for how you might remix and transform your essay in another genre — perhaps with an entirely different audience in mind.

18

MLA Style

In English and in some humanities classes, you may be asked to use the MLA (Modern Language Association) system for documenting sources. The guidelines in this chapter follow those set forth in the *MLA Handbook*, 9th edition (2021).

Rather than thinking of these guidelines simply as rules to be followed, think of them as guidelines for participating in an academic community—a community in which the exchange of and extension of ideas requires a system. Although this chapter presents a system for citing many different kinds of sources, it doesn't cover everything; and at times you will find that you have to think critically to adapt the guidelines to the source you are using.

18.1 Elements of MLA Citations

MLA documentation consists of in-text citations that refer to a list of works cited at the end of a project. There are often several possible ways to cite a source in the list of works cited. Think carefully about your context for using the source so you can identify the pieces of information that you should include and any other information that might be helpful to your readers. The first step is to identify elements that are commonly found in works that writers cite.

Author and Title

The first two elements, both of which are needed for most sources, are the author's name and the title of the work. Each of these elements is followed by a period.

Author.
Title.

Container

The next step is to identify elements of what MLA calls the "container" for the work—any larger work that contains the source you are citing. The context in which you are discussing the source and the context in which you find the source will help you determine what counts as a container in each case. Some works are self-contained; if you watch a movie in a theater, the movie title is the title of your source, and you won't identify a separate container title. But if you watch the same movie on a streaming service, the container title is the name of the website or application on which you watched the movie. Thinking about a source as nested in larger containers may help you to visualize how a citation works. (Also see the diagram in this section.)

The elements in the "container" part of your citation may include, in order, the title of the container; the name of contributors such as editors or translators; the version or edition; the volume and issue numbers or other numbers such as season and episode; the publisher; the date of publication; and a location such as the page number, DOI (or Digital Object Identifier), permalink, or URL (or web address). These elements are separated by commas, and the end of the container is marked with a period.

Most sources won't include *all* these pieces of information, so include only the elements that are relevant and available for an acceptable citation. If your container is itself a part of some larger container, such as a database, simply add information about the second container after the first one.

Basic container information

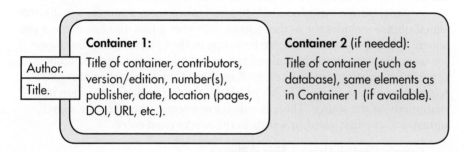

Author.	**Container 1:**	**Container 2** (if needed):
Title.	Title of container, contributors, version/edition, number(s), publisher, date, location (pages, DOI, URL, etc.).	Title of container (such as database), same elements as in Container 1 (if available).

Works Cited Entry, one container (Selection in an anthology)

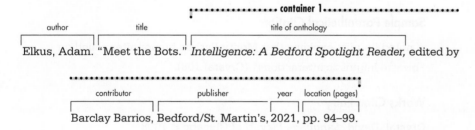

······· container 1 ·······

author · title · title of anthology

Elkus, Adam. "Meet the Bots." *Intelligence: A Bedford Spotlight Reader*, edited by

contributor · publisher · year · location (pages)

Barclay Barrios, Bedford/St. Martin's, 2021, pp. 94–99.

Works Cited Entry, two containers (Article in a journal in a database)

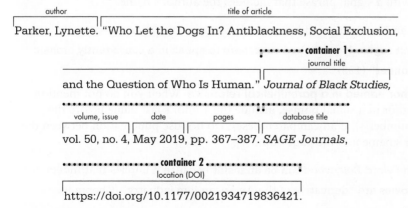

author · title of article

Parker, Lynette. "Who Let the Dogs In? Antiblackness, Social Exclusion,

······ container 1 ······
journal title

and the Question of Who Is Human." *Journal of Black Studies,*

volume, issue · date · pages · database title

vol. 50, no. 4, May 2019, pp. 367–387. *SAGE Journals,*

······ container 2 ······
location (DOI)

https://doi.org/10.1177/0021934719836421.

18.2 Creating MLA-style In-Text Citations

MLA style requires you to supply an in-text citation each time you quote, paraphrase, summarize, or otherwise integrate material from a source. In-text citations are made with a combination of signal phrases and parenthetical references and include the information your readers need to locate the full reference in the works cited list at the end of the text.

A signal phrase introduces information taken from a source; usually, the signal phrase includes the author's name — either a first and last name if the source is being mentioned for the first time in the essay or just a last name for later citations. Parenthetical references include at least a page number (except for unpaginated sources, such as those found online) or other locator, such as a time stamp. The list of works cited provides publication information about the source. There is a direct connection between the signal phrase and the first word or words in the works cited entry.

Sample Citation Using a Signal Phrase

In his discussion of Monty Python routines, David Crystal notes that the group relished "breaking the normal rules" of language (107).

Sample Parenthetical Citation

A noted linguist explains that Monty Python humor often relied on "bizarre linguistic interactions" (Crystal 108).

Works Cited Entry

Crystal, David. *Language Play*. U of Chicago P, 1998.

1. Author named in a signal phrase Ordinarily, introduce the material being cited with a signal phrase that includes the author's name.

Stan Lee claims that his comic-book character Thor was actually "the first regularly published superhero to speak in a consistently archaic manner" (199).

2. Author named in a parenthetical reference When you do not mention the author in a signal phrase, include the author's last name before the page number(s), if any, in parentheses. Do not use punctuation between the author's name and the page number(s).

The word *Bollywood* can be an insult because it implies that Indian movies are "derivative of the American film industry" (Chopra 9).

Directory to MLA In-Text Citation Models

3. Digital or nonprint source Give enough information in a signal phrase or in parentheses for readers to locate the source in your list of works cited—at least the author's name or title. If the source lacks page numbers but has numbered paragraphs, sections, or divisions, use those numbers with the appropriate abbreviation in your parenthetical citation. Do not add such numbers if the source itself does not use them.

Digital Source without Stable Page Numbers

As a *Slate* analysis has noted, "Prominent sports psychologists get praised for their successes and don't get grief for their failures" (Engber).

Digital Source with Numbered Chapters

In her newest story, a city is enclosed "by a high white wall" (Rowling, ch. 3).

4. Two authors Name both authors in a signal phrase or in parentheses.

Gilbert and Gubar point out that in the Grimm version of "Snow White," the king "never actually appears in this story at all" (37).

5. Three or more authors In parentheses, use the first author's name followed by et al. ("and others"). In a signal phrase, give the first author's name followed by a phrase such as "and others" or "and colleagues."

> Examining the lives of women expands our understanding of human development (Belenky et al. 7).

> Similarly, as Belenky and colleagues assert, examining the lives of women expands our understanding of human development (7).

6. Organization as author Give the group's full name in a signal phrase; in parentheses, shorten the name to the first noun and any preceding adjectives, removing any articles (*A, An, The*).

> According to a survey by the Girl Scouts of the United States of America, seventy-five percent of young people want to elect more women to Congress.

> One survey reports that seventy-five percent of young people want to elect more women to Congress (Girl Scouts).

7. Unknown author Use the full title of the source if it is brief. If the title is more than a few words, shorten it to the first noun and any preceding adjectives (not including *A, An, or The*) in parentheses. Place the title in quotation marks or italics according to the style used in the list of works cited.

> Some groups are calling for clinical trials to be nationally coordinated ("Virus").

8. Two or more works by the same author Mention the title of the work in the signal phrase or include a short version of the title in the parentheses.

> Gardner shows readers their own silliness in his description of a "pointless, ridiculous monster, crouched in the shadows, stinking of dead men, murdered children, and martyred cows" (*Grendel* 2).

9. Two or more authors with the same last name Include the author's first and last name in the signal phrase or first initial and last name in the parentheses.

> One approach to the problem is to introduce nutrition literacy at the elementary level in public schools (E. Chen 15).

10. Indirect source (source quoted in another source) Use the abbreviation qtd. in to indicate that you are using a source that is cited in another source.

> Jordan "silently marveled" at her Black students' dismissal of Black language in the novel (qtd. in Baker-Bell 24).

11. Multivolume work In the parenthetical citation, note the volume number first (if any) and then the page number(s), with a colon and one space between them.

> Modernist writers prized experimentation and gradually even sought to blur the line between poetry and prose, according to Forster (3: 150).

12. Work in an anthology or a collection Use the name of the author of the work, not the editor of the anthology, but use the page number(s) from the anthology.

> In "How to Write Iranian-America, or the Last Essay," Khakpour details degrading experiences with English language instructors "who look to you with the shine of love but the stench of pity" (3).

In the list of works cited, the work is alphabetized under Khakpour, the author of the story, not under the name of the editor of the anthology.

> Khakpour, Porochista. "How to Write Iranian-America, or the Last Essay." *The Good Immigrant: 26 Writers Reflect on America*, edited by Nikesh Shukla and Chimene Suleyman, Little, Brown, 2019, pp. 3–15.

13. Government source In a signal phrase, include the name of the agency or governing body as given in the works cited list. In a parenthetical citation, shorten the name.

> The National Endowment for the Arts notes that social media and online events play a significant role in "showcasing the importance of the arts to the vitality of the nation" (15).

> Social media and online events play a significant role in "showcasing the importance of the arts to the vitality of the nation" (National Endowment 15).

If you cite more than one agency or department from the same government in your essay, you may choose to standardize the names by beginning with the name of the government (see item 57 in the works cited list section). In that case, when shortening the names, give enough of each one to differentiate the authors: *(United States, National Endowment); (United States, Environmental Protection).*

14. Entire work Use the author's name in a signal phrase or a parenthetical citation.

> Michael Pollan explores the issues surrounding food production and consumption from a political angle.

15. Two or more sources in one citation List the authors (or titles) in alphabetical order and separate them with semicolons.

> Economists recommend that employment be redefined to include unpaid
> domestic labor (Clark 148; Nevins 39).

16. Repeated citations from the same source If you cite a source more than once in a paragraph, you may omit the author's name after the first mention in the paragraph as long as it is clear that you are still referring to the same source.

> Family expectations are at the heart of *Everything I Never Told You*, a
> debut novel in which a daughter shrinks from a mother who forces her
> to read books on science and medicine "to inspire her, to show her what
> she could accomplish" (Ng 73). But teenage Lydia commits herself to
> standing up to her overbearing mother, promising that "she will tell her
> mother: enough" (274).

17. Personal communication or social media source Use the name of the author as given in the works cited list.

> Grammar Girl explains that "Irish English uses many words differently
> from American and British English, and 'myself' is just one example."

18. Literary work Because literary works are often available in many different editions, cite the page number(s) from the edition you used followed by a semicolon; then give other identifying information that will lead readers to the passage in any edition. For a novel, indicate the part or chapter (*175; ch. 4*).

> In utter despair, Dostoyevsky's character Mitya wonders aloud about the
> "terrible tragedies realism inflicts on people" (376; bk. 8, ch. 2).

For a poem, cite the part (if there is one) and line(s), separated by a period.

> Whitman speculates, "All goes onward and outward, nothing
> collapses, / And to die is different from what anyone supposed,
> and luckier" (6.129–30).

If you are citing only line numbers, use the word "line(s)" in the first reference (*lines 21–22*) and the line numbers alone in subsequent references (*34–36*).

> For a play, indicate the page number, then the act and/or scene: (*37; sc. 1*).
> For a verse play, give only the act, scene, and line numbers, separated by
> periods: (*4.2.148–49*).

19. Sacred text The first time you cite the work, give the title of the work as in the works cited entry, followed by the book, chapter, and verse (or their equivalent), separated with periods. Common abbreviations for books of the Bible are acceptable in a parenthetical citation. Omit the source's title from the parentheses in all citations after the first.

> He ignored the warning: "Pride goes before destruction, and a haughty
>
> spirit before a fall" (*New Oxford Annotated Bible*, Prov. 16.18).

20. Encyclopedia or dictionary entry For reference work entries without a named author, give the title of the entry in quotation marks.

> The word *crocodile* has a complex etymology ("Crocodile" 139–40).

21. Visual If you cite information from a numbered visual in a source and do not present the visual in your essay, use the abbreviation "fig." and the original figure number in place of a page number in your parenthetical citation: (*Manning, fig. 4*). If you refer to the figure in your text, spell out the word *figure*. If the visual does not have a figure number in the source, use the visual's title or a description in your text and cite the author and page number as for any other source.

> For visuals that you use in your essay, include a figure or table number and a caption with information about the source (see p. 464).

22. Legal source For a legislative act (law) or court case, name the act or case either in a signal phrase or in parentheses. Italicize the names of cases but not the names of acts.

> The Jones Act of 1917 granted US citizenship to Puerto Ricans.

> *Dred Scott v. Sandford*, which concluded that neither free nor enslaved
>
> Black people could be citizens of the United States, may have been the
>
> US Supreme Court's worst decision.

18.3   Creating an MLA-style List of Works Cited

An alphabetized list of works cited, which appears at the end of your project, gives publication information for each of the sources you have cited. (For more information about preparing the list, see p. 464; for a sample list of works cited, see section 18.5.)

Directory to MLA Works Cited Models

General guidelines for the works cited list

In the list of works cited, include only sources that you have quoted, summarized, or paraphrased in your project. MLA's guidelines are applicable to a wide variety of sources. At times you may find that you have to adapt the guidelines and models in this section to source types you encounter in your research.

Organization of the list

A works cited entry typically includes the following elements, or pieces of information:

- The author (if a work has one)
- The title
- The title of the larger work in which the source is located (MLA calls this a "container")—a collection, a journal, a website, a database, and so on
- As much of the following information as is available about the source and the container, listed in this order:

    Contributor (such as editor, translator, director, performer)

    Version

    Volume and issue numbers or similar numbers

    Publisher or sponsor

    Date of publication

    Location of the source: page numbers, DOI, URL, time stamp

Not all sources will require every element. For more information on identifying and organizing source elements, see pages 438–439. See specific models in this section for more details.

Author

- Arrange the list alphabetically by authors' last names or by titles for works with no authors.
- For the first author, place the last name first, a comma, and the first name. Put a second author's name in typical order (first name followed by last name). Separate two authors' names with "and." For three or more authors, use "et al." after the first author's name.
- Spell out "editor," "translator," "director," and so on.
- For organization authors, list the name as it appears in the source. If the name begins with an article (*A, An, or The*), omit it.

Titles

- In titles of works, capitalize all words except articles (*a, an, the*), prepositions, coordinating conjunctions, and the "to" in infinitives — unless the word is first or last in the title or subtitle.
- Use quotation marks for titles of articles and other short works.
- Italicize titles of books and other long works, including websites.

Publication information

- Use the complete version of publishers' names, except for terms such as *Inc.* and *Co.*; if the name begins with an article (*A, An, or The*), omit it. Retain terms such as *Books* and *Publishers*.
- For a publisher with *University* and *Press* in its name, use *U* and *P* for each word. (Do not abbreviate or omit *Press* if *University* is not also in the publisher's name.)
- For a book, take the name of the publisher from the title page (or from the copyright page if it is not on the title page). For a website, the publisher might be at the bottom of a page or on the "About" page. If a work has two or more publishers, separate the names a forward slash.
- If the title of a website and the publisher are the same or similar, use the title of the site but omit the publisher.

Dates

- For a book, give the most recent year on the title page or the copyright page.
- For an article from a periodical such as a newspaper or a journal, use the most specific date given, whether it is a month and year, a full date, or a season (*spring 2021*).
- For a web source, use the posting date, the copyright date, or the most recent update date. Use the complete date as listed in the source. If a web source has no date, give your date of access at the end of the entry (*Accessed 24 Feb. 2021*).
- Abbreviate all months except May, June, and July and give the date in inverted form: 11 Feb. 2021. Use "Sept." for September.

Page numbers

- For most articles and other short works, give page numbers when they are available in the source, preceded by "p." (or "pp." for more than one page).
- Do not use the page numbers from a printout of a source.

- If an article does not appear on consecutive pages, give the number of the first page followed by a plus sign: 35+.

URLs and DOIs

- Give a DOI (digital object identifier) if a source has one. Include the protocol and host (*https://doi.org/*). (See item 11.)
- If a source does not have a DOI, give a permalink, if possible. Copy the permalink provided by the website.
- If a source does not have a permalink or a DOI, include a URL. Copy the URL directly from your browser. You may remove the protocol (*http://* or *https://*) if you do not need to provide live links for your readers. See also pages 464-465.
- If a URL is longer than three lines in the list of works cited, you may shorten it, leaving at least the website host (for example, *cnn.com* or *www.usda.gov*) in the entry.

General Guidelines for Listing Authors

Alphabetize entries in the list of works cited by authors' last names (or by title if a work has no author). The author's name is important because citations in the text refer to it and readers will therefore look for it to identify the source in the works cited list.

1. Single author Give the author's last name, followed by a comma, then give the first name and any middle initials, followed by a period.

Cronin, David.

2. Two authors List the authors in the order in which the source lists them. Reverse the name of only the first author.

Stiglitz, Joseph E., and Bruce C. Greenwald.

3. Three or more authors List the author whose name appears first in the source followed by "et al." (Latin for "and others").

Lupton, Ellen, et al.

4. Organization or group author When the author is a corporation, a government agency, or some other organization, begin with the name of the organization. Omit an article (*A, An, or The*) that begins the name.

Human Rights Watch.
Coca-Cola Company.

5. Unknown author Begin with the work's title. In general, titles of short works are put in quotation marks and titles of long works are italicized.

"California Sues EPA over Emissions."

Green Vehicle Guide.

6. Author using a pseudonym (pen name) Use the author's name as it appears in the source, followed by the author's real name in brackets, if you know it. Alternatively, if the author's real name is better known, you may start with that name, followed by "published as" and the pen name in brackets.

Saunders, Richard [Benjamin Franklin].

Franklin, Benjamin [*published as* Richard Saunders].

7. Screen name or social media account Start with the account display name, followed by the screen name or handle (if available) in brackets. If the account name is a first and last name, invert it. See items 39 and 40 for more on citing social media.

Gay, Roxane [@rgay].

Pat and Stewart [@grammarphobia].

8. Multiple works by the same author Alphabetize the works by title, ignoring (but not omitting) the article *A, An,* or The at the beginning. Use the author's name for the first entry only. For later entries, use three hyphens or dashes followed by a period. Use three hyphens or dashes even when the author is a government agency or an organization.

Coates, Ta-Nehisi. *Between the World and Me.* Spiegel and Grau, 2015.

---. *We Were Eight Years in Power: An American Tragedy.* One World,
    2018.

9. Multiple works by the same group of authors When you cite multiple sources with the same group of authors (same lead author and coauthors), alphabetize the works by title. For the first entry, use the authors' names in the proper form (see items 1–4). Begin subsequent entries with three hyphens (or dashes) and a period.

Eaton-Robb, Pat, and Susan Haigh. "Pandemic May Lead to Long-Term
    Changes in School Calendar." *AP News,* 15 Apr. 2021, apnews.com
    /article/pandemics-connecticut-ned-lamont-975d41076ae6b9850
    30c133614685f33.

---. "Rock Star Van Zandt Helping Connecticut Students
Re-engage." *AP News*, 20 Apr. 2021, apnews.com/article
/health-music-education-arts-and-entertainment
-entertainment-5b038c218b30863d76031134db46fa5d.

Articles and other short works

10. Article in a magazine Use the complete date given in the source. Give
the volume number and issue number when available.

Owusu, Nadia. "Head Wraps." *The New York Times Magazine*,
7 Mar. 2021, p. 20.

Misner, Rebecca. "How I Became a Joiner." *Condé Nast Traveler*, vol. 5,
2018, pp.55–56..

Stuart, Tessa. "New Study Suggests Burning Fossil Fuels Contributed to 1
in 5 Deaths in 2018." *Rolling Stone*, 17 Feb. 2021, www.rollingstone.com
/politics/politics-news/fossil-fuels-air-pollution-premature-deaths
-statistics-1127586/.

Guerrero, Desirée. "All Genders, Period." *The Advocate*, no. 1105,
Oct.–Nov. 2019, p. 31. *ProQuest*, www-proquest-com.proxy3
.noblenet.org/docview/2488268993.

11. Article in a journal Give the volume number and issue number, if
available, for all journals.

Matchie, Thomas. "Law versus Love in *The Round House*." *Midwest
Quarterly*, vol. 56, no. 4, summer 2015, pp. 353–64.

Bryson, Devin. "The Rise of a New Senegalese Cultural Philosophy?"
African Studies Quarterly, vol. 14, no. 3, Mar. 2014, pp. 33–56, asq
.africa.ufl.edu/files/Volume-14-Issue-3-Bryson.pdf.

Harris, Ashleigh May, and Nicklas Hållén. "African Street Literature: A
Method for an Emergent Form beyond World Literature." *Research
in African Literatures*, vol. 51, no. 2, summer 2020, pp. 1–26. *JSTOR*,
https://doi.org/10.2979/reseafrilite.51.2.01.

12. Article in a daily newspaper

> Camero, Katie. "COVID-19 Is Spreading Faster In Our Homes and More Often Than We Thought." *Fort Worth Star-Telegram*, 2 Nov. 2020, p. 2.
>
> Jones, Ayana. "Chamber of Commerce Program to Boost Black-Owned Businesses." *The Philadelphia Tribune,* 21 Apr. 2021, www .phillytrib.com/news/business/chamber-of-commerce-program -to-boost-black-owned-businesses/article_6b14ae2f-5db2-5a59-8a67 -8bbf974da451.html..

13. Editorial or op-ed Add the word "Editorial" or "Op-ed" to the end of the entry if it is not clear from the author or title of the source.

> Kansas City Star Editorial Board. "Kansas Considers Lowering Concealed Carry Age to 18. Why It's Wrong for Many Reasons." *The Kansas City Star,* 9 Mar. 2021, www.kansascity.com/opinion/editorials /article249793143.html.
>
> Shribman, David M. "Gorman, Summoned to Participate, Is Celebrated." *Pittsburgh Post-Gazette,* 24 Jan. 2021, www.post-gazette.com /opinion/david-shribman/2021/01/24/Gorman-summoned-to -participate-is-celebrated/ stories/202101240042. Op-ed.

14. Letter to the editor If the letter has no title or headline, use "Letter" in place of a title.

> Carasso, Roger. Letter. *The New York Times*, 4 Apr. 2021, Sunday Book Review sec., p. 5.

15. Review If the review is untitled, use the label "Review of" and the title and author or director of the work reviewed. Then add the information for the publication in which the review appears.

> Jopanda, Wayne Silao. Review of *America Is Not the Heart*, by Elaine Castillo. *Alon: Journal for Filipinx American and Diasporic Studies*, vol. 1, no. 1, Mar. 2021, pp. 106–08. *eScholarship*, escholarship.org /uc/item/0d44t8wx.
>
> Bramesco, Charles. "*Honeyland* Couches an Apocalyptic Warning in a Beekeeping Documentary." *The A.V. Club*, G/O Media, 23 July 2019, film.avclub.com/honeyland-couches-an-apocalyptic-warning-in-a -beekeepin-1836624795.

Books and other long works

16. Basic format for a book For most books, supply the author name(s); the title and subtitle, in italics; the name of the publisher; and the year of publication. For an e-book, include "E-book ed." before the publisher.

> Cabral, Amber. *Allies and Advocates: Creating an Inclusive and Equitable Culture.* Wiley, 2021.

> Cabral, Amber. *Allies and Advocates: Creating an Inclusive and Equitable Culture.* E-book ed., Wiley, 2021.

17. Audiobook Give the author name and the title, each followed by a period. After the title, include the phrase "Narrated by" followed by the narrator's full name. If the author and narrator are the same, include only the last name. Then include "audiobook ed.," the publisher, and the year.

> de Hart, Jane Sherron. *Ruth Bader Ginsburg: A Life.* Narrated by Suzanne Toren, audiobook ed., Random House Audio, 2018.

18. Author with an editor or translator

> Ullmann, Regina. *The Country Road: Stories.* Translated by Kurt Beals, New Directions Publishing, 2015.

19. Editor

> Coates, Colin M., and Graeme Wynn, editors. *The Nature of Canada.* On Point Press, 2019.

20. Work in an anthology or a collection Begin with the name of the author of the selection, not with the name of the anthology editor.

> Symanovich, Alaina. "Compatibility." *Ab Terra 2020: A Science Fiction Anthology*, edited by Yen Ooi, Brain Mill Press, 2020, pp. 116–23.

21. Multiple works from the same anthology or collection Provide an entry for the entire anthology (the Ooi entry below) and a shortened entry for each selection. Alphabetize the entries by authors' or editors' last names.

> Challinor, Nels. "Porch Light." Ooi, pp. 107–15.

> Ooi, Yen, editor. *Ab Terra 2020: A Science Fiction Anthology.* Brain Mill Press, 2020.

> Symanovich, Alaina. "Compatibility." Ooi, pp. 116–23.

22. Edition other than the first

Walker, John A. *Art in the Age of Mass Media*. 3rd ed., Pluto Press, 2001.

23. Multivolume work

Include the total number of volumes at the end of the citation. If the volumes were published over several years, give the inclusive dates of publication. If you cite only one of the volumes, include the volume number before the publisher and give the date of publication for that volume.

Brunetti, Ivan, editor. *An Anthology of Graphic Fiction, Cartoons, and True Stories*. Yale UP, 2006–08. 2 vols.

Brunetti, Ivan, editor. *An Anthology of Graphic Fiction, Cartoons, and True Stories*. Vol. 2, Yale UP, 2008.

24. Encyclopedia or dictionary entry

Robinson, Lisa Clayton. "Harlem Writers Guild." *Africana: The Encyclopedia of the African and African American Experience*, edited by Kwame Anthony Appiah and Henry Louis Gates Jr., 2nd ed., Oxford UP, 2005, p. 163.

"House Music." *Wikipedia: The Free Encyclopedia*, Wikimedia Foundation, 8 Apr. 2021, en.wikipedia.org/wiki/House_music.

"Oligarchy, *N.*" *Merriam-Webster*, 2021, www.merriam-webster.com /dictionary/oligarchy.

25. Sacred text

Give the title of the edition of the sacred text (taken from the title page), italicized; the editor's or translator's name (if any); and publication information. Add the name of the version, if there is one, before the publisher.

Quran: The Final Testament. Translated by Rashad Khalifa, Authorized English Version with Arabic Text, Universal Unity, 2000.

The Oxford Annotated Bible with the Apocrypha. Edited by Herbert G. May and Bruce M. Metzger, Revised Standard Version, Oxford UP, 1965.

26. Foreword, introduction, preface, or afterword

Begin with the author of the book part, the part title (if any), and a label for the part. Then give the title of the book, the author or editor preceded by "by" or "edited by," and publication information. If the part author and book author are the same, use only the last name with the book title.

> Coates, Ta-Nehisi. Foreword. *The Origin of Others*, by Toni Morrison,
> Harvard UP, 2017, pp. vii–xvii.

27. Book with a title in its title If the book title contains a title normally italicized, do not italicize the title within the book title. If the book title contains a title normally placed in quotation marks, retain the quotation marks and italicize the entire title.

> Masur, Louis P. *Runaway Dream:* Born to Run *and Bruce Springsteen's*
> *American Vision*. Bloomsbury, 2009.

> Lethem, Jonathan. *"Lucky Alan" and Other Stories*. Doubleday, 2015.

28. Book in a series After the publication information, list the series name and the book's number in the series, if available.

> Denham, A. E., editor. *Plato on Art and Beauty*. Palgrave Macmillan,
> 2012. Philosophers in Depth.

29. Republished book After the title of the book, cite the original publication date, followed by the current publication information.

> de Mille, Agnes. *Dance to the Piper*. 1951. New York Review Books, 2015.

30. More than one publisher named If the book was published by two or more publishers, separate the publishers with a slash, and include a space before and after the slash.

> Acevedo, Elizabeth. *With the Fire on High*. HarperTeen / Quill Tree
> Books, 2019.

31. Graphic narrative or illustrated work If the author and illustrator are the same, cite the work as you would a book with one author (see items 1 and 16). When the author and illustrator are different, begin with the contributor who is most important to your research. List other contributors after the title, labeling their contribution. If there are multiple contributors but you are not discussing a specific contributor's work in your essay, you may begin with the title.

> Martínez, Hugo, illustrator. *Wake: The Hidden History of Women-Led*
> *Slave Revolts*. By Rebecca Hall, Simon and Schuster, 2021.

> *Stealth*. By Mike Costa, illustrated by Nate Bellegarde, colored by Tamra
> Bonvillain, lettered by Sal Cipriano, vol. 1, Image Comics, 2020.

32. Book in a language other than English Capitalize the title according to the book's language. Include an English translation of the title, in brackets, if your readers are not familiar with the book's language.

> Vargas Llosa, Mario. *El sueño del celta [The Dream of the Celt].* Alfaguara
> Ediciones, 2010.

Online sources

33. Entire website If the website does not have an update date or publication date, include your date of access at the end (see the second example in item 34).

> *Lift Every Voice.* Library of America / Schomburg Center for Research in
> Black Culture, 2020, africanamericanpoetry.org/.

34. Short work from a website

> Enzinna, Wes. "Syria's Unknown Revolution." *Pulitzer Center,*
> 24 Nov. 2015, pulitzercenter.org/projects/middle-east-syria
> -enzinna-war-rojava.

> Bali, Karan. "Shashikala." *Upperstall.com,* upperstall.com/profile
> /kishore-kumar/. Accessed 22 Apr. 2021.

35. Online book After the book publication information, include the title of the site in italics, the year of online publication, and the URL for the work. If the book's original publication date is not available, include the date of online publication.

> Euripides. *The Trojan Women.* Translated by Gilbert Murray, Oxford UP,
> 1915. *Internet Sacred Text Archive,* www.sacred-texts.com
> /cla/eurip/troj_w.htm.

36. Entire blog Cite a blog as you would an entire website (see item 33).

> Ng, Amy. *Pikaland.* 2020, www.pikaland.com.

> Horgan, John. *Cross-Check.* Scientific American, 2020, blogs
> .scientificamerican.com/cross-check/.

37. Blog post Cite a blog post as you would a short work from a website (see item 34).

> Horgan, John. "My Quantum Experiment." *Cross-Check,* Scientific
> American, 5 June 2020, blogs.scientificamerican.com/cross-check
> /my-quantum-experiment/.

Edroso, Roy. "No Compassion." *Alicublog*, 18 Mar. 2021, alicublog

.blogspot.com/2021/03/no-compassion.html.

38. Comment on a blog post or an online article List the screen name of the commenter and use the label "Comment on" before the title of the post or article. Include the URL to the comment when possible; otherwise, use the URL for the post or article.

satch. Comment on "No Compassion," by Roy Edroso. *Alicublog*,

20 Mar. 2021, 9:50 a.m., disq.us/p/2fu0ulk.

39. Tweet Give the text of the entire tweet in quotation marks, using the writer's capitalization and punctuation, or a brief description if you are focusing on a visual element of the tweet rather than the text in your work. Follow with "Twitter," italicized, the date, and the URL. See item 7 for how to style screen names.

Abdurraqib, Hanif [@NifMuhammad]. "Tracy Chapman really one

of the greatest Ohio writers." *Twitter*, 30 Mar. 2021, twitter.com

/NifMuhammad/status/1377086355667320836.

40. Other posts on social media Cite as a short work from a website (see item 34). If the post does not have a title, use the text accompanying the post, if it is brief, as the title; if the post is long, use the first few words followed by an ellipsis. If the post has no title or text, or if you are focusing on a visual element rather than the text in your work, provide a description of the post. (See item 7 for how to style screen names.)

ACLU. "Public officials have . . . ." *Facebook*, 10 May 2021, www.facebook

.com/aclu/photos/a.74134381812/10157852911711813.

Rosa, Camila [camixvx]. Illustration of nurses in masks with fists raised.

Instagram, 28 Apr. 2020, www.instagram.com/p/B_h62W9pJaQ/.

Jones, James [@notoriouscree]. "Some traditional hoop teachings

#indigenous #culture #native #powwow." *TikTok*, 6 Apr. 2021,

www.tiktok.com/@notoriouscree/video/6948207430610226438.

Visual, audio, multimedia, and live sources

41. Work of art or photograph Cite the artist's name, the title of the artwork or photograph, italicized; and the date of composition. For works viewed in person, include the institution and the city in which the artwork is located after the date and a comma. For works located online, include the title of the site and the URL of the work after the date.

> Bronzino, Agnolo. *Lodovico Capponi*. 1550-55, Frick Collection, New York.

> Lange, Dorothea. *Migrant Mother, Nipomo, California*. Mar. 1936. *MOMA*, www.moma.org/collection/works/50989.

42. Cartoon or comic strip

> Shiell, Mike. Cartoon. *The Saturday Evening Post*, Jan.–Feb. 2021, p. 8.

> Munroe, Randall. "Heartbleed Explanation." *xkcd*, xkcd.com/1354/. Accessed 10 Oct. 2020.

43. Advertisement

> Advertisement for Better World Club. *Mother Jones*, Mar.–Apr. 2021, p. 2.

> "The Whole Working-from-Home Thing — Apple." *YouTube*, uploaded by Apple, 13 July 2020, www.youtube.com/watch?v=6_pru8U2RmM.

44. Map or chart
If the map or chart is located in another source, cite as a short work within a longer work. If the title does not identify the item as a map or chart, add "Map" or "Chart" at the end of the entry.

> "Australia." *Perry-Castañeda Library Map Collection*, U of Texas Libraries, 2016, legacy.lib.utexas.edu/maps/cia16/australia_sm _2016.gif.

> "New COVID-19 Cases Worldwide." *Coronavirus Resource Center*, Johns Hopkins U and Medicine, 3 May 2021, coronavirus.jhu.edu/data /new-cases. Chart.

45. Musical score

> Beethoven, Ludwig van. *Symphony No. 5 in C Minor, Opus 67*. 1807. Center for Computer Assisted Research in the Humanities, 2008, scores.ccarh.org/beethoven/sym/beethoven-sym5-1.pdf.

46. Music recording
Begin with the name of the person or group you want to emphasize. For a single work from an album or collection, place the title in quotation marks and the album or collection in italics. For a long work, give the title, italicized; the names of pertinent artists and the orchestra and conductor (if relevant). End with the record label and the date. If you listen

to the recording online, include the URL for the recording or the name of the app.

> Bach, Johann Sebastian. *Bach: Violin Concertos*. Performances by Itzhak
>
> Perlman, Pinchas Zukerman, and English Chamber Orchestra, EMI,
>
> 2002.

> Bad Bunny. "Vete." *YHLQMDLG*, Rimas, 2020. *Apple Music* app.

47. Film or movie If you focus on a particular person's work, start with that name. If not, start with the title of the film; then give the director, distributor or production company, and year of release. Other contributors, such as writers or performers, may follow the director. If you viewed the film on a streaming service, include the app or the website name and URL at the end of the entry. See item 53 for how to cite online videos (from *YouTube* or *Vimeo*, for example).

> *Judas and the Black Messiah*. Directed by Shaka King, Warner Bros.
>
> Pictures, 2021.

> Youn, Yuh-Jung, performer. *Minari*. Directed by Lee Isaac Chung, Plan B
>
> Entertainment / A24, 2020. *Amazon Prime Video* app.

> Kubrick, Stanley, director. *A Clockwork Orange*. Hawk Films / Warner
>
> Bros. Pictures, 1971. *Netflix*, www.netflix.com.

48. Supplementary material accompanying a film Begin with the title of the feature, in quotation marks, and the names of any important contributors. End with information about the film, as in item 47, and about the location of the supplementary material.

> "Sweeney's London." Produced by Eric Young. *Sweeney Todd: The Demon
>
> Barber of Fleet Street*, directed by Tim Burton, DreamWorks Pictures,
>
> 2007, disc 2. DVD.

49. Radio or television program If you are citing a particular episode, begin with the title in quotation marks. Then give the program title in italics. List important contributors (narrator, writer, director, actors), if relevant to your writing; the season and episode numbers; the network, distributor, or production company; and the date of broadcast or publication. Unless you viewed or listened to the program on a live broadcast, end with the site or service on which you accessed it (see p. 460).

> "Umbrellas Down." *This American Life*, hosted by Ira Glass, WBEZ, 10
>
> July 2020.

"Shock and Delight." *Bridgerton*, season 1, episode 2, Shondaland /
Netflix, 2020. *Netflix*, www.netflix.com.

Hillary. Directed by Nanette Burstein, Propagate Content / Hulu, 2020.
Hulu app.

50. Radio or television interview Begin with the name of the person who
was interviewed, followed by "Interview by" and the interviewer's name, if
relevant. End with information about the program as in item 49.

Kendi, Ibram X. Interview by Eric Deggans. *Life Kit*, NPR, 24 Oct. 2020.

51. Podcast series or episode Cite a podcast as you would a television series
or episode (see item 49).

"Childish Gambino: *Because the Internet*." *Dissect*, hosted by Cole
Cuchna, season 7, episode 1, Spotify, Sep. 2020. *Spotify* app.

Dolly Parton's America. Hosted by Jad Abumrad, produced and reported
by Shima Oliaee, WNYC Studios, 2019, www.wnycstudios.org
/podcasts/dolly-partons-america.

52. Stand-alone audio segment

"The Past Returns to Gdańsk." Written and narrated by Michael Segalov,
BBC, 26 Apr. 2021, www.bbc.co.uk/sounds/play/m000vh4f.

53. Online video If the video is viewed on a video-sharing site such as
YouTube or *Vimeo*, put the name of the uploader after the name of the
website. If the video emphasizes a single speaker or presenter, as many TED
Talks do (see p. 464), list that person as the author.

"The Art of Single Stroke Painting in Japan." *YouTube*, uploaded
by National Geographic, 13 July 2018, www.youtube.com
/watch?v=g7H8IhGZnpM.

54. Live performance Begin with either the title of the work performed or, if
relevant, the author, composer, or main performer. After the title, include relevant contributors such as the director, the choreographer, the conductor, or
the major performers. End with the theater, ballet, or opera company, if any;
the date of the performance; and the location.

Beethoven, Ludwig van. *Piano Concerto No. 3*. Conducted by Andris
Nelsons, performed by Paul Lewis and Boston Symphony Orchestra,
9 Oct. 2015, Symphony Hall, Boston.

Schreck, Heidi. *What the Constitution Means to Me*. Directed by Oliver
Butler, 16 June 2019, Helen Hayes Theater, New York City.

55. Lecture or public address Cite the speaker's name, followed by the title
of the lecture (if any) in quotation marks; the organization sponsoring the
lecture; the date; and the location. If the lecture or address has no title, use
the label "Lecture" or "Address" after the speaker's name.

Gay, Roxane. "Difficult Women, Bad Feminists and Unruly Bodies."
Beatty Lecture Series, 18 Oct. 2018, McGill University.

56. Personal interview Begin with the name of the person interviewed. Then
describe the type of interview, and end with the date of the interview.

Freedman, Sasha. Video interview with the author. 28 Jan. 2021.

Other sources

57. Government publication Give the name of the author as presented by
the source.

U.S. Bureau of Labor Statistics. "Consumer Expenditures Report 2019."
BLS Reports, Dec. 2020, www.bls.gov/opub/reports/consumer
-expenditures/2019/home.htm.

If you use several government sources, you may want to standardize your
list of works cited by listing the name of the government, spelled out,
followed by the name of any agencies and subagencies.

United States, Department of Labor, Bureau of Labor Statistics.
"Consumer Expenditures Report 2019." *BLS Reports*, Dec. 2020,
www.bls.gov/opub/reports/consumer-expenditures/2019/home.htm.

58. Legal source For a legislative act (law), give the government body, the
Public Law number, and the publication information.

United States, Congress. Public Law 116-136. *United States Statutes
at Large*, vol. 134, 2019, pp. 281–615. *U.S. Government Publishing
Office*, www.govinfo.gov/content/pkg/PLAW-116publ136
/uslmPLAW-116publ136.xml.

For a court case, name the court and then the case. Give the date of the
decision and the publication information.

United States, Supreme Court. *Miller v. Alabama*. 25 June 2012. *Legal
Information Institute,* Cornell Law School, www.law.cornell.edu
/supremecourt/text/10-9646.

59. Pamphlet or brochure

Sierra County Public Health. *Benefits of the COVID-19 Vaccine.* 2021,
    sierracounty.ca.gov/DocumentCenter/View/5522/Benefits-of-the
    -COVID-19-Vaccine-Brochure. Brochure.

60. Dissertation

Kabugi, Magana J. *The Souls of Black Colleges: Cultural Production,
    Ideology, and Identity at Historically Black Colleges and Universities.*
    2020. Vanderbilt U, PhD dissertation. *Vanderbilt University
    Institutional Repository,* hdl.handle.net/1803/16103.

61. Published proceedings of a conference

Zhang, Baosheng, et al., editors. *A Dialogue between Law and History:
    Proceedings of the Second International Conference on Facts and
    Evidence.* Springer, 2021.

62. Published interview See item 56 for a personal interview.

Harjo, Joy. "The First Native American U.S. Poet Laureate on How Poetry
    Can Counter Hate." Interview by Olivia B. Waxman. *Time,* 22 Aug.
    2019, time.com/5658443/joy-harjo-poet-interview/.

63. Personal communication

Primak, Shoshana. Text message to the author. 6 May 2021.

Lewis-Truth, Antoine. E-mail to the Office of Student Financial
    Assistance. 30 Aug. 2020.

64. Classroom materials For materials posted to an online learning management system, include as much information as is available about the source (author, title or description, and any publication information); then give the course, instructor, platform, institution name, date of posting, and URL. For materials delivered in a course pack, include the author and title of the work; the words "Course pack for" with the course number and name; "compiled by" with the instructor's name; the term; and the institution.

Rose, Mike. "Blue-Collar Brilliance." Introduction to College Writing,
    taught by Melanie Li. *Blackboard,* Merrimack College, 9 Sept. 2020,
    blackboard.merrimack.edu/ultra/courses/_25745_1/cl/readings.

18.4 Formatting Student
Papers in MLA Style

The following guidelines are consistent with advice given in the *MLA Handbook*, 9th edition (2021), and with typical requirements for student projects. If you are creating a digital project or have formatting questions, it's always a good idea to check with your instructor before preparing your final draft.

Formatting an MLA Project

Margins and spacing. Leave one-inch margins at the top and bottom and on both sides of each page. Double-space the entire text, including set-off quotations, notes, and the list of works cited. Indent the first line of a paragraph one-half inch.

First page and title page. For a project authored by an individual writer, a title page is not needed. Type each of the following items on a separate double-spaced line on the first page, beginning one inch from the top and aligned with the left margin: your name, the instructor's name, the course name and number, and the date. On the next line, place the title, centered, with no additional spacing above or below the title. See section 18.5 for an example.

For a group project, create a title page with all members' names, the instructor's name, the course, and the date, all left-aligned on separate double-spaced lines. Center the title on a new line a few spaces down.

Page numbers. Include your last name and the page number on each page, one-half inch below the top and aligned with the right margin. For a group project, include all members' last names and the page number; if the names will not all fit on a single line, include only the page number on each page.

Long quotations. Set off a long quotation (more than four typed lines) in block format by starting it on a new line and indenting each line one-half inch from the left margin. Do not enclose the passage in quotation marks.

Headings. While headings are generally not needed for brief essays, readers may find them helpful for long or complex essays. Place level 1 headings, boldfaced, at the left margin without any indent. If you need subheadings (level 2, level 3), be consistent in styling them. Capitalize headings as you would titles. See 18.5 for an example.

Visuals. Place tables, photographs, drawings, charts, graphs, and other figures as near as possible to the relevant text. Tables should have a label and number ("Table 1") and a clear title. For a table that you have borrowed or adapted, give the source below the table in a note like the following:

Source: Boris Groysberg and Michael Slind, "Leadership Is a
Conversation," *Harvard Business Review*, June 2012, p. 83.

All other visuals should be labeled "Figure" (usually abbreviated *Fig.*), numbered, and captioned below the visual. The label and caption should appear on the same line. If your caption includes full source information and you do not cite the source anywhere else in your text, it is not necessary to include an entry in your list of works cited. Remember to refer to each visual in your text, indicating how it contributes to the point you are making: *see table 1; as shown in figure 2.*

Formatting an MLA Works Cited List

Begin the list of works cited on a new page at the end of the project. Center the title "Works Cited" about one inch from the top of the page. Double-space throughout.

Alphabetizing the list. Alphabetize the list by the last names of the authors (or the names of corporate or government authors); if a work has no author, alphabetize by the first word of the title other than *A, An, or The.*

Indenting the entries. Do not indent the first line of each works cited entry, but indent any additional lines one-half inch. This is called a *hanging indent.*

Including URLs. If you include a URL in a works cited entry, copy the URL directly from your browser. If the entire URL moves to another line, creating a short line, you may leave it that way. Do not add any hyphens or spaces.

Kundu, Anindya. "The 'Opportunity Gap' in US Public Education — and
How to Close It." *TED*, May 2019,
https://www.ted.com/talks/anindya_kundu_the_opportunity_gap_
in_us_ public_education_and_how_to_close_it.

Professionally typeset works, such as this book, may introduce line breaks to avoid uneven line displays.

If a URL is longer than three lines in the list of works cited, you may shorten it, leaving at least the website host (for example, *cnn.com* or *www.usda.gov*) in the entry. If you will post your project online or submit it electronically and you want your readers to click on your URLs, do not insert any line breaks, shorten the URL, or delete the protocol (*https://* or *http://*).

18.5 Sample Student Research Writing in MLA Style

Every student research essay is different, of course, but it helps to look at strong models. On the following pages is a research essay on student success, written by Ian Byrne, a student in a first-year writing course. The example that follows, "Making It in College," demonstrates an effective response to the prompt introduced in Chapter 15.

MLA

Essay is formatted with MLA-style heading and margins.

Title is centered.

Writer begins with an engaging opening sentence.

Thesis presents the main point and previews the essay's organization.

Writer uses consistent headings to move the reader through his essay.

Byrne 1

Ian Byrne

Professor Starkey

English 110

5 December 2018

Making It in College

Every college student who has ever sat up all night drinking too many cups of coffee while trying to finish a research paper like this one has probably paused at some point to wonder: *Why?* The answer, of course, is the future, when a college degree will pay off with a good job, a comfortable house, and the freedom to travel and enjoy life. Even in a booming economy like the one we are in now, having a college degree still matters. According to the US Bureau of Labor Statistics, "Among people age 25 and older with a bachelor's degree or more education, the unemployment rate was 2.1 percent" in April 2018, a rate that is almost twice as strong as the "4.3 percent for high school grads" in the same time period. But while these benefits may sound wonderful, not all high school students naturally adjust to the college lifestyle, immediately finding their place on campus, earning a high GPA, finding good internships, and graduating in four consecutive years. While no one solution or strategy can meet the challenges of every student across the country, there are a number of ways to succeed in college. The most effective strategies for a successful college experience are managing money and time effectively, learning how to network, and simply getting enough sleep.

Managing Money

The first and perhaps most obvious challenge of going to college is figuring out how to pay for it. Affordability is in the news every year when students go back to school: some version of *tuition, fees, and room and board have risen again.*

Byrne 2

The accumulation of this rising cost each year has made college virtually unattainable without taking on some debt. It wasn't always like this. According to the National Center for Education Statistics, the average cost of a four-year public education in 2016, the most recent year for which government statistics are available, was $26,120. In 1986, the same education would have cost an average of $5,504, using today's dollars. "Between 2005–06 and 2015–16, prices for undergraduate tuition, fees, room, and board at public institutions rose 34 percent, and prices at private nonprofit institutions rose 26 percent, after adjustment for inflation" ("Tuition Costs").

Unfortunately, federal aid and grants have not been able to keep up with the rising costs as well as students have hoped. The result of this increase has been students incurring more debt in the form of loans and working more hours to cover tuition and living expenses, often at the expense of their college experience. A study by professors Tracey King and Ellynne Bannon found this problem to be particularly widespread:

> Nearly half of all full-time working college students are working enough hours to hurt their academic achievement and the overall quality of their education. At the same time, the majority of these students report that they would not be able to attend college if they did not work . . . 46% of all full-time working students work 25 or more hours per week, and 42% of these students reported that working hurt their grades.

There is an obvious solution that many millennials are asking for: make college free. It was one of the main tenets of the Bernie Sanders campaign in 2016's presidential election. He argued in favor of free tuition at public universities for all students. While this would by no means solve the debt problem

Byrne 3

overnight, it would at least make a meaningful dent in the issue. However, the solution seems to be a long way off; for now, most students will have to rely on smart money management.

Managing money starts by making and keeping more of it. Work study jobs, private scholarships, tax credits, living off campus and/or going to community college are all ways to save a bit of cash, even if they don't pay for school completely. Pell Grants, for example, which are federally funded, can help to take a few thousand off the bill right away. The maximum award for one of these is $6,095, and the awards are determined by need ("Federal Student Aid"). Scholarships are another great way to pay tuition. Again, they are not likely to cover the whole bill, but they can lower costs significantly for high-achieving students, service-oriented students, and athletes.

On- or off-campus jobs are another essential way to fund education, and they can be effective as long as the work doesn't take over academic hours. Work study jobs, which are federally funded, are often well-paying, and many college towns will have part-time positions available at local businesses during the school year. My brother Nathan, for instance, was a student worker at the county court during college. He was able to help a judge with a special project, which meant he earned money and also had an experience that interested him as a criminal justice major. For students who really want to lower their college costs, becoming a resident assistant or its equivalent is another smart move: these positions generally provide free housing, and some may even pay a wage on top of that.

Managing Time

Assuming that the financial component of college can be worked out, though, that still leaves two or four years of busy student life—and it's not all socializing with friends at house

Writer uses material from a personal interview as support.

Second heading, styled like the first, indicates another major section of the essay.

Byrne 4

parties. In addition to time spent in class, students need to make time for homework, preparing for exams, clubs and other extracurricular activities, jobs, laundry, and sleep. To make all these things work together, students need to be able to manage their time effectively. Time management is one of the most difficult things to do in college, when there seems to be a new distraction every day.

The University of Oxford produced a video that includes a number of time management strategies. Even though the 2014 video is a little out of date, one strategy that seems worth developing is learning "to say 'no,' in order to say 'yes' to something more important or pressing" ("Short Guide"). Putting off instant gratification for a higher priority is something many young people have to learn. The video also suggests prioritizing assignments that are due soon, like exams or papers, explaining that "weighing immediacy and importance" are essential to balancing the responsibilities of student life—and having a social life outside of all the work ("Short Guide").

Prioritization is incredibly important to ensuring that everything in a student's schedule gets done. To learn to prioritize, you can use diagrams, a calendar, or keep a simple list of the things that need to be accomplished in a given week. Some people may find organizational diagrams most effective, since they can be used to prioritize tasks not only by urgency or due date, but also by their actual importance. In this way, you can also distinguish between your personal and academic lives, as many personal problems will be important but not as urgent as your work. Students who use tools such as calendars, planners, and diagrams to practice prioritizing have a head start over those who don't.

The writer uses second person "you" occasionally to connect with part of his audience—other students who want to "make it" in college.

Writer introduces a quotation with a signal phrase and includes a page number after the borrowed material.

Visual evidence breaks up the text and supports the writer's points.

Byrne 5

There is another key time management idea to consider: you can't procrastinate if you want to succeed. According to Cynthia Jenkins, a teacher and advisor at University of Texas, procrastination will often happen on big projects or papers, which can seem easy to put off in the short term, but "may catch up with you in the end" (45). Pushing off papers or studying for a test until the last minute is a good way to lose sleep, harm your health, sink into an academic slump, and get caught up in an exhausting cycle of procrastination (fig. 1). Jenkins argues that instead of procrastinating, it may help to set up a schedule showing "fixed" items—such as class times, homework, study sessions, and so on—and then schedule time to relax in between. This turns procrastination into something more essential: recovery time. This period of time provides some freedom to catch up with friends, go to the gym, or just watch a TV show and "detox from academia" (Jenkins 47). School can

Fig. 1. "Time Management." *Allegheny College*, 2021, sites .allegheny.edu/learningcommons/time-management/.

Byrne 6

be exhausting to students who feel like they're always running around; scheduling breaks can make all the difference, while also ensuring that work gets done in a timely manner.

Learning to Network

College is not only about academic work, however. For many people, the main purpose of college is to prepare students for the job market. The preparation will, in theory, make it easier to get a job and earn income after graduation. But there is a gap between being ready and eager for professional life and actually finding professional work, and that gap must be filled by networking. Networking is the developing of professional relationships, and it has become an essential skill to practice, especially as job markets become more competitive with more applicants. There is a saying that many feel describes the way people find internships and jobs during and after college: "It's not what you know, it's who you know." This is not to say, however, that academics are unimportant or less important to developing connections. Bonds-Raacke and others argue that "what you know gets you in the room but it is who you know that will get you a seat at the table."

Networking seems like a tedious thing to make time for, but as a student you can start small by going first to trusted professors. Since professors are often people who have left a certain field to teach it to others, they may have still have ties to that industry. If you develop a relationship with that professor, they may be willing to connect with you on LinkedIn and pass your name and contact information along to someone who could offer an internship or a job.

College campuses are also convenient for networking, as recruiters from companies will often come to schools for specialized events (see fig. 2). Students can generally go to

Fig. 2. Networking is a skill college students should master.
Luis Alvarez. "Businesswomen Handshaking in Auditorium."
Getty Images, www.gettyimages.com/detail/photo
/businesswomen-handshaking-in-auditorium-corridor-royalty
-free-image/1166085433. Accessed 21 Nov. 2018.

these free of charge, and can make connections for internships,
jobs, and even research experiences with professionals in their
field. These events are ones that some students often turn
down, as they can appear time-consuming and "schmoozy,"
but more and more experts are expressing that, as *Washington
Post* journalist Sakina Rangwala puts it, "Networking is not
optional anymore; it is a crucial skill to master." In fact, surveys
of many businesses are showing that employers consistently
rank networking as one of the most important aspects of
finding a job (Rangwala). For a student to succeed in college,
and in the professional world that follows, building a network
of reliable professional contacts can be a massive boost.

Full publication information for
this source is given in a caption,
so no entry is needed in the list
of works cited.

Byrne 8

Getting Enough Sleep

No matter what steps you take to build your academic and professional credentials, they may not mean much if you aren't mentally present and awake during your college years. Of all the factors affecting college life, adequate sleep is perhaps the most important. This may sound unrelated; on the surface, sleep has little to do with college. It's not time that can be spent writing essays or studying for exams, which leads many people to view it as wasted time. But nothing could be further from the truth. In fact, according to researchers Katya Trudeau Potkin and William E. Bunney, "sleep plays an important role in the consolidation of memory. This has been most clearly shown in adults for procedural memory (i.e. skills and procedures) and declarative memory (e.g. recall of facts)." Developing a good sleep cycle leads not only to better recall, but also to better academic performance. A study in the *Journal of Adolescent Health* found that students' test scores improved by more than twenty percent after adequate hours of sleep, compared with those who did not get enough hours, a result that has been replicated in college students and other age groups (Lund et al.).

The drawbacks of losing sleep can be worse than just losing points on a test. Writing in the journal *Nature and Science of Sleep*, researchers Shelley Hershner and Ronald Chervin concluded:

> Daytime sleepiness, sleep deprivation, and irregular sleep schedules are prevalent among college students, as fifty percent report daytime sleepiness and seventy percent attain insufficient sleep. The consequences of sleep deprivation are problematic to college students and can result in lower grade point averages, compromised learning, and impaired mood. (73)

Even a summary of a source is introduced with a signal phrase and cited in the text.

Byrne 9

College presents many reasons to stay up late, whether it be for academic purposes or a night out on the town. A late night here and there is unlikely to hurt a student's overall performance, but in order to sustain academic progress, sleep should be a stable part of any student's schedule. In some studies, regular napping has been shown to be a strategy of many successful college students.

Making It All Work

Following each of the suggestions in this essay will help increase the likelihood that a student completes college, earns a degree, and is ready for the next step. However, what's really important is learning to juggle everything so that nothing gets left out. You might be managing your money well but not getting enough sleep, or you could be doing a good job of networking but not keeping a good handle on your time. I am fortunate to have the example of my brothers in front of me, but I know that so many students are the first in their families to attend college. The juggling act is a different one for every student. Sometimes the "balls" are of different weights; other times an extra one gets thrown in unexpectedly. When students are able to successfully manage their money and time, build relationships, and stay healthy, they have the best chance at a college experience that can be as smooth as a well-practiced act and that can set their whole future in motion.

Conclusion echoes the writer's position and engages with a metaphor.

Byrne 10

Works Cited

Bonds-Raacke, Jennifer, et al. "Should I Be Networking? Exploring the Importance of Networking for Students." *Psychology Student Network*, vol. 5, no. 1, Jan. 2017, www.apa.org/ed/precollege/psn/2017/01/importance -networking.aspx.

Byrne, Nathan. Phone interview with the author. 15 Nov. 2018.

"Federal Student Aid at a Glance." *Feberal Student Aid,* U.S. Department of Education, 2018, studentaid.ed.gov/sa /sites/default/files/aid-glance-2018-19.pdf.

Hershner, Shelley D., and Ronald D. Chervin. "Causes and Consequences of Sleepiness among College Students." *Nature and Science of Sleep*, vol. 6, 2014, pp. 73–84. *PubMed*, https://doi.org/10.2147/NSS.S62907.

Jenkins, Cynthia. *Skills for Success: Developing Effective Study Strategies*. Wadsworth, 2005.

King, Tracey, and Ellynne Bannon. *At What Cost? The Price That Working Students Pay for a College Education*. United States Public Interest Research Group, 1 Apr. 2002. *ERIC*, files.eric.ed.gov/fulltext/ED470026.pdf

Lund, Hannah G., et al. "Sleep Patterns and Predictors of Disturbed Sleep in a Large Population of College Students." *Journal of Adolescent Health*, vol. 46, no. 2, Feb. 2010, pp. 124–32. *PubMed*, https://doi.org/10.1016/j.jadohealth. 2009.06.016.

Potkin, Katya Trudeau, and William E. Bunney. "Sleep Improves Memory: The Effect of Sleep on Long Term Memory in Early Adolescence." *PLoS ONE,* vol. 7, no. 8, 2012. *EBSCOhost*, https://doi.org/10.1371/journal.pone.0042191.

List of works cited is organized alphabetically by author (or by title when no author name is given).

Byrne 11

Rangwala, Sakina. "Networking 101." *The Washington*
    Post, 9 Oct. 2012, www.washingtonpost.com/jobs
    _articles/2012/10/09/dbb7d628-121d-11e2-be82
    -c3411b7680a9_story.html?utm_term=.44a8f5a5cb1e.

"A Short Guide to Managing Your Time." *YouTube*, uploaded
    by U of Oxford, 14 Feb. 2014, www.youtube.com
    /watch?v=gtt9sX4WTYY&feature=youtu.be.

"Tuition Costs of Colleges and Universities." *Fast Facts*,
    National Center for Education Statistics, nces.ed.gov
    /fastfacts/display.asp?id=76. Accessed 18 Nov. 2018.

U.S. Bureau of Labor Statistics, "Unemployment Rate 2.1
    Percent for College Grads, 4.3 Percent for High School
    Grads in April 2018." *TED: The Economics Daily*, U.S.
    Department of Labor, 10 May 2018, www.bls.gov/opub
    /ted/2018/unemployment-rate-2-1-percent-for-college
    -grads-4-3-percent-for-high-school-grads-in-april-2018.htm.

19

APA Style

In classes in the social sciences and in some classes in the sciences and the humanities, you may be asked to use the APA (American Psychological Association) system for documenting sources. The guidelines in this chapter follow those set forth in the *Publication Manual of the American Psychological Association*, 7th edition (2020).

Even though these guidelines present a system for citing many different kinds of sources, they may not cover every type of source you need to cite. At times you may find that you have to think critically to adapt the guidelines to the sources you are using.

19.1 Creating APA-style In-Text Citations

Directory to APA In-Text Citation Models

APA style requires you to supply an in-text citation each time you quote, paraphrase, summarize, or otherwise integrate material from a source. In-text citations are made with a combination of signal phrases and parenthetical references and include the information needed to give credit and for readers to locate the full reference in the list of references at the end of the text.

When citing a source in your text, include the following in a signal phrase or parenthetical citation:

- the author's (or authors') last name(s)

- the year in which the source was published

- a page number or other section locator (for a direct quotation)

In APA style, a page number or other section locator need not be included for a summary or paraphrase, but check with your instructors to make sure you understand their requirements.

There is a direct connection between the in-text citation and the first part of the corresponding entry in the list of references. It is crucial that the name and year mentioned in the in-text citation match the name and year in the reference list. The reference list is alphabetized by authors' last names, and if there is a mistake in the list or in the in-text citation, readers won't easily be able to find the source they are looking for in the list of references.

Sample In-Text Citation

Bruns (2017) argued that by imprisoning men—"which discourages shared responsibility for children, the home, and the household economy—prisons, jails, and justice system processes reproduce gender inequality" (p. 1332).

Reference List Entry

Bruns, A. (2017). Consequences of partner incarceration for women's employment. *Journal of Marriage and Family, 79*(5), 1331–1352. https://doi.org/10.1111/jomf.12412

NOTE: APA style requires the use of the past tense or the present perfect tense in signal phrases introducing cited material: Smith (2020) reported; Smith (2020) has argued.

1. Basic format for a quotation Ordinarily, introduce the quotation with a signal phrase (what the APA calls a "narrative citation") that includes the author's last name and the year of publication in parentheses. Include the page number in parentheses following the quotation.

> Zhang (2019) showed that "when academics are strongly motivated to teach and are satisfied with and take pride in their teaching," their feeling of affiliation with the schools at which they teach increases (p. 1325).

If the author is not named in a signal phrase, include the author's last name, the year of publication, and the page number in parentheses following the quotation:

> ". . ." (Zhang, 2019, p. 1325).

2. Basic format for a summary or a paraphrase As when citing a quotation (see item 1), include the author's last name and the year the work was published either before the borrowed material or in parentheses following it. A page number is not required for a summary or a paraphrase, but include one if it would help readers find the passage in a long work or if your instructor requires it.

> Instructors' positive feelings about teaching carry over into their feelings about the schools at which they teach (Zhang, 2019, p. 211).

3. Quotation from a source without page numbers If your source does not include page numbers, include other information from the source—a section heading, a paragraph number, a figure or table number, a slide number, or a time stamp—to help readers find the cited passage:

> Lopez (2019) has noted that "..." (Symptoms section).

> Myers (2019) extolled the benefits of humility (para. 5).

> Brezinski and Zhang (2017) traced the increase ... (Figure 3).

> The American Immigration Council (2021) has recommended that "..." (Slide 5).

> In a recent TED Talk, Gould (2019) argued that "..." (13:27).

Do not include location numbers for sources in e-book format. If you shorten a lengthy heading, place it in quotation marks: ("What Is It" section).

4. Specific section of a source To cite a specific section of a source, such as a portion of an audio or video recording; a slide in a set of lecture slides; or a dedication, preface, foreword, afterword, or chapter, name the section in your signal phrase.

> In a dedication written while he was in hiding, Salman Rushdie (1991) included an acrostic of his son's name: SAFAR.

If the section was written by someone other than the author, include the section author's name in your signal phrase.

> In his foreword to Anthony Ray Hinton's moving book (2018), Bryan Stevenson wrote ... (p. iv).

In your reference list, include a citation for the work as a whole.

5. Two authors Name both authors in a signal phrase or in the parenthetical citation. In the parenthetical citation, use an ampersand (&) between the authors' names; in the signal phrase, use the word "and."

> Bloomberg and Pope (2017) have argued that with global warming we are facing a "*kairos*: a supreme moment at which one simply must act, however implausible or inconvenient" (p. 12).

> Some have argued that we are facing a watershed moment, or "*kairos,*" in the fight against global warming (Bloomberg & Pope, 2017, p. 12).

6. Three or more authors Use the first author's name followed by "et al." (Latin for "and others") in either a signal phrase or a parenthetical citation.

> Similarly, as Belenky et al. (1986) showed, examining the lives of women expands our understanding of human development.

> Examining the lives of women expands our understanding of human development (Belenky et al., 1986).

7. Organization as author If the author is a government agency or some other organization, give the group's full name in a signal phrase or parenthetical citation the first time you cite the source.

> The Kaiser Family Foundation (2018) found that 11% of children living in Texas were uninsured in 2017.

> In 2017, 11% of children living in Texas were uninsured (Kaiser Family Foundation, 2018).

For an organization with a long name, you may abbreviate the name of the organization in citations after the first. Include the abbreviation—in parentheses in the signal phrase or in brackets in the parenthetical citation—following the organization's full name.

First Citation	The Centers for Disease Control and Prevention (CDC, 2021) found that . . .
	or
	(Centers for Disease Control and Prevention [CDC], 2021)
Later Citations	(CDC, 2021)

For a work by a government agency or large organization with multiple, nested departments, list the most specific agency or department as the author, as in the reference list.

8. Unknown or anonymous author If the author is unknown, include the work's title (shortened if it is long) in the in-text citation.

> As a result of changes in the city's eviction laws, New York's eviction rate dropped by over a third from 2013 to 2018 ("Pushed Out," 2019).

All titles in in-text citations are set in title case: Capitalize the first and last words of a title and subtitle, all significant words, and any words of four letters or more. For books and most stand-alone works (except websites), italicize the title; for most articles and other parts of larger works, set the title in quotation marks.

Only in rare cases, when "Anonymous" is specified as the author, use the word "Anonymous" in the author position: (Anonymous, 2020). (Also use the word "Anonymous" at the start of the reference list entry.)

NOTE: Titles are treated differently in reference list entries. See the "Title" and "Source" sections of "Elements of APA reference list entries" on pages 485 and 486.

9. Two or more works by the same author in the same year In your reference list, use lowercase letters ("a," "b," and so on) with the year to order the entries. Use the same letter in your in-text citation. (See item 12 in the reference list section, p. 492.)

> Soot-free flames can be produced by stripping the air of nitrogen and then adding that nitrogen to the fuel (Conover, 2019b).

10. Two or more authors with the same last name To avoid confusion, use the authors' initials in the in-text references.

> K. Yi (2019) has demonstrated . . .
> D. Yi (2017) has shown that . . .

If the authors share the same initials, spell out each author's first name:

> Kim Yi (2019) has demonstrated . . .
> Kenneth Yi (2017) has shown that . . .

11. Indirect source (source quoted in another source) It's often best to find and use the original source. If that is not possible (for example, if the source has not been translated), cite the original source and then include "as cited in" plus the author's name and the date of the secondary source.

> One reviewer commended the author's "sure understanding of the thoughts of young people" (Brailsford, 1990, as cited in Chow, 2019, para. 9).

If you mention the original author in a signal phrase, just include "as cited in" plus the secondary source in the parenthetical citation.

12. Two or more works in the same parentheses When your parenthetical citation names two or more works, put the citations in alphabetical order, separated by semicolons.

> So far, studies of pharmacological treatments for childhood obesity have been inconclusive (Barbour et al., 2018; Xu & Xue, 2016).

13. Work available in multiple versions Some works may be available in more than one version. For example, an article may be reprinted in a collection or anthology, an older work may have been republished, or a translated work may be available in both the original language and other languages. If you consulted a reprinted, republished, or translated work, include both the date of original publication and the date of the version you used, and separate the dates with a slash: (Padura, 2009/2014).

14. Sacred or classical text For a religious work (such as the Bible, the Torah, or the Qur'an), include the title of the version you consulted, the year of that version's publication, and the chapter, verse, and line numbers.

> (*New International Version Bible,* 1978/2011, Proverbs 16:18).

For a classic of poetry or drama, provide the author, year (or years) of publication, and the relevant numbered sections: For poetry, use canto, book, or other section names or numbers, and line numbers; for plays, use act, scene, and line numbers.

> (Milton, 1667/2017, 1.263)
>
> (Shakespeare, 1595/2010, 1.1.134)

See also item 34, "Sacred or classical text," in the reference list section (p. 498).

15. Website, software, or app Most references to digital works or works published online can be cited in the text of your paper using one of the other models in this section:

- If author and publication date are supplied, use the usual author-date format: (Smith, 2019).
- If the reference list entry uses "n.d." ("no date"), use that in your in-text citation: (Smith, n.d.).
- If the source is listed by the organization's name in the reference list, use the organization as author: (Greenpeace, 2019).

Whichever format you use, be sure that your in-text citation matches what you have used in your reference list entry. For example, if you quote, paraphrase, or summarize a tweet, include either the actual name or the screen name of the author in your text, depending on what appears in the author position in your reference list. (See item 61 in the reference list section, p. 505.)

However, if you merely refer to a website, a type of software, or an app in your text without citing specific information from that work, then no formal in-text citation (or reference list entry) is needed. Just mention the work, and include the URL (that is, the Universal Resource Locator, or web address).

16. Audiovisual or multimedia works In the "Author" position, include the name of the person (or people) primarily responsible for producing the work and the date it was created or released. For example, to cite a work in a museum, include the artist's name and the date the work was created: (O'Keeffe, 1931).

To cite a film, include the director's name and the date the film was released: (Peele, 2019).

See the "Author" section (p. 485) in "Elements of APA reference list entries" and the introductory portion of "Multimedia sources" (p. 499) for more about whom to include in the "Author" position.

17. Personal communications Personal communications include a variety of source types, from text messages and emails you received to interviews and oral histories you recorded and live classes you attended. Cite personal communications that cannot be accessed by your readers in the text only; they should not be included in the list of references.

> Some have argued that advertisers should design ads responsibly for younger viewers (F. Johnson, personal communication, May 20, 2019).

Include any other information in the text that readers would need to understand the reference, such as the tribal membership of your source in a work that draws on oral traditions of Indigenous Peoples.

> (H. Powers, Onondaga Nation, personal communication, April 2, 2021).

19.2 Creating APA-style Reference List Entries

For an APA-style research project, you will develop a "References" list, an alphabetical list of the works you cite throughout your project. Place the list of references at the end of your paper or project. For advice on preparing the reference list, see "Formatting Student Papers in APA Style" (p. 506). For a sample reference list, see section 19.5.

Elements of APA Reference List Entries

An APA-style reference consists of four parts:

- The **author**'s (or authors') name(s)
- The **date** of publication
- The **title** of the work
- The **source** of the work (the retrieval information)

Insert a period following each of these four parts.

author   date   title

Gazzaniga, M. S. (2019). *The consciousness instinct: Unraveling the mystery*

source information

of how the brain makes the mind. Farrar, Straus and Giroux.

In general, the first two elements—author and date of publication—appear in both in-text citations and reference list entries. The title and source information often appear only in the reference list entry.

Author
The author is the person or people most responsible for the work:

- For a book or article, the author is the person (or people) who wrote it.
- For a movie, the person most responsible is the director.
- For a government report, the author might be the specific agency that produced the report.
- For a company's annual report, the author is probably the corporation that produced the report.

If the role of the individual who produced the work is not that of author, include a brief description in parentheses identifying the role, such as "Ed." for "Editor." (For more about listing authors, see "General Guidelines for Listing Authors," p. 489.)

Date of Publication
In the in-text citation, the date of publication is the year the item appeared; in the reference list entry, the date may be the year alone, or it may be more specific:

- For a daily newspaper, weekly magazine, podcast episode, or blog or social media post, include the year, month, and day: (2019, February 10).
- For a monthly magazine, include the year and month: (2019, May).
- For a book or scholarly journal, include the year: (2019).
- For a multivolume work or TV series, include a range of years: (2011–2019).

For some works—such as a translation or a work that was reprinted in another source or republished at a later date—you may need to supply two dates. (See item 33, p. 498.) If no date is given, include "(n.d.)" for "no date" in your in-text citation.

Title
The title is the name of the specific part of the work you consulted. This can be a bit tricky to determine, so it may help to consider whether the work is

- a stand-alone item, such as a novel, a movie, a one-time TV special (such as the 2019 Grammy Awards), or a one-off podcast, *or*
- part of a larger whole, such as an article in a journal, a chapter in a book, or an episode in a weekly podcast or TV series.

If the item you consulted is a separate work, then your title is just the title of that work. Set it in italics. Type the titles of stand-alone works in sentence case (capitalize only the first word of the title and subtitle and any proper nouns):

> *Culture code: The secrets of highly successful groups.*
>
> *Out east: Memoir of a Montauk summer.*

If the item you consulted is part of a larger whole, then set the title of the part you consulted in regular font (without quotation marks or italics), in sentence case:

> Why we believe in conspiracy theories.
>
> Robert Caro reflects on Robert Moses, L.B.J., and his own career in nonfiction.

If you are citing a nonacademic source or one that is not peer-reviewed (such as a newsletter or press release), or if you think the type of source you are citing will not be clear to your readers, include a bracketed label (like "[Newsletter]" or "[Video]") following the title.

> *One Night in Miami* [Film].

Source

The source section of a reference entry supplies the information readers need to identify and locate the source:

- For a stand-alone work, like a book, the source information is the publication information: the publisher and, if the work was accessed online, a DOI (or digital object identifier) or direct-link URL.

- For a work that is part of a larger work, such as an article in a journal or a chapter in a collection or an edited book, the source information is information about the larger work, such as the publisher (for a book) and the volume, issue, and page numbers and a DOI or URL (for a journal article).

Source title Titles of periodicals and books are set in italics; the names of websites are set in regular font. Periodical titles (journals, magazines, newspapers) and website names are set in title case (capitalize all words of four or more letters and all significant words):

> *Journal of Applied Psychology.*
>
> *The Wall Street Journal.*

Book titles are set in sentence case (capitalize the first word of the title and subtitle and any proper nouns):

> *The Oxford encyclopedia of psychology and aging.*

Publisher (for books) For books, include the full name of the publisher following the title. Omit terms that indicate corporate structure, like "Inc." or "Ltd.," but otherwise set the publisher's name as it appears on the book itself. (The publisher's location is not included.)

Volume and issue number (for periodicals) Scholarly journals and some magazines are published in "volumes" (all the issues published in a single year) and "issues" (the periodical published each week, month, or quarter). If available, include volume and issue numbers after the periodical's title. (Newspapers and many magazines are published simply by date.) Volume numbers are italicized; issue numbers (which appear in parentheses) are not: *12*(3).

Page numbers For a selection that appears in a book, include the page number(s) for the part you consulted following the collection or anthology title, after the abbreviation "p." (for "page") or "pp." For an article that appears in a periodical, include the page numbers (with no "p." or "pp.") after the issue number, or after the periodical's title if no volume or issue number is available. (See items 13, 14, and 15 on pp. 492 and 493.)

DOIs and URLs If a digital object identifier (DOI) is available, include it at the end of the citation with no period at the end. If there is no DOI but you can supply a direct-link URL, do so; if not, omit the URL. If the DOI or URL is long, you can include a shortened form by using a site like shortdoi. org or bitly.com. Some sites (the *New York Times,* for example) provide shortened permalinks.

Include the DOI as a link. The APA recommends using the International DOI Foundation's current format.

https://doi.org/10.1037/apl0000377

If you encounter a DOI in a different format, change the beginning to "https://doi.org/" and add the DOI number for the specific work (with no space between the slash and the DOI).

Now let's put this all together and look at a couple of examples of reference entries.

If you read an article in a journal, your reference entry consists of the author's name, the article's title, and information about the source (the journal in which the article appeared):

Reference List Entry for an Article in a Journal

author	(date)	title	source title	volume (issue)	pages

Becker, G. S. (1995). The economics of crime. *Cross Sections*, *12*(3), 8–15.

However, if you read the same article in a collection of essays, then the author and title remain the same, but the source section now includes information about the collection in which the article appeared. Information about the original publication appears at the end of the citation.

Reference List Entry For An Article From A Collection

author	(date of collection)	article title	editors

Becker, G. S. (2018). The economics of crime. In A. Walsh & C. Hemmens (Eds.),

source title	(edition number, pages)

Introduction to criminology: A text/reader (4th ed., pp. 101–107).

publisher	previous publication year

SAGE Publications. (Original work published 1995)

If you can't find all the information you need to write a complete citation, do your best to provide the information needed to credit your source and lead your readers to it.

Directory to APA Reference List Models

General Guidelines for Listing Authors

In APA style, all authors' names are written with the last name first, and initials are used in place of first and middle names. If an author's last name is hyphenated or if an author has a two-part last name, include both names.

Johnson-Sheehan, R.

García Márquez, G.

If the first name is hyphenated, include a hyphen with no spaces between the initials.

Kang, D.-W.

If an author's name has a suffix, such as "Jr.," include it after the initials.

> Foreman, G., Jr.

The first element is important because citations in the text refer to it. In-text citations point readers to complete references in an alphabetized reference list.

1. One author Give the author's last name, followed by a comma, and then give the first and middle initials (if provided in the source), each followed by a period.

> Gazzaniga, M. S.

2. Two to twenty authors List up to twenty authors, each one last name first, followed by any initials. Include a comma after each author and an ampersand (&) before the last author.

> Wiegand, I., Seidel, C., & Wolfe, J.

3. Twenty-one or more authors For twenty-one or more authors, list the first nineteen, followed by an ellipsis mark (. . .) and the last author, without an ampersand (&) before the last author.

> Sharon, G., Cruz, N. J., Kang, D.-W., Gandal, M. J., Wang, B., Kim, Y.-M.,
> Zink, E. M., Casey, C. P., Taylor, B. C., Lane, C. J., Bramer, L. M.,
> Isern, N. G., Hoyt, D. W., Noecker, C., Sweredoski, M. J., Moradian,
> A., Borenstein, E., Jansson, J. K., Knight, R., . . . Mazmanian, S. K.

4. Organization as author When the author is a corporation, a government agency, or some other organization, begin with the name of the organization.

> American Psychiatric Association.

> National Highway Traffic Safety Administration.

For works by government agencies, list the most specific organization as the author. For a work by the National Highway Traffic Safety Administration, for example, the NHTSA would be listed as the author, and the U.S. Department of Transportation would be listed as the publisher of the source.

5. Pseudonym or screen name If you know the writer's actual name, provide it in inverted order, with the screen name or handle following in square brackets.

> King, L. [@kingsthings].

If you do not know the writer's actual name, provide the full screen name, not inverted.

> Trinity Resists.

6. Author with a one- or two-word name If the author uses a single name (like "Prince" or "Sophocles") or a two-part name in which the two parts are both essential (like "Snoop Dogg" or "Cardi B"), include that name in the author position.

> Plato. (2016). *The republic* (B. Jowett, Trans.). Project Gutenberg. http://www.gutenberg.org/files/1497/1497-h/1497-h.htm (Original work published ca. 380 B.C.E.)

7. Unknown author Unless the author is listed on the work as "Anonymous," begin the reference list entry with the work's title. For a stand-alone work, put the title in italics.

> *Atlas of the world.* (2019). Oxford University Press.

For a work that is part of a larger whole, put the title in the regular font, with no quotation marks or italics.

> Pushed out. (2019, August 24). *The Economist, 432*(9157), 19–20.

8. Author and editor Include the editor's name, in parentheses, following the title, plus the label "Ed." (for "Editor") or "Eds." (for "Editors").

> Sontag, S. (2018). *Debriefing: Collected stories* (B. Taylor, Ed.). Picador.

9. Editor For an edited work, put the editor's name in the author position, followed by the label "(Ed.)" for "Editor."

> Yeh, K.-H. (Ed.). (2019). *Asian indigenous psychologies in the global context*. Palgrave Macmillan.

If there are multiple editors, use the abbreviation "(Eds.)."

10. Translator

> Calasso, R. (2019). *The unnamable present* (R. Dixon, Trans.). Farrar, Straus and Giroux. (Original work published 2017)

11. Editor and translator

> Weber, M. (2020). *Charisma and disenchantment: The vocation lectures* (P. Reitter & C. Wellmon, Eds.; D. Searls, Trans.). NYRB Classics. (Original work published 1919)

12. Two or more works by the same author in the same year Insert lowercase letters following the year in the order in which the sources appear in the reference list ("a" for the first item, "b" for the second item, "c" for the third item, and so on). Works that include only the year (such as books and articles in scholarly journals) precede works that include a year, month, and day (such as articles in newspapers and magazines).

> Gladwell, M. (2019a). *Talking to strangers: What we should know about the people we don't know.* Little, Brown and Company.
>
> Gladwell, M. (2019b, January 14). Is marijuana as safe as we think? *The New Yorker.* https://www.newyorker.com/magazine/2019/01/14/is-marijuana-as-safe-as-we-think

If both works use a more specific date, arrange the citations chronologically.

> Conover, E. (2019a, June 8). Gold's origins tied to collapsars. *Science News, 195*(10), 10. https://bit.ly/31JTgKD
>
> Conover, E. (2019b, June 22). Space flames may hold secrets to soot-free fire. *Science News, 195*(11), 5. https://bit.ly/2p0Xj89

If both works use the year alone or use the same more complete date, then alphabetize the citations by title (ignoring "A," "An," or "The" at the start of a title) before assigning a lowercase letter to each.

Articles and Other Parts of Larger Works

If you are using an article from a periodical (journal, magazine, newspaper) or a section from a book or other text-based longer work, use one of the models in this section. (For stand-alone works such as books, audiovisual or multimedia works, or social media, see the sections that follow.) Also refer to the "Title" and "Source" sections of "Elements of APA reference list entries" on pages 485–86.

13. Journal article

> Ganegoda, D. B., & Bordia, P. (2019). I can be happy for you, but not all the time: A contingency model of envy and positive empathy in the workplace. *Journal of Applied Psychology, 104*(6), 776–795. https://doi.org/10.1037/apl0000377
>
> Hung, J. (2018). Educational investment and sociopsychological wellbeing among rural Chinese women. *Inquiries Journal, 10*(05). http://www.inquiriesjournal.com/a?id=1736

Le Texier, T. (2019). Debunking the Stanford Prison Experiment. *American Psychologist*, 74(7), 823–839. https://doi.org/10.1037/amp0000401

Notice that "Stanford Prison Experiment" is capitalized in the last example because it is a proper noun.

14. Magazine article

Vlahos, J. (2019, March). Alexa, I want answers. *Wired*, 58–65. https://www.wired.com/story/amazon-alexa-search-for-the-one-perfect-answer/

If the magazine supplies a DOI or uses volume and issue numbers, include that information as well.

Greengard, S. (2019, August). The algorithm that changed quantum machine learning. *Communications of the ACM*, 62(8), 15–17. https://doi.org/10.1145/3339458

If you lack a direct-link URL (for example, if you accessed the magazine through an academic research database) or if you read the article in print, omit the URL.

Koch, C. (2019, October). Is death reversible? *Scientific American*, 321(4), 34–37.

15. Newspaper article Include a direct-link URL if available.

Daly, J. (2019, August 2). Duquesne's med school plan part of national trend to train more doctors. *Pittsburgh Post-Gazette*. https://www.post-gazette.com/news/health/2019/08/02/Duquesne-med-school-national-trend-doctors-osteopathic-medicine-pittsburgh/stories/201908010181

If the direct-link URL is long, you can include a shortened form. (See p. 487 for more about using DOIs and URLs in reference list entries.)

Daly, J. (2019, August 2). Duquesne's med school plan part of national trend to train more doctors. *Pittsburgh Post-Gazette*. https://bit.ly/2Vzrm2l

If you accessed the article using a database or read it in print, omit the URL and include the page number (if available) following the newspaper name.

Finucane, M. (2019, September 25). Americans still eating too many low-quality carbs. *The Boston Globe*, B2.

For news from a website such as BBC News, cite the article as you would a web page (see item 25, p. 496).

16. Newsletter article

> Bond, G. (2018, Fall). Celebrities as epidemiologists. *American College of Epidemiology Online Member Newsletter, 4–5.* https://www .acepidemiology.org/assets/ACE_Newsletter_Fall_2018%20FINAL.pdf

If it will not be clear that you are citing a newsletter, you may include the label "[Newsletter]" following the title.

17. Comment on an online article In square brackets following the commenter's name (or screen name) and the comment date and title, include the words "Comment on the article" and then the title of the online article in quotation marks. If the comment is untitled, use up to the first twenty words of the comment itself in the title position. (See also item 5, "Pseudonym or screen name," on p. 490.) Provide a direct URL to the comment if one is available. If not, link to the article.

> lolly12. (2019, September 25). My husband works in IT in a major city down South. He is a permanent employee now, but for years [Comment on the article "The Google workers who voted to unionize in Pittsburgh are part of tech's huge contractor workforce"]. *Slate.* https://fyre.it/0RT8HmeL.4

18. Selection in a collection or anthology, or a chapter in an edited book Include the page numbers for the section following the source title.

> Pettigrew, D. (2018). The suppression of cultural memory and identity in Bosnia and Herzegovina. In J. Lindert & A. T. Marsoobian (Eds.), *Multidisciplinary perspectives on genocide and memory* (pp. 187–198). Springer.

19. Abstract Best practice is to cite the original source, rather than just the abstract of the source. But if you accessed only the abstract, include "[Abstract]" following the article's title.

> Brey, E., & Pauker, K. (2019, December). Teachers' nonverbal behaviors influence children's stereotypic beliefs [Abstract]. *Journal of Experimental Child Psychology, 188.* https://doi.org/10.1016/j. jecp.2019.104671

20. Article with a title in its title If the internal title is italicized, retain the italics, but set it in sentence case: Capitalize only the first word of the title and subtitle and any proper nouns.

> Fernandez, M. E. (2019, July 30). How *Orange is the new black* said goodbye to the Litchfield inmates. *Vulture.* https://www.vulture. com/2019/07/orange-is-the-new-black-character-endings.html

21. Editorial or letter to the editor Include a label in square brackets following the title to make clear the type of source you are citing.

> Gavin Newsom wants to stop rent gouging. Will lawmakers finally stand up for tenants? [Editorial]. (2019, September 4). *Los Angeles Times.* https://lat.ms/2lBlRm1

> Sanchez, L. (2020, December 17). Enforce social distancing, close bars [Letter to the editor]. *El Paso Times.* https://www.elpasotimes.com/ story/opinion/2020/12/17/enforce-social-distancing-close-bars-reader -letters-to-the-editor/3913747001/

22. Review After the review's title, include "[Review of the]" plus the type of production being reviewed (book, film), followed by the title of the work being reviewed and the name of the author or director or other major contributor. If the review is untitled, include the bracketed description in the title position.

> Douthat, R. (2019, October 14). A hustle gone wrong [Review of the film *Hustlers,* by L. Scafaria, Dir.]. *National Review, 71*(18), 47.

> Hall, W. (2019). [Review of the book *How to change your mind: The new science of psychedelics,* by M. Pollan]. *Addiction, 114*(10), 1892–1893. https://doi.org/10.1111/add.14702

23. Published interview The format of the citation depends on the source type in which the interview appears. For an interview published in print, include the interviewer in the "author" position.

> Remnick, D. (2019, July 1). Robert Caro reflects on Robert Moses, L.B.J., and his own career in nonfiction. *The New Yorker.* https://bit. ly/2Lukm3X

Typically, the interview subject will be named in the title of a work published in print, but if not, work the interview subject's name into your text in a signal phrase. (To cite a recorded interview, see item 54, "Lecture, speech, address, or recorded interview," p. 503.)

24. Entry in a reference work Treat an entry in a reference work like a selection in a collection or anthology, or a chapter in an edited book (see item 18, p. 494).

> Brue, A. W., & Wilmshurst, L. (2018). Adaptive behavior assessments. In B. B. Frey (Ed.), *The SAGE encyclopedia of educational research, measurement, and evaluation* (pp. 40–44). SAGE Publications. https://doi.org/10.4135/9781506326139.n21

If a source is intended to be updated regularly, include a retrieval date.

> Merriam-Webster. (n.d.). Racism. In *Merriam-Webster.com dictionary*. Retrieved November 5, 2020, from https://www.merriam-webster. com/dictionary/racism

Since Wikipedia makes archived versions available, you need not include a retrieval date. Instead, include the URL from the "View history" tab for the version you used.

> Behaviorism. (2019, October 11). In *Wikipedia*. https://en.wikipedia. org/w/index.php?title=Behaviorism&oldid=915544724

25. Web page or document on a website Many documents published on websites fall into other categories included in this guide and can be cited using models in other sections. For articles in an online newspaper, for example, follow item 15, "Newspaper article" (p. 493), and for an entry in an online dictionary, follow item 24, "Entry in a reference work." Use one of the models below only when your source doesn't fit in any other category. In these items, the website name follows the title unless author and website name are the same.

> Albright, A. (2019, July 25). *The global education challenge: Scaling up to tackle the learning crisis*. The Brookings Institution. https://www .brookings.edu/wp-content/uploads/2019/07/Brookings_Blum_2019 _education.pdf

> National Institute of Mental Health. (2016, March). *Seasonal affective disorder*. National Institutes of Health. https://www.nimh.nih.gov/ health/topics/seasonal-affective-disorder/index.shtml

> BBC News. (2019, October 31). *Goats help save Ronald Reagan Presidential Library*. https://www.bbc.com/news/world-us -canada-50248549

Books and Other Stand-Alone Works

26. Basic format for a book For most books, include the author's name, the year of publication, the title (in sentence case and italics), the name of the publisher (no location needed), and, if accessed online, the book's DOI or direct-link URL.

> Treuer, D. (2019). *The heartbeat of Wounded Knee: Native America from 1890 to the present*. Riverhead Books.

> Kilby, P. (2019). *The green revolution: Narratives of politics, technology and gender*. Routledge. https://doi.org/10.4324/9780429200823

27. Edition other than the first Include the edition number, in parentheses, following the book's title; the period follows the edition number.

> Dessler, A. E., & Parson, E. A. (2019). *The science and politics of global climate change: A guide to the debate* (3rd ed.). Cambridge University Press.

28. Collection or anthology Include the name(s) of the editor(s) followed by the abbreviation "Ed." (for "Editor") or "Eds." (for "Editors") in the author position. For a selection in a collection or anthology, or a chapter in an edited book, see item 18 (p. 494).

> Lindert, J., & Marsoobian, A. T. (Eds.). (2018). *Multidisciplinary perspectives on genocide and memory*. Springer.

29. Multivolume work (all volumes)

> Zeigler-Hill, V., & Shackelford, T. K. (Eds.). (2018). *The SAGE handbook of personality and individual differences* (Vols. I–III). SAGE Publications.

30. Multivolume work (single volume) If the volume has its own title, insert a colon following the series title and then the volume number, a period, and the title of the volume, all in italics.

> Zeigler-Hill, V., & Shackelford, T. K. (Eds.). (2018). *The SAGE handbook of personality and individual differences: Vol. II. Origins of personality and individual differences.* SAGE Publications.

If the volume you used has its own editor, use that name (rather than the name of the series editor) in the author position. If it is untitled, insert the number of the volume you used, in parentheses and in the regular font, following the series title.

31. Book with a title in its title If the book's title includes another title, neither italicize the internal title nor place it in quotation marks.

> Miller, K. (2018). *I'll be there for you: The one about* Friends. Hanover Square Press.

32. Book in a language other than English If you consulted the book in its original language, put the title, translated into English, in brackets following the title in its original language.

> Díaz de Villegas, N. (2019). *De donde son los gusanos: Crónica de un regreso a Cuba después de 37 años de exilio* [Where the worms are: Chronicle of a return to Cuba after 37 years of exile]. Vintage Español.

33. Republished book Include the original publication date following the citation. (See also item 13, "Work available in multiple versions," in the in-text citation section, p. 482.)

> Fremlin, C. (2017). *The hours before dawn*. Dover Publications. (Original work published 1958)

34. Sacred or classical text Cite sacred and classical texts like books. Sacred texts typically do not list an author, but you should give the title of the edition you used, the year it was published, the translator's name (if any), and any other source information available for the version you used. For an annotated version, include the editor in the author position. If an original date is known, include it at the end of the citation; if the date is approximate, include "ca." (for "circa"). Include "B.C.E." (for "before the common era") for ancient texts.

> *New International Version Bible*. (2011). Biblica. https://www.biblica.com/bible/ (Original work published 1978)

> Homer. (2018). *The Odyssey* (E. Wilson, Trans.). W. W. Norton & Company. (Original work published ca. 675–725 B.C.E.)

> Aurelius, M. (1994). *The meditations* (G. Long, Trans.). The Internet Classics Archive. http://classics.mit.edu/Antoninus/meditations.html (Original work published ca. 167)

35. Government document If no author is listed, include the department that produced the document in the author position. Any broader organization can be included as the publisher of the document. If a specific report number is provided, include it after the title.

> National Park Service. (2019, April 11). *Travel where women made history: Ordinary and extraordinary places of American women*. U.S. Department of the Interior. https://www.nps.gov/subjects/travelwomenshistory/index.htm

> Berchick, E. R., Barnett, J. C., & Upton, R. D. (2019, September 10). *Health insurance coverage in the United States: 2018* (Report No. P60-267). U.S. Census Bureau. https://www.census.gov/library/publications/2019/demo/p60-267.html

36. Report from a private organization

> Ford Foundation International Fellowships Program. (2019). *Leveraging higher education to promote social justice: Evidence from the IFP alumni tracking study*. https://p.widencdn.net/kei61u/IFP-Alumni-Tracking-Study-Report-5

37. Brochure or fact sheet

National Council of State Boards of Nursing. (2018). *A nurse manager's guide to substance use disorder in nursing* [Brochure].

World Health Organization. (2019, July 15). *Immunization coverage* [Fact sheet]. https://www.who.int/news-room/fact-sheets/detail/immunization-coverage

38. Press release

New York University. (2019, September 5). *NYU Oral Cancer Center awarded $2.5 million NIH grant to study cancer pain* [Press release]. https://www.nyu.edu/about/news-publications/news/2019/september/nyu-oral-cancer-center-awarded--2-5-million-nih-grant-to-study-c.html

39. Website Include a citation to an entire website only if you borrow ideas or information from its home page. (If you merely refer to a website in your paper, without discussing any specific information or ideas, you do not need to include a citation to that website in your reference list.) If you retrieved information that is subject to change, also include the date you accessed the source.

U.S. debt clock. Retrieved October 21, 2019, from https://www.usdebtclock.org/

Multimedia Sources

List the person or people most responsible for an audiovisual or multimedia work in the author position, with a label (in parentheses) to clarify their role. Who is "most responsible" depends in large part on the source type: For movies, include the director; for a streaming video, include the person who uploaded it; for a photograph or a work of art, include the photographer or artist; for TV or podcast episodes, include the writer and director or the episode host.

Do not include information about how you experienced the material—in a movie theater, on broadcast television, or on a streaming service—unless you watched or listened to a special version, such as a director's cut. This information can be included in square brackets following the title or combined with other bracketed information already included after the title.

40. Blog post Treat a blog post as you would an article in a magazine or newspaper (items 14 and 15, pp. 493).

Fister, B. (2019, February 14). Information literacy's third wave. *Library Babel Fish*. https://www.insidehighered.com/blogs/library-babel-fish/information-literacy%E2%80%99s-third-wave

41. Comment on a blog post Treat a comment on a blog post as you would a comment on an online article (see item 17, p. 494).

> Mollie F. (2019, February 14). It's a daunting task, isn't it? Last year, I got a course on Scholarly Communication and Information Literacy approved for [Comment on the blog post "Information literacy's third wave"]. *Library Babel Fish.* https://disq.us/p/1zr92uc

42. Podcast If you merely mention the podcast's name in your text, you need not cite it in your reference list. If you discuss characteristics of the podcast as a whole, however, include an entry.

> Boilen, B. (Host). (2008–present). *Tiny desk concerts* [Video podcast]. NPR. https://www.npr.org/series/tiny-desk-concerts/

> Abumrad, J., & Krulwich, R. (Hosts). (2002–present). *Radiolab* [Audio podcast]. WNYC Studios. https://www.wnycstudios.org/podcasts/radiolab/podcasts

43. Episode of a podcast If the episodes are numbered, include the podcast number following the title, in parentheses. If the host of an individual episode differs from the host(s) of the podcast in general, put the episode host's name in the author position, and include the series host(s) in the source information.

> West, S. (Host). (2018, July 27). Logical positivism (No. 120) [Audio podcast episode]. In *Philosophize this!* https://philosophizethis.org/logical-positivists/

> Longoria, J. (Host & Producer). (2019, April 19). Americanish [Audio podcast episode]. In J. Abumrad & R. Krulwich (Hosts), *Radiolab.* WNYC Studios. https://www.wnycstudios.org/podcasts/radiolab/articles/americanish

44. Online video or audio Think of the author of an online video or audio file as the person or organization that posted it. For a TED Talk, for example, the presenter is the author if the video was accessed on the TED site. However, if the TED Talk was accessed on YouTube, then TED becomes the author because the TED organization posted the video.

> Wray, B. (2019, May). *How climate change affects your mental health* [Video]. TED Conferences. https://www.ted.com/talks/britt_wray_how_climate_change_affects_your_mental_health

TED. (2019, September 20). *Britt Wray: How climate change affects your mental health* [Video]. YouTube. https://www.youtube.com/watch?v=IlDkCEvsYw

When deciding whether to italicize the title of the video or audio file, consider whether it is part of a series (regular font) or a stand-alone item (italics).

BBC. (2018, November 19). Why do bad managers flourish? [Audio]. In *Business Matters*. https://www.bbc.co.uk/programmes/p06s8752

The New York Times. (2018, January 9). *Taking a knee and taking down a monument* [Video]. YouTube. https://www.youtube.com/watch?v=qY34DQCdUvQ

45. Transcript of an online video or audio file

Gopnik, A. (2019, July 10). *A separate kind of intelligence* [Video transcript]. Edge. https://www.edge.org/conversation/alison_gopnik-a-separate-kind-of-intelligence

Glass, I. (2019, August 23). Ten sessions (No. 682) [Audio podcast episode transcript]. In *This American life*. WBEZ. https://www.thisamericanlife.org/682/transcript

46. Film Include the production company after the title. Separate multiple production companies with semicolons.

Peele, J. (Director). (2017). *Get out* [Film]. Universal Pictures.

Hitchcock, A. (Director). (1959). *The essentials collection: North by northwest* [Film; five-disc special ed. on DVD]. Metro-Goldwyn-Mayer; Universal Pictures Home Entertainment.

47. Television or radio series

Waller-Bridge, P., Williams, H., & Williams, J. (Executive Producers). (2016–2019). *Fleabag TV series*. Two Brothers Pictures; BBC.

48. Episode from a television or radio series

Waller-Bridge, P. (Writer), & Bradbeer, H. (Director). (2019, March 18). The provocative request (Season 2, Episode 3) [TV series episode]. In P. Waller-Bridge, H. Williams, & J. Williams (Executive Producers), *Fleabag*. Two Brothers Pictures; BBC.

49. Work of art in a museum Include information about the museum following the artwork's title. If a photograph of the image is available on the museum's website, include the direct-link URL.

> O'Keeffe, G. (1931). *Cow's skull: Red, white, and blue* [Painting].
> Metropolitan Museum of Art, New York, NY, United States.
> https://www.metmuseum.org/art/collection/search/488694

> *Helmet mask (kakaparaga)* [Artifact]. (ca. late 19th century). Museum of
> Fine Arts, Boston, MA, United States.

50. Photograph For a photograph that is available outside of a museum's collection, include the title of the photograph (if any), followed by the label "Photograph" in brackets. If the photograph is untitled, include a bracketed description that includes the word "photograph" in the title position. In the source position, include the name of the site you used to access the photograph.

> Browne, M. (1963). *The burning monk* [Photograph]. *Time.* http://
> 100photos.time.com/photos/malcolm-browne-burning-monk

> Liittschwager, D. (2019). [Photograph series of octopuses]. National
> Geographic. https://www.nationalgeographic.com/animals
> /2019/10/pet-octopuses-are-a-problem/#/01-pet-octopus-trade
> -nationalgeographic_2474095.jpg

51. Map

> Desjardins, J. (2017, November 17). *Walmart nation: Mapping the largest
> employers in the U.S.* [Map]. Visual Capitalist. https://www
> .visualcapitalist.com/walmart-nation-mapping-largest-employers-u-s/

52. Advertisement Use the model for the source in which the advertisement appears.

> America's Biopharmaceutical Companies [Advertisement]. (2018,
> September). *The Atlantic, 322*(2), 2.

> Centers for Disease Control and Prevention. (n.d.). *A tip from a former
> smoker: Beatrice* [Advertisement]. U.S. Department of Health and
> Human Services. https://www.cdc.gov/tobacco/campaign/tips/
> resources/ads/pdf-print-ads/beatrices-tip-print-ad-7x10.pdf

53. Music recording For classical works, put the composer in the author position, and provide information about the performer in brackets after the title. For popular works, put the performer in the author position. Include multiple record labels separated by semicolons.

Nielsen, C. (2014). *Carl Nielsen: Symphonies 1 & 4* [Album recorded by New York Philharmonic Orchestra]. Dacapo Records. (Original work published 1892–1916)

Carlile, B. (2018). *By the way, I forgive you* [Album]. Low Country Sound; Elektra.

Carlile, B. (2018). The mother [Song]. On *By the way, I forgive you*. Low Country Sound; Elektra.

54. Lecture, speech, address, or recorded interview

Grigas, A. (2019, October 8). *The new geopolitics of energy* [Address]. Freeman Spogli Institute for International Studies, Stanford University, Stanford, CA, United States.

Parrado, N. (2011, March 27). *Nando Parrado, plane crash survivor* [Interview with C. Gracie; audio file]. The Interview Archive; BBC World Service. https://www.bbc.co.uk/programmes/p00fhjnb

For an interview in an archive, put the person interviewed in the author position.

55. Paper or poster presented at a conference

Include all those involved with the conference presentation, even if only one person was actually at the conference; the full dates of the conference or meeting (not just the presentation date); the title of the presentation or poster, followed by a label (in brackets) stating the nature of the presentation (as described in conference materials); and the name and location of the conference. If there is a link to the presentation or poster, include it at the end of the reference list entry.

Wood, M. (2019, January 3–6). *The effects of an adult development course on students' perceptions of aging* [Poster session]. Forty-First Annual National Institute on the Teaching of Psychology, St. Pete Beach, FL, United States. https://nitop.org/resources/Documents/2019%20 Poster%20Session%20II.pdf

56. Video game

ConcernedApe. (2016). *Stardew Valley* [Video game]. Chucklefish.

57. Mobile app If you merely mention the app, include an in-text citation only; include a reference list entry only if you discuss the app in a significant way.

> Google LLC. (2019). *Google earth* (Version 9.3.3) [Mobile app]. App Store. https://apps.apple.com/us/app/google-earth/id293622097

58. Presentation slides If the presentation is inaccessible to your readers, cite it only in the text of your paper.

> Centers for Disease Control and Prevention. (2019, April 16). *Building local response capacity to protect families from emerging health threats* [Presentation slides]. CDC Stacks. https://stacks.cdc.gov/view/cdc/77687

Social Media Sources

If a social media source is not accessible to all readers, cite the post in the text of your paper only. For any social media sources that are accessible to your readers, use the author's real name, if given, followed by the pseudonym or screen name in brackets, exactly as in the source. If you know only the screen name, begin with that name without brackets. If the posting is undated, use "n.d." in parentheses. If untitled, include up to the first twenty words of the post or caption, or use a description of the post in square brackets. Include any emojis, hashtags, and links from the post if possible (each counts as one word), and keep unconventional spelling or capitalization as is. If you cannot use an actual emoji (😘), then include its name in square brackets ("[kissing face emoji]") instead. Describe images, or recordings, and the type of post in brackets following the title. Include an access date only if the post is not archived or if the content is likely to change.

59. Profile

> National Science Foundation [@NSF]. (n.d.). *Tweets* [Twitter profile]. Twitter. Retrieved October 15, 2019, from https://twitter.com/NSF

60. Facebook post

> Georgia Aquarium. (2019, October 10). *Meet the bigfin reef squid* [Video]. Facebook. https://www.facebook.com/GeorgiaAquarium/videos/2471961729567512/

> Georgia Aquarium. (2019, June 25). *True love* 💕 *Charlie and Lizzy are a bonded pair of African penguins who have been together for more than* [Image attached] [Status update]. Facebook. https://www.facebook.com/GeorgiaAquarium/photos/a.163898398123/10156900637543124/?type=3&theater

61. Tweet

Schiller, Caitlin [@caitlinschiller]. (2019, September 26). *Season 6 of*
Simplify is here! Today we launch with the one and only @susancain,
author of Quiet [Thumbnail with link attached] [Tweet]. Twitter.
http://twitter.com/caitlinschiller/status/1177214094191026176

62. Instagram post or highlight

Smithsonian [@smithsonian]. (2019, October 7). *You're looking at a ureilite*
meteorite under a microscope. When illuminated with polarized light,
they appear in dazzling colors, influenced [Photograph]. Instagram.
https://www.instagram.com/p/B3VI27yHLQG/

Smithsonian [@smithsonian]. (n.d.). *#Apollo50* [Highlight]. Instagram.
Retrieved October 15, 2019, from https://www.instagram.com/
stories/highlights/17902787752343364/

63. Online forum post

ScienceModerator. (2018, November 16). *Science discussion: We are*
researchers working with some of the largest and most innovative
companies using DNA to help people [Online forum post].
Reddit. https://www.reddit.com/r/science/comments/9xlnm2/
science_discussion_we_are_researchers_working/

Other Sources

64. Data set or graphic representation of data (graph, chart, table)

Reid, L. (2019). *Smarter homes: Experiences of living in low carbon homes*
2013–2018 [Data set]. UK Data Service. http://doi.org/10.5255/
UKDA-SN-853485

NPR. (2021, April 23). *Total cases and weekly trends, by state and territory*
[Chart]. https://www.npr.org/sections/health-shots/2020/09/01
/816707182/map-tracking-the-spread-of-the-coronavirus-in-the-u-s

65. Legal source The title of a court case is not italicized in the reference
list, though it is italicized in the in-text citation.

Sweatt v. Painter, 339 U.S. 629 (1950). http://www.law.cornell.edu/supct/
html/historics/USSC_CR_0339_0629_ZS.html

66. Personal communications Omit personal communications—letters, text messages, or email messages you have received, lecture notes that you took or that are posted only on a server your readers cannot access, and so on—from your reference list. Describe them only in the text of your paper. (See item 17 in the section on in-text citations, p. 484.)

19.3 Formatting Student Papers in APA Style

The following guidelines for formatting a student paper and preparing a reference list are consistent with advice given in the *Publication Manual of the American Psychological Association*, 7th ed. (2020).

Formatting a Project in APA Style

Margins and fonts Use one-inch margins on all sides (the default setting in most word processing programs). Use a 10- to 12-point font that is accessible to readers, such as Arial, Times New Roman, or Calibri. Some instructors may have their own font requirements. With the exception of any footnotes, which should be set in 10-point type, set the whole paper in the same font size.

Indents For the text of the paper, use paragraph indents of one-half inch. Quotations of forty or more words should be indented one-half inch from the left margin, but they do not use a paragraph indent unless the quotation is more than one paragraph long.

Footnotes (or endnotes) Footnotes appear at the bottom of the page on which they are called out, and endnotes are gathered up at the end of the paper, following the reference list. Footnotes typically add information that is relevant and informative but that does not fit into the body of the essay. If you need to include them, set them single-spaced in a 10-point font, using the footnote function in your word processor to number them consecutively with arabic numbers (1, 2, 3, etc.).

Line spacing Except for any footnotes or tables, double-space your whole paper, including the title page and reference list. Set footnotes single-spaced, and set tables single-spaced, one-and-a-half-spaced, or double-spaced, depending on what is easiest to read and understand.

Page numbering Number all pages in the upper right-hand corner, one-half inch from the top of the page and one inch from the right margin. The title page is page 1. Do not include the title or your name at the top of each page, unless your instructor requires it.

Headings Not all papers need headings, but if you are writing a long or complex paper and headings would help guide your reader, insert them. All headings use title case: Capitalize the first and last words, all other significant words, and any words of four or more letters.

First-Level Heading (centered, boldface)

Second-Level Heading (left-aligned, boldface)

Third-Level Heading (left-aligned, boldface, italics)

Title page Unless your instructor directs you otherwise, your title page should include the following information, centered on the page:

- the title of the paper in boldface type, three or four double-spaced lines from the top margin
- your name and the names of any coauthors, one blank double-spaced line below the title
- your school and the department in which the course is offered
- the course number and name (using the format shown in the catalog or on other school sites)
- your instructor's name (check to see how your instructor would like to be addressed: for example, as "Professor" or "Dr.")
- the assignment due date (in the date format of the country you are in)

Preparing the Reference List

Begin the reference list on a new page at the end of the paper. Center the heading "References" one inch from the top of the page, and set it in boldface type. Double-space the entire reference list.

Alphabetizing the list Alphabetize the reference list by the authors' (or editors') last names; if a work has no author or editor, alphabetize it by the first word of the title other than "A," "An," or "The."

   If you used more than one work by the same author, order those works by date, from earliest to latest. If you used more than one work by the same author in the same year, see item 9 in the in-text citation section (p. 482) and item 12 in the reference list section (p. 492).

Formatting the entries Start the first line of each entry at the left margin; indent lines after the first one-half inch (a "hanging indent"). Use your word processor settings to make the hanging indent.

DOIs and URLs If a DOI or URL is long, you can include a shortened form by using a site like shortdoi.org or bitly.com. Permalinks (provided by some publications, such as *The New York Times*) are often short, so use those if available. Do not manually add line breaks to URLs or DOIs. If your word processor inserts line breaks automatically or moves a DOI or URL to its own line, you can accept that formatting.

19.4 Additional Sections for Professional Papers

The following elements are not required for student papers; they are typical requirements for professional papers intended for publication. Your instructor may request that you use some or all of these elements (an abstract for a long or complex paper, for instance). If so, these guidelines will help you format those sections.

Author note Set an author note (titled "Author Note" in boldface font) at the bottom of the title page. In the first paragraph, include any acknowledgments (such as thanks for assistance) or disclosures (such as of conflicts of interest); in the second paragraph, include your contact information. Begin each paragraph at the left margin, with the first line indented one-half inch.

Abstract An abstract is a one-paragraph summary (fewer than 250 words) of the main points of the paper. If your instructor requests one, use the following format:

- Place the abstract on its own page, after the title page.
- Center the heading "Abstract" (in boldface type) at the top of the page.
- Start the abstract itself one double-spaced line below the heading.
- Do not indent the first line of the paragraph.

Keywords Keywords are terms for indexing the paper in databases. If your instructor asks you to supply them, they should be typed one double-spaced line below the abstract. Begin the line with "*Keywords:*" (in italics), indented one-half inch; then type the keywords in lowercase letters (except for proper nouns), separated by commas, and with no period at the end of the list.

Running heads On every page of the paper, including the title page, type the title of the paper (shortened to no more than fifty characters), flush with the left margin in all capital letters. On the same line, flush with the right margin, type the page number. Number all pages, including the title page.

19.5 Sample Student Research Writing in APA Style

On the following pages is a partial research paper on student-centered learning and educational technology, written by April Bo Wang, a student in an early education class. All pages of the student paper appear in the e-book.

The paper is adapted from Hacker and Sommers, *A Writer's Reference*, 10th ed., Bedford/St. Martin's (c) 2021.

1

Technology and the Shift From Teacher-Delivered to Student-Centered Learning: A Review of the Literature

April Bo Wang

Department of Education, Glen County Community College

EDU 107: Education, Technology, and Media

Dr. Julien Gomez

October 29, 2019

All pages are numbered, starting with the title page.

Paper title is boldface, followed by one blank (double-spaced) line. Writer's name, department and school, course, instructor, and date follow on separate double-spaced lines.

Marginal annotations indicate APA-style formatting and effective writing.

APA

Sources provide background information and context.

In-text citation for a quotation from a source without page numbers includes a paragraph number or another locator.

Wang sets up her organization by posing three questions.

Wang states her thesis.

2

**Technology and the Shift From Teacher-Delivered to
Student-Centered Learning: A Review of the Literature**

In the United States, most public school systems are struggling with teacher shortages, which are projected to worsen as the number of applicants to education schools decreases (Donitsa-Schmidt & Zuzovsky, 2014, p. 420). Citing federal data, *The New York Times* reported a 30% drop in "people entering teacher preparation programs" between 2010 and 2014 (Rich, 2015, para. 10). Especially in science and math fields, the teacher shortage is projected to escalate in the next 10 years (Hutchison, 2012). In recent decades, instructors and administrators have viewed the practice of student-centered learning as one promising solution. Unlike traditional teacher-delivered (also called "transmissive") instruction, student-centered learning allows students to help direct their own education by setting their own goals and selecting appropriate resources for achieving those goals. Though student-centered learning might once have been viewed as an experimental solution in understaffed schools, it is gaining credibility as an effective pedagogical practice. What is also gaining momentum is the idea that technology might play a significant role in fostering student-centered learning. This literature review will examine three key questions:

1. In what ways is student-centered learning effective?
2. Can educational technology help students drive their own learning?
3. How can public schools effectively combine teacher talent and educational technology?

In the face of mounting teacher shortages, public schools should embrace educational technology that promotes student-centered learning in order to help all students become engaged and successful learners.

APA

3

In What Ways Is Student-Centered Learning Effective?

According to the International Society for Technology in Education (2016), "Student-centered learning moves students from passive receivers of information to active participants in their own discovery process. What students learn, how they learn it, and how their learning is assessed are all driven by each individual student's needs and abilities" (What Is It? section). The results of student-centered learning have been positive, not only for academic achievement but also for student self-esteem. In this model of instruction, the teacher acts as a facilitator, and the students actively participate in the process of learning and teaching. With guidance, students decide on the learning goals most pertinent to themselves, they devise a learning plan that will most likely help them achieve those goals, they direct themselves in carrying out that learning plan, and they assess how much they learned (Çubukçu, 2012, Introduction section). The major differences between student-centered learning and instructor-centered learning are summarized in Table 1.

Bell (2010) has argued that the chief benefit of student-centered learning is that it can connect students with "real-world tasks," thus making learning more engaging as well as more comprehensive (p. 42). For example, Bell observed a group of middle-school students who wanted to build a social justice monument for their school. They researched social justice issues, selected several to focus on, and then designed a three-dimensional playground to represent those issues. In doing so, they achieved learning goals in the areas of social studies, physics, and mathematics and practiced research and teamwork. Students engaged in this kind of learning performed better on both project-based assessments and standardized tests (Bell, 2010).

Headings, centered and boldface, help readers follow the organization.

Wang uses a source to define the key term "student-centered learning."

Locator (section title) is included for a paraphrase to help readers find the source in a long article without page numbers.

Student text continues for three more pages before her conclusion. Not all pages are shown here.

Wang creates a table to compare and contrast two key concepts for her readers.

4

Table 1

Comparison of Two Approaches to Teaching and Learning

Teaching and learning period	Instructor-centered approach	Student-centered approach
Before class	• Instructor prepares lecture/instruction on new topic. • Students complete homework on previous topic.	• Students read and view new material, practice new concepts, and prepare questions ahead of class. • Instructor views student work, identifies learning opportunities.
During class	• Instructor delivers new material in a lecture or prepared discussion. • Students—unprepared—listen, watch, take notes, and try to follow along with the new material.	• Students lead discussions of the new material or practice applying the concepts or skills in an active environment. • Instructor answers student questions and provides feedback.
After class	• Instructor grades homework and gives feedback about the previous lesson. • Students work independently to practice or apply the new concepts.	• Students apply concepts/skills to more complex tasks individually and in groups. • Instructor posts additional resources to help students.

Note. Adapted from *The Flipped Class Demystified,* by New York University, n.d. (https://www.nyu.edu/faculty/teaching-and-learning-resources/instructional-technology-support/instructional-design-assessment/flipped-classes/the-flipped-class-demystified.html).

5

A Stanford study came to a similar conclusion; researchers examined four schools that had moved from teacher-driven instruction to student-centered learning (Friedlaender et al., 2014). The study focused on students from a mix of racial, cultural, and socioeconomic backgrounds, with varying levels of English-language proficiency. The researchers predicted that this mix of students, representing differing levels of academic ability, would benefit from a student-centered approach. Through interviews, surveys, and classroom observations, the researchers identified key characteristics of the new student-centered learning environments at the four schools:

- teachers who prioritized building relationships with students
- support structures for teachers to improve and collaborate on instruction
- a shift in classroom activity from lectures and tests to projects and performance-based assessments (pp. 5–7)

After the schools designed their curriculum to be personalized to individual students rather than standardized across a diverse student body and to be inclusive of skills such as persistence as well as traditional academic skills, students outperformed peers on state tests and increased their rates of high school and college graduation (Friedlaender et al., 2014, p. 3).

Can Educational Technology Help Students Drive Their Own Learning?

When students engage in self-directed learning, they rely less on teachers to deliver information and require less face-to-face time with teachers. For content delivery, many school districts have begun to use educational technology resources that, in recent years, have become more available,

Page number or other locator is not necessary for a paraphrase from a short article.

In a citation of a work with three or more authors, the first author's name, followed by "et al.," is given in parentheses or in a signal phrase.

Authors and year are given earlier in the paragraph, so only page numbers are provided at the end of the paraphrase.

6

more affordable, and easier to use. For the purposes of
this paper, the term "educational technology resources"
encompasses the following: distance learning, by which
students learn from a remote instructor online; other online
education programming such as slide shows and video or
audio lectures; interactive online activities, such as quizzing
or games; and the use of computers, tablets, smartphones,
SMART Boards, or other such devices for coursework.

Much like student-centered learning, the use of
educational technology began in many places as a temporary
measure to keep classes running despite teacher shortages.
A Horn and Staker study (2011) examined the major patterns
over time for students who subscribed to distance learning,
for example. A decade ago, students who enrolled in distance
learning often fell into one of the following categories:
They lived in a rural community that had no alternative
for learning; they attended a school where there were not
enough qualified teachers to teach certain subjects; or they
were homeschooled or homebound. But faced with tighter
budgets, teacher shortages, increasingly diverse student
populations, and rigorous state standards, schools recognized
the need and the potential for distance learning across the
board.

As the teacher shortage has intensified, educational
technology resources have become more tailored to student
needs and more affordable. Pens that convert handwritten
notes to digital text and organize them, backpacks that charge
electronic devices, and apps that create audiovisual flash
cards are just a few of the more recent innovations. According
to Svokos (2015), some educational technology resources

Wang develops her thesis.

In a signal phrase, the word "and" links the names of two authors; the date is given in parentheses.

entertain students while supporting student-centered
learning:

> GlassLab, a nonprofit that was launched with
> grants from the Bill & Melinda Gates and MacArthur
> Foundations, creates educational games that are now
> being used in more than 6,000 classrooms across the
> country. Some of the company's games are education
> versions of existing ones—for example, its first
> release was SimCity EDU—while others are originals.
> Teachers get real-time updates on students' progress
> as well as suggestions on what subjects they need to
> spend more time perfecting. (5. Educational Games
> section)

Many of the companies behind these products offer
institutional discounts to schools where such devices are used
widely by students and teachers.

Horn and Staker (2011) concluded that the chief benefit of
technological learning was that it could adapt to the individual
student in a way that whole-class delivery by a single teacher
could not. Their study examined various schools where
technology enabled student-centered learning. For example,
Carpe Diem High School in Yuma, Arizona, hired only six
certified subject teachers and then outfitted its classrooms
with 280 computers connected to online learning programs.
The programs included software that offered "continual
feedback, assessment, and incremental victory in a way that
a face-to-face teacher with a class of 30 students never could.
After each win, students continue to move forward at their
own pace" (p. 9). Students alternated between personalized
55-minute courses online and 55-minute courses with one of

Quotation of 40 or more words
is indented without quotation
marks.

Locator (section title) is used
for a direct quotation from
an online source with no page
numbers.

Student text continues for
three more pages before her
conclusion. Not all pages are
shown here.

Tone of the conclusion is objective and presents answers to Wang's three organizational questions.

11

However, rather than having students identify their own learning goals and design their own curriculum around those goals, CCA uses educational technology as an assessment tool to identify areas of student weakness. It then partners students with teachers to address those areas (pp. 8–9).

Conclusion

Public education faces the opportunity for a shift from the model of teacher-delivered instruction that has characterized American public schools since their foundation to a student-centered learning model. Not only has student-centered learning proved effective in improving student academic and developmental outcomes, but it can also synchronize with technological learning for widespread adaptability across schools. Because it relies on student direction rather than an established curriculum, student-centered learning supported by educational technology can adapt to the different needs of individual students and a variety of learning environments—urban and rural, well funded and underfunded. Similarly, when student-centered learning relies on technology rather than a corps of uniformly trained teachers, it holds promise for schools that would otherwise suffer from a lack of human or financial resources.

12

References

Bell, S. (2010). Project-based learning for the 21st century: Skills for the future. *The Clearing House, 83*(2), 39–43.

Çubukçu, Z. (2012). Teachers' evaluation of student-centered learning environments. *Education, 133*(1).

Demski, J. (2012, January). This time it's personal. *THE Journal (Technological Horizons in Education), 39*(1), 32–36.

Donitsa-Schmidt, S., & Zuzovsky, R. (2014). Teacher supply and demand: The school level perspective. *American Journal of Educational Research, 2*(6), 420–429. https://doi.org/10.12691/education-2-6-14

Friedlaender, D., Burns, D., Lewis-Charp, H., Cook-Harvey, C. M., & Darling-Hammond, L. (2014). *Student-centered schools: Closing the opportunity gap* [Research brief]. Stanford Center for Opportunity Policy in Education. https://edpolicy.stanford.edu/sites/default/files/scope-pub-student-centered-research-brief.pdf

Horn, M. B., & Staker, H. (2011). *The rise of K-12 blended learning*. Innosight Institute. http://www.christenseninstitute.org/wp-content/uploads/2013/04/The-rise-of-K-12-blended-learning.pdf

Hutchison, L. F. (2012). Addressing the STEM teacher shortage in American schools: Ways to recruit and retain effective STEM teachers. *Action in Teacher Education, 34*(5/6), 541–550. https://doi.org/10.1080/01626620.2012.729483

International Society for Technology in Education. (2016). *Student-centered learning*. http://www.iste.org/connected/standards/essential-conditions/student-centered-learning

List of references begins on a new page. Heading is centered and boldface.

List is alphabetized by authors' last names. All authors' names are inverted.

First line of an entry is at the left margin; subsequent lines indent one half-inch.

Double-spacing is used throughout.

13

Mitra, S. (2013, February). *Build a school in the cloud* [Video].
TED. https://www.ted.com/talks/sugata_mitra_build
_a_school_in_the_cloud?language=en

Moeller, B., & Reitzes, T. (2011, July). *Integrating technology with
student-centered learning*. Nellie Mae Education Foundation.
http://www.nmefoundation.org/research/personalization/
integrating-technology-with-student-centered-learn

Rich, M. (2015, August 9). Teacher shortages spur a
nationwide hiring scramble (credentials optional).
The New York Times. https://nyti.ms/1WaaV7a

Svokos, A. (2015, May 7). 5 innovations from the past decade
that aim to change the American classroom *Huffpost*.
https://www.huffpost.com/entry/technology-changes
-classrooms_n_7190910

Watson, J. (2008, January). *Blended learning: The convergence
of online and face-to-face education*. North American
Council for Online Learning. http://www.inacol.org/
wp-content/uploads/2015/02/NACOL_PP-BlendedLearning
-lr.pdf

APPENDIX 1
Keeping a Portfolio

As you create a body of work over the course of a semester, you'll find yourself growing as a writer and possibly wanting to return to earlier essays to make them better. To make that emphasis on process and revision central to the composition course, some colleges have moved toward a portfolio model of grading.

The portfolio method, borrowed from studio art classes, requires that writers write, rewrite, experiment, and improve all semester long—and then end the semester by selecting their best pieces to be graded. Of course, there are variations on the process, but most composition courses follow a similar track for portfolios:

Portfolio Process

- Students compose and turn in an essay.

- The instructor provides feedback for revision but does *not* assign a grade.

- Students continue to revise the essay until the end of the term, keeping track of their progress in a separate journal.

- Other essays are assigned, turned in, and receive instructor feedback that is designed to help the student revise each essay over the course of the semester.

- At the end of the term, students submit a portfolio of *revised* versions of their best essays, which are graded.

- The portfolio normally contains all drafts of every assigned essay, as well as a reflective essay that appraises the student's progress over the course of the semester.

Portfolios are normally collected in a digital format. (If you draft by hand or if some of your drafts contain handwritten comments, you might be asked to scan copies of these early drafts.) Whether yours is an electronic or paper portfolio, several pieces of advice are likely to apply:

Tips for Keeping a Portfolio

- **Hold on to everything.** If your instructor or peer reviewers have marked your draft—either digitally or by hand—then that draft should become part of your portfolio. Basically, retain any document with feedback.

- **Keep a journal of your progress as a writer.** You'll want to keep track of your challenges and successes over the course the semester. This material will not just be helpful in composing a reflective essay on your portfolio (see below); it will also help you to improve as a writer each time you compose a new essay.

- **Make sure you turn in everything that's required.** Just as you would check and recheck a prompt before submitting an essay, be certain you carefully follow the directions for your portfolio provided by your instructor. If you are turning in an e-portfolio, double-check every link to ensure that everything works as you expect it to. If possible, test the link(s) or the attachment(s) from a computer other than the one you typically use.

- **Consider the life of your portfolio *after* the semester is over.** Yes, your portfolio exists primarily because it is a class requirement. However—especially if the collection of your writing will inhabit an online space—think about who else might read your portfolio in the future. More and more, employers are asking to see samples of writing by potential employees, and an outstanding portfolio could end up being your ticket to a good job.

One of the most significant pieces of the portfolio puzzle is the reflective or introductory essay that accompanies your revised drafts. Pay attention to your instructor's specific instructions, of course; but remember that most reflective essays will ask you to think rhetorically, just as you do with any essay.

Creating Your Reflective Introductory Essay

- **Know your audience.** Sometimes the only person who sees your writing portfolio is your own instructor. Ideally, over the course of a semester, you've come to know that person well enough to realize what to leave in and what to take out. Some portfolios, however, are assessed by other instructors, whom you may never have met and who know nothing about you. If that's the case, remember all you've learned about good writing practices to effectively connect with anonymous reviewers of your work.

- **Discuss the composition and revision of each essay.** Just as you've been asked to be specific throughout the semester in your essay writing, use concrete examples as evidence in the reflective essay on your overall portfolio. Focus on the details of your own writing in this introduction to your work. Quote selectively from your essays in the same way you would if you were analyzing a text by another writer.

- **Reflect on your progress over the course of the semester.** It's important to be thinking about your portfolio *throughout* the semester, not just at the very end. If you've been keeping a journal, consult it frequently to show how your attitudes, skills, and habits have changed during your time in class.

- **Be honest.** Think through what *really* transpired over the course of the semester. Students writing a reflective essay might assume their instructors want to see a straight line of progress, but instructors, who are usually writers themselves, know that's not the way a writer's development usually happens. Yes, you want to come across as someone who's worked hard and improved, but don't make claims that aren't supported by the essays that are actually in your portfolio. If you made gains, then losses, then more gains, there's nothing wrong with charting that.

- **Help your instructor see your writing as you see it yourself.** Part of being honest about your writing is helping your instructor see the composing process through your eyes. What *particular* challenges have you faced that your instructor might not know about? How have you overcome them?

- **Talk about what's next for you as a writer.** Writing is a process. Your reflective essay should not only take stock of how far you've come, it should also reflect on what's ahead for you as a writer. What elements of your writing still need improvement? What have you learned that you can carry with you, no matter what writing situation lies ahead?

DIY A1: Reflect on Your Writing

Wherever you happen to be in the semester — and whether or not your class is using portfolios — write about the writing challenges you've faced so far and what you've learned. Use the guidelines above to discuss the essays that you've already turned in, being as specific as possible in your references to each one.

APPENDIX 2
Writing Timed and In-Class Essays

The writing process you've been learning about up to this point has been recursive. You were encouraged to think and annotate and prewrite and draft and revise and edit and to come back to that process over and over until it's time for a final proofread. The process approach to composition is based on extensive research and generally produces the best results—you should follow it whenever possible.

Sometimes, however, you don't have days and weeks to work on a piece of writing. Instead, you have to produce it on demand, in a short amount of time, in class or in an online setting. This type of writing requires you to think and work quickly and efficiently. Your prewriting may be only a few notes and a scratch outline. Your thesis will probably be fairly simple and direct, and there won't be much time for editing, much less a deep revision.

Ideally, you'll first encounter timed writing in a low-stakes situation, similar to those found in the many DIY (Do-it-yourself) assignments in this book. In addition to the help they provide you with whatever project you are working on, ungraded timed writing activities also offer opportunities to practice for graded timed writing assignments like midterms and finals.

When you sit down for a midterm or a final, you rarely know *exactly* what you will encounter, which makes essay exams excellent examples of the need for writing with flexibility. Still, even if there's nearly always an element of surprise involved in these assignments, you can help yourself succeed by taking the following steps:

Preparing for and Writing Timed Essays

- **Be prepared.** If you've been advised to look at an assigned reading, read it. If your instructor has given you a practice exam, take it. Any preparation you can do *before* you begin the timed writing will increase your confidence and your likelihood of success.

- **Take advantage of every legitimate resource.** If your timed essay is designated as "open book" or "open notes," then, by all means, take advantage of this opportunity to expand the depth and quality of your response.

- **Read and reread the prompt.** Usually your instructor will give the class at least a hint of what's going to be on a timed essay exam, but sometimes the prompt may seem to come straight out of the blue. If that's the case, *stay calm* and read the assignment again. Often during your second read-through, you'll realize that the assignment is closer to what you expected than you initially thought. Even if the prompt is basically what you were expecting, make sure you respond *exactly* to the prompt that's actually on the page. Never assume you know what you will be writing about until you see your assumptions confirmed in the exam instructions.

- **Make a scratch outline that includes a thesis statement.** Drafts written quickly tend to go off track. Keep your essay organized and focused by writing a working outline and a thesis statement. Take some time to collect your thoughts and write out an essay plan. After each paragraph, take another look at your outline and thesis to make sure you're still doing what you set out to do.

- **Find your pace.** You may be tempted to rush or to procrastinate. Try to find a happy medium between the two so that you can make steady progress. Above all, write at the pace that best suits you. If you should happen to be in a classroom or in a Zoom meeting, where you can see some or all of the other students, don't worry about those who start writing immediately. Instead, make sure you have a pretty good idea of what *you* want to say before you begin.

- **Allow time for proofreading.** Writing until the very last minute is not a good idea. Imagine that the exam ends ten minutes before it actually does and finish early. Then carefully reread your essay, correcting errors as you go. If you finish more than ten minutes early, make sure you've said everything you need to say before you exit the exam.

- **Follow the rules of the assignment.** With more and more timed writing assignments taking place online, some colleges are using proctor services, which do everything from watching students via their computer's video cameras to recording every single keystroke that a student makes during an exam. While some of these proctor services are relatively unobtrusive, others may use facial-recognition or eye-tracking software. Whatever situation you find yourself in when you are writing a timed essay, remember that if you are following the rules set out by your instructor, you have nothing to worry about. Take a deep breath, relax, and write well!

Acknowledgments

Bethany Brookshire, "Why People Don't Vote, and What to Do about It," *Science News*, November 4, 2016. Used with permission.

Emily Chamlee-Wright, "The Presumption of Good Faith in Campus Conversations," *Inside Higher Ed*, August 13, 2019. Copyright © 2019 by Emily Chamlee-Wright. All rights reserved. Used with permission.

Manohla Dargis, "Before He Was 'King Arthur,' He Was a Guy Ritchie Lad," *The New York Times*, May 11, 2017. Copyright © 2017 by The New York Times. All rights reserved. Used under license. https://nytimes.com

Carol S. Dweck, "Chapter 1: The Mindsets" from *MINDSET: THE NEW PSYCHOLOGY OF SUCCESS* by Carol S. Dweck, Ph.D., copyright © 2006, 2016, by Carol S. Dweck, Ph.D. Used by permission of Random House, an imprint and division of Penguin Random House LLC. All rights reserved.

John Gardner and Betsy Barefoot, excerpt from *Your College Experience: Strategies for Success*, 12e. Copyright © 2016 by Bedford/St. Martin's Press. Used with permission.

Ylonda Gault Caviness, excerpt from "We Go Way Back," *The Meaning of Michelle*, by Veronica Chambers. Copyright © 2017 by Veronica Chambers. Used with permission.

Nikole Hannah-Jones, excerpt from "The 1619 Project: 'The Idea of America,'" *The New York Times*, August 2019. Copyright © 2019 by The New York Times. All rights reserved. Used under license. https://nytimes.com

David Leonhardt, "Is College Worth It? (Clearly, New Data Say)," *The New York Times*, May 27, 2014. Copyright © 2014 by The New York Times. All rights reserved. Used under license. https://nytimes.com

"Analysis of Oprah Winfrey's Speech at the 75th Golden Globes," by Curran McCrory. Used with permission.

John Otis, "Becoming a Confident College Student, With the Help of an 'Angel,'" *The New York Times*, January 10, 2017. Copyright © 2017 by The New York Times. All rights reserved. Used under license. https://nytimes.com

William Safire, "A Spirit Reborn," *The New York Times*, September 11, 2002. Copyright © 2002 by William Safire. All rights reserved. Used with permission.

Kurt Streeter, "South L.A. Student Finds a Different World at Cal," *Los Angeles Times*, August 26, 2013. Copyright © 2013 by Los Angeles Times. Used with permission.

Gary Suarez, "Bad Bunny's 'Las Que No Iban a Salir' Turns Self-Isolation into a Global Party," *Rolling Stone*, May 20, 2020. Copyright © 2020 and Trademark ® Rolling Stone LLC. All rights reserved. Used by permission.

Marlene Towns, "The New Gillette Commercial: The Best an Ad Can Get," *The Hill*, January 20, 2019. Copyright © 2019 by The Hill. Used with permission.

Index

B

List of Activities in *Hello, Writer*

Working Together Activities

Applying What You Know Activities